Westview Special Studies on Latin America and the Caribbean

Revolution and Counterrevolution in Central America and the Caribbean
edited by Donald E. Schulz and Douglas H. Graham

A detailed examination of the roots of revolution and counter-revolution in Central America and the Caribbean, this book draws on the research of an interdisciplinary team of noted scholars. The authors give special attention to the institutional and structural causes of stability and instability--in particular, the traditional role of the United States; the current economic crisis; the changing role of the Roman Catholic church; the influence of the military and security forces, the oligarchy, and the business sector; the problems of instituting socioeconomic reform; the politics of subsistence; and the revolutionary opposition. Following the thematic chapters, a country-by-country focus is employed to assess the situations in El Salvador, Guatemala, Nicaragua, Honduras, Costa Rica, and Jamaica, and a section devoted to the international dimensions of the crisis looks at Mexican, Soviet, Cuban, and U.S. policies toward the region. The editors' concluding chapter explores prospects for the future of this troubled area.

Donald E. Schulz is assistant professor of political science at the University of Tampa. He is coeditor (with Jan S. Adams) of *Political Participation in Communist Systems* (1981) and author of *Communist Policy Toward Southeast Asia, 1954-1969* (1970). Douglas H. Graham is professor of agricultural economics and director of the Latin American Studies program at the Undergraduate Center for International Studies, Ohio State University. He is coauthor (with Thomas W. Merrick) of *Population and Economic Development in Brazil, 1800 to the Present* (1979).

Revolution and Counterrevolution in Central America and the Caribbean

edited by Donald E. Schulz
and Douglas H. Graham

Westview Press / Boulder and London

Westview Special Studies on Latin America and the Caribbean

Copyright © 1984 by Westview Press, Inc.

Published in 1984 in the United States of America by Westview Press, Inc.,
5500 Central Avenue, Boulder, Colorado 80301; Frederick A. Praeger, Publisher

Library of Congress Catalog Card Number: 84-50988
ISBN: 0-86531-550-7
ISBN: 0-86531-551-5 (pbk.)

Composition for this book was provided by the editors
Printed and bound in the United States of America

10   9   8   7   6   5   4   3   2

Contents

Preface

Americans are a fashionable people. They exchange their crises like last year's old clothes, responding to the latest political advertisements, infatuated by such catchy slogans as "domino theory," "another Vietnam," "window of vulnerability," "supply-side economics," and so on.

But the crisis in the Caribbean Basin cannot be summed up in a slogan. It is multidimensional—social as well as economic, political as well as military, historical as well as current. It cannot be understood solely in terms of either domestic causation or foreign intervention. Rather, all of these interrelated facets of the problem must be considered if we are to have any realistic chance of pursuing U.S. interests in an effective and constructive manner in this region of extraordinary turmoil. At the same time, it is necessary to recognize that the standard ideologies—conservative, liberal, and radical—have failed to provide an adequate frame of reference. At best, they have offered partial truths; at worst, they have seriously distorted reality by engaging in wholesale selective perception.

This book is based on two assumptions. The first is that any reasonably comprehensive treatment of the current crisis must be multidisciplinary in nature. The crisis in the Caribbean Basin is far too complex to be reduced to its political or military dimensions. Thus, we have brought together historians, political scientists, journalists, economists, and a career diplomat in an attempt to provide a diverse range of professional perspectives. Beyond this, however, we have also tried to be multi-ideological. No single weltanschauung holds the key to truth; conservatism, liberalism, and radicalism all contain important insights, as well as significant limitations. By soliciting contributions from representatives of all three schools, we hope to provide the volume with a comprehensiveness and diversity ordinarily lacking in mono-ideological interpretations.

Stated another way, our contributors tend to complement each other not only by concentrating on different problems but also by focusing on similar problems in different ways.

The text is divided into three sections. In the first of these, we deal with the structural and institutional sources of stability and instability--the changing roles of historical actors (the United States, the Roman Catholic Church, the oligarchy, and the military), the rise of new political forces (the middle class, proletariat, and peasantry), and the impact of the international economic system (especially the economic shocks experienced by the region in recent years). Some of these factors are dealt with at chapter length, others through subsections. In addition, a number of distinct theories and concepts (e.g., the theories of economic and political development, "competitive exclusion," the "population explosion," the "domino theory," the "dialectic of revolution") have been advanced in the academic and popular literature in an attempt to explain the sources and dynamics of change. These will be examined at length in an introductory overview chapter by one of the editors.

The second section will employ a country focus. Here the primary emphasis will be on Central America-- namely, El Salvador, Guatemala, Nicaragua, Honduras, and Costa Rica. Of the Caribbean island-states, only Jamaica, the most sophisticated, advanced, and instructive of the British Commonwealth countries, will be at least briefly treated in other chapters. The focus, in short, will be on the most important countries--in particular, those that have undergone, are currently undergoing, or are likely to undergo revolutionary turmoil. The Central American focus is justified in no more complex terms than that is where most of the action is.

The third section deals with the international dimension of the crisis. We have chosen to concentrate on the crucial outside actors: the United States, the Soviet Union, Cuba, and Mexico. The U.S. role, in particular, is decisive. If, as is argued explicitly in the chapters by Schulz and implicitly by several other contributors, the United States has become a major destabilizing force in Central America, one fears for the future. A short postscript by Schulz suggests a possible alternative, but without much optimism that the necessary changes in policy will be adopted.

For convenience, the term American will be used interchangeably with the United States throughout the text, even though, obviously, all of the hemisphere could claim the name American.

Due to the limitations of our word-processing system, we were not able to insert diacritical marks such

as accents and the like. We hope that the reader is not
inconvenienced by their omission.

Finally, a note of thanks should be extended to all
those who made this work possible. The Department of
Agricultural Economics and Rural Sociology of The Ohio
State University provided staff and facilities for the
preparation of the final manuscript. The University of
Tampa granted Donald Schulz a generous sum of money
through its Faculty Development Program for the editing
and indexing. Barbara Lee and Phyllis Seidel did the
typing. Jill Loar was responsible for getting the
material onto the word processor. Mrs. Lee coordinated
the preparation of the manuscript and did much of the
proofreading. These ladies are to be commended for their
efforts and patience in putting up with all the frustrations that accompanied the assembling of this work.

Donald E. Schulz
Douglas H. Graham

Part 1

Structural and Institutional Sources of Stability and Instability

1
Ten Theories in Search
of Central American Reality

Donald E. Schulz

If hell, as Thomas Hobbes once said, is truth seen too late, then the recent belated discovery of Central America by the United States suggests the hazards of engaging in a quagmire whose origins are only dimly understood and whose dimensions can as yet be only guessed. Prior to the 1978-79 Nicaraguan revolution, few areas of the world were taken more for granted by the State Department and the public. An obscure backwater of the international system, the region (with the notable exception of Costa Rica) seemed perennially somnolent under the rule of traditional oligarchies and military dictatorships. Today all that has changed. Civil strife wracks El Salvador and Guatemala and threatens to spread to Honduras. Counterrevolutionary exiles, organized, trained, and equipped by the United States and Honduras, attack Nicaragua from sanctuaries in southern Honduras. Rumors of impending war dominate cafe conversation in Managua and Tegucigalpa. The possibility of inter-nationalization and regionalization--of a great brushfire of violence sweeping the isthmus from Mexico to Colombia, drawing in the United States and Cuba in support of their respective clients--remains the ultimate nightmare. Only time will tell whether the specter will become a reality.

How is one to understand these developments? As so frequently happens in highly politicized settings, attempts to explain often obscure as much as they reveal. Complex phenomena are force-fit into Procrustean ideological molds. Reductionism and selective perception abound. The first casualty is truth.

In recent years, a number of theories and arguments have been set forth in an attempt to provide a handle to Central American realities. Some have been presented as monocausal or mutually exclusive, others as links in an interrelated web. ("Everything," Viron Vaky once remarked, "is part of everything else.")[1] This introduction will examine the most prominent of these explanations. Although some are seriously flawed and none are adequate to grasp the full complexity of the Central

American crisis, together, viewed critically, they
provide a reasonably comprehensive, multidimensional
frame of reference, with significant policy implications
for the future.

(1) THE THEORY OF ECONOMIC DEVELOPMENT: COMPETITIVE
     EXCLUSION AND RURAL-URBAN UNDEREMPLOYMENT

     One of the curiosities of recent U.S. political life
is how theories and ideas long discredited in both academia and the "real world" have reemerged and again become
politically fashionable. A striking example is provided
by the Reagan administration's Caribbean Basin Initiative
(CBI). In February 1982, the president unveiled a long-
range development program consisting primarily of proposals for (1) a one-way free-trade arrangement whereby
exports from the affected countries would be allowed to
enter the United States duty-free for a period of twelve
years, (2) tax incentives for U.S. firms investing in the
region, and (3) a supplemental FY 1982 appropriation of
$350 million, much of which would be concentrated in the
private sector to "help foster the spirit of enterprise
necessary to take advantage of the trade and investment
portions of the program."[2] Technical assistance and
training would be provided to Basin entrepreneurs. Among
other things, the proposed legislation would prohibit
recipient governments from imposing confiscatory conditions on U.S. businesses or limiting American access to
Caribbean markets and commodities. Rather, the "magic of
the marketplace" would be the key to generating self-
sustaining growth.
     The program itself was quite modest--87 percent of
Caribbean exports already entered the United States duty-
free and another 5 percent (textiles) were excluded from
the plan. Clearly, this was no Alliance for Progress.
Yet much of the impetus, spirit, and rationale smacked
strongly of that earlier, ill-fated effort. Notwithstanding the technical problems associated with the two
projects, both were based on the dubious proposition that
economic growth is a cure for poverty and the revolutionary discontent that it spawns: Create wealth and,
even if it is not distributed equitably, some will
"trickle down" to the masses.[3]
     Unfortunately, the theory fails to take into account
the fundamentally exploitative nature of the socioeconomic and political structures plaguing most Central
American countries. It is not simply a question of
wealth generated in highly inegalitarian societies
flowing disproportionately to those who already have
riches, power, and status. That is only part of the
iceberg; equally important, the poor have often grown
poorer: Newly generated wealth and the promise thereof

have whetted the appetites of the rich and powerful,
inspiring them not only to make better use of their own
economic resources, but also to encroach on those of
their less powerful and more impoverished countrymen.
The consequence has been the conversion of "trickle-down"
theory into "trickle-up" economics.

Although the specifics vary from country to country,
the general pattern is fairly clear: Economic
"development," through the transformation of subsistence
agricultural into agro-export economies, set in motion a
process of "competitive exclusion,"[4] which reinforced and
deepened existing inequalities and led to the progressive
immiseration of large segments of the rural population.
In El Salvador, Guatemala, and Nicaragua, during the
latter part of the nineteenth century, this involved the
conversion of Indian communal and private lands into
coffee latifundios and the attendant dispossession of
numerous peasants, as small holdings were bought up,
"grabbed," or otherwise consolidated into larger units.
Subsequently, in the 1950s and 1960s, as cotton, sugar,
and other commodities began to challenge the dominance of
coffee, many additional lands were converted to those
crops.

The social consequences were formidable: In El
Salvador, there was a dramatic decrease in colono
arrangements (from 55,000 in 1960 to 17,000 a decade
later), as planters increasingly resorted to temporary
landless workers and mechanization to cultivate and
harvest their crops. The number of landless peasants
grew from 12 percent in 1960 to 41 percent in 1975. Only
about 6 percent of rural households had access to enough
land to meet the subsistence needs of the average family.
Over 50 percent of the agricultural labor force was
unemployed more than two-thirds of the year.

Similarly, in Guatemala, the modernization of agriculture gave rise to a "qualitative redistribution of
rural misery."[5] Between 1964 and 1979, the number of
farms too small to provide a subsistence living increased
from 364,879 to 547,572 (reflecting the subdivision and
parcelling out of existing holdings from generation to
generation), while their proportion of total farmland
declined from 18.6 to 16.2 percent. Conversely, the
largest 2.1 percent of the farms increased their total
land from 2.2 to 2.75 million hectares. Even as peasant
holdings were losing 26 percent of their acreage in the
1970s, the area devoted to export agriculture swelled by
45 percent. Rural unemployment grew accordingly. In the
1960s agricultural employment grew .1 percent per year,
while the rural population expanded by 2.6 percent.
Currently, some 500,000 men, women, and children are
forced by poverty and tenancy arrangements to migrate to
the Pacific Coast to harvest coffee, cotton, and sugar
cane on the large estates, the great majority at no more

than the minimum wage of $3.20 a day. In spite of a
remarkable agricultural-export performance, domestic food
production failed to keep pace with population growth.
The result has been increasing malnutrition. (Life
expectancy among the rural Indian populace is only 49
years.)[6]

In Nicaragua, too, land concentration was accelerated, most notably in the Pacific zone, where subsistence farmers were increasingly displaced, with an
attendant rise in rural and urban unemployment. In the
1950s alone, growing production had forced some 180,000
peasants from small farms into seasonal plantation work.
After the mid-1960s, agricultural unemployment climbed
steadily, reaching 16 percent in 1977 and 32 percent in
1979. (The latter figure, of course, is largely a
reflection of the civil war.) At the same time, real
wages and income declined. In turn, the rural poor
increasingly expressed their anger through land seizures,
strikes, and the formation in 1977 of the Association of
Rural Workers.[7]

Meanwhile, in Honduras, the least developed country
in the region, the expansion of commercial agriculture--
mainly coffee, cotton, and cattle--for the first time
began to seriously disrupt communal forms of property-
holding. Between 1952 and 1965, competitive exclusion
produced a 39 percent decrease in _ejido_ land (not to mention the impact on national and _ocupante_ holdings). As
elsewhere, the large _haciendas_ often expanded through the
simple expedient of enclosing new lands with barbed wire,
thereby denying access to peasants whose families had
worked these plots for generations. In southern
Honduras, for instance, two estates added some 54,000
acres to their holdings through such practices.
Nevertheless, employment opportunities in the expanding
capitalist agricultural sector and the continuing availability of colonizable land absorbed most of the surplus
labor force until the late 1970s: "In combination with
the agrarian reform programs of the early 1970s, these
factors meant that rural Hondurans overall did not
experience a sharp, real deterioration of their incomes,
wealth, or control over their livelihoods in degrees or
at rates anywhere approaching the declines affecting many
rural Nicaraguans, Guatemalans, and Salvadorans."[8]

This is a crucial point. Moreover, these less
exclusionary conditions were mirrored in Costa Rica,
where land reform, colonization, and the continued growth
of the banana industry absorbed many of the small-holders
displaced in the 1960s and early 1970s. Thus, the two
countries in which the impact of competitive exclusion
was least devastating were the most politically stable in
the region.

And what of industrialization? Clearly, it was not
a panacea for the social crisis spawned by agricultural

modernization. Modern factories were built and expensive
machinery imported. A small minority of the population
was enriched, and a certain number co-opted into the
rising middle class. The vast majority, however, were
excluded. Since industrialization was capital-intensive,
relatively few jobs were created. By one estimate, only
about one out of every five people entering the Central
American labor market between 1970 and 1975 was able to
obtain employment.[9] In El Salvador, for instance, the
manufacturing sector grew by 24 percent between 1961 and
1971, while the number of people it employed increased by
only 6 percent. Indeed, the number of workers employed
in manufacturing as a percentage of the economically
active population actually declined. The ranks of the
marginally employed mushroomed. Forty-two percent of
urban jobs paid below the official poverty level; about a
quarter of the workforce was unemployed or underemployed.[10]

In short, industrial expansion was fundamentally
incapable of absorbing the growing urban workforce being
created by rapid population growth and the influx of
underemployed immigrants from the countryside. The
growth potential in the Central American Common Market
was limited, while the high-cost industries created
behind the Common Market tariff barriers were unable to
compete in the more rapidly growing world market for
light manufactured goods. Thus, employment opportunities
were restricted by industrial policies moving these
countries too far from their prospective comparative
advantage, producing for the wrong (i.e., more slowly
growing) market and with inappropriate, high-cost technology. This set of policy errors reinforced and
deepened socioeconomic polarization and helped pave the
way for the political crises of the late 1970s and early
1980s.

Will the Caribbean Basin Initiative (CBI) alleviate
these conditions, or will it intensify the crisis by
exacerbating the very socioeconomic conditions that it is
intended to ameliorate? The outlook is problematic, at
best. In the 1960s, Central American leaders embraced
programs like the Alliance for Progress (its idealistic
rhetoric notwithstanding) and the Central American Common
Market partly because they were thought to obviate the
need for basic structural reforms: It was unnecessary to
create a domestic market for their industrial products by
raising mass living standards when an external demand
could be generated through the Common Market. Workers
would thus continue to serve the economy as cheap sources
of labor, rather than as consumers wielding economic
power of their own. Development, as it occurred in
country after country, became part of the problem of
political instability, rather than a solution to it.

8

The central issue has scarcely changed. Agrarian reform has been truncated in El Salvador and is floundering in Honduras. In Guatemala, the land colonization program in El Peten has been subverted by the rush of speculators and generals to acquire properties whose value has escalated due to the exploitation of oil and nickel deposits in the region. At the same time, the CBI does not guarantee the kind of efficient, labor-intensive industrialization, capable of competing on the world market, that will be necessary to cope with the critical problem of unemployment. The provision of credit for new investments in plants and equipment favors capital-intensive, rather than labor-intensive, investments, when, indeed, it is the latter that the region most urgently needs. Large-scale U.S. economic penetration, moreover, could well lead to an anti-American backlash down the line. Finally, by placing its emphasis on industrialization and neglecting agriculture, the CBI is likely to intensify the crises in food production, urban migration, and unemployment. The pressures for emigration would accelerate at the very time that Congress is moving to restrict immigration into the United States.[11] The result could be the bottling-up of social tensions in the countries of their origin.

(2) DEMOGRAPHIC THEORY: THE POPULATION EXPLOSION

> Paddock: What is going to happen in Salvador?
> Westcott: Salvador is now striving to increase agricultural production by 3 percent. Even if it succeeds, which is doubtful, this is a losing battle because the population growth is probably over 4 percent.
> Paddock: Yes, but what is going to happen?
> Westcott: . . . Well, if you pin me down like that, it is, of course, obvious. There is going to be an explosion.[12]

Land usage or population growth? Clearly, both are major contributors to the Central American dilemma. Until recently, the conventional wisdom tended to stress the latter over the former. El Salvador was the classic example: As the most densely populated mainland country in the Western Hemisphere, with a rate of population growth averaging over 3.4 percent a year and a doubling time of about twenty years, it was widely regarded as a demographic disaster (see Tables 1.1 and 1.2). In the words of Paddock and Paddock: "One draws back in consternation, wondering how a nation, any nation, can keep from sinking into complete anarchy when, just to stand still, it must double all its facilities--power

TABLE 1.1

Population in Four Central American Countries

	El Salvador	Guatemala	Honduras	Nicaragua
Population[a]	4.9	7.0	3.2	3.2
Density[b]	590	190	78[d]	40
Rate of Growth[c]	2.9	3.0	3.4	3.4

Sources: Thomas P. Anderson, Politics in Central America (New York: Praeger, 1982), p. 3; World Bank, World Development Report 1982 (Oxford: Oxford University Press, 1982).

[a]In millions (1979)

[b]Inhabitants per square mile (1979)

[c]In percentages (1970-80)

[d]A cautionary note should be entered here, for statistics can be misleading. Thus, when one takes into account such factors as the amount of land under cultivation, the fertility of the soil, and the actual number of people engaged in agriculture, "underpopulated" Honduras turns out to be not all that much better off than "overpopulated" El Salvador. See William Durham, Scarcity and Survival in Central America (Stanford: Stanford University Press, 1979), pp. 102-110.

supply, housing, potable water, schools, medical facilities--in the next nineteen years."[13]

From the 1950s onward, El Salvador's "parabola of misery"[14] steadily worsened, as population growth persistently outran food supply. As agriculture expanded beyond the "carrying capacity" of the land, soils were depleted. The per capita land base for food crops steadily decreased. In an attempt to increase the amount of acreage under cultivation, more and more marginal lands were given over to food crops, leading one authority to conclude that "the area devoted to subsistence crops has virtually reached its absolute maximum and may . . . be expected to decline in the near future. Food crops are currently being cultivated on slopes which cannot withstand permanent cultivation. The productivity of such land, already marginal, will be destroyed within

TABLE 1.2

El Salvador: Population Growth

Year	Population	Rate of Growth[a]
1920	1,165,000	--
1950	1,855,917	1.3
1961	2,510,984	2.8
1971	3,554,648	3.4
1977	4,205,000[b]	3.1
2000	9,427,100[c]	3.4
	8,332,600[c]	3.0
	7,730,400[c]	2.7
	6,954,100[c]	2.4

Source: El Salvador: Demographic Issues and Prospects (Washington, D.C.: World Bank, 1979), pp. 1, 35.

[a]In percentages.

[b]Estimated by applying a 3.1 percent growth rate to the 1971 census population.

[c]Estimates based on the probable range of the growth rate, 1970-2000.

a few years."[15] Meanwhile, the quality of rural diets deteriorated, as sorghum, a crop that grew relatively well in such conditions, became an important human food. The rapid deforestation and erosion of the countryside, already widely in evidence in the 1940s, continued apace.
     This demographic growth had social and political consequences: Decreasing access to land led to a reduced capacity for survival. Malnutrition flourished. Peasants and agricultural laborers increasingly migrated to the San Salvador Metropolitan Area, where they swelled the ranks of the unemployed and underemployed and aggra- vated all of the problems of housing, education, medical care, and other social services already strained by the

TABLE 1.3

Population Growth in the San Salvador
Metropolitan Area

1950	1961	1971
213,363	352,299	564,967

Source: El Salvador: Demographic Issues and
Prospects (Washington, D.C.: World Bank,
1979, p. 52).

push toward industrialization (see Table 1.3). Among
other things, the resulting psychosocial stress contributed to the highest national homicide rate in the world.
Meanwhile, tens of thousands of peasants left the country
for Honduras in search of land and employment.

Thus was the stage set for the 1969 "futbol war"
between El Salvador and Honduras--and for the forcible
repatriatation of some 130,000 Salvadorans who were
driven back into their native land, aggravating all of
the socioeconomic conditions that were already paving the
way for the political unrest of the 1970s.

The question remains: What has been the relative
importance of population pressures vis-a-vis non-
Malthusian causes of resource scarcity? In a careful
statistical study of the Salvadoran problem, William
Durham clearly established that the population-food
production imbalance that developed in the 1950s and
1960s was not simply a consequence of agriculture
expanding to its physical limits: In fact, total agricultural production kept pretty much abreast with
population growth. Large increases in export production
occurred in the face of growing food shortages. In
essence, food crops "consistently lost out to more profitable export crops in the competition for land. . . .
Large expanses of fertile land have been converted to the
production of export crops at the expense of domestic
food production."[16]

More specifically, Durham calculated that

the effects of land concentration (the distribution
factor) have been greater than the effects of rapid
population growth . . . for a full 50.8 percent of
the agricultural population of El Salvador. For
these people, the hypothetical 1892 land base of
7.41 hectares shrank to an average of .38 hectare

or less by 1971--a 19.5-fold decrease in land availability. Distributional dynamics figured larger than population dynamics in that change by a ratio of 1.34:1 . . ., or more.[17]

In short, it was not so much rapid population growth that created land scarcity as it was the simultaneous trend toward land concentration. The population explosion was an important factor, but a secondary one. Distribution was a more crucial issue.

It is difficult to say whether the Durham thesis also holds for Guatemala, Nicaragua, and Honduras, since comparable studies have not been conducted. Although population growth rates in all three countries surpassed those of El Salvador in the 1970s, their densities remained far lower. (However, in the case of Honduras, at least, this is rather misleading, as is noted in Table 1.1.) In any case, it is impossible to calculate with precision the extent to which competitive exclusion or population growth stimulated the insurgencies of the late 1970s and early 1980s. The translation of objective socioeconomic conditions into rebellion is not automatic. One can merely hypothesize that here, too, increasing land concentration may have been the more potent factor. Peasants pushed off their lands through force or fraud would seem more likely candidates for revolutionary violence than those who were victims of the more subtle and impersonal forces of population pressure.

Finally, it is important to note that these civil wars have created important shifts in the locus of population growth--shifts that carry important implications, especially for those countries that have not yet experienced insurgencies. The issue here is not natural increase but migration. Hundreds of thousands of Salvadorans, Guatemalans, and Nicaraguans have fled their homelands, alleviating population pressures in the countries of their origin while aggravating them in the countries of their destination. Over 80,000 have thus far flocked to Mexico, 40,000 to Honduras, and 14,000 to Costa Rica. The continued flow of tens of thousands of highly politicized, alienated, and unassimilated foreigners into these countries, already plagued by severe socioeconomic problems, will severely strain local resources (housing, health, and educational facilities, employment opportunities, etc.) and may well become a major factor in spreading social and political unrest to these lands.

(3) PSYCHOECONOMIC THEORY: RELATIVE DEPRIVATION, RISING EXPECTATIONS, AND ECONOMIC CRISIS

" . . . [W]e know that revolutions . . . are caused not by social injustice . . . [b]ut by revolutionaries,

and revolutionaries are people. They are not social
forces; they are people with guns."
So says Jeane Kirkpatrick.[18] More realistically,
socioeconomic and political circumstances help shape the
motivations of revolutionaries and those who support them
and often serve as catalysts for rebellion. Over the
years, social scientists have attempted to construct an
integrated theory of political violence linking environ-
mental and psychological factors to behavior. Rooted in
classic frustration-aggression theory, this explanation
holds that obstructions to the satisfaction of basic
human drives (e.g., the need for food, shelter, security,
and self esteem) lead to frustration-induced tensions
that, in turn, are released through aggressive behavior.
Sometimes this aggression is internalized in the form of
self-inflicted violence (suicide, drug addiction, etc.);
sometimes it is directed against individuals or organizations perceived, rightly or wrongly, to be the source of
the resented deprivation; occasionally, it is translated
into political action in the form of turmoil, conspiracy,
or internal war. Whether one mode of violence or another
is chosen is largely a function of perceptions (and
misperceptions), anticipated gains, opportunities, and
fear of retribution. In general, however, the greater
the frustration, the greater the amount of aggression;
and the greater the intensity of deprivation, the greater
the magnitude of political violence.[19]
Yet, deprivation is a subjective as well as
objective phenomenon. As John Booth has noted: "Were
absolute deprivation or poverty alone the root of
rebellion, the world's poor and the poorest nations would
be constantly in revolt. . . . [T]hose who rebel are
seldom the most abjectly poor, and the nations with
turmoil are often those where there has been economic
growth. . . ."[20]
In short, it is "discontent arising from the
perception of relative deprivation" [emphases added] that
"is the basic, instigating condition for participants in
collective violence."[21] The gap between people's expectations, desires, and beliefs in terms of what they are
entitled to, on the one hand, and their perceived
circumstances and capabilities, on the other, is the
generator of revolutionary discontent. The larger the
gap, the greater the potential for revolt.
Thus, political rebellions are frequently preceded
by a "revolution of rising expectations," often borne of
economic growth and the spread of mass communications, in
which desires and expectations rise faster than they can
be satisfied. This in itself is enough to create
considerable frustration and discontent. But if such
circumstances are accompanied or followed by a decline in
the socioeconomic well-being of a substantial portion of
the population, the resultant skyrocketing relative

deprivation (RD) could set in motion aggressive behavior that may tear society apart. Moreover, even among those who have not experienced rising expectations, growing socioeconomic hardship will increase RD as the gap between traditionally modest expectations and the emerging unpleasant reality widens.

The most ambitious attempt to compare levels and effects of relative deprivation in various Central American countries is Booth's study, "Toward Explaining Regional Crisis in Central America: Socio-economic and Political Roots of Rebellion." Although his research is limited by incomplete data, he nevertheless assembles substantial evidence to support his contention that rapid socioeconomic change, especially since the mid-1970s, seriously undermined the living standards and economic interests of major segments of the Salvadoran, Nicaraguan, and Guatemalan populations, leading to growing frustration, anger, and mass mobilization. In large part, this was a product of the increasing economic inequality and hardship wrought by the competitive exclusion and population pressures discussed in preceding sections of this chapter. Beyond this, however, he examines trends in consumer prices, real wages, unemployment, employment as a percentage of national income, and government expenditures on human services to draw a more complex portrait of the nature of the deprivation. In turn, these trends are related to the increasing politicization of disadvantaged elements in the form of union organization, industrial disturbances, political demonstrations, and other forms of aggressive behavior. Although hard data on psychological states, perceptions, and opinions is unavailable, a fairly strong circumstantial case is made that substantive differences in RD levels account in significant part for the growing turmoil in Nicaragua, El Salvador, and Guatemala and the relative quiescence in Costa Rica and Honduras.

By traditional measures, Central American economies performed well in the three decades prior to the 1980s. Annual gross national products (GNPs) grew more than 5 percent a year; per capita income doubled; exports rose sixteen-fold.[22] Clearly, wealth was being created, and some people profited considerably. Under such circumstances, rising expectations were almost inevitable for those who benefited or hoped to. After 1973, however, these gains began to erode. The OPEC oil embargo and the subsequent rapid rise in oil prices led to an inflationary spiral that continued throughout the decade. In Guatemala, for instance, the average annual change in the consumer price index rose from .7 percent (1963-72) to 12.3 percent (1973-79) per annum. The comparable figures for Costa Rica were 2.6 and 12.2 percent. And the other three countries experienced similar increases (see Table 1.4). As a consequence, real wages

TABLE 1.4

Percent Change in Consumer Prices, 1963-79

Year	Costa Rica	El Salvador	Guatemala	Honduras	Nicaragua
1963	3.0	.9	.1	2.9	.8
1964	3.3	1.8	-0.2	4.6	9.6
1965	-0.7	0	-0.7	3.2	3.9
1966	0.2	-0.9	.6	.2	3.9
1967	1.1	1.8	.5	1.2	1.6
1968	4.0	1.8	1.8	2.6	3.1
1969	2.8	0	2.2	1.8	0
1970	4.6	2.6	2.4	2.9	5.9
1971	3.1	.3	-0.5	3.1	5.6
1972	4.6	1.7	.5	3.4	3.3[a]
1973	15.2	6.4	14.4	4.7	16.8[a]
1974	30.1	16.9	15.9	12.9	20.5[a]
1975	17.4	19.1	13.1	8.1	1.8
1976	3.5	7.0	10.7	5.0	2.9
1977	4.2	11.9	12.6	8.6	11.4
1978	6.0	13.3	7.9	5.7	4.6
1979	9.2	15.9	11.5	8.8	48.5

Source: James W. Wilkie and Stephen Haber, eds., Statistical
Abstract of Latin America (Los Angeles: University of
California Latin American Center Publications, 1981),
Tables 2605, 2608, 2609, 2611, 2613.

[a]Estimates based on Central Bank or other data. See John Booth,
The End and the Beginning: The Nicaraguan Revolution (Boulder,
Colo.: Westview Press, 1982), p. 79.

sharply declined. In El Salvador and Nicaragua, they
recovered somewhat around 1976, then continued their
plunge downward. By 1977, they had fallen 12 percent
from 1973 levels in the former and more than 29 percent
from 1967 levels in the latter. Meanwhile, in Guatemala,
erosion was steady--over 32 percent between 1972 and
1977. In contrast, though Honduras experienced a steep
decline (29 percent) between 1973 and 1974, by 1978 wages
had more than recovered their 1973 level. And in Costa
Rica, after a sharp drop between 1974 and 1975, they
quickly shot up 13 percent by 1977 over 1973 figures. In
Booth's words: "This contrast strongly suggests that
while relative deprivation based upon declining real
incomes among Nicaraguan, Salvadoran, and Guatemalan
workers probably intensified in the middle and late
1970s, in Costa Rica and in Honduras the workers'
recovery of their purchasing power . . . likely . . .
defused feelings of deprivation based upon diminishing
earning capacity."[23]

These trends were reinforced by growing
unemployment. The problem was particularly acute in El
Salvador and Nicaragua. In the former, about 25 percent
of the workforce was unemployed or underemployed by the
late 1970s.[24] In the latter, joblessness rose from 3.6
percent in 1971 to 20 percent in 1978. In contrast,
unemployment in Honduras was significantly lower and
comparatively stable, fluctuating between 6.9 and 9.4
percent from 1971 to 1978. Meanwhile, Costa Rican
unemployment remained low and stable, rising from 4.4
percent in 1976 to 4.6 percent in 1978.[25]

Again, these patterns must be placed within the
broader context of a growing shift of wealth away from
the lower classes toward the large landowning and
business sectors. As we have seen, increasing
landlessness and concentration of landownership were
major factors in El Salvador, Guatemala, and Nicaragua,
but of lesser significance in Honduras and Costa Rica.
At the same time, the available data on real wages,
unemployment, and employee compensation as percentages of
national income[26] suggest a serious deterioration in the
position of the working class in all countries except
Costa Rica and, to a lesser extent, Honduras (see Table
1.5). Clearly, some people were losing in relative
terms, some absolutely, and some both.

The resulting frustration and discontent had
behavioral consequences. Although it did not lead
directly to large guerrilla movements, it did produce new
strategies and forms of political, social, and economic
organization as part of a growing effort to mobilize
workers and peasants to redress their grievances.

As real wages declined, the number of industrial
disputes rose (see Figure 1.1). In Nicaragua, the long-
suppressed labor movement stepped up its organizational

TABLE 1.5

Real Working Class Wage Indices

Year	Costa Rica	El Salvador[a]	Guatemala[b]	Honduras[c]	Nicaragua[d]
1963	80	90	–	–	92
1967	–	105	112	–	137
1970	96	96	113	–	121
1971	107	94	115	–	119
1972	103	98	115	96	114
1973	100	100	100	100	100
1974	108	92	91	71	100
1975	91	90	84	82	106
1976	103	95	81	94	106
1977	113	88	78	88	97
1978	–	87	–	103	–

Source: John A. Booth, "Toward Explaining Regional Crisis in Central
America: The Socio-economic and Political Roots of
Rebellion" (paper presented to the 44th International
Congress of Americanists, Manchester, England,
September 6-10, 1982). Based on Wilkie and Haber, eds.,
Statistical Abstract, Tables 1400, 1401, 1402, 1403, and
consumer price-index data in Table 1.4 of this chapter.
Values of indices represent an unweighted average of wages
in manufacturing, construction, transport, storage and
communication, and agriculture, corrected for consumer
price changes.

[a]Includes agriculture (mean for men and women), manufacturing, and
construction only.

[b]Includes wages in manufacturing only.

[c]Includes wages in manufacturing and construction only.

[d]Includes wages in manufacturing, transportation, and construction.

18

FIGURE 1.1

Real Working-Class Wages Versus Number of Industrial Disputes:
Costa Rica, El Salvador, Guatemala

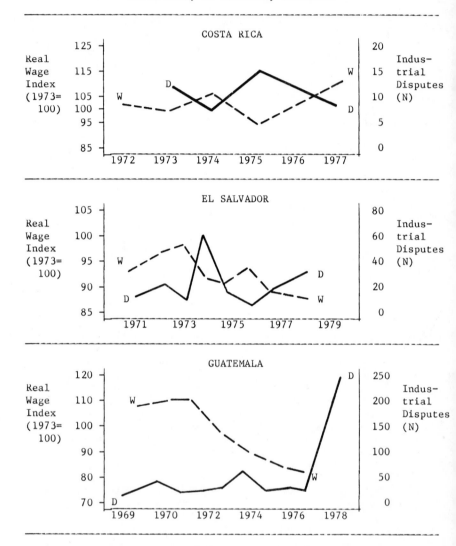

Source: John A. Booth, "Toward Explaining Regional Crisis in Central
          America: The Socio-economic and Political Roots of
          Rebellion" (paper presented to the 44th International
          Congress of Americanists, Manchester, England,
          September 6-10, 1982).
D = Industrial Disputes = _____
W = Real Wage Index   = - - - - - - - -

efforts: Strikes and work stoppages proliferated.
Catholic priests and social workers organized the rural
and urban poor into community self-help groups; peasant
unions began to gain momentum. Moreover, as many small
businesses and commercial jobs were wiped out by the 1972
Managua earthquake and inflation eroded middle-class
living standards, unionization and strike actions spread
to white-collar employees. The beneficiaries of the
economic growth of the 1960s now began to join the
disadvantaged in protesting their economic decline. Even
the bourgeoisie--increasingly disturbed by the Somoza
regime's corruption and the growing political and labor
unrest--began to desert the dynasty and call for reforms.
    Similarly, in El Salvador, industrial conflicts rose
dramatically in 1974 as real wages plunged, ebbed in
1975-76 as wages momentarily improved, then escalated
rapidly in 1977-78 as wages dropped once again. In the
process, labor organizations grew in size and militance.
Illegal peasant unions aggressively pressed for land
reforms and higher agricultural wages. Christian base
communities organized the poor in urban and rural areas.
By the late 1970s, mass organizations, mobilizing tens of
thousands of disenchanted peasants, workers, teachers,
students, and professionals, were rapidly radicalizing
the Salvadoran political scene. Between 1977 and 1979,
these groups engaged in widespread civil disobedience,
demonstrations, and takeovers of government buildings,
churches, and foreign embassies in order to dramatize
their demands.
    Guatemala, too, experienced a marked growth of labor
and peasant unrest, though mobilization there lagged
somewhat behind developments in Nicaragua and El
Salvador. Again, a sharp decline in real wages spurred
unionization and gave rise to a substantial increase in
industrial disputes in 1973-74. Moreover, in 1976, a
devastating earthquake caused severe damage to lower-
class housing and led slumdwellers to form confederations
that pressed the government for assistance and initiated
a transport strike in 1978. Here, too, Catholic religious workers played a major role in rural areas in mobilizing the traditionally passive and fatalistic Indian
masses into cooperatives and other bodies through which
they could assert themselves in pursuit of their economic
interests. By the latter part of the decade, the Indians
were organizing politically as well. In 1978, a
Committee for Peasant Unity was formed that two years
later led a successful strike for higher wages by some
75,000 sugar cane workers. After years of suppression,
the labor movement burst forth in 1978 with over 200
industrial disputes.
    In short, there is substantial evidence that growing
relative socioeconomic deprivation led to a dramatic
increase in lower-class mobilization and politicization

in the 1970s. It did not in itself create full-scale insurgencies. Though low-level guerrilla wars simmered in all three countries, other catalysts would be required before these nascent movements would be transformed into major threats. Thus RD, as we have here defined it, was only one element in the equation—a necessary but not sufficient condition for revolution. This was but the initial stage in a process.

And what of Costa Rica and Honduras? Again, the contrast was striking. Although neither country was free from mass mobilizations, strikes, and other forms of labor turmoil, the levels of disturbance were much lower than elsewhere. In the former, militance was largely diffused by the proletariat's success in winning higher wages. In Costa Rica, wealth filtered down to the masses to a degree unprecedented in Central American societies. In large part, this was the product of a democratic social welfare system and prosperity generated by high international coffee prices. As for Honduras, though considerable mobilization occurred among peasants and within the large and powerful union movement, discontent was contained relatively well by a modest land reform and the proletariat's recovery of much of the earning power it had lost between 1973 and 1974 (see Table 1.5).

Finally, it is necessary to note that, since the outbreak of revolutionary turmoil in the late 1970s, economic conditions have worsened considerably. In 1982, gross national products decreased in all five of the Central American countries considered in this chapter (see Table 1.6). The causes were multiple and, in part, interrelated: Hence, the 1979 increase in the price of oil imports was accompanied by a decline in the international price of coffee and other Central American exports, which in combination led to increased overseas borrowing at high interest rates these countries could ill afford. The financial crisis, moreover, was compounded by a massive outflow of foreign capital as investors fleeing growing political chaos sought to transfer their wealth to more secure havens. In response to pressures from the IMF and other lenders, governments were forced to impose stringent austerity measures as the price for renegotiating their debts. Meanwhile, guerrilla economic sabotage aggravated the decline of the Salvadoran, Guatemalan, and (more recently) Nicaraguan economies.

The upshot has been rapidly escalating socioeconomic deprivation, growing frustration and discontent, and the continuing spread of political violence. Clearly, there are elements of a self-perpetuating process in all this. The economic crisis has structured RD into these societies in such a way as to reinforce the revolutionary conditions this deprivation helped create in the first place. In turn, political violence has worsened the

TABLE 1.6

Decline in Growth of Central American Gross
National Product, 1977-82 (In percentages)

	1977	1978	1979	1980	1981	1982
Costa Rica •	8.9	6.3	4.9	.6	-3.6	-5.9
Guatemala	6.8	5.0	4.7	3.5	1.0	-3.5
El Salvador	6.1	3.9	-1.5	-9.6	-9.5	-1.0
Honduras	8.7	7.0	6.6	2.6	0.3	-1.4
Nicaragua	0.9	-5.4	-25.9	10.0	9.0	-2.5

Sources: Statistics compiled by Douglas H. Graham from
          World Bank and Interamerican Development Bank
          sources and Economic Report of the President
          (1983). See Chapter 5, Table 5.1 in this text.

economic situation by deterring investments, stimulating
capital flight, and otherwise disrupting the stability
needed to foster economic growth. The process is more
advanced in El Salvador and Guatemala than in Honduras
and Costa Rica. In Nicaragua, it has come full circle,
so that rising RD has become an important factor in the
growth of counterrevolutionary opposition to the
Sandinista regime.

(4) THE THEORY OF POLITICAL DEVELOPMENT: STRUCTURAL
     PETRIFICATION AND POLITICAL DECAY

     Economic growth often leads to destabilizing
results. The kind of "development" pursued in Central
America during the 1950s-1970s was especially disruptive
because it impacted negatively on a substantial portion
of the populace, heightening inequalities and margina-
lizing sectors of the work force, which in turn no longer
had a raison d'etre in terms of the economic systems that
were emerging. But there were other respects, also, in
which growth was disruptive. As Mancur Olson has argued,
winners, too, can be a destabilizing force.[27] For some,
appetites and expectations are whetted beyond any
possibility of satisfaction; others, though gaining in
absolute terms, become anguished when their relative
position erodes vis-a-vis that of more rapidly advancing

neighbors. Perhaps most important in the Central American context, economic growth and industrialization gave rise to new socioeconomic groups—in particular, a middle class and urban and rural proletariats—that for the first time began making demands on the political structures of the Old Order. At that point, the critical question became one of how those structures would respond. On the one hand, they could attempt to co-opt these new actors, thus initiating a process of political evolution through the "creation of political institutions sufficiently adaptable, complex, autonomous and coherent to absorb and to order the participation of these new groups and to promote social and economic change in the society."[28] On the other, they could respond with repression, in effect seeking to deny change by paralyzing or destroying all current and potential sources of opposition.

The distinction is between political development and political decay, the suggestion being that, without the former, socio-economic modernization tends to produce political disintegration. Central America is a classic case. Most of these societies were little more than "living museums"—petrified polities governed by political dinosaurs whose mode of rule would have been more appropriate to the nineteenth century than the 1970s. The traditional rules of the political game permitted change, but only in a very limited sense—namely, that which did not threaten the position of established elites. New actors were admitted to the arena of reciprocally recognized elites, provided they were willing to abide by this basic principle and could demonstrate a significant power capability.[29] In the 1960s and 1970s, however, co-optation began to break down. Under pressures generated by economic development, there was a marked rise in elite-challenging behavior by labor unions, rural cooperatives, Catholic base communities, opposition political parties, and other organizations representing the growing and increasingly politicized middle and lower classes. The threat posed by these groups cannot be overstated: Civilian political parties endangered the military's traditional dominance of the political arena. Labor unions and rural co-ops threatened (by their demands for higher wages and agrarian reform) the economic base of both traditional oligarchs and modernizing industrialists. Rather than adapting to these inputs (or demonstrations of power capability) with structural reforms, Central American elites and institutions remained inflexible. Structural petrification, reinforced by official and semi-official violence, effectively denied these newly emerging social forces access to the political system. The consequence was a monumental crisis of legitimacy, with growing numbers of the politically alienated choosing to opt out

of the system and pursue change through alternative
structures and strategies.

In El Salvador, Guatemala, and Nicaragua,
continuismo was especially blatant. Thus, in the 1972
Salvadoran presidential elections, the apparent victory
of the Christian Democratic reform candidate, Jose
Napoleon Duarte, was annulled by the simple expedient of
halting the broadcast of election returns; the next day,
it was announced that the government candidate had won.
Two years later, in Guatemala, a Christian Democrat-
backed coalition rallied around a centrist military
officer, Efrain Rios Montt, who proceeded to win the
balloting only to be barred from power by more conservative colleagues. (Subsequent elections in both
countries were marked by flagrant fraud, thus ensuring
continued political domination by the military.)
Meanwhile, in Nicaragua, Anastasio Somoza had decided
that one term in the presidency was not enough. Though
the constitution forbade him from continuing in office, a
tortuous political arrangement, including the temporary
handing over of "power" to a triumvirate of liberals and
conservatives and the amendment and subsequent rewriting
of the constitution, enabled him to reemerge as president
in 1974, with a term formally scheduled to last until
1981. (This was to become a "matter of principle" to
Somoza during his last desperate months in power, when he
refused to resign under mounting pressure, since he was,
after all, "constitutional" president.)

Each of these countries would experience major labor
unrest, massive government violence, and full-scale
insurgencies in the late 1970s and early 1980s. In
contrast, neighboring Honduras would remain relatively
stable. (This notwithstanding chronic golpes, which are
less a sign of instability than that of "business as
usual.")[30] As of this writing, guerrilla activity has
been minimal. In part, this quiescence may be attributed
to a greater flexibility on the part of Honduran elites.
A modest land reform was implemented in the mid-1970s.
Democratic elections were held in late 1981. Government
repression has been comparatively restrained. Finally,
often overlooked is the fact that Honduras is the
poorest, least economically developed country in Central
America. Such development as has occurred has yet to
produce the kind of massively destabilizing socioeconomic
changes witnessed in El Salvador, Guatemala, and
Nicaragua.

(5) ELITES AND INTEREST GROUPS: LIBERATION THEOLOGIANS,
     REACTIONARY DESPOTS, AND REVOLUTIONARY ZEALOTS

     Still another focus of attention has been on the
elites and interest groups in conflict. Here one must

stress the importance of leadership and organization.
Revolutions are rarely made spontaneously, through mass
uprisings. Most frequently, disenchanted elements from
the bourgeoisie or petit bourgeoisie become declasse and
provide the intellectual, inspirational, and organizational guidance necessary to mobilize traditionally
fatalistic and passive lower classes behind the revolutionary cause. This is not, of course, to suggest that
leaders do not sometimes emerge from the peasantry and
proletariat--Salvador Cayetano Carpio is an obvious
example--but that these are the exceptions, rather than
the rule. Indeed, Gabriel Zaid has gone so far as to
argue that the Salvadoran conflict is essentially a
struggle between elites: "Those on top cannot agree on
how to treat those on the bottom: This is the conflict,
in which those on the bottom are both subject and
victims.³¹

There is much truth in Zaid's remark, though like
most generalizations about the Central American tragedy,
it should not be pushed too far. It is too easy for
partisans (or cynics) to reduce the issues to a mere
struggle for power in which one side or the other (or
both) terrorizes and manipulates the populace for its own
ends. Although such interpretations may capture an
essential part of these conflicts, they often over-
simplify a more complex reality. Neither revolutionary
nor counterrevolutionary coalitions are monolithic, and
in the cases of El Salvador and Nicaragua, they encompass
a wide variety of political opinions. (In the former,
for instance, social democrats coexist uneasily with
Marxist-Leninists and Christian Democrats with fascists.)
Motives are diverse and often mixed: Some play the game
for power or spoils; others pursue the communist utopia;
still others believe in democracy and/or social reform.
Moreover, if violence is widely employed by both sides,
it is equally true that hundreds of thousands of
Salvadorans, Guatemalans, and Nicaraguans align themselves with one camp or the other voluntarily, sometimes
with fervor. Contrary to assertions by the Reagan
administration, the Salvadoran and Guatemalan guerrillas
are not without popular support. Nor, for that matter,
are the regimes they are fighting--which is one reason
they have not yet been overthrown.

It has often been argued that these revolutions are
largely the products of the rise of modernizing groups
and their challenge to the traditional order. Industrial
bourgeoisies, middle-class Christian Democrats, labor and
student movements have all played significant roles.³²
Just as important, however, have been the changes that
have occurred within the traditional establishment--most
notably, within the Roman Catholic Church.

The 1960s witnessed a veritable revolution in the
Church. Whereas previously it had almost everywhere been

allied with existing regimes, Vatican II (1962-65), strongly influenced by the social encyclicals of Pope John XXIII, produced a marked shift in both doctrine and behavior. Thus, in 1968, the Latin American bishops convened their Second Episcopal Conference (CELAM II) in Medellin, Colombia, in what has been called "one of the major political events of the century," a meeting that "shattered the centuries-old alliance of church, military, and the rich elites."[33] From this point on, the clergy would make a "preferential option for the poor" and seek to defend the rights of the oppressed through Christian base communities (comunidades de base).

In Chapter 4 of this text, Penny Lernoux has described the deep divisions these changes brought within the Church. For our purposes, it is enough to note that the "consciousness-raising" educational activities of the comunidades had a profound socializing effect on their membership. Self-esteem rose markedly; fatalism and passivity disappeared, as peasants began participating in and accepting responsibility for decisions in major areas of their lives where they had previously exercised little control. Moreover, religious and social actions quickly spilled over into the economic and political sectors: Unions were formed and strikes and demonstrations waged, as the poor organized to defend their interests in the face of the increasingly debilitating effects of "competitive exclusion," rampant unemployment, and subsistence wages. In turn, the oligarchy and the military, perceiving (quite accurately) that this grass-roots movement constituted a major threat to their power and interests, responded with massive violence: Dozens of priests and nuns and hundreds of lay preachers were assassinated, as the reactionary coalition sought to behead the monster before it was too late.

And what was the nature of the elite system with which these reformers came into conflict? Baloyra has termed it "reactionary despotism": an alliance of agriculture sector capitalists and military officers whose primary objective has been the "preservation of privilege. This includes a historical monopoly of public roles and of the entrepreneurial function, which makes them question the legitimacy and advisability of allowing others to share in these functions whether in the public or private spheres."[34] The coalition arose in the 1930s in an attempt to prevent the victory of nationalist or populist alliances, which might have promoted the evolution of democracy by checking arbitrary rulers, replacing arbitrary rules with just and rational ones, and allowing the masses to share in the making of the latter.[35] The coalition's nature is best illustrated by its reaction to the demands of the newly emerging sectors:

This is not merely a question of whether the
government should not bend too much in the direction
of unions, spend too much on welfare, conduct public
policy in demagogic terms to attract votes, or try
to push taxes beyond reasonable limits. This is
normally the complaint agenda of loyal conservatives
who accept the suffrage and are willing to use the
power of the private sector to defend themselves and
countervail the power of the mass electorate, acting
through responsible institutions. The dominant
actors of the reactionary coalitions of Central
America do not believe in the suffrage, . . . in
paying taxes, . . . in acting through responsible
institutions when they perceive defeat. Their basic
premise is that the government should exist to
protect them from other social groups in order to
continue to accumulate capital without the
restraints created by labor unions, competition,
and government regulation. In short, they demand
total deference to their version of the capitalist
system.

More specifically, the "core elements" of the
reactionary coalition" include:

the largest agricultural planters who monopolize
the control of the sectoral associations, cattle
ranchers, large merchants with linkages to
agricultural interests, financiers and bankers whose
main creditors or "factors" are engaged in the
export trade and in real estate speculation, former
government officials and retired military officers
who have embezzled public resources, and individuals
connected to the repression of opposition elements
either in an official or in a paramilitary
capacity.[36]

These are the elements who have the most to lose
from any transition to democracy. Though they have not
always directly controlled the government, they have
until recently exercised at least veto power in
Nicaragua, El Salvador, and Guatemala. Although original
oligarchies have splintered, the industrial bourgeoisies
that emerged never gained enough leverage to successfully
challenge the older groups. Thus, they remained
peripheral, rather than core actors in the "living
museum." The capitalist state was maintained
"unreformed." Whenever a democratic transition appeared
to be paving the way for a more enlightened version of
capitalism, the core reactionaries blocked the process
through "hysterical campaigns, threats to repatriate
capital, conspiracies and, in the case of Guatemala

a generation ago and of El Salvador today, counter-revolution.[37]

The precise nature of the coalition varied from country to country. In Nicaragua, it was much smaller and less stable than elsewhere. The inability or unwillingness of other economic elites to challenge the political hegemony of the Somoza clan relegated them to a subordinate position in what was essentially a personalistic and patrimonial form of despotism. There, as well as in El Salvador, the military served as a junior partner and guarantor of the oligarchy. In Salvador, however, the power of the officers was greater: They dominated the political arena through their "official" party and their control of the presidency. From time to time, modernizing elements even introduced modest reforms in the face of oligarchical opposition. None of this, however, fundamentally changed the system. When an "agrarian transformation" was attempted in the mid-1970s, the oligarchy still had enough influence to effect, in league with the most conservative elements in the military, a reactionary restoration (albeit an unstable and temporary one).[39]

But it was in Guatemala that the ideal of reactionary despotism came closest to finding its real-world counterpart. There the military became the senior partner in the ruling coalition. Whereas in El Salvador officers were comparatively discrete in their corruption, their Guatemalan counterparts used gangster-like violence and rampant illegality to enrich themselves. The decade of the 1970s witnessed the creation of a materialistic "order of the samurai" in which the most influential military leaders also became the economic leaders of the country. In the process, numerous fortunes were made, as officers seized lands and manipulated "development" projects in the Northern Transversal Strip and the Peten. Dozens of military-dominated, semi-autonomous state institutions were set up, as the army invaded spheres of activity traditionally reserved for civilians.[39]

Given the above alignment of reformist and reactionary elites and interest groups and the fundamental incompatibility of their values and interests, it should not be surprising that growing mobilization of the masses would be met with large scale and often indiscriminate repression. In the process, the Central American militaries, traditional guardians of stability, would themselves become major sources of destabilization.

(6) THE THEORY OF PROCESS: REFORM, REPRESSION, AND THE
     DIALECTIC OF REVOLUTION

Central American societies are sorely in need of structural reforms. Yet, it is quite another matter to

argue--as is often done in both government and academic
circles--that such programs are the key to peaceful
change. Revolutions, it is said, can be avoided, if only
we can win the "hearts and minds" of the people through
agrarian reform and other measures, thus undercutting the
guerrillas' appeal to the masses.

The evidence to date is far from reassuring. The
experience of countries like Nicaragua, Guatemala, and El
Salvador suggests that attempts to introduce such change
into highly rigid, violence-prone political systems are
as likely as not to have repressive and destabilizing
consequences. Clearly, it is not enough to appreciate
the socioeconomic and political preconditions of
revolution; there is also a dynamic element involved.
Revolution is a process involving an extended sequence of
actions and reactions, a "dialectic" of threat and
retaliation: Thus, pressures for reform (for the most
part, nonviolent ones) give rise to resistance (often
violent) on the part of those supporting the status quo.
Conservative obstruction and repression, in turn,
radicalize the proponents of reform, who increasingly opt
out of the system, frequently to seek power through the
barrel of a gun. The portrait is one of self-
intensifying and mutually destructive violence:
Revolutionary terror heightens counterrevolutionary
repression, which further radicalizes the opposition,
driving a growing number of moderates and uncommitted
into the arms of the extreme left. The dialectic
continues, gaining a life of its own, increasingly
polarizing society until one side is able to muster
enough effective coercion to disable or destroy the
other. Within the context of the previously-discussed
theories, this process may be viewed schematically in
terms of the stages indicated in Table 1.7.

Although this model, like all ideal types, over-
simplifies a more complex and subtle reality, something
of this nature has clearly taken place: "As the political spectrum broadened and the impact of new ideologies
and the labor movement . . . began to be felt, the far
right introduced the strategy of polarization."[40] The
handmaiden of polarization was terror. By attempting to
destroy or paralyze the opposition through indiscriminate
violence, these regimes enormously increased relative
deprivation (defined here in political terms) as they
transformed themselves into direct threats to their
citizens' security. The consequences were predictable:
Reform movements were turned into full-scale insurrec-
tions.

In Nicaragua, the process developed to its logical
conclusion, with one side decisively triumphing over the
other. The origins may be traced back to the earthquake
that devastated Managua in 1972. In response to the
rampant corruption that followed, both moderates and

TABLE 1.7

The Dialectic of Revolution

Stage I	Stage II	Stage III	Stage IV	Stage V	Stage VI
Increasing RD generated by development-induced poverty, rising expectations, population pressures, and economic crises	Socioeconomic and political mobilization and pressure for reform	Conservative obstruction and repression	Escalating RD (political as well as socio-economic) leading to growing frustration, radicalization, and revolutionary violence	Heightened counter-revolutionary violence	An ongoing process culminating in the eventual victory of either revolutionary or counter-revolutionary forces

radicals stepped up their opposition to the Somoza
regime. In December 1974, the editor of La Prensa, Pedro
Joaquin Chamorro, organized a number of opposition
parties and labor confederations into the Democratic
Liberation Union (UDEL). That same month, the Sandinista
National Liberation Front (FSLN) raided an elite
Christmas party in the capital, capturing and successfully holding for ransom a dozen of the country's most
prominent business and political leaders. In retaliation, the regime launched a war of extermination,
creating a virtual reign of terror in Zelaya, Matagalpa,
and Segovia. In the words of William LeoGrande: "For
two years, peasants in those areas were subjected to a
systematic campaign of torture and mass execution. To
deprive the FSLN of support, eighty percent of the rural
population was uprooted and herded into resettlement
camps. The countryside then became a free-fire zone."[41]
    This was only the beginning. Massive human rights
abuses led to widespread domestic and international
condemnation. Organizations originally created to pursue
narrow economist goals--higher wages, better working
conditions, and so forth--became increasingly radicalized. U.S. pressure on Somoza to lift the state of
siege, including restrictions on military and economic
aid, only emboldened the opposition, paving the way for a
broad anti-government alliance. In October 1977 the FSLN
reappeared, launching small-scale attacks throughout the
country. At the same time, "The Twelve," a group of
respected business, professional, and religious leaders,
praised the Sandinistas as a legitimate political force
that would have to be included in any solution to the
crisis.
    In response to this growing resistance, the regime
made a fatal mistake: In January 1978, Pedro Joaquin
Chamorro was assassinated. This was the spark that
provided the opposition with a broad mass base. The
nation erupted in a wave of spontaneous riots.
Nicaraguan business leaders called a general strike,
demanding Somoza's resignation. But the government was
still far too strong to be toppled; it countered with
massive repression. In the department of Chontales, over
350 peasant families were killed in a period of two
months. In Monimbo, an Indian barrio in Masaya, National
Guard violence ignited a full-scale insurrection. In
response, the Guard devastated the neighborhood; hundreds
were killed, arrested, or "disappeared."
    The next round in the dialectic occurred the
following August. In a daring assault on the National
Palace when congress was in session, the Sandinistas took
over 1,500 hostages. The dramatic move caught the imagi-
nation of the nation. Thousands lined the streets to
cheer the triumphant commandos as they left the country
on a safe passage, along with several dozen released

political prisoners. Another general strike followed.
When the FSLN launched another series of attacks, mass
uprisings were sparked in over half a dozen cities.
Again, the National Guard retaliated with massive
violence. To "save" cities from the rebels, it was
necessary to destroy whole neighborhoods. In the
process, some 3,000 to 5,000 people were killed. When
the guerrillas withdrew, they took with them thousands of
new recruits.

The climax of this process came in June-July 1979,
with the launching of the Sandinistas' final offensive
and the collapse of the Somoza regime. In less than a
year, FSLN forces had increased about five-fold, largely
in response to the indiscriminate repression of the
National Guard and the growing public perception that
momentum was on the guerrillas' side. The revolution was
triumphant, but at a terrible cost: Some 50,000 people
had been killed and another 100,000 wounded; one-fifth of
the population had been left homeless and a third of the
workforce unemployed. This in a country of only 2.5
million people. (A comparable death toll in the United
States would be 5 million.)

In contrast to Nicaragua, the revolutionary processes in El Salvador and Guatemala have not yet been
resolved. In the former, the origins of the dialectic
may be traced back to the political and labor turmoil of
the late 1960s to early 1970s. Even before the 1972
electoral fraud, the first insurgent organizations were
being formed. Simultaneously, Catholic and Christian
Democratic activists encouraged the creation of agricultural labor unions and Christian base communities. By
the mid-1970s, the continuing frustration of reform and
increasing government and paramilitary repression led to
an unprecedented proliferation and alliance of militant
opposition groups. Guerrilla bands conducted sporadic
acts of terrorism. Mass organizations, encompassing tens
of thousands of union members, pressed their demands with
growing fervor. In turn, right-wing "death squads"
launched a wave of assassinations, with the progressive
clergy becoming a major target. As in Nicaragua, the
dialectic acquired a momentum of its own. The ranks of
both extreme left and extreme right swelled;
increasingly, they vied with one another to see who could
conduct the most spectacular acts of violence.
Ultimately, this growing chaos culminated in the collapse
of the Romero dictatorship in October 1979.

But the overthrow of the ancien regime did not end
the process; indeed, it intensified it. In the weeks
that followed, both left and right systematically sought
to undermine the new reform junta through competitive
acts of revolutionary and counterrevolutionary terror.
The tactic worked. Within a few weeks the junta
collapsed. A second was formed, but shortly that also

disintegrated, as growing numbers of moderates and
leftists fled the regime in protest against the violence
being waged by its security forces. Still, the dialectic
continued. With the initiation of a sweeping land reform
in spring 1980, the military and security agencies
sharply escalated the repression. In turn, terror was
met by terror. Month after month, the process gained
momentum, as the guerrillas, now semi-unified in the
Farabundo Marti National Liberation Front (FMLN), began
the drive toward their "final offensive."

That assault came in January 1981, and it failed
miserably. The insurgents had greatly overestimated
their popular support, while underestimating the strength
of government forces. Since then the violence, though
fluctuating considerably, has generally declined.
Although estimates vary from source to source, all
suggest that the number of civilians killed in 1982 was
substantially less than in the previous year. The Reagan
administration has attributed this decline to its human
rights policy, but other factors are clearly more important. For one thing, the kind of massive demonstrations
that wracked San Salvador in the late 1970s and 1980 are
now a thing of the past. The human costs (in terms of
government repression) became prohibitive. As a consequence, the opposition shifted the struggle away from
the cities to the countryside where civilian supporters
were easier to protect. Since January 1981, moreover,
the guerrillas have chosen to concentrate on economic
sabotage, rather than engage in grandiose general offensives against forces vastly better armed than their own.
Finally--and perhaps most important--there has been the
serious demoralization and decay of the Salvadoran military. Government offensives, a major cause of civilian
casualties, have become infrequent. The army seems far
more intent on <u>avoiding</u> the insurgents than combatting
them. Thus, for instance, when the latter seized the
strategic city of Berlin in Usulatan department in
February 1983, some 6,000 of the government's best troops
were taking a stroll in Morazan, to the northeast.
Civilian casualties have indeed declined, but for reasons
having little to do with any enhanced respect for human
rights.

But though the momentum of the dialectic has ebbed,
the process continues and the death toll remains high--
over 5,000 in 1982, according to the Roman Catholic
Archdiocese. At this writing, the military situation
continues to deteriorate. The army is increasingly
factionalized and demoralized, and the economy remains in
decline. Under such circumstances, the long-range
outlook is not in the government's favor. It is a
primary tenet of guerrilla warfare that if the insurgents
do not lose they will eventually win. Barring a negotiated settlement, the conflict may be expected to heat

up again. By the same token, should the military regain
the initiative--and U.S. advisers are pressing it to do
just that--one may anticipate a major reescalation of the
bloodshed. If the extreme right emerges triumphant in
the power struggle currently underway in the armed forces
and goes on to win the elections scheduled for March
1984, civilian casualties will be maximized.

In Guatemala, by contrast, the military advantage
clearly rests with the government, at least in the short
run. Nevertheless, the roots of the revolutionary
process run long and deep, extending all the way back to
the 1954 CIA-directed overthrow of the democratically
elected reform government of Jacobo Arbenz. Since then,
the country has never been the same.

Thus, the Arbenz-Arevalo reforms were abruptly
cancelled and a military dictatorship imposed, which,
over the past three decades, has been responsible for the
deaths of tens of thousands of Guatemalans. In the
1960s, this action-reaction process led to a full-scale
guerrilla war. The response by the extreme right was
swift and devastating: Vigilante bands were formed and
joined the military in a massive campaign of extermination. Secret societies, paramilitary organizations,
and death lists proliferated. Targets included
unionists, student leaders, and center-left politicians,
as well as the guerrillas and suspected peasant sympathizers. Violence led to counterviolence in extended
sequence, with the government--assisted by death squads
and U.S. military advisers--eventually prevailing. All
in all, some 3,000 to 8,000 people are believed to have
died in the Zacapa-Izabal counterinsurgency campaign of
1966-68.

Yet, even then, the dialectic did not cease. The
late 1970s produced still another round: Deteriorating
real wages, growing economic inequality, and increasing
frustration on the part of the political opposition led
to renewed mass mobilization. Waves of strikes occurred;
the center-left opposition began to organize a reform
coalition in preparation for the 1982 elections. In
response, the government unleashed a massive wave of
terror. Hundreds of Christian Democratic politicians,
union leaders, university students, and faculty were
assassinated. In the countryside, repeated massacres of
the Indian population--especially those who participated
in rural cooperative, literacy, health, and other
development programs or who protested being pushed off
their land--systematically sought to destroy all sources
of actual and potential opposition. The result was to
drive many of the survivors into the arms of what had
previously been a very small and ineffective guerrilla
movement.

Hence, the reappearance of a major insurgency in the
early 1980s. Only with the overthrow of Lucas Garcia and

his replacement by Efrain Rios Montt in March 1982 was
the tide reversed. In the months that followed, Rios
Montt brought urban violence under control by reorgan-
izing the national police detective corps, which had
been responsible for many of the killings, and prohibiting anyone but uniformed security forces from carrying
weapons. The activities of the death squads immediately
stopped. The public reaction, as clearly reflected in my
extensive summer 1982 conversations with several dozen
Guatemala City residents from all walks of life, was a
collective sigh of relief, tempered only by an occasional
expression of fear about what was going on in the
countryside. There, a carrot-stick strategy combining
massive terror (including "scorched earth" tactics
against selected villages) with a civic action and self-
defense program ("fusiles y frijoles") was enjoying
considerable success in intimidating or winning over
Indians who had previously been either sympathetic to the
guerrillas or neutral. Again, the human costs were
considerable: According to Amnesty International, 2,600
Indians were killed in the first half year of Rios
Montt's rule. Since then, the killings in the countryside have continued at rates comparable to those of the
preceding period.[42]
    Whether the military has permanently turned the tide
or the successes of the past year and a half are only
temporary is impossible to say with certainty. What
remains clear is that the guerrillas have not yet been
defeated. Although their clandestine support organizations have been hard hit, they have reportedly lost few
combatants. The socioeconomic and political conditions
that gave rise to the insurgency remain unchanged. And
the loyalty of those Indians who have been forcibly
dragooned into government self-defense patrols is highly
suspect. In short, though the dialectic has been rather
one-sided during Rios Montt's first year in power, there
is reason to believe that the revolutionary process is
far from over. [In August 1983, Rios Montt was
overthrown by his Minister of Defense, General Mejia
Victores; there followed a marked resurgence of urban
death squad activities.]
    And what of Honduras? Has a comparable revolu-
tionary process already begun? At this writing,
increased acts of guerrilla terrorism are producing
growing military and paramilitary repression. "The practice of arresting individuals for political reasons and
then refusing to acknowledge their whereabouts and status
seems to have become established," reported Americas
Watch in late 1982. Since January 1981, some forty-six
Hondurans and fifty non-Hondurans had been abducted in
this fashion. A few subsequently reappeared and left the
country; others were found dead; most simply
"disappeared." Moreover, the situation was rapidly

growing worse: Thirty-one of the forty-six Honduran
victims had been seized after the inauguration of a
civilian government in January 1982.[43] During 1983, the
repression continued apace.
Though the revolutionary process has just begun, the
signs are ominous. In the past, the Honduran military
has been relatively restrained in its use of violence--
compared, that is, to its counterparts in Nicaragua, El
Salvador, and Guatemala. But the Honduran social structure is now being seriously strained by the same economic
crises that have ravaged its neighbors. And the very
fact that the government has been at least formally
returned to civilian hands has, ironically enough, aggravated the situation by raising expectations that are
unlikely to be fulfilled. The result has been growing
disillusionment and unrest. Nor are matters helped by
the continuing hegemonic role of the military, encouraged
as it is by the Reagan administration's attempts to
transform Honduras into an anti-communist military
bastion. The power of the civilian president remains
acutely limited. General Alvarez has established himself
as the effective caudillo. And he is by temperament
bellicose with regard to security matters, both domestic
and regional. Indeed, some of the recent guerrilla
activity in Honduras has been instigated from abroad in
retaliation for Honduran military operations in El
Salvador and Honduran-based counterrevolutionary attacks
into Nicaragua. Should war break out between Managua and
Tegucigalpa, one may anticipate a serious worsening of
the domestic security problem.

(7)   THE DOMINO THEORY: FOREIGN COMMUNIST AGGRESSION
      OR MUTUAL ESCALATION?

    Not since Vietnam has the domino theory been debated
with as much intensity as it is being debated today.
High government officials have defended it in
congressional hearings. A State Department "White Paper"
and documents allegedly captured from the Salvadoran
guerrillas have been widely publicized in an attempt to
demonstrate the existence of a "textbook case of indirect
armed aggression by communist powers through Cuba."[44]
Should El Salvador fall, it is argued, Guatemala will be
next. Then Honduras, Costa Rica, Panama, Mexico, and so
on until the United States' southern flank becomes a
veritable sea of hostile regimes allied with the Soviet
Union and Cuba and endangering U.S. security.
    Like the debate of two decades past, the current
argument has generated more heat than clarity. Critics
were quick to discount the White Paper as grievously
flawed. Not only was it said to distort the basic causes
of the Central American turmoil, but the "captured

documents" presented in support of the administration's
case were themselves highly suspect. Even if authentic--
and some suggested that they might be doctored or
forged--they were inconclusive. In some instances, they
had been attributed to authors who clearly did not write
them; in others, there had been significant mistransla-
tions; in still others, administration statistics on arms
traffic, supposedly drawn directly from the documents,
had been extrapolated in dubious ways. The State
Department, moreover, had released only those materials
that supported its position; those that did not were
studiously ignored. When the department's Jon Glassman,
who had been given the major credit for the White Paper,
was so impolitic as to admit that parts of it were
"misleading" and "overembellished" and that there had
been "mistakes" and guesses by the government analysts
who had translated and explained the captured documents,
the administration's credibility gap widened
considerably.[45] In the words of William LeoGrande:
"Only the demonstration effect gives limited truth to the
domino theory. When the Salvadorans saw the Nicaraguan
people succeed at deposing their dictatorship, they were
encouraged in their efforts to do the same."[46]
     Yet, for all the errors, dubious extrapolations,
questionable interpretations, and selective evidencing,
one cannot escape the impression that the critics have
themselves engaged in selective perception. Though their
criticisms have damaged the administration's case, they
have by no means destroyed it. These are glancing blows,
not direct hits. In spite of much initial skepticism,
this writer has come to the conclusion that if the
crucial materials are forgeries, they are very good ones.
Among other things, they do not support some of the
administration's most cherished arguments: The Soviets
do not come off as having a "hit list" in Central
America. On the contrary, they seem to have dragged
their feet at every turn, agreeing "in principle" while
procrastinating in practice regarding the provision of
transportation for the weapons supplied to the Salvadoran
insurgents by Vietnam. Thus, the Salvadoran guerrilla
emissary who arranged the arms flow repeatedly complained
about his inability to meet high-level Soviet officials.
Concern was expressed as to the effect that Moscow's
indecision might have on the participation of other
parties. His trip report ends on an inconclusive note,
with the Kremlin's reply still unreceived. Further
documentation on the "Soviet connection" is conspicuously
absent.
     Nor do the Sandinistas appear to be all that
dedicated to promoting the revolution in El Salvador.
Indeed, the complaints of Salvadoran guerrilla
representatives in Managua supply rare insight into the
relations between the insurgents and their foreign

sponsors. Clearly the Nicaraguans, though interested, were much more concerned with their own survival. The guerrillas complained that the Sandinistas undervalued and ignored them, made unilateral decisions that they had to respect, placed obstacles in the way of their political work, and "had a tendency to look down on the situation" in El Salvador and to "protect the Nicaraguan Revolution." This was not "a relationship of mutual respect, but rather one of imposition." At one point, the Salvadorans, in frustration, declared: "Gentlemen, all right, we understand that Nicaragua must be protected, but for that there is an art and a science which is called 'CONSPIRACY.' Let us conspire together."[47]

Such accounts have the ring of truth. An expert forger, of course, might inject such contradictions into the documents to throw off the wary critic. The Reagan administration, however, is not noted for its subtlety. Fabricated evidence would almost certainly have made a much stronger, less ambiguous case. Assuming the authenticity of the documents, the only thing they establish so far as Soviet complicity is concerned is that Moscow financed the Salvadoran guerrilla emissary's trip to Vietnam and that subsequently some 10 tons of weapons (not 200 tons, as the State Department charged) made it across the border into El Salvador.

No doubt this traffic was but the tip of the iceberg. Though some critics have pointed to such limitations as evidence of Soviet/Cuban/Nicaraguan noninvolvement, these claims seem naive. The desire to discredit the administration's position has led to serious perceptual distortions and a tendency to minimize or deny foreign communist complicity. Thus, definitive evidence is demanded, and when it is unavailable (as is almost invariably the case in such situations) the charges are dismissed out of hand. No matter that Castro has a long history of attempting to export revolution or that the Cubans themselves have tacitly admitted their involvement on more than one occasion.[48] Or that a Costa Rican congressional committee has provided extensive evidence of massive Cuban participation in the international effort to supply the Sandinistas in the last months of the anti-Somoza struggle. (According to this legislative report, about 60 percent of the 450 tons of arms believed to have entered Costa Rica prior to July 1979 came from Cuba.)[49] It would appear that, to those with a psychological investment in disbelief, reason and evidence are irrelevant.

The real question, then, is not whether there has been foreign communist military intervention, but how much, when, and what are the implications. There is strong evidence that, in the aftermath of the Salvadoran guerrillas' unsuccessful "final offensive" of January

1981, the Cubans and Nicaraguans reevaluated their policies. Weapons shipments sharply declined, as both governments signalled their desire to improve relations with the United States. Though acknowledging that there had been a significant drop in the flow of arms to the insurgents, the Reagan administration, enamored with visions of military victory, rejected these feelers and launched a sustained offensive designed to intimidate Havana and Managua into withdrawing all aid--political as well as military--to the guerrillas. Over the next three years, repeated overtures from the Cubans, Nicaraguans, and the Salvadoran opposition to seek negotiated solutions to the Central American crises were systematically ignored or rejected.[50]

Recently, the issue of foreign communist intervention has again been raised. In early 1983, the military situation in El Salvador deteriorated significantly, and the administration moved to bolster the regime with $110 million in military aid. Testifying before Congress, Secretary of State Shultz and others resurrected the domino theory. The flow of arms from Nicaragua, it was claimed, had increased markedly. Intelligence reports showed that the guerrillas were now being supplied continually by helicopters and light aircraft. They had no shortage of arms--mostly U.S. M-16s, Soviet and East German demolition equipment, and American-made mortars.

The question must be asked: Is this for real? Or is it a convenient fantasy designed to pry more arms from a reluctant Congress? The available evidence suggests that there has been no major influx of arms from Nicaragua in the nearly three years that have followed the Salvadoran guerrillas' January 1981 offensive. If the administration had evidence to the contrary, it would almost certainly have made it public. Even the Hondurans have not been able to detect such traffic. The Honduran Army controls all border crossings from Nicaragua and patrols the border in El Salvador, yet as of February 1982 it had not intercepted any major arms shipments to El Salvador since January of the previous year.[51]

Nor have more recent efforts found notable escalations. It is significant that U.S. diplomatic and military personnel in the field see little evidence of large-scale Nicaraguan arms traffic; some say quite candidly that the flow has dwindled to a trickle and that most of the guerrillas' weapons now come from supplies captured or purchased from the Salvadoran military. (According to a Salvadoran opposition source, 1,826 rifles and 99 heavier weapons were captured during the first seven months of 1983. Another source, moreover, reports that the major army/air force ammunition dump at Ilopango Air Force Base has become a "guerrilla supply warehouse.") Neither the U.S. Embassy nor the Salvadoran government has been able to display any evidence to the

contrary. There has not been a single report of an
aircraft originating in Nicaragua being shot down or even
seen by government forces. Not even Salvadoran officers
claim that supplies from abroad are any longer a major
factor in the war.[52]
    Still, the problem cannot be dismissed altogether.
Some weapons--and, more important, ammunition and
communications equipment--apparently still get through.
And this traffic may very well increase in the future.
The danger is that the U.S./Honduran/Nicaraguan exile war
against the Sandinistas may become so intensified that it
may lose its deterrent effect and produce a Sandinista
counterattack. In short, the danger stems less from any
unilateral "armed intervention" by the communist powers
than from a self-intensifying spiral of mutual escalation
that could spread the current conflicts throughout the
region. Should the Salvadoran revolutionaries emerge
victorious from their struggle, the pressure on the
remaining bastions of counterrevolution--the regimes in
Honduras and Guatemala--would become enormous. The
domino theory might then very well become a reality.

(8) THEORIES OF AUTHORITARIANISM AND TOTALITARIANISM:
    IS NICARAGUA "ANOTHER CUBA"?

    "Only intellectual fashion and the tyranny of
Right/Left thinking prevent intelligent men of good will
from perceiving the facts that traditional authoritarian
governments are less repressive than revolutionary
autocracies, that they are more susceptible of liberalization, and that they are more compatible with U.S.
interests."[53]
    The argument, of course, is hardly new. The idea
that there are systemic differences between authoritarian
and totalitarian polities was an almost universally
accepted tenet of the Cold War scholarship of the 1950s.
Assumptions that the latter were inherently "frozen"--
i.e., incapable of within-system change--and were much
more prone to massive human rights violations seemed
justified by both the historical experience of the Soviet
and Nazi regimes and by the structural characteristics of
such systems: the existence of pervasive party and
police controls capable of reaching into all sectors of
society, down to the grassroots, penetrating all
autonomous interest groups and transforming them into
transmission belts of the party-state apparatus through
which the masses could be mobilized and manipulated and
opposition (both actual and potential) eliminated.[54]
    On a purely abstract level, the idea of totali-
tarianism had--and continues to have--considerable
intellectual power. The question is how well it captures
the realities of the regimes it purports to describe.

Put simply, the model is an ideal type that real-world systems only approximate. Over the past twenty years, a vast array of research, much of it based on field experience, has uncovered considerable diversity both within and among communist polities, as well as elements of systemic change unaccountable under the totalitarian paradigm.[55]

Thus when Jeane Kirkpatrick suggests that "the history of this century provides no grounds for expecting that radical totalitarian regimes will transform themselves" into democracies,[56] she is skating on very thin ice. In fact, both Hungary in 1956 and Czechoslovakia in 1968 provide clear evidence of the democratizing potentials within at least some real-world communist systems. That the Soviet Army intervened in both instances to reverse those trends only underscores the fact that systemic change was indeed occurring--in spite of the totalitarian origins of both polities. More recently, the rise of the independent trade union Solidarity bears witness to the transformation of Polish totalitarianism into a particularly incompetent and corrupt form of bureaucratic authoritarianism. (The latter has since been replaced by a military dictatorship--again, largely the product of Soviet pressures to avert democratization.) In short, there is nothing inevitably "frozen" about such regimes. The totalitarian structure may be expected to resist systemic alterations, but it is far from omnipotent. Pressures for change exist and are often formidable.[57]

Nor should one accept uncritically Kirkpatrick's argument that systemic differences make totalitarian systems far more repressive, since they "claim jurisdiction over the whole life of the society and make demands for change that so violate internalized values and habits" that people flee "by the millions." In contrast, traditional authoritarian regimes do not "disturb the habitual rhythms of work and leisure, habitual places of residence, habitual patterns of family and personal relations. . . . Such societies create no refugees."[58]

Again, on a purely abstract level, the argument makes much sense. The problem comes when one examines the real world. Although it may well be that totalitarian regimes are generally more repressive than authoritarian ones, there are at the very least many exceptions: Is totalitarian Yugoslavia really more repressive than authoritarian Guatemala? One may doubt it. Perhaps the ultimate (though certainly not the only) measure of repression is body count. Since 1954, tens of thousands of Guatemalan citizens have been assassinated in an unprecedented wave of state terrorism. Nothing remotely approaching this level of repression has been witnessed in the Eastern European communist systems during this period. Or, one might add, Castro's Cuba, or

Sandinista Nicaragua. Nor is Guatemala alone. Over the
past four years, some 40,000 Salvadoran civilians have
been killed, the vast majority by government military and
security forces and allied "death squads."
Nor is Kirkpatrick correct when she suggests that
such societies create no refugees. Some do; some don't.
As of late 1982, an estimated 51,000-69,000 Salvadorans
had fled their homeland for Mexico and other Central
American countries. Another 250,000-500,000 were thought
to have entered the United States illegally, and 250,000
more had fled their rural homes for urban areas.
Meanwhile, in Guatemala, close to a million people--
mostly Indian campesinos--have become refugees in their
own country. Some 70,000-100,000 have fled into Mexico
to escape the military's massive counterinsurgency
campaign.[59] Yet, Kirkpatrick would have the United
States cultivate the friendship of the Guatemalan and
Salvadoran regimes, while castigating the Cubans and
Nicaraguans as "more repressive."
(Lest anyone misconstrue the above as an apology for
Cuba and Nicaragua, let me hasten to add that the human
rights performances of those governments leave much to be
desired. In the early and mid-1960s, there were tens of
thousands of political prisoners in Cuban jails, often
living in primitive conditions and subjected to
brutality. Subsequently, most were released, and prison
conditions improved considerably. Even today, however,
there are still perhaps a thousand political prisoners.
And, of course, more than a million Cubans have fled the
island--for economic as well as political reasons--since
Castro came to power.
By the same token, in Nicaragua, under the current
state of emergency, human rights have steadily
deteriorated. In the face of exile raids from Honduras,
over 15,000 people, mostly Mosquito Indians, have been
forcibly evacuated from areas along Nicaragua's northern
border for security reasons; a comparable number have
fled into Honduras. In the process, several hundred have
been injured, imprisoned, or killed. Arrests have become
increasingly arbitrary. Opposition politicians, parties,
unions, and the newspaper La Prensa have been repeatedly
harassed by pro-government mobs. In one notorious case,
a Catholic priest was stripped and paraded naked in the
streets, while Sandinista television recorded his
humiliation. The situation, in short, has gotten very
nasty and will probably get worse. Even so, there is a
qualitative difference between these kinds of abuses and
the indiscriminate mass murder one encounters in
Guatemala and El Salvador.)[60]
There are other problems: Kirkpatrick prefers
traditional autocrats because they merely "tolerate"
social inequities and poverty; totalitarians, she says,
create them.[61] Again, the facts are most inconvenient

for her thesis. In Central America, military-oligarchical dictatorships (and their Spanish predecessors) have been major causes of poverty and inequality; in recent decades, moreover, these features have been aggravated by capital-intensive industrialization, export-oriented agricultural development, and the competitive exclusion and unemployment that have accompanied them. In contrast, the Sandinista regime in Nicaragua has attempted to reduce such inequities through major socioeconomic reforms--including land redistribution, extended medical facilities and social security benefits, a massive literacy campaign, and many other measures.[62]

In point of fact, there is no evidence that revolutionary autocracies are any more likely to create poverty and social injustice than are traditional dictatorships. Indeed, the very state intervention Kirkpatrick so dislikes may often be designed to alleviate such inequities. The case of Cuba is instructive: Whatever the negative features of this particular brand of totalitarianism, and there are many, it is difficult to argue that there is more poverty and social injustice now than under Batista. Serious scholars, many with no love for Castro, have long recognized that the Revolution brought vast opportunities for upward socioeconomic mobility to the lower classes.[63] The gross discrepancies between rich and poor that existed in the prerevolutionary era have been largely eliminated. Millions of people have gained access to housing, health, education, and recreational facilities that they did not have previously. Unemployment, if not eliminated, has been at least minimized. And if life is austere, nobody is starving. In this respect, the contrast between Cuba and most other Latin American societies is striking: One does not find in Cuba the grinding poverty that exists almost everywhere else in the region.

It is precisely this redistributive thrust and the class conflict that accompanies it that are largely responsible for the outpouring of refugees that Ms. Kirkpatrick so deplores. One should not infer from this, however, that those staying behind are worse off than before. Some are. But many others may benefit--often at the expense of those who leave. The calculus is not nearly as clear-cut and negative as Kirkpatrick suggests.

The name of the game is selective perception, and it can be played equally well by both liberals and conservatives. The point is that it is fundamentally dishonest: One can no more "prove" that totalitarian regimes are more repressive than authoritarian ones by dredging up the memories of Stalin, Mao, or Pol Pot than one can demonstrate the opposite by citing the examples of Guatemala, El Salvador, or Uganda. Nor is it all that clear that one system-type or the other is more likely to

"create" poverty and inequality. Clearly, conditions
vary more from regime to regime than they do from system
to system. One must look at the specifics of the
particular countries being compared.

In my judgment, finally, Kirkpatrick's relentlessly
one-dimensional analysis is less a reflection of the real
world than a symptom of her own mindset. I would characterize her intentions as quintessentially political: By
obscuring reality in a cloak of abstract theory, she
provides a coherent and powerful critique of liberal
democratic (Carter administration) foreign policy. No
matter that this critique is highly selective in both its
logic and evidence, it struck a responsive chord--as may
be seen both from the howls of indignation from the left
and the wild applause from the right. And it certainly
did wonders for her career.

But gamesmanship has its price. The trouble with
ideological perspectives is that they all too often
force-fit reality into the procrustean mold of
preconceived doctrine, with disastrous consequences for
policy, not to mention national interest.

Nicaragua is a case in point. Was it programmed to
become "another Cuba" the moment the Sandinistas came
into power, as Kirkpatrick and her admirers contend? Or
was the situation more complex than that? One need not
downplay the totalitarian proclivities in the Sandinista
movement to recognize that the new Nicaraguan elite is
not monolithic. Not all elements are Marxist-Leninist,
and those that are vary in their degrees of pragmatism or
dogmatism. More important, Nicaragua is not Cuba. In
the latter, an enormously popular charismatic leader
faced few serious constraints to the establishment of a
totalitarian system. The Soviets agreed fairly early on
to serve as the island's economic patron. Washington
obligingly provided the specter of an external threat,
enabling Castro to wrap himself in the flag of besieged
nationalism and to mobilize the Cuban populace behind his
leadership and policies. In contrast, there is no such
charismatic personality among the Sandinistas. Moscow
has been unwilling to subsidize their revolution, which
remains heavily dependent on western sources of finance.
Opposition parties and interest groups, though imperiled,
are still active and vocal participants in the political
process. La Prensa, by far the most popular newspaper in
the country, continues to criticize the regime, as does
the widely respected archbishop of Managua, Miguel Obando
y Bravo. At the same time, a large portion of the
economy (officially, 60 percent, though this is somewhat
misleading) remains in the hands of the private sector.

Thus, while it is difficult to imagine the
Sandinistas establishing a liberal democracy or voluntarily relinquishing power through elections, the precise
nature of the Nicaraguan system has yet to be determined.

Soviet - Nicaragua

Even if the Marxist strain predominates, as seems likely,
the regime need not necessarily be totalitarian or
repressive. Nor need it inevitably be anti-American.
The Sandinistas desperately need economic aid, and the
United States is in a position to provide at least some
of it, both directly and through international lending
agencies. By employing the carrot, as well as the stick,
Washington may still be able to take advantage of its
inherently strong bargaining position to loosen the
Sandinistas' embrace of the Soviet Union and Cuba. The
goal of U.S. policy should be a genuinely nonaligned
Nicaragua. With the skillful use of diplomacy and
economic aid, we may yet induce that country to become a
Central American Yugoslavia. (Even a Mexican-style one-
party hegemonic system is not out of the question.)
    The other possibility, of course, is that Nicaragua
may indeed go the way of Cuba. If we persist in
repeating the mistakes of the past and leave the
Sandinistas no alternative to a hostile relationship with
the United States, that will most certainly happen. That
is the Kirkpatrick option.

(9)   THE UNITED STATES AS A DESTABILIZING FORCE:
      THE STRATEGY OF CONFLICT AND THE POLITICS OF
      COUNTERPRODUCTIVITY

      "The quintessence of incompetence lies not in the
inability to effectuate one's intentions (ineffectuality,
after all, is often a product of forces beyond our
control), but rather in having an effect that is
precisely the opposite of what is intended and required
by one's interests and values. Counterproductivity,
rather than impotence, is the cardinal sin in foreign
policy.[64]
      One of the most significant phenomena associated
with the Central American crisis has been the
transformation of traditionally stabilizing actors into
destabilizing ones. The church and the military are two
prominent examples; the United States is a third.
Historically, the United States has been a predominantly
stabilizing force in the region. North American
interventions in the Imperialist Era (1898-1934) were
primarily designed to restore political and economic
order in societies plagued by civil strife, financial
instability, and rampant corruption. There were, of
course, exceptions. Like the Soviet Union later in
Eastern Europe, Washington was anxious, for reasons of
national security and economic interest, to foster a zone
of client states. Thus, when revolutionary or
nationalist elites threatened to disrupt this structure
of domination, the "Big Stick" would be used to restore a
pro-U.S. equilibrium. North American policy during this

era was characterized by frequent, lengthy military occupations and direct involvement in the details of internal rule.[65]

The "Good Neighbor Policy" (1934) changed much of this. Henceforth, a more subtle and indirect form of control--hegemony--would be established, designed to maintain regional stability by means other than the costly and discredited techniques of "Gunboat Diplomacy." For over four decades, this new system worked reasonably well. Though U.S. client states were often illegitimate and repressive, they were usually able to maintain order. On those rare occasions when all else failed, Washington would intervene for the purpose of reestablishing pro-American regimes through surrogates (Castillo Armas. in Guatemala, Brigade 2506 in Cuba) or multilateral "peacekeeping" forces (the OAS in the Dominican Republic), which obscured and legitimized the nature of U.S. actions. Only in Cuba, with the rise of Castro and his defection to the Soviet camp, did hegemony break down.

Yet for all its short- and intermediate-range success, the system contained the seeds of its own destruction. As Schlesinger and Kinzer point out in their study of the CIA-sponsored overthrow of the Arbenz regime, "the 1954 coup showed other countries in Central America that the United States was more interested in unquestioning allies than democratic ones. As a result, movements toward peaceful reform in the region were set back, dictators were strengthened and encouraged, and activists today look to guerrilla warfare rather than elections as the only way to produce changes."[66]

We are now reaping the fruits of that harvest. The hegemonic system has broken down, a disintegration accelerated by the inability of both Republican and Democratic administrations to adjust to the realities of regional political decay. That U.S. policy has been maladaptive has been widely accepted by critics of both conservative and liberal persuasion, though there is little agreement on alternative strategies that might have preserved North American influence and regional stability while minimizing the opportunities for Cuban and Soviet expansionism. Thus, for instance, the conservative Ms. Kirkpatrick has criticized the Carter administration for actively destabilizing the friendly and, in her view, relatively benign Somoza regime and paving the way for the hostile and repressive Sandinista dictatorship. In contrast, the liberal LeoGrande has argued that selective perception led Washington to adopt policies that were too little, too late. The U.S. sin was not in undermining Somoza, but in not doing it sooner and more effectively, so that the moderate opposition might establish a viable transition regime that would prevent more radical forces from coming to power.[67]

Since the Reagan administration assumed office,
the criticism has broadened and intensified. Though
different critics have focused on different issues,[68]
there is a widespread feeling that the president and his
key advisers misperceive the sources of the turmoil--that
they seriously overestimate the importance of
Cuban/Soviet/Nicaraguan interference and underestimate
the domestic causes (e.g., widespread social injustice,
massive human rights violations on the part of
governmental and nongovernmental elites, the frustration
of democratic reform). At the same time, they have been
wed to a strategy of conflict in which force and the
threat of force are seen as crucial determinants in the
struggle. Thus, El Salvador was initially perceived less
as a threat than as an opportunity to establish U.S.
resolve. This was "one we could win." The United States
would wipe out the memory of Vietnam and send a message
to the world. The failure of the guerrillas' January
1981 offensive had graphically demonstrated their
weakness. With proper assistance, the Salvadoran Army
would mop up the insurgents in short order, with minimum
risk and cost to the United States. Meanwhile, Cuba
would be deterred from supplying the guerrillas by
threats to "go to the source" of the problem.[69]
    Subsequently, the Reagan team would turn its
attention to Nicaragua. With Honduran and Argentine
military cooperation, anti-Sandinista forces would be
organized, trained, and equipped to wage guerrilla war
against the Managua government. Although the ostensible
purpose of these operations would be to disrupt Cuban
activities and guerrilla supply lines and keep the
Sandinistas off balance, their primary function would be
to soften up the regime for a major guerrilla campaign.
In the words of one U.S. military adviser: "We are
hoping the Sandinistas will make the same mistake Somoza
did. If we can provoke them into retaliation against
opposition leaders and civilians, that will drive more
and more people to take up arms. This revolution is
reversible!"[70] Indeed, by May 1983, administration
enthusiasm for the "secret war" had become so great that
the president was openly referring to the anti-Sandinista
forces as "freedom fighters." The CIA director and the
assistant secretary of state for Inter-American Affairs
were reportedly telling congressmen that the Managua
government might be overthrown before the year was
out.[71]
    It is within this context that the administration's
"political solutions" to the Central American crisis must
be viewed. In El Salvador, Mr. Reagan has reversed the
Godfather's dictum by making the guerrillas an offer they
cannot possibly accept: They must lay down their arms
(in effect, surrender) and participate in government-
organized elections. This notwithstanding the fact that

when opposition leaders have made themselves similarly
vulnerable in the past, they have often been assassinated
by the very security forces whose ostensible job it was
to provide them with protection. In any case, the
guerrillas have little faith in the electoral process.
Even if they were able to win at the polls (assuming
there were honest elections and they were able to
campaign freely), few observers believe they would be
allowed to take office. There has been too much
bloodshed and bitterness. Existing elites are unlikely
to surrender their power and spoils so easily.
    The administration is fully aware of these problems.
Thus, its proposals must be viewed primarily as a public
relations exercise--a counter to repeated calls for a
"dialogue" from everyone from the Salvadoran opposition
to the Mexican government to the pope.[72] The U.S.
Congress and public are the primary audiences. To the
extent that such statements are aimed at the opposition
at all, their targets are not the guerrillas, but rather
their civilian allies. The idea is to separate moderates
from radicals, the better to isolate and defeat the
latter. Divide and conquer. In this sense, the function
of the proposed "political solution" is not to end the
fighting, but rather to continue it on more favorable
terms.[73]
    In short, Washington is still very much committed to
military solutions. Yet, strangely enough, the United
States and its Salvadoran ally have as yet formulated no
coherent strategy. As in Vietnam, policy seems aimed
more at preventing a guerrilla victory in the short run,
at minimum cost, than winning the long-range conflict.
Indeed, it is difficult to escape the impression that
U.S. policy has once again become hostage to forces
beyond its control, forces that have a vested interest in
indefinitely increasing the magnitude of the North
American military and economic commitment. In the 1960s,
the Saigon government was able to induce ever-greater
levels of U.S. involvement by repeatedly threatening to
collapse. One gets the uneasy feeling that history is
repeating itself. There are influential elements on the
Salvadoran right who believe that the United States can
be "hooked" into pulling their chestnuts out of the fire.
They point to the "Hinton episode" to support their
argument: In November 1982, the U.S. Ambassador to El
Salvador publicly condemned the rightist "mafia" as being
as much of a threat to the country as the guerrillas.
Unless human rights abuses were stopped, he warned, aid
might be suspended. A few days later, the White House
unceremoniously instructed him to cool it. Subsequently,
Assistant Secretary of State Thomas Enders, who had
approved Hinton's remarks and proposed a "two-track"
strategy in which the United States would seek negotiations with the guerrillas, while continuing to support

the Salvadoran government, was relieved of the day-to-day
direction of Central American policy and eventually
pushed out of his post altogether. (At the same time,
Hinton was also replaced.)

The message, which roughly coincided with a decision
to restore military aid to Guatemala, seemed clear and
unequivocal: Washington was so obsessed with preventing
a communist victory that it would excuse even massive
human rights violations. Shortly thereafter, this
impression was reinforced when the administration
announced it would seek a substantial increase in supple-
mentary assistance to El Salvador. If approved, the
request would have brought total U.S. military and
economic aid to that country to $136.3 million and $227.1
million, respectively, for 1983. Thus, step by
incremental step, the United States was once again
proceeding up the ladder of escalation. Where the path
would lead, no one could say.

The point, of course, is that rather than solving
the problem, the United States has become part of it. In
the past, Washington has been a selectively stabilizing
influence, reinforcing friendly regimes and undermining
those perceived to be hostile. Now, however, a new
dimension has been added. Policy has become increasingly
counterproductive. Poorly conceived actions are having
unintended and destabilizing consequences. Rather than
returning peace to El Salvador, such actions have
prolonged the conflict. Rather than strengthening the
moderate Christian Democrats and weakening the far right,
they have had precisely the opposite effect. Nor has a
massive influx of U.S. aid enabled the Salvadoran
military to gain the upper hand against the insurgents.
On the contrary, riven through with incompetence and
corruption, increasingly on the defensive against an
enemy that is larger, more experienced, and better
equipped than ever before, the army finds itself in a
significantly weaker position than it was when the Reagan
administration came into power--and for reasons that are
partially the result of administration policy.
Ironically, the United States has now become the
insurgents' primary source of arms. The Salvadoran
military is a sieve through which weapons readily flow
into guerrilla hands. Many are captured; others are
purchased from corrupt officers. The upshot is that the
United States is now arming the FMLN more generously than
Cuba ever did.

Nor is the problem restricted to Salvador. By
promoting hostilities between Nicaragua and its
neighbors, Washington risks internationalizing and
regionalizing the conflict, even as it induces the
Sandinista government to take increasingly repressive
measures domestically to bolster national defense. There
is a strong element here of the self-fulfilling prophecy.

Initially, the administration justified the adoption of
an antagonistic stance on the ground that the Sandinistas
were funnelling a massive amount of weapons to the
Salvadoran guerrillas. Yet, when that flood dwindled to
a trickle, it made no difference. U.S. policy continued
to be cast in an inflexible mold of iron. The
consequence was the reinforcement of the most totalitarian and destructive propensities in the Nicaraguan
leadership. Those who were predisposed to believe that
"North American imperialism and its domestic serviteurs"
were simply doing what they were inevitably programmed to
do found their beliefs reinforced and their political
hand strengthened. Those who held more moderate
positions were effectively undermined. At the same time,
the democratic forces within Nicaragua were seriously
weakened. It was almost as if Washington had written off
the democratic opposition as doomed--unless of course it
took up arms. Yet, the growing North American-Somocista
threat made it increasingly difficult for the latter to
take such a course. Anti-Sandinista Nicaraguan
nationalists found themselves in much the same position
as anti-Castro Cuban nationalists during the Bay of Pigs
incident. No matter how much they might dislike the
Marxist regime, the thought of becoming North American
pawns and allying themselves with the hated Somocistas
has been more than most could stomach. Thus trapped
between unacceptable alternatives, their future is highly
tenuous. In a besieged fortress, moderates become an
endangered species.

In short, the United States has fallen into the trap
of playing Goliath to the Sandinistas' David. By
providing Daniel Ortega and company with the specter of
an external threat, Washington has enabled them to wrap
themselves in the cloak of besieged nationalism and to
justify the revolution's increasing militarization. A
degree of unity and control has thus been maintained that
might have been impossible under other circumstances.

Nor do administration policies bode well for the
future of countries like Honduras, Costa Rica, and
Belize. Though Mr. Reagan has professed a desire to
foster democracy in the region, his policies seem to be
having the opposite effect. By encouraging the militarization of Honduras, the administration has bolstered the
most anti-democratic elements in that country. If voters
had any single message in mind when they elected the
liberals to office in November 1981, it was that the
Honduran military--one of the most corrupt in Central
America--should get out of politics. That has not
happened. Indeed, two weeks before the elections, senior
officers met with the candidates of both major parties
and extracted debilitating political concessions. The
net effect has been to reduce President Suazo Cordova to
the status of a figurehead. The military, under the

leadership of General Gustavo Alvarez Martinez, has
severely defined the limits within the civilian government makes and administers policy. In the process human
rights violations have excalated, the quality of
pluralism has declined, and Honduras has become
increasingly involved militarily in the internal affairs
of Nicaragua and El Salvador. In retaliation, foreign-
supported guerrilla activities are for the first time
jeopardizing Honduran domestic security, even as the
prospects of war with Nicaragua loom increasingly large.
     The turmoil, moreover, has begun to spread to Costa
Rica in the form of frequent border incidents and a
growing influx of Nicaraguan refugees. Meanwhile, the
activities of former Sandinista commander Eden Pastora
have raised the problem of Costa Rican territory once
again being used to launch attacks into Nicaragua.
Whether the government can prevent such actions remains
to be seen. In any case, the country has major socioeconomic problems of its own, which are likely to subject
its democratic system to serious strains in the years to
come.[74] Within this context, U.S. efforts to bolster
Costa Rica militarily contain the danger of encouraging
that nation to resurrect an armed force, something it has
been blessed without for three-and-a-half decades.
Again, the point must be stressed: Central American
militaries tend to be parasitic and destabilizing institutions. They are a large part of the reason why El
Salvador and Guatemala are torn by strife and Costa Rica
and Belize are not.
     Finally, the administration's attempted embrace of
the Guatemalan military government runs the risk of
encouraging those bellicose generals to fulfill their
expansionist ambitions with regard to tiny, non-
militarized, democratic Belize. This is understood all
too well by the British, who have the responsibility for
defending that country in the short run.
     In sum, the problem with U.S. policy is fundamental:
By fostering regional militarization, Washington has
fueled and spread the turmoil, rather than contained it.
The Central American militaries are no longer stabilizing
institutions; indeed, they have become profoundly
destabilizing. Whether in Guatemala City, San Salvador,
Tegucigalpa, or the contra base camps in southern
Honduras, these are the forces that have posed the
greatest threat to order, democracy, and social justice.
Not only do they have a vested interest in increasing
levels of U.S. military and economic involvement, but
they are an active force promoting the internationalization and regionalization of the violence.

(10)   THE QUAGMIRE THESIS: THE INTERNATIONALIZATION AND REGIONALIZATION OF CONFLICT

"Those who cannot remember the past are condemned to repeat it."[75]

El Salvador is not Vietnam. It is smaller, both in terms of geography and population, and much nearer the United States. The logistical problems of a military engagement would be comparatively minor. The guerrilla opponent would be smaller, less organized, and less experienced, with no dense jungle to hide in. Since this would be primarily a revolutionary or class conflict, rather than an anti-colonial war of national liberation, nationalism would presumably be a less potent weapon for the insurgent side. Nor would there be a land border with a neighboring communist state supplying the guerrillas en masse with troop reinforcements. Or so the argument goes.

At first glance, the situation would appear to have all the ingredients of a "splendid little war" that could be wrapped up in short order at minimum cost. On closer examination, however, there are balancing factors that make the scenario less reassuring. For one thing, the domestic constraints on U.S. policy are much greater today than they were during the early years of the Vietnam involvement. It is doubtful whether the United States can concentrate its military and economic resources in Central America the way it did in Southeast Asia. Would Congress accept the idea of sending 100,000 troops to that besieged isthmus? Or 50,000? Or even 10,000? If so, under what circumstances? And with what results? In Vietnam, various U.S. administrations suffered from the illusion that they could control events through incremental escalations of American military power. They forgot that the United States was not the only party capable of escalation.

The critical issue is whether the fighting, which has thus far been relatively contained in El Salvador, Guatemala, and the Nicaraguan-Honduran border region, will spread, drawing in the United States and its allies on one side and the Cubans and their friends on the other. There are several scenarios in which this could happen. By far the most probable and dangerous involve Nicaragua.

Increasingly besieged by CIA-sponsored guerrilla forces, the Sandinista government will come under growing pressure to take extraordinary measures to defend the revolution. Not only will the Nicaraguan military buildup be accelerated, along with its dependence on communist bloc arms, but the Cubans may very well be asked to send several thousand additional military advisers--and, if the situation grows bad enough, combat troops--to bolster the country's defenses. Though Castro

is acutely aware of the dangers and is most anxious to
avoid war with the United States, he would probably
comply with a request for more advisers. Nor can one
discount the possibility that combat troops may be sent.
Havana's commitment to the Sandinistas is far stronger
than its commitments to its Angolan and Ethiopian allies
at the time of those engagements. The destruction of the
Nicaraguan revolution would be a tremendous political and
psychological blow for Castro, one he may not be able to
accept. Ironically, in its zeal to destabilize
Nicaragua, the Reagan administration may simply
accelerate that country's militarization, while provoking
the very Cuban involvement it desires to prevent.[76]
    Under such circumstances, the Soviets might not be
far behind. Although they have thus far been quite
cautious on the Nicaraguan issue, pressure from Castro to
fulfill their internationalist obligations (at a minimum,
to increase the flow of military aid, including the
delivery of MiG jet fighters) and inducements by the
Sandinistas (the promise of future military bases?) might
just turn the tide. One should not forget that it was
during a similar period of United States-Soviet tension
(in the aftermath of the U-2 incident and the collapse of
the Paris summit conference) that Moscow forged its
commitment to the Castro regime. Through its unbridled
hostility, the Reagan administration has largely
destroyed what positive incentives it had to work with
(especially the inducements of arms control) to restrain
the Soviets from attempting to penetrate the region.
Although one does not anticipate the large-scale introduction of military personnel a la Cuba--that would
probably be too risky--increased political, economic, and
military aid of the sort that is commonly accepted as the
legitimate prerogative of nation-states is entirely
possible, even likely. (Even so, there have already been
hints that Soviet nuclear missiles might be introduced in
retaliation for the emplacement of U.S. Pershing and
Cruise missiles in Europe. But this I take for bluff.)
    As the external pressure on the Sandinistas grows,
moreover, so will the danger of war between Nicaragua and
its neighbors. Recent moves to resurrect the Central
American Defense Council (CONDECA)--accompanied by much
talk of war against Nicaragua--are ominous. Should the
Honduran-based contra threat, aided by the Honduran
military, continue to escalate as anticipated, the
temptation to launch a retaliatory strike against that
country may prove overwhelming. Frustration and anger
breed aggression. Similar moves might also be made
against Costa Rica should that government prove unwilling
or unable to prevent insurgent raids from its territory.
In either case, military action might take a number of
forms--for example, the encouragement and supply of
Honduran guerrilla movements, the infiltration of

Nicaraguan insurgents, a conventional invasion, air
strikes, or some combination of the above. It might be
relatively limited, seeking merely to destroy base camps,
or more ambitious, aimed at destabilizing or displacing
the Honduran and Costa Rican governments. Suffice it to
say that the Nicaraguan regime has the capability of
posing a major threat to both countries, through
conventional or unconventional means. Two thousand
battle-hardened Sandinista guerrillas infiltrated into
Honduras could turn the Honduran military's worst nightmares into a reality.

(As this chapter goes to press, there are signs that
a low-level Nicaraguan counterescalation may already be
underway. Thus, for instance, Defense Minister Humberto
Ortega recently warned that, if his country continued to
be attacked from Honduran territory, Honduran revolutionaries might engage in rear-guard military actions.
"They are disposed to support the Nicaraguan revolution
with all their resources." Although "peaceful
coexistence is what we seek--if governments like that of
Honduras choose to support aggression, they will face
reverberations inside their own countries." A few days
earlier, Nicaraguan newspapers had carried the text of a
communique signed by six Honduran leftist groups, calling
for the creation of a unified front against the Honduran
regime.[77] Subsequently, a column of 100 insurgents
trained and sent from Nicaragua moved across the border
to begin guerrilla war. The unit, however, was wiped out
by the Honduran Army.)

What would the United States do in such a situation?
It is not at all clear. The Reagan administration's
instinctive reaction would be to send in the marines.
The "Soviet option"--direct intervention in the manner of
Hungary (1956), Czechoslovakia (1968), and Afghanistan
(1979)--is a distinct possibility. The president would
no doubt argue that aggression must not be appeased, that
these developments simply confirmed everything the State
Department had been saying about the Nicaraguan/Cuban/
Soviet threat, the domino theory, and all that. It is
just possible that Congress might buy the message. If
the fear is sufficient, the Tonkin Gulf syndrome will be
resurrected. Again, however, this is not 1964. At least
some would rejoin that the administration had once again
engaged in a self-fulfilling prophecy--that Nicaraguan
"aggression" was a consequence of and reaction to acts of
war on the part of forces encouraged and nurtured by the
United States.

Much depends on the nature of the threat. A limited
Nicaraguan military action against Honduran or Costa
Rican base camps might not lead to all-out war. The U.S.
response might be restricted to attempts to intimidate
Nicaragua and Cuba and a major increase of military aid
(including advisers) to the endangered allies in

question. The situation might restabilize. The CIA
might even pressure the Hondurans and the contras to
refrain from their aggressive activities against
Nicaragua. A cutoff of aid could be threatened, and if
necessary carried out, to make the point. (How much
leverage the United States could exercise over the
contras, who are already armed to the teeth and have
their own agenda, is subject to question, however.) On
the other hand, the more serious the Sandinista/Cuban/
Soviet threat is perceived to be, the more likely that
the United States will become directly involved in the
fighting and/or escalate its indirect war against
Nicaragua. A full-scale Nicaraguan invasion of Honduras,
for instance, might well act as a lightning rod for
American troops and retaliatory strikes. So might the
introduction of Cuban combat troops--even if they were
restricted to performing defensive functions in
Nicaragua.

Moreover, even if Congress prohibits the introduction of combat troops or otherwise restricts U.S.
involvement, there is still the very real possibility of
indirect intervention through surrogates. Argentina and
Israel are already involved and might be willing to
substantially increase their commitments. The Guatemalan
military might well be tempted to step in with combat
forces. A multinational CONDECA intervention is quite
possible. (The most reactionary elements in Guatemala,
Salvador, and Honduras are all convinced that the
Sandinista virus will have to be exterminated sooner or
later; the commitment to sooner, rather than later, could
come at any time.) Under such circumstances, the lines
between "aggression" and "defense" would become
increasingly blurred, restraints on all sides seriously
eroded, and the prospects for a generalized Central
American war substantially increased. As the threat to
Nicaragua continued to escalate, Cuban involvement would
probably grow, along with the flow of arms (and perhaps
personnel) into Salvador, Guatemala, Honduras, and Costa
Rica. Panama and Mexico might also be affected. Should
the United States become directly involved in the
fighting, the resultant nationalistic and leftist
backlash might cause the domino theorists' worst-case
scenarios to come true: Sabotage against the
(indefensible) Panama Canal? A spillover of the violence
into southern Mexico, threatening the oil fields? The
Cambodianization of Central America, with guerrillas
being pushed from one country to another by U.S.
intervention forces? The ultimate nightmare would find
internationalist brigades roaming up and down the isthmus
in a great brushfire of violence that would make the
current conflicts look like tea parties.[78] That such a
conflagration might produce millions of refugees and lead

to a whole series of anti-U.S., pro-Cuban/Soviet regimes is a distinct possibility.
This is not, of course, the only conceivable outcome. Theoretically, a wide range of scenarios can be imagined, including the "best-case" visions of the Reagan administration. It is conceivable--though not very likely--that El Salvador and Guatemala will be definitively pacified and the Sandinistas overthrown. It is even possible that a U.S. blockade of Cuba--an attempt to go to the "source" of the problem--might cut off that route of supplies, modest though it appears to be at this point. It would also, of course, create other problems: U.S. action against Cuba could raise the possibility of war with the Soviet Union. It might also result in Moscow's retaliation against areas of our own strategic vulnerability--for example, Berlin, the Middle East, and southwest Asia (Iran/Pakistan). The proverbial people who live in glass houses should avoid throwing stones.

THE UNITED STATES AND CENTRAL AMERICA: ON ILLUSIONS, REALITIES, AND NO-WIN SITUATIONS

> President Castillo Armas' objective, "to do more for the people in two years than the communists were able to do in ten years," is very important. This is the first instance in history where a communist government has been replaced by a free one. The whole world is watching to see which does the better job.
>
> --Richard M. Nixon[79]

The human capacity for self-deception is virtually infinite. Almost thirty years after the CIA-engineered overthrow of the democratic, socialist, reform government of Guatemala, U.S. leaders are still trying to reconcile the irreconcilable by embracing repressive and corrupt elites while simultaneously attempting to foster democracy and social justice. By now, this has assumed a classic pattern: A perceived revolutionary threat to U.S. hegemony and security jolts Washington out of its usual complacence and neglect of Latin America. A strategy of "reform with repression" is adopted. The CIA is unleashed against the offending government (Guatemala, Cuba, Nicaragua). Military and economic aid to friendly regimes is stepped up. Counterinsurgency and civic action programs are promoted hand-in-hand. Agrarian reform and democracy are pushed in an attempt to win the "hearts and minds" of the people. When it becomes clear, however, that our allies have no interest in any but paper reforms (one must at least go through the motions to ensure the continued flow of aid) and no intention of sharing their power, democracy and social justice are sacrificed for the sake of political expediency. In Guatemala, the cost can be partially measured in the tens of thousands of civilians killed in the state terrorism conducted by Castillo Armas and his successors.

There are some who will say that times have changed--that in El Salvador we have at last taken a stand in favor of democracy and reform. But this is a refrain that has been heard too often in the past to be accepted uncritically. The historical record suggests that the American commitment is primarily tactical and instrumental, designed to defuse the insurgency and legitimize U.S. policy before Congress, the public, and the international audience. (Indeed, it is highly unlikely that Congress would have continued to fund our Salvadoran policy had not the Carter and Reagan administrations wrapped themselves in the cloak of reform.) Unfortunately, such commitments tend to be superficial and short-lived. Once the danger is over (and sometimes even before), things revert to normal. It is no accident that when the Castroite guerrilla threat disappeared in the late 1960s, so did the Alliance for Progress. As for El Salvador, the much vaunted land reform was long ago truncated; it is now struggling for survival. And although elections are scheduled for March 1984, they are as likely to return the oligarchy as the Christian Democrats to power. Whatever the short-run outcome, the long-range prospects for democracy-- especially once the United States withdraws from the country--are not bright.

One is struck by the nature of American illusions. President Reagan may think of the anti-Sandinista guerrillas as "freedom fighters"--and some of them are-- but the Somocistas whom the CIA has chosen to embrace include some of the most violent, corrupt, and discredited elements of the Old Order. Should they win, the consequences would be predictable. In the words of one contra officer: "Come the counterrevolution, there will be a massacre in Nicaragua. We have a lot of scores to settle. There will be bodies from the border to Managua."80

"Why don't they behave like us?" one U.S. officer recently complained to me in San Salvador. He was genuinely perplexed that Salvadoran troops were reluctant to fight for "their" government, that officers were selling U.S.-supplied arms to the guerrillas, and that nobody seemed very interested in bringing to justice soldiers who had committed human rights violations. His reaction was not unusual. Americans, it appears, are as culture-bound in Central America as they were in Vietnam. Our insistence on force-fitting alien realities into a U.S. frame of reference, projecting our own values onto others, and ignoring evidence that does not fit our preconceived stereotypes has led to a policy that is both ineffective and dangerous. When our initial attempts fail, we escalate rather than reevaluate. To little good. It does not help to endlessly threaten the Nicaraguans and Cubans if the basic causes of the Salvadoran conflict are Salvadoran. The hope that by raising the ante we can pressure the Sandinistas into calling off the Salvadoran revolution is a desperate pipe dream. They do not have the capability, even if they wanted to. As the situation in El Salvador continues to deteriorate, the United States will at some point have to make a difficult decision: to commit combat troops, seek a negotiated solution, or accept the overthrow of the Salvadoran government.

There are no easy choices. Americans have been socialized to believe that every problem has a solution. Yet, there are many circumstances in the real world in which there are no solutions—at least in the ideal sense. Often, indeed, the choice is between different ways of losing, some less painful than others. We may now be at just such a juncture. It is time that Americans gave serious thought not just to winning, but to minimizing losses and risks. A negotiated solution to the Salvadoran crisis, with the emergence of a genuine reform regime neither hostile to the United States nor aligned with the Soviet bloc, may still be a feasible alternative to escalation. But the longer we wait, the poorer our bargaining position is likely to be. If we procrastinate too long, the opportunity may well pass us by altogether. Or at best, as in Vietnam, the settlement that does emerge will be merely a thinly veiled cover for surrender.

NOTES

1. Viron P. Vaky, "Hemispheric Relations: 'Everything is a Part of Everything Else,'" Foreign Affairs, 59, 3 (1981), pp. 617-647.
2. U.S., Department of State, "Caribbean Basin Initiative" (Washington, D.C.: Government Printing Office, February 24, 1982), p. 4.
3. The Alliance, of course, also contained a substantial reformist thrust, centered primarily on the concept of agrarian reform. But this was widely ignored in practice.
4. See, especially, William H. Durham, Scarcity and Survival in Central America (Stanford, Calif.: Stanford University Press, 1979), pp. 21-54.
5. Edelberto Torres-Rivas, "Guatemala--Crisis and Political Violence," NACLA Report on the Americas, 14, 1 (January/February 1980), p. 20.

6. Shelton H. Davis and Julie Hodson, Witnesses to Political Violence in Guatemala, Oxfam: Impact Audit 2 (1982), p. 45; John A. Booth, "Toward Explaining Regional Crisis in Central America: Socio-economic and Political Roots of Rebellion" (Paper delivered to the 44th International Congress of Americanists, September 1982), pp. 12-13; George Black, "Garrison Guatemala," NACLA Report on the Americas, 17, 1 (January/February 1983), p. 17; Jerry Stilkind, "Guatemala's Unstable and Uncertain Future" (Washington, D.C.: Center for Development Policy, February 19, 1982), p. 4.

7. John A. Booth, The End and the Beginning (Boulder, Colo.: Westview Press, 1982), p. 84, and Booth, "Toward Explaining Regional Crisis," pp. 10-11; George Black, Triumph of the People (London: Zed Press, 1981), pp. 37, 69.

8. Booth, "Toward Explaining Regional Crisis," p. 15. See also Rafael del Cid, "Las Clases Sociales y su Dinamica en el Agro Hondureno," Estudios Sociales Centroamericanos, 18 (September/December 1977), p. 144; Durham, Scarcity and Survival, pp. 117-123; and Steven Volk, "Honduras: On the Border of War," NACLA Report on the Americas, 15, 6 (November/December 1981), pp. 13-14.

9. Edelberto Torres-Rivas, "The Central American Model of Growth: Crisis for Whom?" Latin American Perspectives, 7, 2-3 (Spring/Summer 1980), p. 35.

10. Similarly, in Nicaragua, at the height of industrial growth from 1963 to 1973, some 15,000 agricultural jobs were lost but only 13,000 new positions created in modern, capital-intensive factories. See Black, Triumph of the People, p. 68. For sources on El Salvador, see Chapter 6 of this text.

11. For more thorough critiques, see Robert Pastor, "Sinking in the Caribbean Basin," Foreign Affairs, 60, 5 (Summer 1982), pp. 1038-1058; and the forum on the "Caribbean Basin Initiative," in Foreign Policy, 47 (Summer 1982), pp. 114-138.

12. William and Elizabeth Paddock, We Don't Know How: An Independent Audit of What They Call Success in Foreign Assistance (Ames, Iowa: Iowa State University Press, 1973), p. 107.

13. Ibid., p. 285.

14. The term is William Vogt's, cited in Durham, Scarcity and Survival, p. 21.

15. Howard E. Daugherty, "Man-induced Ecological Change in El Salvador" (Ph.D. dissertation, University of California, Los Angeles, 1969), p. 85.

16. Durham, Scarcity and Survival, pp. 30-38.

17. Ibid., p. 47.

18. Text of speech to the Conservative Political Action Conference, Washington, D.C., March 21, 1981.

19. See, especially, Ted Robert Gurr, Why Men Rebel (Princeton, N.J.: Princeton University Press, 1970).

This literature is so extensive as to prohibit a listing
of specific sources. For a recent overview and extensive
bibliography, see Ted Robert Gurr, ed., Handbook of
Political Conflict (New York: Free Press, 1980).
    20. Booth, "Toward Explaining Regional Crisis," p. 2.
    21. Gurr, Why Men Rebel, p. 13.
    22. U.S., Congress, House, Prepared Statement of
Richard E. Feinberg Before the Subcommittee on
Inter-American Affairs, Committee on Foreign Affairs,
July 21, 1981.
    23. Booth, "Toward Explaining Regional Crisis,"
pp. 8-9 and Tables 3 and 4. Most of Booth's statistics
are from James W. Wilkie and Stephen Haber, eds.,
Statistical Abstract of Latin America (Los Angeles:
University of California Latin American Center
Publications, 1981).
    24. El Salvador: An Inquiry into Urban Poverty
(Washington, D.C.: World Bank, 1980), pp. 8-9.
    25. Booth, "Toward Explaining Regional Crisis,"
Table 5.
    26. The following is based primarily on Ibid.,
pp. 15-20.
    27. Mancur Olson, "Rapid Growth as a Destabilizing
Force," Journal of Economic History, 23, 4 (December
1963), pp. 529-552.
    28. Samuel P. Huntington, Political Order in Changing
Societies (New Haven, Conn.: Yale University Press,
1968), p. 266.
    29. For an elaboration of the "living museum" thesis,
see Charles W. Anderson, Politics and Economic Change in
Latin America (Princeton, N.J.: Van Nostrand, 1967),
pp. 87-114. For an application of the thesis to El
Salvador, see Chapter 6 in this text.
    30. Thus, the waggish reference to the Honduran
capital of "Tegucigolpe."
    31. Gabriel Zaid, "Enemy Colleagues: A Reading of
the Salvadoran Tragedy," Dissent (Winter 1982), p. 38.
    32. See, for example, Stephen Webre, Jose Napoleon
Duarte and the Christian Democratic Party in Salvadoran
Politics, 1960-72 (Baton Rouge: Louisiana State
University Press, 1979); Eduardo Colindres, Fundamentos
Economicos de la Burguesia Salvadorena (San Salvador:
University of Central America, 1977); Samuel Stone, Las
Convulsiones del Istmo Centroamericano (San Jose: CIAPA,
1979); Susanne Jonas and David Tobis, eds., Guatemala
(New York: NACLA, 1974); and Alistair White, El Salvador
(New York: Praeger, 1973). Journals such as Estudios
Centroamericanos and Latin American Perspectives also
contain much useful research on elites and interest
groups.
    33. Penny Lernoux, Cry of the People (New York:
Doubleday, 1980), p. 37. See also Tommie Sue Montgomery,
Revolution in El Salvador (Boulder, Colo.: Westview

Press, 1982), pp. 97-117; and Margaret E. Crahan,
"International Aspects of the Role of the Catholic Church
in Central America," in Richard E. Feinberg, ed., Central
America: International Dimensions of the Crisis (New
York: Holmes and Meier, 1982), pp. 213-238.
    34. Enrique Baloyra, "The Deterioration and Breakdown
of Reactionary Despotism in Central America" (Paper
delivered at the 44th International Congress of
Americanists, September 1982), p. 34. This article is
scheduled to appear in a forthcoming issue of the
Journal of Latin American Studies.
    35. Barrington Moore, Jr., Social Origins of
Dictatorship and Democracy (Boston: Beacon Press, 1966),
p. 414.
    36. Baloyra, "Deterioration and Breakdown,"
pp. 35, 41.
    37. Ibid., p. 36.
    38. For a detailed analysis of "reactionary
despotism" in El Salvador, see Enrique Baloyra's El
Salvador in Transition (Chapel Hill: University of North
Carolina Press, 1982).
    39. See, for example, Gordon Bowen's chapter in this
volume. See also George Black's two-part study,
"Garrison Guatemala" and "Guatemela--The War is Not
Over," in NACLA Report on the Americas, 17, 1 and 2
(January/February and March/April 1983).
    40. Francisco Villagran Kramer, "The Background to
the Current Political Crisis in Central America," in
Feinberg, ed., Central America, p. 20.
    41. William LeoGrande, "The Revolution in Nicaragua:
Another Cuba?" Foreign Affairs, 58, 1 (Fall 1979),
p. 31.
    42. If anything, according to Americas Watch (AW),
the situation has deteriorated. See "Creating a
Desolation and Calling it Peace," the May 1983 supplement
to the AW report on Guatemala, excerpts from which
appeared in the New York Review of Books, 30, 9 (June 2,
1983); "Human Rights in Central America: A Report on El
Salvador, Guatemala, Honduras, and Nicaragua" (New York:
Americas Watch, April 27, 1983).
    43. "Human Rights in Honduras: Signs of 'The
Argentine Method'" (New York: Americas Watch, December
1982), pp. 5-8.
    44. U.S., Department of State, "Communist
Interference in El Salvador" (Washington D.C.:
Government Printing Office, February 23, 1981), p. 8.
More recent State Department reports include "Cuba's
Renewed Support for Violence in the Hemisphere" (1981),
"Cuban and Nicaraguan Support for the Salvadoran
Insurgency" (1982), and "Background Paper: Central
America" (1983).
    45. For critiques of the "White Paper," see
Washington Post (June 6, 1981); Wall Street Journal

(June 8, 1981); Walter Poelchau, White Paper, Whitewash (New York: Deep Cover Books, 1981), pp. 75-101; James Petras, "Blots on the White Paper: The Reinvention of the Red Menace," in Marvin E. Gettleman, Patrick Lacefield, Louis Menache, David Mermelstein, and Ronald Radosh, eds., El Salvador: Central America and the Cold War (New York: Grove Press, 1981), pp. 242-253; and Ralph McGhee, "The CIA and the White Paper on El Salvador," The Nation (April 11, 1981).
46. New York Times (March 9, 1983).
47. U.S., Department of State, "Communist Interference in El Salvador: Documents Demonstrating Communist Support of the Salvadoran Insurgency" (Washington, D.C.: Government Printing Office, February 23, 1981), Document G.
48. See, for example, Castro's interview with Hans-Jurgen Wischnewski, as reported in the New York Times (April 25, 1981); also Jorge I. Dominguez, "Cuba's Relations with Caribbean and Central American Countries" (Paper delivered at the conference on "Stability/ Instability in the Caribbean Basin in the 1980s," University of Pittsburgh, October 1982), pp. 13-15.
49. New York Times (May 21, 1981).
50. For the details of some of these overtures, from a foreign service officer who was in a position to know, see Wayne Smith, "Dateline Havana: Myopic Diplomacy," Foreign Policy, 48 (Fall 1982), pp. 160-169. See also Luis Burstin, "My Talks with the Cubans," New Republic (February 13, 1984); Chapters 6 and 14 in this text; Dominguez, "Cuba's Relations," pp. 13-14 and 17. For the most recent overtures, see Latin America Weekly Report (August 5, September 9 and 23, November 25, December 2 and 9, 1983); and Latin America Regional Report (August 19, October 28, and December 2, 1983).
51. New York Times (February 5, 1982).
52. Ibid. (March 9, April 3 and 25, and July 31, 1983).
53. Jeane Kirkpatrick, Dictatorships and Double Standards (New York: Simon and Schuster, 1982), p. 49.
54. See, especially, Carl J. Friedrich and Zbigniew K. Brezinski, Totalitarian Dictatorship and Autocracy (New York: Praeger, 1956); and Bertram D. Wolfe, "The Durability of Soviet Totalitarianism," in Alex Inkeles and Kent Geiger, eds., Soviet Society (Boston: Houghton Mifflin, 1961), pp. 648-659.
55. See, especially, Donald E. Schulz and Jan S. Adams, Political Participation in Communist Systems (New York: Pergamon Press, 1981).
56. Kirkpatrick, Dictatorships, p. 51.
57. This may be seen in somewhat more subtle form in the Soviet Union itself, especially in the transition from the Stalin era to that of Khrushchev. Compare, for example, Merle Fainsod's How Russia is Ruled (Cambridge:

Harvard University Press, 1963) with Jerry Hough's
updated version of that classic, How the Soviet Union is
Governed (Cambridge: Harvard University Press, 1979).
   58. Kirkpatrick, Dictatorships, pp. 49-50.
   59. New York Times (January 23, 1983); and the
Americas Watch reports cited in Note 42.
   60. According to the State Department, there were
fifteen to twenty credible reports of deaths at the hands
of the Nicaraguan security forces in 1982--this in
contrast to thousands in Salvador and Guatemala. See
U.S., Department of State, Country Reports on Human
Right Practices for 1982 (Washington, D.C.: Government
Printing Office, February 1983).
   61. Kirkpatrick, Dictatorships, p. 49.
   62. See, for example, Booth's chapter in this text;
see also Carmen Diana Deere, "Agrarian Reform in Central
America and U.S. Foreign Policy: El Salvador and
Nicaragua" (Paper delivered at the 1982 meeting of the
Latin American Studies Association, March 1982); and
Thomas W. Walker, ed., Nicaragua in Revolution (New York:
Praeger, 1982).

   63. The most sophisticated and objective analyses,
which go to considerable lengths to point out Cuban
failures as well as successes, are: Jorge I. Dominguez,
Cuba: Order and Revolution (Cambridge: Belknap Press,
1978), pp. 173-190 and 218-229; and Carmelo Mesa-Lago,
The Economy of Socialist Cuba: A Two-Decade Appraisal
(Albuquerque: University of New Mexico Press, 1981),
pp. 109-174, 187-198.
   64. Donald E. Schulz, "The Strategy of Conflict and
the Politics of Counterproductivity," Orbis, 25, 3 (Fall
1981), p. 679.
   65. On the U.S. role during the eras of imperialism
and hegemony, see Karnes' chapter in this text; see also
James Kurth, "The United States and Central America:
Hegemony in Historical and Comparative Perspective," in
Feinberg, ed., Central America, pp. 39-57. For a
detailed treatment of the imperialist and hegemonic eras
in U.S.-Cuban relations, see Dominguez, Cuba, pp. 11-109.
   66. Stephen Schlesinger and Stephen Kinzer, Bitter
Fruit (New York: Doubleday, 1982), p. 254.
   67. Kirkpatrick, Dictatorships, pp. 23-90; LeoGrande,
"The Revolution in Nicaragua," pp. 33-38.
   68. For substantive critiques, see William M.
LeoGrande and Carla Anne Robbins, "Oligarchs and
Officers: The Crisis in El Salvador," Foreign Affairs,
58, 5 (Summer 1980), pp. 1084-1103; and LeoGrande, "A
Splendid Little War: Drawing the Line in El Salvador,"
in Marvin Gettleman et al., eds., El Salvador,
pp. 360-79; Richard E. Feinberg, "Central America: No
Easy Answers," Foreign Affairs, 59, 5 (Summer 1981),
pp. 1121-1146; Robert Leiken, "Reconstructing Central
American Policy," Washington Quarterly, 5, 1 (Winter

63

1982), pp. 47-60; Piero Gleijeses, "Tilting at Windmills: Reagan in Central America" (Washington, D.C.: Johns Hopkins Foreign Policy Institute, 1982); Max Singer, "The Record in Latin America," Commentary, 74, 6 (December 1982), pp. 43-49; Tom J. Farer, "Managing the Revolution?" Foreign Policy, 52 (Fall 1983), pp. 96-117; Smith, "Dateline Havana"; Schulz, "The Strategy of Conflict."

69. Reportedly, Secretary Haig promised the president a quick victory. See New York Times (March 4, 1982).

70. Conversation with this author at a contra base camp in southern Honduras, December 1982.

71. Subsequently, Director Casey denied having made these comments. It appears that this may have been an informal "off-the-record" statement, rather than formal testimony before Congress. Regardless, CIA officials had been making similar "not for attribution" assessments to reporters for some time. At the very least, it was clear that the prospect of a Sandinista ouster was viewed with considerable glee. See New York Times (May 23 and 24, 1983).

72. In the words of an April 1982 National Security Council document, it was necessary to co-opt "cut-and-run negotiation strategies by demonstrating a reasonable but firm approach to negotiations and compromise on our terms" (emphasis added). See Ibid. (April 7, 1983).

73. In the words of Undersecretary of Defense Fred Ikle: "We do not seek a military stalemate. We seek victory for the forces of democracy" (Speech before the Baltimore Council on Foreign Affairs, September 12, 1983).

74. See, especially, the chapter by Gonzalez-Vega in this text.

75. George Santayana, Reason and Common Sense (New York: Dover, 1980), p. 284.

76. Recent CIA reports suggest that the Cubans may already be stepping up their military involvement in Nicaragua. Most notable is the reported presence in that country of General Arnaldo Ochoa Sanchez, deputy to the Cuban Minister of the Armed Forces, who is said to have been "secretly assigned to duty"--perhaps for the purpose of organizing a large-scale move into Nicaragua. Ochoa played a similar role in Angola and Ethiopia. See New York Times (June 19, 1983). On this issue, see also Schulz's comments in the section on Nicaragua and Cuba in Chapter 15.

77. Ibid. (April 10, 1983).

78. In the aforementioned warning, Humberto Ortega noted that the Nicaraguan government had received "dozens and even hundreds" of offers of military help from supporters in Latin America and Europe. Nicaragua's response to those offers, he proclaimed, "will be made known at the appropriate moment." See Ibid.

79. Richard M. Nixon, "What I Learned in Latin America," This Week (August 7, 1955).

80. Newsweek (November 8, 1982).

2
The United States
and the Caribbean Basin
in Historical Perspective

Thomas L. Karnes

For nearly two hundred years the United States has maintained a presence in the Caribbean, from the tentative days when George Washington sought the trade of the British West Indies until the present. It should not be surprising that U.S. policy has not always exhibited continuity, and perhaps it is too much to expect any great nation to behave consistently toward several disparate states over so many decades. By examining the short-range programs of several individual administrations, however, one can find some threads of continuity. As American history passes through its eras of Monroe Doctrine, Corollaries, Dollar Diplomacy, Watchful Waiting, Good Neighbors, Alliance for Progress, and so on, guidelines become a little clearer and reveal something more than Uncle Sam thrashing about whenever anarchy or some obnoxious dictatorship becomes too irksome for the American public to tolerate.

This reading will focus on certain recurring themes in our history that may help us understand our leaders and what they were trying to do (then and now) a bit better. The first of these themes was strongly highlighted in 1982. Throughout much of the preceding two years, assassinations and bloody civil strife in Central America marked the headlines of U.S. newspapers. Yet, when war broke out between Great Britain and Argentina over the Falkland Islands, Central American news moved several pages back from the front. Soon thereafter Israel invaded Lebanon, and Central America seemed to disappear from press interest altogether. The area's problems, of course, had not gone away. Little, in fact, had changed at all. What so clearly was being demonstrated was the low priority Central America and the Caribbean hold in U.S. public interest. Unfortunately that scale of precedence closely parallels the attitude of the State Department, which traditionally places its concerns with Europe, Asia and the Middle East ahead of those with Latin America.

Moreover, policy is made much more diffuse because the region itself has little unity. The Caribbean is a loose geographic area, whose definition often depends on the purpose of the definer. (El Salvador, for instance, does not touch the Caribbean, but American presidents tend to ignore this.) The region contains colonies and states, both old and new. Some are governed badly and some well, some by dictators and some by progressive democrats. Their people are of all races, occupying tiny islands or mid-sized states. Some have great wealth; most suffer indescribable poverty. No single policy should be expected to accommodate such diversity.

Third, it should be recognized that all of these relationships are badly proportioned. The United States is vastly superior to all of the Caribbean neighbors in size, wealth, natural resources, and population. Yet the Caribbean countries often possess resources of great value to the United States. In a political sense the nations of the hemisphere vowed their juridical equality in 1933 and several times since, and Washington was a willing signatory to these pacts. But sheer size belies this equality. With the best of intentions the United States can inadvertently destroy an economy or overthrow an administration merely by changing its buying or consumption habits. Other major nations, such as the United Kingdom, France, and the USSR, have also possessed this great power/small power advantage, and comparisons would be instructive, had we the purpose and space here.

Fourth, U.S. policy has always contained a variety of motives. Good intentions and bad have coexisted; highly benevolent, selfless actions have been followed by exploitation. Some motives have been purely economic, others political or strategic. Often they are so mixed as to defy disentanglement. These motives may change with the needs of the times, but the nation's security is never far from the minds of U.S. policymakers, for the Caribbean is regularly described in Churchillian terms as America's soft underbelly, irrespective of other problems.

Finally, it is obvious that some policy trends have occurred through the years. In the nineteenth century, the United States faced enormous problems at home and often exhibited only minimal interest in the Caribbean. Expansionism occurred on a large scale, but primarily into adjacent regions, and Americans generally had yet to accept the doctrine that overseas territories might be a part of the U.S. destiny. At the close of the nineteenth century events thrust themselves quickly upon us, and a great debate took place over the propriety of having an overseas empire. Proponents of a Greater America won readily, and the Caribbean became our lake and the heart of a worldwide empire. That empire reached its geographic peak by the 1930s, but by no means had

America's influence begun its decline. The change was in concerns and interests and the method in which we set about achieving and protecting them.

This chapter will trace that pattern and describe U.S. policy toward the Caribbean in terms of nineteenth century Manifest Destiny, early twentieth-century imperialism, and hegemony from the 1930s until the present.

THE UNITED STATES AND THE CARIBBEAN BASIN IN THE NINETEENTH CENTURY

The U.S. attitude toward the lands and peoples of the Caribbean Basin (an expression not used until the 1980s) is older than the Panama Canal, older than the Monroe Doctrine, older even than the nation itself. It sprang from the ambitions of the American people, the descendants of those Anglo-Saxons who, having faced the ocean and the wilderness, grew apart from the mother country and fought a war to secure their independence. Early successes and prosperity made the new American nation cocky, and its citizens began to think of themselves as a chosen people in a rich land set aside just for them. Before them lay a vast continent, empty and available.

In the way stood the Indian, but as a "heathen" he could justifiably be pushed aside. The neighboring Spaniard (and his successor, the Mexican) possessed a higher culture, but this culture was still backward, undemocratic, and priest-ridden and therefore needed help from the Anglo-Saxon--through force, if necessary. Somehow, God had saved the Western Hemisphere (precisely how much of it was an issue often debated in Congress) for this particular breed of Anglo-Saxon and had mandated to him the responsibility for bringing enlightenment to the cultures that happened to be in the path of empire. Thus obligation and opportunity became inextricably linked. By the time the American republic had reached its fiftieth birthday, this mystique had permeated society and acquired the name of Manifest Destiny. A war with Mexico brought the United States to its "natural borders," the ocean and the Gulf; a terrible civil war delayed the movement only a few years before the Americans began to talk of the mission beyond the mainland.

Though arguments frequently ensued about the propriety, not to mention probable success, of absorbing insular territories occupied by darker races, many Americans had lusted after Cuba from the earliest days of the nineteenth century. When the other principal Spanish colonies in the New World initiated independence movements, Cuba remained testily loyal. Alarmed by the

interest that major European states displayed in the
island, Congress in 1808 resolved a no-transfer
principle, warning Spain and other interested powers that
although Cuba in weak Spanish hands concerned Americans
little, her transfer to a stronger nation would be
inimical to U.S. interests and thus viewed with
considerable apprehension. Successive administrations
offered to purchase the colony, and some unofficially
even threatened to "wrest" the land from the reluctant
mother country--in the words of the Ostend Manifesto.

The other major island in the Caribbean, named
Espanola by Columbus, secured its freedom from both Spain
and France early in the nineteenth century and promptly
split into two mutually threatening, inchoate republics
called Haiti and Santo Domingo (later the Dominican
Republic). Discouraged by their widespread poverty and
Black populations, the American people held little early
interest in them until, like Cuba, the republics began to
be coveted by European foreign offices and investors.
Once again, the U.S. State Department warned the
foreigner away. The Lincoln administration went so far
as to challenge Spain's right to reannex certain portions
of the island. In the 1870s, land scandals touching
close followers of President Grant were exposed by the
Senate, probably preventing the annexation of naval bases
if not the entire island.

On the mainland, U.S. interests unfolded at an
uneven rate. American pioneers and other restless souls
were invited into Texas by unthinking Mexican officials,
and between 1820 and 1850 the Americans acquired more
than half of Mexico, while occupying the Mississippi
Valley, crossing the Rockies and absorbing much of Oregon
country by sheer force of numbers. Great Britain evened
up some of her loss in Oregon by taking advantage of U.S.
preoccupation to extend English influence into British
Honduras, the Mosquito Coast of Honduras and Nicaragua,
Guatemala, Costa Rica, and various points key to possible
canal sites. The British government did little more than
passively support the private individuals and corporations who bore the expense and danger of these extensions
of English influence, and few crown colonies resulted.
Always in the background, however, prowled British naval
strength, never reluctant to defy the Monroe Doctrine.
Most of these adventures occurred before 1850. In that
year, the U.S. took first serious notice of increasing
British arrogance when the interests of the two states
collided in the strategic Gulf of Fonseca on the Pacific
side of Central America. To prevent a third Anglo-
American war, Washington and London concluded a
deliberately vague cooling off measure called the
Clayton-Bulwer Treaty. Though the British held that the
pact did not require relinquishment of any of their
holdings or investments, their active expansion in the

Caribbean came to a halt. Before the end of the century, interests in Asia and Africa turned England permanently away from competition with the United States in the Caribbean; instead, it began relying on American might to protect the interests of both nations.

Meanwhile, after 1850 U.S. pretensions had grown, stimulated by filibusters, small merchants, and the California gold rush, which prompted a railroad across Panama. Major entrepreneurs such as Cornelius Vanderbilt and adventurers such as William Walker frightened the Central Americans with their investments and mercenaries. Nevertheless, the United States acquired no Central American possessions and absorbed no Central American state in the years from 1850 to 1898.

By the close of the century, U.S. policy had been strengthened by a firmer stand toward Great Britain, but it still remained little more than a blending of the Monroe Doctrine and Manifest Destiny. In practice, this policy meant continued resistance to European intervention of any sort and sporadic concern for immediate neighbors when they got into trouble with aliens from another hemisphere. But after 1898 a new United States burst upon the world.

THE ERA OF IMPERIALISM

The choice of 1898 as the beginning date of Imperial America is an arbitrary one. Signs that the United States was acquiring the trappings of a great power were visible as early as the Civil War, and by the 1880s such evidence had become most impressive. The United States was second only to Russia in population among the industrialized states; it was the world leader in wheat production and nearly so in coal, iron, and steel. Indeed, it was the leader or rapidly overtaking the leader in almost every measure of industrial or commercial vitality by the 1890s. In military terms the nation still lagged, but an urgent naval building program toward the end of the century promised to overcome that deficiency. But the year 1898 brought some of the most fateful changes in American history, including the commencement of imperial democracy. Cuba occupied center stage.

The island's long movement toward independence resurged in the 1890s and crested in 1898. The inhumane and unhygienic conditions accompanying the bitter war of liberation against Spain distressed the American people, who could scarcely ignore the bloodbath on their doorstep. The stages by which the United States entered the fighting need not concern us here; war came. Already in an expansive mood, the public welcomed the conflict for many reasons and waged it in an upbeat tempo with

religious enthusiasm strongly resembling the Manifest
Destiny of the 1840s.

The declaration of war against Spain contained an
unusual disclaimer. The United States asserted its
determination to leave the government and control of Cuba
to its people when the fighting ended. This promise,
called the Teller Amendment, surprised world leaders and
brought much complication to the issue when the Spanish
were defeated.

No one could have predicted Spain's total military
failure; few wars with such vast results have been won so
easily. After less than four months of combat, the
United States acquired the Philippines and Guam from
Spain, absorbed Hawaii and Samoa from native rulers, and
thrust the American flag far across the Pacific. But
more central to our theme, the United States now
possessed Puerto Rico and occupied Cuba militarily while
trying to sort out its future relationship with the
island.

Ready or not, the American people now had an empire,
with all the responsibility of governing many diverse
peoples, some backward, some advanced. These new
subjects had to be protected. That meant new military
and naval expansion, coaling stations, free access to the
seas, a canal, perhaps through Panama or somewhere in
Central America. These measures, in turn, required more
military power to protect them. New markets would be
opening to U.S. business, and there would be greater
opportunities to invest, produce, and buy. Bullish
America reacted; in the years of the first military occupation of Cuba--1898-1902--nearly 200 corporations were
founded in the United States, dozens of them expecting to
do most of their business in the new empire. They
included two sugar trusts, the American Tobacco Company,
International Harvester, Bethlehem Steel, and the United
Fruit Company, all of which invested in Cuba.[1]

But how should the island be governed? Given the
Greater America feeling of so much of the nation, would
the Teller Amendment prove an embarrassment to be quietly
tossed aside? The unusual combination of sugar beet
interests, bond sellers, and the noble-minded brought
some soul-searching, particularly when military occupation revealed the economic and political immaturity of
the Cuban people. At this juncture a variety of forces
and philosophies exerted their influence upon American
policy: pure imperialists touting mercantilism;
disciples of Alfred Mahan demanding naval bases, not
necessarily encumbered by colonies; men such as Elihu
Root, Roosevelt's secretary of war, who feared German
intervention in the Caribbean and sought some means to
hold the island in a protectorate; anti-imperialists who
wanted a completely free Cuba; Roosevelt himself, who
warned the Cubans of the consequences of misgovernment;

and those ambivalent Americans who might have wanted a colony but deplored the inability of dark-skinned "natives" to be absorbed into a democracy.

The resulting compromise brought about the first U.S. protectorate in the Caribbean--a Cuba free, but not quite free. Although never precisely copied again, the procedure served as the basis of similar relationships throughout the region for the next thirty years. The instrument providing this bit of legerdemain was the Platt Amendment, constituting first simply an addition to an army appropriations bill, then an appendix to the Cuban constitution, and ultimately the heart of a treaty between the two states. The measure would serve as the cornerstone of Washington's Caribbean policy until the 1930s.

The amendment's major terms included restrictions on Cuba's right to borrow funds elsewhere than in the United States; severe restrictions on Cuba's right to make treaties with nations other than the United States; the right of the latter to lease and maintain lands necessary for coaling or naval stations (ultimately, the United States retained only Guantanamo Bay); and, in the most significant restriction of all, Cuba's granting to the United States the right of intervention to preserve life, liberty, and property and to carry out obligations imposed on the United States by the Treaty of Paris.

A few Cubans supported the amendment. Some considered it better than a military occupation, if that were the alternative. But most recognized the document for what it was--a severe limitation on sovereignty and a method of making them second-class citizens in their own country. No one could estimate its full impact.

From 1902 to 1934 Cubans labored under the restraints of the Platt Amendment. U.S. troops assisted in the inauguration of Tomas Estrada Palma as the island's first president, then withdrew in May 1902. Commencing his term with patriotic fervor, in the flush of military victory and a balanced budget (thanks to the American military government's performance), Estrada Palma's early years proved productive. Yet when he sought a second term, his rivals promptly used force to prevent the extension, and Estrada Palma turned to the United States for support. Theodore Roosevelt first sent a personal emissary, but when that accomplished little, he initiated a full-scale intervention by the marines. In a fashion all too familiar to former colonists of Spain, Estrada Palma was set aside for Roosevelt's representative, Charles Magoon. Magoon and the marines remained from 1906-09, leaving the island a bit more quiet and solvent again, but in many ways psychologically weaker.

Other interventions lasted a few months; one dragged out from 1917 until 1922. Together they helped develop

among the Cuban people a Platt Amendment syndrome—a
tendency to pass on difficult decisions and problems to
the United States, along with the blame when things went
wrong. Administrations in trouble found it easy to
appeal for help and get more tenure from an Uncle Sam
seeking peace. The biographer of Jose Marti complained
that the amendment "favored the growth of general civic
indolence, a tepid indifference to national dangers."[2]
Nationalism and national pride found harsh soil in which
to grow, a condition made no better by the entrenched
position of many Spaniards left from colonial times or
arriving in the wave of new immigration to the island.
Political immorality, bad enough under Spain, now seemed
epidemic. After World War I, gangster money and thrill-
seeking tourists moved with ease from the United States
to Cuba. The fleshpots, the Mafia casinos, and the
rum-running trade assaulted Cuban pride, not to mention
virtue. As the price of New York bank loans in 1922, an
"Honest Cabinet" was imposed upon the government by the
U.S. overseer, Enoch Crowder. (The irony escaped few
Cubans.) And, above all, the tyrant sugar extended its
reign, with boom and bust, underemployment, undernourish-
ment, and absentee ownership all serving as court
attendants.

Historians once spoke of a "benevolent protectorate"
and the "myth" of intervention, and saw the United States
holding strategic motives rather than the economic objectives stressed by most modern writers. Suchlicki refers
to this period as that of the "Platt Amendment Republic."
Langley terms it the "Years of Paternalism." Whitney
Perkins speaks of "Commitment and Exercise of Control."
Dominguez calls it "Governing through Pluralization."[3]
Probably it is safe to conclude that the American people,
with mixed intentions, no worse than other nations and
better than many, had taken on an imperial status with
which they proved uncomfortable.

Of the four other protectorates established during
the Imperialist Era, the most important was Panama.
French and American interest in this isthmian canal, the
lobbying in New York and Washington, Colombian obdurate-
ness, Theodore Roosevelt, Philippe Bunau-Varilla, and the
revolt of the Panamanian firemen flesh out a story known
even to the proverbial schoolboy. Not only was a canal
zone created, but a new republic called Panama acquired
life. How much freedom would it have?

A comparison of Panama's status with that of Cuba is
instructive. Given the almost identical birthdates of
the Platt Amendment and the Hay-Bunau-Varilla Treaty, one
might expect considerable similarity in their philosophy
and language. But such is not the case. The former
specifically spelled out the instances in which Cuba
could exert its sovereignty and under which the United
States might legally intervene in its affairs. In

contrast, the word <u>intervene</u> does not occur in the
Hay-Bunau-Varilla Treaty. Of course, Panama's relations
could not be extricated from canal matters and the
American presence in the Canal Zone, which the United
States would possess and exercise "as if it were the
sovereign of the territory." But Panama granted the
United States "in perpetuity" a <u>carte blanche</u> to use any
Panamanian lands <u>outside</u> the Zone needed for construction, operation, or protection of the canal. Under this
proviso, Colon and Panama City, which are outside the
Zone, fell within American jurisdiction. Since these
were the only likely centers of political uprisings, the
proviso gave the United States considerable leverage to
control dissidents.

In brief, by concordat Cuba might expect American
intervention--if something went "wrong." Panamanians, on
the other hand, could anticipate that the U.S. presence
would be a constant, the legal basis being Article One of
the Hay-Bunau-Varilla Treaty: "The United States guarantee and will maintain the independence of the Republic of
Panama." Emphasis, probably not needed, came from
Article Twenty-three, which added that if the United
States should ever have to use force for the protection
of the canal, it could do so, and could also construct
such permanent fortifications as needed.[4] Essentially
this arrangement remained until 1937.

A different set of circumstances brought about
America's third protectorate, that of the Dominican
Republic, in 1904. This lovely, unhappy land dates its
written history from the colony founded by Columbus in
1493 and can boast the oldest European city in the
hemisphere. The Dominican Republic occupies some sixty
percent of the island of Espanola, which it shares with
Haiti. The two domains also share a bloody history.
Half a century after the death of Columbus Spain lost
interest in the island and began tolerating the
intrusions of pirates and French settlers. By the end of
the seventeenth century, the latter had acquired legal
title to the western third of the island and turned it
into a prosperous sugar colony based on African slavery.
(This portion was to call itself Haiti.) Spain ceded her
remaining share to France in 1795, and it was against
France that the first movement for independence succeeded
in the Caribbean--Haiti becoming free in 1804, the
Dominicans in 1809. The Spanish then returned, but in
time they too were overthrown. After a brutal racial
struggle, the Dominicans succumbed to the Haitians, who
ruled them from 1822 until 1844, when the Dominican
Republic achieved sovereignty. Tensions between the two
have never completely disappeared.

Conditions in independence proved little better than
under Haiti, which attempted repeated invasions. These
threats, plus chronic poverty and tyranny, caused the

little republic to offer itself and some of its natural
resources for sale to several major powers. From the
U.S. perspective, the most serious incident occurred in
1861, when, taking advantage of the American Civil War,
Spain reincorporated the nation as a province. But the
venture proved too costly, and the queen, Isabella II,
withdrew her forces.

The episode excited many Americans, and both
President Johnson and President Grant made overtures
toward annexation. Grant would have settled for a lease
on the vast Bay of Samana, but rumors of scandal and land
fraud reached Washington, and the Senate rejected his
plan. The last two decades of the century witnessed the
dictatorship of Ulises Heureaux, whose efforts to
modernize the Dominican Republic grossly exacerbated its
financial plight. Heureaux had to borrow to pay off old
loans, the interest rates apparently ranging from 120 to
several hundred percent for short-term notes, owed
primarily to European investors. Broke, the nation
offered itself to the United States in 1899. Rebuffed by
Secretary of State John Hay, the Dominicans gave a group
of foreign bondholders control of much of the customs
collection, the nation's chief source of revenue.
Meanwhile, these creditors badgered their respective
governments to force complete repayment. In 1904, the
Dominican president announced his intention to let the
United States assume his country's financial burdens.

Again, Theodore Roosevelt appeared on stage. Just
three years before, he had been most conciliatory toward
several European states when they inquired about using
force to collect debts owed by Venezuela. At that time,
he had replied that the Monroe Doctrine did not
"guarantee any state against punishment if it misconducts
itself, provided the punishment does not take the form of
the acquisition of territory by any non-American power."
Britain and Germany responded by instituting a blockade
and did considerable damage to Venezuelan shipping and
other property. Venezuela then agreed to arbitration,
and the claims issue went to the Permanent Court of
Arbitration at The Hague. When that tribunal ruled that
the nations doing the blockading should get preference in
the claims settlement, Roosevelt changed his mind and his
policy, announcing what became known as the Roosevelt
Corollary to the Monroe Doctrine. In his 1904 annual
message, he declared that "chronic wrongdoing" by another
American state might require punishment by some
"civilized nation." Under the Monroe Doctrine that would
have had to be the United States, since it could not have
permitted any other state to perform that disciplinary
function.[5]

So the Dominican Republic was not to be let off with
a bombardment and a Hague judgment or some similar
penance. Something new would be tried.

Roosevelt took advantage of the simplistic tax structure that the Dominicans had inherited from colonial Spain, which relied almost totally on export and import taxes for the national revenue. In 1906, while an American fleet ominously patrolled Dominican waters, President Ramon Caceres concluded an executive agreement with Roosevelt on the use of the customs to liquidate the Dominican debt. (The agreement was used to bypass the Senate because Roosevelt sought a stronger commitment than that body would accept.) The terms did not require a U.S. occupation in any military sense; a handful of advisers--usually Ivy League economists--assumed responsibility for collecting the taxes, withholding 55 percent for the repayment of the foreign debt, plus advisers' expenses, and doling out the remaining 45 percent to the Dominican government for its operations. Under these arrangements many bondholders were willing to settle and leave, so net shares varied substantially across creditors. Most bondholders, however, were satisfied. Curiously, the Dominican government found itself with more cash on its hands than before the fiscal intervention (when its own agents did the collecting). The national debt dropped from $40 million to $17 million. In 1907 compromise made possible the solidification of the arrangements in a treaty. For about five years the system worked, the little nation stabilized itself, and Roosevelt and his successor felt satisfied with the Corollary.

But peace never lasts on Espanola. A revolution broke out in 1911, wiping out the surplus; President Caceres, who achieved office by assassination, left the same way. That same year, President Taft found it necessary to lend money once again to the Dominicans and even to supply several hundred marines to maintain peace. By 1916 the Wilson administration reluctantly ordered a full-scale occupation, which lasted until 1924. The receivership, somewhat modified, continued until 1941. Customs collecting for U.S. protectorates had little long-term success.

The fourth protectorate to be considered is Nicaragua, whose tiny size and relative unimportance in international affairs belie the intensity of its relations with the United States. These relations have extended over more than a century, long before the Panama Canal aggravated every Nicaraguan issue.

As early as 1826, American investors sought and obtained a concession to construct a canal through Nicaragua but let it lapse. Before mid-century, representatives of several European states had had the same experience. The peak of British interest coincided with the end of the Mexican War and the discovery of gold in California, which thrust Nicaragua dramatically onto the American stage. To profit from the Argonauts' need for

safe transportation across the isthmus, Cornelius
Vanderbilt and his partners secured a contract with
Nicaragua in 1849 for the right to build a canal and a
rail and carriage road. The canal itself had to be
postponed, but Vanderbilt profited by turning a
combination of boats, burros, and carriages into a
network that linked steamers on both the Atlantic and the
Pacific shores.
    This system functioned for four years until William
Walker and his forces sided with Vanderbilt's rivals to
take it over. The rivalry merged into a Nicaraguan civil
war and something of a Central American war against
Walker, who was driven off the isthmus and later killed.
But Vanderbilt also lost out with the completion of the
Panama Railroad in 1855.
    All this activity on the part of private investors
and foreign governments finally caught the attention of
the United States, where popular assumption held that
Nicaragua possessed the best canal route. Between 1849
and 1914, the two states negotiated ten different
treaties on the subject of canal rights. Several tilted
in the direction of a protectorate, but before any such
protectorate could be consummated, world attention
shifted to Panama and the ill-fated French attempt to
pierce the land there. Ultimately, of course, the
Americans replaced the French and succeeded in completing
the canal.
    But U.S. concern for Nicaragua did not die with the
shift to Panama. The reality of a canal anywhere in
Central America necessitated interest in Nicaragua.
Nowhere had factions struggled more bitterly and less
fruitfully. At heart lay a senseless regionalism,
simplistically labeled "liberalism versus conservatism,"
controlled only when the current strong man was strong
enough. In the administration of the liberal general
Jose Santos Zelaya (1893-1909), these conditions marked
the beginning of Nicaragua's major involvement with the
world. Brutal, but more progressive than his predecessors, Zelaya meddled in the affairs of his neighbors
as he sought to revive the old Central American federation, until the wrath of Washington fell upon him. He
had enemies enough to provoke rebellion in any year, but
in 1909 certain conservatives, embittered fellow-
liberals, the State Department, and foreign businessmen
who had been locked out by the dictator combined to
remove him, the precipitating action being his execution
of two mercenaries who happened to be American citizens.
His resignation made it possible for the U.S. marines to
ensure the installation of a conservative friendly to the
United States, after which they departed.
    The next few years provided endless chaos for
Nicaragua. The liberals were probably the more popular
party, whereas the conservatives enjoyed U.S. support.

77

Both groups factionalized constantly. A special American agent worked out an agreement among the politicians over the presidency and customs (a la the Dominican Republic), plus New York bank loans to replace the overdue loans from Europe. Again, the U.S. Senate would not concur, so President Taft arranged an executive agreement with the new Nicaraguan President, Adolfo Diaz. Almost immediately the liberals rebelled, and the marines returned--this time to stay.

American marines, varying in number from 100 to about 2,000, occupied Nicaragua for nineteen of the next twenty years from 1912 to 1933. In 1916, to further strengthen this relationship, the two nations ratified the Bryan-Chamorro Treaty, which gave the United States certain canal and other territorial rights in return for $3 million. (The canal was never built. American officials determined that most of the $3 million should be used to repay creditors, and the treaty so threatened the security of Nicaragua's neighbors that they took the matter to court.) In 1925 the marines were removed during a period of peace and sent back when civil war broke out again. In 1927, the United States, eager to aid Diaz, supported the marines with a show of battleships and grants of arms and money. Embarrassed by the opposition to the protectorate, President Coolidge dispatched Henry Stimson as special representative to negotiate a peace of permanence. He accomplished an election, won by Diaz's opponent, and a truce among factions. Ultimate stability was to rest with a constabulary or national guard trained by the marines.

But one group of partisans refused to lay down their arms and continued to wage guerrilla war. Their leader, Augusto Cesar Sandino, led hit-and-run campaigns against both American business outposts and the Nicaraguan government. His successes were more symbolic than real. In 1934 he ended his campaign and was treacherously murdered by the new ruler, Anastasio Somoza. The defeat of Sandino and what he appeared to stand for, and the rising power of the Guardia Nacional and its boss, Somoza, mark the watershed of American imperialism in Nicaragua. By the 1930s the United States no longer sought to interfere in Nicaraguan affairs but felt it could trust the new regime to support its wishes.

In many ways the U.S. experience in Nicaragua duplicated that in the Dominican Republic. In both cases the protectorate included military occupation, customs collections, and loans. In Nicaragua, the emphasis on loans was greater and more purposeful. Roosevelt had used loans only to pay off the Dominican's foreign obligations in order to reduce the danger of European intervention. Taft's policy, which he unfortunately labeled "Dollar Diplomacy" (a term too well remembered by Latin Americans), intended an active, as contrasted with

Roosevelt's re-active, program of investment for stability's sake. Taft, in short, anticipated the developmental loan of a later day.

The fifth and last Caribbean protectorate established by the United States, and the only one initiated by a Democratic president, was Haiti, the most forlorn of American republics. Today Haiti's per capita gross domestic product amounts to one-half of Bolivia's, one-third of Paraguay's, and one-fourth of that of its neighbor, the Dominican Republic--all poverty-stricken lands. As an eighteenth-century colony, Haiti produced great wealth from its sugar plantations, but little for the slaves and their descendants once the French army and landowners had been overthrown and banished. Shortly after independence in 1804, regionalism, racism, and political ignorance took over. Illiterate masses supported greedy rulers in the face of grinding poverty. Only a despot could hold office, and then not for long. Before 1915, only two presidents left office at the time scheduled by law.

Because of the slavery issue, the United States traditionally exhibited little regard for Haiti and did not extend diplomatic recognition until 1862, when the slaveowners had left Washington. The Mole St. Nicolas, a sturdy breakwater protecting a fine harbor on Haiti's northwest coast, proved to be the only exception, and after the 1860s Haitian and American presidents frequently discussed the prospect of a lease or sale. Nothing came of these proffers, and when the Platt Amendment assured the Americans control of Guantanamo Bay, and thereby domination of the Windward Passage, the Mole's value largely disappeared.

Toward the end of the nineteenth century, the increasing presence of European commerce kindled U.S. interest, often reflected in visits by American warships to remove non-Haitians whose lives and property were threatened by the regular rebellions on the isle. French and German economic interests became more substantial in Haiti than in any other nation of the Caribbean. French money dominated the lending, export, and banking businesses, but the United States feared the Germans more for their ownership of utilities and shipping lines and their reputations for financing uprisings. The latter were also believed to have designs on the Mole, since they had no Caribbean coaling station.[6]

By the outbreak of World War I, international tensions over the control of Haiti had increased dramatically. German interests at home stimulated an uncertain withdrawal program from the Caribbean, and the Americans and French found themselves in almost total control of Haitian finances and customs through ownership of the Haitian National Bank. Near anarchy forced the two powers to ask for American marines to guard the shipping by warships of some $500,000 of the bank's resources to New York for safekeeping.

An uprising in July 1915 prompted the new president, Vilbrun Guillaume Sam, to order the slaughter of a number of political prisoners, many of them influential. In retribution, a mob tore him from his hiding place in the French Embassy and dismembered his body in the streets of Port-au-Prince. The U.S. marines, who had warned the Haitians about further disorders, immediately landed, took the capital and, within a few weeks, the entire nation. President Wilson established a protectorate, with the Navy Department governing through puppet Haitian officials. The Haitians were required to accept this protectorate in the form of a ten-year treaty, subsequently extended another decade. When the Haitian congress refused to ratify a U.S.-made constitution, the Marines conducted their own plebiscite and secured its easy passage.

The protectorate, probably the bloodiest in all of the Caribbean, endured until 1934 when the marines left, but the receivership continued until 1941, as in the Dominican Republic.

Between 1903 and 1915, the U.S. government, by force or threat of force, had intervened substantially in the domestic and foreign affairs of five Caribbean states--Cuba, Panama, the Dominican Republic, Nicaragua, and Haiti. The reasons for each involvement included a complex set of strategic, financial, commercial, and humane motives. Each instance was defined by significant periods of military occupation, but not necessarily for the duration of the entire intervention. No effort has been made in this reading to include cases in which a marine detachment landed briefly to evacuate endangered American citizens (or others), temporarily protect property, or merely "show the flag."

Nor is there space to include instances in which demonstrations--usually by warships--were used to bring about some end other than a protectorate, to show support for an administration, to discourage rebels, and so on. These activities have often taken place so briefly that they do not show up in official records. At times they occurred at the request of an American consul or naval commander without official sanction from Washington until later. They compose another portion of the imperial story, less well-known and difficult to categorize as much more than another source of Yankee-phobia.

It should be noted in passing that the nation geographically closest to the United States, Mexico, has never suffered the indignity of an American protectorate, although, of course, it lost substantial territory through warfare and purchase. Relations between the two countries were severely strained during the early years of the Mexican Revolution, and President Wilson used troops to occupy Vera Cruz in 1914. Again, in 1916-17, he dispatched the army under General John Pershing into Chihuahua on a punitive expedition. For nearly a year and a half (1913-14), he withheld diplomatic recognition on moral grounds from the administration of President Victoriano Huerta, until other factions overturned Huerta. These are clearly other forms of intervention, but the United States made no effort to run the Mexican government or occupy its territory as would be the case in a true protectorate. Mexico's revolution continued for many years, and tensions between the two states eased only a little before World War II. But the many claims, questions, and other disputes during the 1920s and 1930s led to no more military occupations or interventions.

Not solely by armed or fiscal intervention did the United States attempt to stabilize the Caribbean. Less eye-catching but more imaginative were the State Department's diplomatic measures, the most noteworthy being the Central American treaties of 1907 and 1923. Not surprisingly, Theodore Roosevelt planned the first of these, bringing the Central American representatives to Washington for plans to end their ceaseless meddling in one another's business. The resulting treaties included provision for noninterference, neutrality under specific circumstances of Central American warfare, peace machinery, and two dramatic innovations--the compulsory settlement of international disputes and a Central American Court of Justice to perform that miracle. The court handled minor affairs effectively, but its judges always voted along national lines. Eventually, it failed to get the support of the United States on a crucial matter concerning Nicaragua, and so it died. The 1923 treaties contained much of the same philosophy as their predecessors, but created a weaker tribunal. They reduced the chronic interference, but only when U.S. might stood squarely behind the agreements, and the machinery could not handle the many rebellions of the 1930s triggered by the Depression. By 1940 all of the five Central American republics had denounced the treaties, with no objection from the United States.

THE ERA OF HEGEMONY

Prior to Franklin Roosevelt, no American president had ever renounced the practice of maintaining Caribbean protectorates (roughly 1898-1933). Abandonment of that policy resulted from the recognition that occupation produced ill will, little permanent good, and often not even short-term peace. On Espanola, local resistance to the two interventions became increasingly bitter after World War I, and reports of brutal (admittedly often retaliatory) behavior by American troops brought sharp

criticism from the National Association for the
Advancement of Colored People (NAACP) and investigations
by both Congress and the Navy. The Navy Department
produced no whitewash. The reports greatly distressed
President Wilson, and he set the machinery in motion to
disengage from the Dominican Republic, the first operation of this kind. Military concerns delayed matters,
and it was not until 1924 that Calvin Coolidge could
announce the final withdrawal of American troops.

In the 1920s renewed American feelings of
isolationism were strengthened by unsavory reports of
events in Nicaragua and Mexico, and President Hoover
received much popular support from Latin Americans when
he expressed his distaste at the representation abroad of
his nation in this fashion. A Pan American meeting at
Havana in 1928 marked the beginning of official Latin
American protests over U.S. interventions, and much of
this complaint was directed to Franklin Roosevelt even
before his inauguration. As a result, when in the 1933
Inter-American Conference at Montevideo the matter of
prohibiting intervention reached the agenda for the first
time, Secretary of State Cordell Hull--with only mild
reservations--concurred and signed a treaty recognizing
the equality of states. Further agreements followed,
specifically prohibiting the interference by any American
state in the affairs of another.

Nonintervention became the cornerstone of the Good
Neighbor Policy, and between 1933 and 1939 Roosevelt
brought to an end all four of the remaining Caribbean
protectorates. He even refused to exert diplomatic
pressure on Mexico when that nation expropriated vast
petroleum and land resources from foreigners in 1937, and
he insisted that the owners take their protests to
Mexican courts, not to the U.S. State Department.
Nonintervention and the near-unity of the hemisphere
resulting from Axis aggression greatly enhanced the aura
of the Good Neighbor Policy. For the first time Latin
Americans had been treated--legally, at least--as equals,
capable of managing their own affairs. Throughout the
hemisphere it was widely assumed that this attitude,
reflecting the best in U.S. behavior, would be policy for
decades to come. How much of an aberration did the Good
Neighbor Policy represent?

We do not know. Just before World War II, the Axis
powers appeared to pose serious dangers to all the
hemisphere (even though Argentina and Chile questioned
this for their own reasons). For the first time since
James Monroe, most Americans, North and South, perceived
the same enemy, already sweeping everything in its path
in Europe and Asia. Roosevelt represented the last
defense against that enemy, and the Latin Americans
rallied behind him. They also trusted him. So far, at
least, nothing had occurred to provoke his intervention

or his need to "spank" some little state (to use the words of his distant cousin). What if some European nation were to menace the stability of the Caribbean, as in the old days? Roosevelt had anticipated that possibility.

In July 1940, more than a year before the United States went to war, Roosevelt had asked for and received authority from all the Latin American republics to protect the colonies in the Caribbean from German attack and occupation. This "Act of Havana" gave the American states together--or any state acting alone--the right to use force to maintain existing ownership (i.e., to protect colonial status). Although the measure seemed to accomplish a multilateralization of the Monroe Doctrine, the signatories recognized that only the United States would have the power to enforce the measure. Argentina expressed its suspicions, but generally the pact was well received. (It spoke only of colonies, but one would have to assume that the agreement would have been identical if the independence of a small republic were jeopardized).

Today, scholars are examining aspects of the Good Neighbor era and finding more self-interest than did earlier historians. It just may be that the Axis threat and a happy coincidence of circumstances permitted Roosevelt the luxury of enjoying a Carribean less disturbed than it had ever been before or since. Given similar circumstances, perhaps he would have intervened as much as his predecessors and successors did.

But history cannot be written that way. The facts are that Roosevelt had dissolved much of the American empire and brought about a new relationship of closer diplomacy, the first substantial government loans to Latin American states, attractive trade agreements, cultural ties, vast investments, and military pacts. The relationship would never be the same again. Most writers call this new dependence "hegemony," and the word suits, in part because of its imprecision. What difference would it make to the relationship with Roosevelt gone and new enemies arising in the world? The emergence of the Cold War marked the end of the Good Neighbor.

Western Hemisphere nations assumed that their wartime agreements were temporary, and that permanent security measures would be concluded after the war. U.S. problems with Argentina delayed matters for a while, but in 1947 nineteen Pan American nations convened their delegates at Quitandinha in the state of Rio de Janeiro. (Ultimately all twenty-one states ratified the agreements reached.) The aim was to achieve a mutual security pact, and there was little disagreement as to its appropriateness. The Rio Treaty (or more correctly, the Inter-American Treaty of Reciprocal Assistance) created the machinery for resistance against armed attack from outside or within the hemisphere, consultation concerning

forms of aggression other than armed attack, and the
means of accomplishing such defense.

President Truman saw the pact as a means to secure
the hemisphere against Soviet aggression, whereas the
Latin states seemed more interested in reordering the
Inter-American system. Ironically, the treaty also
marked the departure of Latin America from the forefront
of U.S. national interest, for the discussions and decisions at Rio coincided with the Truman Doctrine and the
Marshall Plan. These contradictions were most clearly
expressed in the Inter-American Conference at Bogota in
1948, when all sorts of legal codifications for the
pursuit of peace were drafted, but the Latin Americans
were told of the impossibility of developing an economic-
assistance plan comparable to those for Europe. Lacking
serious communist threat, Latin America would get little
aid.

But when Soviet strength became more ominous, the
next three American presidents, Dwight Eisenhower, John
Kennedy, and Lyndon Johnson, all used the executive power
to try to destabilize unfriendly governments or suppress
rebellions in the name of anti-communism. Eisenhower
first resumed this pre-Good Neighbor practice, but tipped
his hat in the direction of world public opinion by using
covert methods rather than the blunt openness of "Gunboat
Diplomacy."

The occasion was the presence in Guatemala of
successive left-wing reform governments, the second of
which, under Colonel Jacobo Arbenz, frightened
Washington, especially when its land reform program led
to the confiscation of extensive landholdings of the
United Fruit Company, the old bete noire of Latin
America. The United States had developed clandestine
methods during World War II. Earlier in his administration, Eisenhower had used the CIA to help destroy the
Iranian foreign minister who had nationalized British oil
holdings and threatened the rule of the Shah. Now these
devices would be applied in Central America.

It is still unclear as to how seriously Eisenhower
considered the overt use of American forces to eliminate
Arbenz. He and Truman had both briefly flirted with
utilizing the ever-available Somoza to overthrow the
Guatemalan government. But Ike preferred the covert
tools of Iran--threats, a bought press, military aid to
the beseiged country's neighbors, and powerful propaganda
campaigns. In combination, these measures critically
weakened the Guatemalan Army. Assistance to Arbenz's
enemies at home and abroad promised a slick success.
Bewildered, the Guatemalan Army did little to oppose the
small invasion force under the leadership of Colonel
Carlos Castillo Armas, who became the new president,
dutifully beholden to Washington. A revolution had
ended.

The secrecy of the overthrow eliminated the possibility of much immediate public debate about the morality of the action; but challenged, Eisenhower would undoubtedly have ducked behind the Monroe Doctrine and declared the action justified in the face of a foreign threat to the security of the hemisphere and the United States. Nearly a generation was to pass before this hypothesis would be tested by American scholarship and found wanting.[7]

In 1959 Fidel Castro's rise to power initially created mixed feelings of fear and support in Washington. Before two years had elapsed, however, two administrations had decided that his regime posed a critical threat to all the Americas. Still touchy about "intervention," both the Eisenhower and Kennedy governments considered means of overthrowing Castro without the use of U.S. troops. Willing Cuban refugees abounded, and the CIA, flushed with its victories in Iran and Guatemala, promised a cheap and easy success. But this time everything went wrong. Miscalculations, false assumptions, bad intelligence, and presidential indecision made the 1961 Bay of Pigs invasion a byword for failure. In his embarrassment, President Kennedy could only protest that he had not used American forces to interfere in Cuban affairs, an interesting effort to bathe in what remained of the Good Neighbor halo. Predictably, Cuban morale tightened and Yankee-phobia intensified.

Lyndon Johnson, too, had his turn with communist threats in the Caribbean. Since 1931 the Dominican Republic had been tyrannized by a bloody dictator, Rafael Trujillo. By the 1950s his behavior began to distress Washington, which shed few tears when he was murdered in 1961. Two years later, Juan Bosch came into office by election, only to face awesome reconstruction, Trujillo holdovers, and the usual Latin American problems. When he attempted reforms, the conservatives packed him off into exile. In April 1965 a bewildering revolt broke out, possibly supporting Bosch, though this is uncertain. The Dominican government and the American Embassy both cried for help to protect U.S. citizens and property, making it sound as if Castro had provoked the uprising. Johnson sent the marines, initially to protect lives. Then, in a welter of confused intelligence reports, the president declared that American intervention was necessary to prevent the establishment of another communist regime in the hemisphere. In the face of substantial criticism, Johnson sought the support of the Organization of American States (OAS). Five governments voted against the United States, but he got his majority. Several countries, including Brazil, contributed troops to an OAS "peacekeeping" force. In 1966 a provisional regime was installed, backed militarily and financially by Washington, and the OAS troops were withdrawn. A presidential election was held, and the Dominicans chose Johnson's candidate, Joaquin Balaguer, over Bosch. Balaguer then had himself reelected two more times. Nicaragua revived. Balaguer finally lost in 1982.

The unpopularity of interventions is reflected in the fact that all three presidents after Truman-- Eisenhower, Kennedy, and Johnson--declined to use U.S. forces in overt fashion as in the pre-Good Neighbor days. The first two resorted to covert action, hoping that the world would not detect the support given to insurgent groups; Johnson, on the other hand, made no secret of American presence, but tried to create the impression that the Dominican invasion was a regional effort in which the United States was only one of the participants.

Since the Dominican affair, U.S. troops have not been used to intervene in Latin America--at least, not in the usual sense of the word. Yet in the past fifteen years the Caribbean nations have probably never been more troublesome. In an earlier time, the almost constant state of war in El Salvador and Guatemala, the thousands of kidnappings and assassinations aggravated by near-bankruptcy in some states, would have provoked the mobilization of the U.S. marines many times over. But the most significant U.S. action in those years was the commencement of a withdrawal from the most important spot in the region--the Panama Canal.

In a sense this change began, however slowly, back in the days of the Good Neighbor Policy and continued until the Carter administration. In the 1930s, the United States recognized Panama's growing nationalism by ending the protectorate and various other privileges and increasing the annuity paid to Panama. Another treaty in 1955 substantially raised the annuity again and made minor concessions to assuage Panamanian pride. Eisenhower conceded that Panama held some form of residual sovereignty, and Kennedy acknowledged something of the same sort when he permitted the flying of the two national flags together in the Canal Zone. Egypt's seizure of Suez could scarcely pass unnoticed, and Johnson, too, felt compelled to seek new routes to forestall sabotage and other dangers.

But all these changes could not conceal the increased yearning of the Panamanians for complete ownership. At first, U.S. public opinion was unyielding, even in the face of frequent riots. Gradually a combination of fear for the canal's safety, recognition that it was indefensible against sabotage, its increasing inadequacy for world trade, and acceptance of the Panamanian legal position led successive presidents (Johnson, Nixon, and Ford) to carry on new treaty nego- tiations. The work was completed by President Carter and Panama's chief of state, Omar Torrijos. The fight in the U.S. Senate was bitter, but unexpected support from some conservatives pushed it through. The new treaty, in effect as of 1979, completely changed the relationship of the two nations toward the canal. A joint interim commission will manage the facility until 1999, with the United States holding a five-to-four majority until 1990, when the arrangement will be reversed. By the year 2000 the canal will be entirely Panama's. Meanwhile, the two nations share defense responsibilities, while Panama assumes jurisdiction over crime and control over the railway. Certain measures were also taken to aid American citizens who were employed at the canal and who wished to retire or leave the Zone, and to train Panamanian replacements.

The Canal Treaty amply demonstrates the complexities of U.S. policy in the Caribbean, as the presidents whose actions made possible the final work of Jimmy Carter had all taken hard lines on maintaining an American presence. Should the disposal of the Panama Canal be regarded as a late blooming of the Good Neighbor Policy or an aberration in the new era of hegemony? Opposition to the treaty was bitter and vocal, yet the favorable vote in the Senate was sixty-eight to thirty-two, a bipartisan, two-thirds majority. Was this a growing recognition of the improprieties of the 1903 rebellion, a touch of magnanimity, a sop to Latin America, a sign of fear? Future studies may better answer these questions, but for now it would seem that the action at least provided a clear-cut late-blooming retreat from imperialism.

CONCLUSION

From 1898 until 1933, the United States maintained a Caribbean empire, even if not always recognized as such by American citizens. This dominion usually came about through presidential use of military powers to avoid requests for war declarations that would not be forth-coming and executive agreements signed to avoid treaties that would not be ratified. The Good Neighbor-World War II era has traditionally been described as ending that empire and marking the transition to better days. That interpretation may not be totally correct, but change did occur. Although still retaining some insular colonies, the United States withdrew its troops and promised not to return them.

But the Cold War all too soon ended that honeymoon and brought a return to interventionism. The new methods are more sophisticated, often secret, technologically too advanced for Theodore Roosevelt's time, and they reflect a dominance acquired through political, economic, and military strength. Although hegemony does not permit complete freedom of the client state, it does entail a greater degree of initiative than was the case during the Imperialist Era.

Under present-day hegemony, the danger exists that Congress may play an even weaker role in determining policy. Every passing decade has seen presidents reaffirm their right to independent action in the Caribbean. Secrecy becomes more possible, and the public is often poorly informed of the issues and merits of intervention. Loans, diplomatic recognition, military sales, and grants can accomplish stability--or its absence. Belated efforts to regain its constitutional authority can be seen in the restrictions Congress has placed on aid that can be given Central American states accused of human rights violations.

Aside from protecting U.S. security--an issue not likely to go away soon--what issues remain that might provoke future interventions or occupations? The older question of the protection of American lives and property has lost some of its urgency. Citizens abroad can now be evacuated so quickly by air that the use of troops becomes irrelevant. Property seizure is more complex. It is difficult to generalize about the amount of U.S. foreign investment today compared with the pre-1933 period because of inflation, secrecy, and complicated ownership patterns. With the abrogation of the Platt Amendment, for instance, American investment in Cuba declined sharply. By contrast, in Panama and the Dominican Republic it multiplied many times, long after the protectorates had ended. Perhaps more important is the fact that the amount of tangible property has generally declined. The multinational banana companies, for example, own far less land now than they did a generation or two ago, but they have vastly increased production by dealing with local growers. It is unlikely today that a president would justify an intervention on the grounds that he had to save the real estate of Amalgamated Whatever. Politics have shifted at least that much.

The entire history of American policy in the Caribbean can be analyzed in terms of fear of foreign powers or their systems. Obviously neither James Monroe nor Theodore Roosevelt had addressed himself to the question of communism, but Monroe and his generation worried, inordinately it seems today, about the transfer of a foreign political system--monarchism--to the Western Hemisphere. Roosevelt's generation fretted not so much about a system as about the penetration of a major external power or the expansion of a power already established in the region. Americans of World War II days showed considerable alarm in the face of German fascism, which seemed to be entrenching itself through commerce, bases, and spies. Since the 1950s, they have expressed even greater distress that the extension of

another foreign political system--this time labeled
communism--would be dangerous to our peace and security.
The name of what we fear changes, but the thread of
insecurity continues to be woven through our history.
Crowded Europe has always had tense borders; spacious
America has faced the matter only sporadically and hence
is more frightened by its appearance. Security still
lies at the heart of the matter; today we are repeatedly
warned that civil war in El Salvador or Guatemala
threatens our own safety.

Back in 1900 the Americans debated the propriety of
a democracy holding an empire; but that issue has
probably disappeared with the empire. Perhaps now we
need a thoughtful discussion of the value of hegemony.
We know that our interventions throughout the Imperialist
Era proved a mixed bag. Usually American force could
reestablish peace (though not necessarily permanent
peace); but they brought us no friends worth having.
Only in the short run have we aided economies; and
certainly we have been unable to teach democracy of our
sort to anyone. In short, even with the highest and
lowest of motives (and there have been both), American
intervention has done little to make the intervened any
better off than before. Sometimes intervention has ended
dramatically--as in Cuba and Panama--with a significant
change in legal status. On other occasions, the United
States has simply wearied of the affair and withdrawn, as
in Haiti and the Dominican Republic.

Always mixed, often confused, and certainly slow to
be heard, American public opinion increasingly becomes
the greater arbiter, the strongest force for justice, and
that is as it should be. Among the developing nations,
nationalism continues to grow wildly. Inevitably, U.S.
control will become looser, the leash will grow longer,
the connection less visible. We must accept that.

NOTES

1. Samuel Eliot Morison and Henry Steele Commager,
The Growth of the American Republic (New York: Oxford
University Press, 1962), Vol. II, p. 208. On the
economic penetration of Cuba during the first military
occupation, see especially Philip S. Foner, The Spanish-
Cuban-American War and the Birth of American Imperialism
(New York: Monthly Review Press, 1972), Vol. II, Ch. 21.
2. Jaime Suchlicki, Cuba from Columbus to Castro
(New York: Charles Scribner's Sons, 1974), p. 105.
3. Suchlicki, Cuba, p. 103; Lester D. Langley, The
Cuban Policy of the United States (New York: John Wiley,
1968), p. 115; Whitney T. Perkins, Constraint of Empire
(Westport, Connecticut: Greenwood Press, 1981), p. 1;

Jorge I. Dominguez, Cuba: Order and Revolution (Cambridge: Belknap Press, 1978), p. 11.

4. Gustave Anguizola, Philippe Bunau-Varilla (Chicago: Nelson-Hall, 1980), pp. 349-358.

5. Thomas L. Karnes, The Latin American Policy of the United States (Tucson: University of Arizona Press, 1972), pp. 190-191

6. Dana G. Munro, Intervention and Dollar Diplomacy in the Caribbean, 1900-1921 (Princeton, N.J.: Princeton University Press, 1964), pp. 326-327.

7. Richard H. Immerman, The C.I.A. in Guatemala (Austin: University of Texas Press, 1982). Implicates Eisenhower to a much greater degree than do previous studies.

3
Autumn of the Oligarchs

Paul Heath Hoeffel

Although the recent revolutionary upheavals in Central America have taken much of the world by surprise, one of their most remarkable and tragic aspects is that they did not happen sooner. The power struggles in El Salvador, in Guatemala, and during the 1970s in Nicaragua have revealed the extraordinary obsolescence of those social orders, characterized by brutal, restrictive rule by oligarchs in coalition with military officers. It is the nature of this reactionary coalition that lies at the root of the conflicts, a simple but inescapable fact that has been obscured, at least in the United States, by the specter of an East-West struggle. The single most important reason for the urgency, bitterness, and extremity of the continuing conflicts in El Salvador and Guatemala arises from the long-standing oligarchic stranglehold on these economies and the intransigence of these elites in the face of legitimate demands for social, political, and economic change.

What is striking about the oligarchs of El Salvador and Guatemala is not their wealth, which pales in comparison to elites in larger Latin American countries,[1] or even the misery that their self-serving rule has meant for the majority of Guatemalans and Salvadorans. Nor are they unique in their greed, though their proportional shares of national incomes are among the highest in Latin America: In both countries they represent less than 2 percent of the population and absorb 25 percent of the GNP.[2] What is astonishing is that they have been able to maintain their constrictive, highly class-conscious rule with so few compromises so far into the twentieth century--and that they have every intention of continuing it, whatever the cost for the Guatemalan and Salvadoran peoples.

Elsewhere in Latin America the hold of the oligarchies was broken, to lesser and greater degrees, either by an emerging bourgeoisie or by irrepressible popular movements, almost always giving way to more dynamic forms of economic development and, occasionally, even democratic rule. In most cases this breakthrough was accomplished by the first part of this century, though in Colombia, for example, where coffee too has been king, it did not come until the late 1940s.

As for the neighbors of Guatemala and El Salvador, which will be discussed only to counterpoint the experience in these two countries, Mexico broke its oligarchy in the revolution of 1910; Costa Rica's oligarchy gave way in the 1920s; in Honduras, political differences and the advent of the oligopolistic fruit companies effectively subsumed the elite; and in Nicaragua, the Somoza dynasty in alliance with the National Guard effectively short-circuited traditional oligarchic rule since the 1930s, only to form a very narrow (and consequently extremely vulnerable) oligarchy, which was overthrown in July 1979.

The Sandinista victory over the regime of Anastasio Somoza Debayle and the subsequent dismantling of the despised National Guard in Nicaragua sparked frantic and bitter debate among the ruling circles in Guatemala and El Salvador. By October 1979, a reformist military coup in Salvador ousted General Carlos Humberto Romero, a typical exponent of the decades-old oligarchic-military alliance. In Washington it was believed that the drastic agrarian and financial reforms decreed by the new junta would be sufficient to snap the spine of oligarchic rule, clearing the way for centrist forces excluded for so long from political life. Policymakers ignored repeated experiences with the ferocity and resilience of the oligarchs, who had met such challenges before. Four years later, far from having its stranglehold on El Salvador broken, the oligarchy has managed to reassert itself into the struggle. It watches with swelling confidence as its traditional solution to crisis, the military option, becomes implemented as de facto state policy.

In Guatemala, whose oligarchy makes the Salvadorans look enlightened, a scramble of elections and coups eliminated an untenable military-oligarchic arrangement under General Lucas Garcia, bringing in a born-again general to stem the tide of revolution by restoring credibility to the badly tarnished military rule. Here, even more than in El Salvador, there is no room for halfway measures, and, indeed, there never has been. Guatemalans know the present struggle will be a fight to the bitter end.

Most historians mark the beginning of oligarchic rule in El Salvador and Guatemala with the introduction of widespread coffee production in the 1870s. This is indeed a crucial juncture in the histories of both these countries, but the oligarchic roots go far deeper and are far more pervasive than that. The essential character of

oligarchic rule was established 400 years ago. It is a
rule that arguably has lowered the standard of living of
the vast majority of the rural population continuously
since the advent of the Spanish conquistadores.

THE ANTECEDENTS

After the violent conquest of Central America in the
early sixteenth century, the self-contained Indian
communities of the isthmus were forcibly restructured to
fit the economic needs of Castilian Spain. With time,
their hispanicization would reflect the mother country's
autocratic social and religious character as well. An
entire elite was imported to administer the colony and
oversee this process. The fanatical conquistadores,
military men who were rewarded with titles and enormous
tracts of land, cleared the way for the Spanish viceroys,
magistrates, friars, and priests who worked together to
pacify the surviving population and put them to work to
generate wealth for king and church.

Official representatives of imperial Spain, these
colonists differed fundamentally from those who were soon
to be sailing for North America from northern Europe.
The Spanish crown and its merchants were very careful
about who would represent them in a far-off land.
According to one historian, the official emigrants were
handpicked to ensure their religious conformity, "the
purity of Spanish ruling stock," and above all that the
wealth of the new territories would faithfully be
returned to Spain.[3]

It is also notable that these administrators were
the representatives of a monarchy that was in the midst
of expelling hundreds of thousands of Jews and Moslem
infidels and of a church under the spell of the
Inquisition. The grasping, narrow intolerance of both
would be transplanted to the New World. Rules governing
human decency were suspended to facilitate the control of
the new lands. As Spanish women were not allowed to
emigrate to prevent the depopulation of the peninsula,
colonists (clergy included) were permitted to have
dozens, even hundreds, of Indian concubines in order to
reduce, as quickly as possible, the dangerous dispropor-
tion of Spaniards to Indians.

The Vice-Royalty of Guatemala, which governed most
of what is Central America today, was considered one of
the backwaters of the Empire, since, unlike Mexico and
Peru, it yielded little gold or silver. Still, it was
administered with care and subject to elaborate economic
controls. Administrators were given a percentage of the
taxes and tributes they extracted from the Indians who
now worked their lands as serfs. The alcaldes, or
village mayors, became the merchants for the few consumer

goods imported from Spain, in effect establishing
monopolies over the retail general stores. Those who
excelled in repatriation of wealth were rewarded with
land grants.

Though in competition for fertile land and the
limited labor force, the clergy and magistrates worked
hand in hand to bring the indigenous population under
control. Theirs was a natural alliance. Not a great
deal of money, however, was to be made in Central
America. Lacking precious metals, agriculture became the
sole definition of wealth.[4] Superexploitation of the
small labor force was necessary from the start.
Surpluses had to include taxes for the Crown, tithes for
the church (one tenth of all agricultural production), as
well as a percentage for the local administrators, and,
last of all, subsistence for the workers. Those capable
of labor were frequently worked to death, and the abuses
threatened the extermination of the Indians rather than
their conversion into a god-fearing, reliable labor
force.

A protest over the slaughter by Bishop Bartolome de
las Casas prompted Holy Roman Emperor Charles V to decree
the Indian Laws in the mid-sixteenth century. These
statutes set aside communal lands, or ejidos, for the
Indians and laid down the rules for their serfdom, which
remained a centerpiece of colonial governance. They also
established the humanity of the natives. (The debate
over the existence of the Indian soul consumed much
time.) Still, the Indian's uncooperativeness, paganism,
nakedness, ignorance, disease, and sexual and social
mores were generally repugnant, if not alarming, to the
colonists. Las Casas suggested that the work force be
supplemented by Africans, thus prompting the beginning of
the slave trade in the Americas.

A profoundly racist social system grew up around
these attitudes, establishing a fundamental and ongoing
social premise: Those who owned land were automatically
assumed to be part of the ruling class. This was (and
remains) a caste with a separate legal system, access to
education, the right to participate in politics,
decisionmaking (if only at the local level), and, with
severe restrictions, commerce. In contrast, those who
did not own land were born to work and could assume no
such rights. It is a distinction that remains deeply
ingrained in Central American society, particularly
discriminating against Indians.

Although the Indian Laws greatly slowed the
expropriation of communal Indian lands (and, it can be
argued, saved them from the near-extermination suffered
by the North American Indians), the process of privatiza-
tion continued. The main crop that Spain had assigned to
the Central American backwater was anil, or indigo, a
rich blue dye extracted from plants. By 1800, one-third

of the land and one-fourth of El Salvador's population of
some 165,000 was producing indigo on increasingly larger
farms. The entire population of what now comprises
Guatemala, Honduras, El Salvador, Nicaragua, and Costa
Rica was around 800,000.[5]

INDEPENDENCE

Independence from Spain, which came to Central
America virtually by default in 1821, held significance
only for the tiny elite. For the Spanish administrators,
the handful of merchants who operated monopolies over the
import-export trade, and the higher clergy (the church
had by now become the largest landowner and holder of
slaves in Central America), the collapse of Spain's
mercantilist scheme spelled trouble.

By the nineteenth century, the Spanish administration of the colonies had become totally corrupt. The
highest positions were still held by Spaniards, and
lucrative administrative offices were frequently sold to
the highest bidder. Inter-regional trade had been
outlawed, stunting the development of the criollo, or
native-born elites, despite their common interests and
needs. Landowners were poorly paid for their crops,
which disappeared into the commercial network controlled
entirely by Spain. For the criollo landowners who grew
indigo, tobacco, and sugar, independence boiled down to
the promise of free trade--free from the oppressive
taxation and controls imposed by the parasitic Royal
administration. The progressive ideas transforming
Europe and the United States found echo among a sector of
the elite, splitting them between traditionalist conservatives and modernizing liberals, the latter largely
criollo landowners who also favored a Central American
Union of the former colonies, which was formed shortly
after independence.

The conservatives, most of them clustered around the
colonial hub of Guatemala City, were strong enough to
resist the liberal challenge and retain power. This
liberal defeat, after several years of confused and
sporadic warfare, reflected the continuing power and
persistence of the reactionary elite, whose counterparts
elsewhere in the Americas and Europe had succumbed to the
onslaught of history. Far from eclipse, the conservatives were able to extend their backward rule, including
the restoration of full colonial privileges to the
church, for another three decades.

The instrument of conservative salvation was an
unlikely caudillo named Rafael Carrera, a shrewd ladino
pig farmer in his early twenties who was inspired to
rally an Indian army against the liberals, led by General
Francisco Morazan, whom the clergy had convincingly

denounced as the anti-Christ.[6]   Key to the Indian support
for the conservatives was the latter's recognition of the
ejidos, which the liberals promised to abolish along with
church lands as running counter to a free market system.

As it turned out, Carrera became the antithesis of
what the conservatives wanted as their savior, much less
their absolute and rather competent dictator, until his
death in 1865.   Indeed, they lived in terror lest his
consuming anti-liberal fervor fade, leading him to turn
his Indians against them.

Carrera set a telling precedent.   Other strongmen
embodying the magical combination of military and
religious charisma have emerged during critical moments
in both Guatemalan and Salvadoran history, making this
experience seem less anomalous.   One obvious example was
General Maximiliano Hernandez Martinez, known as El Brujo
(the Sorcerer), who carried out the infamous matanza, or
massacre, of peasants in 1932 for the Salvadoran
oligarchy.   More recently, the emergence of General
Efrain Rios Montt has represented the magic solution to
the deepening Guatemalan crisis.   A fundamentalist born-
again Christian, Rios Montt claimed to have been selected
by God to lead Guatemala out of the crisis of the Old
Order.   Unlike Carrera, however, he relied heavily on the
evangelical appeals of the Protestant fundamentalists,
rather than the reactionary pieties of the Catholic
clergy.   As with Carrera, the Guatemalan elite live in
perpetual fear that this erratic fanatic might turn on
them too.

Only after Carrera's death did the liberals
belatedly wrest power from the conservatives in 1871 and
carry out such reforms as the confiscation of church
lands, separation of church and state, and the implementation of laissez-faire trade policies.   Church lands
were simply divided among the liberals.   The triumph of
the first generation of coffee oligarchs actually marked
a step backwards for the rural peasantry as the privati-
zation of communally held lands accelerated as the
economy was converted to coffee production.   But by this
time, Central American society had been rigidly stamped
in the colonial mold, a mold that has yet to be broken.

THE CENTURY OF THE OLIGARCHS: 1880-1980

The hundred years between 1880 and 1980 will go down
in Guatemalan and Salvadoran history as the century of
the oligarchs.   It was during this period that the
liberal criollo elites, free of Spain if not its legacy,
established free trade with the modern world and
seriously began to accumulate their fortunes.

In Guatemala, the first liberal government (1871-83)
granted more land titles to its friends than had been

granted during the previous thirty-three years. Manuel
Herrera, founder of the large landowning, banking, and
industrial family, received about 2,300 acres of land for
$634 in 1875. Other recipients of enormous grants, such
as the Ibarguen family, are now important industrialists
and financiers as well as coffee growers. The Klee-
Skinner clan, whose founder, George Ure Skinner, a
British merchant based in Guatemala from the first half
of the nineteenth century, and Karl Klee, his German-born
business partner, acquired government and Indian lands
for a song in this period. With few exceptions, such as
the conservative Aycinena family in Guatemala, whose
extensive commercial interests and landholdings originated in the eighteenth century, today's oligarchs
acquired their lands and established their businesses
from the middle of the nineteenth century and onward.[7]

Although there was virtually no industrialization
during this period, the first significant capitalist
development did occur. By the 1850s Europeans had
invented synthetic dyes for their textile mills, quickly
ruining the natural dye (indigo and cochineal, a red dye
produced from insects in Guatemala) markets on which
Central America had depended for foreign exchange. It
was an opportune moment to break away from the mono-crop
production originally imposed by Spain. By 1880,
however, the growing demand for coffee in Europe and the
United States inspired land-owners throughout the isthmus
to replace indigo with coffee. The beans produced
fabulous profits and provided a new opportunity for the
oligarchs to participate in the world economy. Concerns
regarding crop diversification disappeared for another
fifty years.

By the turn of the century, England, France, the
United States, and especially Germany were looking to
virgin territories like Central America for new investment opportunities. The criollo elites, firmly in charge
of political life, found that their rule, however
absolute, extended over little more than a few large
fincas, or farms. Thus, it was not surprising that they
were eager to link their destinies with the big banking
houses and manufacturers of Europe. Many of today's top
families made their start as local distributors for the
early U.S., British, and German multinationals.[8]

But throwing in their lot with the foreigners did
not mean they entered the big time. It meant being the
local representative for General Electric, Singer,
Remington, or Wilkinson. Those oligarchs whose fortunes
originated in commerce and industry were, at best,
producing or distributing minor consumer goods such as
foodstuffs, soft drinks, soap, or crude hardware. Later
they would get the hotel and fast-food franchises and
distribute U.S. farm equipment, insecticides,
fertilizers, or Japanese cars.

Though the predominant landowning group, especially
in El Salvador, eventually transferred its coffee profits
into finance and commerce, the substantial number of
families who made their fortunes with breweries or store
chains emerged as a distinct sector of the oligarchy.
They too would try to buy coffee lands as soon as they
had money, but their outlook was slightly more complex
and therefore more modern than the landbound elite.

The governing elites did, however, negotiate relatively large investments in railroads, communications,
and utilities by foreign capital. These provided the
minimal infrastructure necessary for the transport of
coffee and fruit from the producing areas to the port and
little else. Irresistable sweetheart deals with the
foreigners produced numerous individual fortunes,
especially for the presidents and their ministers and
friends. Very quickly the Central American nations
entered into burdensome debt, while the British and the
Americans acquired profitable and frequently total
control of key utilities and lands. By 1910, enough
coffee profits had accrued to permit the <u>criollo</u> elites
to establish their first independent banks, although even
these were largely staffed by foreigners.

By 1906 the United Fruit Company was well on its way
to establishing a monopoly over Guatemalan banana production, its railroads, and its port facilities. A similar
process would come to dominate the less-developed economy
in neighboring Honduras. By 1915, the banana companies
owned over one million acres of the best coastal land in
Honduras and were rapidly gaining political control of
the country. Their power and the country's sparse
population (by the turn of the century, there were less
than 400,000 Hondurans, whereas El Salvador, with
one-fifth the territory, had a population of 700,000)
help explain the failure of Honduras to develop an
oligarchy as powerful as those of its neighbors.[9]

Along with investment came foreigners. By 1914, 90
percent of Guatemala's export earnings came from coffee,
and over half of the coffee production came from foreign-
owned land, mostly German. (Prior to World War II,
Germany imported 60 percent of Guatemala's coffee.) The
German immigrants were to develop an atypical relationship with Guatemala. They tended to marry Indians in
their isolated stronghold in the northern province of
Verapaz and remained aloof from the Guatemalan elite,
which normally welcomed any Europeans. The price for
their aloofness and pro-Nazi sympathies was the
expropriation of their coffee lands and forced internment
during World War II.

Coffee profits inspired the large landowners to
occupy more land and seek further controls over the labor
force. In El Salvador, where legislation outlawing
communal lands was passed in 1882, the last of the Indian

and government lands had become the private property of the landowners by 1920. Forcing peasants from their lands created a convenient labor pool available to do day work literally for pennies. Landlords had to worry about paying wages only during harvest times--i.e., during two or three months a year.

The governments, enjoying the revenues generated from coffee exports, provided the legislation necessary to streamline and stabilize production. Landowners came to rely on the Guardia Nacional in El Salvador (a rural police force established in 1905, modeled on the Spanish National Guard), which they used like a private constabulary, often directly paying the salaries of guardsmen who served on their fincas. The army in Guatemala was similarly used to control labor problems. A quick call to the local Guardia chief or to the minister of the interior would bring a patrol to a rural village to round up peasants for work in the cotton or coffee fields when labor was scarce. Vagrancy laws, requiring peasants to work for landlords for up to six months a year, were passed in both countries. Finally big money was being made.

The patriarchs of this generation of oligarchs were a tough, dynamic, rapacious bunch. Often they were immigrants. Foreign businessmen with names like De Sola, Schoenberg, Parker, Duke, Dalton, and Hill were accepted into elite circles, what would popularly and erroneously come to be called las catorce familias, the fourteen families, in El Salvador. Intermarriage was a cornerstone of this network, forming blood ties between a substantial number of clans. Today there are around two hundred families (the number varies depending where one draws the line) representing interconnected business interests. The same is true in Guatemala, but on a considerably larger scale--perhaps 600 families in all. Over time, the descendants of the early oligarchs "became almost a new race, differing from the rest of the Salvadoran nation not only in social mores and prejudices, but even in color and other physical characteristics."[10] This racial distinction became more and more exaggerated and important in maintaining the popular notion that somehow these people commanded a superior status in life by virtue of being different.

The immediate offspring of this first generation of coffee oligarchs was generally a spoiled and shiftless lot, content to go off to Europe (mainly France and Germany) for educations and extended holidays. Membership in the elite clubs--like Club Americano or Club Guatemala or Club Salvador--of this time were a reliable listing of the elite and rarely had more than 120 to 200 members.[11]

Thus the fifty years between 1880 and 1930 were a kind of golden age, a period in which the oligarchs were

hegemonic in both countries. Today's much-expanded
second and third generations of the great old patriarchs
look back on those men and times with misty-eyed
reverence and nostalgia.

THE CHALLENGE OF THE DEPRESSION

The Great Depression beginning in 1929 was a
disaster for Central America, where the fragile export-
oriented economies had always been vulnerable to European
depressions and upheavals from the earliest colonial
times. In El Salvador, it was an era of crisis for the
elite. Coffee prices plunged from an average of $15.75
(per hundred kilo bag) in 1928 to $5.97 in 1932. The
oligarchs' callous treatment of a growing body of
landless peasants finally spurred popular revolt. In a
sense, they were facing the logical consequences of their
land and labor policies. Their unmarketable export crops
stood rotting in the fields while hundreds of thousands
of hungry, unemployed peasants were left with no means of
support.

On the other hand, the depression also offered the
big cafetaleros an opportunity to expand their land
holdings considerably as smaller growers went bankrupt.
Large merchants found their chance to buy into coffee
lands. The Asociacion Cafetalera, formed in 1929, was by
far the most powerful organization in El Salvador,
controlled entirely by a handful of big producers despite
a membership of some four thousand growers.

In 1932, the oligarchs' worst nightmares were
realized in a frightening uprising, concentrated in the
western coffee-producing provinces of Ahuachapan and
Sonsonate, by campesinos led by the communist Agustin
Farabundo Marti. Horrified at the murder of a handful of
landowners by the badly organized peasants, the owners
appealed to the army commander, General Maximiliano
Hernandez Martinez, to crush the revolt. Martinez, a
wild-eyed theosophist known as El Brujo, complied in a
manner that traumatized the rural population and
discouraged peasant radicalism for decades. Within two
weeks of the January 22nd uprising, his troops had
executed tens of thousands of peasants.

Jorge Sol Castellanos, an economist born into the
Salvadoran oligarchy, was a high-school student at the
time. He recalls how the young members of the oligarchy
were thrilled by the army's violent suppression of the
uprising and formed their own para-military group called
the "Civic Guard" to help out. Together they slaughtered
thousands. "Today the same policy of extermination is in
effect," says Sol. "They use the same expression:
'Muerto el perro, se acabo la rabia' (Kill the dog and
the rabies is gone.)"[12]

But the price for El Brujo's services was high.
From 1932-44, Martinez remained president in the style of
Rafael Carrera. More importantly, the oligarchs
surrendered their hegemony. It was understood that the
army would continue to retain control of the state
apparatus in exchange for protecting the interests of the
large landowners. After 1932, the oligarchs left the
presidency and virtually all key government offices,
except the foreign ministries and those controlling
banking and finance, to the military. This new alliance
marked a shift in the role of the army in the military-
oligarch equation from subservience to dominance,
culminating in the army's complete takeover in 1979.

The 1932 matanza provided another valuable
instrument for retaining power, namely, the multipurpose
doctrine of anti-communism. Adroitly manipulated
red-baiting justified the scrupulous intolerance of the
slightest divergence from the interests of the elite.
Anti-communists set the practically nonexistent margins
for reform, in effect replacing the role of the
Inquisition of other times. The chilling legacy of
la matanza was revived in recent years with the operations of a death squad called the Maximiliano Hernandez
Martinez Brigade, allegedly financed by hard-line
landowners.

Elsewhere in Central America, the depression also
caused crisis. In Nicaragua, after decades of continuous
battles between liberals and conservatives, the U.S.
marines had occupied the country after 1912 to prop up
unpopular conservative regimes. This occupation, only
briefly interrupted, ended in 1933 with their installation of Anastasio Somoza Garcia as head of the National
Guard that they had trained.

The eventual emergence of the Somoza dynasty was
again a drastic military solution. The Somozas created a
power structure based on the National Guard, which was
beyond the control of the traditional elite. In so
doing, they short-circuited what might have been the
eventual consolidation of the traditional oligarchy or
the emergence of a nationalist government under the rebel
Augusto Cesar Sandino. Instead, they created a narrowly
defined oligarchy of their own, drawing on friends in the
middle class to divide up the country's scant resources.
It was the highly personalized and narrowly based nature
of this elite that brought its demise sooner than
occurred in El Salvador and Guatemala.

In Costa Rica, which was the first Central American
coffee-exporting country, the coffee oligarchy was quite
different from its Salvadoran and Guatemalan counterparts. For one thing, it derived its wealth primarily
from the processing and export of coffee, not from
ownership of the producing lands. For this reason, many
middle-sized producers were able to develop, swelling the

ranks of a substantial bourgeoisie, a group that was slow
to form under the cramped economic conditions in
Guatemala and El Salvador.

In 1917 the Costa Rican oligarchy, together with
foreign oil companies, gambled for hegemony with the
golpe d'estado of General Federico Tinoco Granados in
1917. They lost when Tinoco was chased into exile after
a popular uprising the following year. This episode
convinced the long-standing reformist liberal leadership
to take unusual steps, which included gradual elimination
of the army from Costa Rican life. By 1930, the process
of reform and integration of the middle class into
national life was sufficiently underway to preclude the
monopolization of power by the oligarchy and/or the
military.

The Honduran elite, deeply divided politically into
the Liberal and National parties, also failed to achieve
hegemony over the state apparatus. They even failed to
amass much wealth for themselves. If any group wielded
extraordinary power, it was the banana companies, which
had turned Honduras into the world's largest banana
exporter.

In Guatemala, where controls had always been the
most severe, the oligarchs cast their lot with the
corrupt and heavy-handed dictatorship of Jorge Ubico, a
choice they would shortly regret. With the price of
coffee cut in half, the oligarchy pressured Ubico to
crack down on unrest in the countryside and urban
centers. Ubico complied, executing perhaps a hundred
labor, student, and opposition leaders in 1933 and
producing legislation virtually sanctioning forced labor
among the landless Indian population.

The results of the depression in Central America
varied, but each solution to the crises set the stage for
the next fifty years. Those elites who maintained a
monopoly on power had to bloody their hands in repressive
alliances with the military. Weaker (or more realistic)
elites accepted compromise with broader sectors of
society.

THE MODERN PERIOD: IMPOSING THE IMPOSSIBLE, 1944-84

It was not until well after World War II that the
Salvadoran and Guatemalan elites recovered from the
depression. After 1950, however, several factors ensured
that recovery would come with a vengeance. An abundance
of capital, the implementation of import-substitution
schemes, soaring coffee prices, and the rise of a new
technocratic elite combined to begin the transformation
of the old, landowning oligarchy into a modern, diversified business community. This modernization is a key
factor in the oligarchs' survival as a class.

As adept as they were at responding to the
exigencies of international capital, the Salvadoran and
Guatemalan oligarchs showed little patience or
understanding of the dynamics of change within their own
countries. Consciously, and only with rare hesitation,
they did everything in their power to keep social and
political life from undergoing a corresponding diversification. Labor relations remained stultified, and the
emerging middle classes, not to mention a small urban
proletariat, were able to snatch a moment of democracy
only in the relaxed period at the end of the war when
authoritarian regimes were in disrepute.

Cotton had been the only crop that flourished during
the war, as there had been a demand for cloth within the
isthmus. Salvadoran businessmen like John Wright, who
had come from San Francisco in 1919, began to invest in
large-scale cotton farming along the unsettled Pacific
coast. Similar developments were taking place in the
Guatemalan lowlands where the Garcia Granados clan was
soon to be the biggest cotton grower in Latin America.
This was not just another export cash crop. Unlike
coffee cultivation, which was labor intensive, cotton
required considerable capital investment for machinery,
fertilizer, and insecticides.[13] With cotton production,
the proletarianization of the landless peasant was
accelerated. The highly profitable and productive cultivation stimulated investment in textile mills, and a
small garment industry took root in both countries with
substantial Japanese investment. Within the oligarchies,
the cotton growers were considered upstarts, in search of
the quick buck, and were frowned upon by the old-
fashioned coffee growers.

Moreover, with international demand at a new high,
the price of coffee increased from $10 a bag in the early
1940s to $80 in the 1950s. Coffee profits rose from 30
percent in the 1940s to 45 percent in the 1950s. Coffee
production became more scientific, as agronomists experi-
mented with different varieties in an effort to boost
quality and yield. The cattle industry was not far
behind, and now sugar, too, would take off with the end
of the Cuban sugar quota in 1961. Together, these
developments prompted the emergence of a number of efficient, sophisticated landowners, whose profits permitted
expanding financial and industrial ties, preferably
within their own clans.

With the exception of Costa Rica, Central American
universities were abysmal, a fact that reflected state
policy toward education in general and enabled the
elites, who had always sent their children abroad to
study, to gain exclusive access to decent higher education. From the 1950s onward, they favored the prep
schools and technical and business colleges in the United
States. They soon possessed a generation of agronomists

and economists familiar with Keynes and the International
Monetary Fund, as well as the marvels of North American
consumerism. Yet, democracy did not rub off on these
visitors. "We've always admired the American way of
doing business," explained one oligarch who did not want
to be identified. "It's your political system that we
find unacceptable."

This generation of technocrats would direct the
transfer of money from agriculture to light industries,
commerce, real estate, insurance, and finance. It
quickly became apparent, however, that the market for
consumer goods was severely restricted in countries where
the vast majority of people lived at subsistence levels.

And there always seemed to be problems. In
Guatemala, the oligarchs were paying the price for their
indulgence of Jorge Ubico, a classic caudillo from an old
family. Ubico's fondness for European fascists and his
virulent anti-communism led him to outlaw the words
"labor" and "worker." In 1944, a coalition of middle-
class professionals, workers, and army officers managed
to force his resignation. Subsequently, they held the
first honest elections in Guatemalan history and elected
the progressive governments of Juan Jose Arevalo and, in
1950, Jacobo Arbenz, a former army officer. For ten long
years, the oligarchs suffered what came to be known as
the "October Revolution," a challenge at least as
traumatic as the Salvadoran uprising of 1932. These were
ten years of substantial reform.

In 1952, President Jacobo Arbenz heightened the
pressure on the oligarchy by implementing a significant
agrarian reform. Virtually all large landowners,
including the United Fruit Company, the country's largest
employer, had parcels of unused land--in all, some
100,000 hectares--expropriated. Subsequently, the
Eisenhower administration, prompted by the United Fruit
Company and the local oligarchy, launched a covert
campaign to oust Arbenz--a campaign that bore striking
similarities to recent attempts to overthrow the
Sandinista regime in Nicaragua. (Nicaragua and Honduras
were used as bases for anti-Arbenz forces then. Today,
Costa Rica and Honduras harbor the "freedom fighters" who
attack Nicaragua.)

Accounts of the 1954 overthrow of Arbenz tend to
focus on the overriding role of the United States in this
extraordinary adventure, obscuring the role of the
Guatemalan oligarchy and its allies in Honduras, El
Salvador, and Nicaragua. Yet it is clear that, without
the collaboration of these elites, United Fruit and the
CIA could not have enjoyed their ultimate victory.
Somoza was so enthusiastic about toppling Arbenz that he
ordered his planes to carry out intimidation bombings of
Guatemala City without consulting the CIA directorate.
Roberto Alejos, an oligarch whose interests involved

coffee, sugar, cattle, agricultural equipment, and banking, had land expropriated under the Arbenz reform and became one of the more active conspirators. In 1961, he would let one of his plantations be used as a CIA air base for the Bay of Pigs invasion of Cuba.

Colonel Carlos Castillo Armas, who led the bogus Liberation Army, was yet another example of the deus ex machina macho military man coming to the oligarchy's rescue. Having routed Arbenz, he set about dismantling the reforms that had given hope to Guatemala's peasants and workers. Among his first steps was the annulment of the agrarian reform, returning virtually all of the expropriated properties to their former owners. All but one-half of 1 percent of the peasants were evicted from the lands they had been granted. Hundreds of "communist" peasant and labor leaders were executed. It is telling of the American position in this venture that John Foster Dulles, chief of operations as secretary of state, was anxious that the purge had not been thorough enough.[14]

The Arbenz experience had frightened the Guatemalan oligarchs and convinced them of the efficacy of anti-communism in manipulating the support of the United States. But, like their Salvadoran counterparts, they found themselves in a sticky alliance with the military. Even Castillo Armas could not permit things to revert entirely to the good old days under Ubico.

NEW STRUCTURES

In 1960, the Central American nations liberalized their regional trading policies and formed a common market. This action was initially attractive to the oligarchs (and multinationals), as it meant expanding markets without facing the problems of significant domestic income redistribution. As it turned out, however, credits were made available to the middle class for the first time. The rapid economic expansion and diversification generated by the Common Market placed enormous stress on the old system. The elites opposed the growing middle sectors, which were backed by some U.S. agencies that insisted that the implementation of capitalism required greater social and political flexibility.

Ask the oligarchs where things went wrong, and they will often point to the Alliance for Progress as the destabilizing force that has culminated in today's civil wars. In their opinion, the reforms required under the Alliance opened the door to communism. Another subversive force was an old ally, the Roman Catholic Church. After Vatican II (1962-65) and the conference of Latin American bishops at Medellin (1968), the church, concerned for its future, turned its attention to the

poor and embraced a doctrine of social justice. In El
Salvador and Guatemala, where peasant labor unions (much
less rural collective bargaining) were strictly prohib-
ited, the clergy organized clandestine peasant unions.
Introduction of a minimum wage and a six-day work week
and the organization of peasant unions had to be forced
on the landlords, who were always plagued by the gnawing
suspicion that their scheme of things was being undone.

The oligarchs' rationale for their "scheme" boiled
down to pseudo-free enterprise and a racist interpretation of class relations essentially unchanged since
colonial times. The publisher of one of San Salvador's
conservative dailies reflected the typical view of the
relationship between the paternalistic landowner and the
peasant: "Both . . . love the land. The owner loves his
coffee plants, cares for them, and through them expresses
his innate entrepreneurial spirit," whereas the peasant's
"ties to the land are primal." In short, the peasant is
"an ideal racial mix" who can "adapt equally well to work
in the mountains or in the lowlands." His love for the
land, the publisher explained in defense of the brutal
conditions of rural life, "transcends his need for things
like higher education."[15]

A member of the Llach clan, a businessman who left
for Miami in 1980 (the year of greatest setbacks for the
Salvadoran oligarchy) described the famed productivity of
the Salvadoran worker a little less romantically: "The
Salvadorans are the Japanese of Central America. They
have motivation to work hard because they know that if
they don't work, they'll starve."[16]

Orlando De Sola, an ideologue of the hard-line
oligarchs and scion of patriarch Heriberto De Sola, a
Sephardic Jew who had come from Curacao in 1898, bitterly
opposes the agrarian reform, which in his judgment has
done more to undermine the economy than the early
guerrilla movement. De Sola believes U.S. agencies like
the American Institute for Free Labor Development
(AIFLD), which has directed the agrarian reform in El
Salvador, are obsessed with the idea that everyone must
own land. "The campesinos just want security and work,
not land," he claims. "What we need is to industrialize,
to set up massive free-trade zones like in Singapore and
the Philippines. We've got to have industrial jobs to
relieve our overpopulation."[17]

The reality of rural life in these countries was and
remains appalling. The quality of life and labor
conditions in the Salvadoran and Guatemalan countrysides
has deteriorated at an alarming rate throughout this
period of modernization. In 1978, 67 percent of
Salvadoran coffee was produced by only 4 percent of the
estimated 4,800 coffee growers. About twenty-six clans,
including the Quinonez, Regalados, De Solas, Maganas,
Duenas, and Escalon families, had come to dominate the

main export crops, including sugar and cotton.[18] Phase
Two of the 1980 agrarian reform hoped to readjust this
imbalance by expropriating large coffee _fincas_ and became
the focal point of opposition to the entire reform
project.

In Guatemala, during the fifteen year period from
1965 to 1980, the concentration of land ownership speeded
up enormously. The number of subsistence farm families
more than tripled, from 70,000 to 250,000, according to
an independent study by the Comite Interamericano de
Desarrollo Agricola. These units averaged less than a
third of an hectare in size in a country where CIDA estimated that the average family would need to work fourteen
hectares year round to make a decent living from the
land.[19]

Men like De Sola watched with horror as peasant
unions were formed, Christian and Social Democratic
parties developed, and a strong student movement emerged
during the 1960s and 1970s. The oligarchs' willingness
to characterize the most benign impulse toward reform as
"communist," while appropriate during U.S. Cold War
administrations, only exasperated resident American
diplomats from the early 1960s until the advent of the
Reagan administration.

The first in the long series of kidnappings of
prominent Salvadoran oligarchs (which helped finance the
formation of today's guerrilla groups to the tune of some
$50 million) was the 1972 abduction of a fellow student,
Ernesto Regalado Duenas, by a mixed group of angry
university youths. His death created a martyr for the
Salvadoran elite and fed their bitterness toward the
Christian Democrats, some of whom were among the bungling
kidnappers. "(Jose Napoleon) Duarte is just a
communist," Orlando De Sola declared with deep conviction
during a 1981 interview in which he accurately predicted
the ouster of the Christian Democratic president--"a
communist who happens to believe in God."[20]

The oligarchs, of course, met each popular advance
with their own maneuvers. Indeed, they have successfully
been able to outflank the democratic opposition on nearly
every front through intimidation, fraud, or violence.
Thus, for instance, the attempt at a mild agrarian reform
under the Molina government in the mid-1970s felt their
full weight through the National Association of Private
Enterprise (ANEP), which incorporated the coffee growers
and the American and Salvadoran Chambers of Commerce.
The strength of ANEP, which was sufficient to block the
reform, stemmed from the alignment of middle-class
businessmen with the reactionary elite. This alignment
was duplicated again in 1980 when the oligarchy helped
form the Productive Alliance (AP), which rallied the
landowners and medium-sized business interests against

the reform program and presidency of Jose Napoleon
Duarte.

The oligarchs' effectiveness has always relied
heavily on their control over the media, especially the
newspapers, through which a persistent anti-communist
campaign has been waged for generations, inculcating the
vulnerable middle class with apocalyptic visions of
social change. They are also particularly adept at
manipulating existing organizations and inventing phantom
parties and civic groups to provide the illusion of
broad-based support. This multifaceted campaign to link
the oligarchy with the middle class has been particularly
effective as the economic crisis has worsened over the
past decade. Since 1979, the wooing of the middle class
has effectively sabotaged U.S. efforts to create a
cohesive middle sector capable of pulling the country
back from the brink of civil war.

The officers of the army and the National Guard, who
have come to share the oligarchs' distrust and contempt
for la chusma, the rabble, have willingly been the
instrument of official repression. Sharing power is the
central motive, but their cooperation has always been
partly mercenary. In recent years the oligarchs have
provided funds for the death squads, employing off-duty
military personnel in their campaign to terrorize the
population into quietude. In the late 1960s, the head of
the National Guard created the Democratic Nationalist
Organization (ORDEN), a peasant vigilante group, in an
effort to gain grass-roots control over the rural
populace. Offering small amounts of financial credit and
access to steady work, ORDEN enlisted tens of thousands
of alienated, small landowning peasants to aid the
Guardia in controlling and sometimes massacring more
defiant villagers, those who dared to request better pay
or a plot of land of their own.

THE TURNING POINT

Today, the traditional alliances between the
oligarchies of El Salvador and Guatemala and the
military, church, and foreign business elites are in
flux. Each group has had to weigh the long-term
advantages of close ties with the others. As the
containment of social unrest repeatedly broke down during
the 1960s and 1970s, the long-standing ties between the
army and the landed elite, in which the latter had
increasingly assumed a subordinate role, underwent the
most significant change.

Popular disenfranchisement created a political
vacuum that prompted a greater role for the military in
both societies. Military activity had to be stepped up.
Repression became bloodier. The Salvadoran Army struck

out at Honduras in the Soccer War of 1969. By the early
1970s, the Guatemalans had successfully carried out
counterinsurgency campaigns with the help of U.S. Special
Forces. Systematic extermination of political opponents
and leftists had become an integral part of their
repressive apparatus.

The emergence of the Guatemalan military elite as an
independent force with an appetite for institutional
power increased tensions with the traditional power
structure. Officers were no longer merely concerned with
protecting the narrow interests of a small group of
landowners. They were now governing a country that was
growing crowded with divergent interests and rising
expectations, including their own. Increased state power
meant that favored Guatemalan officers, who had traditionally received gifts of land from the big landowners,
were able to secure titles on their own through such
entities as the National Institute of Agrarian
Transformation (INTA). An Army Bank, which came to have
considerable capital resources and oversaw the new influx
of North American capital, was established, negotiating
important deals directly with U.S. corporations and
promising a favorable investment climate. Today there
are 10,000 North Americans living in Guatemala, many of
them working for 190 U.S. firms (a third of them among
Fortune's 500).

Fred Sherwood, former president of the influential
American Chamber of Commerce, arrived in Guatemala as an
operative in the CIA operation against Arbenz. His views
on whether the State Department should pressure the
Guatemalan government about the use of death squads
against its opponents is chillingly representative of the
attitudes of the business community: "Hell no, why
should we do anything about the death squads? They're
bumping off the commies, our enemies. I'd give them more
power. Hell, I'd give them some cartridges if I could,
and everyone else would, too. They're bumping off our
enemies, which are also the enemies of the United States.
Why should we criticize them?"[21]

By the end of the 1970s, military corruption had
virtually gone wild. Under the regimes of Generals Arana
Osorio and Lucas Garcia, officers had become business
partners with or received bribes from virtually everyone
who wished to do business in Guatemala. Before being
overthrown, Lucas amassed a fortune valued at $10 million
in land alone, somewhere between 81,000 and 135,000
acres, much of it originally destined for peasant families. The schemes revealed the close ties that the
officer corps enjoyed with the oligarchy. One of Lucas's
biggest partners and political backers was his nephew,
Raul Granados Garcia, a member of one of Guatemala's
richest families and founder of the Mano Blanca (White
Hand) death squad, which operated in conjunction with the

counterinsurgency operations from the mid-1960s onward.
Together they owned at least fourteen large farms in the
newly developed Franja, the northern border strip
including the departments of Izabal, Alta Verapaz, Quiche
(a central guerrilla area), and Huehuetenango: "The plum
of Lucas' holdings was the Yalpemech farm . . . which
Lucas and Granandos Garcia purchased in 1975 from the
Dieseldorf coffee barons, the richest family in Alta
Verapaz, for only $175,000. Within a year they revalued
the land at $300,000. And within months, they mortgaged
it to obtain a $750,000 loan from the Bank of America
National Trust and Savings Association."[22]

The Salvadoran elections of 1972 and the Guatemalan
elections of 1974 were turning points in the formation of
opposition to the military-oligarchy alliances. In both
cases, the army simply cancelled the victories of
Christian Democratic candidates, Jose Napoleon Duarte and
Efrain Rios Montt. Protests led to the repression and
exile of many opposition leaders. These episodes marked
the beginning of an inexorable shift from reformist electoral politics to revolutionary strategies within growing
sectors of the progressive forces.

Unity, especially in the face of adversity, is one
of the Salvadoran oligarchy's strongest points.
Remarkably few members of the families have broken ranks,
indicating cohesion attributable to their strong family
and ideological networks. The exceptions, men such as
Archbishop Oscar Romero (highest church officials as well
as army officers have always been honorary members of the
oligarchical elite) and Enrique Alvarez Cordova, a
wealthy cattle farmer whose political conscience led him
to become the head of the Democratic Revolutionary Front
(FDR), are singled out for special treatment by the reactionary forces. Romero was assassinated by a right-wing
hit team while celebrating mass in 1980. Alvarez was
kidnapped, tortured, and mutilated before being executed
by security forces later that year.

But the Salvadoran oligarchy is hardly monolithic.
The differences that separated liberals and conservatives
in the nineteenth century can still be detected today.
The central division is between those elites who have
modernized their agricultural holdings and diversified
their financial base into other sectors of the economy
and those landowners who persist in inefficient and backward exploitation of their lands and whose well-being
depends on the maintenance of a cheap labor supply.
Although this distinction is far from exact, the more
"modern" elites enjoy closer ties with the middle-class
business and industrial interests that have developed
since the 1960s. It is this group that inspired the
formation of the Productive Alliance (AP) in 1980,
subsuming middle-class interests into its own.

Many of these modern families were sharp enough to
foresee the agrarian reform of 1980 and sold their large
landholdings or split them up into smaller parcels to
avoid expropriation. Even in the midst of civil war,
they continue to make money in industry or agricultural
areas free of warfare. Although many have gone into
exile, they view their stay in Guatemala City or Miami as
a temporary security measure and have refused to take all
of their money out of the country. Many visit San
Salvador regularly, slipping in and out of the country
quietly to maintain their contacts and entrepreneurial
interests. In general, they acknowledge that times have
changed and are willing to accept a few alterations--even
the sacrifice of some of their more intransigent
brethren--in the struggle for survival as a class.

The other group is more obviously reactionary.
These are the landowners who were affected by Phase One
of the 1980 agrarian reform in which 276 of the country's
largest estates were expropriated. Their response has
been one of indignant outrage, and much of the death
squad activity that has sown terror in the Salvadoran
countryside since the mid-1970s has been financed by
them. The campaign of terror has prevented many
campesinos from taking over titles to the expropriated
lands, much less occupying them.

Most members of this group have gone into exile,
carting with them their family heirlooms and whatever
capital they could liquidate. Most admit they do not
expect to return. When they participate in national
politics, it is with the intention of turning things back
to the way they were before October 1979. They remain
uncompromising and through their central organization,
the El Salvador Freedom Foundation, have lobbied extensively in Washington, D.C., along with the Productive
Alliance, against political negotiations and for the
reversal of the reforms.

It is this group that most bitterly protests the
betrayal of its former allies--the church, the military,
and the United States. They have been implicated in the
assassination of Archbishop Romero and of many rurally
based priests, perceiving the emergence of radicalized
clergy as one of the most serious betrayals. The loss of
control over the military officer corps and the end to
the benign neglect from Washington that they long enjoyed
are attributed to the international communist conspiracy.
Above all, they feel betrayed by the more flexible
oligarchs who have decided to stick it out in El
Salvador. Members of the Productive Alliance are seen as
opportunists who are willing to make any deals to survive
the present conflict.

Despite their serious reverses, however, many
oligarchs remain convinced that El Salvador's future
could not possibly exclude them. They have, they

believe, the expertise, money, and international contacts
that no government can do without for long. "Our
entrepreneurial spirit is the country's only natural
resource," one matron declared confidently. "Without us
the country will sink into the grave."[23]

The year 1980 was a demoralizing one for the
oligarchy; it marked the low point in its influence.
Both the modern and traditional groups have lost their
close ties with the military elite since the shakeup of
1979. At that time the officer corps, alarmed by the
fate of the Nicaraguan National Guard after the fall of
Somoza, abruptly shifted its allegiance from the
oligarchy to Washington, whose reforms it agreed to carry
out. This shift effectively ousted the oligarchs from
their decisionmaking role. They were left to scheme and
plot from abroad, which further undermined their
credibility.

In Guatemala, the gross excesses of successive
military governments had turned the country into an
international pariah. Their corrupt land policies and
human rights violations had forced the Indian population
to join the guerrillas for the first time. The emergence
of General Rios Montt, the former presidential candidate,
was an amazing stroke of luck for both the ruling elites,
military and civilian. As one Guatemalan exile put it:
"They won the lottery without even buying a number."
Although few believe that Rios Montt can bring the
military corruption under control, his programs have been
at least partially successful in restoring Guatemala's
international image and undercutting Indian support for
the guerrillas.

As with El Salvador, there are splits within the
Guatemalan elite. These grew clearer during the rapid
industrialization, which saw new areas of the economy
open up under the management of a relatively large middle
class since the 1960s. Most influential are the import
trade, agro-export, and traditional monopolistic
industrial sectors. Oligarchic industrialists, old
families in textiles, cement, glass, and so forth, have
come into direct conflict with the military expansionists
who, unlike the multinationals, do not respect traditional monopolies.

The extent of foreign control of Guatemalan agricultural and industrial sectors is much greater than that
in El Salvador. Direct U.S. investment is over $300
million, and imports from the United States represent
some $400 million annually. The Guatemalan elite is just
as eager to participate in joint ventures with foreign
capital as were their forefathers at the turn of the
century.

It is tempting to think of the emergence of the
highly visible military caste and its shady civilian
collaborators as a new oligarchy. But the embezzlement

of state funds and theft of Indian land, while making a
number of officers rich, are not the same thing as the
formation of class consciousness and productive capital.
The military remains a closed caste, but those officers
with ties within the civilian elite now form a kind of
mafia-bourgeoisie that includes some of the most ruthless
and violent members of the Guatemalan ruling sectors.
During a period of crisis, such as Guatemala is
experiencing today, this group takes on special
importance, as it can be relied upon by the more
restrained elites to get the dirty work of repression
done.

CONCLUSION

As promising as the events of 1979 were for change
in Central America, the advent of the Reagan administration and the realignment of reactionary forces in the
region have combined to disrupt the impulse toward
reform, revolutionary or otherwise.
The extraordinary comeback of Salvador's landed
elite since its dark year of 1980 can be traced in the
political career of Major Roberto D'Aubuisson, the most
visible expression of the oligarchy's strategy in the
ongoing, murky struggle for power. Prior to 1979,
D'Aubuisson was in charge of intelligence in the National
Guard, where he acquired a reputation as an organizer of
death squads. After the 1979 reformist coup, he launched
an oligarch-financed barracks crusade, complete with
videotaped speeches, to rally officers against the new
junta. In 1980, he was arrested by progressive officers
for plotting to overthrow the government. Evidence also
pointed to his direct involvement in the assassination of
Archbishop Romero. In a classic showdown of forces, the
military high command stood by D'Aubuisson, and within
weeks it was the reformist officers who were on the run.
In the March 1982 national elections, D'Aubuisson
was elected to the Constituent Assembly at the head of
the ultra right wing Nationalist Republican Alliance
(ARENA). Although this organization had been created
only six months earlier, it had remarkable resources
available for its campaign. Defeated, the Christian
Democratic president, Jose Napoleon Duarte, was ousted
from the junta, and D'Aubuisson, described by former U.S.
Ambassador Robert White as a "pathological killer," was
elected head of the Constituent Assembly. The campaign
to reverse the 1980 reforms went into high gear. In
April 1983, the sole remaining member of the doomed 1979
reform government, Defense Minister Jose Guillermo Garcia,
was forced from power, marking yet another victory for the
oligarchy. Notwithstanding his hard line vis-a-vis the
opposition, Garcia represented the military's commitment

to Washington's land-reform policy. As of this writing, D'Aubuisson is expected to announce his candidacy for the presidential election scheduled for March 1984.

Although the Guatemalan oligarchs harbor resentment toward both men, Presidents Ronald Reagan and Efrain Rios Montt assumed their respective offices just in time to stave off the most serious challenge to military-oligarchic rule to date. These elites, which in 1977 had joined El Salvador, Brazil, and Argentina in rejecting U.S. aid tied to Jimmy Carter's human rights policy, danced in the streets of Guatemala City upon Reagan's election. Since then, however, they have fallen into disillusionment, complaining that the Reagan administration has been slow to come to their aid while pouring money into El Salvador.

Even so, the Guatemalan elite has direct access to the Reagan inner circle. <u>Amigos del Pais</u>, the Guatemalan version of the El Salvador Freedom Foundation, has been lobbying in Washington for years. Until Michael Deaver became one of President Reagan's top advisers, the <u>Amigos</u> paid his public relations firm $13,000 a month to represent their interests. In June 1983, moreover, Richard B. Stone was appointed special envoy to Central America. Stone had previously been registered as a paid lobbyist for Guatemala.

Rios Montt's weekly television broadcasts are a reminder to the oligarchs that they are governed by an erratic and often incoherent religious fanatic whose ultimate allegiance to them is in doubt. Restless Guatemalan businessmen would like to hand government over to a man they can trust, someone like Mario Sandoval Alarcon, head of the ultraright National Liberation Movement (MLN), which calls itself "the party of organized violence." Until a MLN coup is considered feasible, Rios Montt will be allowed to carry out his pacification program of <u>fusiles y frijoles</u> (guns and beans), a campaign that camouflages the continuing massacre of Indians and extermination of the opposition.

Notwithstanding all this, the oligarchs of Guatemala and El Salvador are living on borrowed time. A negotiated solution to the struggle in El Salvador (it can safely be assumed there will never be negotiations with the revolutionaries in Guatemala) would involve carrying out the reforms decreed in 1980 and, with any luck, a restructuring of the military command. Given the serious overpopulation and unemployment problems there, a leftist government would probably seek to reorient El Salvador's capital-intensive industrial structure to make it more labor intensive. A military solution involving the annihilation of the Salvadoran opposition is the only way the oligarchs could bring the country back to the pre-1979 era. Barring full-scale U.S. military intervention, the oligarchy must disappear as a class.

In Guatemala, time has proven that even the harshest repression cannot eliminate the revolutionary opposition in the long run. Continued military-oligarchic rule will face a prolonged guerrilla war. Corruption, fanaticism, and, for the first time in its history, the Indian population, are variables that must be figured into any scenarios for Guatemala's future. Political ideologues aside, the choice faced by both the Guatemalan and Salvadoran peoples is not between democracy and communism; it is between civilization and barbarism. The oligarchs made their choice a long time ago.

NOTES

1. Even relative to richer, larger countries, the Salvadoran oligarchs have managed to amass enormous fortunes. Among the larger ones: the Duenas clan, estimated at between $300 and $400 million; the Regalado clan, at $250 million; the De Sola clan, at $125 million; and the Salavaria family, at $75 million. Any family owning coffee farms producing 40,000 quintales of coffee a year has to be worth at least $10 million in land value alone.

2. Guatemala is Central America's most populous, industrialized, and wealthiest country. Indians make up 55 percent of its 7.2 million people. Mario Monteforte, a Guatemalan sociologist, broke down the population by class: 1.14 percent ruling class, 17 percent middle class, and 81.86 percent popular classes.

3. George Pendle, A History of Latin America (Middlesex: Penguin Books, 1963), p. 53.

4. Rafael Menjivar's Acumulacion Originaria y Desarrollo del Capitalismo en El Salvador (San Jose, Costa Rica: EDUCA, 1980) describes the development of Salvador's monoculture and export-oriented economy. Production of cacao, indigo, tobacco, balsa wood, and, later, sugar, cotton, and coffee were almost entirely dictated by Europe's needs.

5. David Browning, El Salvador: Landscape and Society (Oxford: Clarendon Press, 1971), p. 211.

6. Selden Rodman, The Guatemalan Traveler: A Concise History and Guide (New York: Meredith Press, 1967), p. 39.

7. Susanne Jonas and David Tobis's Guatemala (New York: NACLA, 1974) contains substantial amounts of material on the Guatemalan elite and its relationship to U.S. business interests. In particular, there is a revealing thirty-five-page chart tracing the economic and political interests of twenty of Guatemala's top families.

116

8. Anthony Winston, "Class Structure and Agrarian Transition in Central America," Latin American Perspectives, 19 (Fall 1978), p. 31.
9. Steven Volk, "Honduras: On the Border of War," NACLA Report on the Americas, 15, 6 (November/December, 1981), p. 7. Even today, the Honduran elite does not possess the wealth, narrowness of vision, or rigid political control of its Guatemalan and Salvadoran counterparts.
10. Thomas Anderson, Matanza: El Salvador's Communist Revolt of 1932 (Lincoln: University of Nebraska Press, 1971), p. 14.
11. Interview with Francisco Villagran Kramer, former Guatemalan vice-president, January 1983.
12. Interview with Jorge Sol Castellanos, June 1979.
13. Browning, El Salvador, p. 230.
14. Stephen Schlesinger and Stephen Kinzer, Bitter Fruit: The Untold Story of the American Coup in Guatemala (New York: Doubleday, 1982), pp. 222-223.
15. Interview with Mercedes Altamirano in Miami, April 1981.
16. Interview with Salvadoran businessman/oligarch, who requested his name not be used, in Miami, April 1981.
17. Interview with Orlando De Sola in Miami, April 1981.
18. Enrique Baloyra, El Salvador in Transition (Chapel Hill: University of North Carolina Press, 1982), pp. 25-27.
19. Interview with Edelberto Torres-Rivas in Washington, D.C., January 1983.
20. Interview with Orland De Sola, April 1981.
21. Interview with Alan Nairn, Guatemala City, 1980, in Guatemala in Rebellion: Unfinished History, ed. Jonathan L. Fried, Marvin E. Gettleman, Deborah T. Levenson, and Nancy Peckenham (New York: Grove Press, 1983), p. 90.
22. George Black, "Garrison Guatemala," NACLA Report on the Americas, 17, 1 (January/February, 1983), pp. 14-15.
23. Interview with Mercedes Altamirano in Miami, April 1981.

4
Revolution and Counterrevolution in the Central American Church

Penny Lernoux

Sister Marie Rieckelman listened with alarm to the exchange between the three Salvadoran soldiers and the TACA air stewardess. The only woman on the Miami-bound flight that December afternoon in 1980, the Maryknoll nun was repeatedly questioned about her identity and destination. But it soon became apparent that the soldiers were looking for another nun, possibly Ita Ford or Maura Clarke, two of four Maryknoll sisters based in El Salvador. They had been with Marie at a meeting in Nicaragua of the Maryknoll nuns working in Central America, and had been scheduled to return to San Salvador on the same TACA flight that Marie was taking to Miami. However, at the last minute no seats had been available. Prudently, Marie made no mention of their arrival on the next plane from Nicaragua.

But the Salvadorans appeared to have guessed as much, as shown by a radio message from the airport intercepted and later relayed to the U.S. Embassy: "No, she didn't arrive on that flight; we'll have to wait for the next one."[1]

Waiting for Ita and Maura at San Salvador's isolated international airport were Ursuline Sister Dorothy Kazel and lay missionary Jean Donovan. Good friends of the Maryknoll nuns, the pair often chauffeured the sisters about in their Toyota mini-bus. At the airport they encountered a Canadian religious delegation that had flown in for the funeral of six leaders of the chief opposition party, who had been tortured and murdered by security forces earlier in the week. The Canadians urged the women to drive with them to San Salvador, since the trip from the airport to the capital was known to be dangerous. But the nuns refused. Accustomed to driving about the countryside in search of refugees, Dorothy and Jean were blithe to the pending danger. "Blue-eyed blondes are the safest people in Salvador," the blonde, blue-eyed Dorothy remarked. "They're so American-looking, and no one would kill Americans!"[2]

Two days later the battered corpses of the four
women were found in a shallow grave near the airport.
Each had been shot at least once in the head. One had
her pants on backwards; two had no underwear.

The crime might never have come to light had it not
been for a priest from the nearby village of Santiago
Nonualco, who told his superiors in San Salvador that
several peasants had reported seeing soldiers burying
four women who looked like foreigners. The nuns'
mini-bus had already been found by the military, gutted,
on a dirt road three miles from the airport. But the
authorities did not report the incident to the U.S.
Embassy, despite promises to U.S. Ambassador Robert White
by National Police Chief Carlos Lopez and Defense
Minister Guillermo Garcia to put out an all-points alert
for the women. White had contacted the government after
the nuns' worried co-workers informed the embassy of
their failure to make appointments in San Salvador. But
no alert was sent out. As later events would show,
compelling evidence existed to implicate the military
high command in a cover-up of the slaying, and possibly
in the planning as well. "The message we were getting,"
Ambassador White said later, "was that [an investigation
of the murders] would crack the military wide open, that
it could even cause the government to fall."[3]

The killings set off a wave of revulsion and anger,
forcing the Carter administration to temporarily suspend
economic and military aid to the Salvadoran junta. But
as the grieving Maryknoll sisters pointed out, the nuns
were by no means the first religious victims of the escalating political violence. By the end of 1980, twelve
priests had been murdered, including San Salvador's
outspoken archbishop, Oscar Romero. Hundreds of lay
leaders and catechists had been tortured and assassinated, as well as thousands of peasants and workers
belonging to church organizations. Documentation by
Amnesty International showed that the overwhelming
majority were victims of the security forces or paramilitary groups.[4] But the December slayings were the
first involving American nuns. Moreover, the murders had
been premeditated, and three of the four had been raped.

What had the women done to court such a fate? The
intercepted radio message and statements by Ambassador
White suggest that the principal target was Ita Ford
because of her defense of the poor and her work with
peasant comunidades de base (a type of Christian
grassroots community). But Maura Clarke also was marked
because of her association with Ita. Dorothy Kazel and
Jean Donovan were probably innocent bystanders, killed
because they were in the company of the Maryknoll nuns.
On the other hand, they may also have been targeted for
their work with Salvadoran refugees. As Ita knew, to
"feed the hungry and comfort the poor" was considered

subversive by the military. Or as the colonel of a local regiment told her, the church "is indirectly subversive because it is on the side of the weak."[5]

Ita and Maura worked at a church refugee center in Chalatenango. On the border with Honduras, the area has witnessed some of the worst atrocities in the civil war, including frequent peasant massacres by the army and the arrest and torture of priests. Ita arrived in Chalatenango shortly after Archbishop Romero's murder in March 1980; Maura joined her after Ita's co-worker, Maryknoll Sister Carol Piette, drowned in a flash flood. The women went in response to Maryknoll's call for volunteers, Ita and Carol coming from Chile, Maura from Nicaragua and the United States. Although they knew the dangers, they felt that it was right to be there. In Ita's words: "It is a heavy scene--but if we have a preferential option for the poor, as well as a commitment for justice as a basis for the coming of the Kingdom, we are going to have to take sides in El Salvador-- correction--we have."[6]

Two weeks before the fatal drive from the airport, a note was tacked on the door of the parish house where they worked: "In this house are communists. Everyone who enters here will die. Try it and see."[7] The message was signed by the Mauricio Borgonovo Anti-Communist Brigade, a right-wing death squad. Shortly afterwards, a meeting was held by Defense Minister Garcia in the Blue Room of the presidential palace. According to Carlos Paredes, then Deputy Minister of Planning, Garcia spent a half hour denouncing the nuns and priests in Chalatenango as guerrilla collaborators who were encouraging the people to join the insurrection. Though no evidence existed to support such charges, the authorities have never been bothered by legal technicalities. And it is enough to make such a claim to sentence a person to death.

On the morning of the murders, the parish priest at Chalatenango, Father Efrain Lopez, received a letter so threatening that he decided to close the refugee center and return to San Salvador at once. Any doubts about the danger he was in had been dispelled during a harangue by the Chalatenango garrison commander, who accused him and the nuns of inciting and arming the people against the military. "I was very nervous," Lopez said. "I thought if they believed those things . . . , it was more than sufficient to cause the degenerates who work with them to kill us."[8] Lopez knew the two Maryknoll nuns were arriving in El Salvador that day, and he wanted to warn them not to return to Chalatenango. That evening a member of his parish staff was approached at a cinema by an unknown man who showed him a piece of paper and said: "Here is a list of people we are going to kill--and today, this very night, we will begin." On the list were

the names of Ita, Maura, Father Efrain, and a priest who
worked with them.[9]

A death sentence for work that would be considered
Christian charity in the United States is not unusual in
Latin America these days: El Salvador represents only
one example of a religious persecution that has led to
the imprisonment, exile, torture, and murder of nearly
1,200 bishops, priests, and nuns since the late 1960s,
when the Catholic Church embarked on a new course for
social justice. Most of these modern-day martyrs were
gentle, concerned individuals who abhorred violence--
individuals like Ita, Maura, Jean, and Dorothy.

THE WOMEN

Dorothy Kazel had been in El Salvador since 1974 as
a volunteer with a Cleveland, Ohio, diocesan team working
with refugees. Good-humored and buoyant, she was known
for doing outrageously funny things--like getting an Afro
hairstyle. Though religious, Dorothy had not originally
intended to become a nun. She was studying for a
teaching career and engaged to be married when she first
considered joining the Ursuline order. In the beginning
she fought the vocation, but eventually decided to become
a missionary to the poor. In 1968 she spent a summer
working with American Indians in Arizona, and in
Cleveland she counselled drug addicts. But she was
happiest in El Salvador, despite the dangers, and she
begged to stay on when her six years of service were up.
"If there is a way we can help," she explained, "we
wouldn't want to run out on the people."[10]

Dorothy lived with Jean in the port city of La
Libertad. The pair was known as the "Rescue Squad"
because they were always ready with "wheels" and hospita-
lity for their Maryknoll friends. The daughter of a
wealthy Irish family, Jean never wanted for anything when
growing up. Her life was filled with golf, horses, and
trips abroad. It was during one such journey, to Cork,
Ireland, in 1973, that she "found that money wasn't
everything" and began to consider becoming a lay
missionary. When she joined the Cleveland team in El
Salvador in 1978, she gave up a high-paying job as a
management consultant with Arthur Anderson & Co. A
boisterous woman who loved to party, Jean had another,
lesser-known side to her. Asked to describe the ministry
work she would like, she wrote: "To work with lonely
people who don't realize that God loves them."[11] She was
due to return to the United States in 1981 in time for
her 28th birthday.

The daughter of Irish immigrants, Maura began her
novitiate in 1950, when she was nineteen years old.
Assigned to Nicaragua in 1959 to teach in an American

Capuchin parish in the remote rain forests of Zelaya, she
worked for a decade as teacher, principal, and superior.
From Zelaya, in turn, she went to a poor slum on Lake
Managua's shores that was destroyed in a flood, then to a
Managua parish that was levelled in the 1972 earthquake.
Trapped by a jammed door in the upper floor of their
home, Maura and the other Maryknoll sisters made a rope
of sheets and escaped through a window. Still in their
pyjamas, they went to the aid of their neighbors, digging
out bodies and caring for the injured. Subsequently,
Maura worked with comunidades de base in Managua slums
until her return to the United States in 1976.
Throughout her stay in Nicaragua and later in El
Salvador, she lived in poverty. Her generosity and
freedom from possessions were extraordinary. She gave
away everything she had to the poor, including a monthly
allowance of $15 and her few clothes. The other sisters
had teased her because she had given her only shoes to a
woman who had none. When she died, she was wearing a new
pair--a gift from her eighty-four-year-old mother in New
York.
    Of the four women, Ita was probably the most
politically aware--hence her run-ins with the Salvadoran
military. Small and slender, she had experienced a
childhood of illness. Ita was 21 when she left home to
become a Maryknoll nun in 1961, but she had to give up
missionary work for seven years because of poor health.
In 1971 she went to Chile, to the Santiago slum of La
Bandera, where the chain-smoking "gringa" was deeply
loved by the poor for her good humor and willingness to
share their happiness and suffering. Working with Ita
was Sister Piette, who would later meet a tragic death in
El Salvador. The women lived as poorly as their Chilean
neighbors, without any possessions save a few clothes and
a brightly colored artisan bag that was Ita's hallmark.
Their principal work was to help organize comunidades de
base.

THE AWAKENING

    Countless case studies show that the single most
important reason for the church's persecution in Latin
America is the comunidad de base. Whether in Chile,
Brazil, Guatemala, or El Salvador, the advent of the
comunidades has meant revolutionary change--not in
economic or political structures but in the way poor
people regard themselves.
    Deeply religious and overwhelmingly Catholic, the
Latin American masses had been taught to accept fatalism
and poverty during centuries of indoctrination by a reactionary Iberian church. But after World War II and Fidel
Castro's successful revolution in Cuba, Latin America's

conservative bishops began to have second thoughts about
the social injustices they had helped bring about. The
sweeping reforms spawned by the Second Ecumenical
Council, or Vatican II (1962-65), found an echo in the
region, where bishops and priests began to speak of the
need for change. Though few in number, they represented
the intellectual and organizational leadership of the
Latin American church. And it was thanks to them that
the bishops signed an extraordinary document in 1968 at
their second hemisphere meeting in the Colombian city of
Medellin.

Medellin   The Medellin Documents denounced the "institutionalized violence" of a deeply divided and unjust society,
placing the bishops squarely on the side of the poor and
oppressed--the majority of Latin Americans. In taking up
the cause of social justice, the bishops changed the
course of Latin American history, for no longer would the
church be an ally of the military and the wealthy,
landowning classes. Possessed of singular political,
economic and religious power, the church could not be
dismissed or silenced, as were labor unions, political
parties, newspapers, and student federations. Thus
Medellin posed a serious threat to the oligarchies who
dominated the economics and politics of most Latin
American nations: Not only was Medellin a declaration of
independence, but it also suggested vehicles for change,
the most important of which was the comunidad de base.

The origins of the comunidad can be traced to
Brazil, today home of the most progressive and united
church in Latin America. The first one was started by
Cardinal Agnelo Rossi in the early 1960s in Barra do
Pirai in response to the people's complaint that they
could not attend Mass, even on Christmas day, due to a
shortage of priests. Dom Agnelo organized short, simple
courses for lay leaders, women as well as men, so that
they could perform such functions as baptism and
preaching. On Sundays the people would meet to study the
Bible and discuss its meaning for their own lives. These
Bible-reading sessions soon became the principal focus of
the comunidades, because they encouraged the people to
reflect on their poverty and political disenfranchisement
and, in time, to attempt to overcome these difficulties.
The essential message was that all people were created
equal by God and that poverty and repression were not a
penance inflicted by some distant deity but the result of
unjust economic and political structures.

Such "conscientization," or consciousness-raising,
quickly came to be seen as subversive by the military and
the upper classes: Not only were the comunidades opening
the eyes of the people, they were also telling the masses
that God was on their side. And in a region where religion is so pervasive, affecting every facet of daily
life, that was a powerful and dangerous message. In

addition, the comunidades proved an organizational threat by spawning all sorts of other groups, such as cooperatives, slum mothers' associations, and peasant federations. Although the comunidades preserved their essentially religious character, eschewing any involvement with political movements, many of their members went on to found or join labor, civic, and political organizations, there to apply the principles learned in the comunidades, particularly those of solidarity and self-reliance. Despite severe military persecution, the comunidades flourished, much as did the first Christian communities of the primitive church. By 1982 there were over 150,000 in Latin America; in Brazil alone the membership stood at three million.

The persecution suffered by the comunidades also helped to conscienticize the Latin American bishops. Although only the Colombians refused to approve the Medellin Documents, the majority of the bishops had little or no sense of the explosive declaration they were signing. Many undoubtedly would have ignored the commitment made at Medellin had it not been for military persecution of the institutional church. But when priests, nuns, and bishops were arrested and murdered merely for preaching the Gospel, the bishops were goaded to action. And the more they studied the causes of such persecution, the more they concluded that they had been right after all to take a strong stand at Medellin. By the time the bishops met for their third hemisphere conference, in Puebla, Mexico, in 1979, the majority were prepared to reaffirm their commitment to the poor and to human rights. There was a minority of hold-outs, of course, including most of the bishops from El Salvador, but the thrust was clearly in the direction of social justice. Moreover, the comunidades were singled out as the best means to achieve religious conversion and social change.

Ita Ford's experience in the Santiago slums paralleled the awakening of the bishops. When Salvador Allende was overthrown in a bloody coup in 1973, slum areas were among the hardest hit by repression. Members of the comunidades were rounded up and killed; popular organizations were forcibly disbanded. The poor were also hurt by the elimination of government subsidies and by a sharp increase in unemployment due to the regime's monetarist policies. Ita felt angry and frustrated. "Am I willing to suffer with the people here, the suffering of the powerless, the . . . impotent?" she wondered. "Can I say to my neighbors, I have no solutions . . .? I don't know the answers, but I will walk with you, search with you, be with you."[12]

As observed by many other foreign priests and nuns, the experience of repression, like the experience of living in a slum or a backward village, almost always provides a radical political education. Things that were taken for granted, such as food or freedom, no longer exist, and inevitably one is forced to ask "Why?" It was undoubtedly due to such questioning that Ita lost her life in El Salvador. Had she been content to stay in a convent in pious prayer, she probably would not have been affected by the violence. But like Maura, Jean, Dorothy, and other martyrs in Central America, Ita felt it her duty to serve as a Christian witness to the sufferings of the Salvadoran people. Such also is the mandate of the Maryknoll nuns: Evangelization "not only is proclaiming the Good News with truth, clarity, and challenge, but witnessing it in life and service. We have an urgent call to denounce that which deprives man of his legitimate claims for dignity, equality, sharing, and friendships."[13]

THE INVESTIGATION

Five months after the slaying of the four church-women, six Salvadoran soldiers were arrested. But many doubted that they would ever be brought to trial. As former Ambassador White suggested, the suspects, if prosecuted, might implicate others in the crime: "If all the case involved . . . was savage enlisted soldiers acting on their own, there would have been no problem from the beginning [in punishing them]."[14]

In point of fact, the Salvadoran military did everything in its power to stonewall the investigation. They refused to allow autopsies on the women to recover the bullets, claiming a lack of proper surgical masks. Four FBI agents sent to El Salvador to work on the case were denied permission to interview potential murder witnesses. In addition, the government refused to compare prints found on the women's Toyota bus with the fingerprints of twenty soldiers known to have been in the vicinity at the time of the killings. Instead, a "high-level civilian and military commission" was named to take charge of the case. Its members included two close friends of Defense Minister Garcia and a first cousin of Police Chief Lopez.

The Reagan administration quickly showed its willingness to play the game by sharply increasing military aid and training. Secretary of State Haig even went so far as to tell Congress that the women's murders were accidental, an overreaction by nervous soldiers who "misread the mere traveling down the road [of the nuns' bus] as an effort to run a roadblock."[15]

But Haig's claims did not jibe with Congressional testimony by White: "Haig should have known [about the security forces' involvement in the murders] because it was included in my report. The American churchwomen were picked up by the security forces. The shots that killed them were heard just about an hour's drive away. So the idea that the shooting took place while these women ran a roadblock or something of that nature is absurd." Added Sister Melinda Roper, head of the Maryknoll nuns: "I believe that the deaths of the four women cannot be separated from the general pattern of government persecution of the church in El Salvador and from the deaths of thousands of innocent Salvadorans. Nor do I believe the deaths can be separated from U.S. policy toward that government."[16]

The Salvadoran regime's disinterest in solving the crimes is of a pattern with other unsolved murders of religious people in El Salvador, including Archbishop Romero's death. Moreover, the man who allegedly planned the archbishop's assassination, Major Roberto D'Aubuisson, emerged as an important force in the Salvadoran government elected in March 1982. Rodrigo E. Guerra, a prominent Salvadoran businessman and former government official living in exile, charged that "a close alliance had been worked out between some high-level military commanders and the most backward elements of the Salvadoran right [such as D'Aubuisson]. That is why the assassinations of Archbishop Romero, the American nuns, and others will never be solved."[17]

The murders of Romero and the American women did have one important consequence, however: They galvanized Catholic opinion in the United States to oppose U.S. military aid to El Salvador. Despite strong pressure from Secretary Haig, the U.S. Bishops Conference refused to alter its position against military aid and in favor of a negotiated peace settlement. The bishops further argued that Haig's view of El Salvador as an East-West confrontation was simplistic and not in accordance with the facts. The Salvadoran conflict was not due to Soviet intervention, they said, but to "internal conditions of poverty and the denial of fundamental human rights." They continued, "We believe that any perception of Central America's problems, stated primarily in terms of global security, military response, the transfer of weapons, and the preservation of a society that has not promoted the participation of a majority of the people, is gravely mistaken."[18]

REVOLUTION AND THE CHURCH

Although every Latin American country is different, most of Central America shares a similar political and social history, democratic Costa Rica and the former British colony of Belize being the exceptions. Unlike the larger South American nations, which have had some experience of democracy, democratic elections are

practically unknown in El Salvador, Honduras, Guatemala,
and Nicaragua. Guatemala enjoyed a brief period of
reforms in the early 1950s, but the experiment was cut
short by a CIA-managed coup in 1954. As theologian Pablo
Richard points out: "The oligarchies in Central America
never made the least concession to the people, not even
the smallest reform. And since there was no possibility
of popular participation, conflicts always were resolved
in a violent manner, whether the government against the
people or the people against the government."[19]

Central America also shares a common history of U.S.
military intervention, in contrast to South America,
where intervention has tended to be less overt (as in the
CIA's involvement in the 1973 coup against Allende).
Thus, most of the sixty-nine cases of military intervention in Latin America since 1850 have occurred in Central
America or the Caribbean.

The Central American church also has been affected
by the violence of revolution and counterrevolution.
Although the hierarchy has traditionally tended to be
conservative, there have always been exceptions, even in
colonial times. One of the first martyrs of the Central
American church was Bishop Antonio Valdiviesco, who was
killed by the Spanish colonists for his defense of the
region's Indians. The Guatemalan church, too, suffered
persecution during the late nineteenth century when a
liberal, anticlerical government expelled all bishops and
priests in the country.

Although the specter of communism most concerned the
Central American bishops in the period after World War
II, they were not immune to the influences of Vatican II
and Medellin. As government violence escalated in the
1970s, a number of bishops were moved to protest human
rights violations, notably in Panama and Guatemala. But
it fell to the bishops of Nicaragua, the personal fiefdom
of the Somoza family, to make the historic decision to
support revolution. Citing St. Thomas Aquinas' doctrine
in support of "just wars against tyrants," the Nicaraguan
bishops announced their backing for the Sandinista rebels
in the summer of 1979. The issue, then as now, was
whether all nonviolent alternatives had been exhausted.
In Nicaragua, where the National Guard was bombing cities
and massacring thousands of people, including children,
no alternative to insurrection seemed possible. The
Somoza family had run Nicaragua for its own personal gain
for forty-three years, and almost everyone, including
conservative businessmen, actively supported the
government's overthrow.

The lack of alternatives to armed violence underlines one of the principal differences between Central
and South America. Unlike the Central American nations,
where guerrilla insurrection has proved successful, such
insurrection has failed everywhere in South America,

primarily because the people remain unconvinced that the only alternative to military repression is a Marxist guerrilla revolution. Although democratically elected governments have frequently been overthrown, the people have had experience of successful nonviolent forms of pressure, such as strikes and civic demonstrations.

These differences also color the varying responses of bishops and clergy to the problems of social injustice and repression. With the exception of Colombia, no religious are involved in guerrilla struggles in South America. None belong to a political party or hold government office. In Central America, by contrast, priests hold high government offices in Nicaragua, and several priests and nuns have joined the guerrillas or leftist political movements in El Salvador and Guatemala. Willingly or not, the Central American church has been drawn into an armed struggle, whereas in Brazil and Chile, for example, the church leads a nonviolent one.

The impact of these contrasting roles varies markedly. Much of the innovation in the Latin American church has come from the Brazilian bishops, who have taken a position of leadership in new forms of religious expression and organization as well as active non-violence. But with the lone exception of San Salvador's Archbishop Romero, the Central American bishops have tended to follow or react to situations not of their making. This was true even of the Nicaraguan bishops, who declared their support for revolution a month before Somoza's overthrow, when the outcome of the struggle seemed certain. This lack of vision and innovation helps explain the deep division among the Central American bishops, who often seem paralyzed by indecision and fear of change.

EL SALVADOR

Nowhere are these contradictions more obvious than in El Salvador, where most of the hierarchy supports the government while most of the religious base opposes it. The divisions are not new but go back to the early 1970s, when the San Salvador archdiocese began to support agrarian reform. The four bishops from the provinces had long been at odds with San Salvador's Archbishop Luis Chavez y Gonzalez, partly for jealousy of his perogatives as the church's leader in the capital, but mostly because of his reformist ideas, which attracted the more liberal elements of the Salvadoran clergy. The beginnings of religious persecution in El Salvador can also be traced to the archdiocese's support of agrarian reform. Father Jose Inocencio Alas, an outspoken critic of the peasants' miserable condition and the archdiocese's delegate in 1970 to El Salvador's first agrarian-reform congress, was arrested, drugged, tortured, and left naked in the mountains. Father Alas survived, but another priest, Nicolas Rodriguez, was arrested by the National Guard shortly before the 1972 elections. His body was later found, completely dismembered.

It was not until 1977, however, that persecution began in earnest. It started in the rural region of Aguilares, north of San Salvador, where a team of four Jesuits had developed a network of comunidades de base. Many of the comunidades' members and lay leaders subsequently joined the outlawed Christian Peasants Federation (FECCAS) to demand agrarian reform and better rural wages. The Aguilares experiment also encouraged religious in other parts of the country to support comunidades and the right to join FECCAS.

The landowners called the Jesuits "communists" and the comunidades "cells," and there was talk in the countryside of the need for another massacre on the same scale as the one in 1932 when 30,000 peasants were slaughtered. Or as a conservative lawyer told the New York Times: "Whenever the peasants make the least demand, people begin talking about 1932 again. So the reaction is always to put down the peasants before they get out of control. The discussion among the rich families now is whether 20,000 or 50,000 or 100,000 peasants should be killed to restore peace."[20]

Father Rutilio Grande, the Salvadoran-born leader of the Aguilares team, nevertheless insisted that it was the church's duty to support the downtrodden peasants:

The enslaved masses of our people, those by the side of our road, live in a feudal system six centuries old. They own neither their land nor their own lives. . . . Mouths are full of the word "Democracy," but let us not fool ourselves. There is no democracy when the power of the people is the power of a wealthy minority. . . .

I greatly fear that very soon the Bible and the Gospel will not be allowed within . . . our country. Only the bindings will arrive, nothing else, because all the pages are subversive--they are against sin. And if Jesus were to cross the border . . . they would arrest him. They would . . . accuse him of being unconstitutional and subversive, a revolutionary, a foreign Jew, a concoctor of strange and bizarre ideas contrary to democracy, that is to say, against the minority. They would crucify him again, because they prefer a Christ of the . . . cemetery, a silent Christ . . . , a Christ made to our image and according to our selfish interests. This is not the Christ of the Gospels! This is not the young Christ who at thirty-three years of age died for the most noble cause of humanity.[21]

In December 1976, two ex-Jesuit seminarians working with the Aguilares peasants were expelled, as was a Colombian parish priest; a former Jesuit, Juan Jose Ramirez, was interrogated, beaten, and tortured with electric shocks for ten days. The government also expelled two foreign missionaries working in the San Salvador slums, Belgian Willbrord Denaux and U.S. Maryknoll missioner Bernard Survil. Before being deported, Denaux was shackled to the metal springs of a bed during twenty hours of interrogation.[22]

Three months later, after rigged elections had ensured the presidential succession of a corrupt, ruthless general, Father Grande was shot to death, along with a teenager and a seventy-two-year old peasant, while on his way to Mass at El Paisnal, a town north of Aguilares. According to a church autopsy, the bullets that riddled Grande and the others were of the same 9mm caliber as the Manzer guns used by the police. By "coincidence," all telephone communications in the area were cut off within an hour of the triple assassination. Police patrols normally active in the region mysteriously disappeared.[23]

Between Grande's assassination in March 1977 and the slaying of the four American women in December 1980, ten more priests would die, including Archbishop Romero, who was confronted with Grande's death a few weeks after replacing Chavez y Gonzalez as archbishop.[24] Grande had been a personal friend of Romero, and his murder profoundly shocked the devout prelate, changing him almost overnight from a shy conservative to an outspoken defender of Salvador's peasant and working classes.

Chosen archbishop precisely because he seemed so unexceptional, Romero had occasionally written or spoken piously about the church's social teachings, but he had proven his conservative credentials as auxiliary bishop of San Salvador and editor of the diocesan newspaper, Orientacion. Like most of the Salvadoran bishops, he harbored a deep suspicion of "new Christologies" and worried publicly about the "politicization" of priests. Thus he seemed a safe replacement for Chavez, who, because of his support for the poor and oppressed, had long been a thorn in the oligarchy's side.

The San Salvadoran clergy and Auxiliary Bishop Arturo Rivera y Damas had grave misgivings about Romero, but after Grande's death he surprised them by taking a strong stand against the military government and by encouraging a democratic administration of the arch-diocese. "When I became archbishop, priests were being killed, accused, tortured," Romero explained. "I felt I had to defend the church. Then again, I felt that the people the church has to serve were asking me to defend them."[25] Romero's Sunday sermons in the San Salvador cathedral soon became the most important weekly event in the country. Broadcast by the Catholic radio station, YSAX, and attended by thousands of people, the sermons gave hope and information to his listeners about what was happening in the civil war. He also established a church-sponsored office to investigate human rights violations; encouraged the church newspaper, Orientacion, to speak out against such abuses; and gave his personal support to priests and nuns working with refugee groups and comunidades de base.

All these activities were criticized by the military and the oligarchy, but none so much as Romero's support of popular organizations and his admonition to Salvadoran military recruits not to kill their brothers and sisters. The popular organizations included coalitions of peasants, workers, teachers, students, and other concerned citizens, many of whom also belonged to comunidades de base. Romero defended their legitimacy and right to protest against repression--for example, through labor strikes: "No one can take away, least of all from the poor, the right to organize, because the protection of the weak is the principal purpose of laws and social organizations."[26] The existence of such organizations, particularly labor unions, had always been bitterly opposed by the upper classes; in giving them his support, Romero knew he was courting death. Yet he was not afraid. "If they kill me," he said, "I will rise again in the people of El Salvador."[27] When, in March 1980, Romero urged "peasants in uniform" not to obey orders to kill, he was shot down the next day in a San Salvador chapel while saying Mass. With his death, the masses lost the one unifying voice capable of speaking above the government and guerrilla violence. For many Salvadorans, his funeral marked the end of any hope of a peaceful solution: A bomb thrown into the funeral crowd of more than 5,000 set off a shooting match between soldiers and mourners, leaving 26 dead and 200 wounded.

After the funeral there was a noticeable hardening in the positions of the opposing sides. As in the political arena, where more and more Salvadorans were opting for the extreme right or left--at the expense of middle-of-the-road parties and movements--so, too, in the church. Peasants informed on other peasants who were members of the comunidades in order to obtain privileges from the military. In retaliation, guerrillas assassinated peasant leaders of ORDEN, a rural paramilitary force. Priests would not speak to bishops, and vice versa. Thus, the values of solidarity and forgiveness that Romero had preached were often lost in the growing polarization, proving that the ultimate test for the church in overcoming hatred and corruption had yet to be successfully met.

Romero himself often suffered from the lack of such values in the Salvadoran church. For most of his three

years as archbishop, he was engaged in a guerrilla war of
his own with Papal Nuncio Emmanuele Gerarda and four of
his five fellow bishops. (Only Rivera y Damas, Romero's
auxiliary bishop, consistently supported him.) The
Vatican was constantly misinformed about events in El
Salvador by Gerarda and the other bishops, who mounted a
smear campaign through the good offices of Cardinal
Sebastiano Baggio, the powerful president of the
Pontifical Commission for Latin America. At one point,
Rome even considered asking Romero to resign, but the
political situation in El Salvador seemed too volatile
for such an action. Behind-the-scenes machinations
against the archbishop continued, however--some of them
characterized by extreme pettiness.

Although the divisions in other Latin American
churches usually are nuanced and complex, the confrontation among the Salvadoran hierarchy was simple and
direct: Romero represented the option for the poor and
oppressed so clearly stated by the Latin American bishops
at Medellin and Puebla. His opponents in the hierarchy
stood for the church of old, allied to the military and
the oligarchy. Bishop Benjamin Barrera (Santa Ana) was
over-aged, whereas Bishop Eduardo Alvarez, the military
vicar and a colonel, used his army connections to further
his own ambitions. As for Bishop Pedro Arnoldo Aparicio
(San Vicente), who particularly disliked Romero, a former
Salvadoran military president had dismissed him as a man
who "wags his tail when you give him something." The
fourth bishop, San Salvador Auxiliary Bishop Marco Rene
Revelo, frequently went behind Romero's back to curry
favor with Aparicio and Alvarez, all the while professing
friendship for the archbishop.[28]

But Romero was not without means. When the
conservative bishops prevented him from leading the
Salvadoran delegation to the Puebla conference, he went
anyway--and obtained the support of forty prominent Latin
American bishops, who signed a letter of solidarity,
praising his faithfulness to the Gospel. The archbishop
also received strong support from international opinion,
particularly the U.S. Catholic Church.

Though constantly accused of meddling in politics,
Romero represented no political party or ideology but the
people of El Salvador, the vast majority of whom are
poor. His was "the voice of the voiceless." Though he
opposed violence from any source, such opposition cost
him his life. As the Peruvian liberation theologian
Gustavo Gutierrez observed, his death holds a profound
significance: "Before Romero the church tended to say:
these Christians died for political, not religious
reasons. Now it has been made clear that Romero died for
religious reasons. He was killed not because he defended
the rights of the church, but because he defended the
rights of the poor."[29]

With Romero's passing, responsibility for the arch-diocese fell to Arturo Rivera y Damas, who was appointed to the temporary position of apostolic administrator. Though as progressive in outlook as Romero, Rivera suffered from the dual restraints of a conservative hierarchy and fear of the same fate as Romero. Still supportive of the archdiocese's human rights office, he nevertheless distanced the church from its work. Orientacion was placed under the direction of a priest, Roberto Torruella, formerly chaplain to the National Police. All references to human rights were eliminated from the paper, as well as statements by Romero on the subject. Restraints were also placed on clergy working with the comunidades. Meanwhile, ninety-eight priests were forced to leave the country, stripping the church's progressive sector of much of its clerical support. Yet the work begun by Rutilio Grande, Romero, and others continued in comunidades that went underground to form the "Popular Church," but most particularly through the patient and courageous work of Salvadoran and foreign nuns. Today they are the principal religious promoters in areas bereft of priests, carrying on the legacy left by four American women.

NICARAGUA

As historians have often observed, the most difficult part of a revolution is after it has succeeded. This has been notably so for the Nicaraguan bishops, who have had to deal--without much success--with both a dialogue with Marxists and the political activism of priests.

Unlike earlier revolutionary uprisings in Latin America, the Nicaraguan experience was deeply influenced by Catholicism. Members of the comunidades de base played an important role in support of the Sandinista rebels, and battles with the National Guard were often preceded by prayer and reflection on stories from the Bible. When cities were bombed, mourners responded with religious hymns. Religious songs also became a medium of protest and communication, to keep the people informed of the progress of the war. Nuns and priests were actively involved in the rebellion, although only one priest actually took up arms. Rebel radio stations operated clandestinely from religious houses, and nuns and priests provided protection and aid to thousands of refugees. Father Chico Luis, the founder of an agricultural school for young Central American farmers, was killed by the National Guard while seeking aid for some 300 refugees. In addition, foreign missionaries based in Nicaragua used their contacts in the United States and Europe to obtain support for the revolution.

A profoundly religious people, Nicaraguans took for granted the church's participation in the revolution, which they believed sought the same goals of justice and freedom that they had learned in the comunidades de base. For its part, the church aimed to avoid the mistakes of its counterpart in Cuba, where most of the bishops and clergy had opposed the revolution and abandoned the island in its wake, thus eliminating any possibility of future influence. Managua's Archbishop Miguel Obando y Bravo ignored death threats and continued to criticize the Somoza regime, thereby becoming a hero; on several occasions, the bishops strongly rebuked the government for human rights violations. Their opposition to Somoza, combined with the active support of priests and nuns and the deep religiosity of peasants and workers, had an important impact on the course of the revolution. Indeed, it was largely due to Catholic influence that the guerrillas expanded their ranks from a small group of hard-core Marxists to a broader movement that included many non-Marxists.

But if the church had helped influence the guerrillas, the justice of the latter's cause had also influenced the clergy. Explained Father Miguel D'Escoto, who would become foreign minister after the revolution:

> In the beginning, the Sandinista Front...was Marxist' and anti-clerical, perhaps because a process of Christianization had not yet begun in the Nicaraguan church, and it was identified with the interests of the privileged class. But with our evangelical radicalization, placing ourselves on the side of the poor and oppressed . . . , the Front opened itself to Christians because they believed the church an important factor in the struggle for liberation and because they realized they were wrong in believing that only a Marxist could be a revolutionary. Thus the Front acquired maturity and it became authentically Sandinista.[30]

A young guerrilla on the barricades of Esteli put it another way. "Look at this cross," he shouted at a foreign journalist, waving a revolver in one hand and a cross hanging from his neck in the other. "I am not a communist, as Somoza calls all who fight against his government. I am a Catholic and a Sandinista!"[31]

Once the Sandinistas were in power, however, their honeymoon with the bishops quickly soured. Shortly after the fall of Somoza, in July 1979, the hierarchy issued a surprisingly radical statement in favor of socialism; nevertheless, the bishops cautioned that their support would depend on the maintenance of Christian values, particularly a respect for human rights. Such respect was soon called into question by six of the seven

Nicaraguan bishops, with Obando y Bravo as their
spokesman. (Only Ruben Lopez, the bishop of Esteli,
remained supportive of the revolution.) The bishops
complained about the large number of National Guardsmen
still awaiting trial. They were also critical of press
censorship, particularly the government's periodic shut-
downs of La Prensa, the country's leading newspaper. And
they worried publicly about the failure to define a
political model or set a timetable for elections.
   The bishops' criticisms split the Nicaraguan church
along much the same lines dividing the church in El
Salvador, with the overwhelming majority of priests,
nuns, and lay leaders defiantly supporting the revolution. From hero, Obando y Bravo soon became a "Judas,"
and those who thought like him were characterized as
tools of the Reagan administration.
   Neither side was entirely justified. The bishops
were overly critical of the government; the latter's
supporters were equally uncritical of the revolution's
obvious failings. The essential point missed in the mud-
slinging was that no country can emerge from centuries of
violence and dictatorship with a full-blown democracy.
It had taken the Sandinistas forty-three years of
struggle at the cost of thousands of lives to overthrow
the Somozas, and the hatreds and conflicts born of that
struggle would not soon die--particularly if the Reagan
administration was successful in destabilizing the
Managua government.
   Contrary to U.S. government propaganda, which
claimed the Nicaraguan regime was guilty of massive human
rights violations, American observers who visited the
country found a quite different situation. As documented
by a fact-finding mission (including Congressmen Studds,
Edgar, and Mikulski) sponsored by the Unitarian
Universalist Service Committee, postrevolutionary
Nicaragua was

> one of the most peaceful countries in Central
> America. Except for the sparsely populated regions
> along the border with Honduras, where sporadic
> clashes between government troops and alleged
> Somocistas occur, the nation is virtually free of
> political violence. This is due in part to the
> national exhaustion with death following the civil
> war, but even more important has been the desire of
> the Sandinista leadership to avoid Iranian style
> postrevolutionary executions. . . . The Sandinistas
> have generally fulfilled early pledges to be
> 'implacable in rebellion, but generous in victory.'
> Given the fierceness of the civil war and the
> totality of the revolution which it brought about,
> this has been a remarkable achievement.

As for the government's slowness in processing
imprisoned Guardsmen, the mission reported that it
was on ". . . firm ground in alleging that atrocities were committed on a wide scale by the members
of the Somoza National Guard. In the chaos
following the revolution, however, they had neither
the evidence, nor the legal structure needed to try
individual cases in a systematic, fair, and speedy
manner. As a consequence, they improvised a process
which has included within it the periodic pardoning
of some prisoners, particularly women, the very
young, the old, and people who can provide proof of
their innocence. Those against whom strong evidence
exists have been tried and most convicted and
sentenced to long prison terms (the death penalty
has been abolished). There remain, however, a large
number of prisoners who may or may not have committed serious crimes, individuals waiting to funnel
through the slow, jerry-built system of trials.

Press censorship, the mission found, was a serious
problem, reflecting the lack of any tradition in
Nicaragua of mature dialogue. "The status of the press
in today's Nicaragua is less than secure, but by any
standard reasonably applicable to Third World countries,
it remains at present tolerable. The restrictions cannot
grow more harsh, however, without triggering severe
criticism of the government from both within and outside
of Nicaragua."[32]
Finally, the mission noted that while opposition
political parties were legal and functioning, dissidents
worried about the postponement of elections until 1985.
Government sources candidly admitted that tensions
between Marxists and non-Marxists in the Sandinista
leadership were largely responsible for the failure to
define a political model. But they also pointed to the
presence of four priests in the government; a still
strong private sector; the steadying influence of Mexico,
Nicaragua's most important regional ally; and the
pragmatism of the Sandinista leaders--all of which were
moderating factors. Thus, despite internal and external
pressures and severe economic problems, the government
could still claim that pluralism was alive and well.
The regime could also point to some major social
achievements. A literacy campaign conducted by
Sandinista youths taught nearly half a million people to
read and write, reducing the illiteracy rate from 50.2
percent--among the highest in Latin America--to 12
percent, second only to Cuba. Through community-action
programs, Nicaraguans paved streets and built electrical
lines and houses. Managua's downtown area, destroyed in
the 1972 earthquake and never rebuilt by Somoza, is being

converted to a complex of sports arenas and parks. In
the squalid slums ringing the capital, markets, community
centers, and health centers have sprung up; tin and cardboard shacks have been replaced by solid family homes
built by their occupants with free cement, bricks, and
timber supplied by the government. In the countryside,
where the majority of the people live, more than sixty
thousand peasant families have benefited from land
reform; and, for the first time in Nicaraguan history,
peasants and small farmers have access to low-interest
government loans and modern technology. Minimum wages
have been raised in rural and urban areas and rents have
been halved. Education is free, transportation subsidized. Despite gargantuan economic problems, the
Sandinistas succeeded in transferring 12 percent of the
nation's wealth to the poorest 70 percent of the population within a year and a half of Somoza's overthrow.

In view of such achievements, the Nicaraguan
bishops' criticisms often seemed like nit-picking or,
worse, blind stupidity. Such was the case of an over-
hasty assessment by the hierarchy of the relocation of
some 8,500 Mosquito Indians, a relocation that the
bishops said had led to severe human rights violations.
The Mosquitos were moved in early 1982 from infertile,
often flooded lands along the Honduran border to three
new settlements farther south, where the land is highly
suited to mixed farming and will support citrus and coco-
nuts. In the resettlement area the Indians also have
access to schools, social services, electricity, water,
and health services unavailable in the remote frontier
region.[33]

Yet, the Sandinistas did not move the Indians out of
any deep concern for their welfare--although the government now realizes that wooing the Indians is to its
political advantage. The intent was to secure the
frontiers against possible invasion by U.S.-backed
Somocistas from Honduras. Between July 1980 and the
beginning of 1982, some 200 Nicaraguan frontier guards
were killed by such forces. The Sandinista government
claimed, accurately enough, that it could not protect the
Indians. It also charged the Hondurans with abetting the
Mosquito leader Steadman Fagoth, in promoting rebellion
among a minority of the Indians.

According to Secretary of State Haig the Mosquito
resettlement was a case of "genocide," and he claimed to
have pictures to prove it. But "the pictures" turned out
to be a photograph published by the Paris newspaper Le
Figaro that showed bodies being burned in a city street.
The caption described a massacre by the Nicaraguans of
the Mosquitos. Subsequent inquiries revealed that the
picture had actually been taken more than three years
earlier, during the rebellion against Somoza, when the

Red Cross was burning corpses as a sanitary measure after a National Guard attack.[34]

The Nicaraguan bishops also were left in an awkward position for having denounced human rights violations in the resettlement. None of the bishops had actually gone to the area to verify their charges, despite repeated government invitations. Yet on-the-scene reports by Protestant and Catholic church representatives, as well as foreign correspondents, stated that there had been no massive abuses. On the contrary, they suggested that many Indians were glad to have escaped from frontier dangers and looked forward to better living conditions in their new home.[35]

Charges that the bishops had played into the hands of the counterrevolutionaries had a ring of truth. Just as the English played on the Mosquitos' hatred of the Spaniards in colonial times, U.S. and Honduran agents took advantage of Sandinista mistakes in dealing with the non-Spanish-speaking Indians to stir up trouble. Originally, the government had attempted to incorporate the Indians into the revolutionary process by giving Fagoth a position as Mosquito representative in the Council of State. Fagoth owed his power to his position as preacher in the Moravian Church, the dominant religious influence among the Mosquitos. In February 1981, the government claimed to have uncovered a plot by Fagoth to lead a separatist Indian uprising with the support of Somocista and Honduran troops. Subsequently, the entire leadership of the Indian federation Misurasata, representing the Mosquitos and two other coastal tribes, was arrested. The detentions caused riots in the frontier town of Prinzapolka in the northeastern department of Zelaya, resulting in eight deaths. Five U.S. missionaries working in the area were expelled.

In the aftermath, the Sandinistas publicly recognized that the arrests had been an error. The government also apologized to the Nicaraguan hierarchy for expelling the missionaries and said that they could return. (Only one did.) It further admitted that its plan to integrate Indian territories with the rest of the country smacked of cultural colonialism. And in early 1982 it began to study the possibility of creating an autonomous federal department for the Indians in Zelaya, which would manage the local economy and social services while Managua assumed responsibility for defense, international relations, and foreign trade.

In so hastily denouncing the Mosquito resettlement, without recognizing the government's genuine desire to reach out to the Indians, the Nicaraguan bishops merely reinforced the widespread impression that they were being manipulated. For one thing, the papal nuncio, Bishop

Andres Cordero Lanza, refused to support the hierarchy's
critical statement, suggesting that the Vatican was not
prepared to echo Washington's charges of genocide.
Moreover, the bishops' statement coincided with a visit
by Archbishop Obando y Bravo to the United States to
receive an award from the right-wing Institute on
Religion and Democracy. It also seemed strange that the
bishops had suddenly become champions of the Mosquitos,
when they had never bothered about them before. "The
silicosis and tuberculosis contracted through hard labor
in foreign-owned gold mines . . . and the premature death
of young Mosquitos never merited a document or condemnation by the bishops," noted Justinian Lieb, a former
Capuchin priest with twenty-five years experience in
Zelaya. "When the National Guard transferred thousands
of Mosquitos of the Rio Coco zone to an inhospitable
savanna and Somoza's colonels accumulated great fortunes
usurping aid that had been given for the Indians'
transfer, the Espicopal Conference said not a word."[36]
      The Mosquito affair reopened the question of why the
bishops--Obando y Bravo in particular--had become so
hostile to the Sandinistas when they had backed the
uprising and the overwhelming majority of clergy and
laity still supported the revolution. One explanation
could be found in the pressures brought to bear on the
hierarchy by the Latin American Episcopal Conference
(CELAM), the service organization of the Latin American
bishops. Although CELAM had been responsible for
organizing the Medellin and Puebla conferences, by the
end of the 1970s it had come under the control of the
conservative Colombian bishops, who had always opposed
the Medellin Documents. Led by Alfonso Lopez Trujillo--
archbishop, ironically, of Medellin--CELAM embarked on a
witch hunt of progressives, particularly liberation
theologians. Without influence among the larger, more
mature hierarchies like Brazil, Lopez Trujillo's group
centered its attention on Central America, particularly
El Salvador, where it opposed Archbishop Romero, and
Nicaragua, where it encouraged Obando y Bravo's disaffec-
tion under the guise of money and other material aid for
the Nicaraguan church.
      Despite his initial support of the revolution,
Obando y Bravo had always hoped for the emergence of a
Christian Democratic government; his closest allies were
either connected to the Social Christian Party or COSEP,
the businessmen's association, both in opposition to the
Sandinistas. Washington also considered the Christian
Democratic parties in Latin America a useful antidote to
socialism--movements that could talk reform without
actually changing economic and political structures.
Hence the U.S. support for Allende's Christian Democratic
predecessor in Chile, Eduardo Frei, and for a Christian
Democratic president in the Salvadoran junta. Lopez

*Lopez
Trujillo*

Trujillo's CELAM also backed the Christian Democrats as a supposed "third way" between right and left. Not coincidentally, Lopez' chief adviser, the Belgian Jesuit Roger Vekemans, had close links to the Chilean and Venezuelan Christian Democrats, as well as a history of cooperation with the CIA.[37] Nor was it an accident that one of the major sources of false information on the human rights situation, the so-called Permanent Commission on Human Rights, was chaired by a member of Nicaragua's Social Christian Party.

CELAM also opposed the revolution because it had so clearly contributed to a democratization of the church. The Colombians had often criticized the Brazilian bishops for fraternizing with the masses. In Nicaragua a "Popular Church," democratically run by lay people and clergy, was challenging the hierarchy's privileges. Or as described by the disgruntled Mexican Bishop Genaro Alamilla, who formed part of a CELAM delegation to Nicaragua: "The hierarchy is devalued, just like worthless money. They want this popular church that goes from the bottom to the top, from the people themselves. The nuns are the worst of the lot, just like furies. I said to myself in Nicaragua, thank God, I never married!"[38]

Normally attentive to Lopez Trujillo's point of view because of his benefactor, the influential Cardinal Baggio, the Vatican proved surprisingly unsympathetic. Rome refused to cooperate in ordering the handful of priests in the Sandinista government to resign. Indeed, the Vatican Secretary of State attempted to bridge the gap between hierarchy and government. Cardinal Agostino Casaroli showed sympathy toward priests in government posts during a June 1981 meeting in Rome. Papal Nuncio Cordero also urged the Nicaraguan bishops to establish a dialogue with the priests and the religious orders' federation, CONFER.

But as with the press, neither side seemed willing to compromise. Compounding the problem was the often anarchic style of government at the municipal level, with gangs of overzealous Sandinistas going off on their own. For example, after Interior Minister Tomas Borge attacked conservative Protestant sects with foreign ties as "counterrevolutionaries," Sandinista Defense Committees throughout the country began seizing churches and offices belonging to the Seventh Day Adventists, Mormons, and Jehovah's Witnesses. The government became alarmed at the possible international consequences after a visit by a delegation from the U.S. National Council of Churches, which had favored the revolution. The group told the Sandinista junta that Nicaragua could lose the support of liberals in the United States unless peace between church and state was restored.[39]

The warning came in the wake of the worst incident in church-state relations, in August 1982, when Father

Bismark Carballo, Obando y Bravo's chief assistant, was attacked by an assailant while having lunch with a woman parishioner. Both were forced to strip nude, and while four policemen looked on, a government television crew filmed the pair in the street. Although the incidents leading up to the affair remained confused, many Nicaraguans were shocked by Carballo's treatment and indignant at pictures of the nude priest in the government-controlled media. Student protests in private Catholic high schools led to clashes with pro-Sandinista youth. In the deeply religious city of Masaya, south of Managua, a crowd of 500 attacked a police station; in the melee three Nicaraguans were killed and six injured. Five foreign priests involved in the student protests were forced to take refuge in the Costa Rican and Spanish embassies after being threatened by the Sandinistas (one was subsequently deported).[40]

The Carballo affair followed another ugly incident, over the transfer of a popular priest from a Managua parish. The priest, Jose Arias Caldera, had spoken out at a mass rally in memory of fourteen peasant militiamen killed by counterrevolutionaries operating from Honduras. The attackers had painted the slogan "For God and Country--Death to Communism" on the walls of the town, and Arias challenged Obando y Bravo to excommunicate them. Instead, the archbishop transferred Arias as a sign of his disapproval. In protest, progressive Catholics occupied Arias's church. When Obando's auxiliary bishop showed up, he was manhandled, and the locked tabernacle fell to the floor in the scuffle. The following day the archbishop excommunicated everyone involved in the incident.

Although the Sandinistas and their "Popular Church" had played into the hands of the counterrevolutionaries over the Carballo and Arias incidents, in many other cases facts were distorted to make it appear that the church was suffering mass persecution. Thus, a Washington Times article distributed throughout Latin America by the U.S. Information Agency claimed that Bishop Salvador Schlaefer had been violently expelled from the Mosquito settlements in his diocese, even though Schlaefer denied that he had ever been arrested. The article further claimed that Obando y Bravo had been beaten up on several occasions, also untrue.[41]

After John Paul issued a sharp rebuke to the "Popular Church," once again urging that "Christians . . not be divided because of opposing ideologies,"[42] the government and the hierarchy called a truce, finally embarking on a serious dialogue. The Sandinista Defense Committees were ordered not to provoke or be provoked by rightists seeking to use the religious question for political ends. Reaffirming its support for religious freedom, the government told 300 Protestant pastors that

the seized churches would be returned. For its part, the
Catholic hierarchy declared a willingness to work for
better relations between the bishops and the government.

[Subsequently, church-state relations once again
deteriorated. In early March 1983, Pope John Paul
visited Nicaragua as part of his tour through Central
America. Speaking to a crowd of a half million people in
Managua, he warned that the unity of the Nicaraguan
church was being threatened by "unacceptable ideological
commitments." Attacking the idea of a "People's Church"
as "absurd and dangerous," he criticized those priests
holding posts in the Nicaraguan government, saying they
were "acting outside or against the will of the bishops."
During the homily, his words were often drowned out by
pro-Sandinista groups, shouting "Popular Power!" and "We
want peace!" On several occasions, the pope even called
for "Silence!" and was cheered wildly by what seemed like
a majority of the spectators. Subsequently, charges were
made that the Sandinistas had manipulated the electrical
system to enhance the slogans of their supporters. The
president of the Central American Episcopal Secretariat
deplored the behavior of the Sandinista militants as a
"premeditated profanation of the sacramentalized Jesus."
In turn, the Nicaraguan government denied having
organized any provocation, claiming that: "What happened
in the mass was the spontaneous reaction of a people
which has suffered attacks and aggression and is cla-
moring for peace."[43] --Eds.]

GUATEMALA

Of the Central American countries, Guatemala offers
the most typical experience of the changes in the Latin
American church brought about by government repression.
With the exception of Guatemala City's arch-conservative
Cardinal Mario Casariego [since deceased], the hierarchy
has gradually shed its conservative outlook for a more
prophetic tone in response to a state terrorism
unequalled in Latin America. As noted by the Guatemalan
bishops in a November 1981 pastoral letter, Guatemala
stands at a crossroads between "violence and the need for
reforms." "The country has reached a point in its
history where there is no alternative, as pointed out by
Pope John Paul . . .: 'The realization of justice in
this continent faces a clear challenge: Either it is
achieved through profound and courageous reforms . . .
or . . . it will come about through the force of
violence.'"[44]

Since 1954, when the reform government of Jacobo
Arbenz was overthrown in a CIA-directed coup, more than
83,000 people have been killed in Guatemala's political
violence, the vast majority of them Indian peasants slain

142

by the army.[45] Massacres have occurred at Panzos,
Chajul, Cotzal, Santiago Atitlan, Sacala, San Jose
Poaquil, Chuabajito, Coya, Suntelaj, Rabinal, Semuy,
Chupol, and San Antonio Huista--among others. By the end
of 1981, an average of thirty-six people disappeared, or
were kidnapped or assassinated daily. Moreover, the
violence was marked by a cruel, psychopathic style.
Victims were scalped; fetuses of pregnant women were cut
out and thrown to dogs and vultures. . . . "The military
is no longer human," said Julia Esquivel, co-editor of a
Guatemalan church magazine and now in exile. "They cut
out the fetus from a woman, then put her husband's head
in her womb, and sewed her back up."[46] Her story was not
unusual.

     Organized violence against the Catholic Church dates
to 1976, about the time that the Somoza regime in
Nicaragua began to clamp down on comunidades de base.
Between 1976 and March 1982, fifteen priests (including
three Americans) and one nun were murdered by government-
directed paramilitary squads. The bishop of El Quiche
diocese and president of the Guatemalan Episcopal
Conference, Juan Gerardi, was forced to abandon the area
after narrowly escaping assassination. Twenty-five
Sacred Heart missionaries from Spain, as well as a group
of Dominican nuns, also left Quiche because of military
persecution, including the bombing of convents.
Altogether, 105 religious were expelled from the country,
or one-sixth of the priests in Guatemala; sixty-five nuns
also were forced to seek exile. Sixty parishes were left
without priests, including most of Quiche, where there
were only one priest and five nuns to serve one and a
half million people. Four Catholic radio stations were
destroyed or silenced, and ten Catholic high schools and
forty-two centers of religious training were closed.
Several hundred catechists and lay leaders were also
killed. One of the worst examples of the military's
excesses was the kidnapping and torture in 1981 of Jesuit
Luis Pellecer, who became a vegetable. Numerous
Protestant ministers were tortured and killed as well.
"These acts of violence," said the Guatemalan bishops,
"are part of a well-studied plan to frighten the church
and silence its prophetic voice. They also are part of a
climate of irrational terror which our country is
suffering--a terror that has surpassed all limits."[47]
Equally concerned, Pope John Paul publicly chastized the
Guatemalan government for religious persecution and human
rights violations. But the violence continued.

     This was not the church's first experience with
persecution. In the 1870s, when the anti-clerical
liberals came to power, the large landowners confiscated
all its goods and secularized education. (Even today
only 5 percent of the schools are Catholic.) Bishops,
priests, and nuns were expelled from the country; all

religious congregations were suppressed. Not until 1945,
when a reformist, popularly elected government came to
power, did the Guatemalan church recover from the
liberals' blow. Despite U.S. propaganda depicting the
subsequent Arbenz regime as "communist," it encouraged
the church's growth, as none of its "anti-communist"
predecessors had done. Five new dioceses were
established, and for the first time in decades priests
went out to the villages.

The liberal landowners had attempted to justify
their anti-clericalism on ideological grounds, claiming
that the church was opposed to "progress." But because
the landowners themselves so clearly opposed progress (by
the mass of the people), the persecution boomeranged:
Liberal capitalism became identified by the Indian
peasantry with exploitation and repression, whereas
Catholicism was seen as synonymous with justice, freedom,
and equality. Thus, the church had a ready-made base for
evangelization when, in the mid-1950s, priests and nuns
began arriving from the United States and Europe in
response to a Vatican appeal for more missionaries in
Latin America. The foreigners brought new ideas and a
commitment to reform, which survived the 1954 coup and
successive waves of military persecution. Vatican II and
Medellin helped strengthen that commitment, which bore
fruit in comunidades de base, schools for the Indians,
and training centers to develop Indian leadership. In
the Guatemalan context, the church's decision to teach
the Indians to read and write was clearly a political
one: Illiterates were not allowed to vote; they also
were at a disadvantage in any legal dispute.

The conscientization carried out in the comunidades
through study and reflection on the Bible also had a
political impact in developing Indian organizations and
leadership. Religion became the "yeast" of the downtrodden by opening their eyes to their potential to
change themselves and the structures that shackled them.
With church support, Indians began organizing agricultural and consumer cooperatives to reduce dependence
on the large landowners. They also joined a popular
peasant movement known as the Comite de Unidad Campesina.

The landowners were not slow in recognizing this
threat to their economic and political power. Ever since
Arbenz, they had lived in fear of an uprising by the
Indians, who constitute 60 percent of the population.
And now the Indians were awakening, thanks to the
conscientizing work of priests and nuns. As a counterbalance therefore to the emerging "Church of the Poor,"
Guatemalan military governments actively encouraged the
growth of a charismatic movement emphasizing piety and
individualism. They also welcomed such politically
conservative sects as the Mormons and the Jehovah's

Witnesses. But the principal response was, as usual, more violence.

The persecution began in Quiche in the north, where Indian cooperatives were seen as a threat by the region's coffee barons. In March 1976, 200 teachers were ordered to report to the local military base, where they were told by Commander Gregorio Avala: "If you want to keep your jobs, stay out of politics. If you want to stay alive and not be kidnapped or killed, stay away from the church. The military has decided to rid Guatemala of such s---." Ten months later, 150 Quiche catechists were dead, and Maryknoll missionary William Woods had been killed in an airplane crash that many thought had been arranged by the army. One of the catechists who escaped gave a vivid account of the repression: "Soldiers would ask the catechists if they were Catholics; and if they said yes, they were beaten by the soldiers. Houses were searched by the military; and if the soldiers found any Bibles, they would tear them up, stamp on them, and burn them in front of their owners, threatening them with death and telling them it was necessary to 'do away with' the Bible."[48]

The situation came to a violent head in January 1980, when twenty-two Indians from Quiche were burned alive in the Spanish Embassy in Guatemala City. They had occupied the building in a peaceful demonstration to call attention to the peasants' plight; but despite the Spanish ambassador's pleas on their behalf, the military stormed the embassy. The army blamed Spanish priests and nuns working with the Indians for encouraging the occupation; and after two priests were murdered in Quiche, twenty-five nuns and priests fled the province. Bishop Gerardi was to have been assassinated during a trip to officiate at Confirmation ceremonies, but he learned of the plot in time and went to Rome instead. There he told the Pope of the religious persecution in his diocese. When Gerardi returned to Guatemala in October 1980, he was refused re-entry and forced to seek exile in Costa Rica.

Despite the ferocious persecution, Catholicism survives and thrives in Quiche as a church of the catacombs. Some 200 catechists carry on the work of the priests, baptizing, marrying, burying, and "celebrating the Word"--all at great risk to themselves. Groups of four to five families meet secretly in a house to study the Bible. If a meeting is planned for 10 a.m., the first families begin arriving two hours earlier to avoid attracting attention. At these gatherings, the catechists tell stories of daily life. One describes how he was afraid to go into the street to aid his neighbor when he heard calls for help. The next day he found the man's body in a nearby ravine. The catechists say they are afraid to sleep two nights in the same house and tell

ow frightened they are to return home. Yet, they are
also inspired by the parallels between their lives and
those of Christ and the early Christians. They recall
that Jesus, too, was spied on and that some people came
"to trick him with his own words." And they well
remember Judas.[49]

As in other Latin American countries where the
church has suffered persecution, the religious orders in
Guatemala are enjoying a boom in vocations, particularly
the most persecuted, such as the Jesuits and the Belgian
Scheut religious order. Murdered priests are considered
saints. When the Guatemalan priest, Carlos Galvez, was
killed in May 1981, while on his way to baptize a child,
his parishioners circled with rocks and flowers the pool
of blood where he had died. But soon no blood was
visible. It had been reverently gathered up with the
dust of the road and carried home by the grieving
villagers, much as the early Christians had gathered the
blood of their martyrs and the relics of their witness to
Christianity on the sands of Rome's Colosseum.[50]

The blood of martyrs also influenced the Guatemalan
bishops, many of whom suffered persecution in the flesh.
In addition to Gerardi, Mario Rios Montt, the bishop of
Escuintla, went into hiding because of death threats, and
Bishop Gerardo Flores Reyes (Vera Cruz) was blacklisted
by the government. By 1982, twelve of the fifteen
dioceses in Guatemala had opted to follow Medellin's
commitment to the poor and oppressed. Persecution also
helped unite clergy and bishops through regular consul-
tations between the hierarchy and CONFREGUA, the
conference of religious orders in Guatemala.

In response to the bishops' increasingly critical
pastoral letters, the government refused entry to all
foreign priests, including West Germany's Archbishop
Johannes Joachim Degenhardt and his vicar general. It
also increased the harassment of priests and nuns through
kidnappings, torture, and murder.

Nor did the violence stop at Guatemala's borders.
In March 1982, Father Hipolito Cervantes Arceo was found
murdered in his parish house in southern Mexico, sixty-
six miles from the Guatemalan frontier. Cervantes had
given refuge to Guatemalan peasants fleeing military
violence, and his body showed the same marks of torture
that are the hallmark of right-wing death squads.
According to Bishop Samuel Ruiz, whose diocese is located
in the border region of southern Mexico, Guatemala's
extreme right had embarked on a campaign of terror
against Mexican peasants who gave refuge to peasants
fleeing Guatemala.[51]

A month before Cervantes' murder, moreover, twenty
unidentified armed men had stormed the Guadalupe Mission
of the Marist Brothers in the town of Comitan in Chiapas.
The three Marists present were beaten and the mission was

sacked. Like Cervantes, they had been active in promoting comunidades de base and Indian lay leaders. Neither crime was clarified despite demands by the Mexican hierarchy for a thorough investigation. Ruiz's suspicion that the attacks were the work of right-wing Guatemalans was supported by the frequent presence of large numbers of Guatemalan troops that had crossed the border in pursuit of refugees. Although the Mexican foreign ministry admitted to the unauthorized presence o such troops, it refused to give figures for the numbers involved—possibly because it did not have them. Ruiz charged that the Guatemalan military was razing villages in a six-mile-wide swath along the 533-mile-long frontie with Mexico to create a free-fire zone, much as the Salvadoran Army had done along the Honduran border. He said that numerous peasant massacres had occurred in the area, including one in July 1981, when at least twenty corpses were seen floating down the Usumacinta River.[52]

In the crucible of terror, priests and nuns faced a difficult choice. The dilemma was whether they could better serve the people and the church by staying behind as witnesses, thus risking death, or by following the diaspora to Costa Rica, Nicaragua, Mexico, or Colombia, where Guatemalan churchpeople were in exile. Often, the were forced to take the latter course, either under orders from concerned superiors or because they were literally run out of the country at the point of a gun.

Stanley Rother, a forty-six-year-old Oklahoma missionary who worked in the mountain village of Santiag Atitlan, faced such a choice. Because of death threats, he returned to the United States in January 1981. But h could not forget his "people," and in April he went back to continue his fourteen-year mission. "If I have to die," he told his family, "I will die there. I want to be there with my people."[53]

Three months later he was found dead. He had been shot twice, once in the left temple and once in the left cheekbone, by three men wearing ski masks. His body was covered with welts and bruises, suggesting that he had put up a struggle. (Like other priests and nuns in Guatemala, Rother was shocked by the military's brutal torture of Father Pellecer and had sworn that, if the military came for him, they would "not take me alive.")

Affectionately known by his parishioners as "Padre Francisco," Rother had helped build a local hospital, wa active in educational work, and translated the Bible int the local Indian language. Although he scrupulously avoided controversy and was considered conservative by his fellow American priests, Rother was marked for vengeance because he had helped the Indians. He wrote his death warrant in a letter sent to the United States in which he appealed for aid for the widows and orphans

of members of the local <u>comunidad de base</u>. Written in
January 1981, the letter speaks for itself:

> Things have been pretty quiet the past couple
> of weeks until just last Saturday night. Probably
> the most sought after catechist had been staying
> here in the rectory off and on, and almost
> constantly of late. He had been eating and sleeping
> here, and usually visiting his wife and two kids in
> late afternoon.
>
> He had a key to the house, and as he was
> approaching Saturday night about 7:45, he was inter-
> cepted by a group of four kidnappers. Three
> apparently tried to grab him at the far side of the
> church. . . . He got to within 15 feet of the door
> and was holding on to the bannister and yelling for
> help. The other priest heard the ruckus outside and
> stepped out to see them trying to take him.
>
> He considered trying to help, but was scared by
> their height. He called me from the living room
> where I was listening to music but also heard the
> noise, and by the time I realized what was
> happening . . . and got outside, they had taken him
> down the front steps . . . and were putting him in a
> waiting car.
>
> In the process they had broken the bannister
> where the rectory porch joins the church, and I just
> stood there, wanting to jump down and help, but
> knowing that I would be killed or taken along also.
> The car sped off with him yelling for help, but no
> one was able to do so. Then I realized that I had
> just witnessed a kidnapping of someone that we had
> gotten to know and love, and were unable to do
> anything about it. They had his mouth covered, but
> I can still hear his muffled screams. . . .
>
> About 20 minutes after the kidnapping, I went
> to the telephone office and asked the police to
> investigate a car coming their way. I told them it
> was a kidnapping and that they were armed. They
> said they would see about it, but they probably hid
> instead.
>
> We heard yesterday that possibly four or five
> were kidnapped here that same night. . . .
> That makes eleven members of this community
> that have been kidnapped, and all are presumed dead.
> One body has been positively identified and buried
> here; there are possibly three buried in a common
> grave in Chimaltenango. They were picked up in
> Antigua, and the following week I went to all the
> hospitals and morgues in the area and got a list of
> their characteristics and clothing.
>
> For these eleven that are gone, there are eight
> widows and thirty-two children among the group.

> These people are going to need emergency help.
> Others have had to flee to save their lives, and to
> find work in exile is almost impossible. They will
> also need help. [But] be careful about sending
> letters here mentioning relief, etc. We never know
> when the mail may be intercepted and read.[54]

Persecution of the Indians and their religious
supporters drove them into the arms of the left; and for
the first time, large numbers began to join the country's
four guerrilla groups. In several cases, comunidades de
base linked forces with the insurrectionists, as for
example the "Vicente Menchu" Christian Indian column,
named for one of the peasants murdered in the Spanish
Embassy in 1980. A clandestine network of newspapers and
pamphlets helped gain more Indian adherents to the
guerrilla cause. Thus through their refusal to consider
the slightest reform, the landowners and the military had
achieved the thing they feared the most—the marriage of
race and religion in a guerrilla force. "We began to
perceive that all the doors of nonviolent protest were
closing," said Rigoberta Menchu Tun, the daughter of
Vicente Menchu and a well-known Christian Indian leader.
"After a strike or a demonstration, the people would be
massacred. . . . Thus we concluded that the only alternative was war."[55]

The Guatemalan bishops also carried on a war of
their own—against Guatemala City's Cardinal Casariego, a
reactionary Spaniard who consistently supported the military. As cardinal, Casariego represented a powerful
counterbalance to an otherwise united hierarchy concerned
with human rights. He was the principal source of information on Central America for Cardinal Baggio, the
conservative president of the Pontifical Commission for
Latin America and a key figure in Vatican politics.
Thus, he was in a position to soft-peddle the complaints
of men like Bishop Gerardi; he also played an important
role in the smear campaign against Archbishop Romero in
El Salvador. Such has been Casariego's loyalty to the
military that he has frequently supported the expulsion
of foreign priests, although he himself is a foreigner.
Witnesses and sometimes victims of government-sponsored
violence, Guatemela's bishops would like to take a
stronger stand, but they have to do so surreptitiously by
issuing critical statements when Casariego is out of the
country. At one point, tensions between the cardinal and
the bishops were so strained that seven resigned in
protest.

Yet, for all this bitter infighting, none of the
bishops could be remotely described as sympathetic to the
guerrillas. Staunchly anti-communist, they have
repeatedly stated that, in the words of Bishop Gerardi,
"armed struggle is not the answer because we cannot

substitute one unjust system for another." On the other hand, the church cannot remain silent. Not only must it denounce injustices; it must also make clear that no legal redress exists.[56]

Despite a coup by supposed military reformers in March 1982, church sources said that the situation of "institutionalized violence" had not changed. Not only did the coup have the backing of the extreme-right National Liberation Movement, but all the military leaders on the new junta were associated with past repressive governments. The junta's leader, General Efrain Rios Montt, was a born-again Christian and counterinsurgency expert who served as army chief of staff in the early 1970s under President Carlos Arana, better known as the "Butcher of Zacapa." In May 1978, Rios Montt directed the massacre of the Indian communities in Sansirisay, setting a pattern for future military practice.[57]

Despite Rios Montt's frequent allusions to God--"It is time to do as God orders," he vowed shortly after taking power--his rule proved as ruthless as any in Guatemalan history: Amnesty International reported that in the eight months after the coup, the government massacred more than 3,000 peasants. During one five-day period in April, there were five Indian massacres. In early October, the army surrounded 3,500 Indians near the northern town of San Martin Jilotepeque and delivered a chilling ultimatum: Surrender or die. When the Indians gave in, the army butchered 300 and held the rest prisoner in concentration camps resembling the "strategic hamlets" of Vietnam.[58]

In a pastoral letter, Guatemala's bishops condemned the killings as "genocide," but their complaint fell on deaf ears. Even Rios Montt's brother, Bishop Mario Rios Montt, had no influence. Head of the Esquintla prefecture since 1974, and an outspoken defender of the Indian peasants, he was forced to flee the country in the fall of 1982.[59]

Guatemalan religious leaders had no illusions about the future: They would continue to be persecuted as "communists" by the military and the landowners. But as a Guatemalan Quaker minister pointed out: "I am neither pro-communist nor anti-communist. I am a Christian, and Christ is my guide. I have raised my three sons to respect people, to harm no one, to work hard, and to love God. For that they will come some night and take me away."[60]

TABLE 4.1
Martyr Survey:
List of Murdered Bishops, Priests,
Religious, and Laity

The following survey is of necessity a partial list of ecclesiastical and lay martyrs in Central America during the period between 1972 and 1982. Due to censorship and poor communications, particularly in rural areas, detailed information is not available on the thousands of people threatened, arrested, tortured, kidnapped, exiled, or murdered during a time of rising repression. This is particularly true of the laity, many of whom do not figure in official statistics and whose disappearance or death is simply denied by the military.

Symbols:
```
Mgr.............................Bishop
Name without symbol.............Priest (or Pastor)
o ..............................Religious
oo..............................Seminarian
+...............................Layman (+o: woman)
++..............................Ex-priest
```

EL SALVADOR	1972		N. Rodriguez (tortured)
	1977		R. Grande
		+M.	Solorzano
		+N.	R. Lemus
		A.	Navarro Oviedo
		+L.	Torres
		+M.	Baranhona (tortured)
		+F.	Chacon (tortured)
		+S.	Vasquez
	1978	+oF.	Puerta
		+oF.	Delgado (tortured)
		+O.	Guardado
		+M.	Guardado
		+T.	Vasquez
		E.	Barrera (tortured)
	1979	O.	Ortiz
		R.	Palacios
		A.	Macias
	1980	Mgr. O.	Romero
		S.	Spezzotto (Italian)
		M.	Reyes (disappeared & presumed dead)
		E.	Abreyo
		M.	Serrano

(Continued)

TABLE 4.1 (Cont.)

EL SALVADOR	1980	oI. Ford (U.S.)
		oM. Clarke (U.S.)
		oD. Kazel (U.S.)
		+oJ. Donovan (U.S.)
		+ Seven catechists from San Pedro Perulapan (tortured)
		+ & +o 2,816 members of comunidades de base
	1981	J. Salmeron (Evangelist)
		F.A. Lopez (Evangelist)
		+C. Alfaro (Evangelist)
		+G. Perez (Evangelist
		+B. Alfaro (Evangelist)
		+M. Teluda (arrested & presumed dead)
		+oR. Cisnero (Episcopalian)
GUATEMALA	1976	W. Woods (U.S.)
	1977	+ & +o 150 catechists from El Quiche
	1978	H. Lopez
		+ & +o 40 catechists from El Quiche
	1980	+G. Yataz
		S. Jimenez Martinez (Protestant pastor)
		A. Lopez (Protestant pastor)
		F. Villaneuva (Spanish)
		R. Ortiz Morales (Evangelist deacon)
		M.A. Cacao Munoz (Evangelist pastor)
		J.M. Gran Cirera (Spanish)
		W. Voordeckers (Belgian)
		C. de la Cruz (Philippines) (disappeared & presumed dead)
		+H. Cifuentes
		P. Caal (Protestant pastor)
		+P. Leger (Canadian)
		+V. Menchu
	1981	S. Rother (U.S.)
		C. Perez Alonso (Spanish)
		H. Beneti (Italian)

(Continued)

TABLE 4.1 (Cont.)

GUATEMALA	1981		C. Galvez Galindo
			J. Troyer (U.S.)
			(Mennonite missionary)
		+o	Three teachers from Catholic school (disappeared & presumed dead)
			M. Marruzzo (Italina)
		+D.	Quic
			P. Aguilar
			A. Fernandez (Spanish)
			V.H. Hernandez Morales (Protestant pastor) (disappeared & presumed dead)
	1982		J. Miller (U.S.) (Christian Brother)
		oV.	de la Roca
			C. Morales
GUATEMALA/MEXICO	1982		H. Cervantes Arceo
NICARAGUA	1977	+R.	Videa
			G. Garcia (joined guerrilla band)
	1978		C. Luis

NOTES

1. John Dinges, "New Evidence on Missionaries' Deaths in Salvador Suggests Official Plot" (Washington, D.C.: Pacific News Service, n.d.).
2. National Catholic Reporter (Kansas City, Mo.), December 12, 1980.
3. Dinges, "New Evidence."
4. Amnesty International Newsletter (London), January 1981.
5. Robert Armstrong and Janet Shenk, El Salvador: The Face of Revolution (Boston: South End Press, 1982), Galley 97.
6. National Catholic Reporter (Kansas City, Mo.), December 19, 1980.
7. Armstrong and Shenk, El Salvador, Galley 97.
8. Dinges, "New Evidence."
9. Armstrong and Shenk, El Salvador, Galley 98.
10. National Catholic Reporter (Kansas City, Mo.), December 19, 1980.
11. Ibid.

12. Ibid.
13. From the Maryknoll nun's constitution.
14. Dinges, "New Evidence." White was sacked shortly after President Reagan's inauguration; his replacement, Deane Hinton, was head of the Agency for International Development (AID) in Chile from 1969-71, when the Nixon administration blocked international economic aid to the Allende government. Previously, Hinton served as AID director in Guatemala in 1967, where his office assisted the U.S.-backed military regime in counterinsurgency operations. (From 1966 to 1968, the Guatemalan government crushed a guerrilla movement, killing as many as 10,000 peasants, according to a 1981 State Department report.)
15. Ibid.
16. National Catholic Reporter, April 17, 1981.
17. John Dinges, "Investigation Stonewalled," Maryknoll Magazine, December 1981.
18. "La Iglesia y Centroamerica," Revista (Caracas), February 1982, pp. 92-94.
19. O Sao Paulo (Sao Paulo), April 16, 1982.
20. Armstrong and Shenk, El Salvador, Galley 53.
21. Revista (Caracas), April 1977, pp. 170-174, 185-187.
22. "Violence and Fraud in El Salvador" (London: Latin American Bureau, July 1977), p. 21; also "General Romero asume gobierno de El Salvador" (San Salvador: Associated Press, June 30, 1977).
23. La Prensa (Managua), February 21, 1977.
24. Between February and July 1977, seven priests were refused re-entry to El Salvador; eight were expelled; two were killed; one beaten; two imprisoned; and four threatened with death. In July a right-wing death squad calling itself the White Warriors Union announced that the country's forty-seven Jesuits would all be murdered if they did not leave El Salvador within thirty days. "Be a patriot! Kill a priest," urged a series of pamphlets circulating at the time.
25. Penny Lernoux, Cry of the People (New York: Penguin, 1982), p. xviii.
26. "The Church, Political Organization, and Violence" (London: Church in the World, January 1980).
27. Orientacion (San Salvador), April 13, 1980.
28. James R. Brockman, S.J., Oscar Romero, Bishop and Martyr (Maryknoll, N.Y.: Orbis, 1982), Galleys 121 and 132.
29. Lernoux, Cry of the People, p. xviii.
30. Ibid., p. 102.
31. El Tiempo (Bogota), October 9, 1978.
32. "Central American 1981" (Boston: Unitarian Universalist Service Committee, July 1981), pp. 34, 36.
33. Latin America Regional Reports: Mexico and Central America, March 19, 1982.

154

34. Le Monde Diplomatique en Espanol (Mexico City),
April 1982; Time, March 15, 1982; United Press
International (Paris), March 3, 1982; Update Latin
America (Washington, D.C.), March 1982.
35. Latin America Regional Reports: Mexico and
Central America, March 19, 1982; Statement by the Board
of Missions of the Moravian Church of Nicaragua, former
Costa Rican President Jose Figueres, and Congressman Tom
Harkin, in Caribbean Contact (Port of Spain), May 1982;
Letter from Father Tom Rosenberger, OFM, on visit to
Sasha, a relocated Mosquito village; Update Latin
America, March 1982.
36. Latinamerica Press (Lima), March 25, 1982.
37. Lernoux, Cry of the People, pp. 25-28, 289-309.
38. Proceso (Mexico City), March 29, 1982.
39. Latin America Regional Reports: Mexico and
Central America, September 24, 1982.
40. Associated Press (Masaya), August 18, 1982;
Patricia Hynds, "The Ideological Struggle Within the
Catholic Church in Nicaragua" (Managua, September 6,
1982, mimeograph).
41. Hynds, "The Ideological Struggle"; Washington
Times, October 12, 1982.
42. Latinamerica Press, September 9, 1982.
43. New York Times, March 5, 1983; Latin America
Weekly Report, March 18, 1983.
44. Pastoral Letter of the Guatemalan Bishops
Conference, November 14, 1981.
45. Revista Dialogo Social (Panama City), 11, 144
(April, 1982), p. 35. This is also the figure given by
the Guatemalan opposition and verified to me by Arbenz's
foreign minister, Guillermo Toriello, and by Guatemalan
human rights groups in the United States.
46. Joyce Hollyday, "One of Those Rare Treasures,"
Sojourners (February 1982), p. 31.
47. Communique from the Guatemalan Bishops
Conference, July 8, 1981.
48. O Sao Paulo, February 5, 1982.
49. "Human Rights Reports of the Mission:
Guatemala," Pax Christi International (January, 1982),
p. 35.
50. Latinamerica Press, September 3, 1981.
51. Uno mas Uno (Mexico City), March 9, 10, and 11,
1982; also CRIE (Mexico City), March 16, 1982.
52. Uno mas Uno, February 4 and 11, 1982.
53. Time, August 10, 1981.
54. Mary Haynes, "How Come No Media Investigation?"
Between The Lines (August/September 1981).
55. "Testimonio de Rigoberta Menchu Tun," Dialogo
Social (Panama City), 11, 144 (April 1982), pp. 43-45.
56. National Catholic Reporter, April 16, 1982.
57. NISGUA (Washington, D.C.: National Network of
Solidarity with the People of Guatemala, April 1982).

58. <u>Maclean's</u>, November 8, 1982; <u>Latinamerica Press</u>, June 10, 1982.

59. <u>National Catholic Reporter</u>, August 27 and November 12, 1982.

60. Jennifer Flynn, "Being 'There' and North American," <u>Between The Lines</u> (June/July 1981).

5
The Economic Dimensions of Instability and Decline in Central America and the Caribbean

Douglas H. Graham

The recent poor economic performance of the Central American and Caribbean countries reflects the instability and recession characterizing all Latin American countries in the early 1980s. Yet, certain features of the Caribbean Basin setting in the 1970s merit special comment.

This chapter will focus on the small, open economies that make up the majority of the countries in the basin. Thus, Mexico and Venezuela will be excluded since their size and resource endowments reflect a different development pattern and set of issues. At the other extreme, the numerous mini-states of the Eastern Caribbean and Belize in the west will not receive attention, in part because much data is not available for these states and in part because the experience of Jamaica and Barbados, among others, can act as an acceptable proxy for some of the important developmental parameters affecting these smaller island economies. Attention will be focused on the five Central American countries, plus Panama and seven major Caribbean states. The analysis, for the most part, will not be country-specific. Rather, a comparable set of economic and social development indicators wil be presented across all countries, thereby allowing systematic differences and similarities to surface as we interpret the recent patterns of development in the region as a whole.

HISTORICAL LEGACY AND IMPORTANT REGIONAL CONTRASTS

It is useful to keep in mind two distinctive frames of reference in discussing the development performance of these basin countries: First, there are pertinent differences between the English-speaking commonwealth countries and those with a Spanish heritage. Second, there is a sharp contrast in economic performance between the decades of the 1960s and 1970s for the entire set of

countries. The 1960s was the decade of rapid economic
growth while the 1970s (especially the period 1975-80)
registered stagnation and decline.

The English versus Spanish heritage is made up of
some obvious contrasts: racial, historical, and political. The economic implications of these differences are
less clear though, as will be seen shortly, not inconsequential. The legacy of the slave and plantation
economy stands out in the English Caribbean context, with
all the inequalities and weak links for structural transformation associated with this phenomenon.[1] However, the
historical roots of the hacienda economy, with a subordinate indigenous class in much of the Central American
setting, offers a relevant parallel here.

Of greater importance are the historical and
political differences associated with the experience of
independence and the influence of the metropolitan (i.e.
mother) country. In this context the contrasts are
marked and significant, with implications for the
political economy of both regions. Central America's
independence came 150 years ago, and in the intervening
century its development has been heavily conditioned by
the unequal distribution of wealth and the authoritarian
and patrimonial tradition of Iberian culture. By
contrast, independence did not come to the English
Caribbean until the sixth decade of the twentieth
century. Thus, despite the plantation legacy and the
social remnants of chattel slavery, the institutional
framework for independence benefited greatly from the
political ideas and historical setting of the mid-
twentieth century, with its emerging post-colonial style
of development.

The role of the metropolitan country was also
crucial. Great Britain had created a commonwealth
framework within which it was facilitating independence
movements. Mid-twentieth-century political ideas and
traditions were reasonably conducive to constructive and
pragmatic efforts toward independence, although occasional strikes and other acts of resistance speeded up
the process. In the end, the Westminster parliamentary
model prevailed in most of the Commonwealth Caribbean.
Democratic practices, political pluralism, and a loyal
opposition allowing a peaceful transition of power
between political groups has characterized most of the
post-colonial experience in the English Caribbean
setting.[2]

The economic implications of these developments are
clear. In the English Caribbean, political institutions
allow a greater voice to labor unions and urban working-
and middle-class constituencies. Indeed, labor movements
were invariably the political force behind the drive for
independence, and they produced the political leadership
for post-independence political parties and governments.

Consequently, government expenditures and investment priorities for basic needs (especially education and health) and other social welfare programs play a much stronger role in the Commonwealth Caribbean than in the Central American setting, where a less pluralistic and more authoritarian tradition has prevailed.[3] However, exceptions do exist. On the one hand Costa Rica reflects, both politically and economically, a more pluralistic and democratic tradition and a consequent higher investment in basic needs and welfare areas than is characteristic of its Central American neighbors. Within the Caribbean, on the other hand, Guyana and Grenada do not follow a Westminster parliamentary model common to its commonwealth neighbors.

Other contrasts of importance are the different trade and investment channels associated with each sub-region. Not surprisingly, the commonwealth countries have close trade ties (especially exports) with Great Britain, whereas the trade patterns in Central America are dominated by the U.S. economy. Foreign investment patterns have followed a similar line until recently, when American investors, already predominant in Central America, increased their resort hotel and extractive industry investments in the Commonwealth Caribbean. Trade ties are important determinants of export perform-ance and potential. Due to previous colonial linkages, the English-speaking Caribbean countries have been drawn into commonwealth preference schemes in the smaller and more slowly growing market in Britain. At the same time, they were locked out of the politically negotiated sugar quotas and other arrangements in the faster growing American market. Among other things, this European-oriented trade pattern limits the potential of any Caribbean Basin Initiative in these Commonwealth countries. The Central American countries (and the Dominican Republic), on the other hand, are predominantly drawn into the American market and export much less to Europe.

Although such differences are relevant, the simi-larities between these two subregions are still far more important, especially where economic structure and performance are concerned. Countries in both areas reflect the development profile of small, lesser-developed, open market economies adapting to the oppor-tunities and pitfalls of world trade patterns. Foreign trade represents a large proportion of their national output, and consequently foreign trade bonanzas and declines introduce sharp fluctuations in government reve-nues and overall economic activity in these societies. Moreover, given the overwhelming importance of foreign trade activity on the economies of these nations, the foreign exchange rate becomes the single most important price in the economy and foreign trade policies become

160

the most important policy set affecting the economic
welfare of the population.[4]

As already noted, both subregions reflect a
historical legacy of plantation-hacienda structures,
which in varying degrees have been altered by the modern
currents of economic change. Nevertheless, despite these
changes export activity to world markets has concentrated
around traditional export lines, with sugar, bananas,
bauxite, coffee, and tourism predominating. Both subregions have tried to broaden their trade by creating
regional common markets, and both have introduced
protectionist measures to promote import substitution
industrialization (ISI) and some intra-regional trade in
manufactures within these regional associations. For the
most part, neither initiative has proven fruitful and
self-sustaining.[5] The market size was still too limiting
and the industries established too high in cost to permit
competitiveness in larger world markets. This common-
market induced protectionist regime favored intra-
regional trade in high cost manufactures over competitive
exports to world markets and discriminated against
agriculture. An important consequence of these efforts
was some growth in the urban middle class and the small
scale industrial labor force. However, in the end,
limited employment absorption prevailed and there was a
worsening of the distribution of income.

At the same time, the various countries' political
and economic interests were too diverse (and sometimes
antagonistic) to be accommodated within the framework of
a common market with effective mutual obligations and
benefits. This became particularly evident in the late
1970s and early 1980s in Central America, when insurrec-
tions and regional warfare began to grow in size and the
amount of regional trade declined.

During the 1960s and early 1970s, neither region
chose to emulate an East Asian economic model emphasizing
the export of manufactured products to the growing
markets of the developed countries. This failure to
exploit these opportunities was true despite the transportation economies they enjoyed in potentially servicing
nearby developed country markets (especially the United
States). In part, this lack of response was due to a
relative absence of human capital and entrepreneurial
skills (in comparison to the East Asian countries), and
to a less productive and equitable domestic food crop
sector that could lower the relative costs of the urban
wage bill. Most importantly, however, the lack of an
outward oriented export drive and effective promotion of
domestic foodstuffs, was due to the policy-bias of overvalued exchange rates and cheap food policies that
penalized agriculture and emphasized an inward-oriented,
high cost import substitution protectionist regime. In
short, the incentive structure prevented the promotion of

modernized export substitution industrialization (ESI) and turned the internal terms of trade against agriculture.

This policy scenario was unfortunate in several respects. First, an outward-oriented manufactured export strategy would have served a much larger, more rapidly growing, and more self-sustained market than that associated with a smaller, more fragmented, regional common market. The industrial growth potential in the regional market was largely played out in ten to twelve years. Second, the ESI strategy would not have created the disincentives to modernization of the domestic food crop sector that the ISI protectionist strategy had created. Finally, the ESI strategy (as the East Asian experience has shown) is more labor absorptive and less income concentrating than the ISI strategy.[6] In short, the issues of absolute poverty and an improved distribution of income could have been more effectively addressed within the context of an ESI strategy than that of an ISI strategy.

A final set of common features between the Caribbean and Central American regions is a tradition of low inflation compared to the rest of Latin America, though this tradition began to change for selected countries in the late 1970s. Both areas have also recently experienced rising foreign debt, growing balance-of-payments deficits, and an increased rate of growth in the role of the public sector (as well as a comparable decline in the private sector) in shaping the pattern of economic activity throughout the 1970s. This record is documented and discussed in the tables presented in the following section.

THE EMPIRICAL RECORD: TWO DECADES OF GROWTH AND DECLINE

Table 5.1 sets forth the major profile of economic growth over the past two decades for the principal countries in the region. The countries are ranked according to per capita income. They are further classified in terms of per capita income clusters, a classification that highlights the existence of roughly five groups of countries in the region. Haiti stands out as the poorest country, registering a per capita income level well below the others, more in line with the low-income countries of Africa and South Asia. Next come the relatively poor countries in Central America, plus Guyana. In the middle, we find the Dominican Republic, Guatemala, and Jamaica. Substantially above this last group are Panama and Costa Rica. Finally, heading the list are the island economies of Trinidad-Tobago and Barbados, the former an oil-based economy and the latter

TABLE 5.1

Profiles of Aggregate Economic Growth for Caribbean and
Central American Countries for Selected Periods, 1960-82

Countries	1980 GNP Per Capita in 1980 Dollars (1)	1980 Pop. in Millions (2)	Average Annual Growth Rate (GNP)								
			1960-70 (3)	1970-80 (4)	1976 (5)	1977 (6)	1978 (7)	1979 (8)	1980 (9)	1981 (10)	1982 (11)
1. Trinidad-Tobago	$ 4,370	1.2	4.0	5.1	10.8	7.0	6.1	5.3	7.4	6.0	
2. Barbados	3,040	.2	6.2	1.7	-0.1	3.6	4.5	5.5	2.8	-3.1	-4.5
3. Costa Rica	1,730	2.2	6.5	5.8	5.5	8.9	6.3	4.9	0.6	-3.6	-5.9
4. Panama	1,730	1.8	7.0	4.0	-0.3	3.4	3.7	7.1	4.9	3.6	
5. Cuba	1,690	9.7	1.1	6.0a	na	na	na	na	na	na	na
6. Dominican Republic	1,160	5.4	4.5	6.6	6.7	5.0	2.2	4.8	5.5	3.4	1.5
7. Guatemala	1,080	7.3	5.6	5.7	7.4	6.8	5.0	4.7	3.5	1.0	-3.5
8. Jamaica	1,040	2.2	4.4	-1.1	-6.6	-1.6	-0.3	-1.4	-5.4	-1.2	-1.0
9. Nicaragua	740	2.6	7.3	0.9	5.0	0.9	-5.4	-25.9	10.0	9.0	-2.5
10. Guyana	690	.8	3.7	1.6	5.3	-5.0	0.1	-3.8	2.1	1.2	
11. El Salvador	660	4.5	5.9	4.1	4.0	6.1	3.9	-1.5	-9.6	-9.5	-1.0
12. Honduras	560	3.7	5.3	3.6	8.4	8.7	7.0	6.6	2.6	0.3	-1.4
13. Haiti	270	5.0	-0.2a	4.0a	8.4	1.3	5.3	3.6	5.4	0.5	0.1
14. Latin America	1,586	256.0	5.7	5.8	5.3	4.7	4.6	5.8	5.6	-2.5	
15. Middle Income LDCsb	1,580	1,138.8	5.9	5.6	na	4.6	5.0	na	3.5	1.7	
16. U.S.A.	11,360	227.0	3.9	3.2	5.4	5.5	5.0	2.8	-0.4	1.9	-1.8

Sources: Data derived from World Development Indicators Appendix in World Development Report 1982 (World Bank,
Washington, D.C., 1982); Economic and Social Progress in Latin America (Inter-American Development Bank,
Washington, D.C., 1976-82); and Economic Report of the President (U.S. Government Printing Office,
Washington, D.C., 1983).

Notes: a Data refers to 1961-70 and/or 1970-79.
b Refers to 63 LDCs with 1980 per capita incomes above $410. This includes all Latin American countries
except Haiti. See World Development Report 1982, p. 103.

a tourist-affluent society with a very small population base compared to the other countries in the region.

It has been difficult to include Cuba in this framework with any systematic cross country statistical comparisons. In part, the difficulty lies in the unavailability of data; in part, in a different economic accounting framework that makes inter-country economic comparisons difficult or misleading. Moreover, frequent revisions of past time series create doubt and uncertainty about these various series.

Five generalizations, however, can be safely made about the performance of the Cuban economy in the last two decades. First, in terms of per capita income, Cuba clearly belongs in the upper half of Table 5.1. It was already in this position prior to Castro's revolutionary era. Second, the decade of the 1960s saw a decline in income growth associated with the various stages of radical restructuring of economic policy and social and political mobilization. The economic stagnation produced by the Sino-Guevarist policies changed in the early 1970s when the unproductive economic experiments, emphasizing moral over material work incentives, was altered. To overcome the institutional instability that led to the economic decline of the 1960s, the revolution was consolidated in the early 1970s under Soviet guidelines and control. This restructuring of economic policies with substantially increased Soviet economic aid and technicians, more stable planning methods, and better management of state activity also contributed to the improvement in income growth along with the rise in sugar prices in world markets from 1970 to 1975.[7]

Third, by the latter half of the decade, the decline in sugar prices, the droughts, the poor agricultural harvests, and the resource drain of the African campaigns took their toll, with the economy experiencing low growth, poor foreign exchange earnings, and increased foreign indebtedness to non-Soviet sources. Fourth, in terms of basic needs (public health and education), the current Cuban regime clearly has improved the access of important basic services to a wide range of the population. In addition, it has carried out a substantial leveling of economic assets through the confiscation of most private property in the early 1960s. A final feature that merits comment is the continuing monoculture and economic dependency associated with the present pattern of development. Following the failure of the Sino-Guevarist policies promoting economic diversification in the 1960s, sugar returned to predominate in the export portfolio; Soviet trade exercises a preponderant role in both exports and imports; and, in per capita terms, Cuba very likely receives more foreign aid (in this case from Soviet sources) than any country in the world, regardless of source. Beyond these points,

generalizations, particularly in a comparable inter-
country sense, are difficult to develop; thus the
remainder of the article will focus on the performance
and patterns of economic growth of the other countries in
the region.

Several important features stand out in the process
of generalizing the growth records for these countries in
the recent past: (1) The decade of the 1960s (Table 5.1,
column 3) registered a much more impressive growth record
than did the 1970s (column 4), reflecting the initial
success of the import substitution industrialization
strategy in the early years of the respective regional
common markets; (2) eight of the countries recorded lower
rates of growth in the 1970s than in the 1960s and five
(Barbados, Jamaica, Panama, Nicaragua, and Guyana)
experienced sharp declines; (3) the decline of the 1970s
has continued into the early 1980s with an even more
pronounced spread of economic stagnation among all
countries, reflecting the world recession (columns 10 and
11) and political insurrection (for El Salvador and
Nicaragua); and finally, (4) the countries of the basin
area experienced more severe declines in economic growth
than did the rest of Latin America during the 1970s.
This last point is driven home when one looks at the relative share of total GDP of Latin America accounted for by
the Central American and Caribbean countries constituting
our study. In 1970, this subgroup's share of total Latin
American GDP was 6.3 percent. In 1981, this figure fell
to 4.8 percent, a fairly substantial decline (i.e., 31
percent in relative terms) in such a short period. (This
share had not changed between 1960 and 1970.)

The remainder of this chapter will address the principal reasons for the collective decline noted earlier.
In brief, the post-1973 energy crisis took a heavy toll
on most of these countries, which (except for Trinidad)
are all oil importers. Upon closer inspection, however,
we begin to see that various compensatory export booms
occurred in selected primary product areas (sugar, coffee
and cacao), thereby giving some countries various options
to offset the rising costs of imports. What stands out
is a cumulative process of inappropriate policy decisions
undertaken to deal with the growing instability of the
region's terms of trade. These decisions frequently
worsened, rather than improving adjustments to the
fluctuating trends in world prices.

Two final features of the region's growth performance merit attention. First, it is clear that the
Caribbean countries (with the exception of Trinidad)
experienced a much more severe economic decline than did
the Central American countries during this period.
Second, this generalized decline was associated with
sharply different experiences for the various countries
involved. The two nations that illustrate this contrast

in the extreme are Jamaica and the Dominican Republic.
In 1960 and 1970, Jamaica ranked second in per capita
income among all the countries in the region. By 1980,
however, it had fallen to the eighth position, a
remarkable relative decline probably not equaled by any
other country in the Third World during this period. The
factors behind this prolonged stagnation in Jamaica are
reported at length by Carl Stone in Chapter 11 of this
volume. The Dominican Republic, on the other hand,
experienced a sharp relative increase from tenth to sixth
position in per capita income. Among the ironies of this
contrast is that both countries have democratic political
regimes, and both economies are sugar based. However,
the Dominican Republic has a much more productive export
sector. Dominican policymakers contained the tendency to
engage heavily in the high cost and inefficient import
substitution industrialization strategy common to many of
the other countries. Hence the policy signals did not
distort incentives against exports and agriculture. The
country has also experienced less political instability
and has controlled inflationary budgetary pressures. In
short it has exhibited a more intelligent and flexible
policy response to the fluctuating terms of trade of the
1970s. Some of the important features of this policy
response for the region as a whole can be seen through
the ensuing tables and analysis.

ECONOMIC CHANGE AND POLICY RESPONSE: EVIDENCE AND ISSUES

The decline in growth registered in the 1970s was
associated with rising inflation rates, rapidly growing
government deficits, balance of payments disequalibria,
and a serious deterioration in agricultural output and
productivity. Tables 5.2 through 5.6 document this
worsening syndrome for the countries in the region.
Table 5.2 sets forth the record on inflation.
Several conclusions can be highlighted. First, the
decade of the 1960s was an unusually stable, almost
inflation-free period for the countries in the region.
This outcome stands in sharp contrast to the performance
of many countries in South America, which experienced
hyper or near-hyper rates of price increase. Second, the
1970s saw a visible rise in the annual rate of
inflation. This situation grew more severe in the latter
1970s and early 1980s, with many countries registering
rates in the high teens or lower twenties and, in the
case of Costa Rica, reaching a characteristically
"southern cone" level of 110 percent. On the whole,
these rates (with the exception of that for Costa Rica)
are still well below the South American average in the
mid- to late 1970s (see columns 3 and 4, line 13).
However, they do represent a serious problem for small,

166

TABLE 5.2

Rates of Inflation for Caribbean and
Central American Countries for Selected Periods, 1960-81

Countries	Average Annual Rate of Inflation (CPI)						
	1960-70 (1)	1970-80 (2)	1976 (3)	1979 (4)	1980 (5)	1981 (6)	1982 (7)
1. Trinidad-Tobago	3.2	18.5	10.5	14.7	17.5	14.3	-
2. Barbados	3.0	-	5.0	13.2	14.4	14.6	10.0
3. Costa Rica	1.9	15.2	3.5	9.2	18.1	37.0	110.0
4. Panama	1.6	7.4	4.0	7.9	13.8	7.3	-
5. Dominican Republic	2.1	9.0	7.8	9.2	16.3	7.5	7.6
6. Guatemala	0.3	10.4	10.7	11.5	10.7	11.4	8.0
7. Jamaica	4.0	17.0	9.6	29.1	27.1	12.8	7.0
8. Nicaragua	1.8	13.1	2.8	48.1	35.3	23.9	30.0
9. Guyana	2.3	-	9.0	17.7	14.1	24.7	-
10. El Salvador	0.5	11.3	7.0	15.9	17.4	14.8	20.0
11. Honduras	2.9	8.9	4.9	12.5	15.6	10.6	10.0
12. Haiti	4.0	9.4	7.0	13.0	17.9	16.0	18.0
13. Latin America	-	-	50.5	59.5	-	-	-
14. Middle Income LDCs	2.7	13.2	-	-	-	-	-
15. U.S.A.a	2.7	7.8	4.8	13.3	12.4	8.9	3.9

Source: World Development Report 1982, The World Bank, Washington, D.C., 1982, Table 1, pp. 110-11;
Economic and Social Progress in Latin America, 1980-81 Report (Inter-American Development Bank,
Washington, D.C., 1981), p. 12; and Economic and Social Progress in Latin America, 1982 Report
(Inter-American Development Bank, Washington, D.C., 1982), country profile tables.

open-market economies that are integrated into the world trade network.

Large domestic market economies, in which foreign trade represents a relatively small percent of the GDP (Brazil, Argentina, Colombia, and Mexico), can, to some extent, afford to absorb the distortions of protectionist policies and inflation. Countries with small, open economies, on the other hand, in which foreign trade represents 30 to 50 percent of the GDP, cannot ignore the discipline of the world market. They must attempt to adjust their economies and their relative prices to changing world market conditions and, in the process, control domestic inflationary pressures that make it impossible for them to compete in world markets and introduce disequilibria into their balance of payments. Failure to adjust brings in its wake the stagnation and decline in growth that we see in most of these countries from the mid 1970s onward. This failure to adjust, with its high social costs, stands out particularly in the case of Jamaica and Costa Rica (as analyzed in detail by Carl Stone and Claudio Gonzalez-Vega later in this volume).

Table 5.3 illustrates the principal policy set that lies behind this high-inflation, low-growth syndrome. The scenario is associated with a rapid increase in the growth of the public sector and a concomitant decline in private-sector activity. Central government expenditures as a percent of the GDP grew substantially from 1970 to 1980 in most of these countries (column 1) and in some (Jamaica, Trinidad, and Guyana), remarkably so. Unfortunately, the growth in expenditures in these extreme cases was not associated with any growth-enhancing investment activity (column 5). In short, most of this deficit spending did not add appreciably to the countries' capital stock, but rather to public-sector consumption.[8]

Of equal interest here is the growing role of the public sector in total domestic credit in the economy (columns 8-10). Whereas private sector credit activity dominated the financial scene in the early 1970s (column 8), by 1980 this picture had changed in many countries (column 10). Except for Panama and Haiti, the share of private-sector credit in total credit had declined. This outcome reflects the growth in public-sector financing of the growing fiscal deficit through the issue of government bonds and notes and by direct government sector borrowing from commercial banks. To a large extent, the acceptance of this public debt on the part of the debt holders was involuntary in that the government obliges commercial banks to hold an increasing portion of their rising reserve requirements in the form of public debt instruments. This action effectively rechannels the use of the banks' mobilized private demand and savings

TABLE 5.3

Selected Domestic Policy Indicators for Public and Private Sector Activity in Caribbean and Central American Countries, 1970-80

Countries	Central Govt Expend/GDP		Central Govt Deficit/GDP		Avg. Annual Rate of Growth of Gross Domestic Investment in 1980 Dollars	Avg. Annual Rate of Growth of Public and Pvt. Sector Consumption		Share of Private Sector Credit Activity of Total Domestic Credit		
						Public Sector	Private Sector			
	1970	1980	1970	1980	1970-1980	1970-1980	1970-1980	1970	1975	1980
	(1)	(2)	(3)	(4)	(5)	(6)	(7)	(8)	(9)	(10)
1. Trinidad-Tobago	22.5	41.3	-4.4	-1.7	0.1	na	na	na	na	na
2. Barbados	29.8	32.6	-3.5	-5.5	3.4	na	na	100	82	73
3. Costa Rica	13.7	19.6	-0.1	-6.1	7.5	5.9	5.2	77	75	52
4. Panama	20.0	25.0	-4.7	-4.6	3.0	5.8	3.0	na	82	85
5. Dominican Republic	17.7	15.5	-1.6	-2.7	9.9	2.2	6.0	64	62	57
6. Guatemala	9.9	14.2	-1.3	-4.7	5.1	6.4	5.3	76	70	71
7. Jamaica	22.9	43.3	-5.0	-18.1	-9.3	6.7	-1.0	88	66	32
8. Nicaragua	12.1	27.9	-1.4	-8.4	0.7	9.7	0.6	88	94	63
9. Guyana	31.9	64.5	-6.6	-33.5	-2.0	na	na	61	36	13
10. El Salvador	11.9	17.1	-0.5	-5.3	1.8	6.7	5.3	86	84	75
11. Honduras	15.4	22.8	-3.1	-7.8	7.8	7.6	4.1	75	72	64
12. Haiti	15.9	16.3	-0.7	-2.3	7.9	na	3.5	29	49	44
13. Latin America	na	na	na	na	7.4	na	na	na	na	na

Sources: Columns 1 through 5 drawn from Tables 20, 21, and 5, respectively, from the statistical appendix in Economic and Social Progress in Latin America 1982 Report (Washington, D.C.: Inter-American Development Bank, 1983); columns 6 and 7 drawn from Table 4 in World Development Indicators Appendix in World Development Report 1982 (The World Bank, Washington, D.C., 1983); columns 8-10 derived from financial data recorded in International Financial Statistics (International Monetary Fund, Washington, D.C., 1983), various issues, 1970 to 1980.

deposits from private- to public-sector loan activity.
In effect, this policy is an unconventional form of taxation that finances the fiscal deficit. In the process,
the public sector grows in relative importance in the
economy, and the private sector is marginalized as credit
markets are forced to finance growing fiscal deficits of
the public sector. The high social cost associated with
this indirect form of taxation is discussed in Chapter 10
of this volume.

Another important dimension of economic activity
conditioning the growth performance of these nations lies
in the area of foreign trade. Table 5.4 underscores the
remarkable increase in trade dependency, measured in
terms of exports plus imports as a percent of GDP, from
1970 to 1980. At the same time, columns 3 and 4 show
that for most countries the growth of exports was less in
the 1970s than in the 1960s. This sharp increase in
trade dependency was due largely to the growth of
imports, particularly in the post-1973 energy shortage
era. Since, with the exception of Trinidad, all of these
countries are oil-importing less developed countries
(LDCs), they experienced a sharp rise in the cost of fuel
and fuel related products. Instead of cutting back on
imports, they allowed their current account deficits to
grow (column 6) from the mid-1970s to 1980 as export
earnings failed to keep pace with import costs.

Finally, columns 8 and 9 clearly indicate the rise
in foreign indebtedness to which these countries resorted
in order to finance their current account deficits. Only
Guatemala, Barbados, and Haiti have relatively low debt
burdens. The remaining countries are struggling with
rising debt burdens and, more often than not, are in
continual negotiations with the International Monetary
Fund (IMF) over stabilization schemes. Several countries
have been engaged in prolonged debt renegotiations (e.g.,
Jamaica, Costa Rica, Guyana, and to a lesser extent
Honduras and the Dominican Republic) and are facing the
bleak prospect of having to channel more of their
stagnant export earnings to service past debts rather
than current import needs.

The growing instability of world trade in the 1970s
has created serious problems of readjustment, particularly for these small, open economies. Nevertheless,
some economies have fared better than others by
developing a more productive or diversified export sector
and/or containing the urge to over-import beyond the
means of servicing their foreign debt. The lesson of the
1970s is that a more adept and flexible policy response
is called for in the face of rapidly changing conditions.
Unfortunately, as pointed out in the chapters on Costa
Rica and Jamaica, many countries have found it difficult
to accomplish this task.

TABLE 5.4

Selected Indicators of Foreign Trade and External Debt Performance
for Caribbean and Central American Countries in Recent Periods

Countries	Trade Dependency Ratio (Exp & Imp/GDP)		Avg. Annual Growth Rate of Exports of Goods & Services		Current Account Deficit as % of GDP		External Gross Public Sector Debt/GDP		Indebtedness Public & Pvt Sector Debt/GDP
	1970	1980	1960-70	1970-80	1974-5	1980	1970	1980	1980
	(1)	(2)	(3)	(4)	(5)	(6)	(7)	(8)	(9)
1. Trinidad-Tobago	91	201	-0.7	1.8	+20.9	+10.6	12.5	9.0	24.4
2. Barbados	89	181	8.1	7.4	- 5.8	- 4.1	na	12.0	18.3
3. Costa Rica	63	90	11.7	6.1	-13.8	-19.0	13.8	34.3	62.8
4. Panama	71	196	9.8	7.9	- 9.9	- 8.6	19.0	70.1	76.7
5. Dominican Republic	43	60	1.5	7.6	- 5.5	-14.1	14.5	17.5	28.0
6. Guatemala	29	47	8.5	6.5	- 2.0	- 1.9	5.7	6.9	13.8
7. Jamaica	72	107	4.2	-1.1	- 7.4	- 5.9	11.5	43.0	54.0
8. Nicaragua	52	74	9.3	4.2	-14.0	-20.9	20.7	83.0	71.6
9. Guyana	15	154	3.3	-0.6	- 3.4	-20.8	na	89.0	102.7
10. El Salvador	42	74	6.1	4.1	- 5.9	- 1.8	8.6	15.3	25.5
11. Honduras	59	96	9.2	4.6	- 9.4	-13.6	12.8	36.9	55.9
12. Haiti	27	54	-1.8	8.1	- 3.1	- 5.6	10.3	18.5	21.2
13. Ave. for Latin America	26	50	4.9	4.8	-	-	-	-	38.3

Sources: Columns 1 and 2 from Economic and Social Progress in Latin America 1982 Report (Inter-American Development Bank, Washington, D.C., 1983), p. 24; columns 3 and 4 derived from Table 6, p. 353; columns 5 and 6, p. 51 and column 9, p. 73 from same source. Columns 7 and 8 from World Development Report 1982 (The World Bank, Washington, D.C., 1983), p. 138-139.

In terms of macroeconomic policy performance (promising economic growth, moderate to low inflation, and tolerable balance-of-payments deficits and levels of foreign debt), Panama, Trinidad, and the Dominican Republic rank highest. Next in order of performance are those countries with a mixed record, tending toward deterioration in recent years (Costa Rica, Haiti, Honduras, Guatemala, and Barbados). Then come the countries that experienced insurrection and civil war, events that produced sharp fluctuations in their macroeconomic performance (El Salvador and Nicaragua), especially in the latter 1970s and early 1980s. Last are the countries that experienced prolonged stagnation during the last decade, Jamaica and Guyana. These are countries that attempted to implement democratic and authoritarian socialism, respectively, in this period. Curiously, the growth performances just set forth contrast sharply with certain features of basic needs performance, the topic of the next section.

THE BASIC NEEDS DIMENSION AND AGRICULTURE

Tables 5.5, 5.6, and 5.7 round out this comparative review of economic performance for the basin countries. Underscored in these tables are their efforts in the area of basic needs and the performance of their agricultural sectors. Several striking features stand out in the basic needs record. The English-speaking Caribbean countries have strikingly lower birth rates, a factor that contributes to a markedly lower rate of population growth than those rates registered for the Spanish-speaking countries. The non-Catholic religious framework may also play a role in this contrast, allowing for more explicit family-planning practices in the English Caribbean. At the same time, the health and education benchmarks are much more impressive in these countries, where life expectancy and infant mortality are much lower and adult literacy and age-cohort school attendance ratios are much higher. This promising performance no doubt grows out of the pluralistic parliamentary tradition emphasizing the legitimacy and importance of serving the needs of the working class with wide access to important public services. This feature is much less common and less developed in the Spanish-speaking countries in the basin area, with the exception of Costa Rica.

The performance of the agricultural sector offers additional insights into the dimension of recent economic decline. Table 5.6 highlights the continuing importance of agriculture as a source of livelihood, especially in Central America. Anywhere from 30 to 60 percent of the total labor force gain their income from this sector

TABLE 5.5
Demographic and Basic Needs Indicators for
Caribbean and Central American Countries for Recent Years

Countries	Rate of Pop. Gwth 1970-1980	Gross Birth Rate per 1,000 1980	Gross Death Rate per 1,000 1980	Life Expectancy from Birth 1980	Infant Mortality per 1,000 births 1980	Adult Literacy Rate 1977	Enrollment as % of Relevant Age Group 1979 Primary	Secondary
	(1)	(2)	(3)	(4)	(5)	(6)	(7)	(8)
1. Trinidad-Tobago	1.3	23	5	72 years	24	95	96	56
2. Barbados	0.3	17	8	71	21	98	100 (1972)	51 (1972)
3. Costa Rica	2.5	29	5	70	24	90	107	48
4. Panama	2.3	31	6	70	22	79 (1970)	115	66
5. Dominican Republic	3.0	36	9	61	68	67	96	28
6. Guatemala	3.0	40	11	59	70	45 (1973)	69	15
7. Jamaica	1.5	29	6	71	16	90	99	58
8. Nicaragua	3.4	45	12	56	91	90	85	27
9. Guyana	1.7	29	7	68	45	86	93 (1972)	57 (1972)
10. El Salvador	2.9	41	9	63	78	62	82	26
11. Honduras	3.4	45	11	58	88	60	89	21
12. Haiti	1.7	36	14	53	115	23	62	15

Sources: Data for all countries except Guyana and Barbados from World Development Report 1982 (The World Bank, Washington, D.C., 1983), World Development Indicators Appendix, Tables 18, 21, and 23; data for Guyana and Barbados from country specific profile data in Economic and Social Progress 1980-81 (Inter-American Development Bank, Washington, D.C., 1982).

TABLE 5.6

Selected Performance Indicators for the Agricultural Sector for
Caribbean and Central American Countries for Selected Recent Periods

	Annual Growth Rate Agricultural Sector					Percent of Labor Force in Agric. 1980	% Ag. GDP / % Ag. Labor	Per Capita Food Prod. 1970-79	Agric. Exports 1970-79	Agric. Imports 1970-79
Countries	1960-70 (1)	1970-80 (2)	1979 (3)	1980 (4)	1981 (5)	(6)	(7)	(8)	(9)	(10)
1. Trinidad-Tobago	-0.2	-1.4	-2.4	-7.5	-2.6	16	.21	-2.1	7.0	16.2
2. Barbados	2.7	-2.6	7.4	3.5	-21.4	–	–	–	7.4	11.3
3. Costa Rica	5.7	2.5	0.5	-0.8	2.3	29	.59	1.1	14.1	12.0
4. Panama	5.7	1.9	-1.8	1.1	-1.2	27	.53	-0.6	6.0	13.6
5. Dominican Republic	2.1	3.1	1.1	4.7	5.0	49	.37	0.3	12.3	17.9
6. Guatemala	4.3	4.6	2.8	1.8	1.4	55	.46	1.2	18.4	16.3
7. Jamaica	1.5	0.7	-10.9	-2.9	0.6	21	.38	-1.1	5.7	10.0
8. Nicaragua	7.8	3.1	-15.3	-10.1	14.3	39	.59	-0.6	17.6	12.1
9. Guyana	1.0	0.9	-9.6	0.4	2.3	–	–	-1.1	11.4	13.0
10. El Salvador	3.0	2.8	1.5	-5.9	-4.3	50	.54	0.3	19.0	14.9
11. Honduras	5.7	1.5	7.4	-2.8	1.0	63	.49	-1.1	17.4	24.4
12. Haiti	-0.6	2.2	-0.6	5.1	-2.1	74	.53	-2.1	14.6	24.6
13. Latin America	3.4	3.4	2.6	2.9	–	–	–	1.0	14.8	19.2

Sources: Agricultural growth rate information for 1960-70 and 1970-80 (columns 1 and 2) for Trinidad-Tobago, Barbados, Guyana, and Latin America as a whole drawn from Economic and Social Progress in Latin America 1980-81 Report, (Inter-American Development Bank, Washington, D.C., 1982), p. 18, updated for all countries for 1979, 1980, and 1981 from country profile tables in Economic and Social Progress in Latin America 1982 Report (Inter-American Development Bank, Washington, D.C., 1983). Growth data for 1960-70 and 1970-80 for other countries drawn from Table 2 in World Development Indicators Appendix, World Development Report 1982 (The World Bank, Washington, D.C., 1983). Columns 6 through 10 derived from Tables 3 and 19 from World Development Indicators Appendix in World Development Report 1982 (The World Bank, Washington, D.C., 1983), and from Tables I-6, I-8, and I-9 on pages 16, 19, and 21 in Economic and Social Progress 1980-1 Report (Inter-American Development Bank, Washington, D.C., 1982).

TABLE 5.7

Distributional Profiles of Agricultural Landholdings for
Selected Central American Countries During the Decade of the 1960s

Size Class (In Hectares)	El Salvador (1971)		Guatemala (1964)		Nicaragua (1963)		Honduras (1966)		Costa Rica (1963)	
	No. Farms	Area	No. Farms	Area	No. Farms	Area	No. Farms	Area	No. Farms	Area
Under 1 to 5 ha.	86.9	19.6	87.4	18.7	50.8	3.5	67.5	12.4	36.0	2.0
5 ha. to 10 ha.	5.8	7.7	8.9[a]	13.0[a]	13.0	3.2	15.2	10.4	16.7	2.9
10 ha. to 20 ha.	3.3	8.7			25.1[c]	20.5[c]	14.8[d]	29.4[d]	14.2	5.1
20 ha. to 50 ha.	2.5	14.5	1.6	5.9					26.6[e]	27.8[e]
50 ha. to 100 ha.	.8	10.6	2.1[b]	62.4[b]	6.2	14.1	1.4	9.4		
Over 100 ha.	.7	38.9			4.9	58.7	1.1	38.4	6.5	62.2
	100.0	100.0	100.0	100.0	100.0	100.0	100.0	100.0	100.0	100.0

Source: James Wilkie et al. (eds.), Statistical Abstract of Latin America, Vol. 21 (Los Angeles, University of California, Los Angeles, 1981) pp. 58-59.

a From 5 to 20 hectares.
b Over 50 hectares.
c From 10 to 50 hectares.
d From 10 to 50 hectare.
e From 20 to 100 hectares.

(column 6). These percentages are much smaller for the smaller island economies of the English Caribbean, where tourism and other services play a larger role.

The profile of poverty can be deduced from column 7, where the relative income per worker of the agricultural labor force (i.e., the share of agricultural income in total income divided by the share of the agricultural labor force in the total labor force) is set forth. In most countries, agricultural income per worker is only 40 to 50 percent of the national average (which is equal to 1.00). When this finding is combined with a high percentage of the labor force in agriculture, pervasive rural poverty is reflected. Such poverty characterizes Haiti, Honduras, and El Salvador in particular, but is evident in other countries as well.

Column 8 underscores another weakness in these economies: the stagnant food-producing sector. Per capita food production in the 1970s registered negative growth in seven countries and was low in all the rest. Only Costa Rica and Guatemala recorded an acceptable performance in this category. Negative growth rates of per capita food production imply that food output is not keeping up with population growth, much less servicing the increased demand for food derived from the growth of income.[9] Column 2 shows that aggregate growth of the agricultural sector as a whole was generally lower in the 1970s than in the 1960s for most of the countries in the region, implying a worsening trend in more recent years. Associated with this decline in the growth of agricultural output has been a rise in agricultural imports. It is not surprising to note that for almost all countries registering negative per capita food production, there was a faster rate of growth of agricultural imports over exports (columns 10 versus 9). A persistent negative trade balance of this nature is invariably associated with growing disincentives for local agricultural producers and growing rural poverty.

The principal pricing disincentives are as follows: (1) overvalued exchange rates (which penalize agricultural export producers and those earning income from these producers, such as tenants and sharecroppers) and (2) a cheap food policy built around urban retail price controls on foodstuffs and/or cheap food imports through foreign aid programs (i.e., P.L. 480) or commercial food imports, implicitly subsidized through overvalued exchange rates. In these cases, domestic producers of basic grains face unfair competition and experience a decline in both the value of their output and the level of their income.

In addition to these pricing disincentives affecting private producers there has been a serious underinvestment by the public sector in the institutional capacity and human capital within the sector. The lack of effective land reform, the poorly financed agricultural research and extension activities and gross neglect of the rural landless and small holders through lack of investment in rural human capital (i.e. access to public education and public health facilities) explain the low productivity and growing poverty in many of these settings. In short, agriculture has received a low priority in the pricing policies and public sector investment strategies of policymakers in these countries. As a result the internal terms of trade for agriculture have largely been unfavorable with policy instruments emphasizing surplus extraction rather than surplus generation and growth in productivity for the majority of rural producers.

Several additional features merit comment here. The English Caribbean countries recorded a strikingly poor performance in their agricultural sectors in both decades. This outcome has grown out of a combination of discriminatory foreign trade pricing policies penalizing agricultural products and investment policies that have generally favored industry and penalized agriculture, either explicitly or implicitly.[10] The results for the Central American countries, while not as poor as in the Commonwealth Caribbean, show a decline for more recent years. Also significant are the sharp fluctuations in growth that characterize the sector's performance (columns 3-5). This element introduces great uncertainty into income expectations for participants in this sector and places producers at a severe disadvantage relative to those dependent upon urban industrial activity.[11]

Finally, Table 5.7 underlines the structural dimensions of inequality associated with the distribution of land in the five Central American countries. Nothing highlights this point more than the large number of landless and near landless in El Salvador and Guatemala, where roughly 90 percent of the farms operate on less than 20 percent of the land. At the other end of the spectrum, 1-2 percent of the farms control 50-60 percent of the area. Costa Rica, on the other hand, reflects a considerably less concentrated landholding pattern. At the same time, there is a substantially smaller percentage of the labor force in agriculture in that country (29 percent). In short, Guatemala, El Salvador, and Honduras record high percentages of their labor forces in agriculture and high indices of inequality in landholdings. Honduras and El Salvador record a low level of relative product per worker in agriculture and a poor performance in per capita food production and aggregate agricultural growth. These factors underlie the high incidence of absolute poverty found in these settings, and in the case of Guatemala and El Salvador, this structural dimension of inequality is an important factor explaining the rural unrest found in these societies.

SUMMARY AND CONCLUSIONS: DOMESTIC POLICY REFORMS AND
THE LIMITATIONS OF EXTENSIVE FOREIGN AID

In the 1970s, all countries in the Caribbean Basin
reflected the problems and performance of small, oil-
importing, open economies facing unstable world markets.
In the face of rising energy-related costs and increased
world inflation, these countries experienced rising
inflation from the mid-1970s onward. Fluctuating export
revenues contributed to growing balance-of-payment
deficits. Attempts to maintain high levels of imports
and high living standards for the middle classes in the
face of declining export earnings led to increased
foreign indebtedness. These externally generated
factors, in part, induced a set of domestic policy
decisions that greatly increased the relative role of the
public sector in allocating and controlling resource
flows in the economies. Finally, this scenario of
instability and institutional policy change was associated with a decline (and, in some countries, prolonged
stagnation) in the trends of economic growth. All of
these experiences represented a sharp change from the
previous decade when a high to moderate growth scenario
with low inflation and a stable balance of payments was
more common.

This recent history raises questions concerning the
relative role of external events and domestic policies in
generating the low-growth trend of the 1970s. The
eclectic answer that both factors played a role is both
obvious and unhelpful. Some countries clearly fared
better than others. Export booms (especially in coffee)
characterized the economic environment as much as did
energy-related import crises. The issue here is the
appropriateness of the domestic policy responses to the
external events of the decade.

To place this issue in context, we may find it
instructive to remember that in the 1960s much debate
centered around the alleged need for government intervention to promote industrial growth and to redress the
plantation and hacienda legacy characterizing these
economies.[12] By the early to mid-1970s, this interventionist scenario was reinforced by a growing pressure to
meet the basic needs of the poor through public sector
budgets. These various forms of intervention reached
large proportions in some of these countries (especially
Jamaica, Costa Rica and Guyana), generating substantial
fiscal deficits and inflationary pressures that became
less easy to control as various political constituencies
exercised pressure to prevent the government from
reducing the distortions and subsidies supporting their
interests.

The alarming trend of growing fiscal deficits,
rising inflation, and balance-of-payments deficits seen

178

earlier for all countries in Tables 5.2-5.4 are in large part the end result of growing government policy intervention in trade and finance or lack of adjustment to changing world market conditions to avoid short-run political costs. In either case, internal policy errors predominate. Countries that have carried these forms of policy intervention and lack of adjustment to the extreme are Jamaica, Costa Rica, and Guyana; however, all the remaining countries as well have indulged to some extent in these errors.[13]

The most unproductive forms of intervention have proven to be the high cost parastatal or government enterprises set up in these countries in the wake of import substitution industrialization policies. Almost without exception they have proven to be unprofitable drains on the budget, thus preventing a more meaningful use of public resources in other activities.

Other forms of intervention and failures of policy adjustment surround the temporary export bonanzas that rapidly increased government revenues and foreign exchange earnings. The sugar boom in the early 1970s and the coffee boom in the mid-1970s illustrate this phenomenon. Many governments launched grandiose development programs that became import intensive and required additional foreign borrowing. These efforts enhanced the political patronage of the given party in power but proved to be overly ambitious and unrealistic.

Despite the known instability of world commodity markets and the inevitable decline of earlier rises in prices, political leaders frequently lose their contact with economic reality and refuse to exercise caution and discipline. Such leaders often assume the boom will continue forever (or at least for their term in office) and spend accordingly, as discussed in the chapters on Costa Rica and Jamaica in this volume. Unfortunately, when the export boom declines the spending continues, the deficits and foreign debts accumulate, and the crisis deepens in the face of declining foreign exchange earnings. Austerity measures eventually become inevitable, protracted and painful, with concomitant debt renegotiations and difficult stabilization programs extracting a high social cost on the population and a regressive impact on income distribution.

Within this scenario illustrating the lack of adjustment to changing economic conditions lie two classic economic distortions that worsen the distribution of income and economic efficiency: (1) a growing overvaluation of the exchange rate and (2) negative real rates of interest in financial markets (i.e., nominal interest rates on loans and deposits below the rate of inflation). The first distortion penalizes agricultural producers by implicitly taxing agricultural exporters and subsidizing agricultural grain imports to the detriment

of domestic foodstuff producers (i.e., the peasant
class); the second distortion favors a limited number of
borrowers with a large element of implicit subsidy in
their credit transactions while taxing a much larger
number of small savers with rates of interest well below
the rate of inflation, and penalizing an even larger
number of producers who have no access to formal credit
markets and therefore are unable to enjoy the credit
subsidy.

This latter distortion is very widespread and
damaging in these countries.[14] It very likely accounts
for the greatest amount of regressive income transfer in
these societies. Moreover, it is insidious (in the sense
of being hidden or implicit in nature) and is rarely
estimated. Yet it is clear that if only 10 to 15 percent
of the producers in a country have access to formal
credit, as is common in Latin America, (and therefore 85
to 90 percent do not) and this credit is priced well
below the going inflation rate (i.e., a negative real
rate of interest), a substantial subsidy is being transferred to a limited subset of better-off producers, thus
worsening the distribution of income and wealth in these
societies. This hidden and implicit form of income
transfer becomes overwhelming in a society experiencing a
rapid growth in inflation, since nominal interest rates
are rarely adjusted upward as rapidly as are inflation
rates. As we saw in Table 5.2, inflation grew rapidly in
the later 1970s in most of these countries, with serious
regressive implications for income distribution through
the operation of interest rate ceilings in inflationary
settings.[15]

Continued policy interventions of this nature in
trade and financial markets are clearly not in the
interests of these countries, and for the forseeable
future efforts will have to be directed toward reducing
their fiscal deficits, minimizing public-sector dominance
of financial markets, and reforming foreign trade
policies in more liberalizing and less protectionist
directions. As earlier noted, the past tendencies to tax
and increasingly control and channel resources and
manipulate relative prices through exchange rates and
interest rates have created a more burdensome pattern of
inefficiency and a worsened distribution of income than a
less interventionist policy would have produced.

The exceptions to the aforementioned caveats on the
high economic costs of intervention center on the unusual
levels of inequality and poverty associated with the
distribution of land holdings in El Salvador and
Guatemala. The structural dimensions of inequality and
poverty in these societies need to be redressed by interventionist strategies of intelligently designed land
reforms.[16] However, and this is of crucial importance,
once these reforms have been launched, complementary

policies that promote a net transfer of resources to the agricultural sector are necessary. The implication is that negative pricing policies (such as protectionist industrialization strategies and cheap food policies favoring urban industrial interests) should be reduced or eliminated so as to favor the income and productivity potential of the reformed agricultural sector. Public investment criteria should emphasize agricultural research and extension, expanded rural education, feeder roads, and marketing infrastructure to reduce the costs and risks of farming. All too often, ambitious land reform efforts in Latin America have been compromised or destroyed by maintenance of adverse terms of trade against agriculture during the reform effort through pricing and investment policies that favor inefficient, subsidized activities in the urban industrial sphere.

Unfortunately, the political movement necessary to achieve substantial land reform in Latin America is also associated with antiprivate sector and antimarket ideologies. Hence, the agarian reform efforts are frequently compromised by price, trade, and investment policies that promote inefficient public-sector enterprises, unproductive public-sector employment, and discriminatory pricing policies that turn the terms of trade against the reformed agricultural sector. Unfortunately this appears to be the pattern unfolding in Nicaragua.[17]

On the other hand, many political constituencies that believe in the competitive possibilities of a healthy private sector and the growth potential behind the strength of market forces are unfortunately indifferent and frequently hostile to legitimate governmental initiatives that engage in any form of asset redistribution in order to redress glaring structural inequalities in land holdings or markedly increased public investment in human capital for the majority of the population.

Contrary to the conventional wisdom about development that prevailed in the 1960s and 1970s, the reform and modernization of the agricultural sector is today an essential feature of self-sustained economic development in Central America. It is only through policies directed toward this sector that one can directly address the issues of absolute poverty and an improved distribution of income. Improved productivity of both export and domestic food crop production is necessary to create the economic surplus that can eventually lead to an efficient, labor-absorptive path of export-oriented industrialization. Such a strategy will not be easy. Among other things, it requires that policymakers shake off the inefficient and inequitable protectionist biases that have clouded their vision in the past decade and, at the same time, that they acquire the political will to promote effective land reforms and investments in human

capital that address the issues of equity and productivity in the agricultural sector in such countries as
Guatemala and El Salvador. Moreover, in carrying out
these reforms it is important not to distort economic
incentives (by destroying the competitive drive of
healthy market forces), since these forces can play a
valuable role in rendering the reforms successful in the
long run.
     Finally, it is important to note the limitations of
large capital transfers associated with the growing
references to a Marshall Plan for the Caribbean Basin.
This approach worked for a war-torn Europe because the
societies involved were relatively homogeneous and strong
in human capital endowment and managerial capacity;
moreover, they had relatively sophisticated political
institutions and a strong societal consensus on recovery
plans and the distribution of the fruits of this aid.
     These attributes do not exist in the Caribbean Basin
where the effective absorptive capacity for capital
transfers is limited. Here the problem is one not of
recovery but of development. Large amounts of foreign
aid can be disruptive in several ways to self-sustained
economic development. First, it is unlikely that any
initial momentum for large aid transfers could be
maintained. This decline in momentum would create an
abrupt decline in the capital inflows similar to the
decline in export revenues in the late 1970s, thus
disrupting budgetary allocations and development plans in
these countries, with all the attendant declines in
income and employment. False expectations with regard to
the continuity of this aid transfer could create real
economic problems in the future as the state of the world
economy and the mood of the American taxpayer and U.S.
Congress continue to shift.
     Second, any large infusions of funds into these
societies, beyond their limited capacity to absorb and
utilize them effectively, will lead to a sharp increase
in corruption, capital flight to Miami bank accounts and
a misallocation of resources that could prove detrimental
to development. Third, and most importantly, large aid
flows will remove any incentive toward the restructuring
and reforming of the wide range of inefficient and
inequitable economic policies currently in place in many
of these countries. As earlier noted in this chapter,
there exists a wide array of policy-induced distortions
in those economies that are antidevelopmental. Large aid
flows remove the need to correct these distortions, as
they temporarily hide or mask the growing inequities and
serious resource misallocations associated with
inappropriate domestic policies. In the end there would
be no incentive to redesign domestic financial, fiscal
and trade policies to mobilize domestic resources for
development. Local political leaders and policymakers

182

will choose to avoid the difficult and costly political
challenge of increasing and reforming their local tax
bases, reforming financial policies to mobilize domestic
savings and investing in their agricultural sectors
(since subsidized foreign aid food imports would be
available). Large foreign income transfers would become
a comfortable narcotic weakening any resolve to reform
and restructure domestic policies to promote self-
sustained development.[18]

The economic recovery of the Caribbean and Central
American economies will depend upon a revitalization of
U.S. economic growth and world trade. Liberalization of
financial, exchange rate, and trade policies are also
clearly called for in most of these economies to remove
the serious distortions in financial markets and foreign
trade. Structural reforms in land holdings and greater
investment in human capital, rural infrastructure and
productivity enhancing agricultural research and extension activities are necessary but not sufficient
conditions for promoting more productive and equitable
growth. Also called for are a reduction in the role of
the public sector in directly productive activities and a
greater role for undistorted market forces to eliminate
the anti-agricultural bias inherent in many pricing
policies. A modest but uninterrupted flow of foreign aid
could prove helpful in achieving developmental goals in
public sector or rural investment activities. Finally, a
careful readjustment of outstanding debt obligations and
a reduction of protectionist barriers in the U.S.
allowing greater opening of the American market to
traditional export lines (such as sugar) and new export
areas (such as textiles) could help immeasurably in
stimulating economic recovery.

NOTES

1. For a historical review of the plantation legacy
in the Caribbean area see George Beckford, Persistent
Poverty: Underdevelopment in Plantation Economies of the
Third World, Oxford University Press, 1972.
2. Two useful references clarifying these features
in the Caribbean Commonwealth setting are Carl Stone,
Democracy and Clientelism in Jamaica, Transactions Press,
1980; Abraham F. Lowenthal, "The Caribbean" in The Wilson
Quarterly, Vol. IV (Spring 1982), pp. 112-145.
3. A recent study substantiating this point for the
Caribbean Commonwealth countries is Kenneth P. Jameson,
"Socialist Cuba and the Intermediate Regimes of Jamaica
and Guyana" in World Development, Vol. 9, (September/
October 1981), Special Issue, pp. 871-888.

4. Many recent mimeographs have highlighted the overwhelming role of foreign trade policies and exchange rate regimes in small, open economies and the need to manage those policies well to promote successful development. For example see Bela Balassa, The Newly Industrializing Countries in the World Economy, Pergamon Press, 1981 and Anne O. Krueger, Foreign Trade Regimes and Economic Development: Liberalization Attempts and Consequences (Cambridge, Ballinger 1978).

5. An early classic work in the field defending the possibilities for development through regional common markets is William G. Demas, The Economics of Development in Small Countries, McGill University Press, Montreal, 1965. A useful reference documenting the early experience of the Central American Common Market is William R. Cline and E. Delgado, Economic Integration in Central America, the Brookings Institution, Washington, D.C., 1978. More recent works, however, document the growing negative consequences of the high cost, inefficient industrialization, the anti-export and anti-agricultural bias and the worsening distribution of income generated in these regional common market efforts. For a critical review of the Commonwealth Caribbean experience see Caribbean Community in the 1980s, Report by a group of Caribbean experts, Caribbean Community Secretariat, Georgetown, Guyana, 1980. For a critical review of the Central American experience see Claudio Gonzalez Vega, Eduardo Lizano and Minor Sagot, Costa Rica y el Mercado Comun Centroamericano, Editorial Studium, San Jose (forthcoming 1984).

6. For an excellent review of the benefits of an outward oriented export substitution strategy see the references in footnote 4.

7. Two excellent recent sources documenting and analyzing Cuban economic growth are Jorge I. Dominguez, Cuba: Order and Revolution, Harvard University Press, 1978 and Carmelo Mesa-Lago, The Economy of Socialist Cuba: A Two Decade Appraisal, University of New Mexico Press, 1981.

8. For a description of this emphasis promoting government consumption over government investment in Jamaica see Compton Bourne, "Government Foreign Borrowing and Jamaican Economic Growth," Social and Economic Studies, Vol. 30, No. 4 (December 1981), pp. 52-74.

9. The important role of rapid population growth and the social and economic consequences of rapidly expanding rural labor is discussed in Clark Reynolds, "Fissures in the Volcano? Central American Economic Prospects" in Latin America and World Economy: A Changing International Order, Latin American International Affairs Series, Vol. 2, Sage Publications, Beverly Hills, 1978, pp. 195-224.

184

10. Recent studies illustrating how distorted
economic incentives compromised the growth of domestic
foodstuffs and export agriculture in Jamaica are Compton
Bourne and Douglas H. Graham, "Economic Disequalibria and
Rural Financial Market Performance in Developing
Countries" in Canadian Journal of Agricultural Economics,
Vol. 31, No. 1 (March 1983), pp. 59-76; Stephen Pollard
and Douglas H. Graham, "The Performance of the Food
Producing Sector in Jamaica 1962-1979: A Policy
Analysis," in Economic Development and Cultural Change
(forthcoming); and Stephen Pollard and Douglas H. Graham,
"Price Policy and Agricultural Export Performance in
Jamaica," Economics and Sociology Occasional Paper
No. 953, Department of Agricultural Economics and Rural
Sociology, The Ohio State University, 1982.

11. An interesting and thought provoking analysis of
the structural inequalities in Latin American agriculture
and the alleged dynamic chain of exploitative relations
producing generalized rural poverty in Latin America can
be found in Alain de Janvry, "The Political Economy of
Rural Development in Latin America: An Interpretation,"
American Journal of Agricultural Economics, Vol. 59,
No. 3 (1975), pp. 490-499. For an interesting critique of
de Janvry's interpretation see G. Edward Schuh, "The
Political Economy of Rural Development in Latin America:
Comment," in Agriculture in the Third World, edited by
Carl Eicher and John Staatz, George Allen and Unwin,
Boston, 1984.

12. For example see Norman Girvan, Foreign Capital
and Economic Underdevelopment, Institute of Social and
Economic Research, The University of the West Indies,
Kingston, 1972.

13. One frequently hears about the negative impact of
the worsening international terms of trade on the
Caribbean countries. However, this reasoning ignores the
fact that most of the Caribbean Commonwealth countries
are unable to fulfill generous export quotas granted to
them by Great Britain. The factors worsening the export
performance of these countries are essentially domestic
in origin (i.e., a result of overvalued exchange rates,
heavy export taxation by government marketing boards,
poor estate management and deteriorating labor relations
and ineffective research and extension). On some of
these issues see Compton Bourne, "Export Performance and
Prospects for the Commonwealth Caribbean" in Latin
American Trade and Economic Growth, edited by Jorge
Salazar (Pergamon Press, New York, 1983), and the
references cited in footnote 10.

14. There is a growing literature documenting the
remarkably high levels of inefficiency and inequity
associated with the conventional cheap or subsidized
agricultural credit policies common to all these
countries. In many instances subsidized credit is the

single most important distortion harming the poor, contrary to what is conventionally thought. On these issues see Claudio Gonzalez-Vega and Hugo Cespedes, Growth and Equity: Changes in Income Distribution in Costa Rica, United Nations, DIESA/DRPA, New York, 1983; Claudio Gonzalez-Vega, "Small Farmer Credit in Costa Rica, The Juntas Rurales" in Small Farmer Credit in Costa Rica, AID Spring Review of Small Farmer Credit, Vol. II, Agency for International Development, Washington, D.C., 1973; Claudio Gonzalez-Vega, "Interest Rate Restrictions and Income Distributions," American Journal of Agricultural Economics, Vol. 59 (1977), pp. 973-976; Robert Vogel, "The Effect of Subsidized Agricultural Credit on Income Distribution in Costa Rica" in Undermining Rural Development with Cheap Credit, edited by Dale W Adams, Douglas H. Graham and J.D. Von Pischke, Westview Press (forthcoming); and Dale W Adams, "Are the Arguments for Cheap Agricultural Credit Sound?" in Undermining Rural Development with Cheap Credit, edited by Dale W Adams, Douglas H. Graham and J.D. Von Pischke, Westview Press (forthcoming).

15. See especially the references by Gonzalez-Vega and Vogel in the previous footnote.

16. A recent detailed analysis of the progess in the controversial land reform program in El Salvador has been prepared by a team of specialists from the Land Tenure Center of the University of Wisconsin. This was completed as a consulting report for the Agency for International Development in 1983. See Agrarian Reform in El Salvador, a report prepared for the Agency for International Development by Checchi and Company, Washington, D.C., January 1983.

17. This scenario occurred in Allende's Chile and in reform-minded Peru in the early 1970s. Apparently the same scenario is being repeated by the Sandinista government in Nicaragua. Early reports on the progress of the land reform efforts of the new Nicaraguan regime were optimistic and encouraging as reported in Carmen Diana Deere and Peter Marchetti, "The Worker Peasant Alliance in the First Year of the Nicaraguan Agrarian Reform," Latin American Perspectives, Vol. 8, No. 2 (Spring 1981), pp. 40-73 and David Kaimowitz and Joseph R. Thome, "Nicaragua's Agrarian Reform: The First Year (1979-80) in Nicaragua in Revolution, edited by Thomas Walker, Praeger Press, 1981. More recent analyses, however, point out how the internal terms of trade are turning severely against the interests of peasant producers and government pricing, wage, investment and foreign exchange policies are taking a heavy toll on the rural laborers as well as on peasant producers. On this see Forest D. Colburn, "Theory and Practice in Nicaragua: The Economics of Class Dynamics," in Caribbean Review, Vol. XII, No. 3 (Summer 1983), pp. 7-9, 40-42; Forest D.

Colburn, "Nicaragua's Agrarian Reform," paper presented
at meeting of the Latin American Studies Association,
Mexico City, September 1983; and Forest D. Colburn,
"Rural Labor and the State in Post Revolutionary
Nicaragua," Latin American Research Review (forthcoming).

18. Large foreign aid inflows also remove the need
for the recipient country to correct an overvalued
exchange rate to earn more foreign exchange; hence,
foreign aid flows play a direct role in promoting the
continued and growing implicit taxation of agricultural
exports and, at the same time, encourage the imports of
foodstuffs through an artificially low exchange rate. In
this sense foreign aid directly harms agricultural
producers, the constituency foreign donors are allegedly
trying to help. Furthermore, there is no adequate
compensation to offset these negative effects since only
a limited number of producers will benefit from any AID
financed input subsidy programs. However, all producers,
large or small, are affected by the product price distortions generated by an overvalued exchange rate.

Part 2

Stability and Instability:
A Country Focus

6
El Salvador:
Revolution and Counterrevolution in the Living Museum

Donald E. Schulz

Some years ago, Charles Anderson described the Latin American political system as one in which new actors were admitted into the arena of reciprocally recognized elites only when they had demonstrated a significant power capability and provided assurances that they would not jeopardize the position of established elites. In effect, new power contenders could be added to the system, but old ones could not be eliminated. Change was permitted, but only within a limited context. The result was a kind of "living museum": "While, in the history of the West, revolutionary experiences or secular change have sequentially eliminated various forms of power capability, . . . [in Latin America] all the forms of political authority of the Western historic experience continue to exist and operate, interacting one with another in a pageant that seems to violate all the rules of sequence and change involved in our understanding of the growth of Western civilization."[1]

Nowhere in Central America did this description seem more apropos than El Salvador. Although oligarchs and officers had run the country in a practical division of labor since the early 1930s, the processes of modernization had effectively splintered that coalition. Following World War II, a small industrial bourgeoisie had arisen and, in alliance with military modernizers, technocrats, and a sector of the coffee oligarchy (primarily those elements engaged in the export business), had set out to modernize Salvadoran capitalism through industrialization, agricultural diversification, and political reform. As was so often the case elsewhere, this new industrial elite did not supplant the coffee oligarchs; rather, with the aid of young military reformers, it forced them to accept it as a legitimate power contender--just as many years earlier the coffee growers had forced the feudal lords of the latifundia to recognize and share power with them. In turn, instead of creating an internal market for their industrial products by raising the living standards of the masses through structural reforms (thus threatening the interests of the oligarchy), the modernizers sought to generate an external demand in the form of the Central American Common Market.

For a while, the strategy worked. By the 1960s, however, economic growth and industrialization had led to the rise of new power contenders. In the cities, bourgeois political parties and labor unions began to demand a share of the pie. By the end of the decade, the capacity of the system to co-opt these new participants and accommodate change was being seriously strained. Meanwhile, in the countryside, economic and political developments were setting the stage for the growing politicization of the peasantry. As in the volcanos for which El Salvador is so famous, pressure was slowly building to the point of explosion.

STRUCTURAL PETRIFICATION AND THE CRISIS OF "DEVELOPMENT": THE SOCIOECONOMIC DIMENSION

Why an explosion, rather than continued piecemeal co-optation and evolution? Certainly, part of the answer lies in the combination of extreme poverty, inequality, and exploitation that has for so long marked the Salvadoran socioeconomic order and in the structural rigidity which has effectively locked the lower classes into deprivation. El Salvador has been burdened with one of the most rigid class systems and unequal income distributions in Latin America. For over a century, social and economic life had been dominated by a small landed elite--"fourteen families" (las catorce) according to popular mythology. Although in reality this network of family clans was considerably larger (244 by some accounts), about 2 percent of the population owned 60 percent of the land and received a third of the national income. Seventy-eight percent of coffee profits went to less than 6.5 percent of the growers; a mere 145 estates held 20 percent of the land; and a few thousand people controlled the banking system, industry, foreign trade, and the mass media.[2]

The gap between haves and have-nots was enormous. At one end of the spectrum were the affluent neighbor-hoods of the elite. (The Duenas-Regalado clan, for instance, is said to have had a fortune of almost $300 million.) At the other was abject poverty. Thus, a 1981 AID report, based on a 1977-78 random sample of 1,366 Salvadoran households (excluding metropolitan San Salvador), found that 49 percent of household heads had no formal education and another 30 percent were func-tionally illiterate; the median educational level for family members over eighteen years of age was two years

nationwide and zero for rural areas; 52 percent of the
households had no access to farmland and of those that
did, 49 percent had less than one hectare; 94 percent had
less than ten hectares (the minimum necessary to provide
subsistence for an average family of six is nine
hectares); the median annual per capita income was 494
colones ($197), less than the AID poverty line of 668
colones ($267); and 62 percent of national households and
71 percent of rural households lived in poverty, with
most having no access to electricity, potable water, or
toilet and bath facilities.[3] Similarly, other AID
studies found that 73.4 percent of children under five
showed signs of malnutrition;[4] that infant mortality was
60 per 1,000, three times as great as in the United
States; and that life expectancy was fifty-eight years,
compared to seventy-two in the United States.[5] All in
all, noted the authors of the first report, it was "very
difficult to speak of profiles of the poor" since the
population was so "homogeneously impoverished."[6]

But deprivation and inequality alone are not enough
to make a revolution. Other factors are involved. In El
Salvador, there were too many people and not enough land.
With over 570 inhabitants per square mile, population
density was the highest in Latin America. And it was
rapidly getting worse. With an accelerating annual
growth rate of almost 3.5 percent, the population was
doubling every twenty years. In 1930, it had been 1.4
million; in 1961, 2.5 million; in 1971, 3.6 million; and
by 1981, around 5 million. Since some 70 percent of the
land surface was already absorbed in farms,[7] there were
few unclaimed frontiers left where campesinos could
expand their food crops. Accordingly, they had taken to
sowing their corn in any vacant area they could find,
even on the slopes of active volcanoes. The consequence
of this intensive pressure on the land was rapid
deforestation, soil erosion, and habitat destruction.
Peasants were too poor to let their lands lie fallow. So
year after year, the soil was overworked and became ever
more infertile. By one estimate, around 77 percent of
the land suffered from accelerated erosion.[8]

There were few escape valves. True, by the late
1960s, some 300,000 Salvadorans had migrated to Honduras
in search of land and employment. But that channel was
closed indefinitely by the 1969 "futbol war." Indeed, at
that time, some 130,000 Salvadorans had been driven back
into their native land, further aggravating the
increasingly difficult situation in the countryside.

Yet, if overpopulation and land scarcity were major
problems, they were less critical than the issue of land
distribution. Here is a touch of irony. North American
policymakers (and academics) have so often equated
economic development with high growth rates and assumed
the benevolent nature of this process that they have

tended to forget that wealth generated in highly inegalitarian societies gets distributed very inequitably. In the Central American context, the "trickle down" theory has been largely a myth. In El Salvador, in fact, wealth "trickled up." "Development" brought increasing inequality and immiseration. The rich grew richer, and the poor grew poorer.

The crucial concept here is competitive exclusion.[9] During the second half of the sixteenth century, the decline of cacao and the introduction and commercial production of indigo initiated the first of several stages of competition between subsistence cultivators and hacendados. In order to make room for more indigo cultivation and increase their grazing lands, the latter often extended their holdings at the Indians' expense. By the end of the colonial era, according to one conservative estimate, nearly a third of the colony's land area had been appropriated by the Spanish.[10] Even so, many Indian villages managed to retain their communal lands through the colonial period and into the first decades of the Republic. As late as 1879, the villages still considered over a quarter of the country to be their domain.

With the introduction of coffee production in the mid-nineteenth century, however, a second stage of development began. In response to rising international prices, farmers began to shift from indigo to coffee. A radical program of "land reform" was initiated by the government, designed to transform a countryside devoted to subsistence agriculture into one dominated by cash crops. Indian communal lands became a prime target. Municipalities were encouraged to convert their collectively held lands into private holdings. In 1881-82, the traditional communal and ejidal land systems were abolished as impediments to agricultural development. Between 1880 and 1912, numerous peasants were dispossessed, as small land parcels were bought up, "grabbed," or otherwise consolidated into large units. The resulting social dislocation was severe, with many former owners becoming landless wanderers, seeking work as hired laborers on the coffee farms and haciendas. The upshot was a series of uprisings in those areas where coffee was expanding most rapidly. Subsequently, in the late 1920s, a sharp drop in coffee prices set off a new wave of transfers, as many small owners lost their properties because of loan defaults and other debts. Simultaneously, production, employment, and wages plunged. Deprived of communal holdings to fall back on, the Indians once again resorted to violence. The resulting reaction, popularly referred to as la matanza (the massacre), would shape the course of Salvadoran politics for decades to come.

The most recent stage of development and exclusion had its origins in the Great Depression. With coffee

prices faltering, an attempt was made to diversify
agricultural exports. In the 1950s and 1960s, large
regions of the Pacific lowlands were converted into
cotton plantations; sugar production was expanded in
middle altitude areas inappropriate for raising coffee or
cotton. Again, many peasants were displaced. Nor were
matters helped by the introduction of a minimum wage law
in 1965. Planters merely compensated by reducing the
number of permanent resident laborers (colonos) to the
amount required at the slowest times of the year, relying
on temporary workers as needed for specific, short-term
tasks. Whereas previously much work had been done by
women and children, most of these "inefficient" laborers
were now dismissed. All in all, perhaps half of the
permanently employed workers may have lost their regular
jobs, and many their dwellings, as a result of the minimum wage. Nor were meals, on which planters had spent
about 50 cents a day per worker, any longer provided.[11]

The portrait is one of progressive marginalization
and immiseration. The period from 1960 to 1980 witnessed
a dramatic decline in the number of colonos, as more and
more planters resorted to landless temporary workers and
mechanization. Whereas some 55,000 landholdings had had
colono arrangements in 1961, that number had fallen to
17,000 one decade later.[12] The number of landless (i.e.,
those who were neither owners, renters, nor
sharecroppers) had veritably exploded: from 12 percent
in 1960 to 41 percent in 1975.[13] And although rentals
had increased from 33,000 to 76,000 between 1950 and
1971, over 98 percent of these arrangements involved
parcels of under five hectares of land--substantially
less than the subsistence requirements of the average
peasant family.[14] Added to all this, of course, was the
specter of rural unemployment: Over 50 percent of the
labor force was unemployed more than two-thirds of the
year; only 35 percent worked continuously.[15]

Conditions in the cities were far better. Still, as
Alistair White has noted, "development policy . . . , by
encouraging the building of modern factories with expensive imported equipment . . . , tends to impoverish . . .
the majority of the population, but enriches the top 10
to 15 percent and draws a certain proportion of others up
from the masses to form a 'new middle class'. . . ."[16]
Capital-intensive industrialization generated relatively
few jobs. Between 1961 and 1971, the manufacturing
sector grew by 24 percent, whereas the number of people
it employed increased by only 6 percent. Indeed, the
number of people employed in manufacturing as a percentage of the economically active population actually
dropped from about 13 percent in 1961 to around 10
percent in 1971 and 1975. Moreover, by 1975, real
industrial wages, which had risen in the early 1970s, had
fallen back to 1965 levels.[17] The ranks of the

marginally employed--street vendors, shoe-shiners, lottery-ticket salesmen, maids, prostitutes, and so forth--mushroomed. Forty-two percent of urban jobs paid below the official poverty level; roughly 25 percent of the work force was either unemployed or underemployed.[18]

All this had predictable social consequences: About 56 percent of urban families lived in overcrowded dwellings. Forty percent of the housing did not meet minimum standards of habitability. Sixty percent had only one room; 25 percent lacked sanitary facilities; 15 percent had no water.[19] In San Salvador alone, some 150,000 people lived in communal compounds (mesones), most of which were in a state of progressive decay. Seventy-five thousand lived in shanty towns (tugurios), made from tin, scrap, lumber, cardboard, and any other materials that could be acquired. Another 175,000 resided in the "illegal colony" on tiny parcels of land lacking basic facilities. Between 1935 and 1971, the Department of Housing had supervised the construction of only 20,309 units--one-seventh the amount needed--and these benefited primarily the middle and upper working classes, rather than the poor.[20]

STRUCTURAL PETRIFICATION AND THE CRISIS OF "DEVELOPMENT": THE POLITICAL DIMENSION

Yet, development is not merely a socioeconomic phenomenon; it has political implications as well. Industrialization and modernization give rise to new socioeconomic groups--especially the urban middle and working classes; these sectors, in turn, make economic and political demands. The crucial question is this: How does the system respond? A politically modernizing society will adjust to these pressures through the "creation of political institutions sufficiently adaptable, complex, autonomous, and coherent to absorb and to order the participation of these new groups and to promote social and economic change in the society."[21] A failure on this count, however, may well lead to growing alienation and a crisis of legitimacy. Without political development, socioeconomic modernization tends to produce political decay.

El Salvador is a classic case in point. The system has suffered from acute structural petrification. The rules of the political game permitted change, but only very limited change--namely, that which did not threaten the position of established elites. By the late 1960s, however, the pressures generated by economic development led to a marked growth of elite-challenging behavior. In the cities, labor unions became increasingly organized and vocal; strikes and demonstrations proliferated. At the same time, bourgeois political parties--especially

the Christian Democrats--began to assume a serious
oppositional role. Meanwhile, in the countryside, the
growing displacement and immiseration of the peasantry
was paving the way for major agrarian unrest. Clearly,
fundamental structural changes were needed if the
pressures that were building were to be contained short
of an explosion.

But structural change was something that the system
was woefully ill-equipped to handle. In the "living
museum," the dinosaurs had veto power. Measures such as
democratic elections, agrarian reform, the unionization
of peasants and agricultural laborers, and the nationalization of foreign trade implied a major redistribution of
political power and wealth; they violated the rules of
the game. Although reforms might sometimes be used to
siphon off popular discontent, such measures were
employed with great caution. Reforms, after all, could
be dangerous; they could raise expectations and create
demands for additional concessions. Presidents who went
too far in this direction invited a golpe d'estado (coup
d'etat). Not surprisingly, then, such changes tended to
be more facade than substance. Repression and the threat
of repression were the primary glues that held the system
together.

This was a strategy born of experience. Once
before, the volcano had erupted. In the midst of the
Great Depression, with coffee prices and wages plunging
and unemployment rampant, the tentative and modest
reforms of President Arturo Araujo had whetted appetites
and fostered disillusionment. Efforts to suppress the
growing unrest proved ineffective. As popular revolutionary organizations swelled with new recruits and the
economic situation continued to deteriorate, the military
stepped in, deposed Araujo, and installed in his place
General Maximiliano Hernandez Martinez. Subsequently,
when the communists, under the leadership of Agustin
Farabundo Marti, were denied the seats they had
apparently won in the January 1932 municipal elections,
they launched an uprising in the western departments.
Thousands of Indians, armed mainly with machetes,
descended into the towns, looting, burning, and killing
about three dozen civilians. In turn, the military and
security forces declared open season on the Indian
population. Some 10 to 20,000 were slaughtered.[22]

It is difficult to understate the impact that this
event had on the Salvadoran political culture. The
specter of 1932 continues to haunt the country to this
day. Over the years, an elaborate mythology, replete
with stories of blood-crazed mobs butchering thousands of
well-to-do Salvadorans, has been carefully nurtured and
used to justify the status quo. Even the mildest
attempts at reform have invariably been denounced as
communist-inspired. By the same token, fear of another

uprising helped legitimize the ongoing political hegemony
of the Salvadoran military. Before 1931, the oligarchy
"that in effect owned the country also governed it";
since then--until October 1979, in any case--"elements of
the military . . . , with only momentary and inconsequential exceptions, never failed to control both the presidency and the portfolio of defense."[23] In effect, the
army protected the property of the oligarchy, even as
senior officers used their positions of power to acquire
economic wealth themselves. (Under this division of
labor, the military controlled the important political
ministries, whereas the "key positions in economic policy
were filled by representatives of the bourgeoisie, and in
part completely withdrawn from state control."[24] The
memory of 1932, moreover, has justified the resort to
unrestrained violence, when necessary, to maintain order.
     Only recently, however, has coercion on the scale of
1932 been required. The traumatic impact of la matanza
effectively paralyzed the peasantry for decades. As the
situation cooled, politics came to be marked by a certain
balance (by no means equal) between repression and
reform.[25] Indeed, the system took on the appearance of a
homeostatic mechanism. Efforts at reform were limited by
repression whenever they threatened to destroy the
established rules of the game. Yet, the pressure for
change also constrained the use of violence. When
Martinez was finally overthrown in 1944, it was largely
because a growing number of Salvadoran leaders, both
military and civilian, felt that repression was no longer
necessary or desirable. Furthermore, with World War II
and the return of prosperity, the rising industrial
bourgeoisie had grown increasingly unhappy with a regime
that continued to view coffee as the sole key to economic
well-being. Reform was in the air. The question was
whether, and to what degree, it could be effectuated.
There followed an extended period of fluctuation. In
1944, the new industrial bourgeoisie united with military
reformers, students, workers, and the middle class in
opposition to the coffee oligarchy and military conservatives. A provisional government was formed under
General Andres Menendez, with the intent of restoring
democracy. That, however, meant allowing the communists
to organize. (Indeed, during the brief period of
political freedom from May to October 1944, the radical
National Workers' Union grew to embrace some 50,000
members.) As conservative elites watched in horror, it
became increasingly evident that elections would bring a
reform government to power. Accordingly, the armed
forces and oligarchy moved to preempt such an eventuality. In October, Menendez was overthrown.
Subsequently, the military's candidate, Salvador
Castaneda Castro, was "elected" president. And while he
did not resort to the extreme violence of the Martinez

era, he did not make many political or economic
concessions either.

Thus <u>completed was the first in an ongoing sequence</u>
of cycles <u>that would characterize the Salvadoran</u>
<u>political process from 1932 to this day</u>. Time and again,
"reactionary despotism"--the alliance of agriculture
sector capitalists, military officers, and other ultraconservative elements dedicated to the "preservation of
privilege"[26]--would respond to the voices of change with
repression. In turn, dissent would grow within both,
culminating in a <u>golpe</u> by progressive young officers.
Various reforms would be promulgated. In turn, this
would lead to the reemergence of the most conservative
sectors of the army, which would then proceed to
consolidate their hegemony, halt the reforms, and repress
the opposition--hence fueling the continuation of the
process.[27]

The <u>rise of Castaneda Castro</u> (1944) marked the
beginning of the second cycle. By 1948, however,
pressure for reform had once again begun to mount. The
economy had taken a turn for the worse; the masses were
becoming restless. When Castaneda Castro made known his
intention to continue in power, he was overthrown by a
group of modernization-oriented young officers in revolt
against the older generation of commanders. From this
point on, the <u>industrial bourgeoisie would become</u> very
influential. Under the <u>presidency of Oscar Osorio</u>
(1950-56), <u>the military institutionalized a strategy of</u>
<u>repression with reform</u>. While revolutionaries continued
to be outlawed, <u>moderates were co-opted into the system</u>.
Urban workers were allowed to organize unions; opposition
groups were given more freedom than at any time since
1944. By fostering industrial development, jobs were
created for the new middle class. Meanwhile, government
programs, including social security, housing, and
agrarian credit, gave rise to relatively privileged
sectors within the peasantry and proletariat.

In perspective, <u>these benefits were quite limited.</u>
The <u>military maintained its political hegemony through an</u>
"<u>official</u>" party, the Revolutionary Party of Democratic
Unity (PRUD), and <u>rigged elections</u>. Social reforms
helped <u>only a small sector of the poor</u>. In accordance
with the rules of the political game, <u>agrarian or other</u>
<u>structural reforms that would have threatened the</u>
<u>economic position of the traditional elite were not</u>
attempted. Even so, the oligarchy remained recalcitrant.
Industrialization implied the creation of an internal
market and the raising of agricultural workers' living
standards. And that was intolerable. Accordingly, after
1956, <u>resistance from the coffee growers and their allies</u>
<u>eroded what modest social gains had been made</u>. Once
again, <u>a new cycle was beginning</u>. The presidency of Jose

Maria Lemus (1956-60) would be notable mainly for the
repression it perpetrated.

And so the process continued. By 1960, Lemus'
strong-arm tactics had produced vocal opposition in both
military and civilian sectors. An increasingly militant
left was well on its way to rejuvenation; the Communist
Party had become a political force for the first time
since 1932. When the police were sent into the national
university, injuring a number of students and faculty,
the move was widely condemned. Two tension-filled months
later, Lemus fell victim to a golpe.

There followed a replay of 1944. A Governing Junta
was set up and began preparing for elections, which were
to include the radical left. The junta was promptly
overthrown. In its place was established a Civil-
Military Directorate, which quickly moved to restore the
system created by the "revolution of 1948." Again,
substantial freedom was granted for ineffectual political
participation, while more dangerous activities were ruth-
lessly crushed. A new "official" party, the Party of
National Conciliation (PCN), was formed, and its
candidate, Julio Rivera, became "constitutional" president in the uncontested election of 1962.

In the beginning, at least, things went fairly well.
The creation of a Central American Common Market in the
early 1960s generated economic growth, even as it had
seemingly obviated the need for structural reforms to
create an internal market for Salvadoran industrial
goods. The regime was able to render its foes impotent
by co-opting them into the formal political structure.
As the decade progressed, however, serious opposition
began to arise. Proportional representation, introduced
under the liberalizing influence of the Alliance for
Progress, facilitated the growth of alternative parties.
The moderately reformist Christian Democrats (PDC), based
largely in the growing middle class being created by
industrialization, steadily expanded their support in the
cities. From thirty-seven municipalities and fourteen
seats in the Legislative Assembly in the 1964 elections,
the PDC won seventy-eight municipalities and nineteen
seats in 1968. The municipalities of San Salvador, Santa
Ana, and San Miguel, the three largest cities in the
country, all fell to the Christian Democrats. Including
six deputies from smaller parties, the opposition
controlled twenty-five seats in the Legislative Assembly,
as compared to twenty-seven for the Party of National
Conciliation.

By 1968, then, the hegemonic position of the official party was in serious jeopardy. Nor was this the
only challenge faced by the regime. Industrialization
was also fueling the growth of the urban proletariat, and
by mid-decade a decline in socioeconomic conditions had
produced serious unrest. Unemployed workers organized

street demonstrations and demanded government action to
alleviate inflation and provide jobs, housing, and land.
Efforts by the new president, Fidel Sanchez Hernandez
(1967-72), to start reform rolling again after several
years of stagnation encountered increasing militancy on
the part of organized labor. In February 1968 the
teachers' union, ANDES,[28] launched an illegal strike,
which quickly threatened to escalate into an insurrection. Some 10,000 teachers barricaded themselves around
the Ministry of Education. The opposition parties, trade
unions, and other organizations were drawn into the
movement. A series of work stoppages was launched,
culminating in the declaration of a general strike and a
demonstration of over 60,000 people in the capital.
Though the teachers' strike was crushed by government
violence, labor unrest did not die. During the first
eight months of 1969, there were no less than thirteen
major strikes and several related job actions, of which
eight were won by the workers outright.
     The pressure was mounting fast. It was at this
point, however, that fate intervened in the form of the
"futbol war." As has so often been noted, few developments are more likely to unify a divided people and rally
support for a besieged leadership than a common external
threat. Such was the case here. The war with Honduras
provided a convenient escape valve for the dangerous
tensions that were accumulating; it "stopped dead the
development of the class struggle."[29] So effectively did
it undercut the political opposition that when municipal
and Legislative Assembly elections were held in March
1970 the result was a resounding victory for the
government: Nearly 60 percent of the vote went to the
Party of National Conciliation (PCN). The PCN won 34 of
the 52 seats in the assembly and 252 of the 261 municipalities. The Christian Democrats, who had won 78
municipalities two years earlier, were now reduced to 8,
of which only San Salvador was important.
     Yet, this was at best a quick fix. As months
passed, all the old political, economic, and social
problems began to reemerge, aggravated by the effects of
the war itself. Not only had El Salvador lost its lucrative Honduran market, but its access to Nicaragua and
Costa Rica was temporarily impeded as well. The
demographic safety valve that Honduras had provided for
El Salvador's excess population was closed indefinitely.
Most immediately, the national economy was faced with the
problem of absorbing 130,000 Salvadoran refugees who had
fled Honduras for their homeland. All this put
considerable strain on the country's limited resources,
and particularly on the land.
     It was within this context that both the government
and the political opposition (the former largely to
co-opt the latter's voter support) moved to embrace the

explosive issue of land reform. A National Agrarian Reform Congress was held in early 1970. The reaction of the oligarchy was apoplectic. Moreover, conservative alarm increased following the March elections, when President Sanchez Hernandez made known his intention to push ahead with reforms in agriculture, education, and government administration. A long-delayed irrigation and drainage law was enacted. Implementation, however, was slow. Under heavy pressure, Sanchez Hernandez was forced to moderate his policies for the sake of self-preservation. Even so, conservative displeasure with the government's "irresponsible" and "traitorous" behavior triggered a massive defection from the Party of National Conciliation.

Once again, the hegemony of the PCN was in jeopardy. By the February 1972 presidential election, the oficialistas were facing serious challenges from both the extreme right and the center-left. To make matters worse, the Christian Democrats had succeeded in organizing the latter into a National Opposition Union (UNO), behind the candidacy of Jose Napoleon Duarte, the popular former mayor of San Salvador. Under these circumstances, it became necessary to rely on fraud to ensure a government victory. Athough early returns from the outlying departments gave PCN candidate Arturo Molina a substantial lead, the margin began to dwindle as the totals from more populous areas arrived. In San Salvador, where 30 percent of the country's registered voters lived, Duarte defeated Molina two to one. As the situation worsened and panic began to sweep through PCN headquarters, the government banned the further broadcast of returns. The following afternoon, it was announced that Molina had won by a narrow margin.

There were, of course, protests. The UNO announced its intention to challenge the entire election; the threat of a general strike was issued. In turn, the PCN-dominated Legislative Assembly was hastily convened and elected Molina president. (Since no candidate had gained a majority of the vote, it was up to the assembly to make that decision.) To make matters worse, the PCN-controlled Central Election Council had, on technicalities, earlier tossed out the UNO's slates in San Salvador, San Miguel, and four other departments. The upshot was a devastating defeat for the opposition in the municipal and Legislative Assembly elections held the following month. As the situation rapidly deteriorated, a military revolt was launched by young officers in the Zapote and San Carlos barracks in San Salvador. The support of the political opposition was enlisted. Duarte himself issued a radio appeal to the populace. But it was all for naught. The loyalists soon retook the capital after bloody fighting. Duarte was seized, tortured, and flown into exile.

STRUCTURAL PETRIFICATION AND THE DIALECTIC OF REVOLUTION:
THE DISINTEGRATION OF THE LIVING MUSEUM

The 1972 elections were a watershed. The legitimacy
of the political arrangements created by the "revolution
of 1948" had been seriously damaged, and the notion that
structural reforms could be attained through the ballot
box widely discredited. In effect, these events marked
the beginning of the end of the "living museum." Whereas
previously new power contenders had been admitted into
the political arena providing they demonstrated a power
capability and did not jeopardize the position of
established elites, these rules ceased to be operative in
the 1970s. Reactionary despotism was fundamentally
incapable of accommodating the sociopolitical forces that
had been unleashed by economic development. To the
oligarchs and their military allies, this was a zero sum
game--indeed, a struggle for survival. Civilian political parties threatened the army's dominance of the
political arena. Labor unions and rural cooperatives, by
their demands for higher wages and agrarian reform,
endangered the economic base of both traditional
oligarchs and modernizing industrialists. In the eyes of
the conservative elites, there could be no compromise.
The Christian Democrats were especially dangerous, since
they had demonstrated a substantive power capacity. They
had to be stopped, at any cost, before they threatened
the temples of "civilization" by opening the doors to the
"barbarity" of the lower classes. ("Why should we be
accountable to those toads?" was the way one oligarch
contemptuously put it.)[30]
And so the system became increasingly inflexible,
even as pressures for change continued to intensify.
Unable to effect reforms from within, dissidents
increasingly opted out of the formal political structure
and engaged in antisystemic participation, aimed at its
destruction. In turn, the regime responded in characteristic fashion--with repression. By this time,
however, coercion was no longer sufficient to maintain
order. Indeed, it had precisely the opposite effect:
Violence by the left led to an intensification of right-
wing terror. Slowly, an action-reaction process--a
veritable dialectic of revolutionary and counterrevolutionary violence--began to build, undermining the
political order and paving the way for its disintegration.
The most notable developments during the initial
years of this process were the growing politicization of
the Roman Catholic Church and the peasantry. Inspired by
the changing social doctrines of the 1960s (Mater et
Magistra, Pacem in Terris, Populorum Progressio), Vatican
II, and the Second Latin American Episcopal Conference in
Medellin, increasing numbers of priests and nuns began to

identify with and organize the rural and urban poor.
Peasants were organized into Christian grass-roots
communities (comunidades de base) and encouraged to form
unions, to strike, and to press for agrarian reform
(agricultural unions and strikes were still outlawed).
As Penny Lernoux has pointed out in Chapter 4 of this
text, "conscientization" was a form of revolutionary
pedagogy in that it fundamentally changed the way poor
people viewed themselves, stripping away centuries of
fatalism and passivity and activating them in defense of
their political, economic, and social interests. Against
a background of spiralling immiseration (the number of
landless had more than doubled in the 1960s), illegal
unions, such as the Christian Federation of Salvadoran
Peasants and the Union of Rural Workers, began to take
root.

Conditions were now being created for an unprecedented proliferation and alliance of militant opposition
groups. The situation of the industrial proletariat was
sharply deteriorating. Bourgeois reformists had been
almost entirely cut out of the spoils of politics.
(Electoral fraud was even more blatant in 1974 than 1972;
and in 1976 the opposition abstained altogether, thereby
surrendering every public office it held.) Student unrest
led to a wave of demonstrations and strikes. Guerrilla
bands began to engage in hit-and-run raids, kidnappings,
and bank robberies. To all this the government replied
with violence of its own. Numerous opposition leaders
were jailed or exiled. Paramilitary organizations began
systematically to assassinate peasant activists, trade
unionists, and intellectuals. In late 1974, the National
Guard killed 50 peasants and wounded 200 at La Cayetana,
evoking memories of 1932. This occurrence was followed
early the next year by another peasant massacre and by
the killing of several dozen university students during a
July demonstration.

In the midst of this growing disorder, there was one
last attempt to quell revolution through agrarian
"transformation." (Reform was by this time even too
controversial a term to use.) In late 1974, a law
providing for the forced rental--and in extreme cases
confiscation--of unexploited or underexploited lands was
enacted. The following year, another statute created the
Salvadoran Institute of Agrarian Transformation.
Finally, in mid-1976, the government announced the
formation of an initial zone of 59,000 hectares to be
divided among some 12,000 peasant families. Though quite
modest (only 4 percent of the nation's land was affected;
owners were to be amply compensated), the measure encountered heavy resistance. A massive propaganda campaign
was launched by the National Association of Private
Enterprise, along with various agricultural interests, in
an effort to thwart implementation. The measure was

challenged in court. When the oligarchs began exporting their surplus capital to safer havens, undermining the economy, and threatening the devaluation of the colon, a compromise was worked out that effectively emasculated the law.

The defeat of Transformacion Agraria signalled the eclipse of the military modernizers and industrial bourgeoisie. The homeostatic pendulum between repression and reform now swung back to the former with a vengeance. The PCN candidate in the February 1977 presidential election was the minister of defense, Carlos Humberto Romero, a counterinsurgency expert identified with the most reactionary elements in the elite. A new political cycle began.

By now, however, the political decay had spread out of control. Pressures for reform had been repeatedly frustrated, hopes and expectations alternately raised and dashed. The resulting alienation, intensified immeasurably by the growing repression, had by 1977 given rise to three powerful mass organizations, uniting peasants', workers', teachers', and other unions. These umbrella groups—the Popular Revolutionary Bloc (BPR), the Unified Popular Action Front (FAPU), and the Popular Leagues-28th of February (LP-28)—rejected elections in favor of armed struggle and developed close ties with the three operating guerrilla bands. Their members seized haciendas, factories, radio stations, and embassies, and organized demonstrations on behalf of such economic demands as a minimum wage for coffee workers and housing for slum dwellers. The most important of them, the BPR, soon became the dominant opposition force in the countryside and the largest revolutionary organization in El Salvador, claiming 100,000 members by 1980.

The "election" of Romero was followed by accelerated polarization, with right-wing violence increasingly radicalizing the forces of moderation, pushing them into the arms of the left. Demonstrators protesting the rigging of the election were fired on by the security forces and the paramilitary group ORDEN; over 100 people were killed. "Death squads" stepped up their campaign of assassination, with progressive clergymen now becoming a major target. "Be a patriot, kill a priest," read one series of anonymous circulars. In April, Father Rutilio Grande, a Jesuit whose work had radicalized many of the peasants in Aguilares, was gunned down by unknown assailants. Subsequently, the town was attacked by the military, and an estimated 350 to 400 people were killed. Between February and July 1977, 8 priests were expelled from the country, 7 denied reentry, 2 murdered, 2 imprisoned, 1 beaten, and 4 threatened with death.[31] In June a rightist paramilitary group, the White Warriors Union, gave the country's 47 Jesuit priests a month to leave or face extermination.

Nothing could have been better calculated to undermine the regime domestically than the unleashing of violence against the Church. The new archbishop, Oscar Romero, quickly rallied to the support of his clergy. Almost overnight he was transformed from a conservative cleric into an outspoken critic of government repression and social injustice; his weekly sermons, broadcast over radio from the National Cathedral, inveighed against the system of "institutionalized violence." Indeed, by the time of his assassination in March 1980, Romero would be defending the right of armed revolt, provided that all other paths had been exhausted and that the "evil of the rebellion [did] not become worse than the evil of the status quo."32

At the same time, the government was increasingly isolated and condemned internationally for its violations of human rights. Efforts by the Carter administration to moderate it through carrot-stick diplomacy had only limited effect. Thus, El Salvador joined Brazil, Argentina, and Guatemala in rejecting U.S. military aid because of human rights criticism. And although the activities of the death squads did subside temporarily following an American veto of a $90 million loan from the Inter-American Development Bank (the threatened slaughter of Jesuits did not occur), the subsequent decision to grant the loan as a reward for good behavior backfired: Less than a month later, in November 1977, the regime responded to the assassination of industrialist Raul Molina by instituting a draconian Law for the Defense and Guarantee of Public Order. Press censorship was imposed; antigovernment meetings were outlawed, as were strikes and the distribution of "false and tendentious" information adversely affecting social stability. Mere suspicion was made grounds for arrest.

The measure only accelerated the breakdown of public order. The right was encouraged to step up its terrorist activities; the left responded in kind. Indeed, both extremes seemed almost to be vying with one another to see which one could pull off the most spectacular acts of violence. Prominent members of the oligarchy were targeted for kidnapping and assassination by the guerrillas. (Both Foreign Minister Borgonovo and former president Aguirre y Salinas fell victim to such acts in 1977. The following year, the insurgents turned their attention to foreign businessmen and diplomats.) In turn, the right hit the moderate opposition and the mass organizations. Following a violent street demonstration in March 1978, moreover, ORDEN unleashed a reign of terror against the peasants of San Pedro Perulapan. And so it went, with each side feeding the barbarity of the other.

By the summer of 1979, the handwriting was on the wall. The economy was rapidly deteriorating. Conditions

n the countryside and among the urban unemployed were
becoming increasingly desperate. (From 1974 to 1978, per
capita income had declined 1.6 percent per annum.)[33] The
dialectic of revolution was spiralling out of control.
Even the repeal of the Public Order Law (a gesture to
U.S. sensibilities, more than anything else) failed to
stem the deterioration. In May, the top leaders of the
Popular Revolutionary Bloc were arrested. In protest,
the Metropolitan Cathedral was seized. When the National
Police and National Guard fired on a crowd gathered on
the cathedral steps, killing two dozen demonstrators, the
left retaliated with a wave of assassinations and embassy
occupations. Thus began the bloodiest period of the dictatorship. During the first half of the year, government
forces killed over forty people. The teachers' union,
ANDES, which provided much of the intellectual leadership
of the BPR, was especially hard hit. In turn, the
guerrillas stepped up their attacks on foreign business
executives. Capital flight accelerated; new investments
dried up.[34]

By this time, the Carter administration had
concluded that the situation was untenable. The fall of
the Somoza dynasty had brought the domino theory back
into vogue. If El Salvador were not to go the way of
Nicaragua, something had to be done. But attempts to
pressure Romero into easing the repression and opening a
"dialogue" with the opposition were frustrated by his
recalcitrance and duplicity. Meanwhile, U.S. human
rights policy further undermined the regime. Washington
was still trying to promote a dialogue when, on
October 15th, 1979, it was overtaken by events: A group
of young officers overthrew the dictator and set up a
civilian-military junta pledged to fundamental structural
reforms, including land redistribution.[35] The homeostatic balance between repression and reform had at last
broken down. The question was what would replace it.

THE POLITICS OF REFORM AND THE STRUCTURE OF
COUNTERREVOLUTION

It can be seen in retrospect that the government
formed in the wake of Romero's overthrow represented the
last chance to avert an all-out civil war. At first
glance, its prospects seemed fairly promising. The
initial junta was moderately progressive in composition,
its members including Guillermo Ungo, head of the small
social democratic party (the National Revolutionary
Movement); Roman Mayorga, rector of the Central American
University; Mario Andino, a representative of the
modernizing faction of the business community; Colonel
Adolfo Majano, the reform-minded leader of the Military
Youth (Juventud Militar); and Colonel Jaime Abdul

Gutierrez, a compromise figure who served as a link with
the more conservative elements in the armed forces. The
cabinet, too, was drawn primarily from the center-left,
including Christian Democrats, social democrats,
progressive businessmen, and even a member of the
Communist Party. In addition to agrarian and financial
reforms, the new government declared its commitment to
the freedoms of speech, press, and assembly, and the
right to organize political parties and trade unions.
The security forces were to be reorganized, political
prisoners freed, human rights abuses investigated, and a
dialogue with the left opened.

But the regime lacked the power and legitimacy to
restore order and implement the promised reforms. The
junta itself was divided and ineffectual. There was much
talk and little action. To make matters worse, an excess
of pluralism in the cabinet and ministries led to a
"dangerous fragmentation of authority and responsibility.
Within a ministry, the minister might be from one party,
the vice-minister from another, and their ranking
subordinates yet another. Many officials tended to
pursue their own party interests with little regard for
intra-ministry cohesion or discipline."[36]   In effect, the
situation was one of institutionalized anarchy.

Nor was there much cooperation from the combatants.
"The security forces are repressing in a brutal manner,"
protested Archbishop Romero, "more brutal than the former
regime, because they are trying to prevent the new
government from gaining credibility."[37]

So too the radical left. The popular organizations
that had sprung up in the mid-1970s--the BPR, FAPU, and
LP-28--were not represented in the new government, and
their response was generally negative. Skepticism was
rife. Many considered the junta to be part of an
"imperialist maneuver"--a cynical ploy designed to
isolate the revolutionary left and prevent the formation
of a "genuinely" popular government. Accordingly, there
was little restraint. Though on different occasions both
the BRP and LP-28 agreed to suspend their attacks, more
typically the mass organizations and guerrillas sought to
"unmask" the regime and prevent it from consolidating
power. In the words of Joaquin Villalobos, commander of
the People's Revolutionary Army:

> (W)e had to assess matters on the basis of the prime
> element in the ruling junta, the armed forces, which
> held power and were not about to agree to any deep-
> going radical changes, because their objectives were
> counterrevolutionary: to isolate the people from
> their vanguard and . . . destroy the revolutionary
> political military organizations . . . and so,
> regardless of the good intentions of the per-
> sonalities belonging to that first ruling junta, our

policy consisted of applying constant pressure so
that the military sectors that were really running
the government would be forced to take up the
defense of the true scheme of imperialism, the
oligarchy, and their allies. . . . Militant
pressure by the masses and revolutionary actions of
a military nature speeded up the crisis of the first
ruling junta.[38]

In short, repression was "elicited and forced by
purposeful provocation and violence" by elements of the
extreme left.[39] Calls for a popular uprising were
issued, villages occupied, government ministries seized.
Day after day, the streets were filled with demonstrations. Chaos reigned. As expected, the politics of
confrontation fueled the already-existing terror from the
right. In the first week alone, at least 160 people were
killed in clashes with the security forces. Under such
circumstances, even those disposed toward giving the
government a chance were soon radicalized and driven into
the arms of the extremes.

And so the slaughter began, as each side sought to
undermine the regime through competitive acts of revolutionary or counter-revolutionary violence. Out of this
dialectic there gradually arose a myth--fostered by
successive U.S. and Salvadoran administrations to justify
an escalation of American involvement--that the essence
of the crisis was an assault by the extreme left and
extreme right on a moderate reform regime. This was at
best a half-truth. The reality was that the government
itself was splintered into irreconcilable factions,
spanning the political spectrum from communist to
fascist. Right-wing terrorism and opposition to the
proposed reforms emanated not so much from the infamous
"death squads," ostensibly beyond government control, as
from the military and security forces themselves.

Like the junta and the cabinet, the armed forces
were riven with factionalism. One group, the Reformists,
revolved around the Military Youth. In the late 1960s,
Colonel Majano had organized a training program in the
military academy to acquaint young officers with their
country's social, economic, and political problems. Many
had come away convinced that only basic structural
changes could avert violent revolution. Inevitably,
these views brought them into conflict with older, more
conservative elements in the high command. Under the
leadership of the defense minister, Colonel Jose
Guillermo Garcia, the Conservatives accepted the idea of
reform only grudgingly, under U.S. pressure.
Accordingly, the young officers set up a Permanent
Council of the Armed Forces to ensure that the proclaimed
objectives of the "revolution" were not subverted. In
their view, the older commanders "could not be

trusted . . . , carried the taint of corruption from
preceding days, must be monitored carefully and, if
necessary, would have to be weeded out." Both Garcia and
his undersecretary, Nicolas Carranza, came under heavy
criticism for being reactionary obstructions to progress,
and pressure quickly arose for their removal.[40]
Then there were the Neanderthals. Just as a technocratic sector had developed within the military to meet
the requisites of modernization, so there were specialists in repression, with strong support among the
agrarian bourgeoisie. Many were unabashed admirers of
Hitler and Mussolini. These elements invariably
denounced even the mildest of reforms as Marxist-inspired
and displayed a singular inability to distinguish between
center-of-the-road Christian Democrats and the hard-core
Leninists of the Popular Liberation Forces. (Both were
lumped together under the amorphous label "communist" and
singled out for extermination.) Their ties with the
death squads were especially close, many of their rank-
and-file simply stepping out of uniform to moonlight in
the shadowy world of extra-governmental terrorism. Their
modus operandi often smacked of the psychopathic, with
indiscriminate mass killings and ghoulish tortures being
their trademark.
    (There was also, it is true, a sizeable and
politically important group of Opportunists, who were
largely apathetic to social and political issues and
willing to follow anyone who could ensure the institutional survival of the military. But this group hardly
had enough coherence to be termed a faction.)
    Complicating the problems of factionalism and human
rights abuses was the sheer number of organizations performing security functions. In addition to the regular
military (Army, Navy and Air Force), the National Guard,
National Police, and Treasury Police also came under the
auspices of the Defense Ministry and were normally commanded by military officers. Indeed, some of the most
notorious Neanderthals have been in leadership positions
in the security forces--for example, Roberto D'Aubuisson
(former National Guard major and founder of the White
Warriors Union), retired general Jose "Chele" Medrano
(former commander of the National Guard and father of
ORDEN), and Colonel Francisco Moran (former chief of the
Treasury Police). Although the National Police were
responsible for order in urban areas and for coordinating
criminal investigations throughout the country, the
National Guard was primarily a rural force with units in
most towns and villages. There had long been a
mutualistic relationship between the Guardia and the
large landowners. Guardsmen were often employed on the
estates to maintain the authority of owners and administrators and to stifle protest. (Under a law enacted
during the Hernandez Martinez era and still in force in

he 1960s, they were instructed to capture, at the
acendado's request, anyone who appeared suspicious.)
alcontents were dismissed from work, when not dealt with
n a harsher manner. Supporting the National Guard and
he National Police were the Treasury Police, responsible
or borders, harbors, airports, and (with the assistance
f the Custom's Police) customs duties. Under Francisco
oran, they became the most feared of the security
orces, roaming the countryside out of control, assassi-
ating Christian Democratic mayors, agrarian reform
orkers, peasants, and any other suspected "communists"
hey happened to encounter.

Nor did this exhaust the security network. Mass
rganizations had been created for the purpose of
obilizing the rural populace against subversion. Some
7,000 former soldiers helped patrol the villages and
owns as reservists in the Territorial Service. Many
ere simultaneously members of the Democratic Nationalist
rganization--the notorious ORDEN--formed in the early
960s under the auspices of the National Guard, with a
hain of command leading into the presidential palace
tself. By the 1970s, ORDEN may have embraced as many as
0,000 to 100,000 members, though the vast majority were
ominal. ORDEN cards provided a certain amount of pro-
ection from military abuse and often included economic
rivileges. Members sometimes gained priority access to
mployment, cheap credit, schools, and medical facili-
ies. And, of course, if asked to join, potential
embers would have been unwise to refuse. In every
ommunity, however, a few people--retired soldiers, small
andowners, agricultural workers, thugs, and frightened
embers of the middle class--played a more active role as
nformants and guides for the military and security
orces. An even smaller number--10,000 at most--were
rmed and organized into paramilitary units, many of
hich participated in counterinsurgency operations.

Finally, there were the death squads, financed by
ligarchs terrified of the impending reforms but drawing
ost of their leaders and rank-and-file from the military
nd security forces. According to former Salvadoran Army
aptain Ricardo Fiallos, in testimony before the U.S.
ongress, acts of terrorism attributed to these groups
re often "planned by high ranking military officers."[41]
he escuadrones themselves had only limited autonomy:

> Official forces often work in close cooperation with
> the paramilitary on raids, patrols, and assassina-
> tions. Even when death squads work alone, they must
> have the tolerance or permission of the police and
> army, who keep all others off the streets during
> nighttime curfew hours. At their most independent,
> some . . . represent a particular faction of the
> military and security forces in alliance with

civilian right-wing interests. Otherwise they share
the same fundamental goals and methods as the official forces.[42]

In short, the death squads were a functional part of
a complex, institutionalized structure of state
terrorism. By attributing human rights abuses to groups
"beyond official control," the military could evade
"responsibility for the actions of its own security
forces."[43]

And what of the junta? As the weeks passed, it
became painfully clear that real power lay not in this
"civilian-military" directorate but in the military high
command. And within the latter, the conservatives were
dominant. Efforts by the Juventud Militar to form
soldiers' councils to monitor reactionary officers
strengthened the conservatives' resolve to defend the
military's institutional integrity and esprit de corps.
The minister of defense, Colonel Garcia, began to emerge
as the regime's most powerful figure. Under these
circumstances, reforms were systematically sabotaged.
The repression intensified; the promised land redistribution never got off the ground. Efforts to restructure
the security forces were limited to a few dozen
dismissals and a cosmetic reshuffling of personnel.
Although ORDEN was formally abolished, it was promptly
reconstituted as the Democratic Nationalist Front and
continued to patrol the countryside with the military and
National Guard. Finally, there was the thorny issue of
political prisoners: Though the junta had promised their
release, few could be found. Widespread suspicion that
the desaparecidos had been murdered by the previous
regime led to demands that their killers be arrested and
prosecuted. At this point, the government wavered. An
investigation almost certainly would have implicated
high-ranking military and security officials. That in
turn would have destroyed what little unity remained in
the armed forces--something that even the reformists were
unwilling to accept.

And so nothing was done. The situation continued to
deteriorate. By December, 1979, both the extreme right
and extreme left had abandoned all semblance of
restraint. The revolutionary dialectic was rapidly
escalating. A full-scale civil war seemed just around
the corner.

In the face of this growing turmoil, increasingly
frustrated by the military's recalcitrance, two of the
civilian members in the junta, Guillermo Ungo and Roman
Mayorga, made a last-ditch effort to salvage the
situation. A list of demands was issued, including a
call for junta control over all military appointments and
the resignation of Defense Minister Garcia. But the
gambit failed; the military stood its ground. Thus, on

January 3, Ungo and Mayorga resigned, along with most members of the cabinet. Soon thereafter, the third civilian, Mario Andino, also submitted his resignation, leaving the military in the junta by itself.

Through all this the United States remained, first and foremost, a proponent of "law and order." Escalating human rights abuses were met by official silence. Washington now had higher priorities: The left had to be brought under control and the situation stabilized. At the same time, the U.S. Embassy actively courted the Salvadoran business community, lending moral support to one of the most conservative sectors in the country. In retrospect, this can be seen as a critical mistake. Had the Carter administration firmly placed its influence behind Ungo and Mayorga and insisted that the military and security forces cease their abuses and institute the promised reforms, the junta might have survived. Conceivably, civil war might have been avoided. Instead, Washington sent riot control equipment and advisers. The situation thus defined, El Salvador proceeded to descend into the maelstrom.

REPRESSION WITH REFORM

In perspective, October 15 marked more than the fall of the Romero dictatorship: It was the end of a politi-cal system. The rules of the "living museum"--which among other things had bound together all the established elites and protected each from elimination--had now completely been stripped away. All that remained was power.

Yet, power was something that the first junta and its successors were woefully ill-equipped to deal with. These were weak regimes, riven through with irrecon-cilable conflicts, unable to control the contending forces that had been unleashed. On the other hand, the alliance between the oligarchy and military had been seriously eroded. The latter could no longer be entirely trusted to protect the property of the former; it was divided, with some elements still reliable, others bent on reform, and still others susceptible to U.S. pressures for change. At the same time, the left had achieved an unprecedented degree of mass mobilization and was mili-tantly pressing its demands. Under these circumstances, there emerged a very different relationship between reform and repression. Threatened with extinction, the oligarchs and their allies lashed out with all the violence at their disposal. Whereas, previously, pressure for reform had served as a "homeostatic" counterbalance to repression, now it had precisely the opposite effect--it accelerated the terror dramatically.

The pattern became all too clear in the weeks that followed. In order to preserve the appearance of a civilian-military reform regime, the officers turned to the middle-of-the-road Christian Democrats. PDC leaders Jose Antonio Morales Ehrlich and Hector Dada now joined Majano and Gutierrez in a second junta, along with Jose Avalos, an independent physician. Christian Democrats dominated the cabinet. Simultaneously, the left moved to unify its ranks. On January 11, 1980, the BPR, FAPU, and LP-28 joined two other popular organizations, the Democratic Nationalist Union (UDN) and the Popular Liberation Movement (MPL), in forming the Revolutionary Coordinating Committee of the Masses (CR). Eleven days later, the mass organizations put some 200,000 people into the streets of San Salvador in a peaceful demonstration of popular support. In response, government troops opened fire; 67 demonstrators were killed and 250 injured.

Altogether, some 600 people fell victim to military and paramilitary violence during January and February. In perhaps the most blatant incident, Roberto D'Aubuisson, a cashiered National Guard intelligence officer and leader of the White Warriors' Union, appeared on television to denounce a list of people whom he claimed were connected with the political and military organizations of the left. Among them was Christian Democratic Solicitor General Mario Zamora. Several days later, gunmen broke into Zamora's home and murdered him.

The escalating repression soon led to another crisis--one, this time, for both the government and the Christian Democrats. In early March, Hector Dada resigned from the junta in protest: "We have not been able to stop the repression, and those committing acts of repression . . . go unpunished; the promised dialogue with the popular organizations fails to materialize; the chances for producing reforms . . . are receding beyond reach." Those primarily responsible for the obstruction, he noted, are "encysted in the very structure of the government. The democratic government to be developed is traveling a road towards total perversion."[44] Others soon followed. On March 10, 20 percent of the delegates to the Christian Democratic Party's national convention withdrew in protest of the party's continuing participation in the regime. That same day, seven PDC leaders, including Dada, resigned from the party. And so on it went. By May, the entire left wing of the PDC had resigned. The government was hemorrhaging cabinet ministers. Among those to leave were the ministers of the economy, education, finance, planning, foreign trade, and the presidency.

Still, the government survived, with the help of the remaining Christian Democrats. Jose Napoleon Duarte, the party's candidate in the ill-fated 1972 election, replaced Dada in the junta. <u>Under intense pressure from the United States, the regime announced on March 6 a sweeping land reform and the nationalization of foreign trade and 51 percent of the banking system.</u> At first glance, this seemed an impressive program: Properties over 500 hectares (1,235 acres) were to be expropriated and turned into peasant cooperatives. A second stage, moreover, would affect holdings from 100 to 500 hectares (247 to 1,235 acres), including most of the valuable coffee lands. Finally, in April, a third stage, the "Land to the Tiller" program, was announced, entitling renters to take over the lands they worked, up to 7 hectares (17 acres). The idea, of course, was to win the hearts and minds of the peasantry, thus depriving the guerrillas of the sea in which they swam. In the words of U.S. adviser Roy Prosterman, one of the architects of Stage Three: "<u>There is no one more conservative than a small farmer. We're going to breed capitalists like rabbits.</u>"[45]

The <u>military, however, saw another advantage: Here was a golden opportunity to root out subversives. A state of siege was imposed.</u> A technician from the Salvadoran Institute of Agrarian Transformation (ISTA) described what followed: "The troops came and told the workers the land was theirs now. They could elect their own leaders and run it themselves. The peasants couldn't believe their ears, but they held elections that very night. The next morning the troops came back, and I watched as they shot every one of the elected leaders."[46]

This was not an isolated incident. Rather, <u>it was part and parcel of a massive rural pacification program in which repression was a functional complement to reform.</u> Thus, during the first year of the reform, over 500 peasant leaders were <u>assassinated by the security forces and allied death squads.</u>[47] <u>Dozens of land reform workers and other ISTA officials were "eliminated."</u> Even the pro-government peasant organization, the Union Comunal Salvadorena (UCS), became a target. On July 19, 1980, for instance, "at least 1,000 strongly armed masked men wearing bullet-proof vests, with badges identifying them as members of the Death Squad, accompanied by members of the army and agents of the National Guard, invaded the Hacienda 'Mirador' in which the majority of peasant members belonged to the Union Comunal Salvadorena. . . . Witnesses . . . indicated that agents of the National Guard and masked individuals shot sixty peasants. They were selected beforehand after 300 peasant cooperative members were captured."[48]

Nor were such activities restricted to agrarian reform recipients and administrators. <u>Over 500 military and security force operations were conducted in rural areas in 1980.</u> Most were aimed at suspected "guerrilla sympathizers" in zones in which the mass organizations

214

enjoyed strong support. The northern and eastern departments of Chalatenango, Cabanas, and Morazan were especially hard hit. In the words of the Catholic Church's
Legal Aid Office, "to be a victim . . . it is enough to
be a relative of a militant or to be suspected of having
collaborated with the insurgents. The concept of collective responsibility is being progressively extended to
the individual, family, town, and even province."[49]

And so the casualties mounted. In April, 1980, 480
members of the popular organizations were killed; by
June, the figure was 1,000.[50] In one incident, on
May 14, hundreds of unarmed peasants--mostly women,
children, and old people--were massacred by the army,
National Guard, and ORDEN as they attempted to flee into
Honduras. Those who made it across the river were turned
back by Honduran troops. Over 600 were reportedly
killed. Although the Salvadoran and Honduran authorities
denied that the incident had occurred, eyewitnesses were
not lacking. Under pressure, the military eventually
conceded the gist of the charges, though it sought to
minimize the casualties. In Colonel Garcia's words, the
number killed had not been in "industrial quantities."[51]

These months also witnessed the assassination of
Archbishop Romero and the political eclipse of Colonel
Majano. As early as February, 1980, Romero had called on
President Carter to halt U.S. military aid to the junta
on grounds that it would aggravate the repression.
Increasingly radicalized by government violence, he had
come to accept--albeit with reservations--the right to
insurrection. On March 23, he denounced the "reforms
bathed in blood" and called on soldiers to disobey their
commanders. The following day, he was gunned down while
celebrating mass in the National Cathedral. His funeral
on March 30 provided yet another occasion for gratuitous
bloodletting. Between 60 and 100 people were killed and
several hundred wounded when the mourners were attacked
by security forces. Two days later, the U.S. House
Appropriations Subcommittee on Foreign Operations
approved the reprogramming of $5.7 million in Foreign
Military Sales credits to El Salvador.

If there were any doubts left that the military and
civilian reformers had lost the initiative to the
conservatives in the high command, they were removed one
month later. In early May, Roberto D'Aubuisson, back
from a visit to the United States where he had been the
guest of the American Security Council, attempted an
unsuccessful golpe. On orders from Colonel Majano, he
was arrested, along with twenty-three co-conspirators,
including a number of active-duty officers. A diary was
confiscated, including an entry on a so-called Operation
Pineapple, which provided "compelling, if not 100%
conclusive" evidence that he and his followers were
"responsible for the murder of Archbishop Romero."[52] The

Christian Democrats, who had their own reasons for hating D'Aubuisson, demanded that he be tried and sentenced and threatened to withdraw from the government if higher pressures compelled his release. But this was bluff. The day after D'Aubuisson's seizure, the entire 700-man officer corps met and voted to replace Majano with Colonel Gutierrez as head of the armed forces. (By summer's end, virtually all of Majano's supporters would be removed from command assignments.) A few days later, D'Aubuisson was released due to "insufficient evidence." Nothing more was heard of the incriminating documents that had been captured. The Christian Democrats, of course, remained in the government.

THE OPPOSITION: THE STRUGGLE FOR UNITY AND POWER

And what of the opposition? Here, the contrasts with the Nicaraguan and Cuban experiences are instructive. Unlike those revolutions, where broad multiclass alliances toppled unpopular dictatorships, the Salvadoran struggle has been primarily a class conflict, a war of haves against have-nots. Absent has been the kind of charismatic leadership that gave Castroism wide personalistic appeal. Nor has there been a single ogre-figure, a Batista or Somoza, who could serve as a personal target for the concentrated wrath of the populace. Instead, the conflict has been notable for both the anonymity and the viciousness of the contending forces. In comparison with the hard-core Marxists of the Farabundo Marti National Liberation Front (FMLN), the Nicaraguan and Cuban revolutionaries seem almost romantic idealists.

Two points, in particular, need emphasis. The first is tactical, the second a matter of internal power relations. Both involve a special quality of ruthlessness. With regard to the first: There is a difference between revolutionaries and terrorists, but the line is often very thin. Lenin knew this well; indeed, it was a crucial issue in his dispute with the Socialist Revolutionaries. Unfortunately, the Salvadoran guerrillas—some of them, anyway—seem never to have learned the distinction, and it has hurt them badly. Assassinations, kidnappings, bank robberies, and economic sabotage may have their uses (among other things, the insurgents were said to have accumulated a war chest of some $70 million by 1980), but they are also a liability in that they alienate potential supporters. Many fear that a guerrilla military victory would bring a bloodbath, and with good reason. The precedent of 1932, the widespread practice of executing "ears" (enemy informants), and the creation of lists of regime sympathizers to be "eliminated" do not inspire

confidence.[53] In a war as vicious as this one, revenge
is a powerful motivator. The victors, whoever they might
be, are not likely to be charitable.

    Nor have the insurgents been exempt from internecine
strife. From its very inception, the revolutionary movement has been plagued by factionalism. The oldest of the
guerrilla groups, the Farabundo Marti People's Liberation
Forces (FPL), arose in 1970 as an off-shoot of the
Salvadoran Communist Party (PCS). After years of
internal debate against a "stubborn majority that . . .
blocked the advance towards the political-military
strategy that the people needed,"[54] the party's secretary
general, Salvador Cayetano Carpio, led a dissident
faction out of the PCS and embarked on the road of
"prolonged popular war." Initially, the group engaged in
only minor guerrilla actions. (In fact, for the first
two years of its existence the organization did not even
have a name.) Gradually, however, mass support was built
through the Popular Revolutionary Bloc and grassroots
political work among the peasantry.

    This strategy did not win universal acceptance. In
1971, radicalized Christian Democrats and Roman
Catholics, impatient with the slow, incremental policies
of the FPL and PCS, formed the People's Revolutionary
Army (ERP), a "chaotic" organization composed of
"different groups with different approaches . . . , but
sharing the desire to promote armed struggle. . . ."[55]
In its early years, the ERP was permeated by a spirit of
militarism. Strategy was focused on the short run:
Guerrilla action was conceived as a method of igniting an
insurrection. Little effort was made to create a mass
political base. Although kidnappings, bombings, and
assassinations enabled it to build a lucrative war chest
and gain publicity, such tactics isolated it from the
populace even further. Eventually, too, they led to
internal strains--tactical differences, personal power
struggles, factionalism, and the erosion of internal
democracy--culminating in the execution of the revolutionary poet Roque Dalton in 1975 on trumped-up charges
of being a Soviet-Cuban-CIA agent. Not until the First
Congress of the Party of the Salvadoran Revolution (the
ERP's political arm) two years later was this militarismo
overcome, at least to the extent that the movement began
to seek links with the masses through the Popular
Leagues-28th of February.

    Meanwhile, the execution of Dalton (personally
conducted by the current head of the ERP, Joaquin
Villalobos)[56] had led to the rise of a splinter guerrilla
group, the Armed Forces of National Resistance (FARN),
which proceeded to combine an insurrectionary strategy
with a broad multiclass alliance via the Unified Popular
Action Front. From 1975 onward, the FARN and ERP spent
much of their time trying to exterminate one another.

Indeed, on one occasion the FARN leader, Ernesto Jovel, narrowly escaped assassination after being "sentenced" to death by the ERP. When he died in 1980, it was under mysterious circumstances. (Initially, it was announced that he had been killed in a traffic accident; then it was reported that he had been in a plane crash in which one of the engines had failed and the other had dropped off.) Suffice it to say that the incident gave rise to ugly speculation.

By 1979, however, the triumph of the Nicaraguan Revolution had underlined the importance of unity, even as the disintegration and collapse of the Romero dictatorship raised the prospect of a guerrilla victory. Impressed with the historic opportunity apparently at hand, the opposition began the difficult task of unification. Here the Communist Party played a crucial role. In April 1979, "two years behind the times," the PCS had taken "the step in the direction of armed . . . struggle." At the same time, it recognized that the revolutionary movement needed the democratic opposition if power were to be won. Thus when Romero fell, the PCS decided to "stand beside" the democratic forces by participating in the first junta until "the project met with failure in order to prevent their dispersal after defeat and be able to link them up with the revolutionary movement."[57]   Simultaneously, Cuban help was solicited to unify the various guerrilla movements. In December the PCS, FARN, and FPL forged an agreement in Havana that established the bases on which organizational coordination and unity could begin. As early as January/February 1980, a Warning Appraisal from the U.S. Defense Intelligence Agency reported Cuban (and possibly Nicaraguan) aid to the insurgents. Subsequently, at a meeting in April at the Hungarian Embassy in Mexico City, requests (for arms?) were made to East German, Bulgarian, Polish, Vietnamese, Hungarian, Cuban, and Soviet representatives. Later that month, at a session of the PCS Political Commission, note was taken of the need to secure aid from the socialist camp. The latter's attitude was said to be "magnificent"; the possibilities had not been exploited.[58]

These weeks witnessed the formal unification of most of the political opposition. On April 18 a broad civilian coalition, the Democratic Revolutionary Front (FDR), was created, merging the popular organizations of the Revolutionary Coordinating Committee of the Masses with an array of Social Democrats, dissident Christian Democrats, former government ministers, independent trade unionists, professionals, and other elements. Among the most prominent leaders of the FDR were Guillermo Ungo and Roman Mayorga of the first junta; Ruben Zamora of the second junta; and former minister of agriculture (and renegade member of the "fourteen families") Enrique

Alvarez, who was elected president. The Front
immediately recognized the guerrillas as its vanguard and
issued an "anti-oligarchic, anti-imperialist" platform.
One month later, on May 22, the insurgents followed suit.
Since January the PCS, FPL, and FARN had been coordinating their activities through a joint council. Now
they were joined by the ERP in a Unified Revolutionary
Directorate (DRU), designed to coordinate strategy and
supervise operations. (Later in the year, a fifth small
group, the Revolutionary Party of Central American
Workers, would be added to the DRU.) In turn, the
guerrillas recognized the FDR as the basis for a future
government.

DRU

     Efforts to acquire "internationalist aid" were now
stepped up.[59] Visits to Cuba became frequent. In late
May, a PCS representative (possibly Secretary General
Shafik Handal) left Havana for Moscow on the first leg of
a journey that would take him to Vietnam, East Germany,
Czechoslovakia, Bulgaria, Hungary, Ethiopia, and back to
the Soviet Union. Other envoys were sent to Managua to
meet with Sandinista leaders.

     Their reception was mixed. The Soviets were
evasive: An agreement "in principle" to transport
Vietnamese arms, provision of training for some thirty
Salvadoran youths studying in Moscow who wanted to fight
in the war, a plane ticket to Vietnam for the Salvadoran
emissary. After more than two weeks of footdragging on
the arms transfer issue, the emissary began to express
his concern: Lack of a decision could have a detrimental
effect on the decisions of potential suppliers. The PCS
envoy left, returned, and left Moscow again (the second
time in early August) without a firm commitment or even a
meeting with someone at the "proper level" of authority.

     Meanwhile, the emissaries to Managua were encoun-
tering similar difficulties. Meetings with high-level
officials were postponed because of the first anniversary
celebration of Somoza's overthrow; contacts with visiting
dignitaries were restricted. DRU representatives in the
capital complained to the visitors that the Sandinistas
undervalued and ignored them, and made decisions without
consulting them. This was a relationship not of mutual
respect, but, rather, one of imposition. The
Nicaraguans, they lamented, had grown conservative--much
more interested in defending their own revolution than in
fostering the one next door. They refused to treat the
Salvadorans as "ambassadors" and hindered political work.
(At one point, the frustrated DRU representatives had
retorted: "Gentlemen, all right, we understand that
Nicaragua must be protected, but for that there is an art
and a science which is called 'CONSPIRACY.' Let us
conspire together.") The visitors concluded that the
Sandinistas lacked confidence in the maturity, strength,
and unity of the Salvadoran left.

TABLE 6.1

The Opposition

Farabundo Marti National Liberation Front (FMLN) Formed: November 1980	Democratic Revolutionary Front (FDR) Formed: April 1980	
	Revolutionary Coordinating Committee of the Masses (DRM) Formed: January 1980	Democratic Front Formed: April 1980
1. Popular Forces of Liberation–Farabundo Marti (FPL) Formed: 1970 Military arm: Armed Forces of Popular Liberation (FAPL) Formed: 1979	1. Popular Revolutionary Bloc (BPR) Formed: 1975 Affiliates:[a] –Christian Federation of Salvadoran Peasants (FECCAS) –Union of Rural Workers (UTC) –National Association of Salvadoran Educators (ANDES)	1. National Revolutionary Movement (MNR) 2. Popular Social Christian Movement (MPSC) 3. National University of El Salvador (NES) 4. Association of University Students (AGEUS) 5. Movement of Independent Professionals and Technicians (MIPTES)
2. National Resistance (RN) Formed: 1975 Military arm: Armed Forces of National Resistance (FARN) Formed: 1975	2. United Popular Action Front (FAPU) Formed: 1974 Affiliates:[a] –Revolutionary Campesino Movement (MRC) –United Front of Revolutionary Students Salvador Allende (FUERSA)	6. Association of Bus Companies of El Salvador (AEAS) 7. Federation of Salvadoran Workers (FENASTRAS)
3. Party of the Salvadoran Revolution (PRS) Formed: 1978 Military arm: People's Revolutionary Army (ERP) Formed: 1971	3. Popular Leagues–28th of February (LP–28) Formed: 1977 Affiliates: Organizations of peasants, workers, students, and barrio residents	(Continued)

TABLE 6.1 (Cont.)

4. Salvadoran Communist
   Party (PCS)
   Formed: 1930
   Military arm: Armed
   Forces of Liberation
   (FAL) Formed: 1979

5. Revolutionary Party
   of Central American
   Workers (PRTC)
   Formed: 1979

4. Democratic Nationalist Union (UDN)
   Formed: 1969
   Affiliates:[a]
   -Association of High School
    Students (AES)
   -Association of Farmworkers (ATACES)

5. Popular Liberation Movement (MPL)
   Formed: 1979
   Affiliates:
   Organizations of workers, farmworkers,
   and high-school students

8. Federation of Food,
   Clothing, and Textile
   Workers (FESTIAVTSCES)

9. Revolutionary Federation
   of Unions (FSR)

10. United Federation of
    Salvadoran Unions (FUSS)

11. Union of Social Security
    Workers (STISS)

12. Union of Workers of United
    Industries (STIUSA)

13. University of Central
    America (Observer status)

Source: Robert Armstrong and Janet Shenk, El Salvador: The Face of Revolution (Boston: South End Press,
        1982), pp. 252-253.

[a] Partial listing.

Notwithstanding such difficulties, the available evidence suggests that these efforts were largely successful. By mid-September, 1980, substantial quantities of weapons were en route to Cuba and Nicaragua. On September 26, the guerrilla logistics coordinator in Nicaragua informed his Joint General Staff that 130 tons of arms and other military material had arrived for shipment to El Salvador. These activities did not go unnoticed. Though the Carter administration chose to play down intelligence reports of Nicaraguan complicity,[60] the State Department's James Cheek was dispatched to warn the Sandinista leaders that Washington was aware that arms were being moved through their country. Taken aback, the Nicaraguans decided to suspend operations for a month.

THE "FINAL OFFENSIVE": PRELUDE TO SHOWDOWN

By late summer, the revolutionary movement found itself plagued by severe internal crisis and declining mass support. In August, differences over strategy and tactics had led the FARN to withdraw from the Unified Revolutionary Directorate. To make matters worse, the popular organizations, increasingly decimated by government violence and intimidation, had been effectively neutralized. In June, the closing of the National University had deprived them of their communications and coordination center. In August, a general strike called by the FDR ended in dismal failure: Tens of thousands of government employees and factory workers were threatened with dismissal if they joined the action. Bus lines were militarized. Many unionists (including the entire leadership of the electrical workers' union, a crucial component of the strike) were arrested. Police and soldiers were omnipresent. Lacking protection, the vast majority of employees remained on their jobs.

These months also witnessed a growing consolidation and aggressiveness of the right. In September Colonel García and his allies, fearing defections to the opposition, issued a new "order of battle": A number of Majano's followers were removed from command positions and reassigned to desk jobs or foreign military posts. At the same time, U.S. domestic politics accelerated the spiral of violence. Various sympathizers and advisers of the Republican candidate began touring Latin America, assuring military and business circles that a new administration would be more "realistic" than its predecessor. Human rights would be put on the back burner; the United States would no longer try to change the world in its own image. Only Cuba would be treated as the "enemy." In the aftermath of the November elections, the Reagan transition team proposed a curb on

State Department "social reformers." Among the most
prominent targets of the purge: Robert White and
Lawrence Pezzullo, ambassadors to El Salvador and
Nicaragua, respectively.

The consequences were predictable: The right,
anticipating that a Reagan government would tolerate
increasing repression against the left, stepped up the
terror. The number of mutilated bodies found along the
roadway rose to twenty a day. In October, Maria
Magdalena Henriques, a spokesperson for the Salvadoran
Human Rights Commission, was kidnapped and killed; witnesses testified that two uniformed policemen had been
involved. Even more blatant, in late November, some 200
troops surrounded the Externado San Jose High School,
where five leaders of the Democratic Revolutionary Front
were preparing a press conference. Heavily armed
plainclothesmen were allowed to enter the grounds. The
opposition leaders, including FDR President Enrique
Alvarez, were seized. The next day, their mutilated
bodies were found on the outskirts of the capital.

It is difficult to overstate the psychological
impact of this deed on the remaining leaders of the FDR.
When, sixteen months later, they would decline to take
part in U.S.-sponsored elections for a Constituent
Assembly, Washington would charge that this was just one
more sign of their lack of popular support: They refused
to participate because they knew they could not win.
This claim was, of course, disingenuous. The truth was
that no opposition politician dared campaign for fear of
a similar fate.

But worse was still to come. On December 2, four
American churchwomen were murdered under circumstances
that strongly suggested the involvement of the National
Guard. From Washington's perspective, this was a far
more serious development: It was one thing for
Salvadoran nationals to be murdered; quite another when
the victims were U.S. citizens. The killings threatened
to destroy what public and congressional support existed
for administration policy. According to the State
Department's rationale, the United States was backing a
moderate government against the attacks of the extreme
right and extreme left. Now, it seemed, the regime's
security forces and the right were organically linked.
Worse, members of the Salvadoran high command might be
implicated. Though a hurried investigation headed by
Assistant Secretary of State William Bowdler and former
Under Secretary of State William Rodgers found no
evidence of such involvement, doubts remained. At a
minimum, there was high-level complicity in the cover-up
that followed.

(As of this writing, three years later, no one has
been brought to trial, much less convicted, though the
Salvadoran government has long had five guardsmen

suspected of the killings in custody. Even if they are
eventually brought to justice, the suspicion will remain
that they were mere hirelings. No full investigation
into the possible involvement of senior officers and
officials was ever conducted. When the victims' families
attempted to engage a Salvadoran lawyer to press for such
an inquiry, they were told that anything beyond the case
of the five would be dangerous. Moreover, in August
1982, Julio Valle Espinosa, a former National Guard
private who had witnessed the kidnapping, testified that
he had been told by the sergeant in charge that the
abduction had been ordered by superiors.)[61]

Clearly, something had to be done, and fast, to
salvage the regime's image. There consequently followed
another reorganization: The Christian Democrat, Duarte,
was now elevated to the junta presidency. This was
primarily a symbolic gesture, designed to demonstrate
moderate civilian control. Real power lay elsewhere.
The tip-off came with (1) the designation of Colonel
Gutierrez, the most conservative member of the junta, as
vice-president and commander-in-chief of the armed forces
and (2) the removal of Majano, advocate of reform and
leftist participation in discussions on a peace settlement. (Majano was subsequently arrested and exiled.)

Meanwhile, rumors of a right-wing golpe proliferated. Roberto D'Aubuisson, who had been moving
stealthily back and forth between Guatemala and Salvador
since his release from custody the previous spring, now
suddenly resurfaced, lending credence to suspicions that
his anti-government activities enjoyed at least the tacit
backing of the military. At the same time, Cleto
DiGiovanni, a former CIA officer and supporter of the
U.S. president-elect, also appeared, brandishing a
purported message from the Reagan transition team that
its public opposition to a seizure of power should be
disregarded. (He was promptly disowned by Reagan
spokesmen.) Relations between the transition team and
Ambassador White now deteriorated sharply, with the
latter accusing the Reaganauts of undermining his
authority and striking a "heavy blow" at those seeking a
moderate solution to the crisis.

But the threat from the right was only the most
immediate of White's problems. Even more ominous, the
left had managed to restore at least temporary unity and
was rapidly preparing for a military showdown. In
November, the five guerrilla organizations (including the
FARN, which rejoined the DRU) formed a single command,
the Farabundo Marti National Liberation Front (FMLN).
The Nicaraguan arms connection was resumed; the flow of
weapons now reached unprecedented proportions, severely
straining the capacity of the guerrillas to absorb these
materials. The State Department's "White Paper" would
later charge that some 200 tons of arms were delivered in

the weeks prior to the January Offensive. Whatever be the truth of the numbers--and they are open to serious debate--it is clear that substantial foreign assistance was essential if the rebels were to be victorious in the short run. No one knew how strong the insurgents were in terms of popular support or weaponry. Or whether the Salvadoran military could withstand their assault. Given these uncertainties and the high stakes involved, Washington prepared for the worst.

Had there been any doubts that human rights were a secondary concern in the administration's list of priorities, they were now dispelled. On December 4, following the murder of the four churchwomen, U.S. economic and military aid had been suspended. Nine days later, after the reorganization of the junta and the elevation of Duarte, economic assistance was resumed. Loans amounting to $65.5 million were granted, bringing U.S. aid for 1980 to $150 million. This was the beginning of a process that not even the January 5th murder of two American land reform advisers, Michael Hammer and Mark Pearlman, and the president of the Salvadoran Institute of Agrarian Transformation, Jose Rodolfo Viera, could reverse. On January 14, four days after the start of the guerrillas' "Final Offensive," the Carter administration resumed FY 1981 military assistance--$5 million in Foreign Military Sales credits and $420,000 in Training Funds. On January 17, special executive powers were invoked to send $5 million in emergency lethal military aid. The next day, an additional $5 million in military assistance, including three advisory teams, was approved.

(In October 1982, two former corporals confessed to having killed Hammer, Pearlman, and Viera on the orders of two well-connected military officers and an influential businessman. No matter. Two Salvadoran judges ruled that there was "insufficient evidence" to bring one of the officers to trial. By this time, the two other principals had disappeared. Significantly, these rulings occurred after Roberto D'Aubuisson, by this time president of the Constituent Assembly, had given a public testimony to the officers on national television.)

As for the long-awaited guerrilla offensive, it turned out to be not so "final" after all. There was considerable self-deception on all sides. Reports of an imminent assault had been circulating for weeks, blowing hopes, fears, and expectations out of all proportion to reality. This was no replay of Nicaragua. The Sandinistas had had two years to build their forces for the general insurrection; the Salvadoran insurgents were trying to achieve the same results in less than half that time. In their rush to present the incoming Reagan administration with a fait accompli, they failed to appreciate the extent to which the government repression and their own economic sabotage had eroded their popular

support. To make matters worse, the FMLN was plagued by
organizational and communications problems. In San
Salvador the final call for a general strike, made on a
commandeered radio several days before the offensive,
went largely unheard. Key unions remained weakened by
arrests; lack of protection left strikers exposed to
military retaliation. (Even so, on January 15, about
half the shops in the capital closed, and some 20,000
government workers walked off their jobs.) Finally, in
spite of the influx of arms from the communist countries
and the international black market, the guerrillas
remained at a serious weapons disadvantage. Battlefield
reports suggested widespread shortages and a mixture of
modern and obsolete arms.[62]

In perspective, the January Offensive, though an
embarrassing political defeat for the FMLN-FDR, was no
worse than a military stalemate. The insurgents gained
valuable experience. They learned to coordinate their
activities on a nationwide basis and established credibility as a military force. Relatively few casualties
were suffered. And the army was forced to withdraw from
large areas of the countryside in order to protect the
cities. The significance of this last factor would
become apparent only with time, as the guerrillas faded
into their rural strongholds to rest, regroup, and
rethink their situation, only to appear again some months
later with a new and more formidable strategy.

THE REAGAN ADMINISTRATION AND EL SALVADOR: ON THE
STRATEGY OF CONFLICT AND THE POLITICS OF
COUNTERPRODUCTIVITY

The quintessence of incompetence lies not in the
inability to effectuate one's intentions (ineffectuality,
after all, is often a product of forces beyond our
control), but rather in having an effect that is
precisely the opposite of what is intended and required
by one's interests and values. Counterproductivity,
rather than impotence, is the cardinal sin in foreign
policy.

In January 1981, a new administration came into
power in Washington, armed with a preconceived doctrine
that defined the Salvadoran problem primarily in Cold War
military terms and called for Cold War military solutions. A State Department "White Paper" was soon
released, charging that the crisis was a "textbook case
of indirect armed aggression by the communist powers
through Cuba." Secretary of State Alexander Haig claimed
that the Soviets had a "hit list" in Central America.
His deputy, William Clark, announced that the United
States would "go to the source" with whatever means were
necessary to stop the arms flow to the guerrillas.

Underlying this new policy was a belief that the world--
especially the communist world--needed to be sent a clear
and forceful message: No longer would American policy be
characterized by vacillation and weakness; rather,
resolution and strength would be the hallmark of the
Reagan government.

El Salvador provided a convenient opportunity to
dramatize this change. Here was a "splendid little war"
where the line could be drawn against communist
aggression at minimum risk or cost. The guerrillas were
already on the run. Accordingly, repeated opposition
overtures for a dialogue to end the violence would be
ignored. Military and economic aid would be stepped up
dramatically in an effort to apply the coup de grace.
Plans were now announced to provide $25 million in new
military aid, along with $63 million in economic
assistance and fifty-six advisers to train the Salvadoran
armed forces. During the first four months of 1981, the
junta would be sent more than twice as much weaponry as
the communist nations had allegedly supplied the rebels
in the months prior to the January Offensive. Privately,
administration sources revealed that the game plan was to
win a military victory in sixty to ninety days.[63]

The human capacity for self-deception is virtually
infinite. The gross overestimates of guerrilla strength
that had prevailed during the previous autumn were now
replaced by gross underestimates--in spite of Pentagon
warnings that the Salvadoran Army had no hope of winning
with the resources at hand. (Military theorists have
long held that a conventional army and police must out-
number an insurgent force by roughly ten to one because
the latter have the advantage of surprise. At the time,
the Salvadoran military numbered about 17,000 men,
including administrative and support elements, a ratio of
only a little more than four to one over the estimated
4,000 main force guerrillas.) The upshot would be a
strategy of conflict that would prolong the bloodshed,
undermine the land reform and its Christian Democratic
sponsors, strengthen the neanderthal right, and place
U.S. policy hostage to forces beyond its control--forces
that had no interest in the peaceful resolution of the
fighting; forces, indeed, that would seek its expansion,
along with an attendant intensification of American
involvement.

In retrospect, the early months of the Reagan
administration witnessed a golden opportunity lost. The
repulsion of the January Offensive had placed the U.S.
and Salvadoran governments in what would prove to be a
rare position of bargaining strength vis-a-vis the
guerrillas. Washington's new hard line suggested that
the military advantage would be pressed not only in El
Salvador, but against Nicaragua and Cuba as well. And
this intimidation clearly had an impact. No longer could

the insurgents and their foreign sponsors delude themselves into believing that victory was just around the
corner. The military now had the initiative; the future
was highly uncertain. At best, the struggle would be
long and hard. At worst, it would end in defeat. Now,
moreover, both Castro and the Sandinistas had to worry
about the very real possibility that the Reagan administration might wage war on them. Clearly, the situation
was getting out of control; a reevaluation of policy was
in order. Accordingly, arms shipments to the Salvadoran
insurgents were sharply curtailed, as both Cuba and
Nicaragua signalled their interest in improving relations
with the United States.

These overtures did not go unnoticed, but they were
ignored nevertheless.[64] The administration had the bit
between its teeth, and it was not about to let go.

The most immediate consequence was the strengthening
of the Salvadoran right to the detriment of the center.
As early as the previous September, Jose Napoleon Duarte
and the Christian Democrats had indicated their
willingness to enter into a dialogue with the opposition.
Indeed, in February, Duarte, now president of the junta,
had been prepared to fly to Bonn to meet Guillermo Ungo,
the new president of the Democratic Revolutionary Front,
when the trip had to be cancelled because of an attempted
golpe. By this time, the right had become convinced that
the political tide was decisively in its favor and the
time was ripe to put the hapless "civilian-military"
junta out of its misery. Accordingly, in early March,
the peripatetic Major D'Aubuisson surfaced once again,
accusing Duarte of preparing to negotiate with the left
and calling for the replacement of the government by a
"totally military" regime. D'Aubuisson, it seems, had
met the previous year with two members of the Reagan
transition team, who had left him with the impression
that the administration would support such a move. He
now proceeded to invoke their authority, to the acute
embarrassment of the principals concerned.[65]

The right did not get its way. Cognizant of the
political difficulties such a move would create in the
United States, the Reagan administration rallied to the
support of the junta. The months to come witnessed a
concerted American effort to reconcile the Christian
Democrats and the private sector. But to little avail.
These elements were fundamentally incompatible. Though
the Salvadoran bourgeoisie was somewhat less conservative
and certainly more modernization-oriented than the
traditional oligarchs, it was no less steadfast in its
hatred of Duarte. What followed instead amounted to a
creeping subterranean coup. The private sector demanded
that the government change its economic policies, which,
it claimed, had plunged the country into ruin. (The GNP
declined 9.5 percent in 1981; capital flight may have

been as much as $2 billion for the two-year period
beginning October 1979.)[66] The Christian Democratic
ideology of "communitarianism" was denounced as a "steely
dictatorship only comparable to Marxist tyranny. . . ."[67]
The goal was nothing less than the replacement of the
Christian Democrats in the junta by representatives of
the private sector and the rollback of the "unrealistic"
agrarian and banking reforms. By July, Duarte was
accusing the bourgeoisie of being a greater threat than
the guerrillas: "The private sector is in its final
offensive to overthrow the government," he warned.[68]
Under growing pressure from business, the military, and
the Reagan administration, he retreated from his
previously announced readiness to engage in a dialogue
with the FDR, abandoned all plans to implement Phase Two
of the land reform, and extended the freeze on wages.

The full extent of this erosion did not become clear
for some months. In December, the Union Comunal
Salvadorena (UCS), the largest peasant organization in
the country and a strong supporter of agrarian reform,
issued a report warning that the reform was in "immediate
and imminent danger" of collapse due to military-backed
terror, illegal peasant evictions, and a slow,
"frequently hostile" bureaucracy. More specifically, it
was charged that at least ninety officials of campesino
organizations and a "large number" of beneficiaries had
died in 1981 "at the hands of ex-landlords and their
allies, who are often members of the local security
forces." In addition, thousands of former sharecroppers
and tenant farmers had been forcibly evicted from their
farms, in most cases "with the assistance of members of
the military forces," so that they could not claim
ownership documents. Only about 15,000 families eligible
for individual ownership had been granted provisional
titles to their land. No permanent titles had been
granted to individuals, and only three of the more than
300 peasant cooperatives formed on the confiscated large
estates had received titles.[69] Subsequently, a study by
the University of Central America estimated that less
than half of the peasants who were supposed to become
cooperative members had done so.[70]

These were not, of course, the first indications
that something had gone terribly wrong with the reform.
Although Phase One, which set up cooperatives on the
large estates, had been carried out, only about 15
percent of the country's farmland and an even smaller
percentage of the rural populace had been affected.
Moreover, the program had been accompanied by extensive
corruption. Tens of millions of U.S. dollars had been
poured into the Salvadoran Institute of Agrarian
Transformation without any serious effort to audit the
flow. (AID received information only through government
meetings and written reports; no field work of its own

was conducted because of security conditions.) The consequence, according to the Salvadoran Court of Accounts, was "doubtful investments, exaggerated expenses, others improper, some laughable, and others not legally admissible from an accounting point of view."[71] Meanwhile, out in the field, many cooperatives were being forced to pay tribute to local military commanders, mostly in areas in which there was no serious guerrilla threat. Technical aid, credits, and fertilizer were sparse. All too frequently, illiterate peasants were simply left on their own to make out as best they could. The result was predictable: While some cooperatives prospered, others were plagued by disorganization, inefficiency, and declining production. According to an unpublished Salvadoran government report, about one-fifth of the cooperatives had been abandoned altogether.[72]

Nor was this the most serious problem. In fact, the reform had been crippled almost from the very beginning by the indefinite suspension of Phase Two, the very heart of the program, which would have turned medium-sized farms--including most of the valuable coffee lands--into cooperatives. (Among other things, many of these proper- ties are owned by members of the military and their friends.) Furthermore, those smallholders who had received provisional titles in Phase Three (the "Land to the Tiller" program)--only about 12 percent of the 125,000 alleged potential beneficiaries[73]--had achieved dubious gains, at best. Most of these farms were economically marginal--too small, their lands too infer- tile from perennial overwork, to provide more than a bare subsistence living. Most, indeed, could not do even that.

Given all this, it was not surprising that many Salvadorans considered the reform a "cruel hoax intended to buy time and divert international attention from the counterinsurgency campaigns terrorizing the population."[74] It was no secret that many military officers had accepted these measures only grudgingly, under U.S. pressure, as a temporary tactical device designed to alleviate popular discontent, and still hoped that they could be reversed once the insurgency was under control.

The erosion of the reform had predictable consequen- ces. Whereas the initial promise and reality of redistribution had significantly undercut peasant support for the guerrillas, the failure to continue the process led to increasing frustration, disappointment, and cyni- cism. This was no small part of the reason why the military was unable to follow up its success in repelling the January offensive (1981) with a sustained and effec- tive counterinsurgency campaign--in spite of the massive influx of U.S. aid. During spring and early summer, the guerrillas recuperated, reorganized, and reevaluated

their situation in remote and relatively secure base
areas. In late July, they struck again.

In August 1981, FMLN forces overran the National
Guard garrison in Perquin, capturing and holding the town
for ten days before withdrawing with minimum losses.
This was the beginning of a new offensive and a new
strategy. Insurrection would now be replaced by prolonged popular war. The objective was to gradually wear
down the enemy through hit-and-run guerrilla operations.
Through pin-prick attacks against provincial towns and
lightning forays on army outposts, the insurgents would
seek to spread government forces thin, the better to pick
them apart. Meanwhile, increasingly ambitious and
sophisticated sabotage would further undermine an already
desperately sick economy, intensifying hardships and
discontent and demonstrating the regime's inability to
maintain order and govern effectively. The destruction
of bridges (especially the strategic Puente de Oro),
buses, power generators, electric pylons, and telephone
poles played havoc with the communications system,
blacking out three-fourths of the country for weeks at a
time and progressively isolating the eastern third from
the rest.

In turn, repeated government offensives floundered.
Between May and December, the military averaged three
campaigns a month, committing 1,500 to 4,500 troops in
each drive. Eight times the army tried to dislodge the
insurgents from the Guazapa Volcano. Five operations
each were launched in Chalatenango and Morazan, four
against the Chinchontepec Volcano in San Vicente, and
three in the Cerros de San Pedro.[75] By the turn of the
year, few, if any, of the government's military objectives had been achieved. Serious demoralization had set
in. Following a daring FMLN commando raid on Ilopango
airport in January 1982, which resulted in the destruction or severe damage of eighteen aircraft, a number of
soldiers were arrested for complicity in the sabotage.
Meanwhile, human rights abuses were increasingly
spreading from the security forces to the regular army.
Some of these were on a massive scale: Thus, in
December, some 900 civilians, including women and
children, were taken from their homes in and around the
village of El Mozote and killed by government troops
during a sweep through Morazan. According to the
Catholic Church's legal aid office, civilian deaths in
1981 had risen to 13,353 from 8,062 the previous year;
the vast majority were victims of the army, security
forces, and allied death squads.[76]

ON STRATEGY: ESCALATION AND THE "DANCE OF CERTIFICATION"

If at first you don't succeed, escalate.
By the end of 1981, the situation in El Salvador had
deteriorated on all fronts. The attempts of Jose
Napoleon Duarte to establish an effective, moderate,
civilian influence in the government had been thwarted.
The land reform was stalled and increasingly in disarray.
The balance of power between guerrillas and army was
shifting: The insurgents were consistently frustrating
the latter's offensives and had begun to seize the
initiative. In turn, the military was increasingly
plagued by demoralization, corruption, and internal
divisiveness. In the words of Lieutenant General Wallace
Nutting, head of the U.S. Southern Command, the situation
was a "stalemate" and "in that kind of war, if you're not
winning, you're losing."[77]
Little of this could be laid at the door of the
Sandinistas or Cubans. Indeed, the Honduran Army, though
controlling all border crossings from Nicaragua and
patrolling the border with El Salvador, had not intercepted a single major arms shipment from Nicaragua to
Salvador since January 1981. Although some U.S. officials argued that weapons were being dropped into
guerrilla-held zones by aircraft or shipped in small
boats across the Gulf of Fonseca, this was mostly
speculation; hard evidence was conspicuously lacking.
(Indeed, the insurgents themselves continued to complain
of arms shortages.)[78] Nevertheless, throughout the fall
and winter of 1981-82, the Reagan administration
assiduously beat the drums in an effort to resurrect the
specter of Cuban/Nicaraguan aggression. Spokesmen warned
that the "hour was late"; Nicaragua was drifting toward
totalitarianism, had become a "platform for intervention," and was engaged in a Cuban/Soviet-sponsored
military buildup that posed a grave threat to the other
countries in the region. Testifying before the House
Foreign Affairs Committee, Secretary Haig refused to rule
out a U.S. attempt to destabilize or overthrow the
Sandinista government.
People tend to see what they are predisposed to see,
and the Reagan administration is no exception. Instead
of reevaluating dubious assumptions and failing policies,
it attempted to force-fit regional realities into preconceived stereotypes. Characteristically, it upped the
ante. Thus, in December, a new "White Paper" ("Cuba's
Renewed Support for Violence in the Hemisphere") was
issued, notably lacking in the kind of documentary

evidence that had lent authenticity to its predecessor.
Congress was informed that some 1,600 Salvadoran soldiers
would soon begin training at U.S. military bases.
Following the FMLN assault on Ilopango airport, the
administration announced that the regime would be sent an
additional $55 million in emergency military assistance,
no congressional approval required. This was the second
time within a year that the president had invoked special
executive authority on such matters, bringing total
emergency aid to $75 million since the previous March.

The crucial issue, however, concerned the matter of
"certification." Congress had stipulated that military
aid (at least, that over which legislative approval was
required) could be continued only after the president had
vouched that the Salvadoran regime had met certain
conditions, namely: (1) increased respect for human
rights; (2) greater civilian control over the armed
forces; (3) continued progress on the economic reforms,
especially land reform; (4) a commitment to hold free
elections; (5) progress in investigating the deaths of
the six U.S. citizens assassinated in December 1980-
January 1981; and (6) a willingness to enter into
discussions with the major parties in the conflict.
Certification would be required twice a year; it would
affect not only the $26 million that had been approved
under the FY 1982 foreign aid bill, but subsequent
requests as well. (For FY 1983, the administration was
asking for another $61.3 million in military aid.)

This requirement had to be countered if U.S.
policies were to have any chance of success. And so on
January 28, 1982, the president duly issued a statement
of certification--notwithstanding the meager evidence in
support of the assumption of progress on any of the
issues in question, with the exception of the commitment
to free elections. Thus, for instance, the claim that
the human rights situation had improved was disputed by
no lesser authorities than Amnesty International, the UN
Human Rights Commission, the American Civil Liberties
Union, and the Salvadoran Catholic Church. The official
U.S. response was extraordinary in its disingenuousness:
According to the U.S. Embassy in San Salvador, only 5,407
civilians had been killed in 1981. Critics were quick to
note that this figure was based on reports in local
newspapers, whose coverage was limited almost entirely to
deaths in the capital and other cities. Killings in
remote rural areas, constituting the majority of deaths
in recent months, usually went unreported or were
reported only to Salvadoran human rights groups. By the
same token, the embassy's attempts to attribute civilian
deaths to the guerrillas or the government were severely
distorted by its practice of excluding the victims of
government military action, while including those from
comparable guerrilla attacks (which were treated as acts

of "terrorism" rather than combat). As one embassy
official candidly admitted, these figures represented
"only a tiny portion of the people killed in El
Salvador."[79] Clearly, the administration was willing to
certify anything necessary to get what it wanted.

Thus was initiated a semi-annual "dance of
certification." Every six months, the president would
vouch that there had been progress on the relevant
issues. On some matters, this could be done in good
faith; on others, it could not. Civilian deaths did
decline significantly in 1982-83, though this seemed more
a consequence of deteriorating military morale than
increased civilian control and respect for human rights.
(As morale declined, the army surrendered the initiative
to the insurgents. There were fewer military offensives,
hence fewer casualties.) Meanwhile, the land reform
would experience continued stagnation and erosion. At
certification time, there would be a flurry of activity
as provisional titles were granted to selected peasants
at highly publicized ceremonies. But this hardly made up
for the continuing displacement and intimidation of
potential Phase Three beneficiaries. As for the investigation and prosecution of the killers of the American
churchwomen and land reform advisers, suffice it to say
that the Salvadoran authorities continued to move at a
glacial pace. Intimidation, procrastination, and evasion
remained the hallmarks of Salvadoran "justice."

Then there was the question of discussions with the
opposition. Congressional and international pressures on
the administration to seek a political solution to the
Salvadoran crisis were growing fast. During the previous
August, Mexico and France had issued a joint declaration
recognizing the FMLN-FDR as "a representative political
force" that must be included in any negotiations to end
the fighting. In October, the opposition issued a "peace
proposal" calling for negotiations with an open agenda
and no preconditions. This was followed in January 1982
by a letter from the guerrilla commanders to President
Reagan calling for a negotiated end to the war. In
response, the administration moved to co-opt "cut-and-run
negotiation strategies by demonstrating a reasonable but
firm approach to negotiations and compromise on our
terms." The object was to "avoid congressionally mandated solutions, which would work against our interests,"
while isolating the Mexicans and European Social
Democrats, mobilizing regional allies through such structures as the Central American Democratic Community
(created in January 1982), and increasing the pressure on
the Cubans and Nicaraguans.[80]

In short, the function of the administration's
"political solution" was to avoid a negotiated settlement. This was an integral part of the strategy of
conflict, the hidden dimensions of which would now be

234

felt full-force by the Sandinistas. In March 1981, the
United States had begun supporting right-wing rebels
against the Nicaraguan regime. Toward the end of the
year, President Reagan approved a $19.9-million CIA
proposal to organize and finance a 500-man paramilitary
force to harass the Nicaraguan regime from bases in
Honduras. (Another group of 1,000 men was to be trained
by Argentine advisers.) Although the "official" goals of
the operation were limited to sabotaging the economy,
cutting the supply line to the Salvadoran guerrillas,
attacking the Cubans and their "infrastructure," and
otherwise keeping the Sandinista government off-balance
and on edge, there was a more ambitious "unofficial"
objective--to soften up the regime for the full-scale
guerrilla war to come. More specifically, it was hoped
that the Sandinistas could be provoked into further
repression of the democratic opposition, thus driving the
latter into the arms of the counterrevolution. If that
happened, as one U.S. official told Newsweek, the
Nicaraguan government would "fall like a house of cards
in a wind."81

     Over the next year and a half, the U.S. role would
steadily increase. The American ambassador to Honduras,
John Negroponte, would come to exercise proconsular
authority as counterrevolutionary activities grew to
involve over 10,000 Nicaraguan insurgents. Military and
economic aid would be poured into Honduras, freeing the
Honduran Army to pass on older equipment to the contras.
The CIA station would be doubled to include some fifty
personnel and supplemented by dozens of operatives,
including retired U.S. military and intelligence
officers. By spring 1983, the administration would be
asking Congress for $80 million (ostensibly to stop the
flow of arms to the Salvadoran guerrillas) to escalate
the destabilization effort. In the process, the operation grew increasingly out of control, bringing Honduras
and Nicaragua to the brink of war and endangering the
stability of the former.

ON STRATEGY: THE ELECTIONS

     In the winter of 1982, however, the operation was
still in its preliminary stages, still semi-secret and
still overshadowed by what was being publicly presented
as the centerpiece of U.S. policy: the March 28th
Salvadoran elections for a Constituent Assembly. Here
was the administration's answer to the "cut-and-run"
political solutions of its critics. Elections would lend
sorely needed legitimacy to the Salvadoran government,
strengthening the Christian Democratic center and
satisfying the U.S. Congress that progress was being made
and the regime humanized. They would not, of course, end

the fighting, but then that was not their purpose.
Rather, this was an exercise in gamesmanship. The
FMLN-FDR would be placed in a no-win situation. In
effect, the Reagan administration was reversing the
"Godfather's" dictum by making the guerrillas an offer
they could not possibly accept: All they had to do to
participate in the balloting was lay down their weapons
(in effect, surrender). If they refused, the onus for
continuing the fighting would be on them. The administration would have demonstrated its willingness to seek a
"political solution," thus disarming the critics and
strengthening its position in the ongoing struggle to
obtain the funding necessary to continue--and eventually
win--the war.

If, on the other hand, the politicians of the FDR
decided to participate, they would be playing in a game
in which the cards were stacked against them. President
Duarte himself admitted that their safety could not be
guaranteed. The previous March, the armed forces had
published a list of over 130 "traitors" in La Prensa
Grafica, including the top leaders of the FMLN-FDR.
Coming in the aftermath of the November 1980 assassination of five FDR leaders, this amounted to a "death
list." Under such circumstances, participation in the
elections was widely held to be suicidal. The FDR
campaign would have to be conducted via television. With
the audience thus limited, the opposition's chances of
winning would be minimal. Having lured the FDR civilians
away from the FMLN commanders, moreover, Washington could
continue the war against the insurgents from a position
of enhanced political strength. The name of the game was
divide and conquer.

The opposition, of course, did not participate. The
elections were held on schedule. Initial reports
suggested they were an overwhelming success. The
enthusiasm of the Salvadoran public took everyone by
surprise. Two days before the vote, U.S. Ambassador
Deane Hinton told journalists that he would consider a
turnout of 600,000 a success. The president of the
Central Elections Council, Jorge Bustamente, was somewhat
more optimistic, anticipating a turnout of 800,000
maximum. The actual number of ballots cast, as officially recorded, was 1,551,680. Everywhere the media
reported long lines of people waiting to vote. The State
Department was jubilant: The elections were a major
achievement in the development of Salvadoran democracy;
the people had decisively rejected the guerrillas; the
United States was on the right course.

Gradually, however, doubts began to arise. A few
ungenerous scribes noted that the number of recorded
votes exceeded the State Department's own estimate of the
number of eligible voters (1.45 million). One hundred
seven percent of the electorate, evidently, had cast

ballots.[82] Others wondered about the lack of polling
places. San Salvador, with a voting age population of
nearly half a million, had only thirteen places to vote.
In Santa Ana, the second largest city, there were nine;
in San Miguel, the third largest, four. Here, at least,
was a partial explanation for the long lines.

There were still other questions: This writer has
been told stories of chemicals being smuggled into the
country to eradicate the indelible ink marks affixed to
voters' thumbs to prevent double-voting. Also reported
were a number of irregularities in the vote tabulation,
most of which were subsequently explained by the
authorities.[83]

But the most sensational charges came from the
Central American University's Center for Documentation
and Information, which calculated that no more than
1,281,600 votes could have been cast (given 4,272 polling
stations, uninterrupted voting for ten hours per station,
and two minutes voting time per person). The actual
number of voters, it claimed, was somewhere between
600,000 and 800,000. There had apparently been a pact
between the United States, the participating political
parties, and the military high command to double the vote
to "prove" that the Salvadoran people were against the
guerrillas. To maintain unity between the conspirators,
the parties received the same percentage of the inflated
vote that they had won at the polls.

Several points must be made about all this. First,
just as the Reagan administration and the Salvadoran
government had a vested interest in demonstrating the
authenticity of the elections, the left had an interest,
both political and psychological, in discrediting them.
No tangible evidence of the kind of conspiracy suggested
by the university was ever uncovered. It seems improbable that fraud of this magnitude, involving so many
mutually suspicious and antagonistic conspirators, could
have been carried out, much less kept secret. This is
especially true in light of the extraordinary publicity
attending these proceedings. In the words of one writer:
"The fact is that hundreds of international observers and
press as well as poll workers and party observers watched
the elections, received tallies from the precincts, and
verified the integrity of the elections. No one has
documented any substantial charge of fraud."[84]

Nor can one have much confidence in the university's
voting estimates. Such calculations are no better than
the assumptions underlying them, and in this case those
assumptions were extremely dubious. There is no reliable
information, for instance, on the average time it took
voters to cast their ballots. It may well have taken
less than two minutes. (The Central Elections Commission
estimated ninety seconds per vote, and its president,
Bustamente, took only 37 seconds--though granted his

voting table was exceptionally well organized.) Moreover,
even if there were reliable information, such calculations overlook the fact that voting was an assembly-line
process. Usually, several people were simultaneously
engaged at various stages from the initial presentation
of their cedulas (identification cards) to the final
acquisition of indelible ink marks after voting. Within
the hypothesized two minute periods two, three, or even
four people may have been able to complete the process.
Since the university researchers were perfectly aware of
this, one is tempted to dismiss their study as a politically motivated hatchet job.

     As to the number of eligible voters, it must be
stressed that accurate information was simply not
available. Nobody really knows what the population of El
Salvador is,[85] what percentage is eighteen years of age
or older (and thus eligible to vote), how many have left
the country or lost their identity cards. The State
Department's estimate of 1.45 million eligibles was a
reasonable one, but it would have been equally reasonable
to have estimated 2 million or more. Given this kind of
range, 1.55 million votes is not implausible. (One must
remember that in El Salvador voting is mandatory.)
Finally, although rumors of fraud were common before,
during, and after the elections, supporting evidence was
scant. El Salvador's long history of electoral corruption has conditioned many to automatically assume the
worst. People tend to believe what they are predisposed
to believe, regardless of the evidence--or the lack of
it.

     In short, although some irregularities did occur,
these seem to have been relatively minor. The crucial
issue had less to do with the integrity of the vote than
with its significance. Why did so many people
participate? Was this a repudiation of the opposition,
as the State Department claimed?

     Clearly, people voted for a variety of reasons.
Some believed in the parties, personalities, and programs
they were voting for. Both the Christian Democrats and
the Party of National Conciliation had traditional
constituencies, formed over the years, that they could
count on. In contrast, the newly created (November 1981)
Nationalist Republican Alliance (ARENA) found a ready-
made power base in the most reactionary sectors of
Salvadoran society. ARENA's leader, Roberto D'Aubuisson,
was easily the most dynamic campaigner, promising to
unleash the military and end the war within a matter of
months. To many war-weary Salvadorans, he seemed the
proverbial "hero on a white horse," an enormously
appealing, even charismatic, personality.

     But if many voted for particular parties or leaders,
others voted against them. Protest votes were common,
especially against the Christian Democrats, who were

blamed for the continuing deterioration of the economy
and their inability to end the bloodshed. Nor was
participation always entirely voluntary. I have talked
to numerous Salvadorans who voted because they were
afraid not to. The election law required the authorities
to "demand evidence" that people had voted during the ten
days following the balloting. Anyone unable to provide
such proof was to be reported to the town mayor. Given
the intense official effort to get out the vote and the
tendency of the authorities to view abstention as a vote
for the guerrillas, participation was often considered
the safest course of action--a form of life insurance, if
you will. In rural areas, where the old landlord/
National Guard/ORDEN alliance had traditionally delivered
the peasant vote to the official party, coercion was not
uncommon.[86]

Still, for all this, it seems clear that the vast
majority of voters participated voluntarily and with
considerable enthusiasm. The ballot box was a unique
opportunity to express their own views, so neglected in
the past, with regard to the issue that mattered most.
This issue was, above all, a vote for peace, a plea to
both sides to resolve their differences through means
other than those employed over the previous two years.

Was it also a vote against the left? Yes--and no.
It was certainly a vote against the violence of the
left--and right. At the same time, it is impossible to
predict with certainty how the electorate would have
voted had the opposition decided to participate. There
is reason to believe that the left could have mustered a
substantial minority--perhaps 25-30 percent--from those
who abstained, defaced their ballots, or voted for other
parties, had it participated and been given the opportunity to campaign freely. To a certain extent, the
elections were an optical illusion. What was an initial
defeat for the opposition might still be turned into a
center-left victory, if the FMLN-FDR is flexible enough
to consider a future coalition with the Christian
Democrats (and vice versa).

In the short run, however, the elections were a
major setback for the left. Not only did they
demonstrate a lack of popular support, but they also
brought out all the old tendencies toward disunity,
confusion, and triunfalismo (triumphalism). Four of the
guerrilla groups felt that the time was ripe to launch
popular uprisings and a mass insurrection. The Popular
Liberation Forces, the largest of the insurgent organizations, disagreed, arguing that the FMLN-FDR was still far
too weak in the cities for such a strategy to succeed.
At the same time, Cuba and Nicaragua, increasingly
concerned that the Reagan administration would blame them
for any disruption of the elections and would retaliate,
urged restraint. The upshot was a confused and poorly

coordinated offensive: In some parts of the country, there were isolated and ineffective attempts to disrupt the balloting; in others, there was no effort at all; in still others, guerrilla attacks made voting impossible. In effect, the FMLN created just enough trouble to provide the government with maximum propaganda mileage (the image of hundreds of thousands of Salvadorans "risking their lives" to vote was enormously effective), but not nearly enough to prevent the elections from being held.

Yet, in the final analysis, the elections, though a tremendous tactical success for the Reagan administration, were a two-edged sword. It had been Washington's intention to strengthen the Christian Democratic center. Ironically, precisely the opposite occurred. In a field of six parties, ranging from the center to the neanderthal right of the political spectrum, the Christian Democrats found themselves isolated. Though polling more votes than any other party, they fell well short of a majority. The clear winners were the parties of the right. This was still another step in the process of derechizacion--the movement to the right--that had begun in reaction to the October 1979 golpe and the reforms and that had been accelerated by the advent of the Reagan administration. It was an integral part of the cyclical pattern of Salvadoran politics. It did not yet represent a full restoration of "reactionary despotism." Nevertheless, the major winner was none other than that quintessential "man on horseback" Roberto D'Aubuisson-- founder of death squads and assassin of archbishops--and the forces he represented. D'Aubuisson now became president of the newly elected Constituent Assembly. His Nationalist Republican Alliance gained three key economic ministries--agriculture, economy, and foreign trade--as well as public health. Under its supervision, the agrarian reform would now be "perfected." Over the next two months, between 5,000 and 12,000 peasant families would be evicted from their land.[87]

MILITARY DISINTEGRATION AND THE STRUGGLE FOR POWER: THE DECLINE AND FALL OF JOSE GUILLERMO GARCIA

As with the defeat of the January 1981 "final offensive," the success of the March 1982 elections was a high point. Almost everything else for months to come would be downhill.

The neanderthal right did not take power--primarily because the Reagan administration, acutely aware that such an event might raise insurmountable problems with Congress, used the full weight of its influence to effectuate a more "moderate" solution. Here, Defense Minister Garcia proved invaluable. A provisional president had to

TABLE 6.2

Final Vote in the Constituent Assembly Elections

Party	Votes	Percentages	Assembly Seats
Christian Democratic Party	546,218	35.5	24
Nationalist Republican Alliance	402,304	25.8	19
National Conciliation Party	261,153	16.8	14
Democratic Action	100,586	6.6	2
Popular Salvadoran Party	39,504	2.6	1
Popular Orientation Party	12,574	.8	0
Null Ballots	131,498	8.6	
Blank Ballots	51,438	3.3	
Challenged Ballots	6,412		
Totals	1,551,687	100.0	

be elected. Both the United States and the conservatives in the Salvadoran military were determined that the post would not go to D'Aubuisson. On the day the newly elected members of the Constituent Assembly convened their first session, they were unceremoniously buzzed by a military helicopter. Representatives of the National Conciliation Party were threatened with physical violence if they failed to vote for the military's candidate, Alvaro Magana. A golpe was threatened. The U.S. Congress withheld $100 million in economic aid to force Christian Democratic participation in the new government. In spite of the bitter opposition of D'Aubuisson's ARENA, Magana was elected president. Vice-presidencies were parcelled out to the three major parties. Christian Democratic participation in the cabinet was accepted.[88]

This was the beginning of a major struggle over power and policy. In the wake of the elections, the Salvadoran Institute of Agrarian Transformation, which administered Phase One of the agrarian reform, lost about sixty key officials, primarily Christian Democrats, most of whom were replaced by ARENA members. The National Financial Institute for Agricultural Lands, in charge of Phase Three, was largely taken over by ARENA. The reform was now, apparently, to be carried out by elements dedicated to its termination.

Under D'Aubuisson's leadership, the Constituent Assembly quickly moved to emasculate the program. Phase Three, the "Land to the Tiller" plan, was suspended; Phase Two, which would have turned some 1,700 medium-sized farms into cooperatives, was abandoned; constitutional provisions prohibiting further expropriations for land redistribution were reinstated. Encouraged by these measures, landowners, often with the help of local military commanders, began evicting peasants by the thousands. When an outraged U.S. Senate Foreign Relations Committee reacted by threatening to withhold aid if the reform were cancelled or gutted, General Garcia moved to placate the Americans. Though staunchly conservative, the minister of defense was a realist. U.S. aid was critical to the war effort--critical, indeed, to the continued survival of the military itself. It could not be jeopardized. Under intense pressure from the armed forces and the United States, the government backed down. Evictions were halted. With the aid of the military, some peasants regained their lands. In June and July, some 4,000 provisional titles were issued just in time for President Reagan's semi-annual certification to Congress.[89]

But the matter was hardly settled. The months to come witnessed an ongoing conflict between the pro- and anti-reform forces. Cumbersome bureaucratic procedures and delays in transferring titles and compensating owners led to continuing illegal evictions. During the last six months of 1982, 4,791 peasants were thrown off lands they were in the process of acquiring. Yet, simultaneously, some 9,000 new title applications were received, and about 2,300 of the evicted were reinstated by the armed forces. The reform, though seriously crippled, was by no means dead.[90]

This period was marked by growing friction between Garcia and D'Aubuisson. The minister of defense had been instrumental in blocking the ARENA leader's bid to become provisional president. He had aligned the military with the land reform effort. To make matters even worse, in D'Aubuisson's view, he was hampering the war effort by bowing to U.S. human rights pressures. And so beginning in July, "Major Bob" began moving to build support within the armed forces to oust Garcia. An intense confrontation ensued. In August and September, officers close to D'Aubuisson attempted a "legal" golpe but fell well short of the votes needed to depose the defense minister. Subsequently Garcia and his followers, in tandem with the Christian Democrats, struck back, trimming D'Aubuisson's powers in the Constituent Assembly and transferring a number of military commanders whose loyalty was in doubt.

Garcia had weathered the storm, but only for the moment. In October, he took advantage of a lull in the fighting to declare that the guerrillas were in their "death throes." This announcement was, to put it mildly, premature. There followed an opposition offensive, which over the next three months left 1,000 government troops dead or wounded. Army morale, poor all along, plunged to a new low. Worse yet, the FMLN instituted a new prisoner policy: Government troops who surrendered and brought their weapons with them would henceforth not be harmed. From October through January, 446 soldiers did just that, providing the guerrillas with substantial armaments. Corruption, always extensive, now became much worse, as officers took advantage of the flood of U.S. military aid to sell their weapons on the black market. Thus did the Reagan administration become the insurgents' primary arms supplier.

Much of the problem was beyond the control of the minister of defense. It is difficult to win wars when your troops lack training and discipline and do not believe in the cause for which they are fighting. Most Salvadoran soldiers were not volunteers. Rather, this was an army built largely on forced-draft conscription. Peasants and workers were dragooned into service, while their middle- and upper-class counterparts continued their education or went into the family business. Though recruits were supposed to be eighteen years of age, in fact many were younger, sometimes no more than fourteen or fifteen. Nor were their officers well equipped to inspire them to action. Salvadoran commanders were fighting a nine-to-five war, five days a week, against an enemy that was active twenty-four hours a day, every day. Only two department commanders were competent to wage an effective counterinsurgency campaign. The others, lacking will, confidence, and a clear strategy, more often than not went through the motions of commanding, just as their troops went through the motions of fighting. The avoidance of conflict had become a major objective of officers and "grunts" alike. Thus, for instance, when the insurgents seized the city of Berlin in early 1983, 1,000 military and security troops remained in their barracks in Usulatan, only twenty miles away. Meanwhile, some 6,000 of the government's best soldiers were taking a "walk in the sun" in Morazan, to the northeast.

In short, the system was rotten to the core. Garcia did not create the rot, but he had certainly done nothing to eliminate it. Inept commanders had been widely retained and promoted for their loyalty to the minister of defense. As the military situation rapidly deteriorated, however, this luxury could no longer be

fforded. More and more officers came to blame Garcia
for mismanaging the war effort.

In January, 1983, this discontent was galvanized by
yet another confrontation. Lieutenant Colonel Sigifredo
Ochoa Perez, commander of Cabanas, declared himself in
rebellion against the defense minister. This was a far
more serious challenge than that facing D'Aubuisson,
though it was hardly unrelated. Ochoa was one of the few
competent department commanders in El Salvador. Since
assuming his position in the autumn of 1981, he had
brought relative tranquility to that previously troubled
territory. In the process, he had acquired considerable
popular support. His revolt had been triggered by
Garcia's attempt to reassign him to Uruguay as a military
attache. This was a political decision, tantamount to
exile. Ochoa was a friend of D'Aubuisson's (though
somewhat less reactionary). For six days, he defied the
defense minister, denouncing him as corrupt, arbitrary,
and capricious--a "little Hitler"--and demanding his
resignation. It soon became apparent that he was not
alone. The heads of the air force and first infantry
battalion refused to join their fellow commanders in
denouncing the rebellion. The crisis was finally
resolved through a mutual face-saving compromise in which
Ochoa accepted a prestigious position in Washington on
the condition that the defense minister resign within
three months.

Still, Garcia lingered on. On March 18, he offered
his resignation to President Magana, only to have it
refused when the other military commanders declined to
take a clear stand on the issue. Magana, who was
beholden to Garcia for his own position, was still under
the impression that the Americans favored the defense
minister because of his support for the land reform and
other issues dear to the heart of the U.S. Embassy. By
this time, however, even the Reagan administration had
had enough. As the military situation continued its
downward spiral, Washington let it be known that Garcia
had to go. When the head of the air force, Colonel Juan
Rafael Bustillo, announced in mid-April that he would
refuse to recognize Garcia's authority if the latter did
not step down, the nettle was finally grasped. After two
days of bitter negotiations between Bustillo and Magana,
the president promised that the defense minister would
resign over the weekend.

FEAR AND LOATHING IN THE REVOLUTIONARY OPPOSITION

And so ended the reign of Jose Guillermo Garcia.
But the struggle over power and policy was not limited to
the military or its conflict with the revolutionary
opposition; it infested the latter as well. On April 6,

Melida Anaya Montes, "Comandante Ana Maria," the second
ranking leader of the Popular Liberation Forces (FPL),
was murdered in Managua in an especially grisly fashion:
A three-man hit squad entered her house while she slept,
stabbing her eighty-two times with a metal spike and
breaking one of her arms before finally finishing her off
with a razor to the neck. Stunned and outraged, the FMLN
and the Sandinistas responded predictably, charging the
CIA with responsibility for the murder. But the investigation conducted by Nicaraguan security uncovered a very
different story. On April 9, Rogelio Bazzaglia
("Marcelo"), member of the FPL political commission and
one of FPL chief Salvador Cayetano Carpio's closest
aides, was arrested and charged with having planned and
organized the murder. Three days later Carpio, reportedly "depressed and grief-stricken by irrefutable
evidence of enemy activity, carried out by a man in whom
he had confidence,"[91] committed suicide.

News of Carpio's death was withheld from the public
for eight days, until the FPL and FMLN had been notified.
When finally announced, it was met with widespread skepticism and speculation. "Hard-core revolutionaries do
not commit suicide, even when their comrades are killed,"
commented one U.S. official.[92] Certainly, the act seemed
out of character. Carpio was a hard nut, no stranger to
prison, torture, and assassination. Some wondered
whether the Cubans and Nicaraguans might have disposed of
him themselves. Carpio was by far the most doctrinaire
and rigid of the comandantes. He had long been an
obstacle in the way of a negotiated settlement of the
Salvadoran conflict, going along with the FMLN-FDR's
October 1982 offer of unconditional peace talks only
under tremendous pressure from the other guerrilla
leaders. At the same time, there were hints that he had
had political differences with Anaya Montes. Some
observers claimed that she had supported an FPL faction
that had favored greater unification of the FMLN and a
more flexible approach toward negotiations. Had Carpio,
perhaps, in some way been responsible for Ana Maria's
death?

The full story of what happened may never be known.
An FPL spokesman subsequently did confirm the existence
of factional strife. According to this official explanation, divisions had become especially tense the previous
January when a hard-line faction, rejecting negotiations
in favor of prolonged popular war, had been outmaneuvered
by another group supporting a more flexible approach and
greater unity within the FMLN. The latter faction
allegedly won over both Anaya Montes and Carpio, leaving
the hardliners and their leader Bazzaglia in the
minority. Subsequently Bazzaglia, by his own testimony,
had killed Anaya Montes "for the good of the revolution"
and had used ice picks and knives to make it look like a

brutal act of the enemy." Carpio, thrown into an
motional crisis by the affair, suffering from asthma,
nd depressed by the battlefield death of another close
riend, then took his own life.[93]

The explanation is plausible, but not very con-
incing. At the funeral of Anaya Montes, Carpio had
ooked tired and sick. He had spoken haltingly and, even
n the intense heat of Managua, had worn a sweater and
acket. It is possible that something had simply
napped, that he had come to the end of himself. Yet,
ne is left with the feeling that not everything has been
old. Why would someone of Carpio's extraordinary
evolutionary discipline have killed himself? Having
esisted negotiations for so long, would he have been
ikely to abandon that position for a more flexible
trategy? Why the long delay before the announcement of
is death? One is struck by the seeming incongruities.
hen, too, there is the memory of another intrigue,
lmost a decade earlier, when Roque Dalton was "executed"
y his comrades in the People's Revolutionary Army (ERP).
hatever the truth about the deaths in Managua,
alvadoran revolutionary politics seems not to have lost
ts Byzantine and bloody character.

[In December 1983, an FPL communique was published
n the official Sandinista newspaper, Barricada, accusing
arpio himself of having ordered the murder of Anaya
ontes. Carpio had developed an "exaggerated view of his
wn importance, which led him to consider himself the
ost important, purest, most irreproachable revolutionary
n our country and the whole region, the only true
nterpreter of the Salvadoran proletariat and our people.
e saw those who did not accept his positions as a danger
o the revolution and as unconscious agents of the
nemy." Angered at being superseded by Anaya Montes, he
ad ordered her death. When his crime was discovered,
he carried out his last act of political cowardice,
suicide, in order to evade responsibility and save his
ame, which is now drenched with the infamy he brought
pon it."][94]

HE POLITICS OF ESCALATION

Pogo once remarked that he had seen the enemy and
he enemy was us. One of the central themes of this
olume is that the United States, long a major source of
olitical stability in Central America, has now become a
rimary source of instability. Rather than solving the
roblem, we have become part of it. This has been
specially evident in El Salvador, and the trend is
etting worse.

In late summer 1982, the Salvadoran government, with
he quiet support of the Reagan administration, began an

246

indirect "dialogue" with the left. On September 3,
President Magana held a secret meeting in San Salvador
with the Costa Rican foreign minister to discuss the
possibility of negotiations with the opposition. (This
on the heels of a meeting between Costa Rican President
Monge and the head of the Democratic Revolutionary Front,
Guillermo Ungo.) Rumors soon spread that Magana was
considering peace proposals from the guerrillas.
Although the president steadfastly denied this, he did
announce that he would soon establish a multiparty
commission to consider whether negotiations should be
opened. Subsequently, on October 26, the FDR and FMLN
issued a formal joint proposal for unconditional negotiations.

This flurry of peace initiatives produced an
immediate and predictable response from the counterrevolutionary right, which denounced the proposed talks
and set out to sabotage them before they got off the
ground. In mid-October, fifteen civilian opposition and
labor leaders, including five key members of the
Democratic Revolutionary Front, "disappeared" in a series
of separate incidents. Though inquiries to the security
forces produced denials of their involvement, few
observers were convinced. From exile, Guillermo Ungo
denounced "government sectors" trying to torpedo the
dialogue with the left. The U.S. ambassador, Deane
Hinton, deplored the seizures as "thoroughly
regrettable," though he professed to be "reasonably
certain" that they had not been committed on Salvadoran
government orders. Most observers assumed that the
missing would never be seen again. (Subsequently, eight
of the fifteen leaders reappeared in the hands of the
armed forces, charged by a secret military tribunal with
having directed "terrorist activities.")

For Ambassador Hinton, this was the last straw.
Salvadoran judges had recently declined to take action
against a politically well-connected military officer
implicated in the January 1981 killing of two U.S. land
reform advisers and the head of the Salvadoran Institute
of Agrarian Transformation. Now there was this.
Together these developments would make the forthcoming
presidential certification requirement embarrassing and
perhaps impossible. Something had to be done. Thus, in
an unusually candid address to several hundred members of
the American Chamber of Commerce--including some of the
most influential businessmen in El Salvador--Hinton gave
the Salvadoran leaders a piece of his mind: This
rightist "mafia" that murdered its political opponents
was as much a threat to the country as the guerrillas.
It had to be stopped. Since 1979, some 30,000
Salvadorans and a number of Americans had been "murdered,
not killed, murdered." Yet, there had been less than 200
convictions for these and other major crimes. Was it any

wonder that much of the world was "predisposed to believe
the worst of a system which almost never brings to
justice either those who perpetuate these acts or those
who order them?" The message was simple: El Salvador
had to clean up its human rights act, or the United
States might be forced to cut off aid.

The audience was not appreciative. Most sat in
stunned silence; a few walked out. Subsequently, the
rightist press unleashed a stream of vitriol against the
ambassador that was reminiscent of past attacks on Robert
White. Never one to be deterred by such assaults, Hinton
reiterated the message in even stronger terms in an
interview (the Salvadoran legal system was "rotten,"
etc.), pointedly noting that his remarks had been
approved by the State Department and were "clearly within
my understanding of Washington's thinking."[95]

He had not asked the president, however. In fact,
Hinton's remarks had not been cleared with the White
House, and they came as a distinctly unpleasant surprise.
Mr. Reagan did not like "hitting allies when they were
down." The ambassador was accordingly ordered to cool
it. Henceforth, human rights criticisms should be voiced
only in private.

This was an extraordinary act of repudiation, and it
had a devastating impact on Hinton's authority and effectiveness. Many Salvadorans had long operated on the
assumption that the Reagan administration was "hooked,"
that it was committed psychologically and in terms of its
prestige to preventing a guerrilla victory and could not
disengage regardless of what human rights violations were
committed. The muzzling of Deane Hinton was taken as
definitive evidence that they were correct. From this
point on, the ambassador could be ignored with impunity.
Nor did they have to go through even the motions of a
dialogue with the left. The FMLN-FDR proposal for
negotiations was accordingly rejected.

This was the beginning of the end for Hinton and his
State Department sponsor, Assistant Secretary for
Inter-American Affairs Thomas Enders. It had been Enders
who had approved the ambassador's speech, and he had to
share the blame for it. Since the resignation of
Secretary of State Haig the previous June, he had become
the primary actor in Latin American policy. Like Hinton,
he was a hard-line conservative. (Enders had been deputy
chief of mission at the U.S. Embassy in Phnom Penh during
the "secret bombing" of Cambodia. Similarly, Hinton had
been head of AID in Chile when the Nixon administration
blocked outside support to the Allende government;
earlier he had been AID director in Guatemala during the
bloody counterinsurgency there in the late 1960s.)
Nevertheless, two years of struggling with the intrica-
cies of Central American politics had tempered Enders
somewhat: He had come to appreciate the need for a

political solution to the crisis and had actively explored the possibility of negotiations. As the administration's primary spokesman before Congress, moreover, he had become acutely aware of the anti-war sentiment there and recognized the need for a certain amount of compromise and conciliation. When the White House sought to release yet another "White Paper" on Central America, Enders resisted on the grounds that it contained nothing new, was too tendentious, and would simply make things more difficult for the administration on Capitol Hill.

Such attitudes rendered Enders and Hinton suspect in the eyes of more hawkish advisers. And it was precisely these forces whose hands were strengthened by the deteriorating military situation in El Salvador. In February 1983, Jeane Kirkpatrick returned from a visit to Central America and delivered an alarming report to the president: Regional leaders were frightened by the worsening situation in El Salvador; a guerrilla victory there would lead to increased insurgent activity throughout the area; Soviet influence was growing rapidly and posed a potential strategic threat to the United States. The report raised the anxiety level in the White House several decibels and set in motion a bitter struggle for power. In the weeks that followed, Central American policy came increasingly under the control of Kirkpatrick and William Clark, the president's national security adviser. In late spring, Enders and Hinton were ousted from their positions altogether. Policy was now firmly in the hands of the militant right.

These months witnessed yet another round in the steady, incremental escalation of U.S. involvement. A concerted attempt would now be made to turn around the war in El Salvador, transform Honduras into a bastion of anti-communism, and oust the Sandinista regime in Nicaragua. These measures required a major increase in military and economic aid. Here, however, the administration met stiff congressional resistance. Congress had, in December 1982, passed the Boland Amendment, prohibiting U.S. funds from being used to overthrow the Nicaraguan government. By spring, it had become abundantly clear that the law was being violated. Reports of American support for anti-Sandinista guerrillas flooded the press. Denials from administration officials, who continued to insist that the U.S. objective was merely harassment and the interdiction of arms, only served to further antagonize critics: Clearly, Congress was being held in contempt. When the administration requested $80 million in covert funds for a major expansion of these activities, the House of Representatives responded with the Boland-Zablocki bill, which would grant the funds overtly to area governments for purposes of halting the arms flow. (The administration objected that this requirement would "cripple" U.S. policy. It would, indeed, since the funds were intended for purposes far beyond those officially declared.) Meanwhile, requests for $110 million in supplemental military aid to El Salvador became bogged down in congressional committees.

U.S. policy was now at a crucial juncture. Even the Department of Defense, increasingly concerned lest the United States become directly engaged in a Central American war, warned the administration of the dangers: U.S. troops must not be committed without well-defined goals and the clear backing of Congress and the public. If American efforts were "hobbled and trimmed back" by opposition, "the chances of failure would be high." A major but insufficient attempt to halt Soviet/Cuban inroads in the region might be more harmful to U.S. long-range interests than a partial disengagement.[96]

But the administration was no longer listening. Instead, it was increasingly on the offensive. If it could not persuade Congress through reason to grant the required aid, it could perhaps frighten it into doing so. Thus, the specter of the Nicaraguan/Cuban threat was once again resurrected. The flow of arms from Nicaragua, it was claimed, had increased markedly. Recent intelligence reports showed that Salvadoran guerrillas were now being supplied continually by helicopters and light aircraft. They had no shortage of arms--mostly U.S. MiG-16s, Soviet and East German demolition equipment, and American-made mortars.

Unfortunately, administration claims were largely unsupported by the available evidence. Reporters were quick to note that U.S. diplomatic and military personnel in the field saw little sign of any large-scale Nicaraguan arms traffic; some said quite candidly that most of the guerrillas' weapons now came from the Salvadoran military. By July, in fact, officials in San Salvador and Washington were reporting that the flow of outside arms had dwindled to a trickle and had been that way for many months. There had not been a single report of an aircraft originating in Nicaragua being shot down or even seen by Salvadoran government forces. Even a senior Reagan administration official admitted that the guerrillas were receiving only small amounts of weapons and ammunition from Nicaragua. On the other hand, the major army/air force ammunition dump at Ilopango Air Force Base had reportedly become a "guerrilla supply warehouse."[97] According to rebel radio reports, the insurgents had captured 1,826 rifles and 99 heavier weapons since January, enough to increase the number of men under arms by perhaps 30 percent.

No matter. President Reagan continued to insist that the "trouble" in Central America was "coming from outside." During these months, he was increasingly active and vocal on these matters, placing his own considerable powers of persuasion and the prestige of his office behind the push for escalation. The message was far from subtle: "I do not believe," he said before a nationally televised joint session of Congress in April, "that a majority of the Congress or the country is prepared to stand by passively while the people of Central America are delivered to totalitarianism and we ourselves are left vulnerable to new dangers."[98] If there were any Democrats who missed the point, he repeated it in even more explicit terms the following month before an audience of Cuban-Americans in Miami:

> If we are immobilized by fear, or apathy, by those who suggest that because our friends are imperfect, we should not help them; if those trying to throw roadblocks in our path succeed and interpose themselves at a time when a crisis could still be averted, the American people will know who is responsible and judge them accordingly.

> Any excuse for not providing our friends the weapons they need to defend themselves is a prescription for disaster. And again, those who advocate ignoring the legitimate defense needs of those under attack will be held accountable if our national security is put in jeopardy. Teddy Roosevelt is known to have said, "Speak softly and carry a big stick." Well, there are plenty of soft speakers around, but that's where the similarity ends.[99]

Now that was persuasion! No more Mr. Nice Guy. If we lose Central America, it is your fault!

Congress is not known for its courage and integrity. It had taken years to stand up to the executive branch on Vietnam. And even though there was widespread unease in response to Mr. Reagan's Central American policy--a palpable feeling that the United States was slipping into another war--there was also a very real fear that a military victory by the left in El Salvador would fan the flames of revolution throughout the region, ultimately endangering the security of both Mexico and the United States. No one wanted to take the blame for such a disaster. (It was symptomatic of the liberals' dilemma that although they were very free with their criticisms, few offered any specific policy alternatives beyond the amorphous but comforting plea for negotiations or a "political solution." Precisely what was to be negotiated or what should be done if the guerrillas proved recalcitrant was rarely discussed.) Elections would be coming up in 1984. A Republican campaign based on the theme of "Who lost El Salvador?" was a distinct possibility, one the Democrats could scarcely look forward to.

Many were quite willing to duck the issue, or at least to see it depoliticized.

President Reagan, too, wanted the subject depoliticized. To a certain extent, he was already vulnerable to the charge that he was dragging the country into "another Vietnam." In any case, the opposition had to be defused, or at least contained, if his Central American policy had any hope of success. Thus would the stick of intimidation be supplemented by the carrot of conciliation. When Representative Clarence Long, chairman of the House Subcommittee on Governmental Operations, demanded (as a condition of continuing U.S. aid to El Salvador) the appointment of a special envoy to explore the possibilities of a political settlement, the president seized the opportunity to nominate former Senator Richard Stone. Subsequently, when Senators Jackson and Mathias urged the formation of a bipartisan commission on Central American policy, Mr. Reagan complied, appointing as its chairman former Secretary of State Henry Kissinger.

These were extraordinary appointments. Two more improbable peacemakers it would be difficult to imagine: Stone, a former lobbyist for the bloody Lucas Garcia regime in Guatemala; Kissinger, the Great Destabilizer of Chile, architect of the "secret bombing" of Cambodia. They are understandable only within the context of the administration's attempts to divert opposition. Put another way, Congress was being "stroked." Stone would continue previous attempts to lure the FDR civilians away from the FMLN guerrillas (divide and conquer), thus effectively avoiding more dangerous kinds of negotiations (e.g., power sharing) and sidetracking congressional pressure for a settlement. The Kissinger panel (appropriately "stacked" with conservative Democrats and Republicans) would enable the president to appear flexible, open to options other than military ones. Kissinger's own hard-line position on Central America was well known; he was unlikely to present any unpleasant surprises or recommend new policy directions. His enormous reputation would lend considerable weight to the commission's conclusions, which could then be presented as a "bipartisan" national consensus, which in turn both Republicans and Democrats could hide behind. In the meantime, the administration would continue to pay lip service to the peace efforts of the Contadora Group (Mexico, Panama, Colombia, and Venezuela), while effectively blocking any negotiations that it deemed detrimental to the national interest.

Put simply, in my judgment, all this was a smokescreen designed to distract critics while the administration got on with the task of escalating American involvement in the region. Mr. Reagan's real intentions soon became apparent. In July, a secret National

Security task force "working paper" that had been leaked
to the New York Times revealed that the White House was
considering a 40 percent increase in military aid to its
Central American allies for the coming year, including a
doubling of security assistance to Costa Rica, an 80
percent increase to Guatemala, and increases of more than
30 percent to El Salvador and Honduras. "The situation
in Central America is nearing a critical point," the
report warned. "It is still possible to accomplish U.S.
objectives without the direct use of U.S. troops
(although the credible threat of such use is needed to
deter overt Soviet/Cuban intervention), provided that the
U.S. takes timely and effective action." Among other
things, the report recommended the prepositioning of
American military equipment in Honduras for use in a
crisis, the improvement of Honduran air and naval
installations, and attacks by Salvadoran troops on
guerrilla sanctuaries in Honduras.[100]

There followed a flurry of activity. On July 19,
administration sources revealed that two large military
exercises were being planned within the next month,
designed to signal Cuba and Nicaragua that the United
States had the means to stop the shipment of military
supplies between those countries. It was noted that the
president had not ruled out the possibility of a military
quarantine around Nicaragua--if other forms of diplomatic
and military pressure did not stop the arms flow. The
following day, the coordinator of the Nicaraguan junta,
Daniel Ortega, announced the willingness of his government to engage in regional negotiations to ease military
tensions, calling for a nonaggression pact between
Nicaragua and Honduras, a freeze on all arms shipments to
El Salvador, and a ban on foreign military bases and
training in the region. This was a reversal of the
Sandinistas' previous objections to regional talks (they
had preferred discussions with Honduras alone) and seemed
to address Washington's concerns over Cuban arms supplies
to Nicaragua and Nicaraguan shipments to the Salvadoran
insurgents. Clearly, the administration's campaign of
intimidation was having an impact. Nevertheless,
Washington's response was decidedly cool: The proposal
was a positive step, but it had serious shortcomings.
Ortega had placed the Salvadoran guerrillas on the same
level as the democratically elected government; he had
not mentioned the need for "true democracy" in Nicaragua,
or dealt with that country's military buildup. Moreover,
there were no clear provisions for verification.
Meanwhile, Jeane Kirkpatrick was telling an anti-
Sandinista group that there was no truth to the Brezhnev
Doctrine that communist regimes were irreversible. At
the same time, press reports revealed that the United
States had secured Israel's cooperation in sending
captured PLO weapons to Honduras for eventual use by the

Nicaraguan contras. These shipments were part of an
enlarged Israeli role in Honduras and Guatemala,
involving mainly arms sales, military training, and
technical aid for intelligence purposes.

On July 21, President Reagan defended U.S. plans for
naval maneuvers off Central America. Though welcoming
Ortega's speech as a "first step," he declared that it
did not go nearly far enough. The Sandinistas had
promised the Organization of American States that they
would institute democratic freedoms and civil liberties;
they had broken their word. It would be extremely
difficult to bring stability to the region as long as
they remained in power. He "hoped" there would be no
need to impose a naval blockade. The following day, it
was learned that the president had approved a plan to
substantially increase U.S. military involvement in
Central America, including preparation for a quarantine
or limited blockade. The scheduled military operations
were intended to lay the groundwork. Officials said that
Mr. Reagan hoped that this show of force would persuade
the Sandinistas to stop shipping arms into El Salvador.
They also noted that highly classified plans drawn up for
the exercises included the installation of new radar and
electronic surveillance posts in the region, the
positioning of large stocks of military equipment in
Honduras, and the first stages of construction of a $150
million air and naval base in Honduras. Financing for
the expanded presence (except for the base) was still
undetermined, though at least some of it would be drawn
from a number of Pentagon accounts in order to limit the
role of Congress. Another report noted the presence of
an unknown number of U.S. freelance pilots and Spanish-
speaking Americans of Cuban and Mexican descent working
with the Nicaraguan contras.

(Senior administration officials also disclosed that
the Pentagon had recommended that President Reagan raise
the number of military advisers in El Salvador and allow
them to accompany government troops into the field.
These proposals had not yet been approved, however.)

On July 25, the New York Times reported that senior
officials had revealed that the administration was
planning a major expansion of covert operations in
Central America, including increased support for the
anti-Sandinista insurgents. CIA-supported rebel forces
in Nicaragua, it was said, would grow significantly
beyond the current total of 10,000. The Pentagon would
provide the "Company" with military equipment and other
supplies. There were expectations that, as operations
increased, the demand for certain assistance would be
great enough to affect the combat-readiness of some
regular U.S. forces.

By this time, the administration was hemorrhaging
leaks. The press was anticipating another Tonkin Gulf

incident. The "decisive struggle" for Central America seemed to be reaching a climax. Through all this, President Reagan continued to insist that the "trouble" in Central America came from "outside" the region in the form of Soviet/Cuban arms. Regardless of whether the House of Representatives voted to cut off aid to the contras, officials asserted, covert support for those operations would go full steam ahead.

THE FUTURE

Where is all this leading? Seemingly the most obvious answer, though not necessarily the correct one, is to a generalized Central American war. In El Salvador, there are a number of hypothetical possibilities: (1) a military victory by the Salvadoran armed forces, accompanied by a transition to a relatively democratic political system; (2) a military victory by the armed forces, accompanied by a restoration of reactionary despotism; (3) an opposition military victory, followed by the establishment of a Marxist dictatorship; (4) a negotiated settlement, leading to the eventual establishment of a Marxist dictatorship; (5) a negotiated settlement, leading to the establishment of a relatively democratic government, whether right or left of center; (6) a negotiated settlement, leading to the restoration of military dictatorship; (7) U.S. military intervention, leading to the defeat of the left and the establishment of a relatively democratic government; (8) U.S. military intervention, leading to the defeat of the left and the restoration of a military dictatorship; (9) U.S. military intervention, accompanied by a protracted insurgency and an eventual victory by the left.

There are, of course, other permutations, but these are the main ones. What are the odds?

The chances of a military victory by the Salvadoran armed forces are remote. Indeed, no amount of military aid is likely to bring victory if officers and enlisted men lack the motivation and discipline to fight. One can increase the size of the Salvadoran Army and arm it to the teeth, but quantity alone is not enough. Rather, the crucial variable is quality. The fact is that the guerrillas are willing to risk their lives for their cause; government soldiers, in general, are not.

Nor does U.S. training alone change this reality. Only half of the 500 officer cadets trained in 1982 and about 20 percent of the soldiers trained in 1981 have reenlisted.[101] In effect, the U.S. program must be continued indefinitely simply to prevent a serious deterioration in competence. Moreover, any attempts to increase the size of the armed forces are likely to erode motivation and discipline even further. Most recruits

are press-ganged into service; their addition will dilute
what little quality currently exists. Under such
conditions, pouring more weapons into the country will
strengthen the armed forces only temporarily. The
military is a sieve through which military aid flows to
the guerrillas, who are the ultimate beneficiaries of the
current strategy of incremental escalation.

In short, although the United States can prevent a
rebel victory in the short run by racheting the level of
aid up another notch, this is not likely to bring
victory. The guerrillas should rebound, stronger than
ever. Washington will then have to make another
"agonizing reappraisal."

This being said, one cannot entirely discount the
possibility that the Salvadoran military may be able to
turn the war around. Bad armies do sometimes improve.
Popular support for the guerrillas is hardly overwhelming. If the administration is able to cut the flow
of arms, ammunition, and communications equipment from
Nicaragua and the regional black market (especially Costa
Rica and Honduras), such action might make a difference.
Though that supply is currently quite modest, it is not
insignificant. If at the same time the Salvadoran
military can be persuaded to purge its own ranks of the
most corrupt, incompetent and brutal officers, while
replacing them with more competent and honest junior
officers, continuing and expanding the agrarian reform
(to include Phase Two lands), and adopting the kind of
tactical changes being pushed by U.S. advisers (small
night patrols rather than massive search-and-destroy
missions; concentrating on the economically vital south
rather than the barren and sparsely populated north;
establishing a permanent presence, with civic action
programs, rather than sweeping through areas and then
abandoning them to the insurgents, etc.), then victory
may yet be achieved.

Make no mistake, however. This is a long shot.
Moreover, even if the war can be won, the prospects for
democracy and human rights are very poor. A military
victory is likely to strengthen the military, not the
civilians. And in a conflict as bitter as this one, the
victors are unlikely to be charitable toward the
vanquished.

In my judgment, the prospects of a government
military victory are no better than 10 percent, and if it
does occur, the odds are perhaps seven out of ten that it
will result in the restoration of some form of reactionary despotism, especially once the United States
lessens its presence.

A guerrilla victory is much more likely. It
probably would have occurred by now had not Washington
intervened. Here the crucial constraint is clearly U.S.
policy. The United States may not be able to win the

war, but it can prevent the rebels from winning--by physical occupation, if necessary. And it may well do just that. It is probable, however, that Congress will prohibit intervention or, failing that, place so many restrictions on policy as to prevent U.S. power from being used effectively--a replay of Vietnam of sorts. If this occurs, the insurgents will win sooner or later, barring a negotiated settlement.

The regime that emerges will be Marxist. Though it will not inevitably be Stalinist nor engage in a blood-bath against its enemies, one should harbor no illusions: The left has its share of psychopaths too. The Dalton and Anaya Montes "executions" are enough to demonstrate that. This tendency is especially strong within the Popular Liberation Forces, elements of which have recently returned to the practice of killing prisoners, much to the dismay of the more pragmatic guerrilla chieftans. It is not at all clear which FMLN faction (or combination of factions) will eventually prevail. It can be anticipated, however, that a long, bloody, bitter struggle ending in a rebel military triumph will enhance the likelihood of revenge and repression.

Still, the victorious guerrillas will also face substantive constraints. They will have to work out a strategy for governing, especially with regard to the crucial issue of national reconstruction. Economic recovery will require large doses of foreign aid. The more unsavory the regime, the less chance that such assistance will be forthcoming. The United States, in particular, could potentially play a crucial role in El Salvador's reconstruction both directly, in terms of economic assistance, and indirectly, through its influence in international lending agencies. In the process, Washington might well be able to have a major moderating effect on the new government. U.S. influence, moreover, would be enhanced by the former guerrillas' awareness of the dangers of perpetuating their hostile relations with the "Colossus of the North." Here the lessons of the Nicaraguan revolution might well be instructive: A guerrilla triumph would very quickly turn sour if it were followed by U.S. economic and para-military warfare against the new regime. Under such circumstances, the victors could enjoy few spoils; the Salvadoran people, including their leaders, could look forward only to continuing economic devastation, war, and insecurity.

This need not happen. A more constructive scenario can easily be imagined. But for that scenario to become a realistic possibility, a great deal of wisdom and flexibility on the part of both the FMLN and Washington would be required. These are qualities that have not been in great abundance on either side in the past. Although the United States has traditionally been generous to the enemies it has defeated in war, the Vietnam precedent suggests that it will probably respond to the defeat of its Salvadoran ally (indirectly, a defeat of itself) with spite--a "plague on your house." A destructive reaction--including economic sanctions and perhaps covert subversion--would effectively close off the possibility that a relatively moderate and humane regime might develop, while maximizing the probability of repression. This is the path of self-fulfilling prophecy.

The prospects of a guerrilla military victory: 30 percent. If such a triumph occurs, moreover, there is a very high probability--perhaps 90 percent--that the regime that emerges will be at least moderately repressive, and a good probability--say, 60 percent--that it will be highly repressive. A U.S. policy that gave the new Salvadoran leaders a strong positive incentive for moderation, while suggesting the high costs of hostility toward the United States and of human rights violations at home, might significantly lower these odds to around 60 percent and 40 percent, respectively.

What about the prospects of a negotiated settlement? Although far from good, such prospects represent less a long shot than a military victory by the Salvadoran Army. The main problem here is the apparent fundamental incompatibility of the primary forces in contention--the guerrillas, on the one hand, and the U.S. government and Salvadoran military, on the other. Both sides <u>claim</u> to want a political solution to the crisis. What they really mean is that they want <u>their</u> solution--one that will ensure their dominance without their having to pay the full costs of a military victory. Thus, the United States and its Salvadoran ally continue to insist that the guerrillas lay down their weapons and participate in elections the latter would be unlikely to win. In turn, the insurgents call for power-sharing prior to any such balloting--in effect, an attempt to gain through political means what they have thus far been unable to win on the battlefield.

Two points, in particular, must be made. First, a negotiated settlement will occur only when a balance has been reached wherein both sides perceive the war to be stalemated and either lose hope of breaking that deadlock and winning a military victory or recognize that the risks and costs of such a triumph are greater than any benefits likely to be obtained. In short, as long as the United States and its Salvadoran ally believe that the war can be won and is worth winning, the conflict will continue.

Second, a negotiated settlement will not end the struggle for power. One of the most naive (or disingenuous) arguments against power-sharing with the left is the claim that the FMLN-FDR would attempt to use

its position in any transitional government to establish
its political dominance. Of course, it will. So will
the parties of the right and the center. A negotiated
settlement does not put an end to politics. The struggle
for power will continue. The point is to shift that
conflict from the military battlefield to the political
arena, where the physical toll is less.

A "political solution" to the civil war (and by this
I do not mean a negotiated surrender) could lead to
several results. One would be the establishment of a
Marxist dictatorship; another would be the creation of a
viable democratic government; a third would be the
restoration of military dictatorship. It is difficult to
single out any of these possible scenarios as being more
probable than the others. Much depends on the conditions
of the settlement. A political solution that seriously
weakened the Salvadoran Army, for instance, would
increase the likelihood of FMLN-FDR hegemony. The
converse, of course, would apply to any settlement that
emasculated the guerrillas while leaving the military
intact. Should the "institutionality" of the armed
forces be preserved, however, and a balance of power
maintained vis-a-vis the guerrillas, there would be a
reasonable chance that a transitional regime would lead
to honest elections and the formation of a democratic
coalition government.

The trick would be to maintain the stability of that
arrangement. It is probable that the "losers"--
presumably the extreme right and/or the extreme left--
would seek to destabilize any government in which they
were not participants. Thus, other measures--including
the introduction of international peacekeeping forces and
the purging of both guerrilla and government armies--
would be necessary if a "negotiated democracy" is to be a
viable scenario. I shall explore this option in more
detail in the final chapter of this text.

For the moment, let us merely consider the odds. I
estimate the chances of a negotiated settlement to be
about 20 percent. The longer the current stalemate drags
on, however, the greater the likelihood that mutual
exhaustion will impel both sides to seek a political
solution. The FMLN-FDR has already expressed its
willingness to explore such an avenue. Moreover, the
recent death of Salvador Cayetano Carpio and the decline
of the ultra-left faction of the FPL should weaken those
intransigent forces in the FMLN that have opposed
negotiations in the past. At this point, the primary
obstacles to a political settlement remain the Reagan
administration and the Salvadoran military. Again, it is
necessary to stress that the "political solution"
currently being proposed by Washington is no solution at
all--merely a tactical device designed to divide the
enemy, the better to continue the war on more favorable

terms. Unless this stance is changed in such a way as to give the guerrillas an incentive to stop fighting, the bloodshed will continue.

In my judgment, the administration will not significantly soften this position. Thus, negotiations will become a hostage of U.S. domestic politics. A Democratic victory in the 1984 presidential elections might break the logjam, opening up the possibility of a political solution. (Though such a development is far from certain. Jimmy Carter's position on "power sharing" was no different from Mr. Reagan's, and none of the major contenders for the Democratic nomination has thus far been willing to come to grips with the issue.) If the president is reelected, on the other hand, the chances of such a settlement will be remote, at least for the next five years.

The most likely scenarios, however, involve U.S. military intervention, either directly or indirectly through local surrogates. It is probable that an invasion would have been launched some time ago had it not been for the constraints imposed by Congress and public opinion. Such a move may still be in the cards should the military situation continue to deteriorate. If, somewhere down the road, the administration is confronted with a choice of either committing American combat troops or accepting a leftist victory, it will choose the former--unless prevented by Congress. In all probability, this moment of truth would not arise until after the 1984 U.S. elections. The guerrillas are not yet close to victory. A new influx of American aid should bolster the Salvadoran military in the short run. In any event, it would be very difficult politically for the president to make such a commitment in the middle of an election campaign.

Difficult--but not impossible. One of the concerns of those critical of the extensive military exercises scheduled for the latter half of 1983 and continuing in 1984 is that they might lead to an "incident"--a Central American equivalent of the Gulf of Tonkin or Battleship Maine--that could be used as a pretext for intervention, allowing the administration to mobilize congressional and public opinion behind an introduction of American combat forces. Such a move might also be attempted should war break out between Nicaragua and her neighbors--an increasing possibility now that the Central American Defense Council (CONDECA) is being resurrected. The purpose could be limited to shoring up threatened allies (Honduras and El Salvador) or, much more ambitious, aimed at crushing the FMLN and overthrowing the Sandinista regime, if necessary by a full-scale U.S. military occupation.

What would be the upshot? Although there is no question that the United States could physically occupy

El Salvador and/or Nicaragua, this is not the same thing as winning a guerrilla war. The chances of a U.S. victory would be maximized if the operation could be restricted to Salvador. The country is small, the terrain relatively favorable. The insurgents are limited to about 7,000 - 10,000 main-force guerrillas (plus militia and other support elements) and have only limited popular allegiance and weaponry. If they can be isolated and cut off from outside aid, the chances of victory would be fairly high. Presumably, the rebels would not try to fight U.S. forces en masse. Rather, they would attempt to fade away, maintaining their infrastructure intact until such time as the "gringos" left and the war could be resumed on more favorable terms.

Unfortunately, it is not at all clear that the insurgency can be quarantined so easily. Such isolation would be especially unlikely if Nicaragua is dragged into the conflict on a large scale. Most disastrous would be a U.S. attempt to occupy that country. An American invasion would be widely perceived as an attempt to restore the Somocistas to power; it would drive virtually every nationalist in Nicaragua into the arms of the Sandinistas. The latter, in turn, would launch a war of national liberation--a veritable holy war--against the occupation forces. Under such circumstances, the odds on a U.S. victory would not be good. The Sandinistas would be far more numerous and better organized and armed than their Salvadoran counterparts; their popular support would be overwhelming. Nor would the nationalistic backlash be limited to Nicaragua. An "imperialist" intervention would strike a raw nerve extending throughout Latin America. One could hardly conceive of a move better calculated to arouse sympathy for the Sandinistas and hatred for the United States--or one more likely to attract foreign leftist intervention. Already there are some 6,000 Cubans in Nicaragua, about a third of them military personnel. Would they remain uninvolved in the face of a U.S. invasion? The formation of inter-nationalist brigades, composed of Latin American "volunteers," is a distinct possibility.

In short, such an intervention would not bring a quick and easy victory. Rather, it would require an indefinite occupation. And not just of Nicaragua. For having nothing left to lose, the Sandinistas would likely free themselves from the self-imposed restraints they have been operating under and really engage in a "revolution without borders." Honduras. El Salvador. Guatemela. Costa Rica. Regionalizing the struggle would make strategic sense. It would prevent the "imperialists" from concentrating their forces in Nicaragua, spread them thin, give the guerrillas maximum terrain in which to roam and hide. Weapons would not be lacking. The Sandinistas are already armed to the teeth.

And the existence of extensive insurgencies in Salvador and Guatemala would provide an organizational infrastructure in those countries capable of absorbing a massive influx of arms and munitions. Meanwhile, Honduras, surrounded by war on three sides, would become rapidly "Cambodianized," as guerrillas of various nationalities moved from one country to another, fleeing attackers, infiltrating insurgents, and otherwise building the nascent Honduran "liberation movement" into a Fourth Anti-imperialist Front.

The point, of course, is that a U.S. intervention in El Salvador could come not only in response to the guerrilla threat in that country but as a side effect of an American assault on Nicaragua. Such an attack need not be direct. The Reagan administration's current policy of indirect, semi-covert subversion through the contra forces in Honduras and northern Nicaragua could easily have the same effect--for example, by embroiling Nicaragua and Honduras in a war against each other or by triggering a Sandinista counterattack in the form of an increased effort to promote guerrilla activity in Honduras and Salvador. In either case, the administration would likely respond to the threats to its allies with increased military involvement in those countries and increased attacks on Nicaragua. "Eventually the United States will have to get involved in the fighting," Edgar Chamorro Coronel, a director of the Nicaraguan Democratic Force, recently remarked, "because sooner or later the United States will have to intervene directly." In terms of "cost-efficiency," he noted, "it is better for the United States to fight now."[102]

This is not an uncommon attitude among our Central American allies. There are many who would like Uncle Sam to pull their chestnuts out of the fire. One recalls George Ball's prophetic objection to our Vietnam intervention. The then under secretary of state warned that the more U.S. troops became involved in the war, the less the South Vietnamese Army would fight. This is likely to be just as true in Central America.

What are the prospects? I estimate the chances of American combat involvement in El Salvador, in response either to a deteriorating military situation there or to an increased threat from Nicaragua, to be about 40 percent. The odds of success, however, are much more difficult to gauge. Much depends on Congress, which could respond with anything from a blank check to a total cutoff of aid. Or, more likely, if one is to judge by U.S. performance of late, something in between: The Department of Defense recently warned that if the U.S. effort is "hobbled and trimmed back" by opposition, the "chances of failure are high." If victory cannot be achieved in the short or intermediate range, the likelihood of an aid cutoff will grow. By the same token, it

will make an enormous difference whether the intervention
is in El Salvador alone or includes Nicaragua, Honduras,
and perhaps other countries. Again, the chances of
success will be much greater if American military power
can be concentrated in Salvador. Finally, there is the
issue of how the invasion is to be effectuated--by a
massive, quick, and decisive occupation or through a
slow, step-by-step escalation to "stave off defeat for
the time being, without any clear strategy for success--
an awkward parallel with Vietnam.[103]

I confess that I am not optimistic on any of these
counts. The pattern thus far is one of incremental
escalation, hobbled by congressional resistance, aimed at
regionalizing the conflict rather than containing and
localizing it. Although the administration's campaign of
intimidation against Nicaragua and Cuba makes sense if
the goal is to deter those countries from interfering in
El Salvador and elsewhere, current evidence suggests that
Washington's actions are not a response to Nicaraguan/
Cuban behavior. Indeed, if anything, the relationship
seems to be an inverse one: The fewer arms the
Nicaraguans and Cubans ship to El Salvador and the more
conciliatory they are toward the United States, the more
threatening becomes the Reagan administration. It is
difficult to escape the impression that American policy
is increasingly the hostage of forces beyond U.S.
control--forces that have a vested interest in drawing
the United States directly into the Central American
conflicts, especially in Nicaragua. If this impression
proves correct, it is a prescription for disaster.

In sum, the odds of a U.S. victory in a generalized
Central American war are not good--substantially less
than 50 percent, in my judgment. And although the
chances of success would be much better if the intervention were restricted to El Salvador, such will probably
not be the case. Moreover, even if Nicaragua and
Salvador are pacified, one should entertain no illusions
about the future. The forces being backed by the United
States are not "freedom fighters." If the Somocistas are
returned to power, they will arrive on a tidal wave of
blood. As for democracy and social reform, these are
essentially alien values in such highly authoritarian and
hierarchical political cultures. The United States can
perhaps impose them (or some facsimile thereof) in the
short run, but they are not likely to prevail once it
withdraws.

One would like to be more optimistic. Americans
have been socialized into believing that every problem
has a solution; they expect stories to have happy
endings. There lies the rub. For many problems have no
solutions, and many tales end in tragedy. This is likely
to be one of them. In such circumstances, the United
States would be wise not to expect too much. A policy

that seeks to minimize costs and risks, both for the United States and for Central Americans, may be preferable to the rigid pursuit of absolute victories. If the United States clings to the latter, it will be precisely those peoples whose welfare it professes to care about who will bear the primary costs of its folly.

NOTES

I am indebted to Richard Piper, Douglas Graham, Joe Decker, and Constance Rynder for their many insightful comments on the first draft of this chapter. Any errors of omission or commission in the final product are, of course, entirely my responsibility.

1. Charles Anderson, Politics and Economic Change in Latin America (Princeton: Van Nostrand, 1967), pp. 104-105.

2. Thomas P. Anderson, The War of the Dispossessed (Lincoln: University of Nebraska Press, 1981), p. 33; Lawrence R. Simon and James Stephens, Jr., El Salvador Land Reform, 1980-81: Impact Audit (Boston: Oxfam, 1981), p. 7; Segundo Montes, "Situacion del Agro Salvadoreno y Sus Implicaciones Sociales," Estudios Centroamericanos, 28, 297-298 (1973), p. 470; Eduardo Colindres, Fundamentos Economicos de la Burguesia Salvadorena (San Salvador: University of Central America, 1977).

3. Linda K. Wright-Romero, Suzanne Vaughn, and William L. Flinn, General Narrative Report of Survey Information: El Salvador Rural Poor Survey, June 1977-May 1978 (Columbus, Ohio: Ohio State University, 1981), pp. i, 23.

4. Agricultural Sector Assessment: El Salvador (Washington, D.C.: Agency for International Development, 1977), p. 20.

5. Agrarian Reform in El Salvador (Washington, D.C.: Agency for International Development, 1981), p. 11.

6. William L. Flinn, Suzanne Vaughn, and Linda K. Wright-Romero, Profiles of Rural Poor and Factors Related to Poverty: El Salvador Rural Poor Survey, June 1977-May 1978 (Columbus, Ohio: Ohio State University, 1982), p. 3.

7. Agrarian Reform, pp. 8-9. Of the farmlands, 45 percent were cultivated and 38 percent were in pasture. The remainder was not in agricultural use.

8. El Salvador: Zonificacion Agricola (Washington, D.C.: Organization of American States, 1974), p. 5.

9. For a careful treatment of this theme, see William H. Durham, Scarcity and Survival in Central America (Stanford, Calif.: Stanford University Press, 1979), pp. 21-54.

10. David Browning, *El Salvador: Landscape and Society* (Oxford: Clarendon Press, 1971), p. 84.

11. Alistair White, *El Salvador* (New York: Praeger, 1973), p. 119.

12. Eduardo Colindres, "La Tenencia de la Tierra en El Salvador," *Estudios Centroamericanos*, 31, 335-336 (1976), p. 466.

13. Melvin Burke, "El Sistema de Plantacion y la Proletarizacion del Trabajo Agricola en El Salvador," *Ibid.*, p. 476.

14. Simon and Stephens, *El Salvador Land Reform*, p. 6.

15. Colindres, "La Tenencia," p. 472.

16. White, *El Salvador*, p. 248.

17. Harald Jung, "Class Struggle and Civil War in El Salvador," in *El Salvador: Central America in the New Cold War*, eds. Marvin E. Gettleman, Patrick Lacefield, Louis Menashe, David Mermelstein, and Ronald Radosh (New York: Grove Press, 1981), pp. 70-72.

18. *El Salvador: An Inquiry into Urban Poverty* (Washington, D.C.: World Bank, 1980), pp. 8-9.

19. Jose Murillo Salinas, "Breve Panorama de la Situacion Habitacional en El Salvador," *Estudios Centroamericanos*, 29, 308-309 (1974), pp. 431-432.

20. *El Salvador: Background to Crisis* (Cambridge: Central America Information Office, 1982), p. 48.

21. Samuel P. Huntington, *Political Order in Changing Societies* (New Haven: Yale University Press, 1968), p. 266.

22. Casualty estimates vary widely. In his thoughtful treatment of the subject, Thomas P. Anderson suggests that the rebels killed about 100 people, including perhaps 35 civilians. Leftist sources often cite 30,000 as the number of Indians killed. See Anderson, *Matanza* (Lincoln: University of Nebraska Press, 1971), p. 136; and Anderson, *War of the Dispossessed*, p. 24.

23. Stephen Webre, *Jose Napoleon Duarte and the Christian Democratic Party in Salvadoran Politics: 1970-74* (Baton Rouge: Louisiana State University Press, 1979), p. 170.

24. Thus, for instance, the Ministry of Agriculture had no power over the management and regulation of the coffee sector. See Jung, "Class Struggle," p. 74.

25. White, *El Salvador*, pp. 95ff.

26. To use Baloyra's term. See Enrique Baloyra, *El Salvador in Transition* (Chapel Hill: University of North Carolina Press, 1982).

27. Tommie Sue Montgomery, *Revolution in El Salvador* (Boulder, Colo.: Westview Press, 1982), p. 55.

28. Asociacion Nacional de Educadores Salvadorenos.

29. Ernesto Richter, "Social Classes, Accumulation, and the Crisis of Overpopulation in El Salvador," *Latin*

American Perspectives, 7, 2-3 (Spring/Summer, 1980), p. 132.

30. Interview with this author, San Salvador, August 1982. For obvious reasons, the subject requested anonymity.

31. Information provided by Penny Lernoux.

32. Patrick Lacefield, "Oscar Romero: Archbishop of the Poor," in El Salvador, eds. Gettleman et al., p. 201.

33. Rafael Guidos Vejar, "La Crisis Politica en El Salvador," Estudios Centroamericanos, 34, 369-70 (1979), p. 511.

34. Robert Armstrong and Janet Shenk, "El Salvador: Why Revolution?" NACLA Report on the Americas, 14, 2 (March/April, 1980), pp. 25-26.

35. Although the U.S. Embassy had been in sporadic contact with the conspirators and was well aware of what was going on, it apparently remained neutral, neither encouraging nor discouraging the plotters. See Montgomery, Revolution in El Salvador, pp. 11-12.

36. Frank J. Devine, El Salvador: Embassy Under Attack (New York: Vantage Press, 1981), pp. 144-145.

37. Quoted in Cynthia Arnson, El Salvador: A Revolution Confronts the United States (Washington, D.C.: Institute for Policy Studies, 1982), p. 43.

38. Granma Weekly Review (May 18, 1980).

39. Devine, El Salvador, p. 193.

40. Ibid., p. 145.

41. Testimony before the Subcommittee on Foreign Operations of the House Appropriations Committee, April 29, 1981, in El Salvador, eds. Gettleman et al., p. 147.

42. El Salvador: Background to Crisis, p. 82.

43. Amnesty International, "Repression in El Salvador," in El Salvador, eds. Gettleman et al., p. 153.

44. Letter of resignation, March 3, 1980.

45. New York Times (March 13, 1980).

46. Robert Armstrong and Janet Shenk, "El Salvador: A Revolution Brews," NACLA Report on the Americas, 14, 4 (July/August, 1980), p. 17.

47. Washington Post (April 5, 1981).

48. James Petras, "The Junta's War Against the People," The Nation, 231, 21 (1980), p. 674.

49. Socorro Juridico, "Report on Repression," in A Report on the Meeting of the Permanent Tribunal of the Peoples on the Violations of Human Rights in El Salvador, eds. V. Navarro, H. Cox, J. Petras, and G. Wald (Washington, D.C.: CISPES, 1981), p. 41.

50. Solidaridad, 13-15 (1980).

51. A Salvadoran cabinet minister gave the figure of 135 dead. Elsewhere, President Duarte admitted that 300 had been killed, "all of them 'communist guerrillas.' " Washington Post (April 29, 1981); Americas Watch Committee/American Civil Liberties Union, Report on

Human Rights in El Salvador (New York: Random House, 1982), p. 169.

52. The troops arrived just in time to find D'Aubuisson trying to swallow the evidence. Testimony of U.S. Ambassador Robert White, in U.S., Congress, Senate, _The Situation in El Salvador_, Hearings before the Committee on Foreign Relations, 97th Congress, 1st Session, March 18 and April 9, 1981 (Washington, D.C.: Government Printing Office, 1981), p. 117. See also _Excelsior_ (May 13, 1982). White later testified that an eyewitness source had described how D'Aubuisson had supervised the drawing of lots for the "honor" of killing Romero. A D'Aubuisson intimate, Lieutenant Francisco Amaya Rosa, had won the draw and had subsequently selected a sharpshooter named Walter Antonio Alvarez to perform the task. Several months later, D'Aubuisson ordered Alvarez's death. _New York Times_ (February 3, 1984).

53. See, for example, the comments of Ernesto Jovel (then head of the Armed Forces of National Resistance) in _Proceso_ (October 6, 1980).

54. Interview with Salvador Cayetano Carpio, in Mario Menendez Rodriguez, _El Salvador: El Por Que de Esta Guerra_ (Bogota: Editorial La Oveja Negra, n.d.), p. 18.

55. Testimony of Joaquin Villalobos, _Granma Weekly Review_ (May 18, 1980).

56. Testimony of Jovel, in _Proceso_ (October 6, 1980).

57. Testimony of Shafik Jorge Handel, in _Granma Weekly Review_ (June 1, 1980).

58. U.S., Department of State, _Communist Interference in El Salvador_ (February 23, 1981), p. 4; U.S., Department of State, _Communist Interference in El Salvador: Documents Demonstrating Communist Support of the Salvadoran Insurgency_ (February 23, 1981), Documents A, B, and C; and U.S., Congress, House, Permanent Select Committee on Intelligence, _U.S. Intelligence Performance on Central America: Achievements and Selected Instances of Concern_, Staff Report, 97th Congress, 2nd Session, September 22, 1982 (Washington, D.C.: Government Printing Office, 1982), p. 6.

59. The following is based on _Communist Interference in El Salvador_, Documents D,E,F,G,H,I, and J.

60. The administration wished to avoid a cutoff of aid, which would have occurred had it failed to give Congress certification that the Sandinista regime was not "aiding, abetting, or supporting acts of violence or terrorism in other countries." See _U.S. Intelligence Performance_, pp. 5-7.

61. _New York Times_ (October 30 and November 16, 1982).

62. See, for example, _Manchester Guardian_ (March 8, 1961); _Financial Times_ (March 9, 1981); and _Newsweek_ (March 16, 1981).

63. Montgomery, Revolution in El Salvador, p. 180.

64. See, especially, Wayne Smith's chapter in this text; see also his "Dateline Havana: Myopic Diplomacy," Foreign Policy, 48 (Fall 1982), p. 161.

65. "Pure fiction" was the way Roger Fontaine described D'Aubuisson's account of their meeting.

66. Arnson, El Salvador, p. 76.

67. Washington Post (June 27, 1981).

68. New York Times (July 2, 1981).

69. Washington Post (January 25, 1982).

70. New York Times (April 19, 1982). For a much more optimistic analysis, see "Agrarian Reform in El Salvador" (Washington, D.C.: Checchi and Company, AID/SOD/PDC-C-0399, December 1981). Yet another, more pessimistic treatment may be found in Simon and Stephens, El Salvador Land Reform, 1980-81, including the "1982 Supplement" by Martin Diskin.

71. Although no proof exists, there is reason to believe that the January 1981 murder of Jose Rodolfo Viera, the president of the Salvadoran Institute of Agrarian Transformation (ISTA), was due to his efforts to expose mismanagement and corruption in the agency. Indeed, he had gone so far as to expose on national television a $40 million fraud he had uncovered, denouncing the military officers responsible.

72. I was shown a copy of this report by an ISTA informant.

73. This is the figure repeatedly given by the State Department and AID. The figure of 12 percent is based on the UCS statistic mentioned earlier. Significantly, in defending U.S. policy against the UCS charges, Ambassador Hinton revised the previous State Department estimate of potential beneficiaries. "Subsequent analysis based on the best available data" indicated that there were only 67,000 potential beneficiaries. This reduction had its bright side, however. Hinton claimed that 20,000 provisional titles had been issued. Thus, 30 percent of the intended beneficiaries, not 12 percent, had benefited. New York Times (January 25, 1982).

74. In the words of Laurence Simon and James Stephens, in Ibid. (January 6, 1981).

75. Montgomery, Revolution in El Salvador, p. 181.

76. These figures find rough confirmation in similar estimates by the Center for Documentation and Information of the University of Central America (13,229 civilians killed in 1981, a 35 percent increase over the previous year) and the Human Rights Commission of El Salvador (16,276 in 1981, a 20 percent increase over 1980). Most estimates suggest that the government and death squads are responsible for 80 percent or more of the killings.

77. Time (September 7, 1981).

78. New York Times (February 5, 1982).

268

79. Washington Post (January 27, 1982); New York Times (February 26, 1982).

80. This information comes from an April 1982 National Security Council summary paper leaked to the New York Times (April 7, 1983). The emphasis in the quotation is mine.

81. Newsweek (November 8, 1982). I was told similar things by U.S. military advisers during a visit to contra base camps in December 1982.

82. Robert Armstrong, "El Salvador--Beyond Elections," NACLA Report on the Americas, 16, 2 (March/April, 1982), p. 10.

83. See, for example, Senator Nancy L. Kassebaum, Report of the U.S. Official Observer Mission to the El Salvador Constituent Assembly Elections of March 28, 1982, a report to the Committee on Foreign Relations, United States Senate (Washington, D.C.: Government Printing Office, 1982), pp. 34-42.

84. Ibid., p. 34.

85. The last census was taken over a decade ago. Estimates of the population growth rate range from the World Bank's 2.9 percent to almost 3.5 percent.

86. I was told of a number of such instances in Cabanas.

87. The first figure is from Jose Morales Ehrlich of the Christian Democrats; the second is from the Popular Democratic Union, a labor and peasant federation.

88. Armstrong, "El Salvador--Beyond Elections," pp. 18-20.

89. New York Times (September 25, 1982).

90. Ibid. (September 25, 1982 and January 22, 1983). See also "Agrarian Reform in El Salvador" (Washington, D.C.: Checchi and Company, AID Contract PDC-1406-I-00-1136-00, January 1983).

91. Granma Weekly Review (May 1, 1983).

92. New York Times (April 22, 1983).

93. Latin American Weekly Report (June 3, 1983).

94. Barricada (December 13, 1983).

95. New York Times (November 3, 1982).

96. Ibid. (July 17, 1983).

97. Ibid. (March 9, April 3 and 25, July 31, 1983).

98. Ibid. (April 28, 1983).

99. Ibid. (May 21, 1983).

100. Ibid. (July 17, 1983).

101. Latin American Weekly Report (June 24, 1983).

102. New York Times (July 30, 1983).

103. Ibid. (July 17, 1983).

7
Guatemala: The Origins and Development of State Terrorism

Gordon L. Bowen

Observers of the human condition in the Third World have long recognized two distinct trends. First, during the latter half of the twentieth century, a great deal of socioeconomic change has occurred, change that, in varying degrees from country to country, has altered those nations' capabilities to meet human needs. Second, there has also been a tremendous growth in the use of coercion by Third World states vis-a-vis their own citizens, often assisted by the superpowers. Frequently these changes are thought of, respectively, as the trend toward "development" and the trend toward denial of "human rights."

Is there a relationship between development and the violation of human rights? If so, what roles do the state and international forces play? This chapter will examine these issues as they pertain to Guatemala. This is a particularly appropriate setting in which to investigate these phenomena, for the violation of human rights in that country is many faceted. It involves the quiet anguish of the eight in ten children who are malnourished; yet it is also acrimonious. Indeed, Amnesty International recently described Guatemala as a nadir of sorts--a peerless cesspool in which official security forces have been engaged in a systematic program of political murder. At this writing, several hundred people a month are victims.

Is such victimization a function of economic deprivation? Do probable changes in Guatemala's economic future portend an end to the nightmare? Or may such changes actually intensify the human rights problems? What role has the United States played, and what is it likely to do in the future?

Understanding Guatemalan development requires recognition of that nation's international position. Throughout the twentieth century, Central America has been in the sphere of influence of the United States. This reality has affected the planning and implementation

of development by narrowing the range of national policy
options. Just how deeply the United States has
influenced domestic and foreign policy in these countries
and how that influence has been wielded are fundamental
issues. By examining the Guatemalan historical
experience, we can approach the larger question of why
the Guatemalan state today behaves as it does toward its
citizens.

Is the violation of human rights a prerequisite for
multinational corporate (hence, U.S. national) advantage,
as many "dependency" scholars have argued? Has the
economic/political power elite that has evolved in
Guatemala been merely a local variant of the social
structural change that accompanies the importation of
technologies appropriate to a type of development
centralized and dependent on an external market? U.S.
business profits and Guatemalan technological dependency
have been part of the historical record.

But there is an alternative explanation as well--one
which looks to the political life cycle of the Guatemalan
state itself. Such a focus can help account for both the
periods of active, direct American influence and those
periods in which U.S. interests and initiatives have been
stymied. We can more clearly appreciate the difficulties
in achieving progress toward human rights by conceiving
of Guatemala both as a neocolony or U.S. "tributary
state" and as a "Frankenstein Monster," largely of our
own creation, now running amok, beyond our control.

THE SOCIOECONOMIC CONTEXT OF GUATEMALAN POLITICS

A superficial reading of the Guatemalan economic
ledger since World War II would seem to suggest that
substantial economic development has occurred. After
all, the gross domestic product (GDP) rose more than 5.5
percent annually from 1960-80. In this same period,
energy consumption per capita increased by over 50
percent and per capita GNP passed $1,000. Some diver-
sification occurred: Whereas primary products made up 95
percent of Guatemalan exports in 1960, today one-fifth of
the value of exports is derived from manufactured goods.
Though in 1960 exports were sent almost entirely to the
industrialized West, nearly 30 percent of their current
value is derived from shipments to the Third World. In
addition, more than 90 percent of Guatemalan exports in
the manufacturing sector go to Third World buyers.[1]

Guatemalan society reflects some of the dynamism
apparent in these macroeconomic changes. Two-thirds of
all workers were in agriculture in 1960, whereas today
nearly one half of the labor force is in the manufacturing or service sectors. Nevertheless, a huge portion
of the society remains outside the labor force,

marginalized by both the plantation economy and by the
limited manufacturing and service job opportunities
beyond these <u>fincas</u>. <u>Meeting the basic needs of this
part of the population has not had high priority</u>. A 1978
study by the UN International Labor Organization calculated that Guatemalans had to earn at least $320 a year
to remain above the poverty line. At the time, 75
percent had per capita annual incomes of less than
$215.[2]

How can one account for this? <u>The dependency</u>
<u>analysis of A. G. Frank places the blame on intrinsic</u>
<u>requisites of international capitalism:</u>

dependency theory exclusion

> The vast bulk of the population . . . consumed the
> few local products that their low income permitted
> them to purchase and/or subconsumed at levels below
> subsistence. Since the market for colonial produc-
> tion was overseas, their purchasing power was not
> necessary for the realization of colonial produc-
> tion. And <u>from the point of view of international</u>
> <u>and national capital as a whole their wages did</u> not
> <u>represent a purchasing power to be increased, but</u>
> <u>only a labor cost to be reduced; and it was</u>. The
> essentials of this situation have remained the same
> in the twentieth century. . . .[3]

One would be <u>hard pressed to deny</u> that Guatemalan
conditions support Frank's analysis. <u>The majority of</u>
<u>rural families receive low wages and are marginal to</u>
<u>national consumption</u>. They work continuously on small
plots and also seasonally as pickers/harvesters for cash.
Survival on the margins of life is accomplished with less
than $80 per year for many families.
<u>Part of development must mean meeting human needs</u>.
<u>What we see in Guatemala is not development but</u>
<u>"underdevelopment." Human needs are not met</u>. The
question posed most starkly by Guatemala: Is it
necessary under capitalism that Guatemalan underdevelopment include infant mortality of 81 per 1,000 and that
malnutrition affect 82 percent of the population under
the age of five?[4]
<u>Racist and classist attitudes are widespread among</u>
<u>the Guatemalan upper class. These conveniently coincide</u>
<u>with, and reinforce, the economic rationale behind the</u>
<u>contempt expressed in relation to the basic needs of</u> poor
and indigenous peoples. The consequences of such
contempt are staggering. Only 15 to 18 percent of rural
housing units have access to safe water.[5] Accordingly,
diseases related to impure water are widespread. Half of
all recorded deaths involve children five years and
under. Among these, intestinal problems top the list of
causes of death.[6] These problems are particularly acute
in the Western Highlands, where six-tenths of the

nation's people live on a hilly fourth of the land. In
the Highlands, high concentrations of indigenous
("Indian") lingual-ethnic groups are found. Altogether
these twenty-two separate groups account for about half
the national population.

Rural people, especially rural indigenous people,
pay a high price for state indifference to human needs.
The typical member of the Guatemalan poor consumes only
56 percent of the minimum protein requirement for human
life. Life expectancy at birth for Indians is 16 years
less than for ladinos.[7] Their infant mortality rate is
1.7 times as great as that for non-Indian children.[8]

Malnutrition contributes to the denial of other
basic needs. It is difficult, if not impossible, to
educate malnourished pupils. Accordingly, more than half
of the population over age ten is illiterate. Among the
indigenous peoples, three out of four people ten and
older are illiterate.[9] The mark of state policy is
stamped on these results: In 1979, Guatemala devoted
12.4 percent of its budget to education. In El Salvador
the figure was 23 percent; in (Somoza's) Nicaragua, 24
percent; and in Costa Rica, 28 percent.[10]

Poor health, malnutrition, illiteracy, and early
death are the results of human decisions regarding
distribution of assets. They are not due to an absolute
shortage of wealth or food. Reduced to its essence, the
problem is that the maldistribution of income prevents
the poor three-fourths of the population from purchasing
goods and services by which they could meet their needs.
In 1948, one-fourth of all Guatemalans, the ladino upper
and "middle" classes, received 60.5 percent of the
national income. By 1970 the figure was 66 percent, and
in 1979, 66.5 percent.[10] Conversely, the poor's share of
the national pie has shrunk, thus leaving a smaller
portion of national income available for distribution to
indigenous peoples and the ladino poor and working
classes. During the "Alliance for Progress" and
"Development Decade" era, distributional inequities
actually increased. In 1979, 89.8 percent of all farm
units were smaller than the size (7 hectares) that the
World Bank suggests is the minimum needed to provide a
subsistence living for their holders.[12] Six hundred
thousand rural families are now without any land of their
own to farm.

Agricultural production for export has grown rapidly
while subsistence agriculture has stagnated. Between
1961 and 1973, average annual growth in acreage devoted
to subsistence food stuffs (corn, wheat, and beans) was 2
percent a year. During the same period, acreage devoted
to export crops (coffee, beef, cotton, bananas, and
sugar) expanded by 6.5 percent per year. Export earnings
(1960-74) grew apace: in coffee, from $74.6 million to
$172.9 million; in sugar, from $100,000 to $49.6 million;

n cotton, from $5.8 million to $71 million; and in eats, from $200,000 to $21.5 million.[13]

These conditions contributed to a growing trade union and cooperative movement, especially in the 1970s. Most campesinos must seek employment as seasonal wage laborers, which typically involves migration from the highlands to the coastal plantations for a period of several weeks to several months. In response to the wage and working condition demands of these crucial seasonal laborers, the government since the 1960s has allowed plantation owners to organize private security forces. These "irregulars" have been used to impress the rural poor into distant "jobs," a practice that resembles slavery. On the plantations, security forces have been used to break unions, squelch peasant demands for enforcement of minimum wage and social security laws, and enforce usurious terms of debt peonage. All such actions have served to further ensnare the rural poor in a social system where their basic needs have no chance of being fulfilled.

In sum, the political responses of the Guatemalan rural peoples in the 1980s are a by-product of several aspects of their socioeconomic experience. Rural unrest grows out of a 400-year racist tradition of state contempt toward the task of meeting the basic human needs of the indigenous population. It stems from short-term strains related to the displacement of subsistence agriculture and the corresponding expansion of export agriculture. It is further stimulated by inflationary fluctuations (1973-84) in the cash market for food purchases upon which the cash-poor rural lower classes have become increasingly dependent. The local price per pound of dried beans, $.18 in 1978, was over $.60 in 1982. Finally, violent rural unrest stems from the legacy of earlier mass-elite political interactions, a subject to which we now turn our attention.

REVOLUTION FROM ABOVE, 1944-54

During the democratically elected presidencies of Juan Jose Arevalo (1945-51) and Colonel Jacobo Arbenz (1951-54), the distribution of wealth did become a significant issue in Guatemalan politics. In this period the centuries-old tradition of authoritarian government was briefly broken, as was the close reliance on the United States. Labor codes and courts were established to permit orderly unionization of urban and rural workers. Illiterate citizens were given trade union and voting rights. Rural cooperatives were organized. Political parties were permitted to establish permanent local organizations. Especially after 1951 (under Arbenz), government officials and members of the communist

Guatemalan Workers' Party used the freedom to speak
publicly and on the radio to heighten the lower classes'
consciousness of their position and the possibilities for
change.

Society responded. Political participation reached
a high point in the early 1950s. The number of voters
soared to more than two-thirds of those eligible.
Membership in urban and rural unions, aligned with the
government but independent, mushroomed. Among the rural
lower classes, receptiveness to pro-government organizations was greatest among regular church-goers and self-
identified Catholics.

Meanwhile, ownership of the means of production
continued to be highly concentrated in the hands of
foreigners. In 1950, the Boston-based multinational
United Fruit Company (UFCO) owned 325 of the 550 tractors
in Guatemala. National railroads were wholly owned by a
UFCO subsidiary, as were major portions of the electric
utilities and port facilities. Moreover, UFCO was the
largest landowner, holding more than 1 million acres,
principally in bananas and coffee. Thus, to demand
resource redistribution was to demand change in
Guatemalan relations with influential groups in the
United States.

A number of U.S. officials had close ties to UFCO.
Eisenhower's secretary of state, John Foster Dulles, was
a senior partner in Sullivan and Cromwell, UFCO's law
firm, as was his brother, Allen Dulles, director of
Central Intelligence. Henry Cabot Lodge, ambassador to
the United Nations, was a major stockholder and had
served on UFCO's board of directors. John Moors Cabot,
assistant secretary of state for Inter-American Affairs,
was also a major stockholder. Thus, when President
Arbenz proposed an agrarian reform involving land
redistribution (Decree 900), American leaders were
personally affected. Despite a vitriolic anti-Guatemala
campaign by UFCO's public relations department, however,
Washington did not immediately act to prevent the
measure.

In the course of the two-year-long land reform,
about 10 percent of Guatemala's productive farmland was
redistributed on lifelong lease-hold to 89,000 families.
Far from being an assault on capitalism or private
property, the law was designed to liquidate the existing
system of feudal holdings in order to develop capitalist
methods of agricultural production. Only fallow lands
were taken; owners were to be compensated through 25-year
government bonds bearing 3 percent interest, with the
value of the land being determined by the owners' own
previous evaluations for tax purposes. Nevertheless,
both Guatemalan owners (who lost more than 350,000 acres)
and UFCO objected strenuously and approached the U.S.

government seeking the overthrow of Arbenz and the return of their property.

The overthrow of Arbenz and the reversal of the decade-long concern for economic redistribution was accomplished through a process of "active penetration."[14] Most elementally, a Guatemalan military coup was stimulated by a broad range of U.S. inducements. American embassy officials met with senior military officers and urged that Arbenz' "communism" be stopped. CIA pilots flew psychologically debilitating leafletting and bombing raids over key cities and military outposts. U.S. radio propaganda confused Arbenz' officials and the populace into believing that a significant force of Guatemalan exiles, led by Colonel Carlos Castillo Armas, had invaded and conquered much of the country. American officials blocked Guatemalan attempts to have charges of aggression heard before the UN Security Council. Responding to Washington's financial inducements, Honduras, El Salvador, and Nicaragua assisted in these deceptions and in the preparation for the invasion. Though none of these efforts objectively prevented Arbenz from continuing in power, the subjective reality inside Guatemala became untenable. A last-minute effort to divert recently purchased Czech arms to civilian supporters was blocked by the army high command. Fearing imminent conquest by (the almost wholly nonexistent) U.S.-financed, armed, and organized "Liberation Army," generals in Guatamala City revolted. Arbenz was driven from power.

Within months, the expropriated lands were returned to their former owners and a new oil development law favorable to exploration by foreign companies was decreed. At the same time, more than half the electorate lost the right to vote, nearly all unions were disbanded, the communist party was outlawed, and several thousand political prisoners were executed. Residual lower-class politicization, however, required that a new form of dictatorship be created.

THE FORMATION OF THE COUNTERREVOLUTIONARY STATE, 1954-66

Elite fragmentation was a substantial problem. Castillo Armas became president only after U.S. Ambassador John Peurifoy engineered his ascent over the objections of the Guatemalan high command. Violence between "Liberationists" and the regular army repeatedly flared during 1955-57. In spite of this, Castillo was able to establish his personal dictatorship through the creation of a secret police and paramilitary secret societies, which reinforced his independence from the armed forces. Here too, American influence played an

important role. "Public safety"/police-training programs
were begun. A political intelligence police, the
so-called Committee of National Defense Against
Communism, was organized with the aid of the CIA and
charged with tracking down and arresting "communists" and
their sympathizers. Vigilante groups were formed. CIA
operative Fred Sherwood told John Chancellor of NBC News
of his role in organizing the secret societies that
flourished in the mid-1950s: "Several of us thought
perhaps we could stop the (communist) movement by
organizing something in the form of vigilantes or
nightraiders. . . . The American government threw their
forces with these small groups and helped [them]
organize."[15]

Washington's assistance to Castillo had other, more
public dimensions as well. During its three-year reign,
the regime became a high-priority client, with economic
aid apparently totalling $46 million (though other
sources place it as high as $90 million).[16] This help
was particularly noteworthy during the first crucial
months. While U.S. grants to Latin America were
declining more than 38 percent between 1954 and 1955,
those to Guatemala grew over 1,800 percent, from $348,000
to $6,604,000. In 1955, Guatemala received more than 21
percent of the grant aid given to South and Central
America and the Caribbean.[17] By 1957, military aid to
Guatemala had surpassed that granted to every Central
American and Caribbean nation, except Trujillo's
Dominican Republic.

Extensive support did not stabilize the political
situation. Without a mass movement, Castillo could not
mobilize society around his incoherent visions. Rule by
terror could not eliminate intra-elite tensions, which
remained high. Beset by plots on every side, Castillo
was assassinated in July 1957 by a member of the
Presidential Palace Guard.

Due to factional divisions in the military, it took
the better part of a year before Colonel Miguel Ydigoras
Fuentes was selected as Castillo's successor. From 1958
to 1963, his personalistic style of rule continued to
impede national unity. Yet, Ydigoras seemed to be
Washington's best bet. He had not been favored by the
United States in the 1958 presidential election, and that
very fact enhanced both his domestic political position
and his ability to sell American policy initiatives.

Such considerations became especially important
after Fidel Castro came to power in 1959. Challenged by
the popular nationalistic revolution in Cuba, American
policymakers sought not to reform social ills or broaden
political participation, but rather to unify conservative, pro-American elites throughout the region. In
Guatemala three goals in particular were pursued: First,
elite unity was sought through the creation of a single

center-right party and the molding of the security forces
into a unified and reliable anti-communist force.
Second, a U.S.-Guatemalan economic accord was sought in
order to facilitate the expansion of American private
investment. Third, Guatemalan policymakers were
encouraged to assume a position of leadership in the
emerging anti-Castro crusade. These objectives were
assumed to be complementary; they were continuous and
were in no significant way affected by the changeover
from the Eisenhower to Kennedy administration in 1961.

Guatemalan foreign policy under Ydigoras responded
to the concerns of the United States. Under the direction of the CIA, a force of Cuban exiles was brought to
the "Helvetia" finca owned by the brother of the
Guatemalan ambassador to the United States. There the
exiles were given military training in preparation for
the ill-fated "Bay of Pigs" invasion. During this
period, Guatemala's relations with Cuba deteriorated
rapidly. In April 1960 diplomatic relations were
severed, and in the following month the Cuban news
agency, Prensa Latina, was expelled from the country. In
combination with the appearance of ex-President Arbenz on
Radio Havana, these actions had divisive effects both
within the Guatemalan political elite and between elites
and non-elites.

Nationalist reactions to Ydigoras' subservient
foreign policy undermined the other U.S. goals.
Hostility toward Cuba eroded the dictator's authority in
the eyes of some military men, since the benefit to
Guatemala was less than clear. This made it less
possible for Washington to achieve its first objective--
namely, unification of the Guatemalan center, right, and
military into a single coherent force. In the absence of
such unity, proposals in pursuit of the second goal (a
U.S.-Guatemalan accord on private investment rights)
found few friendly audiences.

Even more damaging were Ydigoras' domestic policies.
Discontent over inoperative land-reform promises erupted
in riots in 1960. Potential supporters in the upper
class vehemently opposed Ydigoras' plan to tax incomes
for the first time. Yet, although the regime's popular
base gradually narrowed, its fragile institutional
foundation proved sufficient for its survival--with
American help. Thus, in response to the above-mentioned
riots, Washington sent 3,500 tear gas grenades, $500,000
to pay for military overtime, ammunition, machine guns,
and food. U.S. officials were convinced that stability
would be achieved if the military became the "bulwark of
the situation."[18] Nevertheless, the limits of American
control were suggested when a group of U.S.-trained
officers attempted a golpe in November. The move failed
when the bulk of the army rallied after the U.S. Navy
blockaded the Caribbean coast and American Embassy

officials gave Ydigoras $10 million in emergency "budget support."[19]

Fall 1961 is the period often thought of as the flowering of the Alliance for Progress. U.S.-Guatemalan modernization plans, however, were consumed by such pressing needs as another 2,000 vomit gas grenades, 265 extra gas masks,[20] and increased "Public Safety" training for the security forces. In spite of unequivocal American support, intra-elite tensions remained high. It is true that most pro-communist officers had been purged or had left the service to join the remnants of the November 1960 rebels as guerrillas. But the military had been unable to establish a consensus with regard to presidential succession and other major issues. Especially problematic was the unimplemented U.S.-Guatemalan investment guarantee agreement (1960). In contrast to the contingent role assigned to the bourgeoisie in dependency theory, many in the Guatemalan business community opposed the accord on the ground that it contained too many concessions to foreign capital.

Urban unrest in 1962 demonstrated that the repressed labor movement remained a significant potential actor, one with an agenda quite different from those of the contending elite factions. By 1963, Ydigoras favored reopening the political process, a move apparently intended to more effectively manage disunity by allowing an orderly free election. This development raised new problems, however. In December 1961, former President Arevalo had announced his intention to seek office. This prospect proved entirely unacceptable to the minister of defense, Colonel Enrique Peralta. In March 1963, Peralta overthrew Ydigoras, suspended the constitution, and initiated important steps in the consolidation of the counterrevolutionary state. American aid continued. No military advisers were withdrawn. Diplomatic recognition of Peralta's government was granted after a brief delay.

Why did Washington acquiesce to this abortion of electoral politics? Nine years earlier, when Arbenz had been ousted by a U.S.-sponsored coup, geopolitical considerations had been mixed with a desire to protect access for American multinational corporations. The situation was not much different in 1963. Consider, for instance, this secret intelligence analysis of Arevalo's earlier presidency:

> Arevalo, faithful to his platform, insisted upon the maintenance of an open political system; and neither the military, debilitated by internal rivalries, nor self-seeking politicians were able to circumscribe his policy. It was in this atmosphere of laissez-faire that the communists were able to expand their operations and appeal effectively to various sectors of the population.[21]

It was fear of the reemergence of a similar regime--
of history repeating itself--that haunted both Peralta
and U.S. policymakers. Arevalo was not a communist.
Indeed, he had been so lukewarm about the communists when
he was president that the Guatemalan Workers' Party (PGT)
had remained underground until Arbenz had created an
atmosphere in which it felt less exposed. Nevertheless,
by 1963, Arevalo had assumed a far different form in the
minds of American leaders. In the words of Undersecretary of State George Ball, the Department of State
considered "Arevalo's return . . . adverse to U.S.
interest because of [the] documented virulence [of] his
anti-U.S. prejudices and his proven capabilities to take
his country toward communist domination."[22] The
overriding concern was to ensure the continuing rule of
pro-American elites. Promises of socioeconomic reform
and political democracy, rhetorical touchstones of the
Kennedy administration, were mere appetizers for domestic
consumption. Democracy in Guatemala, where support for
radical change grew from the soil, was perceived as being
injurious to U.S. interests. It is clear that from 1954
to 1963 the domestic processes of Guatemalan leadership
and policy selection had been autonomous ultimately only
to the degree that compatibility with American geopolitical and economic interests was achieved. Between 1963
and 1966, the United States and Guatemala took new steps
to ensure that the latter's armed forces were up to the
task. Within a year, the U.S. Military Assistance
Program (MAP) accounted for 21 percent of the Guatemalan
military budget and 92 percent of all force improvement
expenditures. By 1965, 72 percent of MAP aid was
budgeted for internal security and counterinsurgency
warfare training and deployment. More than $46 million
in nonmilitary aid was concurrently extended from 1963 to
1966.[23]

   Within the American government, the impact on any
future prospect for democracy was clearly perceived. The
choices in Guatemala were not democracy or authoritarianism. The latter was a given. The question was
whether it would be North Americans or Guatemalans who
would use force to defend U.S. interests. In a February
1964 cable, Ambassador John Bell starkly underlined the
role being sought for the Guatemalan military: "[I]
would venture [to] point out that we might be able [to]
reduce or eliminate [the] requirement for MAP in Latin
America if we . . . were willing or preferred [to] use
American manpower rather than Latin. If we are not
prepared [to] do this, MAP seems to me [a] relatively
inexpensive means [of] maintaining our interests."[24]

   Efforts were redoubled to create a behemoth in the
service of U.S. foreign policy. Within the first year of
the Peralta dictatorship, steps were taken to perfect the
police state. Financed and designed by AID officials in

late 1963, a plan was developed to link the anti-
subversive efforts of the Guatemalan military and the
several police agencies with the security systems of
neighboring dictatorships. Radio links were to be
established between field units and a communications
center. A computerized subversives' information archive
would relay information on detained suspects to field
officers directly from the Presidential Palace. (This
project became fully operational only after 1970.)[25] As
early as 1964, U.S. military personnel accompanied the
Guatemalan Army on antiguerrilla operations, but as
observers, not co-combatants. Meanwhile, Peralta
declared it a capital offense to illegally possess
weapons and announced severe penalties for the possessio
of socialist literature. Rural military commissioners
were exempted from civil law and were ordered to draft
suspected leftists.

Yet Peralta remained beyond the complete control of
the Americans. Embassy officials repeatedly were unable
to expedite proposed investment projects of U.S. multinationals and could not persuade Peralta to adopt the
complete package of counterinsurgency measures. AID
plans to reorganize government bureaucracies unrelated t
internal security were frustrated by Guatemalan non-
cooperation. Peralta simply refused to become a Central
American Diem.

The central features of the counterrevolutionary
state emerged between 1954 and 1966. With American
assistance, personalistic pseudo-democratic rule,
augmented by unofficial nightriders, gradually gave way
to direct military government. The foundation of this
alliance was the growing perception within the U.S.-
trained Guatemalan military of the need for counterinsurgency warfare, far more so than any consensus on th
"rights" of North American capital. Indeed, Peralta
turned out to be something of a nationalist on that
issue. Political activities by nonelites were tolerated
only so long as the central role of the armed forces wen
unquestioned. The problem of elite fragmentation would
be resolved by remaking the state into a praetorian,
militarized institution. Those who would question this
trend would be crushed.

REVOLUTION FROM BELOW: COUNTERINSURGENCY
GUATEMALAN STYLE, 1966-70

The election of Julio Mendez Montenegro, candidate
of the Revolutionary Party (PR), in 1966 brought an end
to direct military rule, but in no fundamental way did i
change the basic features of the counterrevolutionary
state. Lacking a significant military element, the
Christian Democratic Party (PDC) was barred from elector

participation, as were the communists. Mendez' party had long ago forsaken the connotations of its name, having worked closely with Peralta after being re-legalized in July 1964. Mendez assumed the presidency only after conceding control over internal security policy to the armed forces.

In the Mendez years (1966-70), the armed forces confronted a determined but small guerrilla movement. MAP advisers sought a more systematic Guatemalan response to the unconventional tactics of the guerrillas than either Ydigoras or Peralta had been willing to conduct. Although the several small bands of guerrillas probably never exceeded 450, neither American officials nor the Guatemalan high command could know for certain how much latent support for guerrilla actions existed. Thus, even though National Intelligence Estimates derided guerrilla strength as "unimpressive,"[26] the U.S. country team joined the Guatemalan high command in support of vigorous antiguerrilla efforts, which had been stymied by the nationalistic Peralta for three years.

In Mendez' first year, the military appointed Colonel Carlos Arana Osorio to conduct counterinsurgency operations in the center of guerrilla strength, the eastern departments of Zacapa and Izabal. Arana's military approach was simple: All who were capable of resistance, both guerrillas and civilians, would be crushed as a way of demonstrating the newly expanded capabilities of the Guatemalan armed forces, thereby deterring future rebellions. Simultaneously, para-military groups swung into action against suspected leftists and sympathizers throughout the land. The bloodbath that followed went well beyond conventional military techniques. U.S. Military Attache Colonel John Webber told Time magazine in early 1968 that it had been 'his idea and at his instigation that the technique of counter-terror had been implemented." Paramilitary death squads (the "White Hand" and "Eye for Eye") were organized to chill peasant support for the guerrillas. These organizations represented themselves as 'independent," but a leader of the ultraconservative National Liberation Movement (MLN), Mario Sandoval Alarcon (an ally of Arana), stated in 1967 that "the army was demoralized last year, until we organized the White Hand. . . . The terrorism of the guerrillas . . . has forced the government to adopt a plan of complete illegality, but this has brought results."[27] At least 3,000 and perhaps 8,000 noncombatants died between 1966 and 1968, primarily victims of official executions and paramilitary violence.[28]

American support for this effort took many forms. Between 1957 and 1969 more than 20,000 Guatemalan police were trained under the AID "Public Safety" program, and more than $2.5 million was spent on police training in

282

1966-70 alone. U.S. military training of Guatemalan
officers reached a new high in fiscal year 1967 and
continued to grow in 1968. (More than 2,100 were trained
in 1950-69.) Total MAP spending in 1967-70 was more than
$7.8 million. This was augmented by steadily escalating
AID and Export-Import Bank transfusions of $15.9 million
in 1967, $17.5 million in 1968, $79.1 million in 1969,
and $32.2 million in 1970. Development assistance during
this first stage of counterinsurgency war totalled $144.7
million.[29] Although it has never been corroborated by
any U.S. official, the Guatemalan vice-president,
Clemente Marroquin Rojas, claimed that American jets,
flown by U.S. active-duty pilots based in the Canal Zone,
conducted napalm bombing sorties as part of the
campaign.[30]

Just as these efforts resembled the "search and
destroy" and "Phoenix" programs in Vietnam, so too there
was a superficial "land reform" to win the "hearts and
minds" of the peasantry. In terms of domestic and international opinion, talk of reform served as a velvet glove
covering the mailed fist of rural military repression. A
grand total of 429 families were beneficiaries of land
redistributions in Zacapa, and these came only after
heavy pressure from U.S. officials.[31] The entire topic
was so charged politically that Mendez found it
impossible to make more than token advances. In 1969,
with the arrival in Washington of the Nixon administration, pressure to use this "carrot" to complement the
"stick" of repression was abandoned.

Nevertheless, the guerrilla forces collapsed under
the weight of counterinsurgency warfare. Despite the
1965 publication of a common-position paper by two
guerrilla groups, no real unity existed among the rebels.
At the time of the Zacapa-Izabal campaign, the three
separate revolutionary movements lacked any meaningful
central command. The small communist party had been
beheaded by the March 1966 kidnapping and murder of
twenty-eight of its top leaders. Remnants of the
November 13, 1960 military coup composed the bulk of the
Revolutionary Movement--13th of November (MR-13), which
differed from the Revolutionary Armed Forces (FAR), a
Marxist band that surfaced in 1963, on a host of
ideological and tactical issues. These three groups
lacked a secure base area within which to regroup.
Although the mountainous terrain of Guatemala affords
many opportunities for retreat, the guerrillas were
repeatedly trapped due to the superior intelligence
system of the counter-revolutionary state.

They were also weakened by their low level of
support (both active and passive) from the rural masses.
The post-1954 repression had led to a reduction in lower-
class participation in all types of political organization. This meant that disaffected elements of the

leading Guatemalan groups tended to predominate within
these newer guerrilla organizations. Ideological
differences led to bitter conflicts over tactics and
prevented unification of the vastly outgunned insurgents.
In addition, the guerrillas, being almost all ladinos,
were ethnically and geographically divided from the large
concentrations of unassimilated Indians in the western
highlands. And so they fell.³⁰ By 1970, nearly all the
bands had splintered, and the survivors, in small groups,
sought refuge in the relative anonymity of the cities.

THE INSTITUTIONALIZATION OF STATE TERRORISM, 1970-84

     In 1970 the architect of counterinsurgency, Colonel
Arana, now known as the "butcher of Zacapa," became
president in a three-way "election" among generals. In
this, as in all subsequent ballotings (1974, 1978, 1982),
all parties that opposed any feature of the counterrevolutionary state were banned. During Arana's reign
(1970-74) and that of his hand-picked successor, General
Kjell Laugerud (1974-78), the Guatemalan Armed Forces
reestablished a form of order. Emboldened by success,
they set about to ensure their permanent preeminence by
making those military leaders who were most influential
in the counterrevolutionary state the economic leaders of
the nation as well.
     Arana's first step was to impose a year-long state
of siege, ostensibly to ferret out fleeing guerrillas,
urban leftists, and their supporters. In reality, the
measure had a much broader and more chilling effect.
More than 700 people were executed in the first two
months,³² many of the victims being relatives, neighbors,
or friends of accused leftists. Between 1,000 and 2,000
summary executions were made during the year-long siege
in which the kill ratio favored the government over the
guerrillas by perhaps sixteen to one.³³
     Again, U.S. assistance facilitated the repression.
In fiscal year (FY) 1971, Guatemala received AID public
safety assistance totalling more than $1.12 million, the
highest in Latin America. MAP spending the same year
($6.6 million) was nearly as high as the total for the
preceding four years ($7.8 million).³⁴ A fleet of paddy
wagons was delivered just prior to the state of siege.
In the early 1970s, the AID-financed Regional
Telecommunications Center, with its centralized
subversive files and radio links with all security
forces, became operational. Amnesty International has
charged that the function of this center, located in the
Presidential Palace annex, was to target individuals for
kidnapping by the security forces.³⁵ In nearly all
cases, the "disappeared" were murdered; often their
mutilated bodies were discovered far from the place of

the kidnappings. In the 1970s, then, rule by institutionalized terror grew directly out of the Guatemalan-
U.S. system of military rule established in the previous
decades. By mid-1972 nearly all large-scale manifesta-
tions of antigovernment activity had waned.

The beneficiaries of this deceptive pseudo-stability
included both the Guatemalan generals and U.S. multinationals. In the early 1970s the army established its
own bank, a cement factory, a television station, and
several smaller businesses. The role of American multinational food companies also changed. By the late 1960s,
most multinationals disguised their North American roots
by operating through subsidiaries. Typical of these
mutations was the United Fruit Company, which in 1969
became United Brands. Shortly thereafter, for tax advantages under Guatemalan law, it became two Guatemalan
private companies, Olemca and Numar. Other familiar
multinationals remained visibly engaged in agricultural
extraction operations: Goodyear continued to own rubber
plantations but also developed a tire-making plant. Del
Monte continued to operate some of the former UFCO banana
acreage. Other multinationals created mini-industries.

Most U.S. private investment fell outside the agricultural sector, especially in mining. Between 1959 and
1969, new direct private foreign investment totalled
$29.2 million.[36] Over 86 percent of it was American. In
the 1970s, oil and nickel became the major hubs of
development, especially in the "Transversal del Norte,"
a largely uninhabited region of northern Guatemala.
These large tracts of land came under the ownership of
leading military officers. Much that was profitably
developed thus directly assisted the praetorian caste's
consolidation of rule.

As early as 1960, the International Nickel Company
(INCO) had sought entry into northern Guatemala. In the
years that followed, U.S. Embassy officials attempted to
expedite the project over the nationalistic obstacles
imposed by generals like Peralta. Although the plant was
authorized in 1965 (foreign ownership was granted for
forty years), it only opened in July 1977. INCO (owner
of 80 percent) developed its Guatemalan nickel as a joint
venture with Hannah Mining (owner of 20 percent) through
the subsidiary EXMIBAL (Exploraciones y Explotaciones
Minerales-Izabal). In 1968, EXMIBAL had asked for and
gotten a ten-year tax exemption on the project. The
following year, an ad hoc commission of the Guatemalan
Congress had investigated the project and denounced the
terms as unfavorable. Typical of the fate of those who
question the propriety of decisions over which the
praetorian caste claims authority, by 1971 two of the
three lawyers on the commission had been assassinated,
victims of "death squad" attacks, and the third was in
exile after surviving a gun attack.

Exploitation of EXMIBAL workers also may be explained in terms of the self-interest of the praetorian caste. The Guatemalan military had a direct interest in keeping wages low and profits high. Taxes were to be based on levels of profit. But these revenues would not go to the Guatemalan treasury; rather, they were to be applied as credit against the amount Guatemala owed toward purchase of an eventual 30 percent share of the operations. Thus, only by relatively high EXMIBAL profits could Guatemalan ownership be realized. Despite this cozy arrangement, INCO closed the EXMIBAL project in November 1981, citing high security costs and the need for cheaper energy to make nickel mining and processing profitable.

As internal security improved, foreign investment steadily grew. Net direct private investment in 1970 ($29 million) was far overshadowed by the net direct private investment which occurred in the last year of the decade ($117 million).[37] Public sector reliance on external capital also grew. Nevertheless, Guatemalan dependence on foreign capital can be greatly exaggerated. It is true that in 1979 the government guaranteed or borrowed more than three times the capital ($129 million) that it did in 1970 ($35 million). But repayment of the public-sector debt also slowed. Whereas repayment equalled two-thirds of new borrowing in 1970, by 1979 it was only one-tenth of new borrowing. Total external public debt had more than quadrupled (to $482 million), but it was still relatively low--7 percent of the gross national product. Of all Third World nations, only four had a better GNP to foreign public debt ratio. The minimal cost of servicing this debt, which represented only 2.2 percent of the annual value of exports, reveals that economic development did not lead to the kind of fiscal crisis that so many Third World nations have experienced.[38]

It may be oversimplification to infer that the repression of nonelites (or potential counterelites) was simply a function of the Guatemalan military's efforts to protect its own (and U.S. corporate) economic interests. Government-spawned violence had become far more generalized. By 1976, at least 20,000--and perhaps 30,000--people had died as a result of a decade of covertly sanctioned murders. There is little doubt that the state itself was behind these killings, whether at the hands of the armed forces or of allied death squads. Institutional integration of the death squads became all but official when the founder of the "White Hand," Mario Sandoval Alarcon, was made vice-president (1974-78). In March 1976, the interior minister publicly approved of the death squads' activities. In September 1980, moreover, the Ministry's press secretary defected to the side of the guerrillas, charging that the stationery of a

new death squad, the Secret Anti-Communist Army, was kept
in his ministry and that targets for "disappearance" were
selected by the minister, the army chief of staff, and
the president.[39]

On February 4, 1976, a major earthquake devastated
Guatemala. In its wake 27,000 were dead, 77,000 injured,
and over a million homeless. Atop this calamity of
nature came the malignancies of man. Relief efforts by
local Catholic and international relief organizations,
generous as they were, were met with government inaction
and corruption. Strain on the social order, made even
more acute by the natural calamity, assumed proportions
previously unknown.

Even before the earthquake, major social changes,
stimulated by two decades of economic growth, had given
rise to groups that, under non-communist leadership, had
begun to mobilize the lower classes to defend their
interests and claim a larger share of the national
economic pie. Among such organizations were those
engaged in rural development programs (cooperatives,
literacy, health, etc.) backed by U.S. missionaries,
private voluntary agencies, Peace Corps volunteers,
medical workers, and others. Over 500 agricultural
cooperatives had been organized, encompassing more than
132,000 families. Similarly, by 1975 a new urban trade
union movement had recruited more than 85,000 members.
Union lawyers had helped forge links between these two
distinct, if nascent, lower-class groups. Bonds were
built by assisting peasants to obtain clear titles to
disputed lands and by supporting strikes by mine workers
in the primarily indigenous departments of Alta Verapaz
and Huehuetenango.

The Laugerud government (1974-78) seized the opportunity provided by the earthquake to penetrate and break
up these movements. In the aftermath of the earthquake,
in late February 1976, a major counterinsurgency operation was launched in the department of El Quiche.
Ostensibly established to catch guerrillas, in the next
few months sixty-eight cooperative members were killed in
Ixcan, forty in Chajul, twenty-eight in Cotzal, and
thirty-two in Nebaj. Similar violence against cooperatives became the defining feature of the government of
General Romeo Lucas Garcia (1978-82). By 1980, nearly
one-half of all (private as well as U.S.-funded) rural
development programs had been terminated or substantially
reduced.[40]

This growing repression altered another significant
political relationship--namely, that with the United
States. By 1977, widespread government murders and other
abuses of human rights drove U.S. officials to propose a
cut-off of American military aid. Coming in the wake of
the 1975 discontinuation of Public Safety training,
Guatemalan officials reacted to this "affront" to their

sovereignty by suspending the MAP program. From 1977 to 1983, the level of official U.S. activity in support of the military/police apparatus of the counterrevolutionary state was greatly diminished. AID support was also complicated. A 1981 proposal by the Reagan administration to extend further financial assistance for the Regional Telecommunications Center had to be withdrawn in the face of a congressional threat to take the administration to court for violating U.S. human rights laws.

Yet Guatemala's military capability was only marginally diminished. In 1974, the regime bought fighter aircraft from France. Even after the arms embargo was instituted, Guatemala continued to purchase "civilian model" Bell helicopters from Texas suppliers. These nonmilitary aircraft were subsequently converted to direct combat use. Other weapons were secured from Sweden, Israel, France, Spain, and Brazil. Military training continued to be provided, with Argentine graduates of U.S. counterinsurgency schools conducting the courses. External finance was secured from such diverse sources as Romania and Argentina.

The "Frankenstein Monster" had taken on a life of its own. The Guatemalan regime rejected Washington's prodding on human rights. It had to; such violations were intrinsic to its method of rule. Rather than accept a pluralistic conception of the state and the competing interests within it, Guatemalan rulers have defined as treasonous resistance from all quarters to any policies. Thus, the labor actions of public-sector bus drivers' have met the same brutal response as strikes at the multinational Coca Cola plant. It is no coincidence that President Lucas Garcia declared trade unionism "subversive"[41] on the day after the December 1978 murder of Coca Cola union official Pedro Quevado y Quevado. Union leaders have been repeatedly kidnapped, tortured, and killed by armed forces personnel and off-duty security forces posing as unofficial "death squads." Official investigations, not to mention trials, have been conspicuously absent.[42]

In the early 1970s, state terrorism was fairly random and appears to have been designed to induce a general depoliticization, similar to that which occurred in 1954-56. Accordingly, only about 11 percent of the "disappeared" (1972-76) were persons identified with the political or labor opposition; the vast majority were peasants or workers without opposition ties.[43] Since the post-earthquake repression, the insurgent movement has changed and grown. Especially since guerrilla columns have waged successful, large-scale operations (post-1978), the scope of state terrorism has become enlarged. Two features in particular stand out: First, there was a great surge in selective, targeted disappearances of leaders (and potential leaders) of

288

opposition parties, unions, critical journalists,
clerics, and university personnel (both faculty and
students). Second, reminiscent of the 1966-68 policy of
rural terror, indiscriminate large-scale extermination
operations were resumed in the countryside. These latter
operations followed the model of U.S. counterinsurgency
war but were no longer U.S.-directed. Counterinsurgency
operations were concentrated in areas in which guerrillas
operated, but since rebel organizations had now developed
more diverse ethnic and geographic bases, most departments of rural Guatemala experienced widespread
atrocities committed by official security forces and
allied death squads.

The years after 1978 brought escalating violence and
increased casualties. A very crude measure of the scope
of the suffering can be made by body counts. In 1981
alone, state terrorism and guerrilla violence accounted
for between 4,000 to 9,000 deaths, according to international human rights groups. (The rebels, on the other
hand, claim that 13,500 died in the same period.)[44]
Although significant worker-student demonstrations in the
fall of 1978 may help to explain the regime's ill ease,
the response seemed quite out of proportion to the
threat. Amnesty International reported that over 90
percent of the victims were killed by official forces or
their allies. The OAS Inter-American Commission on Human
Rights concurred, noting that "in the large majority of
the cases, the deaths . . . were due to illegal executions and to the 'disappearances' engineered by the
security forces or paramilitary civilian groups acting in
close collaboration with the governmental authorities."[45]

Targeted disappearances, torture, mutilation, and
murder of current and potential opposition leaders are
designed to render resistence ineffectual. In Chapter 4
of this text, Penny Lernoux has described the repression
of the church and Christian activists. Of equal interest
is the fate of the trade union movement, which has
suffered from decades of official harassment. In one
twelve-month period (May 1978 to May 1979), 9 union
leaders disappeared, 311 postal workers were arrested,
the national nurses' union was decertified and made
illegal, and the Transport Union office was repeatedly
bombed and ultimately destroyed. Dozens of union activists lost their jobs.[46] Amnesty International concluded
that "to be a union leader or active member of a trade
union in Guatemala today means risking one's life."[47]

Moreover, the process continued: In 1980, 110 union
leaders were killed, along with 300 peasant leaders.[48]
Twenty-six of these disappearances occurred in one day,
on June 21st, when police blocked streets so that
plainclothesmen could raid the central offices of the
trade union movement, a block from the Presidential
Palace. This attack in broad daylight was the third on

union headquarters that year and was followed by other
mass kidnappings of labor leaders. In September 1980,
Vice-President Francisco Villagran Kramer resigned his
office, charging that "the union movement and collective
bargaining between capital and labor have been seriously
harmed by the systematic persecution and killing of union
leaders."[49] In July 1982, all union activities were
decreed illegal.

Other opposition leaders suffered as well.
Politicians, university professors, and students who
opposed the repression often became its victims. In the
words of Villagran Kramer: "Death or exile is the fate
of those who fight for justice in Guatemala."[50] Thus,
the Socialist Democratic party founder, Alberto Fuentes
Mohr, a former finance minister under Mendez, was
machine-gunned in January 1979 after numerous death
threats. Four days later, an eyewitness was shot dead.
Fuentes Mohr's killing had followed his demand for an
investigation into the October 1978 murder of student
leader Oliverio Castaneda de Leon, who had been machine-
gunned in the main square adjacent to the Presidential
Palace after delivering a speech to a large, well-policed
assembly of students and workers. (No arrests were
made.) Fuentes Mohr's death was followed by the March
1979 machine-gun murder of the man most likely to have
led the legal opposition in the 1982 elections, Manuel
Colom Argueta, a former mayor of Guatemala City. Eight
days later, a local secretary general of the centrist
Revolutionary Party was killed. Thirty-eight other
student activists and twelve professors were also
murdered by death squads or security forces in the
twelve-month period ending June 1979. Nor did the
following year bring any respite: At least twenty-seven
professors, fifty-three school teachers, seventy-one
university students, and many opposition party officials
were murdered in 1980. From August 1980 to May 1981, no
less than seventy-six Christian Democrat Party officials
were killed.[51]

Journalists attempting to convey the extent of the
killings met similar fates. From mid-1978 to mid-1979,
the offices of the newspaper El Grafico were machine-
gunned four times; two journalists were killed, and two
radio stations were sacked.[52] Subsequently, Amnesty
International reported that fifteen more journalists were
murdered from June 1980 to January 1982 after
"disappearing."[53] Despite the generally pro-regime line
found in the surviving Guatemalan press, after the March
1982 golpe the new government of General Efrain Rios
Montt issued stern directives that the violence must
always be attributed to "terrorists." Unsatisfied with
the results, the regime imposed prior censorship in July
1982, banning even the semblance of a free press.
According to Rios Montt, the ladino population and the

290

Guatemalan government are at war with the Indians.[54]   In
such times, the reporting of any political event, except
those mentioned in official press releases, is cause for
closing down the offending publication.

The second major feature of state terrorism has been
the renewal of rural counterinsurgency warfare. These
operations began around 1975 as small, targeted actions,
designed especially to evict Indians and ladino peasants
from lands in the mineral-rich north. At first, death
squads were used. Whereas only 4 percent of all killings
from death squad actions in 1972-74 occurred in the three
northern departments (Quiche, Peten, and Alta Verapaz),
by 1976 28 percent were in the north.[55] After the earthquake, a new guerrilla organization, the Guerrilla Army
of the Poor (EGP), found large numbers of recruits in
this area. Confronted by increasingly stiff opposition,
the regime deployed regular troops.

The cycle of violence in the north reflected the
significant, broad base of support for the guerrillas
found in the newly politicized Indian minorities. In the
early 1980s there existed a much greater level of mass
support for the insurgents than ever before, a base that
spanned both ethnic groups. In this respect the
insurrection is fundamentally different from the ladino-
centered guerrilla war of 1966-69. Both of the new
guerrilla organizations, EGP and the Organization of the
People in Arms (ORPA), are filled with members of
Guatemala's Indian ethnic groups. In January 1982, these
elements joined forces with two surviving, primarily
ladino guerrilla organizations--the Guatemalan Workers'
Party and the resurgent Revolutionary Armed Forces--to
form a unified guerrilla command, the Guatemalan National
Revolutionary Union. This organization is a seminal
phenomenon in Guatemalan politics, unifying for the first
time the various Indian ethnics, the ladino peasantry,
the working classes, and the communist party.

This mobilization of the indigenous peoples has been
a direct response to the economic marginalization of
these groups and the state terrorism that enforces it.
Indian land ownership rights have repeatedly come into
conflict with concessions granted to mineral companies
and with newly created ranches given by the government to
allied generals. The responses of the organized peasant
and indigenous peoples, such as those advanced since
April 1978 by the Committee for Peasant Unity (CUC), have
met with targeted, then generalized, repression directed
initially at individuals, then entire families, then
whole villages. Especially noteworthy was the May 1978
ambush by government forces at Panzos, a village near the
oil wells at Rubelsanto and ex-President Lucas Garcia's
78,000-acre ranch. Of 800 Kekchi Indians ambushed, over
140 died. Though over 300 were wounded, Red Cross relief
workers were barred from the area.

Yet, the experience at Panzos is but part of a much larger pattern. Although space limitations prevent a comprehensive portrait in these pages, a few examples will illustrate the increasingly large scale of operations. In 1977-78, in the Olopa area of Chiquimula department, three villages were decimated by military police; over 100 people were killed, including 40 children. In the fall of 1978, more than 30 were killed in Solola after CUC organizers were kidnapped. In 1978-79, other incidents of violence against Indians occurred in Peten, Baja Verapaz, San Marcos, El Progreso, Jutiapa, and Huehuetenango departments.

Between August and October 1979, twenty-two members of the village of Uspantan disappeared after protesting to local officials and the National Congress about earlier disappearances in their area. Some reappeared bearing signs of torture, only to be publicly executed at Chajul. In desperation, villagers from Chajul, Uspantan, Cotzal, and Nebaj marched to the capital, occupied the Spanish Embassy, and, over the objections of the Spanish ambassador, were incinerated by a military attack on January 31, 1980. The sole surviving protestor, badly burned, was kidnapped from a hospital and killed.

In March 1980, a day of army occupation at Nebaj, Quiche department, led to a massacre of more than forty, including thirty-five women and children. In May the army occupied San Juan Comalapa. U.S. Peace Corps worker J. Michael Luhan reported that more than fifty residents in the next few months were dragged from their homes, tortured, and killed. The victims included a three-day-old baby and a fifty-five-year-old woman.[56]

By 1981, such events had enabled the EGP to grow to a force of 1,200 guerrillas, and these operated in many areas with visible public support. Yet, the Lucas Garcia regime continued to pursue the old formula of spiralling repression. In preparation for the Spring 1982 election, rural terrorism was intensified. In April 1981, 123 people died in three small villages near the capital of Quiche department. In May, another 24 died at Chuabajito, victims of death squads. In June, government troops slaughtered 36 (including 20 women and children) at San Mateo Ixtatan, Huehuetenango department. Another massacre, at El Arbolito, Peten, that month, left 50 dead and produced 3,500 refugees. In July, nearly 300 died in a day of aerial bombardment in support of ground operations by government troops at Coya, Huehuetenango. Most of the victims were women, children, and elderly people. In August, nearly 1,000 may have been killed in air attacks supporting counterinsurgency operations in and around San Sebastian Lamoa, near the tourism center of Chichicastenango. Yet, in October, EGP forces mounted their largest attack to that date, a simultaneous assault on three separate department capitals.

The carnage continued to mount: In December, approximately 1,000 people died from operations near Chichicastenango; 4,000 more fled as refugees. Ninety-five residents of Xesic, El Quiche, were killed by troops or death squads between September 1981 and mid-January 1982. On February 15, 1982, refugees from Macalbaj and Calante were ambushed by the army; 54 were decapitated, including 14 children and 5 pregnant women. In early March 1982, approximately 200 residents of Zacualpa, El Quiche, were killed and decapitated by the army.

Despite these military excesses throughout the highlands, lasting political control eluded the armed forces. With no end in sight, frustrated junior officers dramatized their dissatisfaction by staging a successful military coup in late March 1982. However, General Efrain Rios Montt, a senior officer who was chosen as figurehead leader of the new junta, quickly consolidated personal power. In 1982, urban "death squad" killings slowed, fueling widespread hopes for reform. These hopes were kindled by Rios' eccentric style: Members of the small Protestant sect, the Church of the Word, became his chief advisers. Moreover, Rios promised a new approach to win the hearts and minds of the poor, while waging counterinsurgency--the "guns and beans" strategy.

In rural Guatemala the conflict quickened. Army massacres were resumed, especially in Chimaltenango, Huehuetenango, and El Quiche departments.[57] Accompanying the killings was a scorched earth policy so conceived as to deny to the guerrillas the fruit of their supporters' production. Refugees--one in seven Guatemalans--fled in all directions.

Highland villages were compelled to form army-directed, paramilitary patrols (Patrullas de Autodefensa Civil, or PACs) or else be annihilated. After making this Hobbesian choice, villagers then were provided beans and other foods, some of which had been confiscated from less pliant villages. Much of the remainder of the food was U.S. financed; in August 1983, $57 million in food and credits for food purchases were extended by the United States.[58]

In combination with ruthless army operations, the PACs helped slow Indian mobilization by mid-1983. These above-ground organizations insulated the army from clear responsibility for the violence, precisely the same function performed by the "death squads" during earlier counterinsurgency campaigns. The PACs channelled many highly localistic indigenous peoples into locality-based groups. Using classic divide-and-conquer tactics, under army compulsion, villages were then turned loose on neighboring villages. Massacres equally as odious as those under Lucas resulted.[59]

A second major objective of the Guatemalan Armed Forces (1982-83) was the reestablishment of solid military relations with the United States. For Rios, a sympathetic ear was found at the American Embassy and State Department: Atrocities began to be reported as having been conducted by the guerrillas or by unknown assailants.[60] The marketing of this highly questionable interpretation was made considerably easier by the fact that the embassy relied on local press reports and that these reports, after July 1982, were required by the government to attribute all murders to the "subversives." Under Rios' state of siege (which remained in effect from July 1, 1982 to August 8, 1983), most civil and nearly all legal rights of Guatemalans were superseded by decrees that (among other things) allowed arrest for subversive ideas; provided the death penalty for political crimes, including acts committed by minors; eliminated the right to assemble; banned political activities by parties and unions; suspended the right of habeas corpus; and pardoned any and all members of the security forces of all alleged crimes, including murder, rape, and torture. To further cover up the tactics of the terrorist state, Rios eliminated all remaining semblance of a free press, launched verbal attacks against Amnesty International, and continued to prohibit entry into Guatemala by the International Committee of the Red Cross.

Despite Rios' excesses, U.S. military aid to Guatemala was restored in January 1983 "in light of human rights improvements," according to the State Department.[61] Reputable international human rights observers saw matters differently. In December 1982, the U.S. National Council of Churches charged that the central role of the Guatemalan Armed Forces in the government policy of gross violation of human rights was continuing.[62] All refugees, adults, and children interviewed in Chiapas, Mexico, in the Spring of 1983 told Americas Watch investigators that it was from army atrocities, not those of the guerrillas, that they had fled.[63] "Massive extrajudicial executions" by the military were reported by Amnesty International and independent journalists.[64] Other human rights organizations charged that more civilian noncombatants per month were killed by government forces under Rios Montt than in any comparable previous period.[65]

Finally, in February 1983, even the State Department could no longer ignore the Guatemalan reality: Ambassador Frederic Chapin was withdrawn, temporarily, after the Guatemalan Army kidnapped, tortured, and killed US Agency for International Development literacy worker

Patricio Ortiz Maldonado and three companions near San
Ildefonso Ixtahuacan, Huehuetenango. (These killings
represented but the gates of that particular corner of
man's hell: Between August 1982 and Ortiz' death more
than 150 victims of government violence fell in that same
small village.)[66]

STATE TERRORISM AND AMERICAN FOREIGN POLICY IN THE 1980s

In August 1983, General Oscar Humberto Mejia
Victores, the defense minister who had withheld for three
weeks the true facts of Ortiz' killing, the man who
earlier had referred to human rights champion Clarence
Long (congressman from Maryland) as a guerrilla
sympathizer, seized power. Mejia was closely associated
with Rios Montt's military campaign of 1982-83, which
from a tactical viewpoint had been quite successful.
After having bludgeoned rural support for the guerrillas,
the high command of the armed forces, influential retired
officers, and the MLN brought Rios down, apparently so as
to place some distance between themselves and the rubble
left over from this slaughter. Press reports indicate
that U.S. officials also supported Mejia by failing to
inform Rios as they learned of the plot, by consulting
with Mejia outside Guatemala the day before the coup, and
by granting swift recognition to his (unconstitutional)
military government.[67]

Thus, the current regime represents a continuation
of long-standing political patterns. It is clear that
the Guatemalan experience can in no way be reconciled
with a foreign policy predicated on the promotion of
human rights. Considering the role the United States
played in the creation and growth of this "Frankenstein
Monster," U.S. policy should be especially sensitive to
this issue. To be otherwise would forsake values that
are central to our national ethos.

Yet, other considerations have always competed for
the attention of American policymakers. Most important,
the pursuit of geopolitical security (vis-a-vis the
Soviet Union and its clients) and U.S. economic health
figure as primary objectives against which the effectiveness of foreign policies have been and will continue
to be judged. In the 1950s and 1960s it was widely
believed--perhaps naively--that all three of these goals
could be successfully pursued simultaneously. Policies
that weakened Guatemalan communists and strengthened
military institutionalization were thought to stem Soviet
influence and encourage economic development to the
advantage of both the United States and Guatemala.
Pro-American regimes, respectful of human rights, would
develop out of a stabilized political environment.

Economic redistribution would occur in a gradual, orderly fashion.

The grisly Guatemalan record underlines the fallacy of such assumptions. The diverse values and objectives in question often proved incompatible with each other. The promotion of an enhanced capability to identify subversives eliminated (in the short run) the need to build a broad societal consensus. In seeking to create a stable foundation for future (rather than current) democratic politics, the United States helped to provide the means for a new totalitarian system. In fostering a regime capable of protecting North American economic interests, Washington contributed to the creation of a materialist "order of the samurai," which pursues its own institutional economic preeminence without regard for distributional inequities that undermine social consensus. By equating pluralism with the road to communism, that regime gave diverse social forces no form of participation other than armed struggle. Thus, the ultimate by-product of U.S.-Guatemalan cooperation (1954-77) has been a broad-based social movement that, although not controlled by the Soviet Union, seeks realization of its visions through assistance from any and all sources, including the USSR and Cuba.

The anti-American potentials in the situation are too obvious to belabor. The Reagan administration's course of action is self-defeating. Despite the genocidal nature of Guatemalan Army policy, atrocities have failed to defeat the guerrillas. Indeed, in the late Spring of 1982, the EGP opened new offensives in the previously "pacified" Izabal and Zacapa departments. The radicalizing, long, dirty war in Central America, so feared by Americans who sought to avoid another Vietnam, is already well under way.

The long-term prospect of achieving U.S. goals through an alliance with the terrorist state are in serious doubt. A resumption of arms shipments and MAP training will merely fan the flames. Already, the profitability of economic activity has been undermined by the vast security costs for American multinationals. Moreover, to the degree that the revolutionary process becomes further internationalized, it will become more difficult to convey a pragmatic U.S. desire for mutual economic cooperation, regional security, and human rights to any and all forces now seeking an end to repression, including the Guatemalan National Revolutionary Union (URNG).

Unfortunately, subjective and perceptual factors impede discussions to this end. A fundamental gap exists in the way the various parties see both the Guatemalan conflict and the world at large. The published communiques of the URNG member organizations hue to the

main tenets of dependency theory. In this view, the
United States and its allied Latin American ruling
classes are seen as being congenitally unable to
transcend the pursuit of economic advantage, which in
turn is seen as inevitably requiring impoverished, even
repressed, masses. Thus, it is a U.S.-Guatemalan (not
merely Guatemalan) state that the guerrillas see to be in
need of eradication. Their view of the adversary appears
to leave little room within which to conduct the search
for common interests.

By the same token, the insurgents denigrate recent
U.S. policy and continue to comingle the American
scientist and his Guatemalan monster. Nor is this view
entirely erroneous. The sharp reduction in U.S.-
Guatemalan military cooperation after 1977 brought no
human rights improvements. Sanctions were inadequate in
pressuring the Guatemalan military to cease repression
and begin national reconciliation. Although major
weapons systems were withheld, American-manufactured
helicopter parts continued to be sold to the regime, and
U.S. active-duty military helicopter trainers prepared
its pilots for combat. Even before the embargo was
lifted, field telephones, army trucks, and jeeps were
sold to the Guatemalan Army. AID support, moreover,
steadily grew as the violence escalated: $3.9 million in
FY 1980, $8 million in FY 1981, and over $30 million in
FY 1982, according to a letter sent by AID officials to
Representative Don Bonker.[68] (In addition, AID
assistance for 1982 was supplemented by $10 million in
Economic Support Funds under the Caribbean Basin
Initiative. This portion of U.S. assistance is slated to
grow to $40 million for FY 1984.)[69] Nor did the March
1982 seizure of power by Rios Montt really change
anything. The situation quickly deteriorated into
repression-as-usual. Virtually the entire military cast
from the Lucas period has been rehabilitated and returned
to active duty.

If the analysis presented in these pages is correct,
it is highly unlikely that the Guatemalan military, as
presently constituted, can participate in a process of
national reconciliation. In order to pursue its long-
range strategic, economic, and human rights objectives,
therefore, the United States should move soon to explore
new ways of achieving American interests. Military and
economic aid should be halted. Contact should be made
with the URNG to explore possible areas of current and
future cooperation. Discussions within the OAS or the
United Nations should pave the way for the deployment of
an international peacekeeping force with which to maintain order and secure human rights during the transition
to a new regime.

The climax of guerrilla war need not always be a
military event, as the case of Zimbabwe has demonstrated.

Nor must the national interests of revolutionary Third
World governments be diametrically opposed to the
interests of American multinationals, as the Gulf Oil
experience with Angola has shown. But building similar
bridges on which common U.S. and Guatemalan interests can
rest may require a level of creative diplomacy not easily
embraced by ideologues on any side. The first step must
be to recognize the U.S.-Guatemalan record. From that
foundation we can then proceed to discuss our common
interests and objectives. Surely these must include an
end to state terrorism in Guatemala.

NOTES

1. World Bank Development Report 1981 (New York:
International Bank for Reconstruction and Development,
1981), pp. 136, 138, 146, 150, 154, 156.
2. Shelton H. Davis and Julie Hodson, Witnesses to
Political Violence in Guatemala: The Suppression of a
Rural Development Movement (Oxfam America: Impact Audit
Two, 1982), pp. 21, 45-46.
3. Andre Gunder Frank, Dependent Accumulation and
Underdevelopment (New York: Monthly Review Press, 1979),
p. 137.
4. Donald Fox, "Human Rights in Guatemala," Report
for the International Commission of Jurists (unpublished,
1979), p. 6.
5. Report on the Situation of Human Rights in the
Republic of Guatemala (Washington, DC: Organization of
American States/Inter-American Commission on Human
Rights, 1981), p. 130. See also Guatemala: Economic
and Social Position and Prospects (Washington, D.C.:
International Bank for Reconstruction and Development,
1978), pp. 23, 60.
6. Report on the Situation, p. 131.
7. Guatemala: Economic and Social Position and
Prospects, p. 9.
8. Davis and Hodson, Witnesses, p. 45.
9. Educational Deficiencies in Latin America
(Washington, D.C.: Organization of American States,
1979), p. 100.
10. Report on the Situation, pp. 130-131.
11. Fox, "Human Rights," p. 6; Report on the
Situation, p. 128.
12. Davis and Hodson, Witnesses, p. 45.
13. Ibid., p. 46.
14. Gordon L. Bowen, "American Foreign Policy Toward
Radical Change: Covert Operations in Guatemala,
1950-54," Latin American Perspectives, 10, 1 (Winter
1983), pp. 88-102.

15. "The Science of Spying," transcript of NBC television program (May 4, 1965).

16. John Foster Dulles, "Memorandum for the President; Subject: Your Meeting with President-elect Ydigoras of Guatemala" (February 25, 1958), in Declassified Documents Reference System [hereafter DDRS] (Arlington, Va.: Carrollton Press, 1976), p. 71-B; New York Times (July 16, 1957).

17. Office of Business Economics, Foreign Grants and Credits (Washington, D.C.: U.S. Government Printing Office, 1955), pp. 21-33.

18. Ambassador John Muccio, "Telegram to Secretary of State No. 44, 5 PM" (July 21, 1960); Muccio, "Telegram to Secretary of State No. 41, 7 PM" (July 20, 1960). Department of State cables were declassified directly to author.

19. U.S., Congress, Senate, Congressional Record, 91st Congress, First Session, September 10, 1969, p. 10417; Muccio, "Telegram to Secretary of State No. 224, 11 PM" (November 13, 1960), declassified to author.

20. Muccio, "Telegram to Secretary of State No. 143, Noon" (October 26, 1961), declassified to author.

21. U.S., Department of State, Office of Intelligence Research, "Communism in Guatemala," DOS Psychological Intelligence Digest, Supplement No. 1, Intelligence Research Report 6712 (July 1, 1955), in OSS/State Department Intelligence and Research Reports (Washington, D.C.: University Publications of America, n.d.), xiv, reel 9.

22. George Ball, "Telegram to all American Diplomatic Posts in Central America. Caracas, Mexico, Panama, and Santo Domingo" (January 5, 1963), declassified to author.

23. Office of the Assistant Secretary of Defense for International Security Affairs, "U.S. Policies Toward Latin American Militaries" (February 25, 1965), in DDRS, p. 32-B; and U.S. Overseas Loans and Grants (Washington, D.C.: Agency for International Development, May 24, 1972), p. 47.

24. Ambassador John Bell, "Cable to Assistant Secretary Mann" (February 26, 1964), declassified to author.

25. Project Appraisal Report: Guatemala, Public Safety (Washington, D.C.: Agency for International Development, July 29, 1969), p. 4.

26. U.S., Department of State, Office of Intelligence Research, "Opportunities for Communist Exploitation in Latin America: INR Contribution to National Intelligence Estimate 80/90-64" (April 7, 1964), in DDRS, p. 286-G.

27. Guatemala (London: Amnesty International, [hereafter AI], 1976), pp. 3-4.

28. Daniel Premo, "Political Assassination in Guatemala," Journal of Inter-American Studies and World Affairs, 23, 4, (November 1981), pp. 436-437.

29. Project Appraisal, pp. 5, 12; U.S. Overseas, p. 47; U.S., Congress, House, Hearings Before the Subcommittee on National Security Policy of the Committee on Foreign Affairs, 91st Congress, Second Session, October and December 1970, p. 14.

30. Eduardo Galeano, "With the Guerrillas in Guatemala," in Latin America: Reform or Revolution, eds. James Petras and Maurice Zeitlan (Greenwich, Conn.: Fawcett Publications, 1968), p. 329.

31. Rural Community Leadership and Modernization: Pilot Plan for the Northeast (Washington, D.C.: Agency for International Development, April 30, 1969), p. 8.

32. Guatemala (1976), p. 5.

33. Fox, "Human Rights," p. 11; Latin American Political Report (October 27, 1978).

34. U.S., Congress, House, Committee on Foreign Affairs, Hearings on Foreign Assistance Act of 1971, Part 2 (Washington, D.C.: 1971), p. 380; U.S. Overseas, p. 47.

35. Guatemala: A Government Program of Political Murder (London: Amnesty International, 1981), pp. 1–9.

36. Alberto Baeza Flores, La Situacion Politica en Guatemala (San Jose, Costa Rica: CEDAL, 1974), p. 24.

37. World Bank Development Report 1981, p. 160.

38. Ibid., pp. 158–162.

39. Guatemala (1976), pp. 1, 7; Guatemala (1981), p. 8; Amnesty International Newsletter (January 1976).

40. Davis and Hodson, "Witnesses," p. 15.

41. "Guatemala Campaign Circular No. 3: Repression of Trade Unionists in Guatemala," in AI, Country Dossiers 1975-79 (Zug, Switzerland: Inter-Documentation Company, 1981), pp. E-2 to E-180.

42. Report on the Situation, p. 22.

43. Guatemala (1976), pp. 9-12; Premo, "Political Assassination," pp. 429-456.

44. Latin America Weekly Report (January 8, 1982).

45. Report on the Situation, p. 132.

46. "Guatemala Campaign Circular No. 3," in AI, Country Dossiers, pp. E-2 to E-180.

47. "News Release of December 5, 1979," in AI, Country Dossiers, pp. E-2 to E-180.

48. Guatemala (1981), pp. 12-13.

49. Report on the Situation, p. 115.

50. Amnesty International Newsletter (May 1979).

51. "Guatemala Campaign Circular No. 10: Repression in the Academic Sector in Guatemala," in AI, Country Dossiers, pp. E-2 to E-180; Amnesty Action, March 1981; Washington Post (May 14, 1981).

52. "Guatemala Campaign Circular No. 9: Repression of Journalists in Guatemala," in AI, Country Dossiers, pp. E-2 to E-180; see also Julia Preston, "Killing Off the News in Guatemala," Columbia Journalism Review, 20, 5 (January/February, 1982).

53. Quoted in Human Rights in Guatemala: No Neutrals Allowed (New York: Americas Watch, 1982), p. 44.

54. Latin America Weekly Report (March 28, 1982); Latin America Regional Report: Mexico and Central America (July 9, 1982); and Washington Post (July 17, 1982).

55. Guatemala (1976), pp. 12-13.

56. "The Next El Salvador," The New Republic, 184, 15 (April 11, 1981), pp. 23-25.

57. AI, "Massive Extrajudicial Executions in Rural Areas Under the Government of Efrain Rios Montt" (London, July 1982), pp. 1-9, i-xi; Americas Watch, Human Rights in Guatemala; National Council of Churches, "Human Rights in Guatemala," Christianity and Crisis, 42 (December 27, 1982); Americas Watch, "Human Rights in Central America" (New York, April 1983); Americas Watch, "Creating a Desolation and Calling It Peace" (New York, May 1983).

58. Washington Post (August 6, 1983).

59. Americas Watch, "Creating a Desolation," pp. 21-27.

60. Americas Watch, Human Rights in Guatemala, pp. 111-133.

61. Manchester Guardian Weekly (January 16, 1983).

62. National Council of Churches, "Human Rights," pp. 425-427.

63. Americas Watch, "Creating a Desolation," pp. 12-13; Americas Watch, "Human Rights in Central America," p. 15.

64. AI, "Massive Extrajudicial Executions," p. 15; Alan Nairn, "The Guns of Guatemala," The New Republic, 188 (April 11, 1983).

65. Manchester Guardian Weekly (January 9, 1983).

66. Latin America Weekly Report (March 18, 1983), p. 12; Americas Watch, "Creating a Desolation," pp. 40-41; Washington Office on Latin America, Update, 8 (March/April 1983), p. 10.

67. Washington Post (August 10 and 11, 1983); Manchester Guardian Weekly (August 14, 1983).

68. Davis and Hodson, Witnesses, p. 53; Americas Watch, Human Rights in Guatemala; and National Council of Churches, "Human Rights in Guatemala," p. 425.

69. Latin America Weekly Report (February 25, 1983).

8
The Revolution in Nicaragua: Through a Frontier of History

John A. Booth

> "Turbulence and unrest mark the frontiers of history. . . ."

H. L. Nieberg[1]

Since the nineteenth century Nicaragua has periodically captured the attention of outside powers both great and small, and struggles between outsiders have often shaped the course of Nicaraguan events. Sadly, such influence has more often harmed than helped the country. Foreign interventions aside, however, Nicaraguans themselves have been politically contentious, so much so that one historian has characterized his nation's history as one of civil war.[2] The frequent external intrusions upon these violently divisive internal politics have sharpened domestic antagonisms, kept Nicaraguans fighting longer than they might have with only their own resources, and severely set back economic and political development.

The bloody 1979 insurrection that overthrew the forty-three-year-old Somoza dynasty and brought to power the Frente Sandinista de Liberacion Nacional (FSLN) was in many ways only an exaggeration of well-established, pathological sociohistorical patterns. Revolutionary politics since 1979 have retained some of the same conflictual nature and also suffer from external manipulation. Yet the new system has also changed in ways that mark a historical frontier. Nicaragua's class system, political arrangements and practices, ruling elites, and political myths have changed profoundly. Lingering vestiges of the old system, however--its classes, leaders, and their traditional foreign allies--threaten the fledgling revolution from both within and without.

INSURRECTION AND REVOLUTION
Origins of the Somoza Dynasty

The roots of the contemporary Nicaraguan revolution
go back to the early nineteenth century, when sharp
economic and political cleavages were developing within
Spanish colonial society. Prior to independence in 1823,
protopartisan factions of liberals and conservatives
clashed over economic privilege and ideology.
Independence and the formation of the Central American
Republic intensified this dispute as the Leon-centered
liberals and the Granada-based conservatives joined
allies from neighboring states in a struggle for control
of provincial and Central American governments and the
rewards of power. The collapse of the Central American
Republic in 1838 failed to end the violent civil struggle
in Nicaragua. The landed elite that dominated both
parties (the liberals had more middle-sector and urban
support than the conservatives) fought again in 1856-57,
when the liberals invited the filibusterer, William
Walker, to assist them and brought about the intervention
of other Central American conservatives to oust the
interloper. The legacy of this period includes militarism, caudillismo, and political violence, which soon
became entrenched in Nicaraguan political culture.
For four decades the conservatives ruled, and
Nicaragua, temporarily ignored by outside powers, began
to develop its coffee industry, government, and public
service infrastructure. The expansion of coffee cultivation and rapid integration of Nicaragua into the world
economy between 1860 and 1900 pushed many subsistence
cultivators off the land and brought about a repressive
system of rural labor control. Commercial and urban
growth brought new support to the liberals, whose Jose
Santos Zelaya captured the presidency in 1893. A dedicated liberal who ruled dictatorially, Zelaya further
accelerated the development of coffee and public service
infrastructure. Most of the ideological differences
between liberals and conservatives had vanished (both by
then shared classic liberal economic theory), so that by
the turn of the century Nicaraguan parties were basically
non-ideological, clan-dominated factions of the landowning plutocracy.
Zelaya's nationalism eventually led to his downfall.
When the United States chose Panama over Nicaragua as the
site for its transisthmian canal in 1903, Zelaya
approached Germany and Japan about constructing a
Nicaraguan waterway. Angered, Washington helped promote
a conservative revolt in 1909. Marines landed to protect
the rebels. The American legation helped install a
conservative government when Zelaya was forced to resign
and in 1914 obtained a canal treaty to ensure a U.S.
monopoly. From 1909 until 1926, the United States nearly

always kept marines in Nicaragua and promoted heavy American private investment there after taking control of major government revenue sources. This period of foreign financial and political tutelage reversed much of the developmental progress made after 1860, badly weakened the Nicaraguan government, and intensified factional resentments.

A revolt by disgruntled liberals, backed by Mexico, led the United States to intervene once again in 1927. A U.S.-organized cease-fire failed to pacify a populist liberal general, Augusto Cesar Sandino, who commenced a six-year guerrilla struggle against vastly superior U.S. forces and a newly formed Nicaraguan National Guard. Frustrated by its failure to defeat Sandino and by the growing Latin American hostility aroused by its Caribbean basin interventions, the United States withdrew its troops in 1933 and left Anastasio Somoza Garcia head of the National Guard. Sandino immediately ended hostilities but was betrayed and assassinated by Somoza's orders in 1934. With upper-class support from both parties, Somoza ousted his uncle from the presidency in 1936 and repressed labor unrest stemming from the worldwide depression and its effects on Nicaragua. With U.S. backing at critical junctures, Somoza ruled Nicaragua for the next two decades from his power base in the National Guard, skillfully mixing repression with co-optation and keeping the opposition divided. Many leaders of the Conservative Party were bought off with graft and potential opponents repressed under a formula the dictator himself summarized as "bucks for my friends, bullets for my enemies."[3] The Somoza family became immensely wealthy as the dictator exploited the state to fatten his coffers. The National Guard, the Liberal Nationalist Party (taken over and so renamed by Somoza), and the backing of the United States provided the major instruments of control. Somoza Garcia had already groomed his oldest son, Luis Somoza Debayle, to head the Liberal Nationalist Party and his youngest son, Anastasio, Jr., to head the National Guard when a disgruntled former liberal assassinated the dictator in 1956.

The bereaved sons conducted a two-year campaign of terror against regime opponents after the assassination. A wave of armed challenges to the government broke out in 1959-61, but with the help of U.S. military aid the Guard crushed most of the rebels. The only insurgent group that survived was the FSLN, formed in 1961 by veteran leftists from a variety of backgrounds. The organization remained small and suffered setbacks in 1963 and 1967, but it slowly grew and developed an urban and rural support network. With Luis Somoza either serving as president or working from behind the throne as head of the party apparatus and Anastasio commanding the Guard, the brothers ruled jointly until the elder's death in

1967. They permitted a largely symbolic political liberalization that encouraged a Christian Democratic movement to emerge as a potential new power contender and also calmed student unrest. After Luis's demise, however, the regime became more corrupt and repressive, frustrating those who advocated elections to promote change.

Socioeconomic Change and the Rise of Opposition

Economic forces began to transform Nicaragua during the 1950s and 1960s. Ownership of land and industry became further concentrated, and more small farmers were pushed from the land to swell the poor urban neighborhoods and increase inequalities in wealth. In 1961 Nicaragua joined the Central American Common Market (CACM), a measure promoted by the United States under the Alliance for Progress in the hopes of preventing Cuban-style revolutions by encouraging economic growth. The CACM brought rapid capital-intensive industrialization and a gradual merger of the economic elite's several investor factions into a more unified capitalist class. This emerging unified national bourgeoisie collaborated with the now immensely wealthy Somoza family and its political and economic cohorts. However, because the CACM boom created relatively few new jobs and the government kept industrial and agricultural wages low, inequalities in wealth grew worse, living standards of the urban and rural poor declined notably, and unemployment steadily rose (see Table 8.1). Ironically, then, the rapid industrial growth of the 1960s and 1970s brought both high aggregate economic growth rates and progressive impoverishment.

In the mid-1970s, a combination of escalating energy prices and government economic mismanagement in the wake of the Managua earthquake projected these growing strains into the political arena. The December 1972 quake killed 10,000 people, destroyed many lower-class homes, small commercial businesses, and cottage industries in Managua's center, hitting the capital's poor and lower middle class especially hard. Government recovery policy increased the work week, froze wages, and set high recovery taxes on wages and salaries. On top of this came the 1973 OPEC oil embargo and escalating energy prices, which pushed up the cost of almost everything Nicaraguans had to purchase. They responded to these pressures with popular mobilization. First came an upsurge in membership of labor unions and peasant groups demanding higher wages or land; then came community-improvement organizations seeking better services. In 1973-74, protests, strikes, and increased FSLN activity occurred. The unification of the bourgeoisie was

TABLE 8.1

Selected Indicators, Nicaragua 1963-79

Year	Percent Growth of GNP (%)	Percent Change in Consumer Prices (%)	Real Wages in Manufacturing, Construction, and Transportation (1973=100)	Compensation of Employees as % of National Income (Index) (1973=100)	Percent Unemployed	U.S. Military Aid and Arms Transfers (in $1000 U.S.): Military Aid	Arms Cost
1963	10.9	0.8	92				
1964	11.7	9.6	—				
1965	9.5	3.9	—	113			
1966	3.3	3.9	—	—			
1967	7.0	1.6	137	114			
1968	1.3	3.1	—	114			
1969	6.7	2.0	—	114			
1970	1.0	5.9	121	114	3.7	1,053	423
1971	4.9	5.6	119	114	3.6	1,165	1,711
1972	3.2	3.3	114	114	6.0	581	272
1973	5.1	16.8	100	121	9.1	1,050	2,252
1974	12.7	20.5	100	102	7.3	994	1,668
1975	2.2	1.8	106	103	—	3,843	1,041
1976	5.0	2.9	106		13.0	3,546	1,535
1977	6.3	11.4	106		20.0	3,176	2,368
1978	-7.2	4.6	97			695	608
1979	-24.8	48.5				97	1

Source: John A. Booth, "Toward Explaining Regional Crisis in Central America: The Socio-economic and Political Roots of Rebellion" (paper presented to the 44th International Congress of Americanists, Manchester, England, September 6-10, 1982).

arrested as capitalists became nervous over government
economic mismanagement and political unrest. Some business leaders cautiously called for reform, and in 1974
the Democratic Liberation Union (UDEL) appeared, encompassing several small opposition parties and union
confederations and led by important businessmen,
including some previously close to the regime.

The Insurrection

The regime responded to demands for reform with
repression. Following an FSLN seizure of hostages in
December 1974 (in which several Sandinista prisoners were
released from jail and a substantial ransom paid),
President Anastasio Somoza Debayle declared a state of
siege that suspended constitutional guarantees and gave
the National Guard a free hand to suppress opponents of
the regime. In the ensuing reign of terror several
thousand peasants were killed in Zelaya department alone,
and thousands more throughout Nicaragua were subjected to
arbitrary arrest and detention, torture, exile, and
murder. This harsh response had a traumatic impact:
Many who had been politically indifferent were now driven
into opposition; others, who had been activists, became
revolutionaries. The fierce repression visited upon
community workers and leaders, unionists, clergy, laity,
private sector groups, opposition parties, and thousands
of innocent bystanders began to unify the opposition into
several broad multiclass organizations in 1978-79. When
President Carter persuaded Somoza to lift the state of
siege in 1977, there ensued a wave of demonstrations,
spontaneous violence, and demands for reform and the
dictator's resignation. On January 10, 1978, assassins
murdered Pedro Joaquin Chamorro, leader of UDEL and
editor of the opposition daily La Prensa. While riots
and protest demonstrations ripped Managua, many upper-
class Nicaraguans who had been loath to oppose the
dictatorship overtly began to rally to the opposition. A
new anti-Somoza coalition, the Broad Opposition Front
(FAO), organized several strikes that sharply cut the
regime's tax revenues. The government responded by
reescalating repression, especially in the cities.
Though the Frente Sandinista, divided into three
factions since 1975, numbered fewer than 500, it was
still able to dominate the armed resistance to the
14,000-man Guard. In August 1978 the Tercerista wing of
the FSLN seized the National Palace and hundreds of high-
ranking officials, ransoming the latter for $500,000, the
freedom of numerous jailed Sandinistas, and free passage
out of Nicaragua. The incident discredited the regime
and spurred spontaneous mass uprisings in several cities
in September and October. This popular rebellion, to

which the Sandinistas provided little leadership, set in motion four critical processes: (1) The brutal three-month National Guard campaign to retake rebel towns--literally a war on the Nicaraguan people--caused such massive civilian casualties that it ripped away the last shreds of popular support for, or indifference toward, the Somoza regime. (2) Surprised by the ferocity of the revolt, the FSLN factions quickly negotiated reunification in order to capitalize on popular elan and capture leadership of the movement. (3) Moderate forces represented by the FAO and backed by the Catholic Church hierarchy attempted to negotiate Somoza's resignation and a government of national reconciliation that would exclude the Sandinistas. However, bad-faith bargaining by Somoza and defections from the FAO (due to its leaders' violation of internal agreements on negotiations) led to the collapse of the initiative by December. (4) International support for the Somoza government declined dramatically. Costa Rica, Panama, and Cuba stepped up assistance to the FSLN, while Mexico and the Andean Group countries began to oppose the regime in the Organization of American States (OAS).

By this time the Carter administration wished to be rid of Somoza and had trimmed U.S. aid, thus further weakening his government (see Table 8.1). Ironically, however, the United States insisted on a "moderate" solution (i.e., one excluding both Somoza's Liberal Nationalist Party and his National Guard) in its mediation between the FAO and the regime. This goal, patently unacceptable to many FAO organizations, caused dissension within the coalition and prevented any agreement. Washington thus ended up prolonging the crisis and further alienating the Sandinistas.[4]

The final assault followed months of FSLN military consolidation and growing opposition alignment with two Sandinista-led coalitions, the United People's Movement and the National Patriotic Front. When the final campaign began on May 30, 1979, the FSLN quickly gained control of much of the northern third of the country. In spite of heavy desertions, the National Guard made a tenacious last stand against the Sandinistas pushing north from Costa Rica. After a bloody, five-week conventional war, however, the Guard had been pushed back almost to Managua, and its defeat was imminent. The United States made one last effort to negotiate a settlement that would exclude the all-but-victorious FSLN, while thousands of regime supporters and many of the remaining National Guard officers fled the country. The U.S. initiative failed because the rebels' shadow government refused to negotiate; Somoza eventually resigned and departed for Miami on July 17th. Two days later, the Sandinistas and their National Reconstruction Junta entered Managua. Scenes of wrenching contrast prevailed as Nicaraguans both danced and wept amidst the rubble of their devastated society.

SANDINISTA NICARAGUA: THE NEW POLITICAL ORDER

The revolutionary government confronted daunting problems. At least 40,000 people had died in the insurrection, thousands more in the repression that preceded it. The public service infrastructure had suffered massive damage, as had much of the nation's industrial plant. Crops had been abandoned and the agricultural cycle damaged. Thousands, among them badly needed managers and technicians, had fled the country to escape violence and repression. Food, fuel, and medicines were critically scarce. Tens of thousands were homeless, jobless, or ill. The national treasury had been looted empty; remaining was a massive $1.6 billion foreign debt owed largely for the arms used by the National Guard. Violence was rife because of criminals and underground Somoza sympathizers, and because the entire police system had collapsed and much of the populace (including many children) was heavily armed. Rebel leaders themselves had little government experience, and the national bureaucracy was rotten with corruption and mismanagement.

The new government's goals were as follows: (1) the abolition of the old regime and its economic power base; (2) the reconstruction of the national economy; (3) the reduction of class inequality and improvement of the living standards and influence of the lower classes; (4) the replacement of public-sector corruption with an ethic of honesty and service; (5) the formation of a popular (but not necessarily liberal) democracy; and (6) the improvement and protection of human rights.

The Revolutionary Government

Presiding over the victorious rebel coalition was the Joint National Directorate (DN) of the Frente Sandinista, whose nine members (mostly veteran military leaders or intellectuals) set guidelines for public policy and shaped the new political order. Not dominated by any single member, the DN made decisions collectively, a tendency that gave its policies a pragmatic and moderate tenor. From the outset DN members occupied key ministerial posts in order to maintain the FSLN's control of the revolutionary process, and during the first year the Frente consolidated its hegemonic position within the regime. DN members occupied the ministries of Defense (Humberto Ortega Saavedra), Interior (Tomas Borge Martinez), Planning (Henry Ruiz), Agrarian Reform and

Agricultural Development (Jaime Wheelock Roman), as well
as the presidencies of the Governing Junta (Daniel Ortega
Saavedra) and the legislature or Council of State (Carlos
Nunez Tellez).

Executive authority rested in the National
Reconstruction Junta, linked to the DN through Daniel
Ortega. A majority of this three-to-five-member body
have always been Sandinistas, but it has also always
included representatives of other parties. The junta
ruled by decree for roughly a year and has since shared
legislative power with the Council of State. Like the
junta, the cabinet and bureaucracy have contained a
variety of partisan viewpoints from within the
anti-Somoza coalition, but cabinet reorganizations have
enhanced FSLN influence in critical parts of the
bureaucracy. Most of the rank-and-file bureaucrats of
the Somoza era remained in their posts, now supervised by
rebel loyalists throughout the government. Early efforts
to forge a new administrative culture stressing public
spirit and honesty appeared successful, but instances of
corruption still occurred. The bureaucracy grew so fast
that in 1982 the junta ordered a 5 percent cutback in the
number of government employees.

The Council of State is a co-legislative body that
reviews the old legal structure, reforms it where
necessary, and evaluates and recommends changes in junta-
drafted laws. The council's membership is corporatist
rather than geographic; it was designed to represent the
major political forces of the anti-Somoza insurrectionary
coalition. In 1980, its representation was augmented by
including representatives of various new labor and
popular organizations established under the new regime.
These additions shifted the balance of power clearly to
the FSLN, prompting the resignation of Alfonso Robelo
from the Junta and leading to the emergence of an identi-
fiable opposition coalition formed by several private-
sector and opposition representatives. The council still
provides the major mechanism for opposition influence on
public policy, as well as a national forum for political
debate.

The courts were thoroughly renovated and most former
judges replaced. In 1980 the right to amparo, judicial
relief from arbitrary or unconstitutional bureaucratic
action, was established and has formed the constitutional
basis for the Supreme Court of Justice to return
illegally nationalized property to owners and redress
citizen grievances against abuses of authority. Other
constitutional rights have also been protected by the
courts, and regime compliance with court orders has
apparently been fairly consistent. Special tribunals
were established outside the regular court system to try
several thousand agents and guardsmen of the ancien
regime. These bodies were highly politicized and aroused

criticism from civil libertarians. Nevertheless, they remained open to the press; prisoners had free public defense and appeared to be in good physical and mental condition. No death sentences were issued (they are unconstitutional), and numerous accused were acquitted.

The security forces of revolutionary Nicaragua derived from the FSLN and remain part of it, a phenomenon that angers opposition spokesmen. The Ministry of Interior, headed by FSLN co-founder Tomas Borge Martinez, includes the police, customs, and prison system. In the beginning, it had much difficulty with new police officers, almost all of whom had assumed their duties untrained and straight from guerrilla ranks. Abuses of authority were a common problem. However, police training by foreign advisers and a vigorous program of discipline weeded out most of the problem officers within a year and greatly increased competence. The armed forces also had to transform guerrillas and untrained, last-minute volunteers into regular military forces. Many of the untrained or problematical were soon demobilized and replaced by new recruits, who were organized, along with veterans, into a Sandinista Air Force (FAS) and Sandinista Popular Army (EPS). Much of the hodgepodge of arms and captured equipment that survived the war has been replaced with new equipment; some 2,000 Cuban military advisers have helped the transition to the military's new role. The threats posed by the rise to power of Ronald Reagan, the subsequent attempts to destabilize Nicaragua, and the growing hostility from Honduras and exiled Nicaraguan counter-revolutionaries have prompted the regime to build the EPS to around 22,000 troops (1982 figures) and acquire some controversial weapons (e.g., twenty-five Soviet-built T-55 tanks). The Sandinista Popular Militia, first promoted in 1979-80 and then allowed to decline, was reemphasized in 1981-82 and expanded to include some 60,000 well-trained and armed members and perhaps another 60,000 poorly-armed and trained members.[5] Military personnel and militia are considered members of the FSLN and receive ideological training.

Public Policy

Human Rights. In a major break with the pattern of most revolutions and with Nicaraguan tradition, the new regime sought to end human rights violations. After some disorder in the first days after victory, FSLN leaders succeeded in preventing the mistreatment of captured Somocistas, and the new Ministry of Interior largely avoided human rights violations in the penal system. Living and sanitary conditions in the prisons (inherited from the old regime) were poor. Procedural due process,

always scarce in revolutionary settings, was often defec-
tive in the special trials held for Somoza agents from
1979-82, but none of the 7,000 accused were executed and
about half were released or acquitted. (The maximum
sentence given was thirty-four years.) Administrative
compliance with court orders based on habeas corpus and
amparo has been generally good.[6]

Press freedom has fluctuated substantially. A
vigorous FSLN-dominated state media network has coexisted
with independent radio stations and one opposition daily,
La Prensa. Journalists and media are subject to strict
licensing and certain regulations under the Press Law.
The state of emergency begun in 1981 implemented prior
censorship of all media for military security reasons.
On several occasions, La Prensa has been suspended for a
few days for publishing unfounded rumors damaging to the
government, and some of its copy has been deleted regularly by the censors. All other media, including the
FSLN's own Barricada, have also experienced censorship,
but it is widely believed that La Prensa has had more
material deleted than other papers. On several occasions, La Prensa has chosen not to publish a daily
edition because of the late return of copy from the
censor or because too much material was cut to permit
recomposing the paper.[7]

There is substantial freedom of religion. Since
1979, numerous Protestant missionaries have entered
Nicaragua to proselytize. In 1981-82, however, a handful
of clerics (both Protestant and Catholic) were expelled
for conducting counterrevolutionary activity under the
guise of religion. The active participation of rank and
file clergy and laity in the insurrection in support of
the FSLN has ensured good relations with the so-called
Popular Church, but the Catholic hierarchy has made clear
its displeasure with the regime. The visit of Pope John
Paul II to Nicaragua in early March 1983 did little to
heal the breach within the Nicaraguan Church or to
improve relations between the hierarchy and the
Sandinistas. The Pope spoke strongly in favor of social
justice and peace, but he rejected violence, "collec-
tivist systems," and Marxism as means for promoting them.
The struggle of both prohierarchy and proregime groups to
capitalize on the Pope's visit led to a chanting
competition between their supporters during the great
outdoor mass in Managua, an incident that generally
brought discredit to the Sandinistas.

Labor unions and anti-Somoza political parties
enjoyed considerable freedom to operate until mid-1981,
when increasing economic problems, internal tensions, and
pressures from abroad led the junta to suspend the right
to strike and clamp down on party activity. Harassment
of Alfonso Robelo's opposition party, the Nicaraguan
Democratic Movement (MDN), by pro-FSLN crowds occurred

several times in 1982, but other opposition leaders
continued to occupy government positions. Although the
OAS, Amnesty International, and others have criticized
the regime for having some prisoners of conscience (both
of the right and left), alarming rumors of genocide
against the Mosquito Indians were debunked by observers
and conceded by the State Department to be fabrications.[8]
On balance, the Sandinista record has been exceptional
regarding right to life, security, and religious freedom,
and fair (but deteriorating under the domestic and international strains of 1981-82) regarding freedom of press,
party, and association.[9]

Culture

The revolutionaries hoped to forge a new national
culture that would replace individualistic striving with
collaboration; integrate women, Indians, peasants, and
urban poor as full members of society; and increase the
economic and psychological well-being of all Nicaraguans
in an environment of economic and political equality and
participation. To these ends, the FSLN conducted a
vigorous multimedia propaganda campaign through its own
organs and the FSLN-dominated Ministry of Culture, which
operated the national television and radio channels and
subsidized artistic and cultural programs. The largest
campaign undertaken was the 1980 Literacy Crusade, which
sought to impart basic education tools to that half of
the populace ten years or older that remained illiterate.
The massive crusade, with its extensive volunteer
participation, employed pro-FSLN messages to teach both
literacy skills and rudiments of the new national
culture. The program was a considerable success,
reducing illiteracy by as much as two-thirds. The effort
to integrate women into society also went well, as the
regime sought to encourage greater female participation
in the armed forces and government. Equality before the
law and in the workplace were improved, as the
Sandinistas sought to undermine traditional sexist values
through propaganda and legislation.
The cultural problem most resistant to solution
involves the Atlantic Zone, an area distinct in its
racial and cultural mix (including black and indigenous
groups of various languages) and in its religious orientation (mainly Moravian Protestant), and long isolated
from the rest of the nation. Atlantic Zone residents
have almost always resented the "Spaniards" from Western
Nicaragua as exploiters, and the Sandinistas and their
new government were no exception. Tensions in the area
developed quickly; protests and riots occurred, and some
Atlantic Zone residents began to participate in counterrevolutionary plots. In 1981, a U.S.-financed

destabilization program began, financed by the Central
Intelligence Agency. This program recruited Mosquitos on
both sides of the Nicaragua-Honduras border to help some
5,000 former National Guardsmen conduct sabotage in
Nicaragua. Because of this collaboration and because
civilians were increasingly subjected to danger from the
escalating military operations, the Sandinista government
decided in 1982 to relocate Mosquito communities
totalling about 8,500 people to new settlements inland
from the border. Most observers of the process agree
that the relocation was warranted for security reasons.
However, implementation was clumsy and aroused
considerable criticism. Some people were forced to walk
the forty miles to the new camps, a few died during the
long trek, and sixty children perished in a helicopter
crash. The new settlements generally provided adequate
facilities and cultivatable land, but the relocation
caused considerable trauma among many of those moved. By
late 1982, the OAS Inter-American Commission on Human
Rights and the Moravian Church had begun to work with the
government and the Mosquitos to resolve the relocation
problems.[10]

Economic Policy

The Sandinistas sought to rebuild Nicaragua's war-
devastated economy, redistribute income toward the lower
classes (thus reducing inequalities), and dismantle the
economic base of the ancien regime. These goals have
transformed the economic role of the state significantly,
with the public-sector share of the GNP growing from 15
percent in 1978 to over 41 percent in 1980, and with
slight increases since. Most of this expansion came
through the nationalization of banking, insurance,
transportation, mineral production, and agricultural
export, and the takeover of enterprises of the Somoza
family and their cohorts. A major problem confronting
the new public sector (the People's Property Area, or
APP) has been a shortage of managers and technicians;
current educational reforms will not be able to fulfill
these needs for several years. Government reorganization
has also led to the development of a planning process
with several avenues for citizen participation, improved
financial management, and greater efficiency in the
operation of many agencies.

Agrarian reform has sought not only to rebuild
production to prewar levels (something still impeded by
credit problems, loss of agribusiness technicians, and
bad weather), but also to better the living conditions of
the rural poor. The Ministry of Agricultural Development
and Agrarian Reform, headed by DN member Jaime Wheelock,
has nationalized fertilizer, seed, and pesticide imports,

promoted some 4,000 credit and marketing cooperatives for small- and medium-sized producers, and reduced by 85 percent ground rents for small renters. In July 1979, the regime nationalized some 2,000 farms belonging to the Somozas or their cohorts--about 20 percent of the nation's agricultural land--and began operating most of them as state-owned farms.

The regime has encouraged many larger private farms and ranches to increase production by supplying credit, barring strikes, and returning to original owners land illegally nationalized in 1979-80. The private sector produces most of the nation's coffee, cotton, rice, and beef. Under the provisions of the Comprehensive Agrarian Reform Law, unutilized and underutilized largeholdings may be expropriated (with compensation). Through 1982 about 440,000 hectares (only 5.3 percent of Nicaragua's agricultural land) had been redistributed to individuals or cooperatives under the agrarian reform law. Between 1980 and 1981, overall production of export crops rose by 29 percent and goods consumed rose by 18 percent. Basic food grain production rose by 40 percent.[11]

In addition, the government has sought to rebuild industrial production, down by roughly one-third from the 1978 level because of war damage. Priority for credit and vital imports has been given to traditionally strong exports and products needed for internal consumption. Although the state itself took over much industrial production through the APP, private capital retained three-quarters of manufacturing, a third of construction, and about half of services. Several multinationals continued to operate, and certain others were encouraged to reopen. Few new nationalizations have occurred since 1980, except for those firms decapitalized by their owners or those whose owners have been linked to armed counterrevolutionary activity.[12] Though the government has repeatedly affirmed its commitment to a mixed economy, made production agreements with private firms, provided credit, and barred workers' strikes (since mid-1981), capitalists have remained ill at ease with the regime, and new private investment has been desultory. Nevertheless, overall growth in GNP in 1980 and 1981 was rapid--10 percent and 8.9 percent, respectively. The military buildup of 1982 and early 1983, however, diverted considerable government spending from industrial redevelopment and contributed to a 4 percent decline in GNP for 1982.[13] Investments in public service infrastructure and social services have been heavy since 1979. Massive construction projects repaired or built new roads, streets, housing, parks, utilities, hospitals, and health centers, and lowered unemployment from 22.9 percent in late 1979 to 13.4 percent in 1982.[14]

Financing the operations of the state has proved difficult. On the positive side, revenues have risen because of reforms that made taxes more progressive, reduced fiscal administration corruption, and increased voluntary tax payment. On the negative side, internally generated revenues have fallen far short of government expenditures and have thus required heavy external borrowing to finance the deficit. The junta agreed to repay most of the debts of the Somoza government in order to reorganize its foreign obligations and obtain critically needed new credit. At first, such aid was ample, but since 1981 the Reagan administration has squeezed Nicaragua's international credit by cutting off U.S. assistance and dissuading multilateral lenders from extending loans. Although this has been a serious set-back for economic recovery and development, the gravity of the financial crises confronting such countries as Poland, Costa Rica, Mexico, Chile, Argentina, and Brazil make Nicaragua's fiscal and foreign-accounts woes seem moderate. In late 1982, the government reported that it would be unable to retire principal on its outstanding loans but would continue to meet interest rates on schedule.

The revolution has sought to substantially improve the living standards of the poor. Among the redistributive policies adopted have been the creation of popular commissaries and pharmacies to distribute needed goods at regulated (and sometimes subsidized) prices, prosecution of hoarders and speculators, encouragement of food production, and improvement of food distribution. Other policies benefitting the working classes include setting and enforcing minimum wages, fixing rent ceilings on housing, and transferring ownership of oft-rented residential property to the renters. The government has also improved public services--there are widespread free health care and nutrition programs, expanded recreational facilities, extensive construction, and greatly expanded rural and adult education.

DOMESTIC POLICY PROBLEMS

Socioeconomic Policy and the Working Classes

The revolutionary government has sought to redistribute goods and services, improve standards of living of the working classes, and increase mass economic and political influence, even as it promotes economic recovery and growth. In general, the policies adopted have been pragmatic. Knotty problems, however, have impeded progress and forced the government to choose between economic recovery and short-run benefits for the poor.

Class struggle emerged very late in the insurrection, having been obscured by the broad coalitional base

of the revolt. FSLN theoreticians wished to promote the
eventual transition of Nicaragua to some form of indigenous socialism that might ensure equitable participation
of all Nicaraguans in economic and political life. The
Sandinistas thus sought to further working class
consciousness, as well as to nationalize key economic
sectors (banking, import-export) and holdings of the
Somoza cohort. But the government also desired quick
economic recovery, which required a revived and healthy
(if carefully controlled) capitalist sector. This led to
encouragement and protection for the remaining private
enterprise, a policy that caused erstwhile allies from
both right and left to misread the regime's economic
strategy. From the left, certain Trotskyites accused the
FSLN of bourgeois reformism because of government
resistance to further land and factory seizures by
workers. When the far left's incitement continued, the
Sandinistas closed a Trotskyite paper, broke up some
leftist organizations, and prosecuted agitators for
disruption. In contrast, the business community had
hoped for a liberal constitutional regime, a neutral
bureaucracy, and a reformed capitalist economy within
which the entrepreners' wealth would give them a definitive political advantage. Instead, they encountered a
Sandinista movement determined to guide Nicaragua toward
more socialism and careful management of the private
sector. The FSLN's consolidation of its political
advantages, its nationalizations, and its Marxist
rhetoric elicited from the business sector and several
opposition parties intense and persistent criticism.

The problem has been far more than a mere theoreti-
cal dispute. Sharp conflicts between the redistributive
goals of the revolution and the practical necessities of
economic reconstruction appeared early on and continued
to bedevil the Sandinistas. The desire to increase mass
participation in the workplace and improve wages and
working conditions led the FSLN to encourage labor
organization and to permit it to develop freely during
1979-81. As a consequence, unionization occurred in
several confederations (Sandinista, Christian, communist,
and others); there were numerous strikes; wages rose.
However, unionization also increased the reluctance of
some entrepreneurs to invest, prompted others to
decapitalize, and contributed to inflation, as higher
wages pushed up prices for scarce goods. Moreover, the
state had become the owner of many firms and wished to
enhance their profitability and production. But strikes
and wage demands jeopardized this goal. In mid-1981,
therefore, the Sandinistas decided to give economic
recovery short-run priority over redistributive benefits.
Strikes were barred, and wage restraints continued. The
FSLN's own Sandinista Workers' Central (CST) followed
this line, and as a result progress toward labor unity

slowed, criticism of the government increased, and the CST suffered embarrassing defections. In 1982, the CST made a strong drive to increase its strength vis-a-vis other unions.

Furthermore, in agriculture the promotion of improved peasant living standards sometimes clashed with the need to keep a healthy private sector. Although many peasants received land through distribution programs and some 63,000 families were integrated into production cooperatives created from confiscated farms and smallholdings, many peasants in the sugar and cotton industries received no land because economic rationality dictated the establishment of state-owned farms for these capital and technology-intensive crops. In contrast, many large ranchers and commercial farmers who had been anti-Somoza kept their lands. Some illegally nationalized or occupied holdings were returned to their owners. Thus, long-run developmental and recovery requisites overrode immediate working class gains.

In addition, accumulation for the promotion of economic development forced the revolutionary government to deprive workers of the higher wages and living standards that they desired and expected to achieve almost overnight. Development requires capital, but Nicaragua's huge debt and empty treasury required further foreign borrowing merely to reorganize the debt and operate the government. As external debt mounted (long- and mid-term debt totalled $2.29 billion in 1982) and the Reagan administration sought to dry up foreign credit, Nicaragua increasingly had to turn to internally generated revenues for government operations and investment. Such funds have been raised through taxation and foregone consumption for most Nicaraguans in the form of public sector wage austerity, decreased food and drug subsidies, price increases for imported consumer items, and new taxes. These policies have prompted much grumbling--especially from the middle classes, whose living standards have suffered most from austerity.

Finally, the effort to promote improved living standards has involved increasing employment opportunities and social services for the poor. Although the 1981-82 defense buildup, under pressure from the United States and Somocista exiles, had a short-run positive effect on unemployment by increasing the size of the armed forces, new military spending forced the regime to reduce the promotion of socioeconomic development so dramatically that the economic growth rate fell to -4 percent (1982). External threats thus forced the regime to give defense priority over development and living standards. Although many Nicaraguans agreed with the assumptions underlying this difficult choice, others merely noticed their straitened circumstances and complained of mismanagement and corruption.

Thus have the contractions between the revolution's long-run redistributive goals and its short-run practical policy constraints led to a certain incongruity between the hopes and material achievements of the poor. Although in many ways life for most Nicaraguans is already materially better than it was under the Somozas (especially in terms of health care, education, opportunities for workplace and community participation, and freedom to associate and organize), progress has been much slower than desired, and some reversals have occurred, especially for the middle class. Although some of the problem lies in the contradictions inherent in the revolution's socioeconomic goals, were there no external threats to national security, progress would almost certainly be much greater and internal tensions and dissent much less. The March 1983 invasion by Honduras-based <u>contras</u> plunged Nicaragua into war and sharply increased both the costs of defense and the strictures on social programs, both dissent and opposition.

The Role of the Private Sector

The effort to promote rapid economic recovery with private-sector cooperation within the framework of a gradual transition to socialism also contains contradictions. Businessmen considering investment alternatives weigh many factors, including the expected availability of elements of production (credit, raw materials, markets, workforce skills), potential profits, the security and stability of the investment environment, and alternative investment opportunities. The Sandinistas' socialist leanings and the turbulence of Nicaraguan society inevitably raised serious doubts among those capitalists who had worked to overthrow Somoza and remained to take part in the reconstruction. Nicaragua was in the midst of social revolution. The rhetoric of class conflict abounded. Unprecedented levels of unionization and strikes were occurring. The Sandinistas spoke of a mixed economy and the continuation of the private sector, but many observers wondered how long such commitment would remain. Would an investor be threatened with nationalization in five years, fifty, or never? Would he be able to pass his property and wealth on to his heirs? Would credit be available from a state-controlled banking system or outside lenders? Would raw material imports be facilitated? What sort of labor relations could owners expect? For the Nicaraguan investor, these were questions with disturbingly uncertain answers.

In the beginning, the anti-Somocista entrepreneurial elite had hoped to emerge from the insurrection in control of the new state or at least as an equal partner in rule. However, the FSLN's quick consolidation of leadership scotched the bourgeoisie's expectations of great influence. Hope faded for a system like those of Mexico or Costa Rica, where private capital exercises great sway over economic policy despite extensive public ownership. Although the FSLN's economic recovery program left almost three-fifths of production in private hands, investors' doubts remained. The regime established recourse to amparo to protect property rights, suspended nationalizations, provided some credit to the private sectors, helped settle certain worker-management disputes (Texaco, La Prensa), and accepted U.S. development loans to the private sector. In 1981, the right of unions to strike was suspended due to the economic emergency, and additional credit and import facilities were extended to private investors. Although such actions undoubtedly encouraged nervous capitalists, other policies had the opposite effect. From the beginning, private investors had a much smaller share of credit and lower priority for imports than APP industries and public investment projects. The government nationalized hundreds of firms in 1979-80 and for nearly a year declined to define clearly the role of private capital. The economic emergency of mid-1981 led to the suspension of amparo for businesses, and several new nationalizations of decapitalized firms occurred the following year. The Reagan administration cut off an Agency for International Development (AID) loan for private business credit. The long delay in passage of a political parties law left the private-sector pressure groups and their allies in political limbo, while harassment of the MDN by pro-FSLN crowds became an increasing cause for concern. All in all, neither the social environment nor regime policies have inspired investor confidence, so that private investment has been far less than either government or business initially hoped.

One additional problem in defining the role of the private sector has involved its links to external political actors. The Sandinistas' need to attract foreign capital led the junta and the DN, as evidence of good faith, to encourage U.S. government links to Nicaraguan investors through the Consejo Superior de la Empresa Privada (COSEP). In 1980 Nicaragua accepted a $75 million AID loan, half of which was to underwrite loans for private businesses. Such openness to U.S. initiatives invited trouble. Washington disagreed with the revolution's economic program and sought to discourage further nationalization. American actions included supporting anti-Sandinista efforts among certain entrepreneurs within Nicaragua and abroad. Several counterrevolutionary incidents involving businessmen--often linked to Somocista exiles--have occurred, discrediting other, loyal business interests and increasing FSLN and popular suspicion of entrepreneurs in general. Ironically, foreign encouragement of capitalist resistance to the revolution's socialist drift has under- mined the very sector it sought to promote. Indeed, President Reagan's cancellation of the remainder of the $75 million AID loan did far more harm to the private sector than to the FSLN.

Political Opposition and Pluralism

Once in power, revolutionary movements rarely tolerate opposition. In Nicaragua, however, the situation has been complicated by the multiclass, ideologically plural nature of the movement that ousted the Somoza dynasty. The revolutionary coalition included a broad array of parties, interest groups, and labor unions, and even though the FSLN had a predominantly Marxist-Leninist leadership, it too included other ideological strains. The Sandinistas' primacy in the military victory ensured that they would become the preeminent force in the new regime. Nevertheless, within the rebel coalition, other elements, including a non-Marxist faction within the FSLN, soon began to form in opposition to the dominant faction's vanguard role. The strains within the anti-Somoza coalition have grown increasingly intense as the class basis and goals of the various movements--some loyal, some disloyal--have been clarified since 1979.

The earliest armed opponents of the Sandinista regime included underground and exiled Somocista counter- revolutionaries, who in 1979-80 formed paramilitary groups in Honduras and the United States. In 1980, the regime discovered conspiracies by the Frente Armada Democratica--an organization of entrepreneurs--and a Mosquito group, both with ties to the Somocista exiles. These initial plots were handled easily, but between 1980 and 1982 other opponents opted to leave Nicaragua and vowed to wage either armed or political struggle against the FSLN government. First came the Fuerzas Armadas Democraticas Nicaraguenses, led by the Conservative Fernando Chamorro Rappacioli. Subsequently, the leader of the Nicaraguan Democratic Movement (MDN), Alfonso Robelo Callejas, broke with the regime and went into voluntary exile, as did elements of the Union Sandinista de Mosquitos, Sumus, and Ramas. Finally appeared the Frente Revolucionario Sandinista, led by former Tercerista commander and Vice-Minister of Defense Eden Pastora Gomez. Pastora's great popularity and extensive ties within the Sandinista security forces represented the most serious potential challenge to FSLN power, but broad support for his movement had yet to emerge within Nicaragua as of this writing. In September 1982, these four groups formed the Alianza Revolucionaria

Democratica (ARDE), dedicated to armed struggle to oust the FSLN's Marxist leadership from its control of the revolution.[15] Ties between ARDE and the Fuerzas Democraticas Nicaraguenses (FDN)--the U.S.-armed, trained, and financed counterrevolutionary forces based in Honduras--appeared limited at the time of the latter's March 1983 invasion of Nicaragua. Pastora had previously refused to cooperate with the predominantly Somocista FDN. By April, however, he was reportedly under growing pressure from other ARDE leaders to open a southern front from Costa Rica lest the FDN gain a decisive position in the anti-Sandinista struggle.

Most of the groups in the rebel coalition have remained within Nicaragua. Several have coalesced into a loyal opposition, the Coordinadora Democratica Nicaraguense (CDN), which includes the MDN, the Social Christian Party (PSCN), the Democratic Conservative Party (PCD), the AFL-CIO-affiliated Council for Union Unity (CUS), and the Christian Democratic Nicaraguan Workers Council (CTN). These elements have frequently engaged in policy debates in the Council of State, demanding clarification of the private sector's role, greater freedom for non-Sandinista labor unions, a new Press Law to reduce controls on the media, approval of a Parties Law, and convocation of elections in 1983. The debate has been seriously complicated by the slowness of economic recovery and the growing external threat that finally broke into open warfare in March 1983. These difficulties led first to a mid-1981 declaration of economic emergency that suspended amparo and the right to strike, and then to the late 1981 state of emergency, suspending further citizen rights, imposing press censorship, and redirecting substantial public expenditures toward a military buildup. These states of emergency have been attacked by the opposition as an FSLN strategem for moving toward totalitarian rule.

After three years of escalating tension, opposition and pro-regime groups began to discuss their major differences in September 1982. Supporting the government and its policies were representatives of the FSLN, the Independent Liberal Party, and the Popular Social Christian Party. Participating from the Coordinadora Democratica were the spokesmen for the PSCN, the Social Democratic Party, the Council for Union Unity, the Nicaraguan Workers Council, the Constitutionalist Liberal Movement, and the five private-sector groups in the Consejo Superior de la Empresa Privada. While recognizing the belligerent external threat to national security, the opposition criticized Nicaragua's drift toward the totalitarian left. The revolution's initial aspirations for liberty, democracy, and national harmony had been frustrated, they claimed:

(1) Freedom of organization, mobilization, and political pluralism do not exist in Nicaragua. Political parties that criticize the conduct of the revolution have been subjected to political repression, their members and sympathizers have been threatened, and their headquarters vandalized and harassed by violent groups.

(2) The rights of Nicaraguans, recognized in treaties and international conventions, have been restricted, including the freedom to publish and distribute thought. Radio news programs and La Prensa are subjected to strong censorship. . . .

(3) Freedoms of personal liberty and respect for citizens' personal integrity have been reduced to a minimum. There is no labor union freedom for workers affiliated with independent union centrals. . . .

(4) Government-affiliated media have expressed disrespect for the religious beliefs of Nicaraguans through a campaign to ridicule pastors, priest, and bishops. Shock groups, misnamed "divine mobs" (turbas divinas) have attacked religious celebrations and interfered in the exercise of ecclesiastical authority.

(5) Nicaragua maintains a clear policy of alignment with the countries of the socialist bloc. . . .

(6) The government has narrowed the arena within which private capital may operate. State intervention, the fragility of property rights, . . . extensive control of commerce, . . . and increased taxes . . . appear aimed to displace the private sector.

(7) The Legislative Power [is not] independent from the Executive [as it] should be in order to guarantee the expression of political pluralism.

(8) The armed forces [have undergone] marked growth with ultramodern armaments; plus [there is] an increasingly large popular militia.[16]

To correct these problems, the opposition parties proposed the following: a statute of citizen rights and guarantees and the abolition of repressive laws; constitutional appeal (via amparo) against laws violating Nicaragua's constitution or international agreements; an independent legislature to which the executive branch would be accountable; municipal autonomy; a fundamental law of property rights assigning roles to the state and the private sector; legal assurance of pluralism in government; convocation in early 1983 of a constituent assembly to draft a constitution; and publication of the general budget of the nation.

Arguing in support of the regime, the Popular Social Christian Party (PPSC) charged that the opposition's statements sought to discredit Nicaragua abroad and characterized the accusations concerning religion as opportunistic. The PPSC called for all parties and unions to recognize the reality of U.S. aggression and to accept the state of emergency as a temporary necessity. It denied that the state of emergency was part of any strategy for assuming totalistic control and recommended that all agree to elections in 1985 among parties represented in the Council of State. The PPSC also urged review of the cases of "war prisoners," subject to definition of that term; the reopening of radio news programs under a new Press Law; an end to censorship of La Prensa; one hour of television time per week for both the regime and the Coordinadora Democratica (CDN); free labor organization in the communications industry; a clarification of the role of the private sector; and the restoration of amparo to property owners.

The FSLN's position paper insisted that all parties should agree that foreign aggression and economic crisis require the continuation of the state of emergency and that Nicaragua must seek unconditional dialogue with the United States, Honduras, or any other nation to prevent an escalation of the Central American conflict. The Sandinistas also proposed ongoing discussions among all social, political, and economic forces and the Council of State about how to confront the economic and international threats to the nation. They affirmed that, the state of emergency notwithstanding, national reconstruction and defense were compatible with political pluralism and the development of democracy. Specific proposals included:

(1) Council of State debate and approval of a Parties Law and election system to be elaborated with the help of experts and international assistance as needed; approval of a revised Press Law during 1982, to become effective when the state of emergency should end.

(2) Elections in 1985 as scheduled, with preparations and campaigns beginning in 1984, to include the parties eligible under the terms of the Parties Law.

(3) Immediate resumption of one independent radio news program over three stations; participation of opposition representatives in state television programs; admission of the Social Democratic Party to the Council of State; and the review of cases of military-political detainees held for minor offenses.

(4) Continuation of the state of emergency while
     necessary.
(5) Establishment of joint delegations of the
     (pro-regime coalition) FPR and the Coordinadora
     Democratica to promote foreign financial aid
     and seek other nations' help in denying
     counterrevolutionary exile groups' freedom to
     operate from their soil.

Although as of late 1982 there remained ample room
for compromise among the proregime and loyal opposition
groups, important differences persisted over the date for
elections, the state of emergency, and the degree of
political freedom to be restored under existing
conditions. In January 1983 the Coordinadora withdrew
from the discussion, complaining about its inability to
publish its positions and objecting to the wording of the
draft Parties Law to the effect that the goal of parties
should be "to participate in public administration"
rather than to win political power. After a period in
which representatives of the CDN travelled abroad to
explain their views and seek foreign support, some of the
coalition's parties appeared to be vacillating about
returning to the ongoing discussions in late March 1983.
The FSLN labelled the CDN's withdrawal and international
pilgrimage as an effort to confuse both domestic and
international opinion.
Future debates in the Council of State over a legal
definition of the role of the private sector, the Parties
Law, and the Press Law promise to be conflict-ridden
since they involve clashes over basic class interests and
the tools for their promotion (e.g., rules of access to
the media and elections). One problem that has troubled
the FSLN since 1979 is the radicalism of the pro-
Sandinista media. Barricada, El Nuevo Diario, and state
television have often taken positions far more extreme
than those of the FSLN Directorate, aggravating fears
among the private sector, independent unions, and political parties as to government intentions. Though the
directorate has often tried to assuage such fears, there
has been much damage to the atmosphere for political
discourse. The pro-Sandinista media's rhetoric and
tendentiousness could well make reconciliation difficult.
Moreover, the FSLN's condonation or use of mob action
against opposition parties, should it continue, would
severely hamper future discussions. On the other side of
the coin, continued links between the private sector and
some political parties and the external foes of the
revolution would promote suspicion of opposition intentions, loyalty, and commitment to reform. What remains
to be seen is the impact of the March 1983 counterrevolutionary invasion and subsequent guerrilla warfare
on the opposition-regime discussions, press freedom, and

party operations. The attacks would make it easier for the FSLN to curtail such activities. Ironically, then, they may have the effect of seriously weakening the opposition.

FOREIGN AFFAIRS

Nicaragua has adopted a foreign policy of nonalign-ment, anti-imperialism, and internationalism. Among other things, the Sandinista government has joined the Non-Aligned Movement; supported the right to independence of Puerto Rico, Belize, Palestine, Namibia, and other occupied peoples; and claimed "solidarity with the democratic nations of Latin America and the rest of the world."[17] Such behavior was entirely consistent with the revolutionaries' gratitude toward nations and groups as diverse as Cuba, the Palestinian liberation movement, Mexico, Panama, and Costa Rica for their support during the insurrection; it also reflected resentment toward the United States, Guatemala, and Israel (which had all supported the Somoza regime to one degree or another). Such a foreign policy, moreover, was consistent with the ideological roots of Sandinismo in the thought of Sandino and the Marxism of FSLN founder Carlos Fonseca and his disciples in the current leadership.

Independence from the United States, the major expression of Nicaraguan anti-imperialism, has been manifested in many ways, from votes in the United Nations to support for Argentina in the Malvinas (Falklands) dispute. The regime's internationalism has led to new or strengthened diplomatic links with nations of diverse ideologies and alignments--from the People's Republic of China to Taiwan, from the USSR to Brazil, from Cuba to Spain, from the German Democratic Republic and the rest of Eastern Europe to the Federal Republic of Germany, Sweden, the Netherlands, and France. The FSLN as a party established links to various international party organi-zations, including the Socialist International, the moderate Permanent Conference of Political Parties of Latin America, and various communist parties. Nicaragua has accepted reconstruction aid from many nations, the most controversial of which, at least from the U.S. perspective, came from Cuba, which sent some 6,000 doctors, nurses, and other technicians, about a third of them military advisers. The Sandinistas have assisted Salvadoran and Guatemalan rebels with sanctuary, weapons supply and transit, and solidarity. Given the previously great American influence over the Somoza regime's foreign and domestic policies, Washington--and in particular the Reagan administration--has regarded these features of Nicaraguan foreign policy with growing apprehension.

U.S. concern was manifested in relatively conciliatory and positive ways under the Carter administration, but veered abruptly with the advent of Ronald Reagan in January 1981. While the former saw the Sandinistas as tractable and subject to positive inducement to moderation and cooperation, the new Republican policymakers viewed Nicaragua as a Soviet tool directly menacing U.S. interests and hemispheric security--a veritable "platform for intervention against its neighbors."[18] American policy toward Nicaragua thus rapidly hardened. President Reagan removed Ambassador Laurence Pezzullo (who worked well with the Sandinistas), suspended the remainder of a $75 million loan, and began to raise objections to aid for Nicaragua from international lending agencies. By 1982, U.S. hostility had escalated to active support for counterrevolutionary exiles operating in Costa Rica, Honduras, and the United States. By early the following year, some $30 million had been spent on the CIA's destabilization effort.[19] This funding underwrote the FDN's terrorist and sabotage raids into Nicaragua and trained, organized, and financed the 1983 invasion. Despite Washington's refusal to admit this support, various news agencies had traced the contras' money and arms directly to the U.S. government. One FDN soldier training in Honduras aptly summed up this support in a CBS News interview broadcast on April 1, 1983. Brandishing his automatic weapon, he thanked the American people for their aid and said: " Aqui estan sus dolares!" ("Here are your dollars!").

Washington also encouraged increased regional pressure on the Sandinista regime by promoting the anti-Nicaraguan Central American Democratic Community (including Honduras, El Salvador, and Costa Rica) and underwriting a massive militarization program for Honduras. The growing North American-orchestrated pressure on the Sandinistas led many observers to predict an overt U.S. or Honduran attack on Nicaragua to coincide with the U.S.-Honduran "Big Pine" joint military maneuvers of February 1983. Instead, the March invasion by as many as 2,000 FDN contras proved to be the next step in the escalating pressure. The invaders joined at least several hundred other counterrevolutionaries already operating clandestinely in Matagalpa, Nueva Segovia, and northern Zelaya departments. Peasant support for the guerrillas was reportedly strong in some areas. Heavy fighting failed to eliminate the invaders and civilian and military casualties had climbed into the low hundreds by early April. Border incidents between Nicaraguan and Honduran troops were increasing, but at the time of this writing neither Nicaragua nor Honduras seemed bent on pressing the potentially explosive clash any further.

The deterioration of Nicaragua's relations with its Central American neighbors, of course, has roots deeper than any U.S. connection. Nicaragua and Costa Rica have long feuded over boundaries and water and fishing rights, and each has a lengthy tradition of intervention in the internal politics of the other. Nicaragua and Honduras have had similar differences: Disputes over territory led Nicaragua to invade Honduras in 1907 and Honduras to return the favor in 1957. Since 1979, each government has protested about various matters to the other, including clashes between security forces along the border. The gravest difficulty between Honduras and Nicaragua, of course, has been Honduran sanctuary and assistance for the FDN counterrevolutionaries.

Nicaragua's military buildup and the emergence of the Marxist-Leninist FSLN as the dominant political force in the country have prompted the fears of other Central American governments that Managua might have aggressive intentions. Such worries grew rapidly in 1981-82, as the Nicaraguan arms expansion accelerated in response to the growing counterrevolutionary threat. Moreover, changes to more conservative administrations in Venezuela (1980), Costa Rica (1980-82) and Mexico (1982) have increased reservations among former strong supporters of the Sandinistas. Such differences aside, however, all available evidence suggests that since 1981 Washington has sought to exacerbate such tensions, heighten fears, and strengthen potential enemies of Nicaragua wherever they may be found.

Nicaragua's response to such pressure has included repeated offers to the United States and various Central American governments to hold conversations to work out differences and reduce tensions. So far, however, such discussions have usually been rebuffed. A graphic example of this was Honduran President Robert Suazo Cordova's cancelling a scheduled meeting with junta member Daniel Ortega in Caracas in September 1982. Nevertheless, Nicaragua has sought continued good relations with other Latin American nations and U.S. allies in Europe in order to prevent its isolation from the West. Despite the growth of North American-orchestrated hostility in 1983, Managua had neither sought nor established formal military treaties with the Soviet Union or its allies. Nicaragua had no foreign military bases in its territory, nor had it forged any international military alliances. It did acquire military equipment from Warsaw Pact nations (including twenty-five tanks, anti-aircraft guns, rockets, and helicopters) and some 2,000 Cuban military advisers. Managua's aid from the USSR was mainly of an economic and technical character. Neither the Soviet Union nor Cuba appear to have encouraged Nicaragua to expand its formal military ties to the communist bloc.

PROSPECTS

In the prevailing international uncertainty and
domestic warfare, Nicaragua's future is difficult to
predict. Despite the existence of substantial domestic
opposition (both loyal and disloyal), through April 1983
the FSLN felt sufficiently secure that it permitted the
continued operation of opposition parties, unions, and
business groups, and continued to discuss differences
with the loyal opposition. Escalating external economic
and political pressure and the outbreak of the 1983 war
have been designed to provoke increased repression by the
regime and thus undermine the FSLN by encouraging popular
revolt. Despite evidence of some popular support for the
invading contras, foreign-inspired aggression could have
the opposite effect intended--for example, by increasing
opposition tolerance for restrictions on human rights for
security reasons and rallying the highly nationalistic
Nicaraguans behind the FSLN, thus strengthening the
regime. External pressures have already contributed to
prolonging the states of economic and military emergency
because, as DN member Victor Tirado so accurately stated
just the week before the counterrevolutionary invasion,
"We still face serious dangers and threats which are
increasing."[20]
    Should Nicaragua avoid embroilment in a war with
Honduras or with the United States, there may be a fair
chance for the passage of a Parties Law, revisions in the
Press Law to liberalize media access for the loyal
opposition, and elections in 1985. The Sandinistas would
most likely emerge from such a contest with an
overwhelming victory. In contrast, the political effects
of a prolonged clash with the contras or war with the
United States or Honduras would likely include postponed
elections and further constraints on civil liberties.
    The speed of Nicaragua's economic recovery and
development will continue to be severely affected by the
U.S.-backed counterrevolutionary rebellion. The 1981-82
military buildup robbed capital from economic and social
programs, and military spending undoubtedly soared with
the March 1983 invasion. War with Honduras--much more
likely due to the invasion and the continued presence in
Honduras of up to 3,000 more FDN troops--or with another
nation would be devastating. Even if foreign and
domestic military tensions should ease, however,
Nicaragua has already lost much ground in terms of
economic recovery by diverting major investments toward
the military sector. Thus, the Sandinistas had already
been forced into a terrible choice--that of jeopardizing
short- and middle-range improvements in living conditions
and political freedoms in order to defend the revolutionary framework that might make such changes possible
in the future.

NOTES

My thanks to Donald Schulz for his editorial
comments on an earlier draft of this chapter.
   1. Political Violence: The Behavioral Process (New
York: St. Martin's Press, 1979), p. 9.
   2. Jose Coronel Urtecho, Reflexiones sobre la
Historia de Nicaragua (de Gainza a Somoza, Tomo I:
Alrededor de la Independencia (Leon, Nicaragua:
Editorial Hospicio, 1962), p. 7.
   3. Quoted in Pedro Joaquin Chamorro C., Los Somoza:
Una Estirpe Sangrienta (Buenos Aires: El Cid Editores,
1979), p. 129.
   4. John A. Booth, The End and the Beginning: The
Nicaraguan Revolution (Boulder, Colo.: Westview Press,
1982), pp. 165-168.
   5. La Nacion Internacional [hereafter cited as LNI]
(October 14-20, 1982), p. 3.
   6. Inter-American Commission on Human Rights,
Report on the Situation of Human Rights in the Republic
of Nicaragua (Washington, D.C.: Organization of American
States, 1981), pp. 168-171.
   7. Washington Report on the Hemisphere [hereafter
cited as WR] (January 12, 1982), p. 5.
   8. The department originally cited as evidence
photos published in Le Figaro in February 1982. Within
days Le Figaro admitted that the photos were in error,
actually dating from the Somoza era, a fact subsequently
recognized by the State Department. See Jenny Pearce,
Under the Eagle: U.S. Intervention in Central America
and the Caribbean (London: Latin America Bureau, 1982),
pp. 264-265.
   9. Lars Schoultz, "Human Rights in Nicaragua,
Latin American Studies Association (LASA) Newsletter
(Fall 1982), pp. 9-13.
   10. Material drawn from the author's conversations
with Laurence R. Simon, Oxfam America, September 9, 1982,
and Galio Gurdian, an official in the relocation program,
on September 9, 1982, both in Manchester, England. Other
sources include the Washington Post (February 3, 1983);
LNI (February 26-March 4, September 23-29, and October
14-20, 1982).
   11. Mesoamerica (March 1983), pp. 9-10.
   12. WR (October 20, 1981), pp. 1, 7.
   13. LNI (September 16-23, 1982), p. 12.
   14. Mesoamerica (November 1982), pp. 6-7.
   15. The following information is largely based on LNI
(September 23-29 and October 7-13, 1982, and February
17-23, 1983).
   16. This quotation and the information in subsequent
passages are from Ibid. (October 7-13, 1982), pp. 4, 6-7.
   17. Programa del Gobierno de Reconstruccion Nacional,
quoted in Alejandro Bendana, "The Foreign Policy of the

330

Nicaraguan Revolution," in Nicaragua in Revolution, ed.
Thomas W. Walker (New York: Praeger, 1982), p. 321.

18. Thomas O. Enders, "The Central American
Challenge," American Enterprise Institute (AEI) Foreign
Policy and Defense Review 4,2 (1982), p. 9.

19. Newsweek (April 11, 1983).

20. Barricada Internacional (March 21, 1983), p. 1.

9
Honduras: Bastion
of Stability or Quagmire?

Mark B. Rosenberg

Political conflict, civil war, and revolution have
done for Central America what years of poverty, deprivation, and authoritarianism could not: They have placed
it squarely on the agenda of important U.S. foreign
policy interests. Nowhere is this better illustrated
than in Honduras. During the past year, the country has
been the subject of unprecedented economic and military
aid, the visit of a U.S. president, countless
congressional, intelligence, and religious officials,
and, of course, the scrutiny of a foreign press, which
put it on the front pages of newspapers throughout the
world. During 1982, Honduras joined the expanding list
of Central American states that are now major foreign
policy preoccupations of the United States.

Honduras joins the list not because of a significant
internal revolutionary challenge or because of a
persistent and deepening trend in the violation of human
rights, or indeed because it is the poorest country in
continental Latin America. Rather, it is included
because of its strategic location. The country, named by
Columbus on his fourth voyage to the Americas, shares
borders with Nicaragua, El Salvador, and Guatemala.
Honduras' traditional ally, the United States, has
significant geopolitical interests in each of these
countries. More importantly, it perceives Central
America and Panama, together with the Hispanic and
non-Hispanic Caribbean, as a critical arena of geopolitical struggle now straining under unprecedented Soviet and
Cuban interference.

Since the Sandinista victory of July 1979, much
thinking and analysis on Central America has tended to
fall into dichotomies: "revolution or counterrevolution,"
"liberation or repression," "socialism or capitalism."
Honduras' geopolitical centrality to the region and to
U.S. policy has similarly provoked the Vietnam syndrome
analogy--"bastion of stability or quagmire," the subject
of this analysis. In fact, the analogy is inadequate

TABLE 9.1

Central America: Changes in Net National
Product, 1978-82 (at constant prices)[a]

	1978	1979	1980	1981[b]	1982[c]
Guatemala	5.0	4.7	3.5	1.0	-3.5
El Salvador	4.0	-1.5	-9.6	-9.5	-0.5-1.5
Honduras	7.0	6.6	2.6	0.3	-1.4
Nicaragua	-7.1	-25.2	8.1	10.9	-2.0-3.0
Costa Rica	6.3	4.9	0.6	-3.6	-5.9
Central America	3.6	-0.04	0.8	0.8	

Source: SIECA, Diario el Tiempo (December 14, 1982).

[a] 1970 as base year
[b] Preliminary
[c] Projections

because it fails to account for the Honduran elite's
needs and priorities within the regional geopolitical
context.   This chapter explores current Honduran-U.S.
relations within the context of North American policy
and, more important, Honduran civil-military relations.

THE REGIONAL SETTING

Central America has now been at war with itself for
six years.   The political decomposition of the region--
both within states and between them--has been widely
chronicled.   Although "winners" are difficult to
identify, there are no lack of losers: over 80,000
casualties and upwards of a million displaced persons or
refugees.   Infrastructural and financial ruin have all
but erased the economic gains of the late 1960s and mid-
1970s.   If Table 9.1 is any indication, economic stagnation, if not decline, now threatens to be an ongoing
regional condition for the foreseeable future.
Despite the regional economic collapse and its
alarming implications for the future, the United States
has given much more sustained attention to the area's
political struggles.   The unmistakable element that the
Reagan administration has added to U.S. policy has been
its militarization, both rhetorically and substantively
in terms of military aid and training.   This militarization has a certain paradox to it: In the cases of El
Salvador and Guatemala, aid is justified as a means to

nd violence and achieve democratization. In Honduras,
t is rationalized as a way to prevent violence and main-
ain democracy. Militarization has also served as a
ubstitute for meaningful bilateral negotiations with
icaragua and as an instrument to force the Sandinistas
o the bargaining table. However, in light of
icaragua's disastrous economic situation, it is likely
hat, were the Reagan administration really committed to
 peaceful solution in that country, militarization as a
olicy response would not have been necessary. By the
ame token, by providing an excuse for Washington to play
ts military game, the Sandinistas have done a disservice
o the quest for moderation and reform throughout Central
merica.

From a regional standpoint, Honduras plays a criti-
al role in the U.S. effort to contain revolution. This
ole was recognized even before the Reagan administration
ook office. It was crystallized by the Department of
tate's William Bowdler who, in testimony before Congress
n mid-1980, asserted that "Honduras' location between
icaragua and El Salvador gives it a key geopolitical
osition in the 'bridge-building' process we hope will
merge in Central America." Bowdler also argued that
onduras should not be exploited as a "conduit" to
upport conflicts in Nicaragua and Salvador.[1] The
ountry's extensive border with the former and rugged
emilitarized zones with the latter were clearly areas of
oncern for both the United States and the Hondurans.
ndeed, U.S. pressure fostered an October 1980
onduran-Salvadoran peace treaty over the disputed border
reas. Honduran willingness to give generous concessions
o their former foes may have been fostered by the naive
elief that more secure border areas would minimize the
ikelihood of guerrilla activity in their own country and
elp bring the Salvadoran conflict to a speedy conclusion. In fact, Honduras' hard line regarding the
alvadoran guerrillas has helped to do just the opposite.
ince 1980 (even before the Reagan administration),
ashington has attempted to use the country in its
ontainment efforts. This strategy has combined politi-
al, diplomatic, and military resources and has involved
he fitful forging of national, regional, and international coalitions designed to bolster coalition
partners and legitimate U.S. policy.

However, just as North American policymakers have
attempted to use Honduras as an instrument of regional
security policy, so Honduran elites have tried to manipulate U.S. policy for their own needs. Thus, although
there has been a notable and at times colonial-like
congruence between the policies of the two countries,
this convergence masks a deeper struggle within Honduras
over control of that political system.

THE RETURN TO CIVILIAN GOVERNMENT IN HONDURAS

In January 1982, a civilian government formally took power, marking the end of a decade-long military control of the presidency. Democratization had its genesis in the growing popular discontent beginning in the mid-1970s, accelerated by the Sandinista victory of 1979, and in subsequent U.S. pressure to return the country to civilian rule. An orgy of corruption among high-level officers of the Honduran Armed Services and rampant government mismanagement contributed to the military's exit. Firm U.S. pressure kept the democratization process moving forward, despite the growing realization by the military that it would be relinquishing control at precisely the time when national defense appeared most threatened. The Salvadoran civil war was spilling into Honduras by incursions of guerrillas (and their Salvadoran pursuers) onto Honduran territory and by threats and perceived threats from a growing Nicaraguan military establishment.

The process of returning formal power to civilians took place in textbook fashion. Constitutional Assembly elections were held in April 1980. An impressive and unexpected voter turnout gave the Liberal Party a slight majority of votes. When the liberals increased their margin of victory in the presidential elections of 1981, the mandate was clear: Eliminate the military and their National Party allies from power, stop the corruption, and reignite the now staggering economy.

In fact, during 1982 few of the civilian government's goals were accomplished. The military emerged as the real winner of the 1981 elections, in essence snatching victory from the jaws of defeat. Although it has often been suggested that the United States was primarily responsible for reinforcing the military's position, this suggestion does not give enough credit to Honduran civil-military dynamics and the threat that the Honduran military perceives from Nicaragua. Consequently, there is much misunderstanding about the congruence of U.S. and Honduran strategies.

By late 1980, most high-level civilian politicians understood that the key to their success depended less on their ability to mobilize popular civilian support than on their relations with important Honduran military figures. The Liberal Party took a calculated risk by associating itself with (then) Colonel Gustavo Alvarez Martinez, who during the pre-1981 presidential election period had occupied successively two of the country's most important military posts: Chief of the San Pedro Sula military garrison and head of the national police forces (FUSEP). By 1979, Alvarez had established himself as a consummate military professional. Benefitting from training in Peru, Argentina, and the United States,

Alvarez' movement through the Honduran officer corps had
distinguished him from other officers. Although he was
stridently anti-communist, he was relatively less
involved in corruption than were his colleagues. And
unlike others, including President Policarpo Paz, Alvarez
was anti-Sandinista, rarely cooperating with the
Nicaraguan revolutionaries either before or after they
came to power.

If the liberals were to attain power, maintain a
semblance of support from influential business and
commercial interests, and protect themselves from the
Sandinistas, Alvarez would be the logical candidate to
become Chief of the Armed Forces in the civilian government of 1982-86. Reagan's electoral victory in November
1980 practically ensured Alvarez' preeminence. And the
fact that the other leading candidates were known to have
veleidades Sandinistas (Sandinista coquettishness)
further solidified the colonel's position.[2] Alvarez'
centrality to the Liberal Party is also important because
he encouraged the emergence of an anti-Sandinista position within the most influential tendency in the party,
the Rodistas, which firmly controlled and continues to
control internal decisionmaking. Thus, independent of
U.S. interests vis-a-vis the outcome of Honduran elections, Alvarez and Liberal Party leaders met each others'
needs. Another important element in this equation is the
fact that Alvarez and Ricardo Zuniga Augustinas, leader
of the National Party, apparently have professional
enmity of significant proportion. Alvarez' manipulation
of the Liberal Party and vice versa would be critical to
neutralizing Zuniga's almost Machiavellian control of
Honduran politics. To date, the formula has been
successful because the National Party has always depended
on its open political alliance with the military to
ensure its hegemony. Now that coalition has been
ruptured, thanks to both the liberals' stealth and
Alvarez' cunning.

Thus, while Alvarez' ascendancy coincided with the
arrival in Tegucigalpa of Reagan ambassadorial appointee,
John D. Negroponte, it was the logic of the liberals'
quest for office that brought the military hardliner into
power, not Washington's search for a reliable martinet
who would loyally execute the U.S. strategy for the
region. In this sense, the military played a critical
role in the consolidation of civilian power--as might be
expected considering the overall weakness of the civilian
political structure and the fact that the military's
influence is not simply a function of its institutional
composition. Civilian elements within the business and
labor communities have often shown a proclivity for
coalitions with the military or sectors within it. This
tendency, manifest in the late 1960s and early 1970s as
well as under the current government, clearly limits the

possibilities for civilian consolidation of power and the establishment of hegemony over the military. Skillful officers, like Alvarez, recognize this and are aware of the need to manipulate influential civilians as a means of minimizing their accountability to civilian rule.

U.S. POLICY AND STABILIZATION THROUGH MILITARIZATION

The Reagan electoral victory brought with it a "new orthodoxy" that has had clear ramifications in Central America. Confronted with an increase in regional instability and the growing complexity of Central America's international relations, the Reagan administration responded in military security terms. The focus of this policy has been El Salvador and Nicaragua and the critical pivot has been Honduras. U.S. policy, employing a melange of "carrot and stick" resources, has reflected a short-term incrementalist logic that shows little sensitivity to the middle-range regional consequences of "stabilization through militarization" and to the short-run costs to Honduras.

Derisively known to many as the "playground" of Central America, Honduras has played a critical role in the four-year U.S. quest for regional stability. As early as 1979 Viron Vaky, Assistant Secretary of State for Inter-American Affairs, pointed out the country's geopolitical centrality. In early 1980, the militarization of policy began when the Department of State proposed a "reprogramming" of aid, arguing that

> the general question of secure frontiers is critical for Honduras, bordering as it does on two countries undergoing rapid change. A greater sense of confidence in Honduras of the government's ability to control its frontiers is key to regional stability. It is important that Honduras not be used as a conduit for the infiltration of men and arms to feed conflicts in neighboring countries. Honduras must also feel secure if it is to resolve its longstanding dispute with El Salvador.[3]

The administration proposed a 1980 Foreign Military Sales (FMS) financing program of $3.53 million and an increase of the International Military Education and Training (IMET) program from $225,000 to $347,000. FMS credits would enhance military mobility and communications capabilities, and ten U.S. Army Uh-1H helicopters were also included on lease for a year. As the administration explained it: "We anticipate that conflict in El Salvador will be reduced soon, and when that happens, the helicopters will be returned to the United States." IMET funds were to be used to support the training of

ondurans in the United States and Panama and to finance
obile training teams in Honduras. Lurking behind the
dministration's argument, however, was the belief that
f El Salvador fell to the Cuban-supported insurgency,
onduras would be "among the next primary targets."[4]
ince 1980, security assistance to Honduras has undergone
 significant increase, as illustrated in Table 9.2.
     Under the Reagan administration the quantity and
uality of military aid changed significantly, particu-
arly in 1982. Emphasis has been on enhancing Honduran
ir Force capabilities through the purchase of six new
-37 planes designed for counterinsurgency warfare. The
nited States has also provided $13 million in military
onstruction funds for the improvement of airport runways
t Palmeroa Air Academy (Comayagua) and at La Ceiba's
olazon Airport. Upgrading is necessary, it is argued,
o provide runway extensions, second access ramps,
evetment structures, and additional fuel storage facili-
ies. The improvements will also provide greater U.S.
.ccess, building on a 1954 Mutual Military Assistance
greement between the two countries.[5]
     The seven-fold increase in U.S. military assistance
.o Honduras coincided with a shift in strategy toward the

TABLE 9.2

U.S. Security Assistance to Honduras, FY 1980-83
(thousands of dollars)

	1980	1981	1982	1982 Supp.	1983
mmunition	422	2,784[a]	14	7,000	6,000
upply/Support	361	1,050	268	800	2,600
pare Parts	631	254	664	4,000	500
ommunications	394	5	–	3,200[e]	750
ir Force	2,861	213[b]	7,229[c]	4,000[c]	–
rmy	–	–	900[d]	–	–
avy	–	–	115	1,000[f]	–
otal	5,078	4,300	9,200	20,000	9,850

Source: U.S. Embassy, Tegucigalpa, November 1982.

[a] Includes weapons (small arms, M-16s, M-79s)
[b] Includes aircraft parts and technical assistance
[c] A-37s and associated spare parts package
[d] Includes four helicopters, automotive spare parts,
   extra engines, and other items
[e] Includes purchase of radio, repair, and survey of needs
[f] Repair and overhaul of existing patrol boats

region. Both the Carter and Reagan administrations
reasoned that the guerrilla war in El Salvador could be
quickly terminated through military means. Thus,
Washington supplied the Salvadoran Army with unprecedented military and economic aid, culminating in the
March 1982 elections, which were designed to give popular
legitimacy to the military-civilian coalition headed by
Jose Napoleon Duarte. Honduras would play a critical
role in choking off the arms supplies allegedly
transshipped from Nicaragua to El Salvador.

However, as it became apparent in late 1981 that the
Salvadoran elections would be inconsequential to the
administration's goal of regional stabilization, a shift
in strategy occurred. Nicaragua's Sandinistas became the
chief target. The U.S. goal was threefold--to shut off
the arms supplies to El Salvador, to weaken the
Sandinista government through harassment from Somocistas,
Mosquitos, and any other antiregime forces that could be
mobilized, and to bring the Sandinistas to the bargaining
table on U.S. terms.

Once again, Honduras was to play a critical role,
particularly given the melange of anti-Sandinistas who
had already taken refuge in the country and the apparent
(pre-Malvinas) willingness of the Argentine military to
play a proxy role in training and logistics. Moreover,
the growing ethnic problems in the Mosquitia provided an
excellent opportunity for harrassment. In December 1981,
President Reagan approved a "minimal" plan for covert
operations against the Sandinistas that utilized Honduras
as its base of operations.

Much has been written about Honduras' role as a base
for regional counterinsurgency operations. It is no
secret in Honduras that the United States is working
closely with anti-Sandinista groups. The American
ambassador there continually emphasizes the country's
need to defend its borders from outside aggression. The
United States has also participated in three military
maneuvers with the Honduran Armed Forces in the last two
years. The most recent joint exercise, in early 1983,
was carried out near the Nicaraguan border. It was the
largest such effort in the region since World War II,
involved about 1,600 U.S. and 4,000 Honduran troops, and
cost at least $5 million. Although Washington claimed
that these maneuvers were merely "defensive" in nature,
their symbolism illustrated well the contradiction of
U.S. policy toward Nicaragua--a strategy best characterized as an effort to "stabilize through destabilization." U.S.-Honduran efforts give the Sandinistas an
important resource--the threat of an external enemy--for
consolidating their control. Other Central American
regimes have found foreign enemies useful for purposes of
bolstering sagging domestic fortunes: Fidel Sanchez
Hernandez of El Salvador in 1969 against Honduras;

Oswaldo Lopez Arellano of Honduras in 1969 against El
Salvador; Rodrigo Carazo Odio of Costa Rica in 1979
against Nicaragua; and now the Nicaraguans against the
Hondurans and vice versa.

Regionally, Washington's policy has led to the
formation of a loose coalition of non-Marxist Caribbean
Basin countries critical of the United States. Mexico,
previously alone in its criticism of U.S. policies, has
now been joined by Colombia, Venezuela, and Panama. This
criticism, coupled with Washington's open support for
Britain in the Malvinas dispute, has seriously reduced
the credibility of U.S. policy throughout the region. As
U.S. credibility diminishes, so does its ability to
achieve results diplomatically, thereby necessitating
even further militarization as a means to leverage
desired outcomes. Indeed, if Washington's policy outcomes are poorly conceptualized and/or poorly understood
(as they have been under both Carter and Reagan), it is
likely that policy will become confused with outcomes.
Thus, militarization would become an end in itself,
rather than a means. This has, in fact, happened with
Reagan policy toward Central America.

UNITED STATES POLICY AND HONDURAN CIVIL-MILITARY
RELATIONS

In Honduras, U.S. policy has been skillfully manipulated by the Honduran military for its own purposes.
General Alvarez' primary concern is to strengthen
Honduran military preparedness as quickly as possible.
He believes that Honduras will inevitably be caught up in
an insurgency.[6] Moreover, many of his fellow officers
feel that war with El Salvador, similar to the 1969
struggle, is less than a decade away. Thus, Alvarez has
cooperated with the United States as a means of rapidly
strengthening Honduran military capabilities. Were he to
reject U.S. aid, he would be ignoring the conventional
military prowess of El Salvador and the growing militarization of Nicaragua.

However, just as Alvarez has manipulated U.S. policy
for purposes of external defense, so has he tightened
internal security. Starting just before the November
1981 presidential elections, there was a noticeable
deterioration in human rights conditions, which
accelerated once the civilian government, with Alvarez as
Chief of Armed Forces, took office.[7] Paling in quantity
and quality compared to the abuses in El Salvador, this
decline has been directly attributed to Alvarez and a
special investigations unit under his control.[8] Indeed,
despite the "political opening" with a democratic government, an uncommon climate of uncertainty and insecurity
exists in the country, partly a result of the fear of

internal subversion and a possible border war with
Nicaragua. It is significant that guerrilla-sponsored
acts of terrorism in Honduras have coincided with
Honduran military cooperation with the Salvadoran Army.
The kidnapping of 100 San Pedro Sula businessmen in late
September 1982 by Cinchonero guerrillas was tied to
demands for the release of Salvadoran guerrillas held in
Honduran jails. Several kidnappings of prominent
Hondurans and the wanton political murder of a San Pedro
businessman in 1981 gave the military the motivation to
stalk local subversives, who were either threatening the
fabric of Honduran political life, supporting the
Salvadoran insurgents, or providing intelligence to the
Sandinistas. U.S. belligerency toward the region, fear
of the Cuban "devil," and efforts to isolate and oust the
Sandinistas provided a convenient cover for the
establishment of a garrison state environment.

General Alvarez has maintained a close relationship
with U.S. Ambassador John D. Negroponte, who is often
portrayed as Alvarez' patron. Both are strong-willed,
ambitious individuals. Both are anti-communists and
believe in the need for a vigorous military defense.
Thus, despite the fact that they do not always agree on
issues, they seem to complement each other nicely.
However, notions that Alvarez is Negroponte's "man" are
mistaken. As noted earlier, Alvarez' position was made
possible by his relationship with President Suazo
Cordova. Indeed, Suazo now faces a difficult problem--
namely, how to demilitarize Honduran politics and
institutionalize civilian rule at a time when the
country's major ally is supporting militarization both
rhetorically and materially, and when both of its neighbors are undergoing significant internal strife, which is
spilling over into Honduras.

Suazo Cordova has allowed the military to control
national security and foreign policymaking, particularly
at the regional level. The military has also been able
to veto cabinet appointments and seems to enjoy virtual
immunity from the National Congress in terms of the
investigation of corruption or human rights violations.
This lack of accountability to civilians is a carryover
from its domination of political life in the 1970s.
Because of the importance that civilian elites give to
the military, it is accorded a status, if not respect,
equal to that of the government. To formalize this,
under the 1981 Constitution, the chief of the armed
forces was given a term of five years, whereas the
president of the country was restricted to four.

Alvarez has made the most of his situation. He is
reportedly behind efforts to rid the National University,
the San Pedro Sula businessmen's association, and one of
the large teachers' unions of their progressive or
leftist leaderships. It is widely believed that he was

ne of the intellectual authors of a summer 1982 split in
he National Party (now resolved) and that he is now
resident of a countrywide business and political
ssociation that, although nascent, has the markings of a
orporativist body.[9]

Nevertheless, the formulation of Honduran security
olicy has not been a matter of complete consensus either
ithin or outside the government. At his inauguration,
uazo Cordova lyrically stated that "Central America
hould be a zone of peace" and that "Honduras desired to
aintain principles of self-determination and noninter-
ention in the affairs of others."[10] Just two months
ater, his foreign minister began a campaign at the
rganization of American States to "internationalize
eace in the region." The plan included six points:

1. regional disarmament and reduction in the size
   of Central American military forces;
2. reduction in the number of foreign military
   advisers in the region;
3. international supervision of border areas;
4. limitation and control of regional arms traffic;
5. maintenance of all border areas; and
6. permanent dialogue of a multilateral character
   designed to strengthen democratic systems and
   ensure public liberties and the right of popular
   expression.[11]

This address and several others made by the foreign
inister and various government officials were designed
o convince the international diplomatic community that
onduras did not seek a confrontation with its neighbors,
articularly Nicaragua. Of even greater importance,
hese speeches were the public manifestation of a growing
ehind-the-scenes struggle within the Honduran government
nd military over just how much the country should become
nvolved in the regional conflict.[12] Chief adversaries
n this struggle have been the foreign minister, Edgardo
az Barnica, and General Alvarez, the former favoring
oderation and compromise and the latter supporting a
ard-line anti-Sandinista policy.

How could such a division emerge so early in the
oung government's tenure? First, Suazo himself is a
eak ruler. Despite his large popular mandate, he has
ot been inclined and is simply not able to remove the
ilitary from decisionmaking. His efforts at civilian
nstitutionalization must be slow and deliberate. Given
he perceived Sandinista and Salvadoran guerrilla threat,
he military will at least have a mission to keep it
ccupied. Second, both the overt and covert aspects of
.S. security policy play directly into the hands of
onduran militarists, who prefer the security state
pparatus and do not trust civilians, especially

politicians. Finally, the moderate argument represents Suazo's electoral mandate. Hondurans did not vote to pursue a war with Nicaragua. They voted for democracy to ensure the military's withdrawal from public life. The threat of war, however, has ensured that the military will continue to play a role in politics. And as the economy continues its slide, an outside enemy helps the government maintain popular support.

The Honduran Congress has been slow to exploit the executive division over foreign policy. Despite (or perhaps because of) the fact that Suazo's party dominates that body, on only one occasion during the 1982 legislative year was there any serious questioning of foreign policy and the military's role. Congress did have an excellent chance to review Alvarez' leadership following his denunciation by dissident Colonel Leonidas Torres Arias from Mexico in September 1982, but the opportunity was lost because it was afraid of being shut down by the military.

No perceptible opposition to the government on foreign policy matters has emerged from the once dominant National Party, which has thirty-five of Congress' eighty-three seats. Intraparty factionalism and the party's traditional alliance with the military diminish the likelihood that it could effectively criticize and reorient foreign policy.

Equally curious about the Honduran response to their militarization and the use of their country by the United States is the muting of almost all popular organizations. Groups sympathetic to the Sandinistas and the Salvadoran insurgents, originally based at the National University, disappeared from public life in July 1982, shortly after the three-day blackout of Tegucigalpa occasioned by guerrilla destruction of an electrical transformer station. Labor unions have focused on internal bargaining and wage questions. Real opposition to the government and its policies has emerged from the dissident Christian Democratic Party of Honduras (PDCH), which managed but one congressional deputy. Thus, it does not have much public support. The climate of insecurity fostered by militarization has actually reduced the quality of pluralism in the society, even in the first year of "democratization."

The most outspoken criticism of the government has come from the Catholic Church. Although the Church was one of the first in Central America to become involved in secular matters in the early 1960s, its militancy diminished after 1975. In that year, several priests were brutally murdered and mutilated as a result of their advocacy of land reform. Yet the Church began its involvement once again in 1980 with a pastoral letter and since then has issued two others. The latest, in October 1982, complements the government for moving ahead on its

pledge to restore honesty to public life; however, it is
critical of the climate of hostility, fear, and
insecurity and calls on the regime to promote greater
social harmony.[13]

Thus, the "new orthodoxy" heralded by the Reagan
administration has had national security implications for
Honduras. The military has skillfully manipulated U.S.
policy to meet its own ends, both military and nonmilitary. Civilian political leadership has been
weakened by the absence of a strong and forceful chief
executive. Suazo prefers to fight his political battles
indirectly rather than frontally.

THE REFUGEE SITUATION

The regional conflict has brought Honduras another
problem. Refugees from three neighboring countries, El
Salvador, Nicaragua, and Guatemala, now reside within its
borders. Although estimates of the total number vary,
the United Nations places the figure at slightly less
than 30,000 (see Table 9.3).

The presence of diverse groups of refugees has
evoked contradictory responses from the Honduran regime;
these responses are the product of its policies toward El
Salvador and Nicaragua. The desire to cooperate with the
Salvadoran government and military, particularly to stop
the penetration of FMLN guerrillas into Honduras, has
dictated a hard-line approach to the issue of Salvadoran
refugees and border security. In fact, joint military
operations between Honduran and Salvadoran troops
resulted in two massacres of fleeing refugees along the
Sumpul and Lempa Rivers in 1980 and 1981.

Salvadorans are generally restricted to their camps,
located at Mesa Grande and Colomoncagua. The former was
relocated from La Virtud, Granaja, and other villages

TABLE 9.3

Refugees in Honduras

	Assisted by UNHCR	Others	Total
Salvadorans	14,800	2,200	17,000
Nicaraguans	10,050	950	11,000
Guatemalans	500	500	1,000

Source: United Nations High Commissioner for Refugees,
Refugees Magazine (September 1982), p. 10.

close to the Salvadoran frontier in April 1982. The
relocation was consistent with the United Nations'
refugee policy prohibiting official assistance to camps
closer than 50 kilometers from the neighboring country.
Honduran and Salvadoran officials also approved this
relocation, for they believed that the La Virtud camp
served as a source of supply and rest for Salvadoran
guerrillas. Relocation also resulted in some Salvadoran
return migration and some dispersal into the general
Honduran population.

Although Mesa Grande is beginning to develop a
permanent infrastructure and provides some schooling and
health care, conditions at Colomoncagua are still
precarious. Just three kilometers from the Salvadoran
border and the conflict-ridden Morazan province,
Colomoncagua contains about 7,000 refugees. This camp
has been the subject of both official brutality and
guerrilla support, and UN officials are hopeful of moving
it away from the border when a suitable site can be
found.

Treatment of Salvadorans should be understood within
the context of the fears of Honduran peasant groups, who
view the refugees as competitors for the scarce good
land available for cultivation. At the time of the 1969
border war, these fears and animosities evoked vicious
treatment of Salvadoran peasants and merchants who had
taken up residence in the country. Honduran fears are
also generated by the widely held belief that Salvadoran
peasants are more industrious and productive than their
Honduran counterparts. Thus, there is little pressure on
the Honduran government and military for a more consid-
erate treatment of Salvadorans. Both (and particularly
the latter) have a great deal of local autonomy in the
treatment of refugees.

Salvadorans have been the subject of extreme control
and movement restrictions, but such is not the case with
Nicaraguan refugees. This differential treatment has
several dimensions. First, the majority of refugees are
in the Department of Gracias a Dios in the isolated
Mosquitia region of Honduras. Arriving in large numbers
across the Rio Coco in early 1981, this group began to
concentrate at Mocoron, about 110 miles from the coast.
Relief efforts were poorly organized and inadequate, in
part because of the stress on existing relief agencies
resulting from the Salvadoran influx and in part because
of the region's isolation.[14]

A second reason for the differential treatment of
Nicaraguan refugees in the Mosquitia derives from the
coincidence of the group's arrival with the U.S. effort
to harass the regime in Managua. Mosquito leaders,
firmly anti-Sandinista, provided a poorly trained but
terrain-wise group of militants quite happy to cooperate.
The Honduran military, which has a greater presence in

the remote regions of the country than does the government, took advantage of the situation. U.S. logistical support was used to move its Fifth Battalion from Comayagua to Mocoron in July 1982, and its naval presence in Puerto Lempira was enhanced with the provision of new fuel-storage facilities. Mocoron is generally regarded as one of the principal Honduran staging sites of anti-Sandinista raids.

The Mosquito presence, coupled with the earlier arrival of refugees from the 1979 Sandinista victory, has recently been further augmented by a third generation of Nicaraguan exiles. Concentrating in the El Paraiso-Danli area of Honduras, this last group began arriving in April 1982 from the Nueva Segovia region of Nicaragua. Numbering about 3,500, it is slowly growing at the rate of about 200 per month. Villages such as La Lodoza, Santa Maria, Las Trojes, and El Porvenir are popular sites of refuge. As of this writing, little organized assistance has reached these new arrivals, and their movement is generally much less restrained than that of the Salvadorans. The government, at both the national and local levels, has made it clear that no assistance is available. The Honduran national coordinator for refugees, Colonel Abraham Garcia Turcios, estimated in September 1982 that the total number of Nicaraguan refugees could be as many as 15,000, a figure about one-third higher than the estimate provided by the United Nations.[15]

Estimates vary as to the number of Guatemalan refugees in the country. One report placed their presence at more than 4,000; however, 1,000 seems more likely. Of this group, about half were assisted by the United Nations, and the rest were dispersed or in hiding. Unlike either the Salvadorans or the Nicaraguans, there is little controversy surrounding this group, mainly because the important zones of conflict in Guatemala are far removed from the Honduran border. However, if the Guatemalan civil strife should shift southward, then Honduras could be deluged by unprecedented numbers of refugees.

Although the Hondurans generally tend to ignore the refugees, their presence has compromised the sovereignty and territorial integrity of the Hondurans on more than one occasion. On the one hand, the ongoing military cooperation with El Salvador is intended to limit both the Salvadoran guerrilla presence in the country and Salvadoran military and paramilitary movement in the border areas. On the other hand, Honduran military support for the estimated 4,000 anti-Sandinista militants scattered throughout the Nicaraguan-Honduran border area is rooted in the desire of the Honduran high command, and particularly General Alvarez, to harass and destabilize a perceived aggressor and in the coincidence of this aim

with U.S. interests. Such a position makes eminent sense
for the military because it has given the military a
rationale with which to enhance arms and training capabilities. This position also provides the armed forces
with leverage over civilian policy and policymakers,
which might not otherwise exist. Perhaps most important,
even if Honduran military and civilian officials were
opposed to the anti-Sandinista presence, it is doubtful
that much could be done to put an end to it. Thus, by
cooperating with the contras, the Honduran Army is able
to monitor and control an activity that might otherwise
be uncontrollable. (The possibility that desperate
Nicaraguan exiles could become an internal security
threat is rarely entertained in Honduras.)

QUAGMIRE OR SIDESHOW?

This chapter has examined the relationship between
United States policy toward Central America and Honduran
civil-military relations. The militarization of U.S.
policy has been the main theme of the Reagan
administration's regional efforts. This militarization
has been ostensibly designed to evoke stabilization by
creating or preserving conditions propitious to
democracy. In Honduras, nascent democracy is to be
preserved through unprecedented military aid and by
making the country the pivot for efforts to bring about
democracy elsewhere. Honduras will secure its western
borders and prevent Salvadoran guerrillas from using its
territory as a staging base, while cutting off arms bound
to those forces from neighboring Nicaragua. It will host
anti-Sandinista guerrillas, opening its borders to their
free movement, and supply them with arms and material to
conduct their clandestine war. Thus, in El Salvador,
democracy will be created through stabilization, whereas
in Nicaragua it will come about through destabilization.
Military struggle rather than diplomacy is the common
element that gives each of these policies a unifying
theme.
Is Honduras the unwilling vehicle for U.S. strategy?
This analysis has shown that Washington's policy has been
manipulated and molded to the particular needs of
Honduran military and civilian elites. If a "quagmire"
thesis is relevant, however, it applies more to the
Hondurans themselves. Several possibilities come to
mind.
First, Honduran cooperation with the Salvadoran Army
has already brought the guerrilla struggle to Honduras,
and this has been costly not only in physical destruction
but also in a growing restriction of civil liberties. If
the Salvadoran insurgents should finally assume power,
one of their natural external enemies will be Honduras.

The willingness of the Honduran Army to engage in mass killings along the Salvadoran border will not be soon forgotten.

Second, Honduran anti-Sandinista activities threaten to escalate into a full-scale border war, or worse, a prolonged insurgency sponsored by each country against the other. Neither economy could sustain such conflict for long, and inevitably the pressure would mount for a final sustained assault, each country against the other. The inevitable losers in either case would be the Honduran people themselves.

A third possibility concerns the anti-Sandinista Nicaraguans in Honduras and the likelihood of their abandonment by the United States. This stateless group would have no choice but to turn on the Hondurans themselves in its effort to survive. Such activity might be camouflaged as a "leftist" threat to the country as a means by which to maintain U.S. resolve and belligerency against the Sandinistas. At best it would be an act of desperation, but certainly not without logic.

In each of these scenarios, the Honduran people would find themselves increasingly dependent on the military, a group that was clearly repudiated in the 1980 and 1981 elections. Each scenario would also be accompanied by further economic decline and increased pressure on the already hard-pressed poor. Such developments would indeed be a quagmire for the Honduran people, one that would severely strain the foundations of the current order.

Finally, there is the central question of the quality of the U.S. commitment. In this regard, Washington may be setting Honduras up for a major disappointment. Many parallels exist between the North American posture on Honduras and its use and abuse of Cambodia during the early 1970s to relieve pressure on South Vietnam. Although Prince Sihanouk had managed to keep Cambodia neutral throughout the long and bitter struggle, U.S. officials in Southeast Asia first illegally bombed and then invaded the country in an effort to destroy North Vietnamese supply lines and command centers. The violation of Cambodian neutrality opened an opportunity for the local communists, the Khmer Rouge, to make their claim. The resulting violence, death, and demographic displacement assumed tragic proportions. Thus, U.S. policy resulted in exactly what it was trying to prevent—the destruction of a fragile political balance and a communist takeover.

Clearly, the Reagan administration's policy is motivated less by what is good for Honduras than by U.S. desires concerning Honduras' neighbors and the role that that country might play in these matters. Unprecedented economic and military aid, out of all proportion relative to what Honduras has received in the past and what it can

reasonably absorb in the short run, an oversized U.S.
embassy staff populated by many with Southeast Asian
experience, and massive joint military maneuvers are
suggestive. Hondurans with an historical memory should
understand that something that has emerged so quickly can
disappear with equal speed, particularly if leadership
changes are affected as a result of forthcoming elections
in the United States.

NOTES

The author gratefully acknowledges travel support
from the Florida International University Foundation and
the research assistance provided by Cecilia Altonaga,
Marcos Carias, and Delores Quintero.

1. U.S., Congress, House, Hearings Before the
Subcommittee on Inter-American Affairs of the Committee
on Foreign Affairs, 96th Congress, Second Session,
April 29 and May 20, 1980, pp. 49-51.
2. This information comes from a variety of
interviews I conducted while in Honduras during
September-December 1982.
3. U.S., Congress, House, Hearings Before the
Subcommittee on Foreign Operations and Related Programs,
Committee on Appropriations, 97th Congress, Second
Session, March 25, 1980, p. 333.
4. Ibid., pp. 334, 340.
5. Council on Hemispheric Affairs, Washington Report
on the Hemisphere (July 13, 1982); Miami Herald (March
20, 1982).
6. See, for example, Diario el Tiempo (July 13,
1982).
7. See Centro de Documentacion de Honduras (CEDOH),
Boletin Informativo, 5, 12 (February and May, 1982);
also, Americas Watch, "Human Rights in Honduras: Signs
of the 'Argentine Method,'" An Americas Watch Report (New
York, 1982).
8. See "El General Alvarez Quiere que Honduras y
Nicaragua Vayan a la Guerra," and "Estoy Dispuesto a
Someterme a una Investigacion: Torres Arias," Panorama
Politico Centroamerica, 10, 109 (September-October,
1982), pp. 50-55.
9. La Prensa (January 20, 1982).
10. "Mensaje del Senor Roberto Suazo Cordova al
Asumir la Presidencia Constitucional de Honduras, 27 de
Enero 1982" (Tegucigalpa: Gobierno de Honduras, 1982),
p. 11.
11. "Planteamiento del Senor Ministro de Relaciones
Exteriores de Honduras, Doctor Edgardo Paz Barnica ante
el Consejo Permanente de la OEA, Washington, D.C.,
23 marzo 1982" (Tegucigalpa: Gobierno de Honduras,
1982), pp. 13-44.

12. This information comes from interviews that I conducted with U.S. and Honduran officials during September-December 1982.

13. *La Prensa* (October 28, 1982); *La Tribuna* (November 5, 1982); and *Tiempo* (November 5, 1982).

14. This information was collected during my interview with an official of the UN High Commissioner for Refugees, November 1982, Tegucigalpa.

15. *El Heraldo* (September 22, 1982).

10
Fear of Adjusting: The Social Costs of Economic Policies in Costa Rica in the 1970s

Claudio Gonzalez-Vega

Like most small and open economies, Costa Rica has always been vulnerable to the influence of external forces. After 1973, however, the country experienced several external shocks that caused much greater disturbance than any suffered during the previous two decades. Since this sequence of sizable shocks took place in a relatively short period of time, it substantially increased the instability of the economy and magnified its adjustment problems. Although the various disturbances differed among themselves in nature, their effects reinforced each other, while rigidities in the economic and political system made adjustment difficult. This chapter examines the nature of these shocks, the problems that they posed, and the ways in which the country dealt with them.

In 1982 Costa Rica found itself in the midst of an acute crisis, characterized by a stagnant economy, growing unemployment, rampant inflation, and a rapid devaluation of its currency. In addition, the country had accumulated a huge foreign debt that it found very difficult to service. Paradoxically, Costa Rica had shown remarkable progress during the previous three decades, in terms of both economic growth and social welfare improvements. Given the country's resource base, particularly its homogeneous and well-educated population, as well as its political stability, a long-standing democratic tradition, a large middle class, and a less uneven distribution of income than most other Latin American countries, many find it difficult to understand the speed with which the economic situation deteriorated and the extent of the damage to the country's economic and political structures. As a recent report claimed, "no one would have predicted the present outcome even as recently as five years ago, when the country was enjoying an extraordinary coffee bonanza."[1] Although the seeds of the crisis had been sown a long time before, one cannot help but be impressed by the degree of change the country

351

has experienced and the speed with which this change has occurred.

This chapter provides a systematic description of the difficult problems of adjustment faced by a small open economy. Although political influences on the evolution of events have been taken into account, no attempt has been made to explain them. The analysis herein suffers from all the biases implicit in an economic approach; moreover, it does not strive for the formal elegance of economic models. The chain of events that took place could have been easily predicted from the perspective of economic theory, but the fact that the Costa Rican political system did not react with the speed, energy, and innovation required to avoid a major crisis suggests that democratic countries may face serious political constraints in adjusting to sharp external shocks. Moreover, I argue that serious mistakes of economic policy management resulted from political attempts to avoid or postpone an appropriate adjustment, and that these errors further complicated the problem and significantly increased the social costs of adjusting. Short-term political gains were thus obtained at a very high price. In turn, the economic crisis that resulted could eventually undermine the country's political system.

THE NATURE OF THE SHOCKS

Economic crisis in Costa Rica has been the consequence of a combination of long-term structural trends, whose unfavorable effects accumulated slowly but steadily, and of particularly unfortunate short-term circumstances, both at home and abroad. These short-term circumstances included dramatic external shocks, followed by slow and faulty policy decisions in response to these shocks.

The major external shocks were (1) the two international oil crises, in 1973-74 and 1978-80; (2) sharp increases and subsequent declines in the international prices of several agricultural commodities, associated with the coffee boom of 1976-77; and (3) changes in the country's access to international capital markets. Easy access to borrowing abroad was made possible in the mid-1970s by the international recycling of oil profits and the country's creditworthiness during the coffee boom. However, high interest rates that eventually resulted from world inflation greatly increased the burden of servicing this debt, at a time when the large capital inflows of the earlier years were abruptly interrupted because of the crisis.

War, insurrection, and political instability in Central America reinforced the unfavorable structural trends implicit in the protectionist strategy of import substitution (as subsequently discussed) and added further sources of external disturbance. Political events in Central America, however, have not been the major cause of the economic crisis in Costa Rica. This crisis would have occurred even in the absence of turmoil in the rest of the isthmus. Although this turmoil has not yet reached Costa Rica, the deterioration of the Central American political situation and the uncertainty about the economic and social policies of regimes in the area have reduced the viability of the Central American Common Market and its attractiveness for Costa Rican exporters. Morover, by reducing confidence and accentuating pessimistic expectations, political developments have contributed to the contraction of domestic investment and to substantial capital outflows. Events in Central America, therefore, have accentuated the crisis and have added further constraints to the adjustment.

STRUCTURAL BACKGROUND

The nature, extent, and duration of the crisis are in part explained by the structural features of the Costa Rican economy. These elements reflect contradictions between some of the country's most basic characteristics and some of the features of the protectionist strategy of import substitution adopted in the late 1950s. Since this strategy has been pursued for almost three decades, its consequences have been incorporated into the country's productive structure. The contradictions reflect a neglect of crucial economic variables, like market size and factor endowments.

Two main characteristics of the Costa Rican economy have been its small size, with the limitations imposed by a poor domestic market, and its high degree of openness to foreign trade, a consequence of small size. With a population of 2.3 million inhabitants and a gross domestic product (GDP) of about 100 billion colones in 1982, Costa Rica is a very small economy.[2] Given a specialized resource base and a small domestic market, traditionally the country has understood that foreign trade must serve as the economy's engine of growth. Thus, much of the impulse for growth during this century has been provided by the export of agricultural commodities. Exports of coffee, bananas, sugar, and beef have raised the levels of domestic output and income, increased the country's import capacity, and yielded many of the dynamic benefits of specialization.

Costa Rica is one of the most open economies in the world. During the past three decades, exports have represented between one-fifth and two-fifths of the GDP and this proportion has increased over time.[3] Imports

have represented between one-quarter and one-half of the
GDP, with a similar increasing trend. About two-thirds
of the country's agricultural output has been exported,
whereas agricultural exports have earned about two-thirds
of its foreign exchange. Trade has also played an
important role in the development of the manufacturing
sector. When Costa Rica joined the Central American
Common Market in 1963, exports of manufactured goods
represented only 4 percent of total exports, but this
grew to 29 percent by 1979. About four-fifths of these
exports, however, have gone to markets in Central America
protected by the regional integration effort, rather than
into competitive world markets.

With its participation in the Central American
Common Market, Costa Rica consolidated its choice of a
protectionist strategy of industrialization via import
substitution. This decision modified the nature of the
economy's external dependence. At the regional level the
strategy involved free trade among the Common Market
partners and the establishment of a common, highly
protective, external tariff barrier for imports from all
other countries. Costa Rica chose to increase the degree
of openness with respect to Central America, while at the
same time reducing openness with respect to the rest of
the world.

Industrialization via import substitution was
adopted in order to reduce dependence on international
markets and to avoid the fluctuations and uncertainties
associated with a concentration on exports of primary
products. It was believed that the regional market
offered a greater growth potential and was safer and more
predictable than the international market. Recent
political events in the isthmus show that this regional
market is no longer secure. Furthermore, it has never
been a large market. Market size is crucial for successful industrialization, because it determines the scope
for the exploitation of economies of scale and the extent
of competition, as well as the degree of viable specialization. Market size also influences the extent to which
inward-oriented industrial development may proceed
without incurring excessive costs. Unfortunately,
regional integration in Central America led to the
establishment of many high cost industries and to limited
competitiveness in international markets.

GRADUAL STAGNATION

The Costa Rican economy grew at a very satisfactory
pace during the past two decades. Between 1960 and 1980,
the GDP, measured in 1966 prices, grew at an average rate
of 5.8 percent per annum. However, although the average
annual rate of GDP growth was 7.0 percent for 1965-70 and

6.0 percent for 1970-75, it was only 5.2 percent for
1975-80. This long-run decline in growth rates has been
accentuated by the recent crisis. From a historical high
of 8.9 percent per annum in 1977, a consequence of the
coffee boom, this rate of growth rapidly dropped and
finally became negative in 1981 and 1982 (-2.3 and -9.1
percent, respectively).

The decline in growth rates has been shared by all
major sectors. The average annual rate of GDP growth in
the agricultural sector, measured in 1966 prices, dropped
from 8.1 percent for 1965-70 and 3.4 percent for 1970-75
to only 1.8 percent for 1975-80, despite the coffee boom.
This deceleration reflected, in part, the penalization of
agriculture and exports that resulted from the import-
substitution strategy of industrialization. The
industrial sector has also stagnated. The average annual
rate of GDP growth in manufacturing, measured in 1966
prices, dropped from 9.3 percent for 1965-70 and 8.9
percent for 1970-75 to 6.0 percent for 1975-80.
Recently, this rate of growth steadily declined from 12.7
percent in 1977 to a negative -0.5 percent in 1981 and
-14.9 in 1982.

The relatively high rates of growth in the manufacturing sector during the 1960s and early 1970s resulted
from the dramatic increase in Central American trade
after the formation of the customs union in 1963. During
this first stage of import substitution, domestic production rose more rapidly than domestic consumption, as it
not only provided for increases in consumption but also
replaced previous imports, which had represented the main
source of supply of manufactures. Eventually, this
"easy" stage of import substitution was exhausted and the
growth rate of manufacturing output declined to the level
of the growth rate of domestic consumption, which in turn
continued to be determined mostly by the country's
exports to international markets. Indeed, an external
shock, the coffee boom, explained why this long-term
trend toward stagnation was temporarily stopped in the
mid-1970s. Otherwise, the strategy's negative impact on
growth would have become evident earlier.

PROTECTIONISM AND RIGIDITY

The setting up of manufacturing industries to serve
a small regional market was based on high protection.
Although very high levels of effective protection were
adopted for most consumer goods, low and even negative
rates of effective protection were granted for the
production of raw materials, intermediate inputs, and
capital goods.[4] Moreover, the effective rates of protection have been characterized by a great dispersion.
Almost half have fallen below 50 percent, whereas for

about one-fifth of the items these rates have been above
200 percent. Although the average legal rate of effective protection has been about 164 percent, it has been
about 231 percent for traditional consumer goods and only
77 percent for intermediate goods and 62 percent for
metal-mechanic industries. Moreover, protection was
accentuated by favorable fiscal treatment, tax
concessions, and other incentives for investment in the
industrial sector, as well as by credit and foreign
exchange policies that implicitly subsidized these
activities. When all the determinants of effective
protection are taken into account, "Costa Rica has been
the most highly protected country in the region."[5]

One of the consequences of this structure of protection has been a very high import intensity in the manufacturing sector. It has been estimated that in order to
produce $100 worth of output, the manufacturing sector
needs $80 of imported inputs. As a result, the Costa
Rican economy has become increasingly dependent on
imported raw materials, intermediate inputs, and capital
goods, and this has led to increasing rigidity in the
economy. That is, not only has the Costa Rican economy
progressively lost its dynamism, but it has also become
less capable of adjusting to the inevitable external
shocks. One of the main reasons for this increased
rigidity has been the high import intensity of its
manufacturing sector. This has been reflected in the
composition of imports, of which less than 20 percent
represent consumer goods. The balance-of-payments
adjustment required after an unfavorable external shock
forces a reduction of imports, mostly of raw materials,
intermediate inputs, and capital goods destined for
industrial firms. Adjustment, therefore, implies a
reduction of the level of activity, investment, and
growth in the manufacturing sector, and eventually
unemployment.

This scenario introduces an important dilemma for
Costa Rican policymakers: Sharp balance-of-payments
adjustments have a negative impact on growth and
employment, particularly in the manufacturing sector.
This impact takes place at a time when export earnings,
due to the external shock, are also contracting. On the
other hand, lack of balance-of-payments adjustment, which
would otherwise be attained through increased foreign
borrowings and the introduction of domestic controls,
worsens the economy's long-term problems and increases
the social costs of the final adjustment.

As the Costa Rican manufacturing sector is
politically strong, delay of the adjustment has also been
associated with attempts to divert the costs of adjusting
to other sectors through increased intervention in the
economy. The government, in turn, has been willing to
respond to these demands that the adjustment be post-

poned, because it has preferred to adopt a short-run
perspective, particularly when elections are near. All
of this has introduced greater rigidity in the choice of
economic policies, has led to a postponement of the
adjustment, and has greatly increased the social costs of
the crisis.

The nonuniform tariff structure associated with the
protectionist strategy of industrialization has also
reflected the permissive attitude associated with
granting protection. Incentives have been provided to
all politically strong investors, including multinational
corporations, and the magnitude of the assistance has
mostly reflected the relative strength of the participants in the political arena. Much entrepreneurial time
and effort has been spent in lobbying rather than in
increasing productivity. As a consequence, specific
activities have been promoted without concern for
comparative advantages within the manufacturing sector.

The distortions and inefficiencies brought about by
this permissive attitude are apparent in the structure of
production, impose high costs on domestic consumers and
increase the rigidity of the economy. A clear example of
inefficiency has been the protection of about a dozen
car-assembling plants, all attempting to supply the
miniscule Costa Rican market and generating negative net
domestic value added. Furthermore, neglect of efficiency
and of comparative advantages has resulted in a limited
capacity on the part of the manufacturing sector to
compete outside the protected Central American Common
Market. When the Common Market finally broke down,
exports of manufactures could not be diverted to other
markets, a factor that also contributed to the stagnation
of the Costa Rican economy.

FACTOR PRICES AND EMPLOYMENT

Another key feature of Costa Rica is its relative
abundance of labor. The protectionist strategy distorted
not only relative commodity prices, turning the domestic
terms-of-trade against agriculture; it also distorted
relative factor prices, thereby underpricing capital and
overpricing labor in the modern sector of the economy.
Minimum wages and substantial payroll taxes, used to
finance several public sector programs, resulted in an
effective cost of labor for employers considerably higher
than the wages actually received by workers. Social
security and other charges mandated by the government
imposed a surcharge of at least 26 percent on all wages
and salaries. Modern sector wages became higher than the
social opportunity cost of labor for the economy as a
whole.

At the same time, several policies underpriced capital for the modern sector. These policies included the tax treatment of investments, which granted tax breaks on physical capital formation but not on human capital or technological development; the fixed, over-valued foreign exchange rate, which set the cost of imported capital below its social opportunity cost; tariff exemption for capital imports, which increased the rate of effective protection of capital-intensive activities; and the credit-rationing policies that resulted from under-equilibrium interest rates in formal financial markets, which have favored relatively capital-intensive activities.

While trade policies have favored manufacturing, the most capital-intensive sector of the economy, factor-price policies have favored capital-intensive techniques in the rapidly growing modern sectors. The result has been limited labor absorption by the private modern sector, where productivity and wages have been higher than those in the traditional sectors. This has forced the public sector to become an active employer in order to avoid higher unemployment. The limited job-generating capacity of the manufacturing sector has been reflected in the fact that during the first decade after Costa Rica joined the Common Market, between the census years of 1963 and 1973, the relative contribution of manufacturing to the GDP increased from 14.3 to 19.7 percent (for a gain of 5.4 points), whereas the proportion of the labor force employed in the manufacturing sector increased from 11.7 to 12.9 percent (for a gain of only 1.2 points). During the second half of the 1970s, the proportion of the labor force employed in manufacturing increased to 16.3 percent (1979), but declined during the crisis to 15.4 percent (1982).

As a consequence, public sector employment increased more rapidly than private sector employment. Between 1950 and 1980, while the latter grew at an average annual rate of 2.7 percent, the former rose at an average annual rate of 7.4 percent. Recently the difference has increased. Between 1973 and 1980 private sector employment grew, on the average, at an annual rate of 3.4 percent, while public sector employment increased more than twice as rapidly, at an average rate of 8.0 percent. This rapid growth of public sector employment, both in the central government and autonomous institutions, meant that the relative share of the public sector in total employment increased from 6.1 percent in 1950, to 15.3 percent in 1973, and to 19.7 percent in 1980. In the second half of the 1970s, about two out of every five new jobs in the economy were created by the public sector, such that today one out of every five workers is employed in this sector.

This explosion of public sector employment has reflected an implicit policy to keep unemployment low, particularly of qualified and professional workers, in the presence of trade and factor-price policies that have reduced the incentives to hire workers in the private sector. On the other hand, the rapid expansion of public sector employment has caused a growing fiscal deficit, which is at the root of the more recent financial crisis. In turn, the importance of wages in public expenditures has made it politically difficult to cut government spending. The concentration of workers in large public institutions has facilitated their unionization. Public-sector unions are the strongest in the country and have managed to maintain higher wages than those for similar occupations in the private sector, while at the same time preventing any reduction in the absolute size of government. Moreover, the competition for resources, particularly credit, has led to the crowding out of the private sector in the portfolio of the banking system and has contributed to the stagnation of the economy.

The fiscal constraint imposed by the recent crisis has resulted in a declining capacity of the public sector to absorb additional workers. Open unemployment increased from 4.1 percent of the labor force in 1950 to 7.3 percent in 1973, and to 9.4 percent in 1982. Economic stagnation and deterioration of the international terms-of-trade have made it impossible for the public sector to maintain a high rate of employment generation. Open unemployment has become a major political problem and has further complicated the process of adjustment.

EQUITY AND THE SIZE OF THE PUBLIC SECTOR

Another major element of Costa Rican development strategy, aside from industrialization and regional integration, has been the emphasis on equity and improvements in the quality of life. This emphasis has been reflected in the major public investment in education, health, nutrition, social welfare assistance to low-income families, social security, and various public-sector services. The concern for equity may be attributed to the nature of the political system. The democratic process has encouraged participation of all citizens in the selection of political leaders and open debate of economic and social issues. There has always been an active vocal opposition party to question government policy. This has been Costa Rica's unique heritage in the region, and successive governments of different political persuasion have preserved and enhanced social equity.

As measured by the performance of most social indicators and the development of a physical infrastructure for the benefit of all Costa Ricans, the results of the equity-oriented policies are outstanding. Progress in health care, for example, has dramatically reduced mortality rates. In Latin America, only in Argentina, Uruguay, or Cuba will a person born today have as high a life expectancy as one born in Costa Rica. In 1978 life expectancy was 73 years in the United States and 72 years in Costa Rica. Since life expectancy in Costa Rica was only 55 years in 1950, much progress was accomplished during the past three decades. Similarly, infant mortality in Costa Rica has experienced a remarkable reduction, from 75 per 1,000 births in 1958 to 19 per 1,000 births in 1980, and has rapidly approached the level of 15 per 1,000 births observed in the United States. Moreover, during the 1970s almost half of secondary-school age children were in school, and one-fifth of the university age cohort were attending an institution of higher education.[6]

The major beneficiaries of the growth experienced during the past decade and of many of these public-sector services have been the middle-income groups. Furthermore, the equity-oriented system has been very expensive, and a large bureaucracy has evolved to administer it. An increasing proportion of available resources has been devoted to paying public-sector employees, while the benefits reaching the respective target population have declined. Since the costs of these social programs have increased rapidly, exceeding the growth rate of public revenues, the government has been forced to borrow domestically and abroad. The political costs associated with any explicit reduction in these programs have been another major obstacle to policy adjustments.

In striving to attain ambitious social and economic development goals, successive governments have initiated numerous programs and built an elaborate array of public institutions to plan, administer, control, and conduct public- and private-sector activities. With large amounts of foreign assistance, Costa Rica built an impressive network of highways and feeder roads, an extensive electric power network, and a large telecommunications system. Although the positive impact of these investments has been great, the costs have also been high. Due to external financing, payment for this investment has been deferred to the future in ways that may continue to be a drain on the economy. Moreover, there has been considerable government intervention in the economy in terms of price controls, credit allocation, and subsidy schemes.[7]

The Costa Rican government has been not only a welfare state and an interventionist state, but an

entrepreneurial state as well. Government ownership of
several basic industries, including public transportation, oil refining and distribution, cement and
fertilizer production, sugar refining, agricultural
exports, insurance and, most importantly, banking has
given the government considerable leverage with which to
channel a large share of resources toward public-sector
enterprises. A conspicuous example is CODESA, a public
investment corporation that has accounted for an
increasing share of total investment, even in manufacturing.

As a consequence of these policies, the public
sector has become too large. Central government
expenditures, which had represented 15.1 percent of the
GDP in 1970, represented 21.8 percent by 1980. The
protectionist strategy, which has relied heavily on tax
exemptions and implicit subsidies, has resulted in an
income-inelastic tax structure. In 1970 central government revenues represented 13.5 percent of the GDP,
whereas by 1980 they represented only 12.7 percent. As
a consequence of this behavior of expenditures and
revenues, the central government deficit increased from
1.6 percent of the GDP in 1970 to 9.1 percent in 1980.
If the rest of the public sector is added, the fiscal
deficit represented 13.9 percent of the GDP by 1980.
Moreover, by this time the public sector was contributing
25.2 percent of the GDP, 38.7 percent of investment, and
6.1 percent of savings, and was receiving 65.1 percent of
the net increments in domestic credit. This size of the
public sector is a substantial burden on a small, open
economy. Adjustment to external shocks thus requires a
reduction in the size of the public sector, a politically
difficult proposition.

An important feature of the Costa Rican economy has
been a high degree of government intervention in the
financial sector. The four nationalized commercial banks
have had a monopoly on demand and savings deposits and
have accounted for over four-fifths of the assets of the
financial system. These banks have been "characterized
as slow, excessively conservative, and incapable of
significantly contributing to the economic development of
the country because of their implicit lending policies
and their inability to mobilize internal savings."[8]
Transaction costs have been high, bank services poor, and
the credit rationing criteria arbitrary and vulnerable to
political pressures. In the absence of competition, the
banking system has been unresponsive to changing private-
sector needs, steadily becoming obsolete, while a
significant portion of its loan portfolio has been frozen
due to default. Interest rate subsidies have resulted in
substantial free transfers of resources to privileged
borrowers, while credit portfolios have been highly
concentrated in the hands of a few large borrowers.

362

During the crisis, as inflation accelerated, the
flows of new loans, measured in real terms, sharply
declined, affecting mostly productive activities. By
1982, the real size of the credit portfolio of the
banking system was about 40 percent of its size a few
years earlier. In addition, the share of the public
sector in the domestic credit flows had increased
substantially, whereas the private sector was crowded
out. As a consequence, the system was not only
mobilizing too few domestic savings; it was also
contributing to their misallocation.

In summary, the structural problems associated with
a conflict between the Costa Rican economy's most salient
characteristics and the main features of the protectionist strategy of import substitution adopted have
resulted in stagnation and rigidity. In addition,
commodity-and-factor-price policies have resulted in
increasing unemployment, while the expansion of the
public sector and the unresponsiveness of the nationalized banking system have contributed to lack of growth
and financial disequilibrium. All of these problems
suggest the need for substantial discrete structural
changes and policy adjustments, in order to reduce the
degree and dispersion of protection, reduce the size of
the public sector, and more effectively mobilize and
allocate domestic savings through the banking system.
Short-term instability and the perception that high
political costs are associated with these reforms have
not facilitated the decisions.

TERMS-OF-TRADE INSTABILITY

During the second half of the 1970s, Costa Rica
experienced a comparatively large fluctuation in its
international terms-of-trade. Although the information
available for the 1950s is not completely reliable, it
seems that during that period the country's terms-of-
trade were more favorable than in the following two
decades. For the 1950-59 period, the simple average of
the annual composite index of export to import prices
stood at 128.8 percent of its base value for 1966. From
a historical high of 148.8 percent in 1954, however, this
index had already declined to 101.1 percent by 1960.
During the 1960s, on the other hand, these terms were
extremely stable. The difference between the highest and
lowest values, of 106.1 percent (1964) and 91.4 percent
(1968), was only 14.7 points, whereas the difference had
been 39.0 points during the 1950s. This stability
continued until 1974, when the index dropped to a low of
76.5 percent of its 1966 base.

This sudden and significant worsening of the
country's international terms-of-trade in 1974 was the

consequence of the first oil crisis. It represented the first instance of an external shock resulting from a change in import prices, rather than a change in export volumes or prices. Given the stability of international prices prior to 1974, as well as Costa Rica's diversified import basket, changes in export prices, particularly those of coffee, cocoa, sugar, bananas, and beef had been the main determinants of changes in the country's terms-of-trade. After a period of almost complete stability, however, the index of import prices jumped by 37 percent in 1974. As a consequence of these changes and the expansionary credit policy that followed, the value of imports climbed from $455 to $720 million (a 58 percent increase in one year), while Costa Rica's trade deficit increased from $111 to $280 million, almost threefold. This was made possible by $13 million of surplus in the rest of the current account; $243 million of capital inflows (in comparison to $130 million the previous year); and a loss of $23 million in international monetary reserves.

This worsening of the country's international terms-of-trade was soon followed, however, by a rapid improvement and a significant growth in the value of exports, as a consequence of the coffee boom. By 1977, the terms-of-trade index had recovered to 114.7 percent—an implied increase of 38.2 points in three years. At the same time, the value of exports had climbed from $493 million in 1975 to $828 million in 1977, whereas the trade deficit had been reduced to $194 million. This deficit would have declined even more had it not been fueled by the expansion of domestic credit and foreign borrowing.

With the end of the coffee boom and the second oil crisis, Costa Rica's terms-of-trade deteriorated again in 1978. The index had dropped to 91.9 percent by 1980, a reduction of 22.8 points in three years. By 1982 the index had further dropped to 72.4 and to 69.5 in 1983. Since the level of the index at the end of the decade was not particularly low by historical standards, the crisis must be primarily associated with the violent fluctuation experienced in a short period of time. This sharp fluctuation required a sharp adjustment.

External shocks are not new to Costa Rica. In the past, however, unfavorable shocks had been followed by favorable ones. The impact of the first oil shock, for instance, was soon followed by the coffee boom. In recent years, however, all the external influences have been unfavorable, while domestic policy responses have been particularly unfortunate. Moreover, the economy has become less flexible, and the social and political costs of the required adjustments have increased.

POLICY RESPONSES

The oil crisis of 1974 imposed on Costa Rica an important adjustment problem. The deterioration of the country's terms-of-trade reduced real incomes and caused a contraction of the economy. The Figueres administration avoided the contraction by increasing the foreign debt and substantially expanding domestic credit. Domestic credit increased by 45.5 percent, leading to a loss of international monetary reserves and contributing to the country's first inflationary experience in half a century. The wholesale price index rose 26.4 percent in 1973 and 38.2 percent in 1974--this in a country where the simple average of the annual change in this index had been only 1.5 percent per annum during the previous twenty-two years. Thus, the main instruments of the Figueres administration to avoid the adjustment--foreign borrowing and domestic credit expansion--resulted in much higher inflation than that induced by international price changes. At the same time, Costa Rica's public external debt increased from $296 million in 1973 to $379 million in 1974 and $511 million in 1975.

In the following years, the large export earnings of the coffee boom made it possible to divert the inflationary pressures that resulted from the continued expansion of domestic credit toward the balance of payments, thus avoiding domestic price increases. By 1977 the annual rate of increase in the wholesale price index had declined to 7.4 percent. The coffee boom had validated, ex post, the gamble of the Figueres administration, and Costa Rica adjusted to the impact of the first oil crisis with relative success.

The extraordinary improvement of the country's terms-of-trade and the rapid expansion of export earnings associated with the coffee boom significantly increased real incomes. A good measure of the country's purchasing power is the gross national income (GNI)--that is, the gross national product corrected by the impact of changes in the terms-of-trade. In 1966 prices, the GNI increased by 12.5 percent in 1976 and by another 18.3 percent in 1977. This exceptional increase in real income made possible a substantial expansion of consumption, imports, and government spending. In 1966 prices, private consumption increased by 13.6 percent, public sector consumption by 8.8 percent, and imports by 25.1 percent during 1977 alone. In real terms, aggregate demand was 25.9 percent higher in 1977 than in 1975.

As a result of this expansion of aggregate demand, the economy became overheated. What was clearly an exceptional episode, in terms of the rate of improvement in real income, was rapidly accepted as the new norm. Coffee power had finally been achieved and this was celebrated with a spending euphoria. What was actually a

transitory increase in income was viewed as a new higher
level of permanent income, and aggregate spending was
augmented accordingly. The Oduber administration made no
effort to avoid this misperception. On the contrary, it
actually stimulated the spending rush. No significant
effort to mobilize domestic savings or increase taxation
took place during the boom. Costa Rica continued to have
one of the lowest ratios of domestic savings to the GDP
in Latin America. Even at the peak of the boom, domestic
savings represented only 12.7 percent of the GDP.

Moreover, given the attractive terms prevailing in
the international capital markets, Costa Rica's foreign
borrowing increased rapidly. The country's public
external debt grew to $646 million in 1976 and to $834
million in 1977. By early 1978 the Oduber government was
still borrowing abroad, at shorter terms and more
restrictive conditions, merely to pile up international
monetary reserves, which mounted to over $300 million by
May 1978 when Carazo came to power. These loans had to
be repaid during the following months. Oduber's
mercantilist policy had exacted a heavy price on the
country. In sum, government behavior led the public to
believe that the new levels of spending could be maintained indefinitely. The international banking community
added to this perception. Foreign lenders were actively
encouraging the government to borrow and confirmed, with
their behavior, the overly optimistic outlook of the
future.

Thus, Costa Rica increased its level of aggregate
spending not only in proportion to the exceptional
revenues from the coffee boom but even beyond, aided by
increasing inflows of foreign debt. By 1978, however,
the country's terms-of-trade began to deteriorate again.
With the same speed with which real purchasing power had
increased during the coffee boom, it now declined.
Between 1978 and 1981, the losses directly due to terms-
of-trade changes increased eightfold, from 334 to 2,830
million colones. The latter loss was equivalent to one-
third of the GDP. Also, the value of exports increased
by only 4.4 percent in 1978 while, as a consequence of
the second oil crisis, the value of imports increased by
14.2 percent. The trade deficit jumped to $301 million,
and a new adjustment was required.

The time had arrived for consumption, imports, and
government spending to return to their historical levels.
Political opposition to the contraction, however, was
fierce. The spending orgy had created all kinds of
expectations, and no one wanted to rectify the earlier
mistakes. The Carazo administration did not help
matters. Based on a weak coalition, it could not control
the efforts of various pressure groups to avoid the
direct impact of the adjustment. Carazo himself wanted
to be remembered for his efforts to expand the country's

physical infrastructure and for his role in the overthrow
of the Somoza regime. Both targets were expensive. He
chose, therefore, to postpone the adjustment. Again, the
main tool for this postponement was borrowing in the
international capital markets. The country's public
external debt increased to $1,735 million by 1980, in per
capita terms the highest in the Third World. In late
1982 this debt represented over one and a half years of
Costa Rica's GDP and amounted to about $1,500 per capita.
The country's private external debt represented about
$1,000 million more.

All social groups struggled to maintain the standard
of living achieved during the coffee boom. As it became
obvious that impoverishment was inevitable, these groups
attempted to maintain at least their relative shares in
the national income. The financial disequilibria were
thereby increased, since the struggle of the social
groups was facilitated by the government's expansionary
credit policies. Domestic-credit expansion accentuated
the balance-of-payments crisis, augmented the size of the
fiscal deficit, and rapidly accelerated inflation.
Between 1978 and 1980 Costa Rica's current account
deficit increased from $363 to $664 million. This last
deficit was financed by $192 million of capital inflows,
a loss of $198 million of international monetary reserves
and $274 million of interest arrears and other special
loans in 1980. Another $100 million of reserves had
already been lost during 1979. At the same time, the
annual rate of increase of the wholesale price index had
already risen to 24.1 percent in 1979, and reached 117.2
percent in 1981.

POSTPONING THE ADJUSTMENT

During the 1970s it became increasingly obvious that
the strategy of import substitution was losing its
dynamism. The early growth of manufacturing, during the
easy stages of import replacement, was becoming more
difficult to sustain, and Costa Rica's inability to
compete in international markets became clear. The
protectionist strategy, by favoring import-competing
activities in the manufacturing sector, had reduced the
relative profitability of exports. Toward the end of the
decade, exports were also being heavily penalized by an
exchange rate that overvalued the domestic currency.
These policies, in the presence of inflationary
pressures, led to a gradual stagnation of export volumes.

The slow growth of exports, in turn, severely
limited the expansion of domestic manufactures, so
dependent on imported inputs. The dynamic opportunities
offered by the protectionist strategy were also
disappearing in the other Central American countries.

insurgencies and political turmoil further contributed to
the breakdown of the Common Market. At the same time, it
became obvious that the fiscal deficit that resulted from
the accelerated expansion of the public sector was
becoming unmanageable. Many people discussed the need
for a structural adjustment, including a sharp revision
of the protectionist strategy, a reduction in the size of
the public sector, and a financial reform. Manufacturers, organized as a powerful Chamber of Industries,
bitterly argued against any reform. The government
claimed that the social costs of the adjustment were too
high and accordingly postponed it. It was believed that
any abandonment of the protectionist strategy would lead
to widespread bankruptcies and that any reduction in the
size of the public sector would bring high unemployment.
The unfavorable short-term circumstances, due to the
external shocks, further added to the perceived social
and political costs of the adjustment.

Toward the end of the decade the current account
deficit was almost nine times greater than at the
beginning, while capital inflows were becoming less and
less capable of financing these deficits. Economic and
political instability in Central America negatively
impacted expectations. Both local and foreign investors
rapidly lost confidence in the future of the region. New
foreign investment disappeared, whereas repatriation of
previous investment accelerated. At the same time, Costa
Ricans increased their investments abroad and substantial
capital flight took place. As a consequence, the country
was faced with a balance-of-payments deficit in both the
current and the capital accounts and rapidly lost international monetary reserves. A balance-of-payments
adjustment was necessary.

The Carazo administration reacted to the external
shock associated with the decline in primary commodity
prices and the second oil crisis by further increasing
foreign borrowing and expanding domestic credit. Growing
inflationary pressures and pessimistic expectations
induced portfolio revisions. Costa Ricans started to
replace their assets denominated in colones (particularly
cash balances and other financial assets) with assets
denominated in foreign currencies, further accentuating
the capital outflow. Unwilling to facilitate an
appropriate adjustment, Carazo refused to devalue the
colon, even after the country's net international
monetary reserves became negative. A huge political cost
was supposedly associated with a devaluation, and the
president himself increased this cost by arguing that a
devaluation would be the worst possible evil and by
repeatedly insisting that he would not devalue. The rate
of exchange was kept at 8.54 colones per dollar until
September 1980, and when it was eventually freed, it
rapidly increased to 38 colones by the end of 1981 and 65

<u>colones</u> by mid-1982.   The adjustment had been postponed
<u>but not</u> avoided.
     Carazo's refusal to devalue is a clear example of
fear of the consequences of adjusting and of the
resulting policy-making paralysis.   It was evident that
the overvalued exchange rate was responsible for the
decline in export volumes and was subsidizing capital
flight.   Most Costa Ricans were firmly convinced that a
devaluation was inevitable, so it was riskless to speculate against the <u>colon</u>.   The extraordinary increase in
foreign borrowing was thus financing this speculation,
further augmenting the demand for foreign currencies as
well as the gap between the official and the equilibrium
exchange rates.   The consequences of this policy were
both predictable and disastrous.
     Carazo's unwillingness to devalue made it necessary
to increase the public external debt beyond any reasonable magnitude.   The future growth of the Costa Rican
economy was compromised by the heavy burden of servicing
this debt.   The speculative demand for foreign currencies, which was promoted by the failure to devalue,
increased the equilibrium level of the exchange rate far
beyond what was necessary, thereby augmenting the magnitude of the price adjustment required.   The substantial
speculative movements that were thus subsidized resulted
in massive redistributions of income, aggravating the
sociopolitical situation.   The delay in adjusting greatly
increased adjustment costs.   Structural changes, beyond
devaluation, became even more difficult to pursue.

IMPOVERISHMENT: THE SOCIAL COSTS OF POLICY PARALYSIS

     Costa Ricans will be much poorer in the 1980s than
they were in the 1970s.   A much lower rate of growth of
output, particularly if structural adjustments do not
occur, combined with a high rate of population growth
will lead to a decline of per capita income during the
first half of the decade and to a slow recovery during
the second half.   It has been estimated that even under
ideal circumstances the 1979 level of per capita income
will not be realized again before 1990.   This would
require an average real rate of growth of GDP of 5.3
percent per annum between 1984 and 1990--albeit a
difficult target to achieve.   Moreover, the continued
deterioration of the country's international terms-of-
trade means that the same GDP generates less purchasing
power over foreign goods than before--this in a country
where such goods have represented up to 50 percent of the
aggregate supply.   Finally, a much larger proportion of
the GDP will have to be devoted to servicing the
country's external debt, instead of to domestic consumption and investment.   Servicing this debt may require

over 50 percent of the value of exports and about 15
percent of the GDP each year.

Costa Ricans will be paying in the future for the
excess consumption of the late 1970s. Moreover, not only
will debt service significantly reduce disposable income,
but the foreign exchange requirement of this service will
impose a drastic constraint on imports. In the absence
of policy changes leading to an adjustment of the structure of production to the new circumstances, a reduction
of imports of raw materials, intermediate inputs, and
capital goods will impose a severe limitation on the
growth rate of the manufacturing sector and, to a smaller
extent, the agricultural sector. This brake on growth,
in turn, may eventually reduce the country's ability to
service the external debt, thus possibly leading to a
continuous and increasingly onerous rescheduling of the
debt and even to formal bankruptcy.

POLITICAL COSTS

Costa Rica is currently experiencing the most
serious crisis in its recent history--a truly major
crisis given its depth, duration, and potential consequences for the country's sociopolitical and institutional framework. This framework has itself increased
the difficulties of adopting the policies required to
pull out of the crisis and minimize its consequences.
Very high social costs, higher than any the country has
had to face before, will be paid before the adjustment is
over. These costs are so great that they pose a difficult test for institutional stability and political
equilibrium. Further delay of policy decisions to
facilitate the appropriate adjustment, although politically attractive in the short run, would pose a major
threat to the system itself.

Costa Rica is an open society, with a long democratic tradition and a high degree of political participation. Numerous interest groups contribute to the
decisionmaking process. The free press has been an
important forum through which competing groups register
their opinions and exercise their influence. The need
for a consensus, however, delays major policy decisions.
Measures have not been adopted with the speed, opportunity, and strength required. The same features that
make the political system so attractive also make it
vulnerable and fragile.

The crisis has increased the vulnerability of the
political system due to the high expectations of Costa
Ricans, already accustomed to a continued improvement in
their standard of living. These expectations were reinforced by the high growth rates of the 1970s and
confirmed by the coffee boom. During the 1980s, however,

the Costa Rican economy will not be in a position to
satisfy the demands generated by these expectations. The
declining dynamism of the economy will make it impossible
not only to guarantee a continued improvement of living
standards, but even to avoid impoverishment.

Moreover, Costa Ricans have become accustomed to an
institutional system that provides a large quantity of
public goods: free education from primary school through
university, free health care, and good nutrition for
everyone. Cheap water and electricity have been introduced in most homes. Substantial income tranfers have
been channeled by the public sector, which in turn has
provided many employment opportunities. Not only will
the economy be unable to continue financing these
services and transfers, but the size of the public sector
itself will inevitably shrink. Many public goods, taken
for granted, will no longer be freely provided. At the
same time, economic stagnation and inflation will further
worsen income distribution. The burden of impoverishment
will be shared more than proportionately by the already
poor. This deterioration of standards of living will be
faced by a generation that has not known adversity
before. The resulting frustration may lead to social
unrest and violence, so conspicuously absent from Costa
Rican history.

Many have claimed that the political costs of
adjusting are too high and so justify their unwillingness
to modify economic policies. I conclude that, if the
long-term deterioration of the political system is to be
avoided, Costa Rica requires a series of sharp, rapid
adjustments induced by bold economic policy revisions,
including a much lower and uniform rate of protection of
import substitution manufacturing, a reduction in the
level of implicit or explicit subsidies, a much smaller
public sector, particularly in productive areas, and a
drastic overhauling of the financial sector, in order to
increase the share of domestic savings in financing
investment. The Costa Rican democracy may not be able to
survive the kind of prolonged crisis that would result
from the continued postponement of this adjustment,
particularly in view of the regional turmoil. Changes
must be undertaken before expectations become even more
pessimistic and before violence and confrontation upset
the country's political fabric. Drastic policy changes
may actually be the signal, for Costa Ricans and for
foreigners, that the country possesses the will and
discipline needed to overcome its crisis.

NOTES

With regard to the issues covered in this chapter
the author acknowledges discussions with Alberto Di Mare

and other colleagues at COUNSEL; with Eduardo Lizano, Victor Hugo Cespedes and Ronulfo Jimenez, at Academia de Centro America; and with Dale Adams, Douglas Graham, Richard Dubick, and Donald Schulz. Nevertheless, the author accepts full and sole responsibility for the ideas contained herein.

1. Robert Pratt et al., Private Sector: Costa Rica. A.I.D. Evaluation Special Study No. 9 (Washington, D.C.: Agency For International Development, March 1983), p. vi.

2. Given the disequilibrium of the foreign exchange market, it is difficult to select an exchange rate to convert colones into U.S. dollars. Under the author's assumption that the equilibrium rate was close to 40 colones per dollar, this figure was equivalent to $2.5 billion.

3. The text of this chapter includes the values of numerous economic variables. Some of these values are either reported in the following Statistical Annex or have been computed from figures in that annex. The remaining data have been obtained from official sources, mostly Central Bank publications, and have been reported also in the following books: Claudio Gonzalez-Vega and Victor Hugo Cespedes, Growth and Equity: Changes in Income Distribution in Costa Rica (New York: United Nations, 1984); Victor Hugo Cespedes, Claudio Gonzalez-Vega, Ronulfo Jimenez, and Thelmo Vargas, Costa Rica: Problemas Economicos para la Decada de los 80s (San Jose: Editorial Studium, 1983); Victor Hugo Cespedes, Claudio Gonzalez-Vega, Ronulfo Jimenez, and Eduardo Lizano, Costa Rica: Una Economia en Crisis (San Jose: Editorial Studium, 1983); Victor Hugo Cespedes, Ronulfo Jimenez, and Eduardo Lizano, Hacia el Empobrecimiento del Pais: Costa Rica en 1982 (San Jose: Academia de Centro America, 1983); and in COUNSEL, Repertorio Economico (several years).

4. Effective rates of protection indicate the extent to which domestic value added can exceed value added at competitive international prices; they also take into account both nominal tariff rates on the product and its imported inputs.

5. Alan I. Rapoport, "Effective Protection Rates in Central America," in Economic Integration in Central America, eds. William R. Cline and Enrique Delgado (Washington, D.C.: Brookings Institution, 1978).

6. Gonzalez-Vega and Cespedes, Growth and Equity.

7. See Pratt et al., Private Sector, p. ix, for details on several of these issues.

8. Ibid., p. 21.

STATISTICAL ANNEX

TABLE 10.1

Costa Rica: Average Annual Rates of Growth,
in Real Terms, of Selected Production
Indicators, 1960-82 (Percentages).

Year	GDP	GNP	GNI	GDP Agricult.	GDP Manufact.	GDP Construct.	GDP Commerce
1960-65	5.1	n.a.	n.a.	3.2	9.2	5.8	5.0
1965-70	7.0	7.0[a]	6.4[a]	8.1	9.3	4.3	6.7
1970-75	6.0	5.8	3.4	3.4	8.9	10.9	3.0
1975-80	5.2	4.7	5.8	1.8	6.0	9.4	6.2
1974	5.5	6.4	- 1.5	-1.7	12.7	7.8	- 0.7
1975	2.1	1.1	3.8	3.0	3.2	5.7	- 4.2
1976	5.5	5.1	12.5	0.5	5.8	20.8	8.9
1977	8.9	9.2	18.3	2.2	12.7	3.9	17.9
1978	6.3	5.5	0.2	6.6	8.2	5.8	4.2
1979	4.9	4.3	- 0.3	0.5	2.7	19.3	4.1
1980	0.8	-0.4	- 0.4	-0.5	0.8	- 1.1	3.0
1981	-2.3	-4.0	-28.9	5.1	-0.5	-21.7	-10.6
1982	-9.1	-10.1	-60.2	-4.9	-14.9	-32.6	-16.8
1983[b]	0.8	n.a.	n.a.	4.4	-1.8	-6.0	-1.0

Notes: Rates of growth have been computed on the basis
of values in constant 1966 prices.
GDP: Gross Domestic Product.
GNP: Gross National Product.
GNI: Gross National Income, as defined in this
chapter.
[a]   For 1966-70.
[b]   Preliminary estimates.

Sources: Banco Central de Costa Rica, Cuentas Nacionales
de Costa Rica (several years); Victor Hugo
Cespedes, Claudio Gonzalez-Vega et al.,
Problemas Economicos en la Decada de los 80
(San Jose: Editorial Studium, 1983); Victor
Hugo Cespedes, Claudio Gonzalez-Vega et al.,
Costa Rica: Una Economia en Crisis (San Jose:
Editorial Studium, 1983); COUNSEL, Repertorio
Economico (several months).

TABLE 10.2

Costa Rica: Average Annual Rates of Growth, in Real Terms, of Selected Macroeconomic Variables, 1960-82 (percentages).

Year	Per Capita GDP	Per Capita Consump.	Private Consump.	Gov't Consump.	Gross Fixed Invest.	Fixed Invest. & Invent.	Exports	Imports
1960-65	1.4	n.a.	n.a.	n.a.	n.a.	n.a.	n.a.	n.a.
1965-70	4.4	3.3a	6.4a	5.3a	10.0a	8.4a	0.5a	13.6a
1970-75	2.7	0.8	3.2	5.4	4.2	6.2	7.4	3.1
1975-80	2.5	2.5	5.2	5.8	9.4	12.6	4.4	9.2
1974	3.4	n.a.	5.2	8.4	9.7	8.6	7.3	9.4
1975	- 1.1	n.a.	2.2	5.7	- 1.2	- 8.9	- 2.0	- 7.3
1976	6.1	n.a.	4.2	7.8	23.7	26.5	5.4	16.2
1977	3.5	10.7	13.6	8.8	12.4	22.8	8.2	25.1
1978	2.2	5.6	8.4	3.7	8.1	- 0.4	9.9	7.5
1979	- 2.0	- 0.3	2.4	7.7	15.3	9.3	3.3	2.9
1980	- 7.1	- 4.5	- 1.8	1.5	- 9.4	7.0	- 4.3	- 3.4
1981	- 5.1	-11.3	- 8.5	-5.6	-24.9	-37.7	11.1	-26.3
1982	-11.9	-12.6	- 9.8	-2.8	-38.7	-48.1	-10.1	-32.0
1983b	- 2.0	- 1.5	1.3	2.7	- 7.3	5.8	0.0	4.3

Notes: Rates of growth have been computed on the basis of values in constant 1966 colones.

  a For 1966-70.
  b Preliminary estimates.

Sources: The same as in Table 10.1.

TABLE 10.3

Costa Rica: Proportions of Gross Domestic
Product for Selected Sectors of Economic
Activity, 1950-82 (percentages).

Year	Agri cult.	Manu- fact.	Central Gov't.	Other	Exports	Imports
Nominal Terms						
1955	38.3	13.3	7.7	40.7	25.0	26.0
1960	26.0	14.2	9.0	50.8	21.4	26.2
1965	23.5	26.8	9.7	50.0	22.8	33.3
1970	22.5	18.3	10.6	48.6	28.2	35.0
1974	19.4	20.3	11.9	48.4	33.5	48.3
1975	20.3	20.4	12.4	46.9	30.4	38.7
1976	20.4	19.7	13.0	46.9	29.4	35.3
1977	21.9	99.0	12.9	46.2	31.1	36.5
1978	20.4	18.8	14.0	46.8	28.4	36.2
1979	18.5	18.3	15.0	48.2	26.9	37.3
1980	17.8	18.6	15.2	48.4	26.5	36.8
1981	23.0	18.9	13.4	44.7	43.3	48.2
1982	24.7	20.3	11.7	43.3	43.3	39.2
1983[a]	23.3	19.9	13.1	43.7	34.5	35.4
Real terms[a]						
1957	24.4	14.1	12.1	49.4	n.a.	n.a.
1960	25.2	13.8	11.3	49.7	n.a.	n.a.
1965	22.9	16.7	10.8	49.6	25.0	30.9
1970	24.1	18.6	9.9	47.4	34.2	39.6
1974	21.0	21.0	10.2	47.8	37.9	37.9
1975	21.2	21.2	10.3	47.3	36.4	34.4
1976	20.2	21.3	10.1	48.4	36.4	37.8
1977	19.0	22.0	9.8	49.2	36.1	43.5
1978	19.0	22.4	9.7	48.9	37.4	44.0
1979	18.2	22.0	9.7	50.1	36.8	43.1
1980	18.0	22.0	10.0	50.0	34.9	41.3
1981	19.3	22.4	10.4	47.9	39.7	31.1
1982	20.2	20.9	11.2	47.7	39.2	23.3
1983[b]	21.0	20.4	11.1	47.5	38.9	24.1

[a] In 1966 prices.
[b] Preliminary estimates

Sources: The same as in Table 10.1.

TABLE 10.4

Costa Rica: Selected Indicators of Population, Employment and Unemployment, 1950-82.

Year	Total Population ('000)	Annual Rates of Growth				Proportion of Labor Force	
		Population	Employment			Unemployment	Un- and Under-Employment
			Total	Private	Public		
1950	858	3.3	n.a.	n.a.	n.a.	4.1	n.a.
1963	1,380	3.7	2.5a	1.9a	8.8a	6.9	n.a.
1973	1,872	3.1	3.6a	3.4a	5.1a	7.3	n.a.
1976	2,018	2.5	4.4a	3.8a	7.7a	6.3	9.0
1977	2,071	2.6	6.4	5.4	11.5	4.6	7.5
1978	2,126	2.7	5.6	4.2	12.1	4.6	7.6
1979	2,184	2.7	3.3	3.6	2.2	4.9	9.6
1980	2,245	2.8	0.9	- 0.6	7.4	5.9	10.5
1981	2,306	2.7	0.5	0.7	0.1	8.7	14.6
1982	2,370	2.7	4.6	7.0	- 5.3	9.4	16.4
1983b	2,434	2.7	1.0	- 0.5	8.0	9.0	n.a.

Notes: Open unemployment: those members of the working force who are looking for a job and can not find one.
Visible underemployment: those members of the working force who can find only a part-time job. (Equivalent rate).

a Annual averages for the 1950-63, 1963-73, and 1973-76 periods.

b Preliminary estimates.

Sources: Direccion General de Estadistica y Censos, Censos de Poblacion (1950, 1963, and 1973); Ministerio de Trabajo y Seguridad Social, Encuesta Nacional de Hogares, Empleo y Desempleo (several years); Victor Hugo Cespedes and Claudio Gonzalez-Vega, Growth and Equity. Changes in Income Distribution in Costa Rica

TABLE 10.5

Costa Rica: Proportions of the Labor Force Employed in
Different Sectors, 1950-82 (percentages).

Year	Agricult.	Manufact.	Construct.	Other	Private	Public	Urban[a]	Rural[a]
1950	54.7	11.3	4.3	29.7	93.9	6.1	36.2	63.8
1963	49.7	11.7	5.5	33.1	86.7	13.3	37.0	63.0
1973	38.2	12.9	6.9	42.0	84.7	15.3	43.4	56.6
1976	34.8	14.6	6.5	44.1	83.2	16.8	46.1	53.9
1977	33.0	15.8	6.4	44.8	82.4	17.6	47.0	53.0
1978	30.3	15.2	7.4	47.1	81.3	18.7	47.5	52.5
1979	28.7	16.3	7.7	47.3	81.5	18.5	47.8	52.2
1980	27.4	16.3	7.8	48.5	80.3	19.7	48.3	51.7
1981	27.8	15.6	6.8	49.8	80.4	19.6	48.8	51.2
1982	30.2	15.4	5.7	48.7	82.3	17.7	48.4	51.6
1983b	28.3	16.4	5.2	50.1	81.0	19.0	49.6	50.4

a Proportions of the total labor force.
b Preliminary estimates.

Sources: The same as in Table 10.4.

TABLE 10.6

Costa Rica: Indexes of Import and Export Prices, International Terms-of-Trade, and Real Wages, 1950–82.

Year	Index			Annual Rates of Change			
	Export Prices	Import Prices	Terms Trade	Export Prices	Import Prices	Terms Trade	Real Wages
1950	98.4	78.8	124.9	n.a.	n.a.	n.a.	n.a.
1955	124.2	104.1	119.3	4.8a	5.7a	- 0.9a	n.a.
1960	96.2	95.1	101.1	- 5.0	- 1.8	- 3.3	n.a.
1965	100.5	99.3	101.3	0.9	0.9	0.0	n.a.
1970	86.7	99.4	87.2	- 2.9	0.0	- 3.0	n.a.
1975	145.2	182.7	79.4	10.9	12.9	- 1.9	n.a.
1980	231.6	252.0	91.9	9.8	6.6	3.0	n.a.
1974	127.7	167.1	76.5	19.9	37.1	-12.5	- 4.4
1975	145.2	182.7	79.4	13.7	9.3	3.8	- 2.6
1976	164.2	173.7	94.5	13.1	- 4.9	19.0	5.6
1977	209.8	182.9	114.7	27.8	5.3	21.4	6.4
1978	195.8	193.7	101.1	- 6.7	5.9	-11.9	7.2
1979	205.2	222.1	92.4	4.8	14.7	- 8.6	6.0
1980	231.6	252.0	91.9	12.9	13.5	- 0.5	- 3.9
1981	211.9	269.2	78.7	- 8.5	6.8	-14.4	- 6.2
1982	210.4	290.8	72.4	- 0.7	8.0	- 8.0	-29.0
1983b	214.2	308.2	69.5	1.8	6.0	- 4.0	n.a.

Notes: Index of export and import prices in U.S. dollars.
Terms-of-trade are the ratio of export to import prices.

a Average annual rates of change for the periods 1950-55, 1955-60, etc.
Rates of change of a real wage index (base year: 1973), when wages are
deflated by the consumer price index.

b Preliminary estimates.

Sources: Banco Central de Costa Rica, Balanza de Pagos (several years);
Claudio Gonzalez-Vega and Victor Hugo Cespedes, Growth and Equity.
Changes in Income Distribution in Costa Rica (New York: United
Nations, 1983). See also sources for Table 4 and for Table 1.

TABLE 10.7

Costa Rica: Annual Rates of Price Changes, Interest Rates,
and Exchange Rates, 1950-82.

| Year | Annual Rates of Change | | | | | Exchange Rate | Real Interest Rate |
	GDP Deflator	Agricult. Deflator	Manufact. Deflator	WPI	CPI		
1950-55	n.a.[a]	n.a.[a]	n.a.[a]	—	2.0	6.63[a]	n.a.[a]
1955-60	- 0.4[b]	- 6.2[b]	1.9[b]	0.4	1.5	6.63	n.a.
1960-65	1.4	3.3	1.0	0.3	1.3	6.63	6.3
1965-70	3.4	1.5	3.0	4.8	3.1	6.63	- 3.3
1970-75	13.9	14.5	13.4	17.4	14.7	8.54	- 2.0
1975-80	13.8	14.5	11.0	13.3	9.7	14.40	- 3.3
1974	23.2	27.0	19.1	38.2	n.a.	8.54	-20.1
1975	24.5	29.3	21.0	14.0	20.5	8.54	- 2.0
1976	16.6	22.7	12.3	7.2	4.4	8.54	4.9
1977	16.9	33.8	8.9	7.4	5.3	8.54	4.5
1978	7.9	0.3	4.6	9.4	8.1	8.54	2.5
1979	9.1	3.3	9.0	24.1	13.2	8.54	- 9.2
1980	18.8	15.8	20.7	19.3	17.8	14.40	- 3.3
1981	44.6	69.7	41.2	117.2	65.1	37.80	-45.2
1982[c]	93.5	91.6	113.4	79.1	81.8	45.20	-32.2

Notes: WPI: Wholesale price index. Base year: 1966.
        CPI: Consumer price index. Base year: 1975.
        Exchange rate: colones per U.S. dollar, at the end of the year.
        Real interest rate on colones term deposits, with respect to WPI.

d At the end of the five-year periods.

b For 1957-1960.

c Preliminary estimates.

Sources: Banco Central de Costa Rica. Cuentas Nacionales and Boletín Estadístico (several years). Dirección General de Estadística y Censos. Indice de Precios al Consumidor de Ingresos Medios y Bajos del Area Metropolitana de San José (several years). COUNSEL, Repertorio Economico (several years).

TABLE 10.8

Costa Rica: Balance of Payments and Public External Debt. (Millions U.S. dollars). 1950-1982.

Year	Exp.	Imp.	Trade Balance	Current Account[a]	Priv. Cap.	Offic. Cap.	Capital Account	Change Net Reserves	Public External Debt
1950	54	46	8	1	n.a.	n.a.	- 2	- 1	29
1955	81	87	- 6	- 7	n.a.	n.a.	11	4	23
1960	84	110	- 26	- 19	n.a.	n.a.	16	3	28
1965	112	178	- 66	- 67	n.a.	n.a.	69	2	148
1970	231	317	- 86	- 74	n.a.	n.a.	58	- 16	164
1974	440	720	-280	-266	168	75	243	- 23	379
1975	493	694	-201	-218	106	133	239	21	511
1976	593	770	-178	-201	137	129	266	65	646
1977	828	1,022	-194	-226	156	178	334	109	834
1978	865	1,166	-301	-363	103	233	336	- 27	1,044
1979	934	1,397	-462	-558	57	400c	457	-100	1,398
1980	1,002	1,524	-522	-664	63d	403c	466	-198	1,735
1981	860	1,209	-200	-409	- 48d	411c	362	- 47	2,743
1982b	1,008	867	-7	-209	49d	298c	347	138	3,438
1983b	803	930	-127	-373	100d	178c	278	- 95	n.a.

a Includes overdue interest on public sector loans, not paid and which amounted to $178.3 (1980), $292.5 (1981), $316.5 (1982), and $412.6 (1983).
b Preliminary estimates.
c Includes IMF loans and other balance-of-payments assistance.
d Includes errors and omissions.

Sources: Banco Central de Costa Rica, Balanza de Pagos (several years); COUNSEL, Repertorio Economico (several months).

TABLE 10.9

Costa Rica: Selected Fiscal, Credit and Monetary Indicators, 1950-1982.

| | Ratios with Respect to GDP | | | | | | Ratio | Proport. |
| | Central Gov't | | | Public Sector Deficit | Money Supply M2 | Domestic Savings | Dom. Savings/ Net inv. | Public Sector Credit |
Year	Expend.	Reven.	Deficit					
1950	n.a.	n.a.	n.a.	n.a.	n.a.	7.9	n.a.	23.1
1955	n.a.	n.a.	n.a.	n.a.	20.5a	3.8	n.a.	5.9
1960	n.a.	n.a.	n.a.	n.a.	22.2	7.5	60.7	12.7
1965	16.1b	12.1b	4.0b	n.a.	22.9	2.2	15.6	14.5
1970	15.1	13.5	1.6	n.a.	24.4	6.9	45.2	19.1
1974	17.6	14.6	3.0	n.a.	3.05	5.1	22.2	19.6
1975	17.5	13.5	4.0	n.a.	33.0	5.7	32.0	20.5
1976	19.2	13.0	6.2	n.a.	35.8	10.7	54.2	23.0
1977	17.7	13.2	4.4	n.a.	36.8	12.7	61.1	26.6
1978	19.6	13.6	6.0	9.0	41.6	8.6	43.4	28.7
1979	20.6	12.6	8.0	11.9	57.3	6.9	31.6	38.0
1980	21.8	12.7	9.1	13.9	42.4	7.1	30.2	44.3
1981	16.6	12.5	4.1	14.0	54.9	11.7	42.7	46.7
1982	16.6	13.2	3.4	9.9	46.6	n.a.	n.a.	n.a.
1983c	19.7	16.5	3.2	n.a.	n.a.	n.a.	n.a.	n.a.

Notes: All ratios of fiscal magnitudes are computed with respect to Gross Domestic Product, except that of Domestic Savings, which is given with respect to National Disposable Income. The proportion of public-sector credit includes the share of domestic credit for the central government and for the rest of the public sector.

a For 1957.

b For 1966.

c Preliminary estimates.

Sources: Banco Central de Costa Rica, Memoria Anual and Credito y Cuentas Monetarias (several years). The same as in Table 1.

11
Jamaica: From Manley to Seaga

Carl Stone

Recent political changes in Jamaica, viewed from the
vantage point of Cold War politics, give the impression
that this Caribbean state has passed from a Cuban-
influenced Marxist orientation to a capitalist counterrevolution. How far that impression distorts or mirrors
the realities of change in Jamaican politics remains to
be examined. Undoubtedly, the defeat of Michael Manley's
socialist and pro-Cuban Peoples National Party (PNP) by
Edward Seaga's pro-U.S. Jamaica Labour Party (JLP) in the
October 1980 parliamentary elections has produced
important political and policy changes during the first
fifteen months of the new government. The precise nature
of these changes, the extent to which they reflect new
ideological currents, and the implications for domestic
class groupings and the balance of forces between
regional capitalist and anticapitalist tendencies will
form the main focus of this chapter.

In many respects, Jamaica presents an interesting
study of the role of ideology in policy formulation in a
developing country. Like some other Third World states
that made the transition from liberal-reformist to more
radical orientations, a dominant left-leaning ideological
tendency was inserted into Jamaican politics in the 1970s
against the background of a severe economic crisis and as
part of a search for an alternative development path
beyond traditional neocolonial policies. The sharpening
of internal ideological divisions that followed increased
the level of external intervention in the domestic
political sphere, as rival Cold War interests (Cuba and
the United States) consolidated ties with local allies
and turned Jamaican politics into an open thoroughfare
for regional ideological rivalries.

The two party leaders see themselves as advocates of
mutually antagonistic ideologies and relate policy
choices to their respective ideological positions with
great evangelical fervor. Manley denounces neocolonialism and capitalism with passion and projects himself as

an apostle of Third World socialism and the liberation
struggle against imperialism and international capitalism. Seaga, on the other hand, articulates a strong
commitment to free enterprise and a deep faith in its
appropriateness as a model for Third World development.
As a small dependent economy, Jamaica is extremely
vulnerable to external economic pressures and manipulation, and both the political elite and the mass public
have a keen sense of the centrality of foreign economic
and political ties. To that extent, foreign relations
have played a major role in Jamaican domestic politics
since the mid-1970s.

Due to the intensive politicization of the Jamaican
electorates that took place in the 1970s as a direct
consequence of the ideological mobilizations and counter-
mobilizations of the period, issues, party images, and
political personalities have come to be perceived through
ideological lenses by large sections of the public.
These ideological tendencies are, in turn, related to
expectations for class benefits and to notions of what
social interests the parties support and how they
influence the management of public affairs.

Both the earlier PNP government and the present JLP
administration have projected their respective ideologies
(socialism and free enterprise) as policy frameworks from
which solutions to Jamaica's economic and social problems
can be formulated. Both governments have experienced
problems and gaps between the assumptions underlying
their ideological and policy prescriptions and the realities of Jamaican political and economic structures. More
importantly, one needs to assess objectively how far
these prescriptions are likely to provide real solutions
for the economic and social problems of this small, open
economy. In this regard the central problems of
indebtedness, balance of payments crises, shortage of
investment capital, unemployment, economic dualism, and
stagnation in agricultural production, as well as inflation, budget deficits, and weak public sector management,
all make Jamaica fairly typical of the syndrome of
problems that face most developing countries not blessed
with oil. Comparatively, Jamaica in the 1970s had
greater difficulty coping with these problems than
similar Third World countries. Why this was so needs to
be fully explored.

An important feature of the Jamaican political
economy is the degree to which the relatively atypical
and evenly balanced two-party system permitted the
playing out of these sharp ideological contests for power
without resort to unconstitutional seizures by any of the
main political groupings. The Jamaican case, therefore,
permits an analysis of the reactions of public opinion to
this yet unfinished drama of clashing ideological forces
that have grown increasingly hostile to each other and

have divided the Jamaican political community to a degree
unprecedented in its four-decade history of parliamentary
politics.

THE PARTIES AND IDEOLOGY

Prior to 1972, when the PNP came to power, the
organization was a typical social democratic party that
had made its peace with capitalism and private ownership
but still sought to achieve social reform. The latter
included land reform, the broadening of educational
opportunity, cooperative ownership within the petty
commodity sector, progressive taxation of the affluent
property-owning class, and the expansion of government
services for workers and peasants.

The JLP represented the typical Caribbean trade
union party, which avoided ideology and embraced pragmatic reforms that responded to the specific social needs
of unionized workers and small peasants. Unlike the PNP,
which justified the need for active involvement of the
state in economic management, the JLP placed its faith in
the more orthodox capitalist system with a dominant
private sector.

Both parties sought support from all classes, shared
a common view of foreign policy as involving close links
with U.S. and Western European global interests, and
accepted a reformist approach to public policy that
supported private business while using government
spending to meet the social needs of the majority
classes. Political liberalism and social reforms in
domestic policies and a unified perception of world
politics provided an anchor of consensus that stabilized
Jamaican politics. The strong continuity in policy
priorities between successive JLP and PNP governments
meant that (over the 1944 to 1972 period) both parties
became center parties with no sharp or fundamental policy
differences between them. Such ideological disputes as
existed were mainly on the symbolic level, as ideological
issues were treated as debating points to promote party
images at election time and had no real implications or
consequence for policy priorities. Even these symbolic
debates receded from the electoral arena between the
early 1950s and 1972, as the parties differentiated themselves more and more in terms of competence, policy
achievements, and leadership qualities.

The only real difference that emerged between the
parties in the policy area was the tendency of the PNP to
increase both public spending and taxation at a faster
rate than that associated with the JLP and consequently
to promote a higher increase in public employment. On
the other hand, most social and economic policies
remained intact after changes in party government.

However, fundamental changes in ideological orientation took place within the PNP after that party came to
power in 1972. Those changes not only transformed the
party system but also redefined the relationships between
technocrats in the civil service, private sector interest
groups and corporate interests, on the one hand, and the
political directorate, on the other. The new PNP leader,
Michael Manley, proceeded to take the party beyond the
bounds of the inherited social democratic tradition by
attempting to dismantle neocolonialism and economic
dependency in Jamaica. His policy was inspired both by a
strong sense of economic nationalism, which saw Jamaicans
assuming greater control and ownership over the local
economy, and by a commitment to Third World socialist
trends.

Manley's thrust toward close relations with leftist
Third World states (Cuba, Tanzania, Mozambique, etc.) and
his initiative in undertaking an activist stance with
regard to North-South issues represented a dramatic break
from the traditional low-profile, pro-western foreign
policy of the previous JLP government. Evidence of this
realignment was reflected in Jamaica's voting in the
United Nations on controversial ideological issues that
divided the western capitalist countries and the United
States, on the one hand, and the communist and radical
Third World countries, on the other. Whereas under the
JLP the Jamaican government tended to vote with the
western bloc, under Manley's PNP it tended to vote with
Cuba and the radical Third World countries.

This radical new direction in foreign policy was
followed by the cementing of close party-to-party ties
with the Communist Party of Cuba and the gradual takeover
of the PNP machinery by a new generation of younger
leaders who, with the full backing of Manley, injected
Marxist terminology into the party's rhetoric and set
itself the task of moving towards a noncapitalist path of
development.

The idea of the noncapitalist path, as articulated
by Soviet theoreticians[1] and some Third World leftists,
does not involve an abrupt break with capitalism but
rather envisions a set of strategies that are designed to
prepare the way for a break sometime in the indefinite
future. It involves the elimination of the monopoly of
political power by the bourgeoisie (local or foreign);
increasing the power of working people; agrarian reform;
cooperative development; creation of a strong state
sector in the economy to check capitalist tendencies;
militant criticism of imperialism; attempts at promoting
social justice; elimination of class exploitation; and
promotion of class consciousness through the dissemina-
tion of Marxism-Leninist ideas.

There was a massive swing of lower-working-class
votes toward the PNP in the 1976 parliamentary elections,

as the party's promises of social justice generated
strong and vocal mass support. After its decisive
victory, the PNP made some initiatives toward a noncapitalist path. However, as the economy deteriorated
and the government was shackled by aid dependence on the
fiscally conservative International Monetary Fund, this
strategy had to be abandoned. Policy directions moved
back to the center, while the rhetoric of the noncapitalist path continued.

Nevertheless, before the IMF influence became
decisive, the PNP took some crucial steps to increase the
role of the state in economic management and to reduce
the political influence of the bourgeoisie and conservative petitbourgeois technocrats in the civil service.
Many bourgeois persons were removed from statutory boards
and key advisory roles, as a small number of radical-left
intellectuals were recruited into the government as
technocrats and advisers. Conservative civil service
economists were pressured out of key positions, and
leftists were recruited to replace them. As the economic
crisis deepened, the state took over a number of private
companies, and the economy was brought under a regime of
tight regulation and control of foreign exchange,
imports, prices, and foreign currency. Although some
business interests remained on close terms with the PNP
and the prime minister, the majority of the merchants,
manufacturers, and big farmers, as well as the affluent
professional class, reacted in panic to these initiatives. Some migrated to Miami, while others exported
foreign currency, closed or scaled down their business
enterprises, or withheld tax payments.

The actual structural changes carried out by the PNP
were not very far reaching, although Marxist rhetoric
from the top leadership and leftist factions gave quite
the opposite impression. Land-reform plans foundered
against the harsh reality of a legal system that
protected property rights and made land acquisitions
expensive. Radical proposals to change the constitution
so as to widen the state's powers to acquire land cheaply
(among other things) were abandoned after the post-1976
decline in the economy weakened support for socialism and
a poll on the subject (carried out by the author on
behalf of the PNP) showed that the majority of the
electorate neither had interest in the constitutional
change nor supported it.

PNP attitudes toward the private sector were ambivalent and vacillating. Patriotic appeals were made to the
bourgeoisie to cooperate in the handling of the economic
crisis, and incentives were offered to stimulate exports
and employment. At the same time, party leaders singled
out local businessmen for ideological attacks that often
trumpeted ultra-leftist declarations to end capitalism.
The inconsistency of these maneuvers only accelerated the

panic and flight of the bourgeoisie. On the one hand, the PNP espoused the creation of a mixed economy in which a reduced private sector would have a place side by side with the state, which was to control the commanding heights of the economy. On the other hand, party spokesmen abused the private sector and talked of an accelerated transition toward the noncapitalist path and, thereafter, full socialism. Close party-to-party ties with Cuba encouraged the development of radical leftist rhetoric, which bore no real relationship to the actual changes carried out by the PNP. The cosmetic of Marxist terminology served to intimidate the bourgeoisie while pushing the government on a collision course with international capitalist agencies, even though no real structural changes were achieved beyond a reduction in capitalist political influence and an expanded role for the state in the management of the economy.

Land-reform programs left most large private holdings intact. Most of the properties obtained for redistribution were marginal lands made available on a leasehold basis. Thus, the impact of the reform was politically and economically negligible, especially as many projects failed miserably from a production or financial standpoint. Neither equity in land allocation nor efficiency in production was attained.

Cooperatives established in the sugar industry ran into financial and management problems, while weak trade union support for worker participation and hostility by employers weakened the PNP's interest in promoting greater working-class power at the workplace. In any event, the main objectives sought from worker participation were industrial peace and the pacification of labor militancy, rather than the promotion of worker power, which would have had the opposite effect by increasing tensions and class antagonisms in an already conflict-prone labor relations situation.

In effect, the PNP seemed not to have the political will to accomplish the difficult task of pulling this conservative and highly pragmatic political culture into the stormy class conflicts that would have inevitably attended more systematic efforts to move toward a noncapitalist path of development. Dependence on the International Monetary Fund (IMF) for balance-of-payments support and the tight conditions attached to IMF loans forced the PNP to scale down its designs to expand state control of the economy, and to use the public sector to redistribute income and social benefits to the poorer classes. The conservative influence of the IMF, however, was only one of several converging forces. As the state's participation in economic management increased through its larger regulatory role and the growing burden of running public enterprises and parastatal corporations, the PNP discovered that its capability to undertake these tasks was embarrassingly limited. Capital was simply not available to finance these enterprises, as against bailing out bankrupt businesses or keeping open (for employment purposes) companies whose owners and managers had joined the exodus of people and capital out of Jamaica. Large-scale migration at a rate of some 25,000 per year in a small population of 2 million left the public as well as the private sectors short of managerial, technocratic, and production skills.

The greatest strides toward the noncapitalist path were achieved in relation to political objectives. The PNP nationalized two of the three largest privately owned mass media. These included a daily newspaper (the <u>Daily News</u>) and a radio station (Radio Jamaica), which were added to the government-owned radio and television station (Jamaica Broadcasting Corporation). These media were extensively used to propagate the PNP's socialist ideology and policies. A high level of mass mobilization was achieved within the party organization, and enthusiastic activists were politicized to articulate the new ideological currents. In the area of foreign policy, the Manley government closely identified with Cuba and the Third World. This government became one of the principal advocates of the New International Economic Order and the Non-Aligned Movement, and mounted verbal attacks on imperialism and capitalism in international forums.

The JLP's reactions to these developments were to mount intense attacks on socialism and communism and to associate leftist policies with the decline in the economy. Beyond that, the JLP projected itself as a party committed to free enterprise. The bourgeoisie, it argued, should be permitted to resume full control of the economy. The expanded economic management role that the PNP had given the state was perceived as having contributed to the economic failures of the 1970s. Government regulation of the economy was portrayed as dysfunctional to economic progress. The JLP advocated that the forces of the free market be restored to provide a more rational mechanism of resource allocation and price determination. Private ownership, it insisted, was more efficient than public ownership. Private investment and entrepreneurial initiative had to be given the necessary incentives to move the economy forward.

In the political sphere, the JLP reaffirmed its strong pro-U.S. international alignment and denounced the PNP link with Cuba as being part of a grand communist conspiracy to overturn liberal democracy in Jamaica. Attempts by the PNP to politicize the society were criticized as paving the way for a communist one-party state in which freedom of speech and civil liberties would be destroyed. The JLP, therefore, put itself forth as a champion of traditional liberal values deeply rooted in the Jamaican political culture.

In sum, then, the JLP assumed the role of defender of orthodox capitalist economic methods, whereas the PNP moved from a center-left social democratic position toward a more leftist posture that aspired to creation of a noncapitalist path of development. In terms of ideological symbolism and party image, the latter projected itself as the party of the poor, dedicated to bringing social justice to the oppressed, while the former embraced the bourgeoisie and its traditional values of stability, gradualism, technocratic efficiency, and responsible financial management.

As this pattern of ideological polarization rapidly replaced the two-party consensus of the earlier period, certain tendencies emerged in both parties. The JLP was traditionally based on an alliance between pragmatic trade union leaders and business interests hostile to the PNP's socialism. As the ideological divisions between the PNP and the JLP sharpened, the latter's business faction assumed dominance over the trade union segment. Under Seaga's leadership, JLP ideology moved increasingly away from traditional labor populism toward a business and technocratic conception of public affairs management. In the PNP, by contrast, the traditional social demo cratic tendencies declined in importance as the anti-imperialist and Third World socialist perspectives swept the party. Moderates who opposed these trends found their influence rapidly diminished.

THE POLICY DIFFERENCES

Faced with the economic crises of the 1970s, under the banner of advancing socialism, the PNP implemented a mix of economic and social policies. Some reflected the party's new ideological thrust, while others mirrored conventional western economic prescriptions derived from Keynesian theories. As private investment declined in the early 1970s, the PNP took steps to increase govern-ment borrowing from private overseas banks to finance capital needs. This trend is shown in Table 11.1, which also outlines the dramatic fall in private foreign investment that coincided with the PNP takeover of the government.

Immediately following the party's reaffirmation of socialism in 1974 and throughout the subsequent period (1975-80) in which radical currents began to dominate, foreign investment dried up. Only after the 1976 parliamentary elections, however, did the more militant minority of leftists in the PNP leadership join the cabinet. Prior to that, ideological moderates enjoyed strong influence over policymaking, while the party machine was left effectively in the hands of the leftists. It was therefore possible for the government

TABLE 11.1

Trends in Foreign Investment and Government
Private Foreign Borrowing

	1970	1971	1972	1973	1974	1975	1976	1977	1978
Private Foreign Investment[a]	134	147	21	20	21	0	0	0	0

	1972	1973	1974	1975	1976	1977	1978	1979
Loans from Foreign Commercial Banks[b]	14	80	136	119	44	-15	15	-11

[a] Millions of Jamaican dollars
[b] Millions of U.S. dollars

Source: Bank of Jamaica, Annual Reports (various years).

to negotiate large loans from private overseas banks up
to that period. These loans financed public-sector
economic activity.

Added to this pattern of large increases in foreign
borrowing was the adoption of Keynesian strategies of
demand management through deficit budgeting. The object
was to expand consumer spending and to maintain a minimal
momentum of economic activity, given that world inflation
and large increases in import costs had severely reduced
the capacity to import. This decline in imports had a
negative effect on the momentum of activity in the
economy due to the high import dependence of both production and consumption.

As can be seen from Table 11.2, the size of the
budget deficit more than doubled after the PNP came to
power in 1972. The impact of this deficit, added to the
large influx of overseas loans, was to increase significantly the aggregate level of government spending over
gross domestic product (GDP). The table also indicates
that the level of public spending doubled as a proportion
of GDP under these expansionary budgets.

The PNP also sought to develop what it defined as
policies of economic self-reliance. These were designed
to stimulate domestic production as substitutes for
imports that could no longer be afforded due to the
balance-of-payments problem. Reduced levels of imports
generated shortages of many consumer goods that were

394

TABLE 11.2

Budget Deficit and Expenditure

	1972	1974	1976	1978	1980
Budget Deficit as Percentage of Expenditure	18	25	44	40	43

	1972			1978	
Government Expenditures as Percentage of GDP	22			42	

Source: Economic and Social Surveys (1972-80), National
Planning Agency, Kingston, Ja.

normally imported or produced locally. These shortages
had two important effects. First, a large number of
higglers or petty traders created an illegal import-
export trade that brought into the island large quantities of consumer goods, some of which were banned from
importation and some of which were brought in without
payment of the requisite import duty. Second, small- and
middle-sized peasants increased domestic food production,
as consumers had to substitute local food items for those
normally imported.

    Out of the economic crisis, therefore, significant
increases in wealth and income flows accrued to the petty
commodity sector. In the commercial centers and
especially in the island's capital city, Kingston,
higglers made significant inroads into the market share
of middle-class merchants. Between 1976 and 1980, food
imports fell from $90 million to $30 million (in 1972
dollars), while domestic food production grew by 26
percent from $68 million to $86 million (in 1969
dollars). Also over that period the farm gate price for
domestic food crops increased more rapidly than the price
index for the economy as a whole, clearly indicating a
net transfer of income to the petty commodity sector.

    The expansion in income accruing to the petty
commodity sector and the parallel decline in the income
flows and market shares controlled by middle-class
merchants were only part of the picture. The promotion
of self-reliance strategies left huge gaps in the supply
of consumer goods. In fact, considerable alienation

toward the government developed over this issue.
Together with unemployment, the cost of living, and the
overall depressed state of the economy, consumer
shortages constituted one of the four major economic
factors identified by voters as being among the most
important election issues.[2]

The PNP attempted to mobilize the labor force
through rhetoric and emotional appeals to patriotism.
This strategy was based on the premise that one could not
rely entirely on market forces and material incentives to
stimulate economic activity and that political mobilization could assist in energizing the people to scaling
great heights of ambitious production targets. But the
policy proved to be both romantic and futile. Whereas
the small and middle peasants responded to market forces
by increasing domestic food production, government-
financed farm projects promoted as self-reliance strategies (which provided inadequate income and material
returns to the participants) resulted in underutilized
land, huge deficits, and poor performance in production,
notwithstanding various efforts at political mobilization.

A program of industrial democracy was attempted
through promotion of worker participation and cooperatives. However, trade union disinterest, management
opposition, and worker apathy paralyzed the participation
initiative. Moreover, although the cooperative movement
scored a political success in establishing worker control
on the island's three largest sugar estates, the experiment was a financial failure that generated worker
dissatisfaction with its economic rewards.

Faced with economic crises, the government
established state ownership and control over key areas of
the economy that were vital either for overall economic
management or for the pursuit of social justice for the
poor. A major foreign bank (Barclays) was nationalized.
Hotels were taken over on a scale that eventually gave
the government a majority ownership of the industry's
hotel rooms. The cement company was nationalized. A
small number of food processing enterprises were
established under government ownership. A State Trading
Corporation was set up with the long-term objective of
permitting government control of most import areas. In
its initial stages, the corporation monopolized the
importation of basic foods, drugs, and lumber, attempting
to pass on cheaper prices to the consumer through bulk
buying. Wage-price and rent controls were established to
restrict the cost of living.

The shortage of foreign exchange necessitated
controls over imports and foreign currency. Imports were
brought under a tight system of licensing, and foreign
exchange was rationed through the Bank of Jamaica. Joint
ownership was established between the government and the

transnational bauxite companies, and the former reestablished ownership over the mined-out bauxite lands. As a response to the acute shortage of foreign exchange, the government imposed a production levy on the bauxite multinationals that generated additional revenue of some $160-180 million. In addition, the major urban bus company was nationalized.

The Jamaican political economy changed in important ways in the 1970s due to the cumulative impact of these policies. From an economy in which the bourgeoisie was overwhelmingly dominant and in which its class interests were treated as synonymous with the interests of the nation, PNP policies significantly altered the balance of class power. The state now assumed a dominant role in economic management, both in the regulation of business transactions and in control over a large proportion of the flow of income. Further, it increased quite significantly the range and number of public enterprises that were producing goods and services, especially in such crucial areas as agriculture, trade, utilities and services, banking, bauxite, construction, tourism, and mass communication.

Table 11.3 classifies independent Caribbean English-speaking states according to levels of government economic intervention and general ideological tendencies under various regimes. Jamaica is a political system in which both ideology and the level of state economic intervention changed in the 1970s. That change was due primarily to the new currents of socialist ideology that emerged in the PNP under the leadership of Michael Manley.

Under the Manley government, Jamaica moved from low to medium levels of state economic intervention. In contrast to Guyana, where development of a Third World socialist ideological framework led to 80 percent state ownership and high levels of intervention in all important economic areas, considerable private-sector economic power and ownership remained intact in Jamaica. Indeed, this residue of private economic power promoted resistance to socialist advances. The intense conflicts between the PNP leftist intellectual leadership (mainly black, colored, and university educated) and the primarily white bourgeoisie (mainly high school educated) generated a climate in which capital flights, tax evasions, the decapitalization of enterprises, and disinterest in investments added to the economic problems of the period. Strong racial undertones colored these tensions as deep antagonisms developed between these elite groups.

In contrast to Guyana, state ownership in Jamaica represented only 20 percent of total production, whereas the medium- and large-scale capitalist-controlled enterprises accounted for approximately 70 percent of

TABLE 11.3

Commonwealth Caribbean States by Ideology and
State Economic Intervention (1970s)

Ideology	State Economic Intervention		
	Low	Medium	High
Liberal-Pragmatic	Barbados	St. Kitts	
	Bahamas		
	Grenada (under Gairy)		
	Jamaica (under JLP)		
	Antigua		
	St. Lucia		
	Dominica		
Nationalist		Trinidad and Tobago	
Socialist		Jamaica (under PNP)	Guyana
		Grenada (under Bishop)	

Source: Carl Stone, Understanding Third World Politics and Economics (Kingston: Earle Publishers, 1980), p. 42.

total output. The petty commodity sector accounted for
only 10 percent of output. During the years of PNP
socialism, some drastic changes occurred in the distribution of the labor force. As private production fell,
labor shifted to the public and petty commodity sectors.
By 1978 the public sector represented 20 percent of the
labor force, the private sector 36 percent, and the petty
commodity sector (including small farmers, higglers, and
artisans) 44 percent. From 1972 to 1978, the public-
sector employment share grew by 48 percent and the
private-sector share declined by 24 percent; at the same

time, the petty commodity sector grew by 33 percent as
workers displaced by layoffs drifted into own-account
activity.

Government overseas borrowing shifted from private
commercial banks to the International Monetary Fund
between the middle and late 1970s. Indeed, it is para-
doxical that after the PNP shifted to the left after the
1976 elections, it got tied into extensive borrowing and
consequent dependence on the conservative IMF, which was
hostile to most of its policies. Further confusion and
ideological antagonism were added to the political
situation, as policy conflicts between the IMF and the
leftists (who increasingly controlled PNP policymaking
after 1976) made it difficult to develop coherent,
consistent, and predictable economic policies.

No clear winner emerged from the IMF-PNP conflicts.
The latter feared the impact of the former's stabilization policies, which included currency devaluation, free
trade, increasing unemployment, removal of subsidies and
price controls, and the scaling down of state economic
intervention. But since the PNP had no alternative
source of foreign exchange support, it had to compromise
on some issues while fighting the IMF on others. The
IMF, in turn, was especially sensitive to its growing
anti-Third World image and tried to compromise its usual
hard-line policies to find a way of working with this
influential Third World country. The real problem was
that no socialist source of international financing
existed to aid the PNP.

The government was able to maintain high budget
deficits during the period of IMF borrowing. Price
controls remained intact, although the list of controlled
items was eventually reduced. In the face of political
and union pressure, the IMF increased the ceiling on wage
controls from a 7 to 15 percent official limit. Some
subsidies were cut while others remained. The PNP
refused to fire or lay off public-sector workers to
reduce the budget deficit. It broke with the IMF over
that issue at a strategically designed meeting five

TABLE 11.4

IMF Borrowing, 1972-79
(Millions of U.S. Dollars)

1972	1973	1974	1975	1976	1977	1978	1979
14	22	16	16	64	22	72	188

Source: Bank of Jamaica, Annual Reports (various years).

months before the 1980 election and proceeded to blame
the IMF for its economic and political problems.

The big question was to what extent the PNP's
policies were able to achieve the objectives set. On
balance, the failures were more pronounced than the
successes. Between 1974 and 1980, real per capita
disposable income fell 30 percent from $1,019 to $717.
Over the same period, per capita consumption expenditure
in real terms fell 25 percent from $737 to $557. Real
per capita wages also fell 25 percent from $588 to $440.
In spite of the big increase in number of persons
employed in the public sector due to the government's
expansionist public-sector spending policies, the
shrinkage of private-sector employment and the overall
decline in the economy increased unemployment from 23
percent in 1972 to 28 percent in 1980.

The self-reliance policies geared to reduce import
dependence achieved modest successes between 1975 and
1977, but these gains were erased between 1978 and 1980
as domestic production declined dramatically. In 1974,
imports represented 46 percent of the GDP, and this
figure was reduced to 33 percent by 1977 due to tight
import restrictions. However, by 1980 imports had
climbed back to 53 percent of the GDP, although their
value in real terms dropped by over 40 percent between
1975 and 1980.

Gross capital formation fell from 35 percent of the
GDP when the JLP was in power to 26 percent in 1975 and
16 percent in 1980, indicating the dramatic decline in
investment activities. Dependence on foreign borrowing
to finance savings increased from 30 percent when the JLP
was in power in 1969 to 63 percent in 1976 and 68 percent
in 1980. In real terms, domestic savings fell by
approximately 35 percent between 1969 and 1980.

As can be seen from Table 11.5, price controls
brought the inflation level down after the impact of the
oil price increase had created double-digit inflation.
But the impact was short-lived, as huge budget deficits,
shortages, black marketeering, excessively high prices in
the informal higgler-controlled markets, devaluation,
private-sector profiteering, and imported inflation
pushed prices back up to high levels. Clearly Jamaica
fared much worse than other trade-dependent economies in
this respect. Countries with tighter controls over
budget deficits (Bahamas, Barbados, and the Dominican
Republic) were much more successful at managing the local
impact of international inflation.

More importantly, the PNP attempt at demand management failed to stimulate production. Due to the absence
of foreign exchange, which is a significant input for
most local production, excess consumer demand induced by
large increases in money supply led to increased inflation rather than increased output. Shortages of imported

TABLE 11.5

Comparative Inflation Levels for Jamaica and Similar Countries
(Annual Percentage Change in Prices, 1970-80)

	1970	1971	1972	1973	1974	1975	1976	1977	1978	1979	1980
Bahamas	6	5	7	5	13	10	4	3	6	9	12
Barbados	8	12	7	17	39	20	5	8	9	13	18
Dominican Republic	4	4	8	15	13	14	8	13	3	9	17
Costa Rica	5	3	5	15	30	17	3	4	6	9	18
Jamaica	10	5	5	20	24	17	10	11	35	29	27

Source: International Monetary Fund, Yearbook, 1981.

raw materials, machinery, equipment, spare parts, tools,
and containers led to production bottlenecks. For the
Keynesian multiplier to work, adequate supplies of
foreign exchange had to be in place.

As the debt burden mounted, more and more overseas
borrowing and foreign exchange earnings had to be used to
service the accumulated private and public foreign debts.
Public debts were paid, but large private trading debts
went unpaid and creditors removed trade credit from their
transactions with Jamaican companies. This factor added
further to the overall decline of the economy.

Subsidies paid by the government increased from $13
million in 1972 to $200 million in 1978. These
represented the cost of financially unprofitable public
enterprises and price subsidies passed on to consumers to
ease the pressures of declining real income and high
inflation. The subsidy-tax burden, however, proved much
too large for an economy in which budget deficits were
climbing, real incomes were falling, and tax revenue was
decreasing in real terms.

Real gains were achieved in the subsidies passed on
to the consumers on basic imported food items and in the
control of rents. A variety of social legislation,
including a national minimum wage and the distribution of
approximately 180,000 acres of farmland to some 46,000
farmers and agricultural workers, assisted social
survival, although the production results were not
spectacular. The State Trading Corporation, in spite of
the corruption that affected its credibility, functioned

s an efficient bulk purchaser of imports which saved
oreign exchange by replacing haphazard private importing
y merchants.
    Although the PNP's socialist initiatives did not
roduce any spectacular results and failed to arrest the
ecline of the economy, it is possible that the more
ctivist role of the state somewhat reduced the economic
nd social pressures on the urban and rural poor (in the
hort run at least) as a result of food subsidies,
reation of employment in special employment works, and
oney circulation through government social projects.
evertheless, the electorate lost confidence in the
arty's ability to manage the economy. As a consequence,
he PNP was voted out of office in October 1980.
    Table 11.6 gives the details of the balance of class
upport that voted the JLP into power. Apart from
killed workers, who gave it only a small majority, the
LP earned large majorities in all other classes and
ocioeconomic groups, especially among small farmers and
usiness and managerial interests.
    The JLP's reaction to the PNP's economic policies
as to devise an alternative package designed to move the
conomy away from socialism and back to a more private-
ector-controlled market economy with low levels of state
conomic intervention. The JLP accepted entirely the
eed for stabilization policies and the removal of
rotectionist barriers so as to create a competitive

TABLE 11.6

Percentage Vote for JLP in 1980 Elections
By Socioeconomic Groups

Socioeconomic Group	Percentage JLP Vote
Urban Unemployed	60
Skilled Workers	52
White Collar Workers	63
Business and Management	86
Farm Labor	58
Small Peasants	65

Source: Author's opinion poll, October 1980
        (N = 944).

economy, freed of government controls and maximizing
profit incentives for foreign capital. It took the view
that budget deficits were an obstacle to proper economic
management and thus had to be reduced. The regulatory
machinery established by the PNP was seen as stifling
bourgeois dynamism and initiative. The trend toward
state ownership was also attacked, and the JLP committed
itself to divesting these businesses. Public enterprise
that had become recipients of subsidies because of an
inability to break even or show profits would have had to
improve their efficiency or be sold to private interests
The State Trading Corporation came under strong attack
and the PNP was criticized for setting up social project
that wasted public funds.

The self-reliance concept was by implication
rejected by the JLP in favor of an open-economy strategy
The promotion of local ownership was replaced with an
emphasis on foreign and joint local-foreign ownership.
Foreign investment was seen as a necessary prerequisite
for economic recovery. Anti-imperialism and a strong
Third World political identity were to be replaced by a
strong U.S. foreign policy connection as a means of moti-
vating American investment. Foreign policy was to be
moved away from radical leftist ideological postures
toward a more pragmatic path that sought concrete gains.
An export emphasis geared to selling products to the
large U.S. market was to be the main economic strategy,
and this was to be carefully planned in collaboration
with the American government, local bourgeois interests,
technocrats, and U.S. corporations.

Where the PNP emphasized political and ideological
mobilization, the JLP stressed market and material
incentives and greater freedom of choice by consumers,
investors, and labor. A more competitive market was seen
as an ideal substitute for government controls to determine price levels and allocate resources. The JLP was
emphatic in pointing the degree to which shortages and
black markets exploited the consumer, and it argued
vehemently for supply increases to induce prices to
decline. Wage controls were criticized as disturbing
free labor bargaining, which was claimed to be preferable
to state regulation. The JLP promised economic freedoms
for all classes. Stricter financial management by the
government, a climate of confidence between government
and private interests, and prospects for replacing
successive years of negative growth and reduced consumption by a new spurt of investment activity, employment
creation, and more adequate consumer supplies would all
reinforce each other and stimulate more positive orientations to production by workers, managers, owners, and
investors.

The JLP, in effect, agreed entirely with the prevailing IMF and World Bank views regarding which economi

trategies were likely to show results in Third World
conomies facing the kinds of problems that were endemic
n Jamaica and other Caribbean territories in the 1970s.
he key to this approach is the idea of Jamaica earning
ts way out of the crisis by a combination of foreign
nvestment and reallocation of resources from import
ubstitution to exports. In its first year in office,
he JLP used this policy framework as its guide. How far
hese objectives have been established, the degree to
hich they have had to be modified, the actual results
roduced so far, the extent to which the political
conomy has been changed by the dismantling of the
artial attempts at a noncapitalist path, and how far the
esults differ from those generated by the PNP must now
e analyzed.

LP POLICIES AND IMPACT

    The JLP government, which came to power in October
980, inherited an economy that had experienced
ontinuous negative growth over the years of PNP
ocialist administration. Jamaica's economic performance
n the 1970s was by far the worst in the entire Latin
merican region, if we exclude Nicaragua in the last
ears of the anti-Somoza struggle. The contrast with
ther trade-dependent open economies in the region, shown
n Table 11.7, points clearly to the difficulty of
ngineering economic recovery in an island economy that
as been experiencing an unbroken trend of negative
rowth (between 1973 and 1980) under socialist economic
nitiatives. The JLP, therefore, identified a restora-
ion of economic growth as its most immediate objective.
    The first task was to negotiate successfully for
alance-of-payments support. The PNP had broken off
elations with the IMF in May 1980 and had been unable to
ecure adequate loans from other sources in spite of
xtensive efforts vis-a-vis private foreign banks and
ocialist and Third World countries. Without such
unding, the manufacturing sector, which employs 80,000
orkers, would have been shut down because of raw
aterial shortages. Basic goods such as drugs, flour,
ornmeal, and building materials could not have been
mported. The foreign exchange shortage was rendered
ven more acute because the PNP had secured and exhausted
he advanced payments of the levy from the multinational
auxite companies, which gave rise to a serious cash flow
roblem for the new government. The pile-up of unpaid
ebts created by the absence of foreign exchange meant
hat, if loan funding could not be secured, Jamaica's
inancial standing would deteriorate because of its
ailure to pay debts incurred by the previous government.

TABLE 11.7

Gross Domestic Product Growth in Jamaica
and Other Small Open Economies that Import Oil
(In Percentages)

Country	1966-70	1971-74	1975	1976	1977	1978	1979	1980
Jamaica	6.3	3.0	-1.0	-6.7	-4.0	-0.3	-2.5	-3.5
Barbados	7.5	2.6	2.5	-0.1	3.6	4.5	4.7	5.4
Bahamas	n.a.	n.a.	n.a.	5.0	1.5	10.8	6.8	6.9
Dominican Republic	7.7	10.0	5.2	6.7	5.0	2.2	4.8	5.6
Costa Rica	7.4	7.1	2.1	5.5	8.9	6.3	3.3	1.9

Source: Inter-American Development Bank, Economic and
Social Progress for Latin America (1980-81).

        The JLP had anticipated an election victory. Public
opinion polls conducted by the author and published
quarterly by the major local newspaper, the Daily
Gleaner, had consistently indicated that the JLP was
likely to win the election by a wide margin. Even before
the change of government and, while it was still the
official opposition party, Edward Seaga had entered into
discussions with both the IMF and U.S. government
officials with a view to shortening the waiting period
for loans once the party was elected to office.
        A new IMF loan of U.S. $625 million was secured over
a three-year period in addition to a U.S. $350 million
loan from the Caribbean Group for Cooperation in Economic
Development, the consortium of western country interests
directed by the World Bank. Close ties established with
the new Republican administration in Washington and JLP
support for U.S. regional foreign policy designs secured
an increase of American economic aid from U.S. $23
million in 1980 to U.S. $93 million in 1981.
        The large increases in non-IMF loans meant that the
JLP had secured enough financing to avoid laying off
public sector workers to reduce the budget deficit (the
center of the IMF-PNP controversy in 1980). The new IMF
agreement did not relax the usual terms. The difference
was that the new administration shared the fiscal and
economic policy thinking of the IMF technocrats, and a
harmonious relationship replaced the antagonisms of the

NP era. This relationship increased the credibility and
redit-worthiness of the government in the eyes of over-
eas investors, bankers, and creditors.

Like the PNP, however, the JLP took the view that
ontinued large-scale overseas borrowing was a necessary
eature of any economic recovery. The regime's
free-enterprise" ideology and its active support by the
eagan administration considerably increased its ability
o borrow from capitalist sources over and above the
ccess to loan funding available to its predecessor. The
mpact of this larger flow of borrowing eased the foreign
xchange shortage in the short run and increased the
mport capacity of the Jamaican economy. The effect over
he first year of the JLP government was a significant
pward trend in economic activity in most sectors.
owever, the long-term implication will be a sharp rise
n the future debt burden, which will require a substan-
ial increase in export earnings to service this debt.

Preliminary estimates indicate a likely 2 percent
rowth in GDP in 1981 and 4 percent in 1982, in contrast
o the successive years of negative growth in the 1970s.
roduction increases were recorded in most sectors of the
conomy in 1981, with the notable exception of mining, in
hich production fell due to declining demand for alumi-
um generated by the recession in the United States.
oth the manufacturing and construction sectors recorded
eal growth in 1981. Domestic food crop production
ontinued to increase, as it had under the PNP govern-
ent, but export agriculture continued to decline. The
omentum of economic activity increased at a faster pace
n the second half of the year as foreign exchange
vailability improved, lines of credit became more
vailable, and private overseas credit was cautiously
estored to importers. These partial indicators of
conomic recovery followed inevitably from the increased
upply of foreign exchange due to the loan program of the
ew government.

The change of administrations raised the confidence
f the Jamaican bourgeoisie, who applauded the takeover
f the government by a prime minister who unapologeti-
ally endorsed a capitalist ideology and treated the task
f public management as if it were a business venture in
hich profitability, sound fiscal management, and effi-
iency were major goals in public-sector activities. A
urvey carried out by the author among business executives in 252 companies between August and September 1981
learly reflected the optimism with which private-sector
interests responded to the change of government. Sixty-
seven percent of the executives interviewed expressed
intentions to expand business activities, subject, of
course, to the availability of foreign exchange. Ninety
percent expressed overall support for the policy directions being pursued by the government. Foreign exchange

availability was seen as the major problem. Although
much more was now available compared to 1980, the changed
business climate and the start-up of new areas of
economic activity increased the demand for foreign
exchange over and above the increased supply. Seventy-
four percent of these executives, therefore, complained
about the inadequacy of foreign exchange as being the
major obstacle to business expansion and their plans for
raising output and employment.

With increased overseas borrowing and especially
more loans from the United States, the Seaga government
quickly secured large increases in imported food and
basic consumer items, thereby removing the persistent
problem of consumer shortages. U.S. PL480 food aid
doubled between 1980 and 1982. Empty shelves in rural
shops and supermarkets filled. The estimated 50 percent
of rural retail and wholesale shops that had closed due
to shortages during the PNP years now reopened as
supplies of consumer goods virtually doubled in volume
and variety between 1980 and 1981.

These increased supplies of consumer goods had two
quite divergent effects on the economy. First, there was
a dramatic fall in food prices as imported food items
competed with locally produced food and bid down the
price of the latter below the overall inflation level.
(In contrast, during the PNP years local food prices
increased at a faster rate than the overall price index.
The balancing of supply with demand by means of this
import policy enabled the JLP to bring down inflation
from 27 to 5 percent, thereby achieving a remarkable
stabilization of prices in the economy and the lowest
level of inflation in Jamaica since 1973.

The other effect was a decline in the income flow to
domestic food producers, since they had to cut prices as
sales dropped and competition from food imports
increased. Urban consumers with this cheap food policy
benefitted at the expense of small farmers. Of course,
the long- or medium-term effect might be an undesirable
decline in local food production by small farmers who
might not be able to shift output to overseas markets.
In the short run, these rural petty commodity producers
have been rendered worse off by JLP policies.

On the other hand, the JLP has been able to
stabilize basic goods prices in urban areas, pacifying
the militancy of unionized workers whose strike levels
doubled during the Manley years. With a lower level of
inflation, the new government has been able to abandon
wage guidelines and induce public-sector workers to
accept modest annual pay increases (15 percent as a
trade-off for no lay-offs). With a few exceptions,
annual wage settlements in the private sector have also
fallen within a 20 to 30 percent limit, although there
are no wage guidelines and workers had experienced a huge

O percent decline in real purchasing power in the 1970s. he number of work stoppages in 1981 approached that in 980, and strikes continue to occur in strategic ndustries such as cement, electricity, and mining. In 981, for the first time in four years, wage increases xceeded the rise in the cost of living, producing a 9 ercent growth in real consumption levels. By spurring n consumer goods supplies and holding down inflation, he government has been able to stabilize production osts by inducing short-run voluntary restraints on wage nd salary increases. This cost stabilization is, of ourse, vital to Seaga's policy of promoting greater ompetitiveness in exports and attracting foreign invest- ent through the inducement of cheaper labor costs ompared to competing North American or Puerto Rican abor markets.

Between mid-1981 and the first quarter of 1982, owever, the incidence of strikes reescalated to 1980 evels, ending a six-month lull in the intensity of ndustrial conflict. To facilitate the availability of ncreased supplies of both producer and consumer goods nd to achieve a lowering of state control over the rivate sector, the JLP extended the granting of import icenses not funded through explicit lines of credit. hese "no funds" licenses were intended to draw on the oreign exchange available on the unofficial parallel urrency market. During the PNP years, this "grey" arket had been subjected to extreme pressures from the overnment's financial intelligence unit, which brought any businessmen before the courts for illegal currency ransactions. The parallel market was financed mainly hrough the Jamaica-U.S. drug trade in marijuana, which ad developed in the 1970s as a major sector of cash and oreign exchange earnings. The JLP legitimized the arket without changing the currency laws, thus opening ccess to foreign exchange by encouraging importers to se the parallel market to finance imports.

Two major problems developed. Vigilant anti-drug strategies by the Reagan administration in the Florida area and a decline in the price of marijuana coming into the United States from Colombia led to increased domestic output of marijuana in the United States, cutting U.S. trade and dollar earnings by Jamaican traders and growers. Secondly, the excess demand for foreign exchange that was underestimated in the allocation of no-funds licenses bid up the price of U.S. dollars on the parallel market well above the official exchange rate. In the competition for parallel market dollars, merchants outbid manufacturers due to their higher profit margins, larger supplies of cash, and faster turnover of profits. Fortunately, the parallel market represents only 15 percent of import financing. Pressure for both consumer and producer goods imports served to aggravate the balance-of-payments problem in the short run, due to the time required to establish an increased capacity to export. The problem should resolve itself if the export strategies develop momentum.

The short-run balance of payments problem was compounded by the decline in the U.S. demand for aluminum during the recession of 1981-82. This meant that bauxite, the major foreign exchange earner, would be unable to provide any increased foreign exchange earnings to assist the export drive, which could be viable only if total foreign exchange earnings expanded sufficiently. Indeed, due to the U.S. recession and the cutback in North American aluminum production, the bauxite multi-nationals operating in Jamaica were planning for a drastic cut in production. The impact on revenue and foreign exchange earnings would have been catastrophic and was only averted by the Reagan administration's decision to stockpile 1.6 million metric tons of bauxite as a temporary stopgap measure until the market improved. Tourist arrivals for the 1981-82 winter season showed a 25 percent increase over the previous year, but the net foreign exchange inflows were not likely to increase by more than 10 percent. With export agriculture on the decline, the balance of payments will remain a big problem until new industries and areas of production are opened up and existing dollar earners expand to increase the revenue side of the foreign exchange budget. Large inflows of private foreign investment will be necessary to facilitate any such development, and there is a great deal of uncertainty about how much long-term capital inflow will be attracted by the JLP's attempts to induce private foreign investment.

Trading on the favorable image projected by his government's enthusiastic support by the Reagan adminis-tration, Seaga set up a joint U.S.-Jamaica promotional committee to attract foreign investment. The committee is chaired jointly by David Rockefeller of Chase Manhattan Bank and prominent Jamaican businessman Carlton Alexander. Between January and June 1981, 217 foreign investment projects and 135 local projects were submitted for feasibility studies. Up to March 1982, the list of prospective foreign projects had grown to 300, with a potential capital inflow of U.S. $600 million. At least a third of these projects are planned for implementation during 1982. If most come to fruition, there should be a modest increase in job creation, mainly in manufacturing, construction, and agriculture.

To date, unemployment remains as high as it was in the final years of the Manley government, and any major initiative to reduce this unemployment will have to await long-term growth in investment activity, which seems most unlikely to unfold on a large scale. The labor force has a high propensity for increasing employment by small-

scale, self-employment activity providing services to
wage and salary earners. For every job that might be
created in the formal sector, indirect employment in the
petty commodity sector will also increase. A vital part
of the JLP's economic recovery strategy therefore turns
on the question of how many jobs can be created through
the multiplier effect of new investment activity and the
corresponding effect on expanding petty-commodity self-
employment as real purchasing power expands within the
aggregate labor force. If the initial momentum of
investment activity is strong enough over the 1982-83
period, a positive effect on job creation will occur. If
the impact is not great enough to create a significant
number of new jobs by direct formal employment in the
range of 30,000 to 40,000 per year, the JLP's entire
economic strategy will be vulnerable to serious attack by
the opposition. At present, investment trends do not
excite optimism toward a major employment effect.

Indications are that the Seaga private investment
program, developed to make Jamaica a major recipient of
U.S. investment, is not likely to succeed. A survey of
key American business leaders conducted by the Washington
Letter on the Caribbean identified Jamaica as the most
highly rated area for U.S. foreign investment in the
region. The Caribbean Basin Initiative announced by
President Reagan offers trade and investment incentives,
which should maximize the flow of such investments. But
the impact will be constrained by fear of militant trade
unions, the country's uncertain political future, and
limited interest in long-term investments.

The JLP has not been able to dismantle the
infrastructure of state regulation of the economy. The
continued shortage of foreign exchange makes licensing of
imports necessary to ration what is available to priority
areas. After the large increase in consumer goods
experienced in the upturn of import levels in 1981, a
decision has been taken to limit further increases in
consumer goods imports and to allocate additional foreign
exchange inflows entirely to capital goods and raw
materials.

The JLP relaxed controls over rents with the result
that middle- and lower-middle income housing prices and
rents (repressed during the PNP era) escalated between
50 and 200 percent. As a result, the government decided
to roll back rentals to pre-election levels in order to
control the impact of the cost of living. The machinery,
however, has yet to be put in place.

In spite of pre-election attacks on the State
Trading Corporation, it continues to function. Indeed,
the JLP leadership has come to recognize its importance
as an efficient bulk buyer of basic food items able to
pass on lower prices to consumers. Pragmatism has
prevailed over ideology, indicating that a degree of

flexibility remains in spite of the ideological polarization of the two political parties.

Divestment of government-owned enterprises was set in motion, but in most cases leasehold rather than sale is being used as a means of passing these enterprises from government to private management. Divestment is not as rapid as was anticipated, with the exception of hotels and a few other commercially viable enterprises. Some of the public enterprises that the government wants to transfer to private management are not likely to be viable and hence are unlikely to be sold successfully.

The government has tightened up on public management by emphasizing the need for public enterprises to be more financially viable and by attempting to be more efficient in tax collection and control of public spending. Compared to the taxes collected in the first three quarters of 1980, when the PNP was in power, the JLP achieved an 18 percent increase in the comparable period for 1981. Sales taxes increased by 44 percent and income taxation by 28 percent, whereas customs duties rose by 40 percent. Greater momentum of business activity combined with more efficient tax collection helped narrow the budget deficit. The JLP expects to completely eliminate that deficit by 1983-84, by means of a combination of wage restraint and control of recurrent costs. Preliminary figures up to June 1981 indicate that it is being lowered even more quickly than projected. Between April and June, an anticipated $80 million deficit on the recurrent account was reduced to $16 million. These gains, however, are threatened by the likely fall in revenue due to the declining demand for aluminum.

The JLP's policies revolve around an attempt to shift the economy from import substitution toward an export orientation combined with an openly competitive flow of import trade. Local entrepreneurs accustomed to operating within protected markets are reluctant to support the policy, and some are hostile. An open economy appears not to be feasible given the continuing shortage of foreign exchange. The necessary entrepreneurial dynamism needed to expand exports does not exist within the local private sector, and foreign investors are unlikely to fill the void.

The JLP government has achieved the important first steps of stabilizing prices, restraining wages, reducing the budget deficit, and providing incentives for investment. These policies need a climate of greater public understanding to give the government more time to manage the structural changes in the economy. If the momentum of economic activity increases, the problem will eventually take care of itself, but the JLP has failed so far to convince either the private sector or the public that its open economy policies can work and thereby offer real solutions to deep-seated economic and social problems.

The big question is whether the JLP can earn enough credibility for its free-market policies to ride out the dislocations that will inevitably occur in the effort to move the economy toward that objective. A second issue concerns the degree to which visible signs of economic progress can become sufficiently evident before the next election to generate hope in an electorate that was demoralized by the economic failures of the PNP's second term. This issue turns on whether the long-term time-table for reconstruction can show adequate results within the shorter five-year span between elections to win mass support in a context of continuing economic hardships. That support will be critical to giving the JLP enough time to carry out the economic task that has been set. Political support and credibility have been diminishing rapidly as the new policies have failed to increase employment or significantly expand production.

Important political shifts followed the change of government. The JLP broke diplomatic ties with Cuba, as Cold War hostilities in the region intensified. Jamaica has moved from a Cuban ally under Manley to a militant and active supporter of the U.S. anti-communist crusade. Its political style has also changed. An emphasis on populism and political mobilization has given way to a stress on technocratic efficiency. The pursuit of long-run economic goals that enhance recovery has been substituted for populist ideological posturing that sought to maximize short-run popularity, often at the expense of rational economic policies.

The JLP has set its sights on trying to remove the legacy of the Manley years, that is, the socialist strategies and infrastructure of state economic management. Given the long-term nature of the necessary structural changes and the clear need for the state to engineer and guide the process, this author feels that what the JLP is likely to leave behind, after it loses power sometime in the future, is not a return to the low level of state economic intervention of the 1960s but continued medium levels of intervention, combined with a state capitalist system in which the government uses its economic power to aid capital accumulation, rather than socialist redistribution as attempted by the PNP under Manley. Free enterprise might have been the objective, but state capitalism is likely to be the result, as the long-term nature of the country's economic problems will continue to require state leadership and intervention.

PUBLIC OPINION REACTIONS TO THE JLP

Based on data drawn from this author's quarterly polls, a profile of public opinion responses will now be presented as an indication of how the Jamaican electorate

412

viewed the policies charted by the JLP in its first year
in office.

For obvious reasons, stabilization policies that
attempt to restructure an economy from inward-looking
import-substitution strategies to an outward-looking
export orientation invariably produce great political
stress. It has been argued that in the Latin American
context militarism is a necessary and probable development in this transition because of the political
instability that is generated. In the Jamaican case,
these stresses have been combined with the trauma of a
reversal of dominant ideological trends in the society,
which has destroyed the integrative force of political
consensus that enhances stability. The degree to which
stability has been achieved in the first year of the
transition reflects important features of the political
culture, features that are mirrored in the following
public reactions to the new policies and ideological
initiatives of the JLP.

My public opinion polls conducted between October
1980 and December 1981 indicate that among voters
expressing preference for one or the other of the two
parties, the JLP's popular support fell from 59 to 55
percent and the PNP's standing increased from 41 to 45
percent. Only 1 percent of the latter's total reflects
radical leftists who support the tiny pro-Moscow and
pro-Cuban communist party. The trend shows that support

TABLE 11.8

Political Opinion Trends, 1980-81

	Percent JLP	Percent PNP	Percent Uncommitted
October 1980	50	37	13
January 1981	46	29	25
May 1981	48	22	30
July 1981	36	32	31
November 1981	41	35	24
December 1981	41	34	25

Source: Survey research done by the author. Sample size
ranges from 944 and 2,000 respondents.

for the JLP stabilized between October 1980 and mid-1981 and declined thereafter.

The drop in JLP support is based on a growing anxiety among sections of the electorate over the fact that economic hardships have not been significantly eased by the new government. Voters complained about restricted purchasing power, unemployment, high rentals in middle income areas, and continued high prices. On the other hand, 59 percent of those interviewed in the November 1981 poll expressed the view that conditions would be worse if the PNP had won the election. Clearly, in spite of some disillusionment with the short-run effects of stabilization and the relatively slow return to economic recovery, the JLP is seen as the party best equipped to lead Jamaica toward economic recovery. Table 11.9 gives a detailed breakdown of responses to the question of whether conditions would be better were the PNP still in power. It is significant that less than half of the PNP supporters think that conditions would be better under a PNP government and that 56 percent of the independents believe that things would be worse were the PNP in power. Opinions are obviously influenced by strong partisan loyalties, but the JLP has clearly developed an image of being the superior of the two parties in economic and public management.

Note that the areas of policy support center on economic initiatives and administrative efficiency, whereas political and ideological factors are not emphasized (as was the case with similar polls done while the PNP was in power). Clearly, the mood of the country has shifted from populist expectations for radical change to a more pragmatic view of what the country needs and an increased respect for technocratic skills and competence in public management.

Two quite contrary images of the two parties emerged from poll findings over this period. The PNP and Manley are seen as champions of the poor but lacking the competence either to govern effectively or to provide sound economic policies. The JLP and Seaga, on the other hand, are perceived as preoccupied with capitalism and relatively weak regarding commitment to social justice but also as efficient managers who provide hope of economic recovery and good government from which voters will reap benefits in the medium and long runs. Those who dislike JLP policies tend to see the party as having sold out the interests of the poor in favor of the rich and affluent minorities. Future shifts in the overall balance between these conflicting opinions will depend on the momentum and magnitude of the economic upturn induced by JLP initiatives. More so than the PNP in the 1970s, the JLP must show economic progress in order to maintain credibility with voters, given the image of the party and its assumed technocratic competence.

TABLE 11.9

Opinions on Whether Conditions Would Be Better or Worse Had the PNP Won the 1980 Election (in Percentages)

Group	Worse	Same	Better	No Opinion
National Opinion	59	21	17	3
JLP Supporters	90	8	0	2
PNP Supporters	18	33	45	4
Independents	56	33	7	4

Source: Survey research done by the author. N = 1,040.

TABLE 11.10

Reactions to JLP Policies in Urban and Rural Parishes (in Percentages)

Kingston		Other Parishes	
Liking JLP Policies	(49)	Liking JLP Policies	(52)
Increased Food	13	Increased Food	14
General Economic Policies	12	Jobs Created	9
Cleaning Up City	5	General Economic Policies	4
Foreign Investment	4	Foreign Investment	4
Jobs Created	4	Foreign Policy	4
Stable Prices	2	Cleaning Streets	3
Reducing Crime	2	Agricultural Policies	2
Efficiency	2	Reducing Crime	2
Good Government	5	Stabilizing Prices	2
		Good Government	10

Source: Survey research done by the author. N = 1,040.

Reactions were also obtained with respect to
specific JLP policies, such as the closing of cooperatives established by the PNP on three of the largest
sugar estates, the diplomatic break with Cuba, IMF
borrowing, close ties with the Reagan administration,
U.S. economic aid, and foreign investment. My January
1981 poll found that 85 percent of the Jamaican public
favored the close Reagan-Seaga friendship, mainly out of
the hope that it would bring increased economic
assistance. Though Manley consistently criticizes U.S.
policies, the majority of PNP supporters see the United
States as a friendly country likely to give important
economic aid. When asked which countries were likely to
give Jamaica the most economic assistance, JLP
supporters, PNP supporters, and independents gave the
answers listed in Table 11.11, indicating the high
expectation and approval of U.S. aid by all political
constituencies.

My July 1981 poll found that 78 percent of the
public endorsed Reagan's plan to aid Caribbean countries
as part of his government's fight against communism and
for democracy. Eighty-one percent felt that Jamaica
should accept aid, while only 12 percent disagreed. The
December survey established that over 90 percent of the
electorate had no objection to foreign investment that
created jobs, while the January poll reported majority
support (53 percent) and minority opposition (19 percent)
to the JLP reopening of IMF borrowing.

Public opinion divided evenly on the JLP closure of
the sugar cooperatives due to their indebtedness and poor
financial and production management. The balance of
opinion was against the diplomatic break with Cuba, with
48 percent disagreeing and 41 percent supporting, due to

TABLE 11.11

Countries Seen as Most Likely to Help Jamaica,
December 1981 (Percentage Mentioning Countries)

	U.S.	UK	Canada	Cuba	Venezuela	West Germany	USSR
JLP Supporters	95	17	38	0	10	4	1
PNP Supporters	81	10	37	14	8	2	4
Independents	88	15	29	8	6	1	3

Source: Survey research done by the author. N = 1,500.

the feeling that the reasons given were not convincing.
Clearly, pragmatism was prevailing over ideological
crusading. In spite of the electorate's anti-communist
tendencies, critical evaluations were being applied to
the government's break in relations with Cuba over allegations of the latter's providing a haven for PNP gunmen.
    The November poll revealed that 53 percent of the
electorate felt that the economy had begun to show
positive signs of recovery, while 40 percent disagreed.
The breakdown of responses, as shown in Table 11.12,
indicates the extent to which these opinions were
influenced by partisan feelings. Significantly, independents were divided on the issue, with a small plurality
leaning toward optimism.
    In spite of the continued economic hardships
confronting the majority classes and the drop in popular
support experienced over the first year after the 1980
election, the polls all show significant support for the
JLP's economic policies and a positive rating of its
capability to undertake the difficult task of economic
reconstruction.

CONCLUSION

    The change of government in Jamaica in 1980 set in
motion profound changes in both policy and ideological
directions. Socialist political and economic strategies
have been replaced by capitalist strategies that are
seeking to address concrete economic problems as well as
to turn the political economy toward a more conservative
direction. These changes have brought together an
alliance of interests around the new JLP government that
includes the Reagan administration, the IMF, the World

TABLE 11.12

Views on Whether the Economy is Recovering,
November 1981 (In Percentages)

	Economy Recovering	Economy Not Recovering	No Opinion
JLP Supporters	88	10	2
PNP Supporters	16	79	5
Independents	39	34	27

Source: Survey research done by the author. N = 1,040.

Bank, western capitalist donor countries, and the local
Jamaican bourgeoisie. Jamaicans are seeking solutions to
economic stagnation and decline, and the essential
pragmatism that prevails within the electorate has given
the new capitalist approach a chance to show results in
areas where the previous administration failed. External
interests are backing the effort to find a model of
successful capitalist transformation as part of the
global offensive against communist and anti-capitalist
approaches to economic management. How far the JLP
effort succeeds will greatly influence the credibility of
capitalism as a development model in the region. The
tendency for some commentators to evaluate the government
entirely in terms of its ideology diverts attention from
the fundamental task of economic reconstruction that is
being attempted in the effort to move the economy from
import substitution to export orientation. If this
effort succeeds, it will write a new chapter in regional
development strategies and redefine the agenda of
political discussion away from ideology and toward
economic management.

The inherent pragmatism of the Jamaican political
culture has permitted a drastic change in ideological
direction to take place within the framework of
parliamentary politics and against a background of
increasing political stability. To that extent, Jamaica
stands in sharp contrast to Central and South America,
where similar changes in ideological direction are
invariably accompanied by internal war, military coups,
and systemic change.

The JLP will encounter serious problems in its
effort to induce economic recovery through a stabilization and export-orientation strategy. Massive public-
sector aid and foreign borrowing have become necessary,
and this addition to the existing debt will drastically
reduce the proportion of export earnings available for
buying imports. The local private sector is suspicious
of foreign capital and fears a foreign takeover of the
economy. It is even more intimidated by the prospect of
losing its market share to imported consumer goods, a
possible consequence of the JLP's free-market strategy.

The government's plan to develop foreign investment
around the current abundance of cheap labor may be on a
collision course with militant trade unions. Such a
strategy will lead to more jobs, but it may also stimulate wage demands that go beyond the bounds of a cheap-
labor view of wages. Pressures from the IMF, the World
Bank, and the United States to open up the economy will
conflict with counterpressures from domestic capitalist
interests to slow down the process and maintain some
protectionist elements. The entire recovery effort could
be jeopardized if interest rates remain high in the
United States and the U.S. post-recession recovery is not

large enough or fast enough to boost investments in
Jamaican export production to the North American market.
The demand for aluminum remains a big problem, affected
by the recession, the high level of aluminum recycling in
the United States, and the collapse of the U.S. automo-
bile industry, as well as by efforts to substitute other
materials for that high-priced product. Washington's
support for Seaga has set in motion further negotiations
for additional U.S. bauxite purchases as part of a stock-
piling program designed to bail out a Jamaican economy
that will surely collapse if industrial earnings fall
significantly below existing levels.

The JLP's tight money policy is hurting small
business and restricting consumer demand for local food
and other production. It limits consumer demand even
below levels that could easily be absorbed by increased
domestic food output. This will diminish the government's credibility with lower-income voters, who are
rapidly growing restive over the lack of improvements in
their living standards. Unemployment remains high, and
although private-sector investment will help, what these
people truly need is a major building program of housing
and physical infrastructure, financed by the state. Such
an initiative, however, would be contrary to the JLP's
objective of scaling down government expenditures.

The major areas in which Jamaica has a comparative
advantage with respect to trade with the United States
lie in agricultural, agro-industrial, and horticultural
products. A substantial capital inflow and infrastructural investment in areas such as irrigation will be
necessary to realize this potential fully. At best, this
is a long-run possibility not likely to bring dramatic
results within the short-run timetable of election
cycles.

Foreign capitalists, while interested in Jamaican
investments, are reluctant to bring large amounts of hard
currency into the economy because of the continuing
uncertainty of future political directions, high interest
rates available in the United States, and the tendency to
cut risks by borrowing local funds for investment
purposes. To date there is no clear indication as to
how much hard currency will accompany the various foreign
investment projects. Such inflows are vital to ease the
foreign exchange cash flow constraint that will be aggravated by an increasing debt burden.

If JLP economic policies falter or fail to move
faster than they did in the first year in office in terms
of visible benefits to the majority classes, the party
may well have difficulty being reelected next time at the
polls. On the other hand, if its private-sector policies
show some success, they are not likely to be reversed by
a successor PNP government. Present indications are that
when the PNP returns to power its domestic policies are

likely to move back toward the center, although its
foreign policy is unlikely to change. Such a development
would reduce policy dislocations attending a change of
government. In any event, all these changes will be
taking place within the framework of a firm national
commitment to electoral democracy, which is inherently at
variance with the PNP's earlier goal of a noncapitalist
path (an objective that is not likely to be resurrected
with the party's return to power). More importantly,
with the massive exodus of refugees from Cuba signalling
deep problems in that economy, with the admission of the
government in Guyana that it is bankrupt, and with the
mounting economic problems developing in Grenada and
Nicaragua, the attractiveness of socialism as an alternative to capitalist economic management is being
increasingly questioned in Jamaica and the wider
Caribbean.

Socialism has developed a popular political program
of extending power to the people and redistributing
income and assets. However, outside of the communist
states with command economies, socialism is in deep
crisis because of its failure to chart a parallel set of
economic policies that either work or offer a better path
than alternative approaches toward economic development
in the Third World. That fact underlies the decline of
socialism in Jamaica in the early 1980s and represents
another phase in the ongoing dialectical conflict between
competing socialist and capitalist ideological
tendencies.

NOTES

1. See R. Ulyanovsky, Socialism and the Newly
Independent Nations (Moscow: Progress Publishers, 1974).
2. See Carl Stone, Jamaica at the Polls: The
Parliamentary Election of October 1980 (Washington, D.C.:
American Enterprise Institute, forthcoming); and
"Jamaica's 1980 Elections," Caribbean Review, 10, 2
(Spring 1981).

Part 3

The International
Dimensions of the Crisis

12
Mexican Policy Toward
Central America and the Caribbean

Dennis M. Hanratty

One of the most significant aspects of the current
Central American and Caribbean crisis has been the high
profile of the Mexican government. Whether one is
focusing on the protracted conflict in El Salvador,
tension between Nicaragua and its Central American neighbors, or the charges and countercharges flying between
Washington and Havana, there is a well-defined and highly
publicized Mexican position on the subject. For better
or worse, Mexico is a key player in the contemporary
politics of the region.

In a number of cases, the Mexican government has
taken positions that many in the United States have found
disconcerting. Such behavior has often been perceived as
counterproductive to vital American interests and has
caused some observers to question Mexico's sympathies.
Indeed, many here see Mexico as a defender of the most
radical elements in the area.

This chapter is an effort to explain current Mexican
policies. At the same time, it is impossible to
understand contemporary actions without an appreciation
of the more general contours of Mexican foreign policy,
particularly insofar as they relate to Latin America.
Accordingly, these contours will be discussed, along with
certain changes instituted by the Echeverria administration (1970-76), changes that have a significant bearing
on current behavior. In the process, I will also seek to
delineate perceptual and strategic differences between
Mexico and the United States. Given the critical
importance of bilateral relations between the two
countries, one must speculate about the effect of those
disagreements. Can Mexico and the United States reconcile their divergent views? Or will their differences
seriously erode the relationship between them?

CRITICAL DETERMINANTS IN THE FORMULATION OF
MEXICAN FOREIGN POLICY

Crucial to an understanding of Mexican policy is a
recognition of the extent to which it has been shaped by
historical developments. From independence in 1821
through the second decade of the twentieth century,
Mexican governments faced the continual prospect of
foreign intervention, through either military or more
subtle machinations. That tumultuous period witnessed
the 1838 French invasion in the so-called Pastry War; the
Mexican-American War of 1846-48, resulting in the loss of
half of the national territory; the landing of French,
British, and Spanish troops in 1861 and the subsequent
installation of Maximillian of Hapsburg as Second Emperor
of Mexico; the American conquest of the Mexican economy
during the regime of Porfirio Diaz; the duplicity of U.S.
Ambassador Henry Lane Wilson, in 1913, which contributed
to the overthrow and assassination of Mexico's president
and vice-president; and the occupation of Veracruz the
following year by American forces.
Given the extent to which the United States
dominated critical sectors of the economy at the time of
the Mexican Revolution, the latter's goals would
inevitably conflict with American interests. Constitutional provisions placing ownership of land and the
natural resources beneath that land in the Mexican nation
rather than with the individual proprietor, as was the
case during the Porfiriato, significantly impacted on
foreign investments. The same was true for the
revolution's emphasis on agrarian reform and the rights
of industrial workers.
In an effort to defend these measures from external
attack, Mexican policymakers sought refuge in principles
of international law stressing nonintervention and
respect for national sovereignty. These principles were
articulated in 1918 by President Venustiano Carranza in a
speech before the Mexican Congress:

> The guiding ideas of the international policy of
> Mexico are few, clear and simple. They are reduced
> to the following proclamation:
> That all nations are equal; nations must mutually
> and scrupulously respect each other's institutions,
> laws and sovereignty;
> That no nation should intervene in any form and for
> any reason in the internal affairs of another
> nation. All nations must comply strictly and
> without exceptions to the universal principle of
> nonintervention; That no foreigner should attempt to
> obtain a better situation than that experienced by
> the citizens of the country, nor should he use his
> foreign status as a title of protection and

privilege. Nationals and foreigners should be equal
before the sovereignty of the country in which they
are located.[1]

Mexican policy thus took on a decidedly defensive
character, designed to limit the intrusion of the United
States into the country's internal affairs. Reliance on
the principles of nonintervention and self-determination
served as an important shield in the effort to survive as
a sovereign nation.

Mexico's noninterventionist attitude was clearly
evident in 1930 when Foreign Minister Genaro Estrada
issued the "Estrada Doctrine." Under this policy, the
government announced that it would cease to make any
judgmental pronouncements regarding new regimes emerging
in states that had already been recognized. In such
situations, Mexican actions would be limited to the
maintenance or withdrawal of diplomatic personnel. In
the government's view, any public judgment as to the
legitimacy or illegitimacy of a new regime would
constitute an intolerable intrusion in the sovereign
affairs of that nation.

The threat of direct American military intervention
declined markedly under the administration of Franklin
Roosevelt. The weakened state of the U.S. economy,
coupled with the American need to be secure on its
southern border against Nazi intervention, permitted
Mexico to engage in actions that might have been
impossible in earlier periods. The clearest expression
of this increased flexibility was, of course, the
decision of President Lazaro Cardenas in 1938 to
expropriate American oil holdings. Yet even as the
United States renounced intentions of intervening
unilaterally in the affairs of its neighbors, the clear
message was that Latin Americans now assumed a collective
responsibility for hemispheric security. Thus, with the
decline of unilateral intervention, the possibility of
joint intervention emerged. Consequently, a fundamental
goal of Mexican policy became the prevention of the
United States from using hemispheric accords to legitimate such interference.

Actually, Mexico was a strong supporter of the
Panamerican concept in the 1940s and endorsed the
creation of the Organization of American States (OAS)
after World War II. At that time, the OAS was envisaged
as a focal point of regional economic development.
During the early 1950s, however, the Mexican attitude
soured when it saw that body being used as an extension
of American foreign policy. In 1954, the OAS approved
the "Declaration of Caracas" authorizing the use of
collective action against a member whose institutions had
allegedly fallen under the control of international
communism. That statement, of course, was primarily an

426

effort to justify covert operations against the
Guatemalan regime of Jacobo Arbenz. The Mexican government refused to endorse the action, contending that it
violated fundamental principles of international law.
Subsequent administrations have tended to remain at the
margin of OAS activities, opposing efforts to expand the
organization's functions and generally attempting to
limit its use of collective action.

Mexican governments have usually employed a
juridical language in their opposition to OAS activities.
In essence, they have argued that as a regional organization, the OAS must operate in accordance with the
statutory provisions of the United Nations Charter. In
their view, the Charter gives primary responsibility to
the Security Council for the maintenance of peace and
thus places limits on the use of force by regional
bodies. In addition, Mexicans have argued on behalf of a
narrow reading of Article 3 of the Rio Treaty, which
states that an armed attack against one member state is
an armed attack against all, thus committing members to
exercise legitimate collective defense. Their view is
that "armed attack" must mean an action that directly and
substantively threatens the sovereignty of a member and
should not be widened to justify collective action for
other reasons.

The principles of nonintervention, respect for
national sovereignty, and the right of each nation to
determine its own affairs have come to assume an almost
sacrosanct character in Mexican foreign policy. Even
when a Mexican government is engaged in actions that
appear to violate these principles, it must simultaneously couch its actions within them. Thus, the
principles place very real limitations on the range of
acceptable positions that can be taken.

Here is a paradox: On the one hand, adherence to
these principles contribute to a defensive and reactive
attitude among Mexican policymakers. At the same time,
however, the Mexican revolutionary experience virtually
propels governments into assuming an activist, nationalist stance designed to demonstrate their independence
from the United States. Ironically, the need for such a
posture has increased in recent decades as Mexico's own
revolutionary character has faded.

Observers of Mexican politics have noted a certain
hardening of the arteries on the part of the dominant
Institutional Revolutionary Party. Since 1940,
successive governments have generally pursued conservative social policies, hardly calculated to redistribute
national wealth. Indeed, the past four decades have seen
a decline in support for the communal ejido system of
land ownership and an increasing concentration of land.
Government-controlled workers' and peasants' unions have
usually been ineffective spokesmen for their constituents.

Rural inequities and a tremendous pressure for land have
resulted in a continual exodus of peasants to the large
cities. Unable to find either employment or suitable
housing in urban centers that are already bursting at the
seams, these migrants become **paracaidistas**, squatters in
large shanty settlements in the least desirable outskirts
of the cities. Overall, the picture since the end of the
Cardenas administration is one of increasing deterioration in the distribution of income.

These domestic policies have left recent Mexican
administrations susceptible to charges that they have
abandoned the goals of the Revolution. Such claims place
the government on the defensive, given both the profound
impact of the Revolution on the Mexican psyche and the
regime's claim to be the legitimate heir of Madero,
Zapata, and Cardenas. It is not at all unusual,
therefore, for the government to respond to left-wing
accusations with some dramatic foreign policy gesture
that seeks to demonstrate its independent and nationalist
character. Such a move not only serves to link the
administration with past glories, but it also provides an
opportunity to rally the party faithful.

In effect, these acts of independence, both symbolic
and substantive, have created certain expectations with
regard to foreign policy. Domestic opinion has become
accustomed to Mexico's somewhat independent stance vis-a-
vis the United States. It is unlikely that a substantive
change would readily be accepted by the public. The
cumulative effect of earlier positions limits the degree
to which any president can be identified with North
American interests.

Yet, despite Mexico's effort to maintain an
independent posture, it cannot escape the realities of
geography. Relations with the United States remain the
cornerstone of foreign policy. Even allowing for the
increased leverage that Mexico has gained through recent
discoveries of petroleum and natural gas, the relationship between the two nations is a distinctly asymmetrical
one. Although pressures for an independent stance do not
permit Mexican policymakers to acknowledge the importance
of U.S. reactions to Mexican positions, those responses
are carefully considered. Mexico's traditional penchant
for relying on juridical explanations of positions
contrary to American desires can be seen as an effort to
soften negative reactions on the part of the "Colossus of
the North."

MEXICAN POLICY TOWARD CUBA, 1960-64

A detailed discussion of the origins and nature of
Mexico's Cuban policy is beyond the scope of this
chapter. This area has already been analyzed extensively

in two excellent studies.[2]   It is important, however, to
note the basic outlines of that policy in order to grasp
the significance of more recent Mexican behavior.
Clearly, the Cuban experience touched a responsive chord
in the nationalistic revolutionary sentiments of the
Mexican public. This was particularly the case with
leftists, who hoped that the Cuban model would ignite an
independent popular movement in their own country. These
sympathies, in turn, were reinforced by the long-standing
and widespread belief that each nation should have the
right to determine its own destiny. As Fidel Castro
strengthened his ties with the Soviet Union and
proclaimed himself to be a Marxist-Leninist, however,
Mexican leaders became increasingly concerned over both
the direction of his revolution and U.S. perception of
Mexican attitudes toward it. After sending reassuring
signals to a nervous American government, Mexico began to
carve out an independent stance.

Throughout 1959-60, the Mexican left expressed
strong support for Castro. Most significantly, former
President Lazaro Cardenas emerged publicly during this
period to laud the Cuban leader. From the government's
perspective, the most ominous aspect of Cardenas'
behavior was his apparent willingness to assist in the
development of an independent movement of the left.
Faced with this challenge, the administration of Adolfo
Lopez Mateos sought to claim the Cuban revolutionary
mantle for itself by indicating its sympathy for the
Castro regime. Consistent with this effort, the Mexican
government defended Cuba at the August 1960 meeting of
OAS Foreign Ministers in San Jose, Costa Rica. Although
they endorsed the "Declaration of San Jose," which
condemned outside intervention in hemispheric affairs,
Mexican representatives made it very clear that their
action should not be seen as a condemnation of Cuba.

Considering the hallowed status given the principle
of nonintervention, it was to be expected that Mexico
would strongly condemn the Bay of Pigs invasion of April
1961. Indeed, Mexico not only denounced it but introduced a resolution at the United Nations calling upon
member states to prohibit the use of their territories as
staging grounds for incursions against Cuba. In spite of
this stand, however, Lopez Mateos increasingly was
concerned over Cuba's drift into the Soviet camp.
Castro's public embrace of Marxist-Leninism later that
year placed the Mexicans in an untenable position.
Continued expressions of support would have threatened
Mexico's economic relations with the United States.
Mexican private investors were already demanding concrete
action to allay American concerns.

The Lopez administration's position at the January
1962 meeting of OAS Foreign Ministers in Punta del Este,
Uruguay, represented an attempt to satisfy these

divergent pressures. Thus the Mexican delegation, headed
by Foreign Secretary Manuel Tello, supported resolutions
declaring the incompatibility of communism and the
Inter-American system, expelling Cuba from the
Inter-American Defense Board, and creating a special
security committee to investigate communist subversion.[3]
At the same time, however, it abstained on measures to
exclude Havana from the inter-American system and to
impose economic sanctions and an arms embargo.

With both the American government and the Mexican
business community thus satisfied, the Lopez Mateos
administration could once again return to an independent
nationalistic stance. This was most evident at the July
1964 meeting of OAS Foreign Ministers in Washington,
where the Mexican delegation voted against resolutions
denouncing Cuban intervention and requiring members to
break diplomatic, consular, trade, and maritime relations
with Havana. As a final gesture of independence, Mexico
announced that it would not comply with these sanctions.
From the summer of 1964 through November 1970, Mexico
would be the only Latin American nation to maintain
diplomatic relations with Cuba.[4]

FOREIGN POLICY SHIFTS UNDER LUIS ECHEVERRIA

The Mexican government drew immediate domestic
benefits from its repudiation of the OAS Cuban stand. It
was able to demonstrate that despite pressure from the
United States, Mexican foreign policy was not formulated
in Washington. In addition, the regime could once again
bask in the revolutionary sunshine. This was the case as
well in 1965, when the new government of Gustavo Diaz
Ordaz resisted Washington's efforts to create an OAS
Inter-American Peacekeeping Force to legitimize military
intervention in the Dominican Republic.

Although public opinion focused on Mexico's
independent stance at the OAS, bilateral relations
between Mexico and Havana remained correct but cool.
Indeed, government statements of support for the Cuban
Revolution all but ceased by the end of 1961. While
Mexico continued to support publicly the right of the
Cuban people to determine their own destiny, formal
government contacts were virtually limited to the
exchange of diplomatic personnel.

This low level of interaction was consistent with
the traditionally passive nature of Mexican foreign
policy. Although relations with the United States were
critically important and consequently assigned a top
priority, Mexico did not aspire to leadership within the
Latin American community. A leadership role might have
forced it to make judgments about particular Latin

American governments--an anathema to the principles on which its policy was still based.

The administration of Luis Echeverria (1970-76) ushered in a new and more activist perspective. The Echeverria government sought to project itself as a leader in the efforts of Third World nations to restructure their economic relations with the industrialized West. The Mexicans now expanded their level of participation in international bodies, such as the UN Food and Agriculture Organization, and opened new diplomatic missions in various countries. Perhaps most significantly, they went beyond the usual juridical statements at the OAS and took concrete initiatives designed to frustrate U.S. policies in the hemisphere.

The Echeverria government's break with the past can be understood as an effort to respond to serious domestic problems. The new president came to power with a tarnished political reputation. As interior minister under President Diaz Ordaz, he had been intimately involved in the 1968 university student crisis and was therefore held culpable by the left for the Tlateloco massacre.[5] Thus, it was particularly important that he break with the conservative policies of his predecessor and demonstrate a conciliatory attitude toward the left. These decisions became even more critical when, in a replay of Tlateloco, government-supported agitators murdered up to 100 student protesters in Mexico City in June 1971.

Whether Echeverria's foreign maneuvers represented a genuine effort to mobilize the left, as some observers have suggested, or were merely efforts to divert attention from the continuing repression and stagnation of the Mexican system, it is clear that they were primarily intended for domestic consumption. Though the administration intensified Mexico's economic and cultural relations with Cuba, culminating in a presidential visit to Havana, its most dramatic gestures involved the Chilean government of Salvadore Allende.

During the two years preceding the September 1973 Chilean military coup, Echeverria relied on his deepening relationship with Allende to enhance his own progressive image. Invoking the memory of Cardenas' actions against American petroleum companies, the Mexican president visited Santiago in April 1972 and defended Allende's expropriation policy. In a series of significant challenges to American interests, Echeverria ordered the immediate sale of 400,000 barrels of petroleum to Chile at a time when Mexico was a petroleum importer, signed an agreement to sell 100,000 tons of sugar for an amount lower than the world price, and extended the Allende government $72 million in credit.

Perhaps the clearest sign of Mexico's break with the past came with the 1973 coup itself. In a significant departure from the Estrada Doctrine, Echeverria condemned the overthrow of Allende, declared three days of national mourning, and cancelled the annual Independence Day reception. The government also assisted the protest efforts of university students.

THE LOPEZ PORTILLO GOVERNMENT: THE QUEST FOR A CENTRAL AMERICAN AND CARIBBEAN POLICY

Echeverria's actions had a significant impact on the administration of Jose Lopez Portillo. Like his predecessor, Lopez Portillo pursued an activist foreign policy and became a leader in the efforts of developing countries to restructure the international economic order. (Indicative of this approach was Mexico's hosting of the North-South discussions in Cancun in August 1981.) At the same time, this activism was by no means a repudiation of Mexican traditions. Although Echeverria had referred during his administration to the need for new policy concepts, even he had not disavowed the principle of nonintervention. On the contrary, his Chilean policies had been justified on the basis of providing assistance to a nation whose sovereignty had been violated, particularly by the United States. Similarly, the Lopez Portillo government consistently stressed its adherence to those principles.

Though one may be tempted to dismiss such statements as lip service to hallowed but irrelevant concepts, I do not believe this to be the case. Rather, one can identify a certain tension in contemporary Mexican foreign policy as decisionmakers respond to the occasionally conflicting demands of activism and noninterventionism.

Mexican foreign policymaking was certainly an easier task when it was primarily defensive in character. All that was required then was for the government to express indignation at the efforts of some countries to influence events in others. When this indignation was directed at the United States, it satisfied not only the regime's commitment to nonintervention, but also its need to demonstrate a nationalistic and independent attitude. The passive nature of this policy enabled successive administrations to avoid thornier matters, such as human rights violations by various Latin American dictatorships. In opting for a more activist approach, however, Mexico must now express positions that collide head-on with the rigid neutrality of the Estrada Doctrine.

This changing character of foreign policy is most evident in Mexico's actions toward its Central American and Caribbean neighbors. Although Mexico significantly expanded its trade relations with Central America in the 1960s, it rather consistently avoided comment on internal political developments in those countries. When, in 1966, Diaz Ordaz made the first Central American visit of any Mexican president, he emphasized that he would not judge the constitutionality of those governments, since to do so would constitute intervention in the affairs of sovereign states. To the extent that Mexico did comment on political events in the region, it was consistent with the principle of nonintervention. Thus, for example, it traditionally challenged Guatemala's territorial claims to Belize, asserting that the latter's citizens had the right to determine their own destiny. Since 1979, however, Mexico has established a very visible and active presence.

It is no coincidence that this activist posture has come in the wake of vast Mexican oil discoveries. Over the last six years, a series of such finds has catapulted Mexico into the ranks of the petroleum superpowers, with reserves estimated at 250 billion barrels. Lopez Portillo believed that oil offered Mexico an historic opportunity to develop the nation's industrial base. Using petroleum both as an export mechanism and as collateral, Mexico dramatically increased the amount of international credits flowing into the country. Total foreign debt increased from less than $30 billion in 1977 to $85 billion by early 1983.

The discovery of vast petroleum reserves clearly changed Mexico's standing in the international community. The country's prestige skyrocketed; almost overnight, it became a major Third World leader. Equally significant, Mexico moved eagerly to assume the mantle. Lopez Portillo gave his industrial development program the grandiose title of the "Global Development Plan." Appearing before the UN General Assembly in 1979, the Mexican leader outlined a "World Energy Plan" that called for, among other things, the establishment of energy financing and development funds for Third World countries, the creation of an international energy institute, the development of nonconventional sources of energy, and international guarantees that nations will regain full sovereignty over their own natural resources.

The emergence of an activist Mexican foreign policy occurred at precisely the time events were coming to a head in Nicaragua. The Lopez Portillo administration avoided dealing directly with the Nicaraguan civil war until May 1979. In the midst of the increasingly successful Sandinista offensive, however, the president dramatically broke relations with the regime of Anastasio Somoza on May 20th. Although the suspension or rupture of diplomatic relations was not unprecedented in the history of Mexican foreign policy, what distinguished Lopez Portillo's actions from previous behavior was his public pronouncement regarding the character of the Somoza government. In calling on other nations to follow

he Mexican example, the president accused the Nicaraguan
eader of a repugnant attack on basic human rights
hrough genocidal atrocities. In a statement issued
arly the following month, he expanded on these
ccusations: Mexico could not, he declared, remain
ndifferent to a trampling of human rights in another
ountry, particularly when the violation was of an
trocious, deliberate, and systematic nature and was
ither condoned or directed by government leaders. It
as impossible to continue relations with a regime
esponsible for crimes against humanity.[6]

Ever sensitive to the significance of its actions,
he Mexican government continued to stress its adherence
o the fundamental principle of nonintervention. Noting
hat Mexico had always been the most zealous guardian of
hat principle, the president argued that the barbarism
f the Nicaraguan situation was so exceptional that he
as forced to act. The new foreign secretary, Jorge
astaneda, stressed that the Nicaraguan decision did not
epresent a new general policy.

The decision to condemn the internal behavior of
nother regime was a significant departure from the
raditional Mexican stance. In contrast, the adminis-
ration's warnings against outside interference were in a
ime-honored tradition. Having announced its decision
egarding Somoza, the government proceeded to engage in a
oncerted campaign against the introduction of foreign
ilitary forces in Nicaragua.

First, Mexico sought to diffuse Somoza's effort to
btain an investigation by the OAS Inter-American Defense
oard of allegations of Costa Rican assistance to the
andinistas. Secretary Castaneda indicated Mexico's
trong opposition and argued that an investigation of
osta Rican actions would be merely a smokescreen to
ivert attention from Somoza's human rights violations.
his position was somewhat inconsistent with traditional
exican calls for noninterventionism, since the Costa
ican government was, in fact, providing assistance to
he Nicaraguan guerrillas.

In an even more significant move, the administration
layed a major role in blocking U.S. efforts to form an
nter-American Peacekeeping Force. By early June, it had
ecome clear that Somoza's position was a desperate one.
n an effort to forestall a radical solution, Washington
roposed before the OAS that Somoza be replaced with a
rovisional government of national reconciliation and
hat an Inter-American Peacekeeping Force be created to
uarantee its democratic and representative nature. This
aneuver was categorically rejected by Castaneda, who
rgued that it would constitute a serious act of inter-
ention. Maintaining that the people of Nicaragua would
ecide their own destiny without the help of the OAS, the
ecretary declared that "the armed rebellion of the

people is the most genuine expression of the democratic
will of a nation."[7] It was soon evident that most of the
OAS agreed with the Mexicans. Faced with the prospect of
defeat, the United States joined the majority in
supporting a resolution that represented a total victory
for the Castaneda position. Characterizing the Somoza
regime as dictatorial and inhuman, the statement called
for its immediate replacement by a democratic government
reflecting the principal opposition forces, along with
guarantees of human rights, free elections, and respect
for the principle of nonintervention.[8]

Throughout this period, the Mexican government kept
up the pressure for a settlement in accordance with the
OAS resolution. Toward the end of June, Lopez Portillo
again stressed the right of the Nicaraguan people to
determine their own destiny. Characterizing as "grave"
reports that some countries were continuing to sell arms
to Somoza, the administration condemned such practices as
contrary to the OAS resolution. At the same time, it
opposed efforts to permit the participation of Somocista
forces in the formation of the Nicaraguan government.
Subsequently, the collapse of the regime enabled Lopez
Portillo to make a symbolic gesture of great importance
to the Mexican left. On July 19th, the Mexican
presidential plane Quetzalcoatl II was dispatched to San
Jose, Costa Rica, to carry the cabinet of the new
Nicaraguan Government of National Reconstruction to its
triumphant arrival in Managua.

Mexico's active role in the Nicaraguan events of
May-July 1979 signaled the emergence of a much more
forceful Central American and Caribbean policy. The same
year, the Lopez Portillo administration began to
strengthen its relations with Fidel Castro. As noted
earlier, the success of the guerrilla movement in Cuba
had been a significant event for the Mexican left. The
latter had hoped that Castro's victory would spark a
popular mobilization within Mexico itself. Although the
anticipated spark did not occur, Cuba continued to be
viewed by many Mexican leftists as the one Latin American
country where the inequities of the capitalist system had
been swept away.

Given this attraction, a Cuban connection plays a
valuable domestic role. First, Mexico is able to project
itself as a staunch defender of a small nation under
siege by a superpower. This stance not only strengthens
the government's "revolutionary credentials," but also
enables it to assume an independent, nationalistic
position vis-a-vis the United States. In addition,
Mexico's revolutionary image is enhanced by strong
expressions of support by Castro himself. For example,
at a May 1979 meeting with Lopez Portillo at Cozumel,
Mexico, the Cuban leader characterized the Mexican
revolution as a profound social revolution, the signifi-

cance of which separated Mexico and Cuba from all other
Latin American nations. Similarly, the following year,
he lent it further legitimacy by asserting that there
were stylistic differences between the Cuban and Mexican
experiences. The Mexican Revolution, he proclaimed, was
the "common property of all progressive men, of all
revolutionary men." Perhaps most significantly, Castro
noted that both nations had suffered grievously at the
hands of the United States.[9]

To an unprecedented extent for a Mexican president,
Lopez Portillo sought to link himself closely with the
Castro regime. At their Cozumel meeting, the two leaders
issued a joint declaration in which they demanded an end
to the U.S. economic embargo against Cuba, called for a
new international economic order, supported Panamanian
efforts to regain control over the Canal, and reaffirmed
their adherence to nonintervention. On a visit to Havana
in August 1980, Lopez Portillo condemned imperialist
forces that threatened to destroy decolonization and
unity, and declared Mexico's support for national liberation movements as well as for Havana's efforts to regain
Guantanamo naval base. After a meeting with a Cuban
delegation the following February, he declared that the
Caribbean Basin faced a challenge from interventionist
external forces. Mexico and Cuba, he proclaimed, should
stand as examples to other nations in their efforts to
resist such intrusions. Referring to Castro as "my
commander," he called Cuba the Latin American nation for
which Mexico had the greatest affection.[10]

Having broken ties with Somoza and expanded links
with Castro in 1979, Lopez Portillo continued to make his
presence felt the following year with the signing of the
"Program of Energy Cooperation for the Countries of
Central America and the Caribbean." This "San Jose
Agreement," a joint venture of Mexico and Venezuela,
committed the two nations to assist area countries in
meeting their petroleum needs by making available a total
of up to 160,000 barrels of oil on a daily basis and
assisting the financing of such purchases. Participating
nations were to be extended five-year credits for 30
percent of their total petroleum purchases at annual
interest rates of 4 percent. However, should the
petroleum be used to foster significant development
projects, especially in the energy field, credits could
be arranged for up to twenty years at an interest rate of
2 percent. The program was made available without regard
to the nature of the political systems in particular
countries, as could be seen from the list of initial
beneficiaries: Barbados, Costa Rica, El Salvador,
Guatemala, Honduras, Jamaica, Nicaragua, Panama, and the
Dominican Republic. Indeed, appearing in Havana on the
same day as the signing of the agreement, Lopez Portillo
even asserted that Cuba could participate if it so chose.

436

He noted, however, that the Castro government already had
a petroleum agreement with the Soviet Union. Given the
strained relations between Venezuela and Cuba, it is
possible that Lopez Portillo's proposal was not shared by
both sponsors.

It was noted earlier that Mexico played a major role
in frustrating American efforts to form an Inter-American
Force in the waning days of the Somoza government.
Despite this, it was not until the beginning of the
Reagan administration that serious differences over
Central America emerged between the two countries. At
issue was alleged Sandinista assistance to the guerrilla
movement in El Salvador. In one of its first foreign
policy pronouncements, the Reagan administration charged
that Nicaragua had become a staging ground for Salvadoran
guerrillas and a conduit for Cuban supplies and armaments. Washington promptly cut off the aid promised
Nicaragua under the Carter presidency.

The position of the Mexican government was clear and
unequivocal: Efforts by the United States to view the
crisis in Central America within an East-West framework
completely distorted the indigenous roots of the
conflict. As the Mexicans saw it, the struggle in El
Salvador, as well as throughout the region, was based on
decades of repression, inequities in land ownership, high
rates of unemployment and underemployment, and other such
miseries. In addition, Mexico focused on threats to the
Nicaraguan regime from both the United States and groups
financed by the American government. The Lopez Portillo
administration viewed U.S. intervention (either covert or
overt) in Nicaragua as a distinct danger; remnants of the
Somocista National Guard were already carrying out
frequent raids in Nicaragua from bases in Honduras.

In the wake of the American suspension of aid to
Nicaragua, Lopez stepped in to fill some of the gap.
During 1981, Mexico signed agreements to assist Nicaragua
in a series of agricultural projects including irrigation
development, rural training programs, production of seeds
and fertilizers, and investments in basic grain improvements. The Mexicans also agreed to help the Nicaraguans
in their efforts to increase electricity production.
These agreements followed similar efforts in 1979-80,
when the Mexicans set up a joint company with the
Sandinistas to develop Nicaragua's forestry resources,
donated thousands of books to the Nicaraguan educational
system, and promised technical assistance in such areas
as banking, urban development, transportation, public
health, and marketing.

Although Lopez Portillo directly challenged American
interests in Nicaragua, his actions were quite popular at
home, where support for the Sandinistas remained strong.
Furthermore, providing assistance to a beleaguered
government threatened by the United States was entirely

consistent with Mexican political traditions. In contrast, Mexico proceeded rather cautiously in dealing with El Salvador. Despite his image in the United States of being eager to throw himself into the Central American fray, Lopez Portillo initially resisted intense domestic pressures for action.

The assassination of the archbishop of San Salvador, Oscar Romero, on March 24th, 1980, and the bloodbath that occurred at his funeral several days later served as a focal point for the demands of the Mexican left. Thus, for instance, Arnaldo Martinez Verdugo, leader of the Communist Party, charged that responsibility for the massacre rested with the Salvadoran government, which was engaged in a violent offensive against its own people and the Salvadoran clergy who were assisting them. Martinez demanded that the government suspend or cancel commercial agreements, including those involving petroleum, with El Salvador and that it recognize the revolutionary forces as "belligerent elements" in the struggle. Similar demands were made by leaders of the Socialist Workers' Party and the Democratic Party. The left's position was enhanced considerably when the demand for a diplomatic break was endorsed by Sergio Mendez Arceo, bishop of Cuernavaca, and Samuel Ruiz Garcia, bishop of San Cristobal las Casas. The two prelates, who are the left's strongest supporters within the Mexican Episcopate, had attended Romero's funeral and were witnesses to the carnage that followed. Both charged that the Salvadoran right had planned the massacre. Subsequently, Bishop Ruiz led a protest march to the Basilica of Our Lady of Guadalupe in Mexico City. In spite of such pressure, the administration affirmed that Mexico's traditional noninterventionist stance would prevail.

In August 1980, the government was again subjected to intense pressure as a result of the murder in El Salvador of a Mexican journalist. Protests involving reporters, students, and various solidarity groups took place outside the Salvadoran Embassy in Mexico City. Again, demands were made for a break in diplomatic relations and a recognition of the guerrillas' belligerent status. Though the administration continued to resist such pressures, it was clearly not immune from the protests. Castaneda characterized relations with El Salvador as "difficult" and indicated that a rupture would depend on future circumstances. A change in Mexican policy might be forthcoming, he suggested, if the insurgents gained control of some territory, thus permitting them to act as a government.

This relatively cautious approach was indicative of the continued significance of nonintervention as a basic principle of Mexican foreign policy. The government maintained a hands-off policy long after being subjected

to strident demands for a more active role. Lopez
Portillo had repeated opportunities during the course of
the year to engage in a dramatic gesture. That he did
not follow through is a reflection of the long-standing
reluctance of Mexican leaders to become embroiled in the
internal affairs of other nations. At the same time, the
government also demonstrated a certain pragmatism toward
the conflict. Irrespective of any yearnings to
demonstrate its independence from the United States, the
administration felt that it would be more prudent to wait
for future developments.

Throughout 1981, however, the Mexican government
became increasingly concerned over the efforts of the
Reagan administration to force-fit the Salvadoran
struggle into an East-West framework. As a result, on
August 28th, Mexico decisively injected itself into the
conflict through a joint declaration with France.
Although noting that only the Salvadoran people could
attain a real solution to the conflict, the two nations
expressed the fear that the crisis might destabilize the
entire region. They proclaimed, therefore, that the
Farabundo Marti National Liberation Front (FMLN) and the
Democratic Revolutionary Front (FDR) constituted a
"representative political force, disposed to assume the
obligations and exercise the rights that are derived from
that fact." The FMLN and FDR should accordingly be
permitted to take part in negotiations to end the
conflict. The two countries also strongly hinted that
the Salvadoran Armed Forces would have to be restructured
prior to the establishment of a lasting political solution.

The declaration engendered strong protests.
Salvadoran President Duarte categorically rejected it,
characterizing it as intervention in the affairs of
another state: It was not the responsibility of Mexico
and France to develop solutions to an internal Salvadoran
question; this was a dangerous precedent that would
threaten the stability of the region. Duarte's position
was supported by the Salvadoran Bishops' Conference,
which argued that the guerrilla movement was supported by
only a small sector of the population. The bishops
claimed that the declaration would in all likelihood
result in a prolongation of the war--with more deaths,
increased destruction of property, and greater radicalization of Salvadoran factions--and a more rapid inter-
nationalization of the conflict. Equally significant was
the joint statement of nine Latin American governments
characterizing the Mexican-French declaration as interventionist. The document, signed by the foreign
ministers of Argentina, Bolivia, Colombia, Chile,
Guatemala, Honduras, Paraguay, the Dominican Republic,
and Venezuela, condemned the action because "it tacitly
invites other foreign entities to declare on behalf of

the extremist elements that are parties to the crisis; for that reason, far from contributing to a solution of the problem, by attempting to internationalize the problem, it has made it worse."[11]

As is typical whenever a Mexican government is chastised by another nation, a variety of public officials and interest groups came to its defense. Governors in various Mexican states cabled their support for the administration's stand. Declarations of solidarity with the president came from the National Peasants' Confederation, the Federation of Agricultural Workers, the Mexican College of Lawyers, the Union of Telephone Workers, and many other sources.

Despite such support, the administration was acutely sensitive to the Latin accusations. Secretary Castaneda appeared before the press and argued that Mexico could not remain aloof when it had witnessed "the uncontrolled activities of groups which, identified with the institutional apparatus, have liquidated hundreds or thousands of persons, many times in a bestial form."[12] He further charged that the United States was the real interventionist in El Salvador. At the same time, however, Castaneda went to great pains to point out that the Salvadoran opposition had not been recognized as a legitimate government, nor even as a belligerent element, but merely as a representative force that must be brought into negotiations. In addition, he categorically rejected the calls of some that Mexico use the oil leverage provided by the San Jose Agreement as a political weapon against repressive nations, among them El Salvador.

These developments illustrate the difficulties of meshing activism and noninterventionism in foreign policy. Clearly, the Mexican government had intervened in the Salvadoran conflict. Yet the nation's long-standing foreign policy principles required its leaders to deny such allegations. Despite Castaneda's assertions regarding the consistency of Mexican behavior, the Mexico of the 1960s would not have recognized insurgents in another country as representative forces.

It is significant that the positions outlined in the Mexican-French declaration have not been applied to the crisis in neighboring Guatemala. This is so in spite of the presence of a strong guerrilla force and repression almost as severe as that found in El Salvador. The bases for this inconsistency are therefore worth examining.

Secretary Castaneda characterized as "stupid" the American claim that Mexican oil fields were the ultimate target of a joint Soviet-Cuban offensive. Despite such assertions, however, the Mexicans are worried about the impact of the fighting in Guatemala on the oil-rich states of the south, in particular Chiapas. Concerns over Chiapas are by no means limited to its vast

petroleum reserves. The state is beset by serious social
problems, including the nation's highest illiteracy rate,
poor health care, inadequate nutrition, and high levels
of land concentration. Efforts by the Mexican left to
organize Chiapas' Indian majority have been met by
authorities with resistance. The left has claimed that
dozens of peasants have been killed over the last five
years in confrontations with police and that the government has not hesitated to overturn municipal election
victories of the Unified Socialist Party of Mexico.

As the Guatemalan government intensified its war
against the guerrillas in 1981, refugees began to pour
across the border. Lopez Portillo's initial reaction was
hardly in keeping with the traditional Mexican stance of
providing safe haven to political dissidents. Instead,
the government deported up to 3,000 Guatemalans. In the
wake of the political outcry that ensued, however, the
administration relented and permitted the construction of
refugee camps in Chiapas.

Reliable figures do not exist as to the number of
Guatemalan refugees. Estimates at the beginning of 1983
ranged from approximately 20,000 to more than 100,000.[13]
The UN High Commissioner for Refugees calculated that
35,000 Guatemalans in 32 camps in Chiapas were receiving
assistance from the United Nations and the Mexican
Commission on Aid to Refugees. However, there may be an
additional 65,000 refugees who are not receiving
assistance of any kind.[14]

Despite the problem, the Lopez Portillo administration did not take any actions threatening to the
Guatemalan regime. On the contrary, the evidence in
early 1982 suggested a substantial collaboration between
the two governments. Reports circulated that the Mexican
minister of defense held a secret meeting with the
Guatemalan Army chief of staff to plot strategy. In
addition, the two countries reportedly conducted joint
military maneuvers.[15]

Mexican fears of political instability were by no
means confined to Guatemala and El Salvador. Lopez
Portillo was particularly concerned about the serious
deterioration of relations between Nicaragua and its
Central American neighbors. In early 1982, Nicaragua
announced the discovery of a plot to destroy the nation's
oil refinery and cement plant and to assassinate key
members of the Sandinista leadership, a scheme it claimed
had been supported by diplomatic and military attaches in
Managua. Throughout the year, Nicaragua and Honduras
continued to exchange charges of subversion. The former
asserted that dozens of attacks had been carried out by
former Somocista Guardsmen based in Honduras. Nicaragua
also noted news reports of U.S. arms shipments and the
upgrading of Honduran military airstrips. In return,
Tegucigalpa charged that Sandinista forces had carried

out various attacks on Honduran soil. Meanwhile, the
Costa Ricans and Nicaraguans were expelling each other's
diplomatic personnel and locking horns over the former's
navigation on the San Juan River. The Costa Rican
government claimed that the Sandinistas were trying to
destabilize Costa Rica, while the Nicaraguans countered
that the Costa Rican leadership was seeking a smokescreen
behind which to hide the country's economic problems from
its people. Perhaps most ominous of all was the formation by Costa Rica, El Salvador, Honduras, and Guatemala
of a so-called Central American Democratic Community, a
body which then charged that Nicaragua was a threat to
the stability of the entire region.

It was in this general context that Lopez Portillo
traveled to Managua in February 1982 for a major foreign
policy address. The president took the opportunity to
assert once again that the Central American crisis should
be understood not within an East-West framework, but
rather as an indigenous response to unjust social structures. The United States would be guilty of "a gigantic
historical error," he warned, if it intervened in the
crisis. Reiterating his position of the previous
September, Lopez argued that a solution to the Salvadoran
conflict required negotiations among all warring
factions. He then proposed a three-step solution to the
Nicaraguan problem: First, the Reagan administration was
urged to refrain from the threat and use of force against
the Sandinistas. Second, in exchange for the disarming
of Somocista forces on the Honduran frontier, the
Nicaraguans should substantially reduce the size of their
military. Third, a series of nonaggression pacts should
be reached between Nicaragua and the United States, and
Nicaragua and its Central American neighbors. Over-
arching the plan was a call for negotiations between the
United States and Cuba, the absence of which was said to
contribute heavily to the problem. Needless to say,
Mexico stood ready to serve as facilitator of communications among the various parties.[16]

The Managua speech represented the definitive
Mexican position on the Central American crisis. Lopez
Portillo was eager to serve as an intermediary between
the United States and either Nicaragua or Cuba, thus
guaranteeing his place in history. Although Secretary
Castaneda and U.S. Secretary of State Alexander Haig met
in the spring of 1982 to discuss the Mexican initiative,
Washington was not enamored by the plan. The Mexican
offer failed to address the flow of arms through
Nicaragua to the Salvadoran guerrillas. In addition, the
United States was suspicious about Lopez Portillo's
support for the Sandinistas and thus questioned the role
he would play as intermediary.

Nevertheless, the Mexican position received a major
boost in mid-1982, as the Venezuelans began to reassess

442

their policy. The Venezuelan government had been a
strong supporter of the Salvadoran regime of Jose
Napoleon Duarte and had initiated the statement
condemning the August 1981 Mexican-French declaration.
Immediately prior to the March 1982 Salvadoran
Constituent Assembly elections, however, President Luis
Herrera Campins expressed his concerns that the United
States was pursuing an interventionist policy in Latin
America. His announced intention to reevaluate his
government's position after the Salvadoran balloting was
reinforced as a result of the Falkland Islands crisis.
In the last century, the Venezuelans had lost the
Essequibo region to British Guyana and thus had their own
historic grievance against the British. They were
dismayed when the United States assisted the British
effort to retake the Falklands. The Cuban government
shrewdly capitalized on the situation by moderating a
declaration of nonaligned nations that would have
endorsed Guyanese control of the Essequibo and rejected
the Venezuelan claim.

As a consequence of the Venezuelan reassessment,
Herrera Campins and Lopez Portillo directed a letter to
Ronald Reagan urging him to resolve the growing tensions
between Nicaragua and Honduras. The two presidents
proposed direct negotiations between Nicaragua and
Honduras, as well as an upgrading of contacts between
Washington and Managua. Though the United States did not
categorically reject the appeal, it made it clear that
negotiations were useless without an end to Cuban and
Nicaraguan support for the insurgents in El Salvador.
The Venezuelan-Mexican initiative was further diluted by
the October 1982 meeting of foreign ministers from Costa
Rica, Belize, El Salvador, Honduras, Jamaica, and
Colombia. The ministers proposed a "Forum for Peace and
Democracy" to study the crisis in Central America and
offered to provide technical assistance on elections to
other nations. The meeting, which excluded Nicaragua but
included U.S. officials, was seen by Mexico as an effort
to divert attention from its own peace initiative.
Despite the desire of the Mexican president to play a
major role in resolving the crisis, Lopez Portillo left
office in December 1982 with only a series of proposals
to show for his efforts.

CONCLUSION AND PROSPECTS FOR THE FUTURE

Mexican policy has been grounded historically in the
principle of nonintervention, a position initially
developed to protect a young revolutionary nation from
external attack. With the development of post-World War
II hemispheric accords, a key goal became that of
preventing the United States from abusing such accords to

legitimate intervention. This was particularly the case
with respect to Mexican actions in the OAS. Although the
emphasis on nonintervention has contributed to a
defensive, reactive policy, this tendency has been
counterbalanced by the Mexican revolutionary experience,
which has influenced successive governments to adopt
activist, nationalistic stances purposefully independent
of the United States. The Echeverria administration
ushered in a new, much more activist orientation, one in
which Mexico went beyond juridical statements and
initiated concrete measures (such as aid to Allende)
designed to frustrate American policies in the region.
The Lopez Portillo government followed in the activist
footsteps of Echeverria, establishing a highly visible
Mexican presence in Central America. At the same time,
however, the noninterventionist Mexican past imposed
limits on both presidents with respect to the range of
permissible actions.

With the presidency now in the hands of Miguel de la
Madrid Hurtado, it is useful to speculate on the future
of Mexican policy and its consequences for relations with
the United States. It is unlikely that de la Madrid will
assume as high a profile as Lopez Portillo in attempting
to resolve the Central American problem. Mexico's
economic crisis--as reflected in the tumbling value of
the peso, the slashing of government expenditures, rising
rates of unemployment and underemployment, and the
inability to meet scheduled payments to international
creditors--is clearly the priority issue for the new
regime. De la Madrid cannot afford to divert his
energies away from the nation's most pressing problem.

Although a somewhat lower profile is probable in the
future, a word of reservation should be expressed. The
enormous scope of the economic crisis facing the president may cause him to look to the foreign policy arena
for success. An active role in the resolution of Central
American tensions might help divert attention from
intractable economic problems. Indeed, it is worth
noting that Lopez Portillo's Managua initiative came only
three days after the Bank of Mexico withdrew from the
foreign exchange markets, thus precipitating the collapse
of the peso. In addition, the potential for social
unrest that flows from the economic crisis makes it more
necessary than ever that a lid be put on the Central
American revolutionary cauldron. Thus, de la Madrid may
decide that Mexico's vital interests require his involvement in foreign policy.

Although the government may adopt a slightly lower
profile, there will not be a substantive change in the
Mexican position. Throughout his presidential campaign,
de la Madrid endorsed Lopez Portillo's Managua
initiative, a proposal that remains very popular. In
January 1983, the new Mexican foreign minister, Bernardo

Sepulveda Amor, met with his counterparts from Venezuela, Colombia, and Panama. The ministers issued a statement of concern regarding direct or indirect interference in the Central American crisis. They also warned against placing the conflict within the context of an East-West confrontation. Indeed, recent events seem to indicate an increasing shift of Latin American attitudes toward the Mexican proposals. Stung by U.S. actions in the Falklands crisis, Argentina has now endorsed the Venezuelan-Mexican plan. In addition, the Costa Rican government has become concerned that its participation in the October 1982 foreign ministers' meeting was widely perceived as an effort to weaken the Mexican proposal. In future meetings, it is likely that Costa Rica will be more sensitive to the Mexican position. Efforts to seek a negotiated settlement in El Salvador also received a boost when Pope John Paul II called for dialogue during his visit there in March 1983. At the same time, however, the reception accorded him in Nicaragua hardly helped Mexican efforts to portray the Sandinista government as a moderate regime.

The most ominous recent development has been the serious deterioration of relations with Guatemala. The Mexican government is quite concerned about evidence that the Guatemalan military has crossed the Mexican border on numerous occasions since October 1982 in search of guerrillas and their supporters. The most serious incidents to date occurred in January 1983 at refugee camps outside the town of La Trinitaria. Refugees claimed that the Guatemalan soldiers repeatedly entered the camps, resulting in the deaths of four inhabitants. Many have fled and sought the safety of the Lacondon forest of Chiapas. The de la Madrid government has vigorously protested these incursions and demanded Guatemalan guarantees that they will not be repeated. The latter has responded by denying any violation of Mexican territory. After the incidents in January, Proceso reported that the Mexican military had established a security cordon designed to prevent acts of sabotage against Chiapas' prisons and oil fields.[17]

Irrespective of these recent developments, the American government is no doubt pleased that the Lopez Portillo era has come to an end. The Reagan administration was not happy with Lopez Portillo's strong support for Castro, the economic assistance he provided to the Sandinistas, and his calls for a negotiated settlement to the Salvadoran conflict. The United States is hoping that Mexican pronouncements on Central America and the Caribbean will decline under the new president. There is more than a touch of deja vu in all this. One need only reflect back to 1976, when Washington eagerly welcomed the "level-headed" Lopez Portillo and bade good riddance to the demagogic and radical Echeverria.

Yet, although Lopez Portillo did challenge certain
U.S. positions in Central America and the Caribbean, the
moderate dimension of his policy is not fully appre-
ciated. He refused to use the San Jose Agreement as a
political weapon and did not hesitate to assist
conservative regimes in the area. It is particularly
noteworthy that despite the controversy surrounding the
Mexican-French declaration, petroleum continued to flow
to El Salvador. Although Lopez Portillo cared little for
the Guatemalan government, he did nothing to threaten its
existence. Mexican support for the Guatemalan insurgents
has not been forthcoming. Finally, sensitive to American
concerns, Lopez risked incurring the displeasure of
Castro by disinviting him to the Cancun conference.
Indeed, there was more convergence in the policies of
Reagan and Lopez Portillo than is generally realized.
Both were after the same goal: stability and peace in
Central America and the Caribbean. Where they differed
was in their interpretation of the causes of regional
conflict (Soviet-Cuban subversion versus indigenous,
structural inequities) and their solution to the problem
(expanded military support to "friendly" regimes versus
negotiation among warring factions).

As de la Madrid begins his presidency, cracks in the
relationship are all too evident. Among recent areas of
concern are rising tides of protectionism in both
countries, Mexican ambivalence regarding participation in
the General Agreement on Tariffs and Trade, controversy
regarding American damage claims from Mexico's massive
oil spill in 1979, increasing fears in Mexico concerning
the penetration of its economy by direct U.S. investment,
the sloppy handling of the natural gas deal by the Carter
administration, the serious ramifications of the peso
devaluation for American border communities, and, of
course, the absence of a solution to the migrant problem.
It would be unfortunate if Mexico's Central American and
Caribbean policy becomes an additional complicating
factor in the relationship. It should not be so. In the
long run, U.S. interests in the region are probably
better served through support of Mexican efforts aimed at
moderating revolutionary tendencies than through support
of rearguard actions grounded in the failures of the
past.

NOTES

1. Antonio Carrillo Flores, "La Politica Exterior de
Mexico," Foro Internacional, 4 (October-December 1965,
January-March 1966), p. 234.
2. See Olga Pellicer de Brody, Mexico y la
Revolucion Cubana (Mexico, D.F.: El Colegio de Mexico,
1972); and Arthur K. Smith, Mexico and the Cuban

Revolution: Foreign Policy-Making in Mexico under President Adolfo Lopez Mateos (Ithaca: Cornell University, 1970).

3. In addition, Mexico would support the U.S. call for the dismantling of offensive weapons in Cuba during the 1962 Missile Crisis.

4. Cuban-Chilean relations were reestablished soon after the inauguration of Chilean President Salvador Allende.

5. On October 2, 1968, military forces opened fire on student demonstrators at the Tlatelolco housing complex in Mexico City. There is considerable dispute as to the actual death toll, with figures ranging from fifty to several hundred. See Elena Poniatowski, *La Noche de Tlatelolco* (Mexico, D.F.: Ediciones E.R.A., 1971).

6. *Excelsior* (May 21 and June 8, 1979).

7. Ibid. (June 22, 1979).

8. Ibid. (June 24, 1979).

9. "Entre las Revoluciones Cubana y Mexicana, solo Diferencias de Estilo: Fidel Castro," *Proceso*, 5 (August 10, 1981), pp. 14, 16.

10. *Excelsior* (May 18, 1979); *El Dia* (August 4, 1980); "Campana de EU contra Mexico; Resalta JLP la Relacion con Cuba," *Proceso*, 5 (February 23, 1981), p. 18.

11. Both the Mexican-French declaration and the Latin American reaction to it are reproduced in "Documentacion," *Estudios Centroamericanos*, 36 (1981), pp. 916-922.

12. *El Dia* (September 5, 1981).

13. See, for example, *Excelsior* (January 9, 30, 31, February 4 and 5, 1983); *Uno Mas Uno* (January 14, February 2 and 3, 1983).

14. Ignacio Ramirez, "Tropas Mexicanas Forman un Cordon de Seguridad, tras el Ataque Guatemalteco," *Proceso*, 7 (February 7, 1983), p. 25.

15. *Proceso*, 6 (March 29, 1982), pp. 6-8, 22 and 6 (April 5, 1982), pp. 14-17; *New York Times* (March 21, 1982).

16. *El Dia* (February 22, 1982).

17. Ramirez, "Tropas Mexicanas," pp. 24-26; and *Excelsior* (January 30 - February 4, 1983).

13
Soviet and Cuban Policy in the Caribbean Basin

Robert S. Leiken

For more than a half century after the Bolshevik Revolution, the Soviets regarded what has lately come to be known as the "Caribbean Basin"[1] as the geopolitical preserve of the United States. The 1962 Soviet installation of ballistic missiles in Cuba did not constitute a break with this tradition. The missiles were installed for global strategic reasons, rather than to penetrate the region itself.

During the 1960s, the Soviets censured Cuban attempts to spread revolution in Latin America. These efforts lacked the most "minimal calculation of the concrete conditions and the actual correlation of forces" and were doomed to "certain destruction".[2] Only in the late 1960s, and especially the 1970s, did the nature and rhythm of Soviet interest in the region begin to shift. Frequent ship visits to Cuba gradually established a regular naval presence. In the late 1970s, Moscow for the first time perceived revolutionary potential in Central America, as well as opportunities for "socialist orientation".[3]

If in 1979-81 Soviet support for armed struggle in Central America signalled a break with the general line of "peaceful transition," policy shifted again in 1982. This second shift, like the first, obeyed global strategic considerations as well as Central American realities. Although there is room for disagreement about the significance of these changes, what seems beyond dispute is the heightening of Soviet interest in the region over the past decade.

THE GEOPOLITICIZATION OF THE CARIBBEAN

In the past thirty years, the Caribbean Basin has become a region of often turbulent political change. Revolutionary movements have attained power in Cuba, Nicaragua, and Grenada. Other such movements have been defeated in Colombia and Venezuela. Large-scale radical political movements have appeared in Jamaica and the Dominican Republic, whereas military coups of a new nationalistic-progressive type have occurred in Grenada and Panama. At present, there are ongoing insurgencies in El Salvador and Guatemala.

In Central America, the economic growth of the 1960s and early 1970s was destabilizing. As the export sector modernized in response to rising prices for sugar and coffee, roads and telephone lines were extended to previously isolated areas. But although the medieval landscape of Central America acquired some of the appurtenances of the twentieth century, and although the old landlords and a small new rural middle class prospered, the direct producers suffered a dramatic deterioration in their living standards. The very success and expansion of the export sector created considerable pressure on generally scarce available land.[4] As productivity increased, large numbers of workers were forced to join the growing class of landless laborers. Many migrated to towns and cities, where capital-intensive technology employed in import substitution industrialization greatly limited the labor absorptive capacity of the urban sector.[5]

The Caribbean Commonwealth countries also grew in gross national product (GNP), but with less structural change and diversification. This growth involved large amounts of foreign investment and technological imports. Economic expansion could not absorb a rapidly expanding labor force, causing unemployment to reach levels of between 20 and 30 percent.[6] Many of the Commonwealth Caribbean nations, fresh from independence from the United Kingdom, began experimenting with various forms of socialism, populism, and economic nationalism. All but Grenada did so within the framework of political institutions carried over from British tutelage. Many normalized relations with Cuba and the Soviet bloc and actively participated in Third World fora.

In Central America, the political response to economic change was more violent than in the Commonwealth nations. The economic growth of the 1960s wrought major changes in class structure. There was now a middle class, an urban working class, rural landless laborers, and masses of impoverished peasants. But these economic changes were not followed by any such "democratic revolution" as took place in the West in the late eighteenth and nineteenth centuries under similar economic pressures. In the absence of democratic alternatives in El Salvador and Nicaragua, leftist-led mass organizations and guerrilla "armies of national liberation" became the spearheads of broad movements for social change.

No small portion of anger was directed at the United States. While students mobilized behind slogans of "Yankee go home," anti-U.S. sentiments also pervaded the armed forces, the Church, and the rising national pride of an emerging industrial and financial middle class. The Cuban "David" became a symbol for the resurgent popular nationalism after the U.S. "Goliath" invaded the Dominican Republic. In the late 1960s and early 1970s, a movement to nationalize the foreign holdings (especially U.S. holdings) swept through Latin America, first southward along the Andes, then northward to Guyana, Venezuela, and the Caribbean. Legislation restricting equity and profit repatriation became widespread in the 1970s, as did protests against discriminatory U.S. commercial legislation. In the universities and international organizations theories arose attributing Latin American underdevelopment and backwardness mainly to dependence on Spain, England, and, especially now, the United States.

The reaction against a "dependent capitalism" promoted by the United States lent socialism prestige and cast Cuba and the Soviet Union in a favorable light. U.S. backing of counterinsurgency and of oppressive regimes in the Third World persuaded many that the United States was the enemy of their aspirations for independence and the Soviet Union their natural ally.

The rise of nationalism and revolution reflected the region's economic dependency, backwardness, and the widening gap between its rich and poor, as well as the deformed and partial nature of its economic development. Yet for all these contradictions, the region remained relatively stable geopolitically for a long time.

In the late 1970s, however, local conflicts became a source of superpower rivalry. The reaction against the "dependent capitalism" and interventionism promoted by the United States has been proud and profound. With Havana and Moscow seeking to take advantage of this discontent, and the United States determined to reassert hegemony, the Caribbean Basin is now the latest in a growing list of Third World regions to become an arena of international conflict.

For its part, the United States has a number of vital strategic interests in the Basin. Stability in this region is essential to the ability of the United

States to move ships, weapons, and troops to Western
Europe and other parts of the world in case of a crisis.
The Panama Canal continues to enhance the military and
commercial value of the region, permitting the United
States to maintain a "two ocean" naval presence with a
"one-and-a-half ocean navy."[7] The Panama Canal and
Caribbean trade routes carry a steadily increasing cargo
of strategic raw materials. The area serves as a trans-
shipment point for Mid-East oil coming to the United
States; its high-density oil routes carry over half of
U.S. oil imports. The Basin also hosts several
indispensable refineries, as well as two of the world's
leading oil producers, Mexico and Venezuela.

In the late 1970s, the security of the Caribbean
Basin became a source of concern for U.S. policymakers.
Although the prospect of a series of revolutionary
changes in the area instilled panic in many, concern was
fueled primarily by events elsewhere. The steady Soviet
military buildup since 1965, overlapping with the U.S.
strategic retreat following the Vietnam War, produced a
major change in what the Soviets call "the global
correlation of forces." Moscow's strategic offensive in
Africa, Southeast Asia, and the Indian Ocean Basin cast a
shadow over maps of the Caribbean Basin in Washington
boardrooms. That offensive seemed directed at the raw
materials lifelines of Western Europe. When these moves
were placed in the context of the strategic and conventional modernization of Warsaw Pact forces, the invasion
of Afghanistan, and the Soviet "peace offensive" in
Western Europe, it seemed apparent that the Soviets were
seeking to weaken and eventually sever the NATO alliance.
An offensive interdiction capability in the Caribbean
would be an additional element of pressure on Western
Europeans already beginning to doubt the efficacy of the
NATO alliance. To cut off Western Europe, the Soviet
Union would have to mount a threat to maritime traffic in
the North and South Atlantic. At any rate, Moscow's
behavior in the Caribbean was viewed by Washington in
that context.

The Soviets apparently seek to establish a naval
presence effective enough to disturb NATO contingency
plans to resupply forces in Western Europe from the large
U.S. ports in the Gulf of Mexico. The Caribbean, the
Panama Canal, the Atlantic Narrows, and the sea lanes
around the southern tip of South America are potential
choke points where Soviet navy and submarine forces could
disrupt the flow of U.S. maritime traffic. A Soviet bloc
naval deployment in the Caribbean with bases in Central
America could eventually constitute a threat to these
vulnerable routes. Moscow's support for internationalization of the Panama Canal, rather than Panamanian
sovereignty, suggests a desire to exercise influence over
this key waterway.

The Soviets offered a glimpse of that potential
during their 1975 worldwide naval exercises. Warships
using facilities in Cuba and the Azores demonstrated a
capacity to obstruct South Atlantic traffic. Cuban-based
Soviet ships participated simultaneously in exercises
designed to interdict the North Atlantic shipping lanes
essential for U.S.-European trade. Already Cuban facilities have lengthened the on-station time of Soviet
ballistic missile-bearing submarines off U.S. coasts,
thereby permitting hunter-killer submarines to operate
more widely. Soviet military analysts recognize publicly
that U.S. strategic freedom in other parts of the globe
depends on stability in the Caribbean. With the U.S.
tied down in its "strategic rear" the Soviet Union would
be freer in 'areas of more immediate strategic interest,
above all the Indian Ocean.[8]

THE EVOLUTION OF SOVIET POLICY

In the 1970s, Soviet theorists and policymakers
abandoned the "geographic fatalism" that previously
conceded the region to the U.S. sphere of influence. In
1971, a Soviet propagandist declared that "the invisible
wall behind which the USA has been keeping Latin America
from the socialist world has virtually collapsed."[9] Most
recently, Latinskaya Amerika, published by Moscow's
Institute on Latin America, devoted a special issue to
Central America in which the growing importance of the
region in the national liberation movement was
emphasized:

> The liberation movement experienced a new upsurge in
> Latin America in the late 1970s and early 1980s.
> Its center moved to Central America, a region
> bordering directly on the United States. Consider-
> ing the geographic location of the sub-region and
> presence of U.S. armed forces in Panama and on the
> military bases in the Caribbean, it would seem that
> the prospects for the revolutionary process in
> Central American states should be minimal.
> Nevertheless, the liberation movement is rapidly
> gaining strength in these countries.[10]

Until 1980, with the exception of Cuba, to whom the title
was only reluctantly and belatedly conceded, only Africa
and Asia were considered by Moscow to be regions spawning
states of "socialist (read: Soviet) orientation." In
November 1980, Central America was added to the list of
regions in which governments likely to align themselves
with the Soviet Union were emerging.[11]

From the late 1950s to the late 1970s, Soviet Latin
American policy developed in a global context of

"peaceful coexistence" and "detente." By the late 1950s the USSR had acquired the aspirations of a superpower, but without sufficient military capacity, industrial base, or overseas resources to rival the United States. Khrushchev's peaceful coexistence policy was designed to shelter the Soviet Union from challenges to its sphere of influence, to promote trade with the West for acquisitions of needed technology, and to stimulate ties with the resource-rich Third World nations. Moscow's endorsement of "the peaceful road to socialism" at the Twentieth Party Congress in February 1956 signalled to the western and Third World governments that the Soviets were prepared to offer accommodation from local communist parties in exchange for state-to-state relations. This in turn facilitated the broad network of diplomatic and commercial ties required to implement the new policy. Peaceful coexistence and peaceful transition were inseparably linked in a Soviet strategy of accumulating force.

The policy of peaceful transition was pursued with singular dedication in Latin America. At the beginning of the 1960s, the Soviet Union enjoyed diplomatic relations with only three Latin American countries (Argentina, Mexico, and Uruguay). By the late 1960s and early 1970s, as Latin American countries expanded their foreign relations and detente diminished U.S. resistance, diplomatic ties increased. By the end of the 1970s, Moscow enjoyed diplomatic relations with nineteen Latin American nations. Soviet-Latin American commercial ties greatly expanded during this period. In 1964, the Soviet Union traded with only four Latin American countries. By 1975, the number had risen to twenty. Despite wide fluctuations, Soviet-Latin American trade increased thirteen-and-a-half times between 1960 and 1977, climbing from $70 million in 1960 to $912 million in 1979, making it "one of the most dynamic segments of the socialist countries' international trade."[12]

The Cuban revolution embarrassed and threatened to disrupt the Soviet tactics. Fidel Castro reviled the policy of peaceful transition and the practice of "socialist governments that give aid to Latin American oligarchies" and "hamper the work of true revolutionaries"--guerrillas implementing Castro's and Che Guevara's "foco" strategy.[13] Soviet theoreticians and the pro-Soviet Latin American communist parties reproached the "new vanguards" who questioned "the leading role of the working class and its party" and sought to replace it with "political-military fronts" modeled on the Cuban July 26th movement.[14]

Peaceful transition led to a number of splits in Latin American communist parties in the 1960s. Supporters of Soviet policy generally retained control of the official party apparatus. Moscow backed them and

urged them to join with the reformist opposition in broad
electoral coalitions. By the early 1970s, the traditional communist parties were participating with
reformists and nationalists in united fronts in Bolivia,
Chile, Ecuador, Peru, and Uruguay--while fostering others
in Venezuela, Argentina, and Mexico.

The electoral victory of the Popular Unity coalition
in Chile was the crowning achievement of the policy of
peaceful transition to socialism. In April 1971, it
received extraordinary attention at the Twenty-Fourth
Congress of the Communist Party of the Soviet Union
(CPSU), where it was hailed as a "new stage" in the Latin
American revolution. Beyond Chile, the Congress saw
bright prospects in "the new type of officers who are
progressive nationalists" and who were "rapidly
strengthening their interests in a number of Latin
American countries."[15] Soviet analysts believed that the
modernization of Latin American armies had given rise to
a new generation of military officers who reflected "a
radical anti-imperialist trend" and who "do not conceal
their admiration for the Soviet Union."[16] Intensive
efforts to foster pro-Soviet military factions soon
followed.

The September 1973 coup in Chile dashed the high
hopes for a peaceful transition to Soviet alignment and
delivered a telling blow to the Soviet line worldwide.
Early Soviet commentators sought to deflect criticism
that could call into question the basic party line and
placed the blame on the Castroite Movimiento de Izquierda
Revolucionaria (MIR) and other "ultra-left" groups.
Nonetheless, seeds of doubt, which were to bear fruit in
the late 1970s, had been planted in the minds of Soviet
analysts. Even at this time, Soviet authorities agreed
that the preservation of links between the Chilean
military and the United States had been fatal.

In an effort to rectify the Chilean failure, Moscow
provided generous amounts of sophisticated military
equipment and technical assistance to Peru's progressive
military regime. In short order, however, the ascension
to power of the pro-U.S. General Morales Bermudez in
1975, and right-wing takeovers in Bolivia, Uruguay, and
Argentina forced Soviet analysts to reexamine their
strategy. G. Mirskii, hitherto one of the most outspoken
enthusiasts for the "patriotic military," noted that the
progressive spirit of the military "reached its limit"
and exclaimed that a "reactionary counteroffensive,
unprecedented in Latin American history," was "swallowing
up one country after another."[17]

What appeared to Soviet academicians as a calamitous
setback in the revolutionary process merely indicated to
the Soviet leadership that a further refining of tactics
was in order. Throughout Europe and the Western
Hemisphere, Soviet propagandists called attention to the

atrocities of Pinochet's Chile--symbol of U.S.
imperialism's revanchism. Yet this period of
"reactionary counteroffensive" in South America was one
in which Moscow stepped up its economic relations with
Bolivia, furnished arms to Peru on a massive scale, and
courted the Argentine military with increased trade and
credit and multiple military missions.

Soviet appreciation of military regimes in South
America was largely--though not entirely--divorced from
any consideration of their "progressiveness." Friendship
with Argentina became the cornerstone of Soviet Southern
Cone policy. That regime's claim to progressiveness
rested exclusively on its booming trade with the Soviet
Union and its toleration of the pro-Soviet Argentine
Communist Party (as all other leftist groups were
prescribed). Nonetheless, the Soviets and their
Argentine followers drew elaborate distinctions between
the "democratic forces" in the Argentine military and the
"pinochetistas" (that is, the anti-Soviets).[18]
Obviously, Moscow's fine discriminations among military
regimes had less to do with progressiveness or the
peaceful transition to socialism than with Soviet efforts
to penetrate the Southern Cone of Latin America.

Unlike the Cuban revolution, the Nicaraguan
revolution, in a very different international environment, did occasion a general revision of Soviet tactics.
"Armed struggle" became a cardinal point of Soviet Latin
American doctrine in 1979. Soviet Latin American experts
now asserted that "the armed road . . . is the most
promising in the specific conditions of most Latin
American countries" and that "only the armed road has led
to victory in Latin America."[19] Coordination or integration with organizations pursuing armed struggle,
previously scorned as "petit-bourgeois" and "ultra-left,"
were now the order of the day. Che Guevara, the bete
noire of both the Soviets and local communist parties in
the 1960s, was rehabilitated along with his main tactical
principles. Guevara's "subjectivist" view that "it is
not always necessary to wait until all the conditions are
ripe for revolution, the foco can create them," was now
lauded as "a fundamental contribution to Latin American
revolutionary movements."[20]

Previously, the Soviets held that self-sufficient
communist parties were "the decisive factor" for the
taking of power, and that dissolution of those parties or
even ideological concessions on their part was
inadmissible.[21] The post-Sandinista Soviet view is that
military political fronts of the July 26th or Sandinista
type "are capable of substituting for political parties
of the proletariat" in the period before the taking of
power.[22] Since the mid-1970s the Soviets had been
supporting such Cuban-style political-military fronts in
Africa.

The Soviets have urged the Frente Sandinista de
Liberacion Nacional (FSLN) to "create its own party and
Sandinista mass organizations."[23] This is an "essential
condition for the organized strengthening of the
Sandinista ranks . . . and for pursuing a uniform
political course."[24] The Moscow-backed Nicaraguan
Socialist Party has been recommending that the junta
pursue a course closely resembling Soviet prescriptions.[25] Moscow seems optimistic that the FSLN will,
under Soviet guidance, eventually evolve into a Soviet-
style party, a necessity for consolidating power.

The 1979 endorsement of armed struggle was not
absolute. In certain countries like Argentina, Brazil,
and Mexico, where prospects for armed struggle are poor
and those for profitable economic relations promising,
the Soviets continue to broaden commercial and governmental ties and to pursue reformist, united-front
tactics. Rather than placing priority on "unity of the
left," the Soviets give emphasis to "unity with the
liberal bourgeoisie, with ruling circles or with traditional parties."[26] Different levels of economic development and various degrees of dependency on the United
States necessitate different "forms of struggle" to
advance the revolutionary process. The "paths and
procedures" of revolutionary struggle also depend on:

> the uneven economic and political development of the
> Latin American countries and the balance of class
> forces in them, which causes the conditions for the
> development of the revolutionary process to mature
> at different times. . . . This is why many communist
> parties in the Latin American countries are now
> concerned mainly with the creation of unified anti-
> imperialist, anti-dictatorial democratic fronts for
> the purpose of uniting all antifascist patriotic and
> democratic forces.[27]

In general, Soviet tactics have corresponded to specific
levels of socioeconomic development. Countries of
greater economic development generally require policies
of peaceful transition; low economic development necessi-
tates armed struggle.

Although Moscow now advocates and assists armed
struggle in certain Latin American countries, it seeks to
do this without sacrificing the gains of the previous
period. As insurgency mounted in Central America, the
Soviet Union remained on the sidelines, cheering,
training, even coaching, but not managing or playing.
Although the Soviets wish to convince revolutionary movements that they are the "natural allies" of these movements, they wish to be so without alienating major Latin
American governments like Argentina, Brazil, Colombia,
Mexico, and Venezuela, which they have courted over the

456

past two decades. Overt Soviet intervention could arouse against Moscow the anti-imperialist sentiment it seeks to direct against the United States. Moscow's relationship with Cuba enables it to identify with revolutionary movements without taking the blame for their activities.

THE SOVIETIZATION OF CUBA

The current Cuban-Soviet relationship did not spring fully formed from the Cuban revolution. It was a decade and a half before Cuba could be said to have been Sovietized. Cuba's autonomy was reduced by Castro's squandering of political and economic resources; unremitting U.S. hostility and Soviet pressure eventually succeeded in driving him into Moscow's arms.

The establishment of links of dependence was a protracted and uneven process. Throughout most of the 1960s an unsteady detente existed between the two countries. Despite Castro's visits to the Soviet Union, his fulsome praise of Soviet leaders, the adoption of certain economic programs in accordance with Soviet policies, and the toning down of Che Guevara's radical anti-Sovietism, Cuba remained essentially independent in the first decade of the revolution. Castro publicly attacked Soviet Vietnam policy and its pursuit of friendly relations with the United States; he refused to sign the partial nuclear test ban treaty or to support publicly the Soviets against China. The two nations also differed sharply, as we have seen, in their policies toward Latin American governments and revolutionary movements. Events came to a head in 1967 when Castro broke with the pro-Soviet Latin American communist parties and accused the Soviet bloc countries of aiding reaction in Latin America via economic ties.[28] The Soviets responded by cutting military assistance and delaying petroleum deliveries.

The year 1968 marked the end of Cuban opposition to the Soviets on major international questions and the beginning of a process in which Cuba would gradually yield one sphere after another of its domestic and foreign policy to Soviet tutelage.

Castro publicly supported the Soviet invasion of Czechoslovakia. Without access to Cuban and Soviet state papers, I cannot provide a precise explanation for Castro's sudden about-face after the invasion. The Brezhnev Doctrine may have represented for Castro a promise of protection for his troubled regime. It may even have been accompanied by private security guarantees. Certainly before the events of 1968, Cuban officials had expressed considerable concern about the U.S. threat (overt and covert). They had also indicated that under prevailing international conditions, "we are

going to fight alone."[29] After 1968, Cuban-Soviet relations warmed apace; visits and contacts multiplied; trade
negotiations prospered; and the customary barbs directed
at the Soviet Union and at Latin American "communist"
parties gradually disappeared from Castro's speeches.

Between 1969 and 1975, a wave of Soviet technicians
and advisers flooded Cuban planning and administrative
offices. Following the unsuccessful 10-million-ton sugar
harvest of 1970, officials trusted by the Soviets, such
as Carlos Rafael Rodriguez and Osvaldo Dorticos, were
given major responsibility for the economy. The old ad
hoc Cuban-Soviet economic relationship was replaced by
formal institutional ties. In 1970, a joint Cuban-Soviet
Intergovernmental Economic, Scientific, and Technical
Co-operation Commission was established, which facilitated Soviet penetration of Cuba's internal decisionmaking bodies. The commission soon became responsible
for the overall planning of the country's centralized
economy. In 1972, Cuba joined the Council on Mutual
Economic Assistance (CMEA), and that same year, Havana
and Moscow signed a series of agreements rescheduling the
Cuban debt, extending further credits, and raising the
prices of Cuban sugar and nickel in bilateral trade.
Provisions were also made for technical aid to Cuban
industry.

By the late 1970s, the Soviets were providing
approximately 80 percent of Cuba's imports and took over
70 percent of its exports. Direct and indirect subsidies
from Moscow total an estimated $8 million per day, or
$2.92 billion per year.

Cuban internal political institutions were restructured along the lines of their Soviet patrons. In 1972
and 1973, more than a dozen delegations of party
officials from Soviet bloc countries visited the island
to advise and monitor the organization of a Soviet-style
communist party. A delegation of Cuban party leaders
travelled to Moscow to receive training. Cuban trade
unions, women's organizations, and elections procedures
were also modified under Soviet guidance. The DGI, the
Cuban intelligence service, was purged of all suspected
anti-Soviet officers and came under the direct supervision of General Vassily Petrovich of the KGB.[30]

In January 1969, the Soviets announced that they had
reequipped the Cuban Armed Forces.[31] The first Russian
naval squadron stopped at the island in July of that year
and by 1972, Soviet warships had visited Cuba ten
times.[32] The Soviets were now establishing a significant
naval presence in the Caribbean by building up the Cuban
navy and through extended ship visits. Cuban territory
today is available to the Soviets for docking facilities,
satellite tracking stations, electronic intelligence-
gathering installations, the refueling of reconnaissance
flights, and the servicing of submarines at Cienfuegos.

458

One purpose of Moscow's upgrading of the Cuban
military arsenal in the 1970s was to prepare a "rapid
deployment force" with legitimacy in the Third World.
Troops from a small Third World country with a comparatively unspoiled revolutionary image could do much in
Africa that Soviet troops could not. Angola was represented as an independent Cuban initiative for the sake of
"proletarian solidarity," but Moscow's role in Africa
became more conspicuous after this initial success.
Subsequently, Cuban activities in Africa and the Middle
East have been coordinated in an integral package
involving other Soviet bloc participants.

The institutionalization of Soviet-Cuban ties signi-
fies a new kind of neocolonial structural dependency for
Cuba. Although this relationship is not necessarily
irreversible (nor was it intentional on Cuba's part), in
a period in which many Latin American countries achieved
a degree of political and economic independence unprecedented in their histories, Cuba, the "first liberated
territory of Latin America," was compelled by the errors
of its leaders and the policies of the superpowers to
march in a different direction from other Latin American
countries.

THE SOVIET UNION AND CUBA IN CENTRAL AMERICA

While the Soviets remained safely in the background,
the Cuban champions of "anti-imperialism" have taken the
risks that "international solidarity" in Central America
requires. As earlier indicated, the revolutionary movements were not created by Havana or Moscow, but are an
inevitable product of Central America's backward,
repressive, dependent, and oligarchical societies. As
instability mounted in the 1970s, Cuba and the Soviet
Union were presented with new opportunities to spread
their influence.

NICARAGUA

Leaders of the small Sandinista movement went to
Cuba in the 1960s for refuge and military training. In
1978, perceiving the domestic and regional isolation of
the Somoza regime, the Cubans began to intervene significantly. In the summer of that year, they mediated
differences among the Sandinista factions and, in March
1979, helped to achieve the latter's unification. They
provided contacts with international arms dealers and
supplied some weapons themselves, often through the good
offices of neighboring countries. As the 1979 uprising
approached, Havana increased direct arms supplies,
organized and armed an internationalist brigade to fight

alongside the FSLN guerrillas, and dispatched military specialists to the field to coordinate efforts. In the spring of 1979, Cuban military advisers from the Department of Special Operations accompanied FSLN forces into battle while maintaining radio communications with Havana. These advisers, led by Julian Lopez Diaz, a covert action expert who became ambassador to Nicaragua, remained in Nicaragua after the Sandinistas took power. Within a week they were joined by several dozen additional Cuban military, security, and intelligence personnel. Key military advisory and intelligence positions were awarded to Cubans. This situation finally led Panama's General Torrijos to withdraw Panamanian military advisers in 1980 and to offer "friendly warnings" against overreliance on Cuba. Intelligence sources estimated Cuban military and security personnel to have reached 2,000 by the spring of 1983. Emphasis on quantitative estimates obscures the more important consideration--the qualitative predominance of Cuban personnel in central advisory posts.[33]

The Soviet bloc effort in Nicaragua has begun to assume the features of a now familiar division of labor employed in places like Ethiopia and Afghanistan, in which the Cubans (aided by the Soviets) mainly attend to military affairs, the East Germans attend to security and intelligence matters, and the Bulgarians concentrate on economics.[34] The Bulgarians recently provided a $140 million credit over three years for the development of a deep water port at El Bluff on Nicaragua's Atlantic coast (capable of handling 28,000-metric-ton oceangoing ships), as well as hydroelectric, agricultural, and industrial projects.[35] Fifty Soviet and thirty-five East German advisers are stationed in Nicaragua on security missions according to the U.S. State Department.[36]

In March 1980, the FSLN signed a mutual support agreement with the Soviet Communist Party. A series of military accords soon followed. To date the Soviets have supplied fifty T-54 and T-55 tanks, several heavy tank ferries providing water-crossing capacity, one thousand military trucks, plus BM-21 mobile multiple rocket launchers, MI-8 helicopters, AK-47 rifles, AN-2 aircraft, armored personnel carriers, 122mm howitzers, and 152mm guns.[37]

The Soviets have sent technicians to instruct the Nicaraguans in the use of these weapons. Nicaraguan pilots and mechanics have been sent to Bulgaria for training.[38] There is evidence that the Nicaraguans have made preparations for the arrival of Soviet MiG fighters. However, these plans appear to have been altered in the face of warnings from Washington.[39]

The Soviet Union has demonstrated a willingness to assist with long-term development projects but not to be a lender of last resort in crises. Facing a serious foreign exchange deficit, Nicaraguan Head of State Daniel Ortega travelled to Moscow in May 1982. He returned with an economic and technical cooperation agreement for $50 million on very favorable terms for the construction of a hydroelectric plant, technical training centers, and a 400-bed hospital complete with 11 Soviet doctors.[40] However, no foreign exchange assistance was forthcoming. An additional $100 million credit has been extended for the purchase of Soviet farm machinery. A receiving station for Soviet telecommunications satellites permitting direct communications with Moscow is expected to be operable by mid-1983.[41] Finally, the Soviets donated a drydock for the port city of San Juan del Sur along with numerous Soviet technicians for construction and maintenance.[42] The Soviets seem interested in establishing a long-term presence in Nicaragua and in gaining ascendency in the political, military, security, and intelligence spheres--but not in sustaining the Nicaraguan economy on a day-to-day basis.

This policy reflects not only Moscow's current economic problems but also evolving long-term Soviet strategy. With the "changed correlation of forces on a world-scale" and the consequent abandonment of "peaceful transition" as a general line, Soviet authorities from the mid-1970s began to assert that under new international conditions "material aid on the part of the socialist states has ceased to be a factor directly promoting the transition to a non-capitalist path." Instead, the main factor had become "the political, military-strategic, and moral influence of the states of the socialist community.[43] In Africa and Southeast Asia, the Soviet Union, often via a complex division of labor with subordinate bloc members and allies, has sought to dominate political and military structures of newly emerging Third World countries while recommending maintenance of the private sector and economic links with the West. Soviet and Cuban actions and counsel in Nicaragua have been consistent with this policy.

EL SALVADOR

Cuba has played a more direct role in the Salvadoran insurgency than in Nicaragua. It has used its influence to establish a support network for the insurgents in neighboring countries via solidarity groups and local communist parties. During 1980, Havana assisted in the acquisition and delivery of considerable military supplies for the "final offensive" of January 1981. These supplies were collected in Eastern Europe, Vietnam, and Ethiopia, and were delivered through surface, sea, and air routes, often via Nicaragua.[44]

really!

Clearly such a complex clandestine operation could not occur without Soviet approval. On June 2, 1980, Shafik Handal, secretary general of the Salvadoran Communist Party (PCS), met with Mikhail Kudachkin, deputy chief of the Central Committee of the Soviet Communist Party, who suggested that Handal travel to Vietnam to acquire arms and offered to pay for the trip. Handal also requested that the thirty students sent by the PCS for study in Moscow receive military training. Six weeks later, upon returning from Vietnam, Handal met with Karen Brutents, chief of the Latin American section, and was told that the Soviet leadership would transport the now promised Vietnamese arms.[45] Moscow kept its involvement indirect but saw that Handal did not return from the East empty-handed.

The Cubans played a role in the unification of the rebel factions, achieved in meetings in Havana in December 1979 and May 1980. Havana expanded its logistic role and began to assist in tactical planning of insurgent military operations, including the January 1981 "final offensive".[46]

Cuba's role in Guatemala

A similar pattern developed in Guatemala. Once again the Cubans played a role in uniting the deeply divided revolutionary groups. Once formal unity was achieved, Havana expanded military assistance and training programs, reportedly coordinating arms shipments from Nicaragua through Honduras. The U.S. State Department has charged that M-16 rifles captured from the Guatemalan guerrillas have been traced to those left by U.S. forces in Vietnam, thus indicating a Cuban and Soviet role.[47]

CUBA IN THE CARIBBEAN

In the latter 1970s, a Cuban political offensive unfolded, aimed at gaining a foothold in one after another of the Eastern Caribbean islands. This campaign made use of Cuban cultural exports and "solidarity brigades" of teachers, doctors, engineers, and advisers to local political groups. Havana's intelligence network was fed by local sympathizers who added color to Cuban propaganda, making it far more effective than the staid Soviet variety. These methods have created a public image of Cuba and its Soviet-bloc allies as revolutionaries in joint struggle against western imperialism.

Havana's task was facilitated by the middle-class character of many of the new nationalist regimes that came to power in the Caribbean during this period. While espousing revolutionary goals, most of these parties achieved power by decidedly unrevolutionary means, lacking the ties to the labor and peasant movements

enjoyed by the populists they succeeded. Given their
narrow popular base and a shortage of resources with
which to fulfill electoral and revolutionary promises,
their identification with Cuba became vital for maintaining power. Although Cuba can supply neither the
model nor the resources for long-run development, it can
furnish, in Anthony Maingot's words, a veneer of
"revolutionary legitimacy while at the same time
providing the arms, intelligence, and training essential
for grabbing power and keeping it." As these new regimes
expand their public sectors, the Cuban connection becomes
"a smokescreen covering up deficiencies and incompetence
of all kinds."[48] In exchange, the Cubans achieve
influence within security and political apparati.

Havana's Caribbean efforts in the late 1970s focused
on reinforcing the left wing of Jamaica's Peoples
National Party (PNP), while simultaneously supporting the
new Workers' Party. After the PNP defeat in the 1981
elections, Grenada became the focus of Cuban attention.
Many of the leaders of the New Jewel Movement, which
seized power in March 1979, hard upon the return of its
leader, Maurice Bishop, from a visit to Cuba, were
middle-class intellectuals educated in England and the
United States. Havana uniformed, armed, and trained a
Grenadan army of 20,000 and kept it in military zones
declared off limits to the local population. With a
total population of only 110,000, Grenada probably has
the highest ratio of troops to civilians of any country
in the world.[49] According to Washington, the Cubans have
600 civilian and 30 military personnel on the island.[50]

The most tumultuous issue underlying U.S.-Grenadan
relations has been the construction of an airport with a
9,800-foot runway at Port Salines by more than 300 Cuban
construction workers using Soviet equipment. The
Grenadan government argues that the airport is needed to
handle jetliners for its tourist industry and that many
Caribbean islands have built similar facilities.
Nonetheless, the airport will accommodate any aircraft in
the Soviet-Cuban arsenal and would extend the combat
radius of Cuban MiGs to northern South America. Aside
from providing the Cubans with an excellent staging area
for operations in the northern tier of South America, it
would solve the problem of obtaining secure refueling
stops for military flights to Africa. According to the
Reagan administration, the Cubans have also built a
batallion-sized military camp in Calivigny, Grenada. The
camp reportedly contains barracks, administration
buildings, vehicle storage sheds, support buildings, and
a training area with a Soviet-style obstacle course,
which could supplement air and naval facilities presently
under construction.[51]

The Soviets, who established an embassy in St.
George's and provided TASS News Service to the island,

extended a $7.5 million credit line to Grenada for the construction of a satellite-tracking station. Radio Free Grenada stopped broadcasting BBC's "World News from London" following a newscast quoting from a U.S. State Department human rights report on Grenada. The Soviets have provided an additional $4.5 million in economic aid for the island's agricultural sector.[52]

The military rulers of Surinam, led by Lieutenant Colonel Desi Bouterse, came to power via a coup d'etat in February 1980, overthrowing the democratically elected government of Henck Arron. Leftists within the junta sought to overcome their narrow base of popular support by initially strengthening ties with Cuba and Grenada. When this action proved even more unpopular, Bouterse appointed pro-Dutch, pro-U.S. Hendrik Chin-A-Sen as president and jailed the leftists, without abandoning his nationalist economic policy.

Following Bouterse's visit to Grenada in the summer of 1981, his policies began to shift leftward. He ousted Chin-A-Sen in February 1982. The freedoms of the press, of speech, and of assembly in groups larger than three people were curtailed and strict government censorship was imposed. In December 1982, fifteen prominent democratic opposition leaders were arrested and later assassinated, further narrowing Bouterse's base support. Bouterse looked more and more to the newly formed Revolutionary People's Front (composed of two tiny leftist parties: the Libyan-style Union of Progressive Workers and Farmers and the pro-Cuban Revolutionary People's Party, led by the architect of the 1980 overtures to Havana, Sargeant Major Badrisen Sital) and to the increasingly divided army for support.

During this period, Surinam's relations with Cuba, Grenada, and Nicaragua grew intimate. Cuba established a trade mission in 1981, opened a diplomatic mission (later upgraded to an embassy) in early 1982, and reached a sugar-rice agreement in the summer of 1982. As an indication of the importance that Cuba places on Surinam, Osvaldo Cardenas, former director of the Caribbean-Central American section of the Cuban Communist Party's Americas Department, was named ambassador. Official, cultural, and sports exchanges have proliferated in recent months. In the spring of 1982 Bouterse reportedly made a secret visit to Cuba and held discussions with Castro.

The Venezuelan Christian Democratic Party has charged that Soviet and Cuban soldiers are organizing a civil guard inside Surinam. Former vice-premier Andre Haakmat alleges that Havana has organized an internal security force for Bouterse.[53] Though these allegations have not been confirmed, Havana radio praised Bouterse's crackdown on democratic rights, claiming that it had saved Surinam from elements seeking to turn the country

464

over to "imperialists and transnational corporations."[54]

Bouterse is depending on Grenadan, Cuban, and Nicaraguan advisers for help in his new economic and political strategy, which focuses on continuing the nationalization of the economy and building mass organizations to correct the three years of "upside-down revolution."[55] Until and unless Bouterse develops a popular base and an effective program, the Cuban connection will serve him as it does the Caribbean middle-class revolutionaries. Given an opportunity to expand its influence, Havana has thus far proven obliging.

REACTION TO CUBAN-SOVIET EXPANSIONISM

Two distinct policy lines have emerged among those seeking to contain Soviet-Cuban influence in the Caribbean Basin. The first, practiced by many Latin American countries, a number of European governments, the Socialist International, and other international bodies, competes with Havana and Moscow while accepting the legitimacy of movements (even revolutionary ones) for social change in the region. Diplomatic recognition, political support, economic aid, and military assistance are extended to revolutionary governments. Opposition to Cuban and Soviet alignment is urged within an overall context of cooperation. This policy opposes intervention by either superpower (or their proxies) in the internal affairs of the Basin countries, or isolation of those favorably disposed to Cuba or the USSR. In contrast, the Reagan administration tends to identify revolutionary movements and anti-U.S. policies with Soviet, Cuban, and Nicaraguan intervention. It seeks to "reward friends and punish enemies" by withdrawing or extending recognition, cutting off or reinstating bilateral and multilateral aid, and supplying military assistance to pro-U.S. governments and counterrevolutionaries.

Brazil's policy toward Surinam provides an example of the first policy. Following the execution of the Surinamese opposition leaders, the Netherlands and the United States terminated all economic assistance. Brazil continued its aid programs with the express purpose of "containing Cuban influence" and maintaining Surinamese ties with the West. Concerned that western isolation of Surinam would offer greater scope for the Cubans, General Dianilo Venturini, special diplomatic assistant to President Figueiredo, stated "it would be bad for a neighboring country to become the ally of nations that could bring problems to Brazil."[56]

Cuban expansionism has strained the friendly relations carefully cultivated during the 1970s. Between 1977 and 1981, Havana's relations with Colombia, Chile,

Costa Rica, Ecuador, Panama, Peru, and Venezuela have soured. In the spring of 1980, the Cubans began providing the Colombian guerrilla organization M-19 with training and help in its unification efforts with other leftist groups in the country, leading the government to break relations with Havana in March of the following year. In May 1981, Cuba attacked Costa Rica in the United Nations for its criticism of Havana's human rights violations, leading San Jose to sever diplomatic relations. Ecuador and Peru both withdrew their ambassadors from Havana in 1980, following Cuban violations of their embassy rights during the refugee exodus to the United States. By early 1981, many patriotic Latin Americans began speaking out against excessive Cuban involvement in Nicaragua. Both the late General Omar Torrijos of Panama and ex-President Carlos Andres Perez of Venezuela voiced strong criticisms. Most of the democratic parties in the region, including leading Latin American members of the Socialist International and the Christian Democratic World Federation, have followed suit.

In 1979, Torrijos started loosening the close ties built with Cuba during the 1970s. Panamanian teachers, students, and popular organizations staged a massive strike in October 1979 against the Ministry of Education, following its proposal to introduce Cuban books and advisers into the school system. Torrijos cancelled pending commercial agreements with the Soviet Union and began criticizing Castro's leadership of the Non-Aligned Movement. Shortly before his death in the spring of 1981, he criticized Cuba for its interference in Central America. The present Panamanian government has continued Torrijos' policy. In an effort to deny the U.S. pretexts for delaying transfer of the Panama Canal, the government has warned Cuba to step down from its activist role in the region even as it has reaffirmed its diplomatic links with Havana.

In 1981, Venezuelan Foreign Minister Jose Alberto Zambrano declared that "Cuban actions in Central America and the Caribbean region are part of the global strategy of the Soviet Union."[57] Alarmed by Soviet and Cuban efforts to penetrate the region and by prospects of superpower confrontation, Venezuela sought to forge a common "Latin American strategy" against outside intervention, tightening diplomatic relations with Argentina, Brazil, and Mexico. Caracas also opposed increased U.S. military deployments in the Caribbean, consistent with its goal of converting the Basin into "a zone of peace, not a strategic target of the big powers."[58]

In the aftermath of the Falklands (Malvinas) conflict, Venezuela has softened its stand toward Cuba at the same time it has sought to distance itself from the United States. State visits were resumed and the Cuban embassy in Caracas was recently reopened. In June 1982

the new foreign minister, Jose Rodriguez, referred to "a
climate of rapprochement positive towards Nicaragua," and
President Luis Herrera Campins appeared at the
revolution's anniversary celebrations the following month
in Managua.[59]

A major if generally unappreciated source of
resistance to Soviet-Cuban hegemonism is located within
the revolutionary movement itself. This is nowhere more
the case than in El Salvador. Four of the five
constituent groups of the Farabundo Marti National
Liberation Front (FMLN) arose originally as dissident
split-offs from the pro-Soviet Salvadoran Communist
Party.

The three main guerrilla groups in El Salvador are
the Popular Liberation Forces (FPL), the People's
Revolutionary Army (ERP), and the Armed Forces of
National Resistance (FARN). The FPL split from the
Salvadoran Communist Party in 1970 after a long and
bitter struggle against positions supported by the Soviet
Union but opposed by Cuba. Subsequently, however, the
FPL, while remaining suspicious of the USSR, adopted
positions congruent with that of Moscow, especially on
international questions. It is also the grouping closest
to the position of the Cubans and the Sandinistas. The
ERP began as a Maoist split from the PCS and was highly
influenced by the Cultural Revolution and the works of
North Korea's Kim il-Sung. In 1975, its military
commission tried and executed the group's leading
intellectual, Roque Dalton, on suspicion of being a
"Soviet-Cuban and CIA double agent." Dalton supporters
subsequently left the ERP to form the FARN.

In 1981, the ERP and FARN grew close once again.
Within the FMLN a "two-line struggle" between the positions of the ERP and the FARN, on the one hand, and those
of the FPL, on the other, became increasingly evident.
The FPL supports a strategy of "protracted people's war."
Although the term is Maoist, the FPL conception bears
little resemblance to the Chinese theory of united front
with middle sectors, flexible tactics, and broad international alliances. The FPL adheres narrowly to a
concept of "worker-peasant alliance versus the
bourgeoisie" and seems to envision an inevitable direct
confrontation with the United States in which its chief
allies would be Cuba and the Soviet Union. It agreed to
support the FMLN-FDR proposals for negotiated settlement
only after its intransigence had rendered it totally
isolated. The FARN, which has provided the political
leadership for the FARN/ERP alliance, like the
Terceristas in Nicaragua, counterposes insurrection to
protracted war. It favors broad alliances with the
middle sectors, including elements in the military
officers' camps. Recent diplomatic exposure and the
evolution of the Nicaraguan Revolution have reinforced

ts Maoist heritage of suspicion toward the Soviet Union
nd Cuba. The FARN has been critical of the Sandinistas'
ailure to preserve the broad alliances of the prerevolu-
ionary period and to integrate the masses organically
nto the revolutionary process. It is also critical of
heir failure to pursue consistently a policy of non-
lignment. The overt Cuban presence in Nicaragua has
aused problems for the FMLN-FDR as a whole and is
nother source of criticism in the FARN-ERP. The FPL, on
he other hand, maintains close relations with the
andinista National Directorate, especially with former
embers of the Protracted Popular War (GPP) faction led
y Tomas Borge and Bayardo Arce. There have been several
eports of tensions between the FSLN and the FARN in
anagua.

Recently the Cubans have been courting the ERP,
hich has remained independent of them up to now. This
ituation represents a danger to the political indepen-
ence of the FMLN, though it is worth noting that the
ubans have quarrelled with the FPL over the latter's
eluctance to support negotiations. In any event, if the
ar drags on, Cuban influence over the ERP and ERP
riumphalism are likely to increase.

Although Salvador is the most graphic case of the
ivision in the Central American left between its non-
ligned and its pro-Soviet wings, this split has also
een manifest elsewhere. The original Tercerista
endency in Nicaragua envisioned a non-aligned course in
hich the country would become equidistant from the two
uperpowers. Tercerism believed in the maximum use of
nternational conditions, in broad alliances within the
ountry, and in a phased revolutionary process in which
he mixed economy and pluralistic democracy would survive
or generations. These positions did not prevail within
he National Directorate; eventually the Tercerist
endency split and one of its leaders, Eden Pastora
Comandante Cero), left the country along with many of
is followers from the Southern Front. Pastora commenced
ilitary operations against the Sandinista government in
pril 1983. A line similar to that of the FPL in El
alvador and associated with the GPP in Nicaragua seems
o be prevailing. However, the old factional groupings
re giving way to those conditioned by the current
truggle among the Sandinistas.

In Guatemala the Revolutionary Armed Forces (FAR) is
n independent, Tercerista-type organization, whereas the
opular Guerrilla Army (EGP) is Cuban oriented. The
evolutionary Organization of the Armed People (ORPA)
tands somewhere between the two orientations just
entioned, whereas the Guatemalan Workers' Party (PGT) is
ssociated with Moscow. In Costa Rica, in the summer of
982, the electoral front called "Pueblo Unido" split
wice over the issues of broad alliances and the Soviet

468

Union. Eric Ardon, the leader of the Revolutionary
Movement of the People (MRP), stated that a major reason
for separating from Vanguardia Popular, the pro-Moscow
party, is that "they are permanently aligned with the
Soviet Union."[60]

Current administration policy disdains such distinctions. The struggle in the Caribbean Basin is between
"democracy" and "totalitarianism" tout court, a superpower conflict in which one must choose his side.
Reliable allies are U.S.-aligned regimes; countries
pursuing independent policies are distrusted. The Reagan
administration has rejected Mexican and French efforts
toward a negotiated solution in El Salvador and, to date
has been publicly supportive but privately obstructive of
those of the Contadora Group (Mexico, Venezuela, Panama,
and Colombia) to reach a regional settlement.

Under congressional pressure the administration has
likewise offered public support for "political
settlements," provided economic assistance, and spoken on
behalf of "political reform." Nonetheless, such gestures
have been at the service of a policy (sometimes
designated as "two-tracked") that is primarily military.
Thus the administration has armed El Salvador and
Honduras and equipped and trained insurgents who seek to
topple the Sandinista government.

Cuba has become a target of the Reagan regional
counteroffensive. Seeking to divert attention from its
activities in the region and suffering from domestic
economic and political difficulties, Havana began making
conciliatory overtures to the United States in November
1981, asking for negotiations. Previous preconditions
were dropped, and on two occasions, high-level Cuban and
U.S. officials held discussions. In March 1983, Castro
authorized Nicaragua's Daniel Ortega to inform the United
Nations Security Council that the Cuban government was
"willing to start talks immediately."[61]

The United States rejected the Cuban overtures,
pointing to increased shipments of Soviet weapons to the
island in 1981-82, Havana's activity on behalf of Central
American insurgents, and the increasing Cuban presence in
Nicaragua. Within three weeks of Ortega's announcement
at the United Nations, Washington tightened the embargo,
restricted U.S. tourist visits, and cut regular flights
to the island from Miami.

Perceiving Cuban economic weakness and recent
concern over the Soviets' inability to underwrite the
island's economy, the Reagan administration has used U.S.
leverage to tighten the economic vise. Heavy borrowing
from western banks and falling world sugar prices left
Cuba unable to meet its debt service requirements in
1982. The Cubans requested a rescheduling of their $3-4
billion debt to Europe and Japan, with $1.1 billion in
short-term liabilities due in September of 1982. For its

ong-term debt, Havana requested postponement of
epayment for ten years with a three-year grace period.
nterest payments and bank transaction fees would be paid
n current terms.[62]

Administration officials sought to dissuade Cuba's
reditors from leniency, urging that rescheduling be tied
o changes in Castro's foreign policy in Central America
nd Africa. Soviet infusions of foreign exchange did not
aterialize, igniting speculation that Cuban-Soviet rela-
ions were cooling. These rumors were somewhat doused
hen Castro travelled to Moscow for Brezhnev's funeral
nd met with Andropov on November 16, 1982. One adminis-
ration official stated that "the fact the meeting did
appen and the very fact that a picture of Castro and
ndropov together was released to the West is a Soviet
ay of saying, especially to the Reagan administration,
Castro is still our boy.' "[63] U.S. policymakers are
onvinced that when the Cubans feel less isolated and
ulnerable, they will revert to their traditional
ggressive posture.

OVIET-CUBAN REACTION TO THE U.S. COUNTEROFFENSIVE

A number of factors have influenced the Soviet
ecision not to confront the American counteroffensive
irectly. Domestic economic problems and the succession
risis have absorbed much of the Soviet leadership's
ttention and undermined its unity. Soviet passivity in
he Falklands and the Lebanese crises suggests that
Moscow is overextended and preoccupied with Afghanistan
nd Eastern Europe. Moscow's diplomatic efforts have
ocused on its "peace offensive" in Europe; its credi-
ility would be impaired by aggressive behavior in the
Western Hemisphere.

By early 1982, the Soviets and Cubans were anxious
to appear as peacemakers in the Caribbean Basin. But
their temporary lowering of sights seems to be a tactical
retrenchment rather than a strategic withdrawal. The
heavy optimism of the 1979-81 period, which "marked the
beginning of a qualitatively new stage in the development
of the Latin American peoples' struggle against
imperialism and oligarchy," has given way to a more
guarded Soviet view of revolutionary possibilities in
Central America.[64] Current Soviet accounts emphasize the
ebb and flow of country-specific situations rather than
an overall regional upsurge. Yet the work of expanding
Soviet and Cuban influence goes on, not only through low-
profile penetrations of security and military channels of
friendly Basin countries but also through long-range
academic and cultural programs intended to form
pro-Soviet political and technological elites. Above
all, Moscow seeks to capitalize on the renewed image of

U.S. interventionism. If military escalation is not viable at present and significant long-term economic aid is too taxing, both Havana and Moscow are positioning themselves for possible future advances.

Moscow now emphasizes "the aggressive U.S. counter-offensive" in Central America, one aspect of a resurgent U.S. "militarism" that constitutes the principal threat to world peace and stability counterposed to the Soviet peace offensive. Soviet analysts see the revolutionary movements reacting defensively to a revitalized and increasingly belligerent American foreign policy:

> The Reagan administration has shown a distinct preference for military solutions to problems in its relations with countries where tension is growing. Its plans naturally include the creation of reactionary regimes, the training of their armies to suppress the liberation movements, and finally the combat training of various renegades and traitors.[65]

The Soviets view such foreign policy as a return to the "big stick diplomacy" of the pre-Vietnam era.

U.S. policy in the Malvinas conflict was an expression of the new aggressive approach. American support for Great Britain "shattered the inventions of imperialist propaganda that the danger for developing countries emanates from the Soviet Union."[66] The Soviets emphasize U.S. disregard for the views of Latin American nations, as well as the conflicts that U.S. policy created with NATO allies. The Soviets portray U.S. policy in the Western Hemisphere as one aspect of a global counteroffensive:

> The present masters of the White House apparently hope to settle their affairs as well as possible and attain political successes precisely under the conditions of conflicts, tensions, military clashes and confrontations. This is how they are acting in the Middle East and this is how they try to act in the South Atlantic.[67]

In Central America, U.S. policy is depicted as an attempt to regain hegemony by suppressing national liberation movements.

> After proclaiming Central America a sphere of its own 'vital interests,' the U.S. has used every means at its disposal to retain political, economic, and military control over this region. At the basis of the Reagan administration's policy . . . lies a strategy which includes the suppression of the national liberation struggles in El Salvador and Guatemala, the destabilization of . . . Nicaragua,

and the institution of other measures of a preven-
tative nature to keep the liberation movement from
developing in depth and breadth.[68]

Moscow views nonmilitary and multilateral aspects of
.S. policy as links to the broader militaristic
trategy. The Caribbean Basin Initiative is bellicose
ue to its "discriminatory character" toward Cuba,
icaragua, and Grenada.[69] It seeks to foster dependency
nd discord among "friendly nations."[70] The Central
merican Democratic Community is an effort to enlist non-
ombatant nations, particularly Honduras and Costa Rica,
n the legitimizing of intervention, and to bolster the
alvadoran government by overcoming its diplomatic
solation.[71]
        Soviet advice to revolutionaries in the region,
articularly in Honduras and Costa Rica, is now much more
autious: "The main objective for progressive forces is
he effective frustration of the plans to turn Honduras
nto the stronghold of a crusade against democracy in
entral America."[72] In Costa Rica, the principal task is
o prevent that country from becoming a "bridgehead for
ttack on neighboring Nicaragua."[73]
        Guatemala is seen as the hinge of Central America; a
ictory for revolutionary forces there will have an even
reater impact on the region than a victory in either
icaragua or El Salvador; "there is not much doubt that
uatemala is on the brink of massive social upheaval" and
the revolutionaries' present strategy has to be peoples'
ar." But this strategy is represented as a reaction to
ligarchic repression orchestrated by the United States,
ather than the result of popular initiative and momen-
um. "The Guatemalan people had no other choice but
rmed struggle for their freedom and rights, that there
as no alternative to exercising their legal right to
ebel."[74]
        For all the Soviet criticism of U.S. policy, no big
oost in direct Soviet aid to the socialist governments
r revolutionary movements appears to be forthcoming.
ven before Washington's efforts to destabilize Nicaragua
ncreased, there had been growing concern in Managua over
oviet willingness and capacity to assist the
andinista's program of socialist construction. As we
aw in May 1982, Daniel Ortega set out for Moscow with
igh hopes of obtaining emergency currency relief to meet
icaragua's balance-of-payments crisis. He came home
ith the developmental assistance mentioned earlier, but
ithout badly needed foreign exchange.
        Moscow appears to be prudently limiting its commit-
ment of military hardware to the region as well. In the
ummer and fall of 1982, Nicaragua sought to purchase
oviet MiGs to bolster its air force. Moscow has not
een forthcoming. In the summer of 1982 the Central

Committee of the Soviet Communist Party reportedly
distributed a secret letter to fraternal parties and
fronts, placing priority on the Soviet peace campaign in
Western Europe. In the wake of Moscow's abandonment of
the PLO, Central American leftists were increasingly
dubious of Soviet commitment in a crunch.

CONCLUSION

The countries of the Caribbean Basin are
experiencing a double-edged crisis: an internal
economic, social, and political crisis and a crisis of
external hegemony. The Soviet Union, primarily via its
Cuban allies, seeks to fish in these troubled waters.
Moscow's immediate objective is not to establish
pro-Soviet regimes but to weaken its chief global
adversary. It has tuned its tactics to the evolving
situation-emphasizing "unity of the left" or broad united
fronts as dictated by local conditions and Washington's
response.

Geographical distance and its own internal and
external contradictions place limits on Moscow's freedom
of action in the Caribbean Basin. Cuban willingness to
cooperate with Moscow compensates to some extent for
geography. Moreover, proximity to a superpower breeds
powerful opposition to it. Recent history in
Afghanistan, Poland, and China, as well as in the
Caribbean Basin, attests to the growing obsolescence of
"spheres of influence."

The Reagan administration has stressed the security
danger in the United States' "backyard." "Backyardism,"
as a policy approach, seems to represent the American
equivalent of the Brezhnev Doctrine of "limited
sovereignty" for the Eastern Bloc. Hence, those
countries with the bad luck to live in the neighborhood
of a superpower are condemned by geographic fatality to
cede some of the prerogatives of sovereignty to their
powerful neighbor.

Backyardism has not been welcomed by the countries
of the American backyard. Mexico, Venezuela, Panama, the
Dominican Republic, and others have opposed U.S. policies
even as they have sought other ways to impede Soviet
penetration. They wish to see the Basin escape the
domination of the two superpowers and to avoid becoming
an arena of confrontation between the superpowers. Thus,
to date the Latin American and U.S. resistance to Soviet
inroads have worked in opposition to one another. Latin
American countries perceive a considerable component of
resurgent U.S. hegemonism in their American position.
Looking to history, they continue to fear their near and
mighty neighbor more than distant Moscow. This presents
a historic challenge for Washington: Can it forego the

presumptions of hegemony <u>in the interests of</u> a more
viable national security <u>policy in the Caribbean</u> Basin?

NOTES

The author wishes to acknowledge the invaluable
assistance of Lawrence Thomas in preparing this article.

1. The Caribbean Basin is a geopolitical concept
that links the economically and politically diverse
nations located in and around the Caribbean Sea. It
includes Central America; the Commonwealth Caribbean;
other island nations; Mexico, Colombia, Venezuela,
Surinam, and Guyana.

2. G. Karstag, "Concerning the Development of the
Revolutionary Process in Latin America," <u>Latinskaya
Amerika</u>, 1 (January-February 1972), Joint Publications
Research Service [hereafter JPRS] Translation No. 55481
(Arlington, Virginia, 1972), p. 71.

3. R. Ulyanovsky, "O Stranakh Sotsialisticheskoi
Orientatsi," <u>Kommunist</u>, 11 (July 1979), p. 74.

4. Rents charged to peasants tripled or quadrupled
during the 1960s. According to the Secretariat of
Central American Integration, by the early 1970s, 70
percent of the region's rural holdings were "minifundia"
of less than 10 acres. At the same time, 6 percent of
rural holdings constituted more than 70 percent of the
total arable land. See Clark Reynolds, "Fissures in the
Volcano? Central American Economic Prospects," in <u>Latin
America and the World Economy: A Changing International
Order</u>, ed. Joseph Grunwald (Beverly Hills: Sage
Publishers, 1981), pp. 203-204.

5. William R. Cline and Enrique Delgado (eds.),
<u>Economic Integration in Central America</u> (Washington,
D.C.: Brookings Institution, 1978), pp. 196, 198,
323-327.

6. W. Marvin Will, "The Struggle for Influence and
Survival: The United States-Microstate Caribbean
Interface," in <u>Colossus Challenged: The Struggle for
Caribbean Influence</u>, eds. H. Michael Erisman and John D.
Martz (Boulder, Colo.: Westview Press, 1982), p. 202.

7. U.S., Congress, House, Committee on Armed
Services, Testimony of Admiral Thomas B. Hayward, Chief
of Naval Operations, "Report of the Subcommittee on Sea
Power and Strategic and Critical Materials of the House
Committee on Armed Services in Fiscal Year 1980 and
1981," <u>Military Posture</u> (Washington, D.C., 1980 and
1981), p. 4.

8. Sergei Gorshkov, <u>Naval Power in Soviet Policy</u>
(Moscow: Voenizdat, 1979), pp. 11-12.

9. V. Vasileyev, "The United States' 'New Approach'
to Latin America," <u>International Affairs</u>, 6 (June 1971),
p. 48.

474

10. M. A. Oborotova, "Foreign Political Conditions of Revolutionary Development," Latinskaya Amerika, 7 (July 1982), JPRS Translation No. 81859, USSR Report, Political and Sociological Affairs No. 1312, Latinskaya Amerika Special Issue on Central American Revolutionary Process (Arlington, Va., September 27, 1982), p. 75.

11. Boris Ponomarev, "Sovmestnaya bor'ba rabochevo i national' no-osvobozhditel'nogo dvishenii protiv imperialisma, za sotsial' nii progress" Kommunist, 16 (November 1980), p. 41.

12. United Nations Commission on Trade and Development, UNCTAD V, TD/24, Supplement 2 (Manila, May 1979), p. 18 (Table 3), based on Soviet national foreign trade handbooks.

13. Granma Weekly Review (August 20, 1967).

14. Karstag, "Concerning the Development," p. 71.

15. J. Kobol, "Concerning Some Peculiarities of the Evolution of the Armies of the Latin American Continent," Latinskaya Amerika, 4 (1971), JPRS Translation (Arlington, Va.).

16. V. Bushuyev, "New Trends in Latin American Armed Forces" Krasnaya Zvezda (October 3, 1972), in JPRS Translation No. 57347 (Arlington, Va., 1972, October 26, 1972), pp. 4-5.

17. Cf. V. Morozov, International Economic Organization of Socialist States (Moscow: Novosti, 1973), p. 15.

18. Oscar Arevalo, "Reactionary Intrigues Notwithstanding," interview in New Times, 31 (Moscow, July 1977), p. 11.

19. Nikolai Leonov, "Nicaragua: Experiencia de una Revolucion Victoriosa," America Latina, 3 (1980), p. 37; Sergei Mikoyan, "Las Particularidades de la Revolucion en Nicaragua y sus Tareas Desde El Punto de Vista de la Teoria y la Practica de Movimiento Liberador," America Latina, 3 (1980), pp. 102-103.

20. Boris Koval, "La Revolucion: Largo Proceso Historico," America Latina, 3 (1980), pp. 76-79; Sergei Mikoyan, "La Creatividad Revolucionaria Abre el Camino Hacia la Victoria," America Latina, 2 (1980), p. 5.

21. Karstag, "Concerning the Development," p. 77.

22. B. Koval, "La Revolucion," pp. 79-80; Sergei Mikoyan, "Las Particularidades de la Revolucion," p. 101.

23. Ilya Bimov, "El Frente Sandinista de Liberacion Nacional: Fuerza Decisiva en la Lucha," America Latina, 3 (1980), p. 32.

24. M. S. Chumakova, "Nicaragua Viewed One Year After the Revolution," Latinskaya Amerika, 26 (July 1980); JPRS Translation No. 76700 (Arlington, Va., October 27, 1980), p. 32.

25. Alvaro Ramirez, "Nicaragua: From Armed Struggle to Construction," World Marxist Review, Vol. 23, No. 1 (January 1980), pp. 52-54; see also R. Ulyanovsky, "O

tranakh Sotsialisticheskoi Orientatsi," pp. 114-123; and oris Ponomarev, "The Cause of Freedom and Socialism is nvincible," World Marxist Review, Vol. 24, No. 1 January 1981), pp. 17-19.

26. S. Mikoyan, "Las Particularidades de la evolucion en Nicaragua," p. 106; see also K. Maidanik, La Unidad: Un Problema Clave," America Latina, 3 1980), p. 44.

27. Victor Volokii, as quoted in A. Sujostat, "Etapa ctual de la Lucha Revolucionaria de Liberacion," merica Latina, 1 (1977), p. 5.

28. William E. Ratliff, Castroism and Communism in atin America 1959-1976 (Washington, D.C.: American nterprise Institute, Hoover Policy Study 19, November 976), p. 44.

29. Granma Weekly Review (July 30, 1967); C.f. Jorge ominguez, "The Armed Forces and Foreign Relations," in ole Blasier and Carmelo Mesa-Lago, Cuba in the World Pittsburg: University of Pittsburg Press, 1979), p. 59.

30. Robert Moss, "Soviet Ambitions in Latin America," n The Southern Oceans and the Security of the Free Jorld, ed. Patrick Wall (London: Spacey International, 977), p. 195.

31. Krasnaya Zvezda (January 1, 1969), cited in Leon oure and Morris Rothenberg, Soviet Penetration of Latin merica (Coral Gables: University of Miami Press, 1975), . 3.

32. Krasnaya Zvezda (December 2, 1969), cited in oure and Rothenberg, Soviet Penetration, p. 31; James D. heberge, Russia in the Caribbean, Part 2 (Washington,).C.: Center for Strategic and International Studies, 1973), Table 7, pp. 103-105.

33. Washington Post (June 19, 1983); U.S., Congress, enate, Foreign Relations Committee, Statement of Thomas). Enders, Assistant Secretary of State for Inter-American Affairs (April 12, 1983).

34. Washington Post (June 19, 1983), p. 1A.

35. Financial Times (London, March 17, 1983).

36. Senate Foreign Relations Committee, Statement of Thomas O. Enders (April 12, 1983), p. 2.

37. See "Soviet Inroads into Latin America," Remarks of Nestor D. Sanchez, Deputy Assistant Secretary of Defense for Inter-American Affairs, before the Defense Forum for National Educators (March 9, 1983), Washington, D.C.; Diario de las Americas (April 25 and June 6, 1981); Washington Post (June 2, 1981, July 29, November 19, and December 15, 1982); Providence Journal (June 9, 1981); Le Monde (July 21, 1981).

38. Senate Foreign Relations Committee, Statement of Thomas O. Enders (April 12, 1983), p. 1.

39. Washington Post (July 29, 1982 and June 19, 1983).

476

40. Foreign Broadcast Information Service [hereafter FBIS]: Latin America (May 11, 1982), p. P-8.

41. Miami Herald (November 28, 1982).

42. FBIS Latin America (March 16, 1983), p. I-8.

43. N. I. Gavtilov and G. B. Starushenko, eds., Africa: Problems of Socialist Orientation (Moscow: Nauka, 1976), pp. 10-11.

44. U.S., Department of State, Communist Interference in El Salvador, Special Report No. 80 (February 23, 1981); U.S., Department of State, Cuba's Renewed Support for Violence, Special Report No. 90 (December 14, 1981), p. 3.

45. Department of State, Communist Interference in El Salvador, Document E.

46. Department of State, Cuba's Renewed Support for Violence, p. 18.

47. Ibid., pp. 7-8; FBIS Latin America (August 4, 1981), p. 8.

48. Anthony P. Maingot, "Cuba and the Commonwealth Caribbean: Playing the Cuban Card," in Caribbean Review, Vol. IX, No. 1 (Winter 1980), pp. 48-49.

49. Diario de las Americas (July 22, 1981).

50. U.S., Department of Defense, "Recent Developments in Central America and the Caribbean" (1982).

51. Washington Post (February 24, 1983).

52. FBIS Latin America (March 15, 1982), p. 58.

53. Miami Herald (December 14, 1982); Diario de las Americas (February 1, 1983).

54. FBIS Latin America (March 1, 1983), p. Q4; New York Times (January 28, 1983).

55. Latin American Regional Report: Caribbean (February 25, 1983), p. 1.

56. New York Times (June 12, 1983).

57. El Nacional (Caracas) (March 1, 1981).

58. FBIS Latin America (March 18, 1981), p. L3-4.

59. Washington Post (August 1, 1982).

60. La Nacion (San Jose) (August 8, 1982).

61. Granma Weekly Review (April 4, 1982).

62. Miami Herald (September 1, 1982).

63. Miami Herald (December 7, 1982).

64. M. F. Gornov, "Latin America: More Intense Struggle Against Imperialism and Oligarchy and for Democracy and Social Progress," in Latinskaya Amerika, 7 (July 1982), JPRS Translation No. 81859, p. 39.

65. Ibid, p. 17.

66. V. Dmitriyev, "The Crisis of Imperialists' Colonial Policy in Latin America," International Affairs, 10 (October 1982), p. 39.

67. Gornov, "Latin America," p. 12.

68. Ibid, p. 14.

69. Izvestia (July 17, 1982).

70. A. Glinkin and P. Yakovlev, "Latin America in the Global Strategy of Imperialism," MEMO, 10 (1982), p. 77.

71. M. L. Mishina, "Central American Democratic Community," <u>Latinskaya Amerika</u>, 7 (July 1982), JPRS Translation No. 81859, p. 47.

72. A. V. Kuz'mischev, "Political Situation in Honduras," <u>Latinskaya Amerika</u>, 7 (July 1982), JPRS Translation No. 81859, p. 47.

73. Alexander Trushin, "There Should Not Be More Policemen Than Teachers," <u>New Times</u>, 23 (June 1982), pp. 24-25.

74. N. S. Leonev, "Guatemala's Worries and Hopes," <u>Latinskaya Amerika</u>, 7 (July 1982), JPRS Translation No. 81859, pp. 30, 32.

14
Reagan's Central American Policy: Disaster in the Making

Wayne S. Smith

Foreign policy is not the Reagan administration's strong suit, as illustrated by, among other things, its clumsy handling of the European-pipeline-sanctions issue and the deterioration of its strategically important relationship with the Chinese People's Republic. (President Reagan continues to insist publicly that all communists are "the enemy," even though the Chinese and Yugoslavs, among others, clearly are not.) Unimpressive as the administration's record is in other areas, however, history will probably record as its most egregious blunders those made in Central America. Certainly it is there that U.S. policies are most sharply questioned--by the American people, by Congress, and by the allies of the United States. Indeed, the United States is virtually isolated. No major government supports its policies in Central America. Its European allies do not; neither do Canada, Mexico, or most other Latin American governments. And it is hardly an accident that as of the end of 1982, three senior American diplomats in the area had left the Foreign Service in disagreement with those policies.

This chapter analyzes the policies that have so complicated the U.S. position in Central America and points to what might have been wiser alternatives. As Larry Pezzullo, the highly respected former U.S. ambassador to Nicaragua, put it recently: "The single positive thing I can think of to say about the Reagan administration's approach in Central America is that it is so lacking in analysis that it confuses everyone, our adversaries as well as our friends."[1]

THE SITUATION AS OF JANUARY 1981

It is in the nature of politics for one administration to blame its problems on its predecessors and then to pass them on to its successors. The Reagan adminis-

tration is no exception. It jeered at Carter's
"weak-kneed" approach and complained of the mess it had
inherited in Central America. A review of the situation
at the time Reagan took office, however, indicates the
situation has worsened, not improved, since January 1981.

In El Salvador, American policy was at last
beginning to have an impact on what had long been a
dreadful situation. For over a century, the military and
oligarchy had run the country as they wished. Anyone who
protested was exiled or murdered. In 1932, the armed
forces slaughtered some 30,000 striking peasants. By the
early 1970s, however, there were signs of change.
Salvadorans placed their hopes in the 1972 presidential
elections, which were supposed to be free and honest.
But when it became clear that the coalition ticket of
Christian Democrat Jose Napoleon Duarte and Social
Democrat Guillermo Ungo was winning, the military stopped
the vote count and declared Colonel Arturo Molina the
winner. The country was thrown into turmoil, which had
subsided little by the 1977 elections. These too were
fraudulent, and the military installed General Carlos
Humberto Romero in the presidency. His rule was
particularly harsh and unenlightened. Violence
escalated. Political order steadily deteriorated.
There was no question as to who was responsible:
the military.

Some hope for a moderate solution appeared in
October 1979 as progressive-minded younger officers led
by Colonel Adolfo Arnoldo Majano overthrew Romero and
formed a new government with civilian participation. The
regime indicated its intention to push for reforms and to
curb the repressive practices of the security forces.
Before the year was out, however, conservative officers
had emasculated the new government. Most of its civilian
members, including Guillermo Ungo, resigned. Eventually,
Majano himself was driven into exile. Salvadorans who up
until then had held out some hopes for a democratic
solution gave them up. The opposition began to coalesce
and increasingly to embrace armed struggle. The civil
war began in earnest. It was not dreamed up in Moscow;
rather, it was the direct result of the fierce resistance
of the military to change.

If Carter administration policy in El Salvador is to
be criticized, it should be for not having taken a
resolute stand in support of the progressive government
in late 1979. Had the U.S. Embassy in December 1979 made
it clear to the Salvadoran military that the junta had
Washington's full support and that any attempts to undermine it would meet with strong U.S. opprobrium, that
might have made the difference. The junta might have
been respected and the civil war avoided.

Even given this initial error, with the arrival of
Ambassador Robert White in March 1980, American policy

began to get on track. As implemented by White, its central thrust was to emphasize to the Salvadoran government and military that, in order to win popular support, they should move ahead vigorously with socioeconomic reforms and curb the excesses of the security forces. Jose Napoleon Duarte, who had joined the junta after its other civilian members had left, was entirely receptive to such views. Indeed, they coincided with his own. The problem was that, when all was said and done, it was still the military, not Duarte, who controlled the situation. Right-wing death squads remained active. Even so, the more popular, democratic tone of the government, and of U.S. policy, was beginning to have some credibility with the Salvadoran people, thus bolstering the position of both the Duarte junta and the United States, which backed it. When the guerrillas launched their "all-out" offensive in January 1981, the Salvadoran government, which at that point was receiving no U.S. military assistance, was able quickly to defeat it.

This record stands in marked contrast to the government's poor showing during the guerrillas' offensive of February-March 1983. Privately, spokesmen for the Reagan administration have tried to explain away this contrast by claiming the insurgents are now better armed. Secretary of State Shultz, indeed, attributed the new offensive to an upsurge in the flow of arms coming from the Soviet Union through Cuba and Nicaragua. But neither assertion bears up to careful scrutiny. Contradicting Shultz, American diplomats and military and intelligence officers in El Salvador were quoted as saying that external support seemed a minor factor. There was no evidence of any increase in outside assistance; on the contrary, the guerrillas were doing very well with arms captured from government troops.[2]

Furthermore, after the hoopla the administration made over arms shipments from the Eastern Bloc in its February 1981 "White Paper" on El Salvador, it was inconsistent to claim two years later that the guerrillas had not been well armed in 1981. The military situation had indeed worsened, but external factors had little to do with it.

In Nicaragua, the Sandinistas had been in power some eighteen months when Reagan took office. There, as in El Salvador, the Carter administration's principal fault had been its early indecisiveness. The Somoza regime was falling of its own weight. Short of propping it up with bayonets, the United States could not have maintained it in power--nor should the United States have wished to do so. Its interests lay in encouraging a rapid transition and filling the vacuum with the most responsible elements possible. A more resolute stance in favor of Somoza's departure in 1978 might have included the Sandinistas, but they need not have been the central force. By summer

1979, however, the situation had polarized, and there was little if any chance of blocking them from sole possession of power.

Again, the Carter administration tried to make the best of a situation it had initially handled poorly. Even the most perfunctory analysis will suggest that the most logical course of action would have been to attempt through diplomatic and economic persuasion to encourage pluralism and moderation. If the United States were not going to remove the Sandinistas from power (and that was an even more unwarranted option in 1979 than it is today), the only sensible alternative was to try to use its influence with them. After all, the United States had considerable leverage, including economic, to bring to bear. Its situation was by no means impossible. Even the Sandinistas expressed interest in a constructive relationship; most other sectors of Nicaraguan society were even more emphatic on this score.

There were many frustrations. It took over a year and a debilitating debate to get the economic assistance package through Congress. Meanwhile, the civil war in El Salvador had broken out in full, and it was clear that the Nicaraguans were giving some degree of support to the guerrillas there. The Sandinistas, moreover, were hardly dedicated democrats. They had their own revolutionary program to carry out and were not worried about due process for those who got in their way. And, of course, Cuban influence was a matter of concern.

Even so, the U.S. policy of patient diplomacy was not without impact, and it still seemed to offer the best hope of eventually returning the situation to a more normal course. For one thing, there were still demo-cratic elements within the Nicaraguan government with whom the United States could work--men such as Arturo Cruz, Alfonso Robelo, Eden Pastora, and Alfredo Cesar. The democratic opposition was virtually unanimous in encouraging the United States to continue its policy of patient engagement. In January 1981, for example, a wide range of non-Sandinista Nicaraguans expressed concern to Ambassador Pezzullo over the impending cutoff of U.S. economic assistance. Catholics, democratic politicians, and leaders of the private sector (COSEP) all warned that such a step would only make matters worse. It would undercut democratic forces working to maintain pluralism and a mixed economy and would deprive the United States of the only instrument through which it could play an effective role. In Pezzullo's own words:

> We were not unaware of the radical tendencies within the Sandinista government, but it was misleading as well as damaging to our interests to label the whole structure Marxist/Leninist and to treat it as such. There were moderate forces within it which wished to

retain a democratic framework. Between the radicals and the moderates there was still, as of early 1981, a dialogue. It was very much in our interests to see that dialogue maintained. Taking an overtly hostile position against the Nicaraguan government could only excite xenophobic fears within Nicaragua, thus almost assuring that the internal dialogue would be broken off. We did and it was.[3]

As the Reagan administration came to office, moreover, the Nicaraguans and Cubans, largely in recognition of the failure of the Salvadoran guerrillas' "final offensive," signalled an interest in discussions with the United States and in political solutions to the Central American conflicts.[4] The Sandinistas appear to have acceded, at least in part, to our demands that they stop cross-border support to the insurgents,[5] thus indicating that they attached considerable value to a relationship with the United States—in other words, that the United States enjoyed considerable leverage with them. The moment was especially propitious for negotiations. The United States appeared to be in an excellent position to bargain from a position of strength. Unfortunately, this advantage was squandered.

THE REAGAN ADMINISTRATION'S PERCEPTIONS

The Reagan administration came to office with a great deal of ideological baggage pointing it away from negotiated solutions. The new president had long espoused a simplistic "we-or-they" approach to the socialist countries and during the campaign had been particularly insistent on taking stern measures against Cuba and Nicaragua. Much of the administration's initial reaction, moreover, was based on a report written by the so-called Santa Fe Committee in 1980.[6] This study projected the problem starkly in terms of East-West conflict. The Americas were under attack; they were threatened by a brutal extracontinental power, the Soviet Union, which was operating through its Cuban surrogate. It was up to the United States to remedy the situation through a series of political and military measures. Regional security arrangements were to be strengthened, the Rio Treaty revitalized, and bilateral military assistance stepped up. Technical and psychological assistance were to be offered to all countries of the hemisphere in the "struggle against terrorism."

Nowhere in the report was there any favorable mention of agrarian reform; nor were there recommendations for other sociostructural changes or the promotion of human rights. On the contrary, the study recommended that the United States "stop targeting its

484

allies" with an inequitably applied human rights program.
There was no suggestion that the Salvadoran or Guatemalan
governments should halt the atrocities of their security
forces. Why should there be? In the view of the Santa
Fe Committee, the problem was one of external aggression,
not internal conflict and social injustice.

As for Cuba, the report urged that "frankly
punitive" measures be taken, including the opening of a
Radio Free Cuba (an idea the administration took up as
Radio Marti). If these steps did not complete the job,
its authors urged that a "war of national liberation" be
launched against the Castro regime.

The views of the Santa Fe Committee were reinforced
by those of Jeane Kirkpatrick, who was shortly to become
ambassador to the United Nations and to whom President
Reagan frequently turned, and still turns, for advice on
Latin American policy. In an article published in
January 1981, she too stressed the Soviet threat to this
hemisphere and charged the Carter administration with
having given more attention to democratic change than to
American security and with being more interested in
bringing about agrarian reform than elections in El
Salvador. The administration, she complained, seemed to
believe events were shaped by social "forces" rather than
by men.[7]

This was a theme Kirkpatrick embellished with a
vengeance after taking office. Speaking to the
Conservative Political Action Conference in March 1981,
she acknowledged that poverty, illiteracy, and unequal
distribution of wealth are prevalent in Central America,
and noted that some people would therefore have us
believe the problems in that region have to do with
social injustice. But, she went on, these conditions
have existed throughout Central America's history, and
one "cannot explain a short-range problem by reference to
a permanent condition." Revolutions, she declared, are
caused "not by social injustice" but "by revolutionaries,
and revolutionaries are people. They are not social
forces, they are people with guns. Revolutions are
caused by violence and terrorism. . . . "[8]

Tom Paine and Patrick Henry would have been puzzled
by her reasoning, which reduces all revolutionaries to
the status of "terrorists" and suggests that, in
addressing today's turmoil in Central America, one would
do better to emphasize military options than agrarian
reform. To stress the point, she stated elsewhere that
she knew of "no country which has ever successfully
carried out reforms while fighting a civil war."[9]

It was against the background of such advice that
the Reagan administration began to formulate its confrontational strategy in Central America. Its analysis of
events also fostered such an approach. The Salvadoran
guerrillas had just suffered a severe setback and during

1981 agreed to begin a dialogue without preconditions. Cuba and Nicaragua were also indicating a willingness to talk. The administration apparently read these overtures as signs of weakness and concluded that an easy victory was within grasp. After all, if the Salvadoran government had halted the guerrilla offensive without U.S. assistance, just think what it might accomplish <u>with</u> such aid. Accordingly, the administration decided to push for an uncompromising political and military victory: The guerrillas would be defeated, the Sandinistas ousted (the Republican campaign platform already hinted at that), and the Cubans humiliated. Secretary of State Haig is said to have promised Reagan a short-term triumph.[10]

This approach was especially attractive, for if communism could be stopped in its tracks in Central America, that would tend to validate the kind of get-tough policies the administration wished to implement on a global basis. Secretary Haig was reported to believe that the United States had to take a hard-line approach in order to demonstrate American resolve. An aide quoted him as saying: "We must demonstrate to everyone--the Russians, our allies, the Third World--that we can win, that we can be successful. We must move decisively and quickly to turn things around in the world or we will be nibbled to death by the Soviets."[11]

THE ADMINISTRATION'S INITIAL APPROACH

Whatever its other failings, the Carter administration had understood that the United States should not be perceived as bolstering or perpetuating repressive dictatorships. The United States might on a pragmatic basis have to deal with them, but its philosophical preferences for pluralism and respect for the integrity of the individual ought always to be clear. Carter's emphasis on human rights and reforms helped make those preferences clear. Not surprisingly, given the Cold War mindset described earlier, the Reagan administration did not continue that emphasis. Rather, its transition team, which blew through Central America just after the November 1980 elections, sharply criticized American ambassadors, especially Robert White in El Salvador, for having been too energetic in promoting human rights and reforms. The transition team called for the downgrading of both. Subsequently, Secretary Haig confirmed that promotion of human rights would receive less attention; defeating terrorism would receive more. Reforms also took a back seat for a time. The external rather than internal nature of the Central American struggle was given priority. At a press briefing on February 13, 1981, the State Department carried this to the extreme of suggesting that the guerrillas in El Salvador "did not represent a native insurgency"--that is, they were directed from Moscow. The same month, the "White Paper" claimed the conflict had become a "textbook case of indirect armed aggression by communist powers through Cuba."[12]

In the face of this "communist aggression," Secretary Haig announced that the United States must draw a line. The turmoil in Central America was a challenge emanating from Moscow; it was a challenge that the United States had to take up and win.

What to do? First, the administration threatened Cuba. The Castro regime had already indicated an interest in discussions about, and political solutions in, Central America, but never mind. The administration did not wish to explore that avenue. It had come to office vowing to get tough and it was determined to do just that, even if there were no objective reason to do so. It was not interested in discussions or negotiations of any kind. Rather, Secretary Haig threatened military action. Speaking on February 27, he declared that "Cuban activity has reached a peak that is no longer acceptable in this hemisphere. . . . El Salvador is a problem emanating first and foremost from Cuba . . . it is our intention to deal with this matter at its source."[13]

Haig did not spell out how this might be done-- whether by blockade, surgical air strikes, invasions, or some other method. He simply noted that no option was excluded. Though his aim was clearly to intimidate, it is a mystery why he expected to succeed. The Cubans, after all, had played David to our Goliath for years. They had seen it all before--threats, exile raids, clandestine radio stations, and so forth. They had not been intimidated in the past and were not likely to be so now.

As the portent of things to come, the clamps were taken off of Cuban exile paramilitary activity. In obvious violation of U.S. neutrality laws (and of the administration's position against terrorism), Alpha-66 and other exile organizations reopened training camps in Florida and openly stated that the purpose was to prepare their members for raids against Cuba. This was not an idle threat. Raids were carried out. They caused no real damage, and the raiders invariably were captured by the Cuban authorities. In the final analysis, such activities caused far more harm to U.S. credibility than they did to Cuba's infrastructure or morale. The administration, however, neither took any measures to curb them nor issued any statements to suggest it did not condone them.

A confrontational approach was also taken with Nicaragua. The Reagan administration came to office determined to get rid of the Sandinista government. There was never any intention of negotiating with it or

using the economic and diplomatic leverage still
available to the United States. In an appearance before
the Senate Foreign Relations Committee in March 1981, the
president authorized a clandestine operation against
Nicaragua.[14] The "secret war" was thus launched after
the new government had been in office less than two
months.

Not surprisingly, in view of its more bellicose
intentions, the Reagan administration was moved not at
all by the fact that Nicaragua had at least partially
acceded to U.S. demands. Economic assistance was cut off
anyway; preparations for the secret war proceeded apace.
In these efforts, Washington showed little political
acumen, picking as allies the Somocista guardsmen exiled
in Honduras. This was a colossal blunder. Not only was
the United States thus identified with the Somocistas and
"a return to the past," but the fact that Managua was
threatened by a Somocista/CIA operation subsequently made
it difficult for more democratic opponents to raise the
banner against the radical Sandinista commanders. As
Eden Pastora (the legendary Comandante Cero) commented to
me in December 1982:

> With the fatherland under attack from the hated
> Somocista counterrevolutionaries, should we true
> revolutionaries lift our hands against the radicals
> in Managua, we might be perceived as betraying the
> nation, or even become identified with the
> Somocistas. Hence, because of Reagan's stupid
> secret war, I feel my hands to be tied. I can only
> sit and wait for some change in the situation.

From almost any perspective, then, the secret war
was counterproductive to U.S. interests. Very little
thought, apparently, had been given to its objectives and
consequences. The fact that it might well touch off a
step-by-step escalation leading to a full-scale regional
war seemed to daunt American policymakers not at all,
probably because no one had thought that far ahead. And
as for objectives, the administration could give no
sensible explanation. After word of these activities
leaked to the surface in late 1982, official spokesmen
first told Congress that their purpose was simply to
interdict arms coming across Honduras from Nicaragua
bound for El Salvador--an explanation that many legis-
lators considered an insult to their intelligence.
Honduras, after all, is friendly territory. Assuming the
United States had sufficient information to make interdiction possible--for example, routes and schedules--it
would have had no need for a paramilitary force or a
secret army to perform the task. It could have simply
called on the Honduran military or police. They have

cooperated with similar efforts in the past and would have been only too pleased to have continued to do so.

The secret war was not confined to operations in Honduras. Training camps for Nicaraguan exiles were also opened in Florida. This was hardly consistent with U.S. demands for a halt in subversive activities in the hemisphere. As the New York Times pointed out:

> The Reagan administration accuses Nicaragua of violating international law by permitting a flow of arms to left-wing comrades in El Salvador, but the administration scuppers its case when it indulges the training of exile armies in Florida--an illegal and provocative act that justifies alarm in Nicaragua. Hector Fabian, a Cuban-born leader of one such private army, puts the legal point frankly: "Under the Carter and Nixon administrations, what we were doing was a crime. With the Reagan administration, no one has bothered us for 10 months." And its not just training. The forthright Mr. Fabian says that at least 100 Nicaraguan exiles have returned to their country to fight against its revolutionary junta.[15]

In El Salvador, the Reagan administration stepped up military assistance in the form of training, advisers, and armaments. Clearly, it was after a military victory. Even though the guerrillas had offered to talk, it encouraged the Salvadoran government to turn aside any suggestion of ending the conflict through negotiations, first by insisting that the insurgents were making unreasonable demands, then by arguing that the March 1982 elections rendered negotiations unnecessary: If the armed opposition wished to participate, they had but to lay down their weapons and do so.

Many observers, including the Mexican government, pointed out that conditions did not exist for elections. Historically, few civil wars have been ended by having one side convoke elections while refusing to discuss with the other conditions for the latter's participation. The administration was warned that under the circumstances, elections were likely to be truncated, inconclusive, and even counterproductive. They were. They produced a government considerably more fragmented than the Duarte-led junta and one generally further to the right. As predicted, the vote solved nothing.

Despite the fact that it is the poorest of the Central American countries, Honduras had remained aloof from the turmoil around it. The military there had never been as repressive as its counterparts in El Salvador and Guatemala; nor was there as great a disparity in wealth. Moreover, democratic elections had been held in 1981, and in early 1982 power was turned over to a civilian government headed by Roberto Suazo Cordova. At the time the Reagan administration took office, there were high hopes for Honduras. It was not embattled, and democracy seemed to have an excellent chance of taking root.

Honduras' chances are not so bright today. By involving Honduras in the war against Nicaragua, the Reagan administration has endangered it: Honduras may now very well become a target for retaliatory actions from the Sandinistas. The possibilities of a regional war are greater than they have been in decades. Further, the logistics and backroom deals necessitated by the secret war have ineluctably strengthened the hand of military hardliners vis-a-vis the civilians, thus diminishing the prospects for survival of Honduran democracy.

Finally, in Guatemala, the Reagan administration chose to ignore the brutal nature of the Lucas Garcia and Rios Montt governments. Appalling human rights violations were simply glossed over. As in El Salvador, the situation was portrayed in terms of East-West conflict. Nothing could have been more absurd, but President Reagan was led to the conclusion that Rios Montt was a fine fellow who had been given a "bum rap" by the media. The administration has consistently pushed to resume military assistance, despite the staggering atrocities of Rios Montt's regime.

RENEWED EMPHASIS ON HUMAN RIGHTS AND SOCIAL REFORMS...

Having initially denigrated Carter's emphasis on human rights and social reforms, the Reagan administration was quickly forced to trim its sails. For one thing, it came to realize that the American people attach considerable importance to the promotion of human rights and that its disavowal of this commitment was not only bad politics but it also deprived its own policies of any higher moral purpose. For another, it became clear that the governments of the region desperately needed and expected economic assistance. Unless there was promise of such help, their willingness to cooperate with the United States would be greatly diminished.

And so the administration reversed itself. Having previously made light of human rights, it now began insisting that it was as interested in their promotion as any previous government. In addition, new attention was given to economic development. President Reagan launched his Caribbean Basin Initiative (CBI). Having claimed at one time that poverty and social injustice had nothing to do with revolutionary turmoil, Ambassador Kirkpatrick evolved to the point of urging, in February 1983, a Marshall Plan for Latin America. But this was too little too late. The economic assistance provided by the CBI

490

was less than $400 million (only some 15 percent of what the Soviet Union provides to a single country, Cuba, every year). As of April 1983, the guts of the CBI, its trade and tariff preferences, remain bogged down in Congress.

As for the greater attention shown for human rights, this emphasis appears to have been for appearances' sake only. Certainly, the administration did nothing to advance the cause anywhere. It criticized leftist regimes but was unwilling to take any action to improve the situation. In Cuba, for example, it refused to honor a prior commitment to process for entry some 1,500-2,000 former political prisoners. In El Salvador it continued to certify progress in human rights even when it knew there had been none. No one has yet been tried for the murders of any of the Americans in that country--all of whom were assassinated by government security forces or allied death squads. Some 3,000 Salvadorans, including hundreds of women and children, were slaughtered in 1982, most of them at the hands of semi-official death squads and the security forces. Not a single person has been brought to trial for this slaughter.

Nor has the administration effectively used the leverage given it by the certification process. In late 1982, the U.S. ambassador in San Salvador, Deane Hinton, did publicly warn the right against repeated human rights violations. But the White House immediately pulled the rug out from under him by, in effect, disavowing his speech. The conclusion drawn by the far right was inevitable: No attention need be paid to such admonitions. Indeed, the right is convinced that the Reagan administration is so totally committed in El Salvador that it could not disengage even if it wanted to. No matter what the barbarities committed there, the rightists believe the administration will continue to support them and will automatically certify, every six months, that there has been improvement in the human rights situation. They are probably right.

...AND A LOWERING OF RHETORIC

Though it reasserted an interest in human rights and reforms, the administration did not alter its basic approach toward Central America or Cuba. In both cases, that approach remained confrontational. Washington did, however, lower its voice, largely because the hard realities of the situation began to call into question the efficacy of harsh rhetoric.

Belatedly, the administration appears to have realized that Castro would not be intimidated by anything short of a full-scale invasion--and despite all its fire and brimstone, it had no intention of going that far.

One can threaten just so long. After a given point, the threats are seen to be empty and damage the initiator more than the recipient. By the end of 1981, the Reagan administration had passed that point with respect to Cuba.

At the same time, the administration was under considerable pressure from Congress and allies of the United States (especially Mexico) to open negotiations with Cuba. Its response was predictable. To turn aside these pressures, it sought to give the impression of a willingness to talk when in fact none existed. In December 1981, Secretary Haig, who was visiting Mexico City, bowed to the insistence of his hosts and talked to Cuban Vice-President Carlos Rafael Rodriguez. Nothing came of this, or was intended to. Haig simply reiterated well-known U.S. positions. The Cubans, however, believed that at least the ice had been broken and that more substantive discussions might follow. To improve the atmosphere for those talks, in late December 1981 they informed the United States through diplomatic channels that they had suspended arms shipments to Nicaragua. Given the intense interest it had earlier evidenced in this flow and the fact that it had no solid evidence to the contrary (as it privately admitted), the administration's failure to show the least interest in this gesture was incomprehensible. It neither explored the possibilities thus implied nor even acknowledged the overture.

In March 1982, General Vernon Walters was sent secretly to Havana to talk to Castro. This initiative was less spontaneous and far more cynical than Haig's reluctant agreement to meet Rodriguez. The Walters' visit did nothing more than enumerate the issues in disagreement between the two sides--Central America, the return of the excludables dumped on the United States during the Mariel boatlift, and so on--and indicated that these would have to be addressed before there could be any improvement in relations.

The Cubans agreed and indicated their willingness to address these matters, though they noted that while bilateral issues could be negotiated, the war in El Salvador could only be discussed.[16] The Cubans were frankly puzzled by the Walters' mission, but they concluded that its purpose had been to establish an agenda for discussions. They were still awaiting some indication as to when the first round of these talks would be held when the United States, in April 1982, announced new measures against Cuba, including the cut-off of U.S. tourism to the island and the abrogation of the bilateral fishing agreement. The administration justified these measures to other governments by noting that it had tried to talk to the Cubans. It had sent General Walters to Havana (a fact it had carefully leaked only days after his return). Walters had found their position so aggressive and unbending that it was clear dialogue would lead nowhere.

It is difficult to see the Walters' visit as anything more than a diversionary tactic. Having side-stepped what might have been constructive discussions, the administration settled back into a policy similar to that pursued by many of its predecessors: encouraging allies to deny credit to Havana, stepping up propaganda efforts, and limiting travel and other contacts between the two countries. Having backed away from threatening to "take it to the source," the administration had no new ideas to offer.

On El Salvador, too, propaganda had to be toned down. For several weeks after the inauguration, Secretary Haig seemed to breathe fire in that direction almost on a daily basis. Conservative journalists were encouraged to focus on the test of wills shaping up between the United States and the Soviet Union in Central America. Predictably, President Reagan at one point suggested that those who disagreed with his policy in El Salvador were being "manipulated by the communists."[17] It began to appear that the United States was on the way back to McCarthyism, if not on the way to World War III. As this strategy diverted attention from other important problems, such as the economy, the administration decided it had overplayed its hand. Accordingly, in a rather bizarre episode, Deputy Assistant Secretary of State John Bushnell was instructed to warn the media that they were making too much of El Salvador. When that raised eyebrows, Bushnell was publicly rebuked by the White House--thereby indicating that the carrying out of questionable instructions too enthusiastically can be a risky business.

CONTINUITY OF BASIC APPROACH

As earlier suggested, however, the central thrust of the U.S. approach in El Salvador remained the same as before. Negotiated solutions were ruled out; military assistance was key. Elections were held in March 1982, but the armed opposition refused to participate, taking the position that there could be no meaningful balloting until adequate conditions had been brought about through negotiations. With right-wing death squads still operating with impunity, the refusal of the left to participate was understandable.

The elections were supposed to give the new Salvadoran government legitimacy, thus strengthening its hand to end the violence. But this was an illusion. The vote solved nothing. Nevertheless, for the remainder of the year the State Department seemed to bask in the illusion that the elections had turned a corner for the

United States. Corridor talk had it that the large voter turnout indicated a lack of support for the guerrillas; popular support now might be expected to gravitate toward the new government. The United States would be able to "build democracy" in El Salvador. Convinced that they were winning the war, both the Salvadoran government and the Reagan administration rejected out of hand an October 1982 FMLN/FDR proposal for discussions without preconditions or prior commitments. Washington also rebuffed Mexican peace proposals and a Mexican-Venezuelan offer to play a mediation role. This behavior was obtuse, for one of the keys to the Central American problem--which is regional in nature--is to engage the other governments of the area in a diplomatic process aimed at ending the fighting and bringing about an equitable settlement.

The administration's optimism was short-lived. By March 1983, its Salvador policy was in tatters and it was beating a tactical retreat. As more objective observers had warned, the elections had complicated rather than improved the situation. Divisions within the army had been heightened, as pointed up by the revolt of Colonel Sigifredo Ochoa in early 1983. And the temporary capture by FMLN guerrillas of Berlin, a major city, underlined the fact that the government's position was deteriorating militarily.

The administration's response was Pavlovian. It blamed the problem on Cuba and the Soviet Union and called on Congress to provide drastically increased military and economic assistance. Secretary Shultz claimed that external support for the guerrillas had increased. As usual, no hard evidence was produced to back up these assertions. Indeed, it could not be produced, since the administration did not have such evidence.

For his part President Reagan, on March 10th, gave one of his worst speeches ever on El Salvador. To hear him tell it, turmoil in Central America was simply the product of Moscow's global strategic plans. The Soviets, he said, wanted to tie down U.S. forces on the southern border of the United States, thus limiting the American capacity to act in more distant places such as Western Europe and the Persian Gulf. He went on:

> The Communist agenda . . . is to exploit human suffering in Central America to strike at the heart of the Western Hemisphere. By preventing reforms and instilling their own brand of totalitarianism, they can threaten freedom and peace and weaken our national security. . . . We have been slow to understand that the defense of the Caribbean and Central America against Marxist-Leninist takeover is vital to our national security.[18]

Noting the Salvadoran Catholic hierarchy's call for
negotiations and a peaceful solution, both Secretary
Shultz and Vice-President Bush expressed irritation that
churchmen should thus play into the hands of the
communists.

But all this backfired. The administration had
cried wolf too many times. Its arguments were uncon-
vincing and seemed to lead toward an ever-expanding
commitment. The stridency with which it pushed its case,
moreover, alienated many who had previously gone along
with the policy. Typical was the reaction of Republican
Senator Dave Durenberger of Minnesota. In a letter to
the president on March 3, 1983, he complained:

> The administration has managed to convey an image of
> hostility, arrogance, and naivete which is crippling
> its policy and eroding its support. . . . As the
> government of El Salvador loses its political cohe-
> sion, and as the situation increasingly becomes one
> of . . . stalemate, senior officials of your
> administration are falling back on the kind of
> comments which led so many people to question our
> goals in the first place.
>
> I find it astonishing that the Secretary of
> State and the Vice President have so little
> understanding of what is at stake . . . and the role
> which the Catholic Church can play in advancing the
> enunciated goals of the administration. I find it
> outrageous that they would suggest that the Church
> would bolster the ends of Marxism. . . .
>
> A willingness to talk does not mean a
> willingness to commit suicide. If there is any
> danger in offering to meet unconditionally, it is
> far less than the danger of continuing to seek a
> military victory. . . . That is why I have decided
> to seek legislation linking any further military
> assistance to El Salvador on a presidential certifi-
> cation that unconditional negotiations among the
> parties to the conflict are either underway or are
> impossible because the insurgents have imposed prior
> conditions.[19]

In the face of such strong and widespread repudiation of its policies, the administration began to shift
ground. Testifying before the Congress on March 16,
Secretary Shultz stressed the role of socioeconomic
assistance in the new U.S. game plan for El Salvador.
Having previously opposed negotiations of any kind with
the armed opposition, he came around to saying that,
although this was a matter for the Salvadorans themselves
to decide, the United States would help in any way it
could to bring about negotiations that would enable all
persuasions to participate in a democratic process.[20]

There was, however, little to suggest any basic reformulation of policy. While paying lip service to the need for negotiations, the administration's actions continued to preclude them. It pressed ahead with military support and still seemed convinced that something could be gained from elections even if the other side did not participate. Thus, it pressured the Salvadorans to advance the date for presidential balloting to December 1983. This could only lead to a dead end, since, as already noted, the FMLN/FDR had already emphasized that it would not participate in any vote not preceded by a negotiating process aimed at bringing about adequate conditions for elections.

As of April 1983, Congress, increasingly suspicious of the administration's mishandling of the Central American crisis, was moving to limit U.S. military assistance and direct involvement and to attach more conditions to aid of all kinds.

The final denouement has yet to be written. What remains clear, however, is that even should the administration at some point seriously explore the negotiating option, it has already waited until very late in the game. The optimum moment came in 1981 in the wake of the failure of the guerrilla offensive. Since then, the conflict has been a stalemate. Should that stalemate be broken in favor of the guerrillas, any hope for a solution satisfactory to all sides would go aglimmering. Such an eventuality has not yet happened. Energetic and imaginative diplomacy might still rescue the situation. In view of the administration's record, however, one cannot be optimistic. The situation may yet deteriorate to the point where it will have the painful choice of either commiting American troops or accepting military defeat.

NICARAGUA

With respect to Nicaragua, the administration did not even bother to tone down its rhetoric. It did, however, go through its standard ploy of feigning a willingness to negotiate. Assistant Secretary of State Enders visited Managua in August 1981, ostensibly to talk things over with the Sandinistas. Nothing came of this; neither side followed up on the proposals set forth. Nevertheless, in spring 1982, the United States presented a number of new proposals, supposedly with a view to encouraging a negotiating process. When the Nicaraguans responded positively, however, Washington quickly backed away. The administration did not even bother to respond to a Nicaraguan diplomatic note of August 13, which offered to discuss all outstanding issues without conditions. And although it had made a major issue of the possible Nicaraguan acquisition of MiG aircraft, when the Sandinistas announced in December that they would forego adding such planes to their inventory, Washington did not respond in any way, not even to the point of describing this conciliatory move as a positive development. This was a mistake. The Nicaraguan announcement had been intended to provide some breathing room and to stimulate negotiations. When it became obvious that the United States had no intention of entering into such discussions, the basis for Nicaraguan inhibitions disappeared.

Meanwhile, Washington had pressed ahead with the secret war against the Sandinistas. By April 1983, this effort had reached alarming proportions. CIA-backed Nicaraguan guerrillas, many of them former Somocista guardsmen, were operating inside Nicaragua. President Reagan did not even deny the support of the United States. He merely insisted that the operation's purpose was not to overthrow the Sandinistas; rather, it was simply to harass them and interdict arms bound for El Salvador.[21] This fooled no one. The guerrillas had already been interviewed by the Washington Post and had made their purpose crystal clear: to overthrow the Managua government.[22]

This course, in addition to being of dubious legality and inconsistent with American values, seemed certain to bring about dangerously heightened tensions. Cuba could not be expected to stand idly by. On the contrary, the chances were high that thousands of additional Cuban military advisers would be sent to Nicaragua. And the Sandinistas might decide to acquire the MiG aircraft after all. If that happened, Washington also could be expected to escalate. No one in the administration seemed worried about the sequence of events that might be touched off by U.S. actions or concerned lest it lead eventually to a superpower confrontation. Their whole approach toward Central America was characterized by extreme insouciance.

CONCLUSIONS

Far from political and military victories at this juncture, the administration's policies have produced only military stalemate and escalating political problems. Nor does the administration give any sign of changing course. If it holds to the policies of its first two years, it may well alienate the entire region.

The administration's principal sin of commission has been to portray and address the situation in Central America as if it were, first and foremost, a battleground of East-West conflict, and as if the violence there resulted primarily from Soviet/Cuban aggression. A more realistic appraisal is that the conflict is essentially internal in nature. With the Old Order having collapsed in Nicaragua, and in the process of collapsing in El Salvador and Guatemala, the struggle is to decide who will fill the vacuum. Cuba, of course, hopes to turn the situation to its advantage. It sympathizes with the more radical elements and has provided limited support and advice--first to the Sandinistas and then to the guerrillas in El Salvador. But this aid has never been the central factor in the equation. Somoza would have been overthrown in Nicaragua and a civil war would be raging in El Salvador even if Cuba did not exist and Moscow were still ruled by the czars. To be sure, many of the FMLN guerrillas are Marxists. But that fact does not translate the situation into an East-West conflict. To suggest that it does so is to deal with shadows rather than substance. It is also to take the problem out of context, with unfortunate consequences in terms of how the United States should address it. The U.S. challenge in Central America is far more complex and requires subtleties of approach beyond the unsophisticated "good-guys-versus-communists" attitude adopted by Mr. Reagan. Such an attitude diverts attention from what should be the principal concern of the United States in the area: economic development coupled with socio-economic reforms. It also discourages negotiations, which are the key to reducing tensions, providing security guarantees, and finding internal solutions satisfactory to all sides.

The East-West context insisted upon by the administration also makes it extremely difficult to appeal to and/or deal with the many noncommunist components of the opposition--whether in El Salvador or Guatemala. If the United States treats the situation as a case of Soviet/Cuban aggression, it will tend to view all those in opposition to regimes it backs as Soviet/Cuban allies. Such a position would cut off the United States from the moderate, democratic elements that constitute its natural partners.

On the other side of the coin, addressing the situation in an East-West context encourages a skewed perception of the repressive governments that, by oppressing and neglecting the welfare of their people, have done more than anyone to bring on today's revolutionary turmoil. Rather than seeing them as the agents of instability, the Reagan administration tends to view them as valued allies in a common struggle against the communists. Thus does the United States become overly identified with repressive regimes, while they believe they have a blank check from Washington. The United States thereby tends to perpetuate, rather than to alleviate, the very causes of the instability that so concern it. As Ambassador Pezzullo has summed it up:

By identifying Cuban/Soviet subversion as the cause
of the Central American turmoil, we shield the
abusive factions from taking responsibility for
their failures, and we lessen the pressure on them
to change. At the same time, we give the Cubans and
Soviets more credit than they deserve among a
populace unhappy with the status quo and pressing
for change. We repeat the historical error of
positioning ourselves, the most change-oriented
society on the globe, as seemingly defending the
status quo.[23]

Taking the situation out of context and addressing
it as if there were some immediate communist threat to
the vital security of the United States may push the
situation in precisely that direction--that is, it may
become a self-fulfilling prophecy. A harsh and
inflexibly confrontational attitude toward the
Sandinistas and the opposition in El Salvador and
Guatemala further polarizes the situation in those
countries in ways unfavorable to U.S. interests. It
drives them in a more radical direction--exactly the
opposite of what the United States wishes to see happen.
There is, moreover, a glaring inconsistency between
the administration's description of the situation and its
limited response--an inconsistency that suggests it does
not believe its own rhetoric. In the same March 10, 1983
speech in which he reaffirmed that what we face in
Central America is a direct threat to U.S. security
emanating from Moscow and Havana, President Reagan also
excluded the possibility of sending American troops to
fight there. One might ask: If Mr. Reagan believed that
our vital security were really threatened, how could he
rule out any measure necessary to protect it? Certainly,
it would be imprudent to do so. One must conclude,
therefore, that either he does not believe what he is
saying or that he takes American security too lightly.
The same inconsistency is apparent in U.S. policy
throughout the region and results in a situation in which
the United States all too often adopts the worst alternatives possible. For example, the administration claims
that Cuba is the source of U.S. problems in Central
America, but after months of empty and demeaning bluster,
it dropped its threat to "go to the source." The
measures it has taken against Havana are not effective
and resolute. They will not force Castro to do anything;
such measures simply irritate the Cubans and rule out any
possibility of securing through diplomatic engagement
what such halfway punitive measures cannot hope to
achieve.
In the same way, the secret war in Nicaragua does
not get rid of the radical Sandinista commanders, but
merely eliminates the possibility of the United States

having any constructive influence with them through diplomatic means.

In El Salvador, also, while effectively ruling out military victory by excluding the possibility of committing U.S. troops, the administration has refused to explore negotiated alternatives.

The result of all this is a region-wide situation in which Washington eschews diplomacy but also fails to take the resolute action that would be indicated if U.S. security were really threatened; the United States has the benefits of neither the one nor the other. However one analyzes it, the Reagan administration deserves the strongest criticism for its handling of the Central American imbroglio. If it takes at face value its own description of the problem--a threat to U.S. security originating in Moscow and Havana--then it deserves reprimand for not taking resolute action to ensure that security and to contain the problem rather than allowing it to fester indefinitely.

If, on the other hand, the administration's alarmist East-West explanation has been a matter of exaggerating for effect in order to make the situation fit its own preconceived Cold War mindset, then it is guilty of having misled the American people, squandering diplomatic opportunities, and needlessly leading the United States toward an extremely dangerous, even explosive, situation.

Whether the one way or the other, the Reagan administration's Central American policies clearly have not served the national interest.

NOTES

1. Lawrence Pezzullo quoted at an Aspen Institute conference in January 1983.

2. New York Times (March 7, 1983); Washington Post (February 21, 1983).

3. As stated to the author by Ambassador Pezzullo.

4. See Wayne S. Smith, "Dateline Havana: Myopic Diplomacy," Foreign Policy, 48 (Fall 1982), pp. 160-161.

5. The statement issued by the State Department on April 2, 1981 acknowledged that there had been movement in the right direction. The United States, it said, had 'no hard evidence of arms trafficking within the last few weeks, and propaganda and other support activities have been curtailed."

6. See L. Francis Bouchey, Roger Fontaine, David C. Jordan, Lt. General Gordon Sumner, and Lewis Tambs, "A New Inter-American Policy for the Eighties" (Washington, D.C.: Council for Inter-American Security, 1980).

7. Jeane Kirkpatrick, "U.S. Security and Latin America," Commentary (January 1981), pp. 29-40.

500

8. See the text of Kirkpatrick's speech before the conference, March 21, 1981.

9. U.S. News & World Report (March 2, 1981).

10. New York Times (March 4, 1982).

11. U.S. News & World Report (April 6, 1981).

12. Transcript of the State Department's noon briefing for February 13, 1981; U.S., Department of State, "Communist Interference in El Salvador" (Washington, D.C.: Bureau of Public Affairs, February 23, 1981), p. 8.

13. As reported by USICA diplomatic correspondent Marie Koening on February 28, 1981.

14. Washington Post (April 3, 1983).

15. New York Times (December 28, 1981).

16. The administration was careful to exclude the author, then Chief of the U.S. Interests Section in Havana, from these talks. Presumably it did not want any witnesses. I subsequently received read-outs, however, from several reliable sources as to what had transpired. Their descriptions were roughly consistent with an account given by General Walters himself. See Miami Herald (January 8, 1983).

17. Washington Post (March 29, 1981).

18. Text of President Reagan's speech of March 10, 1983.

19. Text of Senator Durenberger's letter of March 3, 1983.

20. New York Times (March 17, 1983).

21. Washington Post (April 17, 1983).

22. Washington Post (April 15, 1983).

23. Ibid. (March 20, 1983).

15
Postscript: Toward a New Central American Policy

Donald E. Schulz

Any attempt at policy prescription in a volume such as this must deal with a basic dilemma. If, on the one hand, an editor tries to forge a consensus, he may be left with the lowest common denominator of what his diverse contributors can agree on. All too often, this effort leads to a watered-down prescription, largely inadequate for dealing with the problems faced. On the other hand, if he addresses the issues squarely, seeking what he believes to be the best policies for the particular dilemmas at hand, then he is likely to abandon consensus.

Not all of the contributors will agree with the analysis and recommendations in this chapter. Most, I suspect, would support the basic thrust, while disagreeing on certain specifics. Some may reject the whole package. Readers can make up their own minds as to the wisdom or bias of what follows. I have earlier argued that U.S. policy has been profoundly counter-productive. By supporting those elements--especially the Central American militaries--that have been primary causes of revolutionary turmoil and by seeking to spread that turmoil to Nicaragua, Washington has become a major destabilizing force. The end result may be a region far more hostile to the United States and vulnerable to Soviet/Cuban influence than ever before. (Nor would the damage be limited to Central America. One could make the same statement about Latin America as a whole. Anti-U.S. elements would have a field day.)

In the process, moreover, the United States may once again destabilize itself. Those who advocate the strategy of conflict underestimate the domestic ramifications of an indecisive struggle of protracted duration. Although a U.S. military intervention would be unlikely to entail as many casualties as did the Vietnam conflict, it would not have to be nearly that destructive to regenerate major domestic unrest. This country has not yet recovered from the wounds of that earlier unfortunate

involvement. Even a comparatively modest engagement
would resurrect painful memories and provoke vigorous
resistance within both Congress and the public at large.
In turn, the heavier the resistance, the less likely that
the given war could be prosecuted effectively.

What would be the effect of such a failure on U.S.
credibility elsewhere? The advocates of conflict like to
argue that the United States will no longer be taken
seriously in other parts of the world if it does not hold
the line in Central America. After all, if Americans are
not willing to defend their own backyard, where will they
use their military power? Yet, the "lessons" of the
region, like Vietnam, are not quite so simple. How
credible would U.S. commitments be if the United States
once again demonstrated that it is too rigid to
reevaluate a disasterous course of action? A wise
president will not confuse U.S. manhood with intervention.

My concerns are twofold: that American policy be
both effective <u>and</u> constructive. There is a moral dimension here that <u>must</u> not be ignored or distorted for
partisan purposes. Like many other Great Powers, the
United States has all too often trodden heavily among its
neighbors. The tendency to manipulate and use small
countries for its own purposes, without regard for the
damage to them, characterizes Washington's policy toward
Central America today just as surely as it did in
Cambodia and Vietnam a decade ago. What will be the
implications for Honduras of the U.S.-promoted
militarization? Of the carefully nurtured hostility with
Nicaragua? It takes little foresight to envision the
undermining of the fragile Honduran democracy and the
spread of war to that heretofore relatively peaceful
land. What about the arming of the Nicaragua <u>contras</u>?
They have already become a state within a state. If they
are unable to return to their native country, one anticipates serious problems for their current hosts. The
<u>contras</u> may themselves become a major destabilizing force
within Honduras.

And what of Nicaragua? Let us assume for the sake
of argument that U.S. policy succeeds and the Sandinistas
are overthrown. What then? Notwithstanding President
Reagan's assertions, not all of the <u>contras</u> are freedom
fighters. This is especially true of the Somocistas, for
whom power, spoils, and revenge are primary motivations.
Civil War II would be another bloodbath, one that would
not cease with the defeat of the current government but
which could go on for some time as the Somocistas slaked
their thirst for revenge against a helpless populace.
Nor would the fighting be likely to end. The Sandinistas
would continue the struggle in guerrilla fashion. There
would almost certainly be a falling out of victors. It
is difficult to imagine elements more incompatible than

the Somocistas and the followers of Eden Pastora. The
only thing that unites these two factions of the opposition is their antipathy for the Sandinistas. When that
glue evaporates, their alliance of convenience would
crumble. Then we could look forward to Civil War III.

One could go on at some length with similar
questions about El Salvador, Costa Rica, and Guatemala,
but the point should be clear enough: These are not the
kinds of fates that anyone with any regard for the well-
being of the Central American people would want to
promote. My basic thesis is that the United States
should seek to minimize, rather than maximize, the
bloodshed and the risks thereof by seriously seeking
negotiated solutions to the region's major conflicts.
Such solutions need not exclude an important element of
coercion. Nicaragua, Cuba, and the Soviet Union are
destabilizing forces, and U.S. power should be used to
discourage their adventures. The United States should
not delude itself, however, by seeking foreign scapegoats
for what are essentially domestic problems. These
revolutions will not go away. Even if crushed, they will
reemerge time and again, as long as those in positions of
authority have no regard for their countrymen, hold them
in contempt, and seek only their own power and enrich-
ment.

EL SALVADOR: THE "ZIMBABWE OPTION"

In November 1980, a mysterious, unsigned manuscript,
purportedly a State Department "dissent paper" reflecting
the views of analysts not only in State but also in the
DOD, NSC, and CIA, began circulating within Washington
circles, raising the possibility of a Zimbabwe-type
settlement to the Salvadoran conflict. Just as the
British intervened in Zimbabwe, so, the argument went,
there was an opportunity for the United States to play a
similar role in El Salvador.[1] What was needed, however,
was a clear recognition on the part of the "regionally
dominant power" (i.e., the United States) that a new
status quo was emerging--that an important segment of
Salvadoran opinion supported not the junta but rather the
Democratic Revolutionary Front (FDR), a broad alliance
of moderate to radical left organizations uniting most of
the opposition. Washington's willingness to recognize
el frente as "a legitimate and representative force"--
though not the only one--"in Salvadoran politics" might
be the necessary first step toward a negotiated solution
to the conflict.

Now, this was not the first time that a proposal had
been floated to "allow the left to come in from the
cold."[2] Unfortunately, for both strategic and domestic
political reasons, the option was never given serious

consideration. Within the foreign policy bureaucracies,
criticism and dissent were systematically ignored. The
result was a kind of diplomatic immobilism. Washington
continued to support the junta, while violence mounted
and the left grew stronger. Subsequently, the election
of a conservative, anti-communist U.S. president and the
murder of the _frente_ leaders seized at the Externado San
Jose High School in November 1980 seemed to bury once and
for all the idea of a negotiated settlement of the
conflict.

Yet, appearances are sometimes deceiving.
Ironically, the Reagan administration may now have an
opportunity to pursue the "Zimbabwe option" much more
effectively than would any conceivable Democratic
administration. Certainly, it has been--and still is--in
a much better position to take the controversial measures
that will be necessary to foster regional peace and
stability. The obvious model here is that of the Nixon
presidency: Precisely because of his long-standing
reputation as a staunch conservative and anti-communist,
Mr. Nixon found it much easier to pursue detente with
China and the Soviet Union than Hubert Humphrey would
have. So too Mr. Reagan. Who, after all, would be
better able to convince this conservative Congress to
accept such a settlement and provide substantive aid to
the regime, whatever its ideological complexion, that
emerges out of it?

At the same time, who would be better equipped to
persuade the Cubans, Nicaraguans, and Salvadoran
guerrillas to negotiate, and negotiate seriously? Reagan
has clearly frightened Castro and the Sandinistas, as can
be seen by the recent spate of conciliatory proposals
from those quarters. If he plays his cards right, he may
very well be able to get their cooperation in settling
regional conflicts in ways that do not jeopardize U.S.
security. If such cooperation is to come about, however,
it will require a degree of sophistication and flexibility on the part of Washington that has not yet been in
evidence. It is not enough to employ the stick alone;
one must also have a carrot to offer.

Finally, who would be better suited than Mr. Reagan
to persuade the recalcitrant Salvadoran military that the
United States is _really_ serious about a settlement?
Washington has the means to exert such pressure through
its economic and military aid. It should accordingly
indicate in the strongest possible terms that it will not
support, or even passively accept, a right-wing coup.
The Salvadoran government and military should be informed
that the United States will expect them to enter into
serious negotiations with the opposition. Arrangements
should be made for a cease-fire, to be followed by the
formation of a transitional coalition government,
including the left. The armed forces would be restricted

to their barracks and the guerrillas to their base camps.
An international constabulary would be introduced to
maintain order and prepare the way for internationally
supervised elections in which all political organizations
could participate a la Zimbabwe, with the United States
committed to support whatever outcome the Salvadoran
people might choose. Finally, a new security apparatus
would be formed, composed of both government and
guerrilla forces, purged of the most undesirable elements
from both sides.

For this plan to work, the United States will have
to adopt a flexible, multidimensional approach to the
region's problems. The strategy of conflict, with its
emphasis on confrontation and military force, will have
to be modified in certain crucial respects. Most
important, Washington must disassociate itself from those
sectors, both in and out of the military and security
forces, who have so grossly abused their own countrymen.
As Gleijeses has argued, the military is the "real source
of power on the government side, and . . . moving toward
its reform is a first essential step."[3]

This will not be easy. The United States will have
to exert strong pressure on its Salvadoran ally to ensure
that the desired changes are made. U.S. credibility will
have to be reestablished vis-a-vis the Salvadoran elite,
for the Reagan administration's pusillanimous efforts on
behalf of human rights have convinced too many of that
country's leaders that Washington's pleas and threats can
be ignored with impunity. These leaders will have to be
disabused of this notion. The most direct and effective
way would be through a suspension of military aid. This
action would by no means leave the government defenseless
(at least in the short run), and it would get the point
across in a manner that mere words could never do.
Simultaneously, the United States should let it be known
that unless the appropriate reforms are undertaken and
negotiations begun, it will, after a specified period,
also cut off economic aid.

One may admit that, on the surface, the "Zimbabwe
option" would seem a fairly long shot. (So was the
original Zimbabwe settlement.) The right might very well
refuse to cooperate, calculating that when the chips are
down Washington will cave in and do whatever is necessary
to prevent a leftist victory. By the same token, the
FMLN might use the negotiations to secure a dominant role
in the transitional government in preparation for a
seizure of power. A bloodbath is conceivable. If the
right, for instance, felt it were being abandoned by the
United States, it might no longer feel constrained by any
need for moderation and lash out in a desperate, all-out
war of annihilation. Needless to say, there is little
trust or goodwill on either side. Regardless of who won
the proposed elections, the losers might well resort to

force. The concept of a loyal opposition has no historical precedent in El Salvador.

On the other hand, it could also be argued that the
United States is at a critical juncture. Not only is
there an administration in Washington that has the potential for making hard and controversial decisions on this
matter, but conditions within El Salvador itself may now
favor such a resolution. In spite of the guerrillas'
recent battlefield successes, a military victory is a
long way off. Several more major offensives will be
ncecssary. At best, the prospects are for a Nicaraguan
scenario, with a series of nationwide attacks gradually
building in intensity until the lid finally blows off the
pressure cooker altogether. Even if successful, such a
resolution would be inordinately devastating for all
concerned. And it is by no means certain that the ending
would be successful. In the past, the Reagan administration has demonstrated a willingness to provide the
Salvadoran government with massive military aid. It
could indicate its determination to continue doing so in
the future should the insurgents spurn the olive branch
being proffered. If that failed to do the trick, the
United States could still intervene with combat troops,
if necessary. Thus, the electoral route might well be
preferable. FDR spokesmen have repeatedly indicated
their desire for a political resolution of the conflict.
With the death of Salvador Cayetano Carpio and the
apparent triumph of moderates over the hard-line
prolonged popular war faction of the Popular Liberation
Forces,[4] the FMLN guerrillas, too, seem more willing than
ever to take part in negotiations. The Nicaraguans and
Cubans concur. Both have long been concerned that the
United States, unable to impose a military solution in El
Salvador, might lash out at them in frustration. Castro
and the Sandinistas are no longer willing to jeopardize
their own revolutions by engaging in adventures in El
Salvador. Once the danger of their initial military
involvements became apparent, they pulled back and
recommended a political settlement to the conflict. Most
recently, they have taken to pressuring the Salvadoran
guerrillas to negotiate in order to take some of the
weight off Nicaragua. Finally, a number of regional
actors--most notably, the Contadora group (Mexico,
Venezuela, Colombia, and Panama)--have offered their
services as mediators. In short, the time is ripe. If
the United States treats the proposed negotiations as an
opportunity to achieve such a settlement, rather than as
a mere tactic for ameliorating international and domestic
opinion, dividing the Salvadoran opposition, and
consolidating the position of the Salvadoran government,
then such negotiations will have a modest chance for
success.

By the same token, the indefinite nature of the
conflict gives the United States a major opportunity to
induce the Salvadoran regime to engage in serious negotiations. If Washington continues to provide military
aid, then it will bolster those elements in the armed
forces who maintain that the United States can be drawn
ever deeper into the conflict and a military victory won.
Incentives to find a peaceful solution will be removed
wholesale. In contrast, if Washington makes it very
clear that it is serious about such a settlement and
backs up its words with actions of the kind described
above, then illusions of a military victory will be
undermined and the incentives for a compromise solution
immeasurably enhanced. As for the danger that a
withdrawal of U.S. aid will unleash a spasm of violence
on the part of the extreme right, I believe it to be
exaggerated. Salvador is already experiencing a reign of
terror. How much worse could things get? The truth of
the matter is that the military does not like to fight
very much. Morale is low, and a cutoff of aid would
probably further weaken the desire for combat. The
dominant motives of Salvadoran officers tend to be
personal aggrandizement and loyalty to their military
institution. As Gleijeses has pointed out, both "require
not defiance, but acquiescence to U.S. will."[5]

It is time to test the political waters to ascertain
whether a "Zimbabwe option" is feasible. Before issuing
any ultimatums, however, the United States must find out
whether international support exists for such a strategy.
Again, this should be a multilateral effort. Those non-
communist countries that have been critical of American
policy should be sounded out with regard to such issues
as providing troops for an international peacekeeping
force. (U.S. soldiers would most assuredly not be
involved in such an undertaking.) If such tangible aid
is not available, then of course the feasibility of the
entire enterprise would be called into serious question.
Similarly, the United States must ascertain whether there
are elements in the current Salvadoran regime whose
cooperation could be secured. The most likely candidates
would come from the Christian Democratic Party and,
especially, the remnants of the reformist faction of the
military. Although the young officers who led the
October 1979 golpe--Majano, Guerra y Guerra, and others--
have been driven into exile, the vast majority of their
colleagues are still in the armed forces, relegated to
desk jobs and other positions of noninfluence. Efforts
should be made, as part of the proposed military reform,
to bring back Majano and the other leaders and to open
the ranks of the senior officers to this crucial source
of fresh blood. It is perhaps not yet too late to
resurrect the young officers as a political force and

save their vision of national renovation from the fate to
which it has been consigned.

In the final analysis, the "Zimbabwe option" may
very well be the best chance the United States has of
heading off an impending policy disaster. If it fails to
take advantage of the opportunity for a negotiated
settlement, it is likely to face an agonizing choice, not
too far down the road, between a humiliating withdrawal
and a commitment of American combat troops. One cannot,
of course, predict the nature of the government that
would emerge from this process. It might be Marxist.
That is one of the risks of bringing the FMLN into the
political process. But one thing is for certain: The
struggle for power will not disappear. Such conflict is
the very essence of politics. Accordingly, the U.S.
objective should be to shift the battle away from the
military arena into the political one, where the human
costs and dangers are far less. This cannot be done
without giving the insurgents an incentive to lay down
their arms: Specifically, they will have to be granted a
share of power in the proposed transitional government,
so that they might have confidence in the electoral
process in which they would presumably be participating.
Their candidates, too, must be permitted to organize and
campaign for office. In short, one must allow for the
possibility that the left may come to power through
peaceful means.

You pay your money, and you take your chances.
That, after all, is what democracy is about. While there
is no way of knowing who would win the proposed elections, it seems highly unlikely that any one party could
gain a majority. Coalition politics would almost
certainly be necessary. One anticipates the emergence of
a broadly based government, leaning either to the right
or to the left. (It is impossible to say which is more
probable.) If the latter, such a government would likely
include Christian Democrats, Social Democrats, and
representatives from the other independent opposition
groups, as well as the FMLN. Such a government would not
necessarily be dominated by the guerrillas; nor would it
inevitably be hostile to the United States. (Much, in
fact, would depend on Washington's behavior.) On the
other hand, the longer the United States waits and the
more intense the fighting becomes, the greater the
polarization of the populace and the radicalization of
the opposition. As the guerrillas' military strength
grows, so will their ability to dictate the country's
future. At the same time, the anti-American potentials
inherent in the struggle will be heightened--not to
mention the cost in terms of bloodshed, both during and
after the cessation of formal hostilities. Should
military solutions prevail, the victors--whoever they
might be--would not be merciful.

So, too, the "Zimbabwe option" may be the United States' best chance of preventing the internationalization and spread of the Salvadoran conflict throughout all of Central America, while maintaining its influence in the region at acceptable costs and limiting that of Havana and Moscow. As the aforementioned "dissent paper" quite rightly points out, the Cuban and Soviet potential for expanding their influence lies mainly in their willingness to provide military equipment and training in wartime. "Few developments would open more opportunities for Cuba in Central America and the Caribbean than the regionalization of armed conflict that would follow the escalation of U.S. military involvement in El Salvador.[6] By contrast, the Soviets and Cubans are at a distinct disadvantage in terms of competing with the United States under conditions of peace. Neither is capable of nor interested in displacing the United States as the area's major trade partner and donor of aid. As long as regionalization can be avoided, the United States will be playing in a game in which the cards are stacked in its favor--regardless of the ideological complexion of the regime that emerges in El Salvador. (After all, that government, too, will be dependent on U.S. aid and trade.)

Finally, there is the key issue of internal order. Perhaps the most difficult task will be the creation of a new military establishment, composed of both government and guerrilla forces, purged of the worst elements in both. The United States will be in a fairly strong position, by dint of its ability to grant or withhold military and economic aid, to press for such changes within the Salvadoran armed forces. The same cannot be said, however, for its relationship with the FMLN. Nevertheless, some leverage is possible. El Salvador will require large quantities of economic assistance, and Washington could make that aid conditional on the willingness of the insurgents to cleanse their ranks of the worst offenders. They might just be willing to do this. The ultra-militants lost (in the short run, at least) the recent power struggle within the Popular Liberation Forces; they are increasingly regarded as a liability by the other FMLN commanders, who might well be willing to sacrifice them for the sake of a power-sharing arrangement. Washington could probably get the Nicaraguans and Cubans to use their influence with the guerrillas on this matter. Both fear that the Salvadoran imbroglio might draw them into a regional war and are anxious to avoid this prospect. This would be their opportunity to make a substantive contribution to a political settlement and at the same time foster their own security. The United States could sweeten the pot by offering political asylum to undesirables on both sides, who could then proceed into exile.

510

This solution would not, of course, solve the problem of creating a new military establishment, but it would help. Integration of government and guerrilla units would be a slow and difficult process even under the best of circumstances. Some form of institutional coexistence may be required for several years until the new government can be elected and can establish its authority. In the meantime and for the foreseeable future (four or five years, at a minimum), it will be necessary to maintain an international peacekeeping force in the country to ensure that this exceedingly delicate and unpredictable arrangement does not come apart at the seams.

NICARAGUA AND CUBA: THE STRATEGY OF COEXISTENCE

One-dimensional perceptions lead to one-dimensional, often counterproductive policies. For the United States, that, surely, is the lesson of its recent Central American experience. The Reagan administration came into office with a ready-made ideological explanation for the revolutionary turmoil in El Salvador: It was the product of "outside" forces, especially Cuba, Nicaragua, and the Soviet Union. Since then, Washington has sought to threaten and punish Havana and Managua in an attempt to get them to cease their aggressions. More recently, it has become clear that the administration intends to oust the Sandinistas altogether, if it can.

The threat and use of force have a legitimate place in U.S. foreign policy, but they must be employed carefully lest they backfire. It is one thing to threaten an aggressor in order to deter him from violence, but if, once he ceases his objectionable behavior, the threat continues to intensify, the deterrent effect tends to lose its power. There is a point of diminishing returns beyond which threats become increasingly ineffective and counterproductive. Driven into a corner, the Sandinistas will turn and fight. And the Cubans are likely to be with them. Then the United States will <u>really</u> see a "revolution without borders."

(In the aftermath of the U.S. invasion of Grenada, a reporter asked Castro how far Cuba would support Nicaragua in the event of a similar invasion. His reply was that "we would try to do everything possible for Nicaragua, but we would face the same problem as in Grenada: We lack the naval and air means to send direct assistance to Grenada. Those are the facts: We do not have any other options." He went on to voice his confidence in the ability of the Nicaraguan people to defend themselves.[7])

Some observers have concluded from this and similar statements that Cuba would remain on the sidelines in the

event of such an attack. In my judgment, this is a
dubious interpretation. It overlooks the fact that there
are already some 5,000 to 6,000 Cubans in Nicaragua,
about a third of whom appear to be military or security
personnel. It is highly unlikely that they would remain
uninvolved in the fighting that would accompany an
invasion. Certainly, they were not uninvolved in
Grenada. Castro's comments can perhaps best be
interpreted as (1) a statement of fact and (2) an attempt
to avoid giving the Reagan administration any pretext for
an invasion. That Cuba could not send direct aid in the
form of immediate troop reinforcements is not in doubt.
It is very likely, however, that various kinds of delayed
and indirect aid would be forthcoming--including the
training and equipping of "volunteers" from Cuba and
other Latin American countries to be smuggled into
Nicaragua clandestinely, along with a continuing flow of
arms. The struggle would go on indefinitely in guerrilla
fashion.)

Though the hour is growing very late, there is still
time to avert disaster. As in El Salvador, Ronald Reagan
is in a far better position than any conceivable
Democratic president to put into effect the necessary
policy changes--if he so chooses. Reagan has indeed
frightened Castro and the Sandinistas; hence his credibility is very high. They believe that he would bomb
Cuba and invade Nicaragua. This fear provides the United
States with a source of considerable leverage--if it is
wise enough to take advantage of it. What is needed is a
mutual security pact: "We will not threaten you if you
do not threaten us." More specifically, the United
States would agree to call off the CIA and the Hondurans
and to withdraw military support from the Nicaraguan
contras. The "secret war" against Nicaragua would be
closed down. Simultaneously, the Sandinistas and Cubans
would terminate their military aid to the Salvadoran
guerrillas and use their influence to help bring about a
negotiated settlement of that conflict. A complex of
regional security agreements, including mutual
nonaggression pledges, would be fashioned, which would:
(1) bar, or at least severely limit, the shipment of
weapons, ammunition, and military equipment into
Nicaragua, El Salvador, Honduras, and Costa Rica for a
period of four years (longer, if possible); (2) ban
foreign military bases and training (U.S., Cuban, Soviet,
or others) in Central America; and (3) provide for an
immediate halving of all foreign military and police
personnel, followed by the gradual withdrawal of the
remainder, to be completed over a period of eighteen
months. Demilitarized zones would be created on each
side of the Nicaraguan-Honduran and Nicaraguan-Costa
Rican borders, to be policed by units of the same international peacekeeping force that would be engaged in El

Salvador. Finally, the Sandinistas would agree to ease
some of their domestic controls--for example, by
releasing some political prisoners, permitting greater
press freedom, allowing opposition parties and interest
groups more liberty to organize and pursue their causes,
and holding national elections in 1985. In return, the
United States would restore full commercial relations and
foreign aid.

As with the "Zimbabwe option," there are many
potential problems with this proposal. One would like to
include Guatemala in the security agreements, but it is
doubtful whether the bellicose generals who run that
country would be willing to cooperate. Similarly, the
contras in Honduras have their own agenda. Having armed
them to the teeth, the United States may not find it so
easy to get those weapons back or to prevent their use in
a continuing guerrilla war against the Sandinista regime.
Nor can the United States be sure of the cooperation of
other major parties. General Alvarez may not want to
terminate the Honduran military buildup, and the Israeli
government, for one, might be willing to help him circum-
vent the restrictions on arms and advisers. By the same
token, the Sandinistas might object to any number of
provisions.

Nevertheless, my guess is that some arrangement of
this sort will be necessary if a wider war is to be
avoided. Both the Nicaraguans and Cubans now seem to
understand this, and they have repeatedly indicated their
interest.[8] The United States should take them up on it.
The incentives for Nicaraguan-Cuban cooperation are
considerable: power-sharing for their allies in El
Salvador, increased security for themselves, and the
restoration of economic relations with the United States.
The Sandinistas, especially, need U.S. trade and aid
(including the lifting of American opposition in international lending agencies) if they are to pull the
Nicaraguan economy out of its doldrums and fuel the kind
of growth that would enable the regime to fulfill mass
expectations and desires for improved living standards.
In short, the United States is in a strong bargaining
position. By using the carrot as well as the stick, it
can maximize its leverage, increasing its influence the
more effectively to promote U.S. interests in Nicaragua
itself.

What is being suggested here is that the United
States must make a serious attempt to substitute a
strategy of peaceful coexistence for the strategy of
conflict that has been so vigorously pursued during the
early Reagan years. Washington has too easily fallen
into the trap of assuming that Castro's friends are ipso
facto its enemies. There is no rational reason for the
United States to isolate itself from the Sandinista
government simply because the latter is "Marxist" or

"revolutionary" or because it maintains good relations with Havana. If Washington is concerned about Nicaragua becoming "another Cuba," then it would be well advised to use its economic and diplomatic resources--especially its economic aid--to promote American values and interests in that country.

That opportunity still exists. As in El Salvador, the Soviets and Cubans would be at a distinct disadvantage. They cannot effectively compete in terms of economic aid, and the United States would have foreclosed military competition through the mutual security treaty. Moreover, it is important to keep in mind that Nicaragua is not your conventional Soviet-bloc, totalitarian system. The Sandinistas' commitment to "pluralism," though increasingly strained by the growing tensions between revolutionary and counterrevolutionary sectors, has not yet been completely abandoned. Private enterprise continues to play a major role in the government's economic program. Independent political parties and interest groups still exist and publish their views in La Prensa. Though human rights violations occur, these are for the most part the overreactions of a jittery state security system struggling to combat armed guerrilla attacks and sabotage. Certainly, personal security is incomparably greater in Nicaragua than in, say, El Salvador or Guatemala.

In sum, if the United States is really interested in promoting freedom and human rights in Nicaragua, it should begin by reevaluating current policy, for the strategy of conflict has placed those values in serious jeopardy. Pluralism cannot flourish under a state of siege. Human rights abuses will continue as long as the country is under attack; indeed, they may be expected to grow worse, as U.S./Honduran/contra pressure intensifies. They are in large part a consequence of American policy. Moreover, as long as the United States continues to wage military, economic, and political war against the Sandinistas, it will effectively lock Nicaragua into the Cuban/Soviet embrace. The Reagan administration has made the Soviet bloc penetration of that nation far too easy. It is time, once again, to open Nicaragua to political competition from the United States. A change of strategy need not lead to a withdrawal into isolationism. Rather, constructive engagement--the continuation of the search for hemispheric security through a balanced mix of economic, military, and diplomatic leverage--would reorient American involvement along more effective, more constructive, and less hazardous lines.

Finally, a word about Cuba. For almost a quarter century, the Castro regime and the United States have been locked in a fundamentally pathological relationship, a veritable dialectic of hostility, marked by "mutual fear, suspicion, defensiveness, and aggression. Time and again, provocation and threat have bred retaliation, reinforcing existing antagonisms and leading to an ongoing process of mutal destructiveness. Each side, in effect, has chronically behaved in such a way as to bring out the worst, most destructive tendencies in the other."[9]

It is time that both sides made a serious effort to break out of this deadlock. It will not be easy, for there is an ongoing structure of incompatibility separating Cuba and the United States that is unlikely to disappear in the years ahead. This is not merely a matter of differences in national interest and ideology; domestic political considerations have also served the cause of hostility. Castro, after all, has made a career of playing David to our Goliath, using the specter of an external threat to unite Cubans around his revolutionary leadership. (Unfortunately, the United States has all too often been willing to fall into the trap by performing the assigned role.) Similarly, various U.S. presidents have felt constrained in their initiatives toward Cuba by the need to avoid alienating important domestic political groups or giving the appearance of being "soft" on communism. Many citizens continue to have intense, negative feelings about Castro, as was recently demonstrated by President Reagan's success in rallying Cuban-Americans behind the strategy of conflict. None of these factors will go away overnight. Cuban ideas and policies will continue to compete with those of the United States in the international marketplace; from time to time, Fidel will be his old provocative self. Clearly, the United States must be equipped to protect its interests.

For precisely this reason, Washington needs to stand back and re-evaluate its Cuban policy, for, as the Central American crisis has so clearly demonstrated, the dangers of continuing this mutually destructive symbiosis have become prohibitive. There are signs, too, that Castro understands this situation and is ready to negotiate. Over the past several years, the Cubans have issued numerous feelers, calling for talks on the entire range of issues in contention between the two countries. The United States has nothing to lose and everything to gain by exploring these signals. Where they would lead, no one can say, but if Washington is unwilling even to make an effort, then of course no progress will be possible. The same sterile pattern will continue, with hostility feeding hostility and destructiveness, destructiveness.

In the process of reevaluation, perhaps, the United States will be able to shed some of its long-standing illusions and inject a new element of realism into its Cuban policy. Too often, it has behaved as if it was an actor in a morality play, casting itself in the role of

Good saving the world from the Cuban Devil. Reality is
not so reassuring. While Cuba is hardly a benign force
on the international scene, neither is the United States,
as the latter's record in countries like Guatemala, Iran,
Vietnam, and Chile amply demonstrates. So far as anybody
knows, the Cubans have never plotted to assassinate a
U.S. president or tried to contaminate American livestock
with swine fever. The CIA, however, has engaged in such
activities against Cuba.[10] Perhaps, too, the United
States will eventually come to recognize Fidel not as a
single-minded purveyor of anarchy, committed to the
elimination of the U.S. presence everywhere in the Third
World, but as a more complex figure, capable of serving
as a force for moderation and stability as well as revolutionary change. (The Cubans have been a stabilizing
element in Angola and Ethiopia, though the United States
has been loath to admit it.[11] Early on, they encouraged
the Sandinistas to retain a mixed economy and a non-
aligned foreign policy and to court U.S. aid and foreign
investment. As previously noted, moreover, they have for
some time been advising the Salvadoran guerrillas to seek
a political solution to the civil war in that country.)
Cuban and U.S. interests are not everywhere incompatible;
there are, in fact, significant areas of commonality.
The stability of Central America has now become one of
them. If Washington can work with Castro on this issue--
and it should make a major effort to do just that--then
it can at last begin the long overdue task of allowing
Cuba to come in from the cold.

CONCLUSIONS

Clearly, U.S. actions cannot be limited to El
Salvador or Nicaragua. The United States needs a truly
regional policy. In neighboring Guatemala, political
violence and human rights violations have built to
Salvadoran proportions, and for essentially the same
reasons. In the words of the "dissent paper," U.S.
support for a negotiated settlement in El Salvador would
"serve notice to the Guatemalan hardliners that their
time has run out. The chances for a less radical and
less traumatic transition . . . will be greatly
improved."[12] At the same time, I should make very clear
that I am not speaking here of a wholesale rejection of
right-wing governments. Far from it; the United States
must be ready to support a wide range of regimes, from
conservatives to Marxists and authoritarians to
democrats--providing such regimes can maintain some
semblance of order and legitimacy and refrain from interfering in the internal affairs of their neighbors. This
might well mean, for instance, major increases in
economic aid to conservative, authoritarian Honduras,[13]

as well as democratic Costa Rica and Marxist Nicaragua,
providing they adhere to the criteria just stated. In
short, a "realistic" Latin American policy will have to
recognize and accept diversity, even as it attempts to
promote stable governments capable of effectuating sorely
needed reforms. (Put another way, either the United
States learns to live with the left, or it will face a
future of chronic military interventions to prevent such
regimes from coming to power or, once there, surviving.)

One last note on economic aid. In the past,
Washington has all too often displayed a tendency to
"throw money" at socioeconomic problems. The recent
Kissinger Commission report is a case in point. Under
present circumstances, an $8 billion aid plan for the
region is wildly unrealistic. Not only is it unlikely to
pass Congress, but, even if it does, such measures can do
no more than hold off a total collapse in Central
America. Under conditions of civil war, economic
development is simply not feasible. Massive capital
flight and guerrilla sabotage will continue to undermine
any such program. Indeed, even in peaceful Costa Rica,
the vast majority of all social welfare funds is eaten up
by the bureaucracy. Notions of a regional "Marshall
Plan" ignore the critical cultural, economic, and political differences between Western Europe and Central
America. In the former, the task was to reconstruct
previously advanced economies; in the latter, such
economies will have to be built from the ground up.
Moreover, Europeans had a long tradition of education,
science, technology, and discipline to work with; Central
Americans do not. What one does find in excess in
Central America, however, are corruption and violence.
Unless these tendencies are tamed, the United States will
be pouring its aid down the proverbial rat hole.

In short, the prerequisites for any effective large-
scale economic assistance program for the region are a
restoration of political stability and an improvement in
financial accounting and administrative procedures.
Neither of these requirements is likely to be achieved in
the absence of peace. Accordingly, economic aid should
be part and parcel of a comprehensive strategy designed
to restore regional peace in the short run. On the most
basic level, this aid can be used to maximize U.S.
bargaining leverage with governments of various
ideological persuasions. Only when those regimes
demonstrate a willingness to make concrete commitments to
peace should the U.S. economic spigot be opened.

What is the likelihood of such policy change?

In my judgment, the odds that the Reagan administration will adopt such measures are virtually nil. The
president and his key advisers are simply too rigid, too
locked into an anti-communist frame of reference, too wed
to their particular vision of the primacy of military

force. Nor is it at all clear that a Democratic
president would fundamentally change anything. Carter
policy differed only in degree, not in kind, from Reagan
policy. None of the major Democratic candidates has been
willing to tackle the issue head-on. They may be
critical of the president, but their own statements on El
Salvador are veiled in ambiguity. They offer no alternatives. No one wants to be burned politically by being
too specific.

Moreover, even if a change in direction is
instituted, the power of the United States is limited.
And the mood in Congress is hardly favorable to the kind
of massive increase in economic aid that would be
necessary to restore long-run stability to the region.
Nevertheless, there is a basic fact of life involved
here, and the sooner Washington comes to terms with it
the better: Economic aid is a major tool in the U.S.
foreign policy repertoire. The United States may use
that tool well or poorly, but if it refuses to use it at
all then it deprives itself of an essential means of
furthering its influence in such regions as Central
America. If it does not exercise its influence, then
there will be others who will exercise theirs, and they
may well do so in ways that are threatening to U.S.
interests.

NOTES

1. Anonymous, "Dissent Paper on El Salvador and
Central America" (mimeo). The authenticity of this
document (though, significantly, not its substance) has
been challenged by department officials. It did not come
from authorized dissent channels; its author or authors
remain unknown.

2. To quote William M. LeoGrande and Carla Anne
Robbins, "Oligarchs and Officers: The Crisis in El
Salvador," Foreign Affairs, 58, 5 (Summer 1980), p. 1103.

3. Piero Gleijeses, "The Case for Power Sharing in
El Salvador," Foreign Affairs, LXI, 5 (Summer 1983),
p. 1050.

4. I say "apparent" because the issue has not yet
been definitively settled. In November 1983, a new
guerrilla organization calling itself the Salvador
Cayetano Carpio Revolutionary Workers Movement emerged,
pledging to follow Carpio's radical line.

5. Gleijeses, "The Case for Power Sharing," p. 1057.

6. "Dissent Paper," p. 21.

7. Granma Weekly Review (November 6, 1983).

8. See, especially, James Chace, "The Endless War,"
New York Review of Books, 30, 19 (December 8, 1983).

9. Donald E. Schulz, "The Strategy of Conflict and the Politics of Counterproductivity," Orbis, 25, 3 (Fall 1981), p. 680.

10. Washington Post (January 9, 1977); Donald E. Schulz, "Kennedy and The Cuban Connection," Foreign Policy, 26 (Spring 1977).

11. See, especially, Schulz, "The Strategy of Conflict."

12. "Dissent Paper," p. 22.

13. Honduras, of course, has an elected civilian president. But real power resides in the military, especially in General Alvarez. Suazo Cordova is essentially a figurehead.

Abbreviations

AID	Agency for International Development
ANDES	Asociacion Nacional de Ecuadores Salvadorenos
ANEP	National Association of Private Enterprise
AP	Productive Alliance
APP	People's Property Area
ARDE	Alianza Revolucionaria Democratica
ARENA	Nationalist Republican Alliance
BPR	Popular Revolutionary Bloc
CACM	Central American Common Market
CBI	Caribbean Basin Initiative
CDN	Coordinadora Democratica Nicaraguense
CMEA	Council on Mutual Economic Assistance
CONDECA	Central American Defense Council
CONFER	Confederation of Religious Orders
CONFREGUA	Guatemalan Conference of Religious Orders
COSEP	Superior Council of Private Enterprise
CPSU	Communist Party of the Soviet Union
CR	Revolutionary Coordinating Committee of the Masses
CST	Sandinista Workers' Central
CTN	Christian Democratic Nicaraguan Workers Council
CUC	Committee for Peasant Unity
CUS	Council for Union Unity (AFL-CIO affiliated)
DN	Joint National Directorate
DOS	Department of State
DRF	Democratic Revolutionary Front (also referred to as FDR)
DRU	Unified Revolutionary Directorate
EGP	Popular Guerrilla Army
EPS	Sandinista Popular Army
ERP	People's Revolutionary Army
ESI	Export Substitution Industrialization
EXMIBAL	Exploraciones y Explotaciones Minerales-Isabel

FAO	Broad Opposition Front
FAPU	Unified Popular Action Front
FAR	Revolutionary Armed Forces
FARN	Armed Forces of National Resistance
FAS	Sandinista Air Force
FDN	Fuerzas Democraticas Nicaraguenses
FDR	Democratic Revolutionary Front (also referred to as DRF)
FECCAS	Christian Federation of Salvadoran Peasants
FMLN	Farabundo Marti National Liberation Front
FMS	Foreign Military Sales
FPL	Popular Liberation Forces
FSLN	Frente Sandinista de Liberacion Nacional (Sandinista National Liberation Front)
FUSEP	National Police Force of Honduras
IMET	International Military Education and Training
INCO	International Nickel Company
INTA	National Institute of Agrarian Transformation
ISI	Import Substitution Industrialization
ISTA	Salvadoran Institute of Agrarian Transformation
JLP	Jamaica Labour Party
LNI	La Nacion Internacional
LP-28	Popular Leagues--28th of February
MAP	Military Assistance Program
MDN	Nicaraguan Democratic Movement
MLN	National Liberation Movement
MPL	Popular Liberation Movement
MRP	Revolutionary Movement of the People
OAS	Organization of American States
ORDEN	Democratic Nationalist Organization
ORPA	Revolutionary Organization of the Armed People (People in Arms)
PACs	Patrullas de Autodefensa Civil
PCD	Democratic Conservative Party
PCN	Party of National Conciliation
PCS	Salvadoran Communist Party
PDC	Christian Democratic Party
PDCH	Christian Democratic Party of Honduras
PGT	Guatemalan Workers' Party
PNP	People's National Party
PPSC	Popular Social Christian Party
PR	Revolutionary Party
PRUD	Revolutionary Party of Democratic Unity
PSCN	Social Christian Party
RD	Relative Deprivation

SELAM	Latin American Episcopal Conference
UCS	Union Comunal Salvadorena
UDEL	Democratic Liberation Union
UDN	Democratic Nationalist Union
UFCO	United Fruit Company
UNO	National Opposition Union
URNG	Guatemalan National Revolutionary Union

About the Authors

JOHN A. BOOTH is associate professor of political science at the University of Texas at San Antonio. He is author of The End and The Beginning: The Nicaraguan Revolution and coeditor of Political Participation in Latin America and has published articles in the Latin American Research Review and other scholarly journals.

GORDON L. BOWEN is assistant professor of political science at Mary Baldwin College. He has published articles in Armed Forces and Society and Latin American Perspectives and is currently working on a book on Guatemala.

CLAUDIO GONZALEZ-VEGA is professor of agricultural economics at Ohio State University and professor of economics at the University of Costa Rica. He has published widely in economic and development journals, including the American Journal of Agricultural Economics, Savings and Development, and Development Digest, as well as chapters in Money and Finance in Economic Growth (edited by Ronald McKinnon) and Uses and Abuses of Rural Financial Markets (edited by D. Adams et al.). He has served as consultant to the World Bank, the Inter-American Development Bank, and the United Nations Economic Commission for Latin America.

DOUGLAS H. GRAHAM is professor of agricultural economics and director of the Latin American Studies program at the Undergraduate Center for International Studies at Ohio State University. He is coauthor of Population and Economic Development in Brazil and coeditor of Why Cheap Credit Undermines Rural Development and has published articles in the Latin American Research Review, Economic Development and Cultural Change, and other scholarly journals.

DENNIS HANRATTY is a Latin American analyst with a political risk assessment firm. He has conducted extensive field research in Mexico for his Ph.D. dissertation on "Change and Conflict in the Mexican Catholic Church" and has presented papers before the

Southern Political Science Association and the
International Studies Association Annual Meetings.

PAUL HEATH HOEFFEL is a veteran Latin American
correspondent, whose best-known publications on the
Salvadoran oligarchy and the "disappeared" in Argentina
have appeared in the New York Times Magazine.

THOMAS L. KARNES is professor of history at Arizona
State University. He is author of both Tropical
Enterprise--Standard Fruit and Steamship Company in Latin
America and The Failure of Union: Central America,
1824-1960 and is editor of Readings in the Latin American
Policy of the United States.

ROBERT S. LEIKEN is an Adjunct Senior Fellow and
Director of the Soviet-Latin American Project at
Georgetown University Center for Strategic and
International Studies. He is currently Senior Associate
with the Carnegie Endowment for International Peace at
Washington, D.C. He is author of Soviet Strategy in
Latin America and has published articles in Foreign
Policy and the Washington Quarterly.

PENNY LERNOUX is a veteran Latin American
correspondent and author of Cry of the People. She is a
frequent contributor to The Nation and other journals.

MARK B. ROSENBERG is director of the Latin American
and Caribbean Center at Florida International University.
He has published articles in the Latin American Research
Review, the Hispanic American Historical Review, and
Caribbean Review.

DONALD E. SCHULZ is assistant professor of political
science at the University of Tampa. He is lead editor of
Political Participation in Communist Systems and author
of articles in Foreign Policy, Orbis, and Newsweek.

WAYNE S. SMITH is a Senior Associate with the
Carnegie Endowment for International Peace. As a former
foreign service officer and head of the U.S. Interests
Section in Havana, he resigned from the State Department
in 1982 in protest of the Reagan administration's Cuban
and Central American policies. His best known publication is "Dateline Havana: Myopic Diplomacy," in Foreign
Policy.

CARL STONE is a reader in political economy at the
University of the West Indies in Jamaica. He is author
of Democracy and Clientelism in Jamaica and coeditor of
The Newer Caribbean: Decolonization, Democracy, and
Development and has contributed articles to the Journal
of Inter-American Studies and World Affairs, the Latin
American Research Review, Economic Development and
Cultural Change, Comparative Studies in Society and
History, and many other journals.

Index

Cesar, Alfredo, 482
Chajul (Guatemala), 286, 291
Chalatenango (El Salvador),
119, 214, 230
Chamber of Industries (Costa
Rica), 367
Chamorro, Pedro Joaquin, 30, 306
Chamorro Coronel, Edgar, 261
Chamorro Rappacioli, Fernando, 320
Chancellor, John, 276
Chapin, Frederic, 293
Charles V (Holy Roman Emperor),
94
Chase Manhattan Bank, 408
Chavez y Gonzalez, Luis, 127, 129
Cheek, James, 221
Chiapas (Mexico), 439-440, 444
Chichicastenango (Guatemala),
291, 292
Chihuahua (Mexico), 80
Chile, 81, 121, 123, 126, 127,
138, 315, 430-431, 438,
453, 464
Chimaltenango (Guatemala), 147,
292
Chin-A-Sen, Henrik, 463
Chinchontepec Volcano (El
Salvador), 230
Chontales (Nicaragua), 30
Christian Democratic Nicaraguan
Workers (CTN), 321
Christian Democratic Party
Chile, 138, 139
El Salvador (PDC), 23, 24, 31,
48, 56, 107, 110, 113,
195, 198, 199, 200, 201,
206, 208, 212, 215, 216,
217, 226, 227, 228, 234,
237, 238, 239, 240, 241,
480, 507, 508
Guatemala (PDC), 23, 33, 110,
280
of Honduras (PDCH), 342
Nicaragua, 304
Venezuela, 139, 463
Christian Democratic World
Federation, 465
Christian Federation of
Salvadoran Peasants
(FECCAS), 128, 202
Chuabajito (Guatemala), 291
Church of the Word, 292
Chusma, 108

CIA. See Central Intelligence
Agency
CIDA. See Comite Interamericano
de Desarrollo Agricola
Cienfuegos (Cuba), 457
Clark, William, 225, 248
Clarke, Maura, 117, 118, 119,
120-121, 124
Clayton-Bulwer Treaty (1850), 68
Client states, 44, 45, 86
CMEA. See Council on Mutual
Economic Assistance
Coca Cola (U.S. company), 287
Cochineal, 97
CODESA (Costa Rican investment
corporation), 361
Coffee, 5, 6, 92, 96, 160,
164, 177, 178
prices, 20, 100, 102, 103,
192, 193
See also under Costa Rica;
El Salvador; Guatemala;
Nicaragua
Colom Argueta, Manuel, 289
Colombia, 25, 72, 92, 123, 127,
138, 139, 167, 407, 438,
455, 464, 465. See also
Contadora Group
Colomoncagua refugee camp
(Honduras), 343, 344, 345
Colon (Panama), 73
Colones
Costa Rican, 353, 366,
367-368, 371(n2)
Salvadoran, 191, 203
Colono, 5, 193
Columbus, Christopher, 68, 73,
331
"Comandante Ana Maria." See
Anaya Montes, Melida
Comandante Cero. See Pastora
Gomez, Eden
Comayagua (Honduras), 337
Comitan (Guatemala), 145
Comite de Unidad Campesina. See
Committee for Peasant Unity
Comite Interamericano de Desar-
rollo Agricola (CIDA), 107
Committee for Peasant Unity (CUC)
(Guatemala), 19, 143, 290, 2
Committee of National Defense
Against Communism (Guatemala
276

El Salvador (cont.)
  agricultural production, 8,
    9-10, 11, 173(table), 176,
    181, 191, 192, 193, 229
  arms, 37, 38-39, 48, 56, 204,
    217, 218, 221, 223-224, 225,
    226, 232, 242, 249, 252,
    253, 255, 262, 338, 460,
    461, 481, 487
  Assembly, 198, 199, 200, 239,
    240, 241, 442
  authoritarian, 41
  and basic needs, 172(table),
    191, 194
  birth rate, 172(table)
  capital. See San Salvador
  and Catholic Church, 117-118,
    119, 120, 123, 124, 125,
    127-132, 201-202, 203-204,
    214, 232, 494. See also
    Martyrs
  Chamber of Commerce, 107
  Civic Guard, 100
  Civil Military Directorate, 198
  class system, 190, 199, 215
  coffee, 98, 99, 100, 102, 106,
    107, 189, 192, 193, 195,
    196, 197
  and communism, 101, 107, 108,
    111, 119, 128, 195, 198,
    208. 209. See also Salvadoran
    Communist Party
  consumer price index,
    15(table)
  and Costa Rica, 199, 246
  cotton, 103, 107, 193
  counterrevolution, 27, 207, 246
  coup (1979), 92, 113, 205,
    239, 507
  currency. See Colones,
    Salvadoran
  death rate, 172(table), 191
  death squads, 31, 41, 108, 111,
    113, 119, 203, 204, 207,
    209-210, 213, 230, 235,
    239, 490, 492
  economy, 21, 164, 168(table),
    171, 189-190, 197, 198,
    203, 204-205, 227-228
  education, 172(table), 190-191,
    272
  election (1982), 235-239,
    240(table)

  elites, 24, 26, 27, 47, 98,
    99, 100-101, 102, 103, 106,
    107, 108, 110-112, 113, 114,
    127, 189-190, 194, 196, 197,
    200, 201, 204, 211
  farms, 174(table), 176, 191
  foreign debt, 170(table)
  foreign trade, 170(table), 213
  GDP, 168(table), 170(table)
  GNP, 21(table), 91, 162(table),
    227
  government, 31-32, 56, 91, 101,
    110, 126, 195-197, 198,
    199-200, 201, 203, 204,
    205-215, 222-223, 227, 228,
    231, 239, 257, 480
  and Guatemala, 114
  guerrillas, 20, 24, 31, 32, 35,
    36, 37-38, 39, 46-47, 48,
    51, 56, 107, 127, 202, 203,
    204, 205, 206-207, 213-214,
    215-221, 222, 223, 224-225,
    226, 229-230, 231, 232, 233,
    238-239, 242, 244-245, 246,
    247, 252, 253, 256-258, 259,
    260, 346, 466-467, 481,
    493. See also Contra base
    camps
  homicide rate, 11
  and Honduras, 11, 35, 50, 109,
    191, 199, 259, 333, 339,
    343, 346
  housing, 194, 197, 203
  human rights, 32, 47, 56, 125,
    204, 210, 211, 222, 232-233,
    241, 246-247, 267(n76)
  income, per capita, 191, 205
  income distribution, 190, 192
  Indians, 98, 192, 195
  industrial disputes, 18(fig.),
    19
  industrialization, 11, 103,
    106, 190, 193, 197, 198
  inflation, 166(table)
  and Japan, 103
  Junta, 198, 205-206, 210-211,
    227, 480, 481
  kidnappings, 107, 118, 246
  labor force, 7, 98, 99, 103,
    176, 192, 193-194
  labor movement, 19, 31, 106,
    107, 130, 190, 197,
    198-199, 201, 203, 221

534

Honduras (cont.)
Air Force, 337
arms traffic, 38, 440, 512
bananas, 98
and basic needs, 172(table)
birth rate, 172(table)
borders, 38, 331, 333, 347
capital. See Tegucigalpa
and Catholic Church, 342-343
Congress, 342
consumer price index, 15(table)
counterrevolution, 39
death rate, 172(table)
democracy, 334, 342, 346,
488, 489
economy, 23, 168(table), 171
education, 172(table)
elites, 102, 332, 333
farms, 174(table)
foreign debt, 169, 170(table),
171
GDP, 168(table), 170(table)
GNP, 21(table), 162(table)
government, 23, 34-35, 49-50,
92, 126, 334-335, 336, 340,
342, 343, 488-489
guerrillas, 34, 35, 50, 52,
340, 342
human rights, 50, 339, 340
and immigration, 12
industrial disputes, 21
industrialization, 7
inflation, 166(table), 171
and Israel, 253, 512
labor force, 176
labor movement, 20, 340
life expectancy, 172(table)
military, 34, 35, 49-50, 231,
334, 336, 338, 339, 340,
342, 344-345, 346, 347, 488
Mosquito Coast, 68
National Police Force (FUSEP),
334
net national product,
332(table)
and Nicaragua, 3, 35, 39, 41,
46, 50, 52-53, 54, 104,
136, 137, 140, 231, 252,
261, 310, 323, 326, 327,
335, 339, 341, 347, 440-441,
489, 511, 512
Nicaraguan counterrevolu-
tionaries in, 318, 320, 321,
326, 327, 328, 338, 343,

345-346, 347, 436, 440, 502
peasants, 6, 16, 20
politics, 102, 334, 335, 336,
342
population, 9(table), 12, 98,
162(table), 172(table)
private and public sectors,
168(table)
refugees in, 343-346
rural, 6, 16, 175
unemployment, 16
university. See National
University
wages, 16, 17(table), 20
See also Contra base camps;
San Jose Agreement; under
El Salvador; Guatemala;
Soviet Union; United States
Hoover, Herbert, 81
Huehuetenango Department
(Guatemala), 110, 286, 291,
292, 294
Huerta, Victoriano, 80
Hull, Cordell, 81
Human capital, 160, 175, 176,
180-181
Human rights, 39, 46, 48, 87,
114, 134, 221, 224, 232, 241,
257, 269, 288, 463, 483,
484, 485, 489, 490, 494,
505. See also under
individual countries
Humphrey, Hubert, 504
Hungary, 40, 53, 217, 218

Ibarguen family, 97
Identification cards. See Cedulas
"Illegal colony" (San Salvador),
194
Ilopango Air Force Base (El
Salvador), 38, 249
raid (1982), 230, 232
IMET. See United States,
International Military
Education and Training
IMF. See International Monetary
Fund
Imperialist Era (1898-1934),
44-45, 66, 69-80
Import substitution, 102, 353,
403, 410, 412, 417
Import substitution industrial-
ization (ISI), 160, 161,
164, 165, 178, 354, 355,

542